REGIONALIZATION AND HARMONIZATION IN TVET

PROCEEDINGS OF THE 4TH UPI INTERNATIONAL CONFERENCE ON TECHNICAL AND VOCATIONAL EDUCATION AND TRAINING (TVET 2016), 15–16 NOVEMBER 2016, BANDUNG, INDONESIA

Regionalization and Harmonization in TVET

Editors

Ade Gafar Abdullah & Tutin Aryanti
Universitas Pendidikan Indonesia, Bandung, Indonesia

Agus Setiawan
Universitas Pendidikan Indonesia, Bandung, Indonesia

Maizam Binti Alias
University Tun Hussein Onn, Johor, Malaysia

LONDON AND NEW YORK

Cover illustrations:

Villa Isola.

Villa Isola is one of Bandung's colonial heritage, which was designed by C. Wolff Schoemaker (1882–1949), commissioned by D.W. Berretty (1890–1934) in 1932. It is located in Universitas Pendidikan Indonesia Bumi Siliwangi campus and has served as its landmark. The building, designed using Nieuwe Bouwen style, was originally Berretty's residence but handed over to the university as the university was established as Teachers Education College in 1954.

Photographer: Agus Juhana

Published 2017 by Routledge
2 Park Square, Milton Park, Abingdon, Oxon OX14 4RN
605 Third Avenue, New York, NY 10017

First issued in paperback 2020

Routledge is an imprint of the Taylor & Francis Group, an informa business

© 2017 Taylor & Francis Group, London, UK

Typeset by V Publishing Solutions Pvt Ltd., Chennai, India

ISBN 13: 978-0-367-73601-9 (pbk)
ISBN 13: 978-1-138-05419-6 (hbk)

Published by: CRC Press/Balkema
          Schipholweg 107C, 2316 XC Leiden, The Netherlands
          e-mail: Pub.NL@taylorandfrancis.com
          www.crcpress.com – www.taylorandfrancis.com

Regionalization and Harmonization in TVET – Abdullah et al. (Eds)
© 2017 Taylor & Francis Group, London, ISBN 978-1-138-05419-6

Table of contents

Social and cultural issues

Teaching innovations in TVET

Innovations in engineering and education

Preface

The 4th UPI International Conference on Technical and Vocational Education and Training was held in Bandung (Indonesia) on 15–16 November 2016. The conference is a biannual event, which has been conducted by the Universitas Pendidikan Indonesia's TVET Research Center and the Faculty of Technology and Vocational Education. Like the three previous conferences, this conference received enthusiastic response from scholars and practitioners of TVET around the world. Participants from Malaysia, India, Timor Leste, and many cities in Indonesia attended this year's conference.

Exploring the theme "Regionalization and Harmonization in TVET," the conference featured Prof. Dr. Numyoot Songthanapitak, the president of the Regional Association for Vocational Teacher Education in Asia and the president of Rajamangala University of Technology Lanna, Thailand; Prof. Dr. HC. Thomas Schröder and Dr. Sven Schulte of the Technical University of Dortmund, Germany; Prof. Dr. Maizam Alias of the Universiti Tun Hussein Onn Malaysia; and Dr. Eng. Agus Setiawan of Universitas Pendidikan Indonesia as keynote speakers. Participants presented their papers, which are categorized under subthemes: Standardization in Regionalization and Harmonization, Skill and Personal Development, Social and Cultural Issues, Teaching Innovations in TVET, and Innovations in Engineering and Education.

There were approximately 200 submissions from various countries to the conference. The committee selected 70 papers to be presented in this year's conference. These papers were then selected to be published in TVET@Asia online, and a conference book, published by Taylor & Francis and submitted for indexation in Scopus and Thomson Reuters.

Ade Gafar Abdullah,
Tutin Aryanti,
Agus Setiawan,
Asep Bayu Dani Nandiyanto,
Ari Arifin Danuwijaya
Universitas Pendidikan Indonesia, Bandung, Indonesia

Acknowledgments

Ade Gafar Abdullah, *Universitas Pendidikan Indonesia, Indonesia*
Agus Setiawan, *Universitas Pendidikan Indonesia, Indonesia*
Ana, *Universitas Pendidikan Indonesia, Indonesia*
Asnul Dahar Mingat, *Universiti Teknologi Malaysia, Malaysia*
Budi Mulyanti, *Universitas Pendidikan Indonesia, Indonesia*
Dadang Kurnia, *Deutsche Gesellschaft für Internationale Zusammenarbeit, Germany*
Dewi Cakrawati, *Universitas Pendidikan Indonesia, Indonesia*
Erica Smith, *Federation University, Australia*
Frank Bünning, *University of Magdeburg, Germany*
Hiroyuki Iida, *Japan Advanced Institute of Science and Technology, Japan*
Ida Hamidah, *Universitas Pendidikan Indonesia, Indonesia*
Isma Widiaty, *Universitas Pendidikan Indonesia, Indonesia*
Joachim Dittrich, *Internationale Tourismus-Börse, Germany*
Kamin Sumardi, *Universitas Pendidikan Indonesia, Indonesia*
Lilia Halim, *Universiti Kebangsaan Malaysia, Malaysia*
Luisa Brotas, *London Metropolitan University, United Kingdom*
M. Syaom Barliana, *Universitas Pendidikan Indonesia, Indonesia*
Maizam Alias, *Universiti Tun Hussein Onn Malaysia, Malaysia*
Margarita Pavlova, *Director, UNESCO-UNEVOC Center, Hongkong*
Mohd. Sattar bin Rasul, *Universiti Kebangsaan Malaysia, Malaysia*
Muhammad Sukri Saud, *Universiti Teknologi Malaysia, Malaysia*
Nazeri bin Mohammad, *Insititut Pendidikan Guru Kampus Perlis, Malaysia*
Numyoot Songthanapitak, *President of RAVTE, Thailand*
Ramlee bin Mustapha, *Universiti Pendidikan Sultan Idris, Malaysia*
Sigit Dwiananto Arifwidodo, *Kasetsart University, Thailand*
Sirilak Hanvatananukul, *Rajamangala University of Technology Thanyaburi, Thailand*
Siscka Elvyanti, *Universitas Pendidikan Indonesia, Indonesia*
Tetsu Kubota, *Hiroshima University, Japan*
Thomas Schroder, *Technical University of Dortmund, Germany*
Tutin Aryanti, *Universitas Pendidikan Indonesia, Indonesia*
Usep Surahman, *Universitas Pendidikan Indonesia, Indonesia*

Regionalization and Harmonization in TVET – Abdullah et al. (Eds)
© 2017 Taylor & Francis Group, London, ISBN 978-1-138-05419-6

Organizing committees

ADVISORY COMMITTEE

Assoc. Prof. Muhammad Sukri Saud
Assoc. Prof. Numyoot Songthanapitak
Assoc. Prof. Sirilak Hanvatananukul
Assoc. Prof. Tetsu Kubota
Dr. Asnul Dahar Mingat
Dr. Joachim Dittrich
Dr. Luisa Brotas
Dr. Margarita Pavlova
Dr. Mohd. Sattar bin Rasul
Dr. Nazeri bin Mohammad
Dr. Phil. Dadang Kurnia
Dr. Sigit Dwiananto Arifwidodo
Prof. Erica Smith
Prof. Frank Bünning
Prof. Hiroyuki Iida
Prof. Lilia Halim
Prof. Maizam Alias
Prof. Ramlee bin Mustapha
Prof. Thomas Schröder

CONFERENCE CHAIR

Tutin Aryanti, Ph.D.

ORGANIZING COMMITTEE

Dewi Cakrawati, M.Si.
Dr. Ade Gafar Abdullah
Dr. Isma Widiaty
Dr. Ana
Dr. Eng. Agus Setiawan, M.Si.
Dr. Budi Mulyanti
Dr. Eng. Usep Surahman
Dr. Ida Hamidah
Dr. Kamin Sumardi
Dr. Siscka Elvyanti
Prof. Dr. M. Syaom Barliana
Nia Amelia, S.Pd.
Diky Zakaria, S.Pd.
Agus Juhana, S.Pd.

Standardization in regionalization and harmonization

Integrated competency-based assessment and certification in vocational high school in Indonesia

B. Santosa & M. Muchlas
Ahmad Dahlan University, Yogyakarta, Indonesia

ABSTRACT: The objective of this research is to find a model of Integrated Competency-Based Assessment (ICBA) and certification that is appropriate for implementation in Vocational High School (VHS). The model is a test of competence that is combined with a learning and assessment process. This study used research and development established by Gall et al. The results of this research found that the model of ICBA and certification was feasible for implementation in VHS. The model was created through the aspects of developing competency standards and competency-based training development in work practices. The competency standard was developed through setting standards of competence and suitability needed for the job. The development of vocational learning is achieved through the professionalism of the teacher, the development of learning resources and learning models, evaluation models, and the reporting of learning outcomes in the form of a skills passport. Developing a competency-based assessment was done in the context of the examination system by working on real jobs.

1 INTRODUCTION

Vocational High School (VHS) has the purpose of preparing students for work and/or continuing their studies. The vocational education system should be able to prepare graduates to have competence in accordance with industry standards, both nationally and internationally. VHSs in Indonesia have implemented the concept of a dual system of education. Education and training can be done in schools and in industry, based on program link and match. Students learn the basic theory and practice in vocational school, then study and work at the company as an apprentice. This dual system is based on the view that vocational education will be efficient if the environment in which students are trained is a replica of the environment where they will be working (Prosser & Allen, 1925).

This study sought to establish competency test models that combine the learning process in schools and learning in industry (industrial working practices) with the assessment process. The curriculum was developed according to the needs of industry and standards in the workplace. Learning at school or in the workplace was adapted to the results of curriculum development conducted by the school and industry. The integrated competency test model is a model that combines aspects of the competency test curriculum development, learning at school, and learning in industry through industry working practices with the assessment process/competency test in order to establish the knowledge and skills of students according to the test of competency standards that apply in the workplace.

1.1 Curriculum development

While Finch and Crunkilton (1999, p. 11) state that the curriculum is defined as the number of learning activities and experiences which students are expected to have; it is like the direction of the school. Scott and Sarkees-Wircenski (2004, p. 396) state that the principle of a vocational education curriculum is derived from the needs of the world of work. Given the three definitions above, it can be concluded that the curriculum is the teaching and learning process that aims to improve the knowledge, skills, and experience of students in formal educational institutions, where the curriculum comes from the needs of the working world.

Cumming and Wyatt-Smith (2009, p. 1) state that assessment (and its interface with curriculum, teaching, and learning) has always been a significant component of classroom practice. Their opinion suggests a scoring system linking the curriculum with teaching and learning. Further, that in implementing the curriculum development, the system of learning, teaching and assessment should be considered.

1.2 Competency-Based Training (CBT)

According to Palomba and Banta (1993, p. 30), competence is a knowledge, skill, ability, quality of personal experience, or other characteristic that is applicable to learning and success in school or in work.

According to Gonczi (1998, p. 222):

To reform vocational education and training within a framework of national competency standards cannot succeed without a change in thinking about assessment methods and the conceptualization of competence requires a holistic approach, which integrates knowledge and skills with realistic workplace practices.

This statement implies that the method of assessment should be modified according to the standards of competence that have been determined. In concept, competence requires an integral approach between knowledge and the skills to practice in a real workplace.

1.3 *Competency-Based Assessment (CBA)*

Gonczi (1998, p. 38) states that CBT is characterized by the relationship between education/training and a Competency-Based Assessment (CBA) system. Competence standards are a major benchmark in the implementation of assessment/competency-based testing. On the other hand, CBA can be done while the trainees/students work in the workplace. Someone who is doing industry practice (on-the-job training) may be tested when they have been able to do the job.

Assessment is a process that involves the collection of evidence that is the basis for determining the progress or achievement of a student or trainee in relation to appropriate learning objectives (Hawke & Oliver, 1998, p. 244). As Miller (2008, p. 2) states, assessment is a broader term than test and the general process that includes gathering, synthesizing and interpreting data involves informal and formal data. Furthermore, Finch and Crunkilton (1999, p. 271) stated that the assessment is the determination of the benefit or value derived from the curriculum (or a part of the curriculum). Assessment is the process of gathering, synthesizing and interpreting data about the learning process as the implementation of the curriculum.

1.4 *On-the-Job Training (OJT)*

Van der Klink and Streumer (2006, p. 369) state that On-the-Job Training (OJT) is intended to: (a) increase the flexibility of learning programs in the workplace, (b) facilitate transfer of class-based learning, because the workplace and place of learning is identical, and (c) change the nature of work to provide more possibilities for integration between learning and work. Van der Klink and Streumer are of the opinion that on-the-job training can be described as a workplace learning

program whose aim is to get learning in the classroom and in the workplace closer together so that the existing competence in the world of work can be acquired by the learners.

The importance of OJT to vocational education is that it can add work experience. Thompson (1973, p. 240) states that OJT is very important for high-school students who want to know how it feels to work in certain jobs. This means that OJT can improve skills when students work. So, to get the skills to apply in the workplace, students must perform on-the-job training in industry.

2 RESEARCH METHODS

2.1 *Model development*

This study aims to develop a test model of competence in VHS and is intended to generate a product in the form of a test model of CBA. Thus, in this study there is a product development activity, and therefore this research includes a form of Research and Development (R&D). In this case, the researchers chose an R&D research model developed by Gall et al. (2007, pp. 589–594), modified by Sukmadinata (2011, pp. 184–190).

The steps of this R&D can be described as follows. The first step is a preliminary study that provides: (a) a study of the literature on the aspects studied, whether derived from the theory, research, or field studies related to competency testing, and (b) the drafting of a competency test product based on the literature and expert judgment and conducted through Focus Group Discussion (FGD) with experts/academics and practitioners in educational institutions and industry/associations. The second step is the development of products, which consists of (a) a limited product trial conducted in two VHSs, and (b) expanded product trials conducted in four VHSs. The third step consists of end-product testing and the dissemination of the associated results.

3 RESULTS AND DISCUSSION

3.1 *Result*

This study was conducted in two stages: the first stage is done by taking a vocational course selected with a qualitative approach; the second stage was testing of the model developed on the basis of the research results.

3.1.1 *Practice teaching and learning activities in VHS*

Some of the findings of practices at the VHS were: (a) the teacher is not required to have a certificate of competency or to become an independent assessor; (b) students learn in working groups of four students, each group having a different job; (c) students wrote a report on the practice and at the end of the meeting there was an evaluation; (d) not all of the materials tested practices; (e) students who failed remedial tests; (f) the result of the practices of the students takes the form of report cards.

3.1.2 Industrial Work Practice (IWP) in the workshop

Observations of the times that the students carry out learning in the workplace in the form of working industrial practices revealed that: (a) students are required to follow a program in the practice of industrial work; (b) students are given the freedom to select a location as desired; (c) students work according to the type of work in the workshop with the guidance of a mechanic who was appointed during the performance of the IWP; (d) the students record all of the types of work that have been done in a daily journal; (e) IWP does not provide practice exams for students; (f) students who have qualified will get an IWP certificate signed jointly by the school principal and the leadership of the industry/workshops.

3.1.3 Vocational Practice Exam (VPE)

External assessors of the industry make no judgment directly on the competencies being tested, due to the limited number of industry assessors. The number of external assessors in Yogyakarta VHS for the implementation of this Vocational Practice Exam (VPE) numbers just two people who cannot be fully present for the VPE. Administratively, the student assessment sheet is signed by two assessors, namely external assessors from industry and internal assessors/teachers, but technically the assessment is carried out by the internal assessor/teacher, then external assessors sign the assessment sheet that has been filled in by the internal assessors. At just two people, the number of external assessors is not sufficient compared to the number of VPE tests undertaken.

3.2 Discussion

The opinions of experts regarding these CBA models are analyzed in the discussion, based on the study of the theory and the data obtained. This part mainly consists of two parts. First, it discusses experts' opinions, including existing theories and research results on CBA models. Second, it discusses the final product of CBA models of this study.

3.2.1 Competency standards development

Standard Kompetensi Kerja Nasional Indonesia (SKKNI) is used as a guide in developing competency standards in vocational training because the purpose of vocational education is to prepare students for work. Norton (2008, pp. 17–18) suggests that in a standard task analysis of needs, work begins and ends with the development of competency profiles. Norton's opinion suggests that, in the development of competency standards, there is a need to analyze the needs of the work, which is none other than already stated in SKKNI, and developed into a competence standard.

Another opinion, expressed by Kelly (2000, pp. 14–15), states that in formulating basic standards in vocational education, concepts and basic operations and aspects of humanity, ethics and society need to be developed. Statements by Norton and Moser (2008) and Kelly (2000) confirmed that there needs to be a blend between the curriculum and SKKNI in developing competency standards in VHS.

3.2.2 Curriculum development

Putting a team of experts who are claimed to be experts on curriculum development and subjects in the curriculum is necessary for curriculum development, in addition to considering business and industry elements. Thus, this team ideally consists of: (a) administrators – academics in the field of vocational education; (b) instructional staff – an instructor in engineering fields; (c) support personnel – the developer of the curriculum/program; (d) advisory personnel – a committee of experts/professional associations. The opinion of Norton and Moser (2008) suggests that the members who should be involved so that the curriculum can be developed effectively and efficiently include engineering education experts, curriculum developers, and practitioners.

Rauner (2009, p. 1582) states that in the development of a vocational education curriculum, the occupational form of work is the main point of reference for the development of curricula. Rauner's opinion suggests that in developing the vocational education curriculum, forms of work related to the position/task become a reference in the development of the curriculum. Another opinion that supports consideration of the needs of students and social conditions was expressed by Prosser in Scott and Sarkees-Wircenski (2004, p. 390–391), which states that vocational education as an educational institution must expand opportunities for students to study or work as needed.

3.2.3 Competency-based training development

Input from a team of experts who claim that the module as a source of learning needs to be enriched with other learning resources to give students flexibility, in accordance with the opinion of Norton and Moser (2008, pp. D1–D2), states that learning should be able to provide a program for individual development, and the learning process can take place in the workplace. The learning model needs to be developed in the direction of cooperative learning and in accordance with the demands of the curriculum, in line with the expert opinion of

Dewey in Clark and Winch (2007, pp. 126–127), who states that vocational education has characteristics that include, firstly, a curriculum that demonstrates relevance to the vocational needs and, secondly, the knowledge needed to provide a better approach to the learning process.

3.2.4 *Development of Industrial Work Practice (IWP)*

The expert judgment which states that there needs to be standardization of competence in the IWP program, along with the imposition of performance criteria in the workshop where students practice industrial work, was supported by the opinion of van der Klink and Streumer (2006, p. 375), who suggest that learning in the workplace be based on training design details, such as contained in instructional design theory. The purpose of training is determined according to analysis tasks in the workplace, and learning materials should be developed in accordance with the conditions in the workplace. The standardization of competences, along with their performance criteria, should contribute to the skills passport of vocational students following an IWP program.

3.2.5 *Development of an Integrated Competency-Based Assessment (ICBA)*

According to expert judgment, the development of an ICBA and the use of a first-party professional certification agency (*Lembaga Sertifikasi Profesi Pihak-1* (LSPP-1)) at a VHS should be supported by strong policies and regulations. The ICBA should be carried out by a professional certification institution recognized by the certification body of the relevant profession in order to obtain the recognition of an independent agency. Under the guidelines of the National Professional Certification Board (*Badan Nasional Sertifikasi Profesi* (BNSP)), education and training institutions can seek the presence of LSPP-1. Students are tested by LSPP-1, which has received accreditation from BNSP. ICBAs, in the form of collecting evidence of competence, were conducted by LSPP-1. Students who have demonstrated evidence of competence have been declared competent and certified by LSPP-1. Students who have not been certified competent to work practice in industry, and together with students who want to gain competency, are tested by LSPP-1 using patterns established through work/simulation. Students who have satisfied all competency packages will receive a technician certificate and those who have got the certificate of compliance that they meet a competency have mastered the skill contained in the passport.

3.2.6 *Final development of ICBA model*

Verification is done by LSPP-1 on the results of the ICBAs completed by students during IWP. If the results are in accordance with the standards of competency that have been listed in the skills passport, then LSPP-1 issues a certificate of competence. If the results are not in accordance with the criteria, then the student does not receive a certificate of competence. Students who have not been declared competent by the industry when implementing industrial working practices, are given the opportunity to follow up with a competency test in a work simulation conducted by LSPP-1 at an assessment center in the VHS. The material in the ICBA covers competency clusters that have been listed in the skills passport in accordance with the student's choice. The revised ICBA end models from the final product assessment by the experts can be seen in Figures 1 and 2 (see Appendix).

4 CONCLUSION

Based on the results of data analysis and discussion, the results of this study can be summarized as follows.

1. The model for a competency test was conducted at VHSs in the form of the VPE, which is an integral part of the examination conducted in the context of the National Education Standards.
2. Barriers to ICBA implementation in VHSs are: (a) vocational training has yet to have independent professional certification agencies; (b) the VPE that has been used to date is based on a simulation of real work patterns; (c) the certificates of competency issued by VHSs have not received recognition from an independent professional certification agency.
3. The ICBA model we have developed for VHSs includes: (a) competency standards developed according to a blend of SKKNI for the automotive industry with Standar Kompetensi Lulusan (SKL); (b) synchronization with the syllabus requirements of existing jobs in industry, reviewed regularly every year; (c) components of vocational learning such as teachers becoming independent assessors, students gaining material soft skills through the inculcation of a Kaizen culture, progress reports in the form of skills passports, and VHSs having TUK, and becoming independent professional certification agencies; (d) students carrying out IWP with a focus on clusters of competence, with competency tests conducted on the basis of a real job in the industry.
4. The ICBA model that is feasible in VHSs is a competency test that combines the learning process with a process of assessment/examination conducted when students carry out industrial work practice and based on a pattern of student work on real jobs.

REFERENCES

Clark, L. & Winch, C. (2007). *Vocational education: International approaches, developments and systems.* Abingdon, UK: Routledge.

Cumming, J.J. & Wyatt-Smith, C. (2009). Framing assessment today for the future: issues and challenges. In Wyatt-Smith, C. & Cumming, J.J. (Eds.), *Educational assessment in the 21st century: Connecting theory and practice.* Dordrecht, The Netherlands: Springer.

Finch, C.R. & Crunkilton, J.R. (1999). *Curriculum development in vocational and technical education: Planning, content, and implementation* (5th ed.). Needham Heights, MA: Allyn & Bacon.

Gall, M.D., Gall, J.P. & Borg, W.R. (2007). *Educational research: An introduction* (8th ed.). Boston, MA: Pearson Education.

Gonczi, A. (Ed.) (1998). *Developing a competent workforce: Adult learning strategies for vocational educators and trainers.* Adelaide, Australia: National Centre for Vocational Education Research (NCVER).

Hawke, G. & Oliver, L. (1998). Assessment in modern vocational education. In Gonczi, A. (Ed.), *Developing a competent workforce: Adult learning strategies for vocational educators and trainers.* Adelaide, Australia: NCVER.

Kelly, M.G. (2000). *National educational technology standards for students: Connecting curriculum and technology.* Eugene, OR: International Society for Technology in Education.

Miller, P.W. (2008). *Measurement and teaching.* Munster, IN: Patrick W Miller and Associates.

Norton, R.E. & Moser, J.R. (2008). *DACUM (Developing a curriculum) handbook* (3rd ed.). Columbus, OH: Center on Education and Training for Employment.

Palomba, A.C. & Banta, W.T. (2001). *Assessing student competence in accredited disciplines: Pioneering approaches to assessment in higher education.* Sterling, VA: Stylus Publishing.

Prosser, C.A. & Allen, C.R. (1925). *Vocational education in a democracy.* New York, NY: Century.

Rauner, F. (2009). TVET curriculum development and delivery. In Maclean, R. & Wilson, D. (Eds.), *International handbook of education for the changing world of work: Bridging academic and vocational learning.* Dordrecht, The Netherlands: Springer.

Scott, J.L. & Sarkees-Wircenski, M. (2004). *Overview of career and technical education* (3rd ed.). Homewood, IL: American Technical Publishers.

Sukmadinata, N.S. (2012). *Metode penelitian pendidikan.* Bandung, Indonesia: PT Remaja Rosdakarya.

Thompson, J.F. (1973). *Foundations of vocational education: Social and philosophical concepts.* Englewood Cliffs, NJ: Prentice-Hall.

van der Klink, M.R. & Streumer, J.N. (2006). The effectiveness of OJT in the context of HRD. In Streumer, J.N. (Ed.), *Work-related learning* (pp. 369–392). Dordrecht, The Netherlands: Springer. appendix

APPENDIX

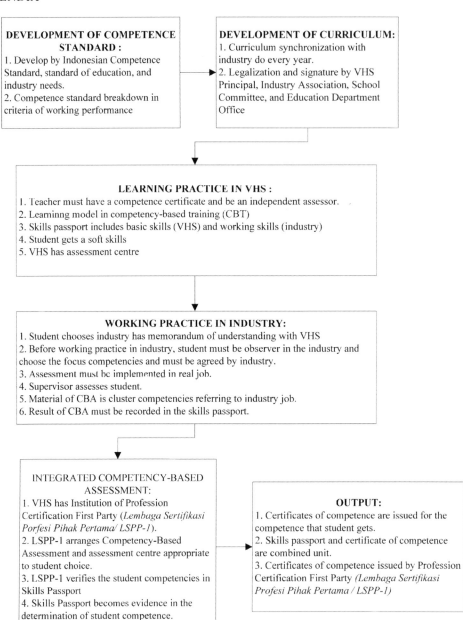

DEVELOPMENT OF COMPETENCE STANDARD :
1. Develop by Indonesian Competence Standard, standard of education, and industry needs.
2. Competence standard breakdown in criteria of working performance

DEVELOPMENT OF CURRICULUM:
1. Curriculum synchronization with industry do every year.
2. Legalization and signature by VHS Principal, Industry Association, School Committee, and Education Department Office

LEARNING PRACTICE IN VHS :
1. Teacher must have a competence certificate and be an independent assessor.
2. Learninng model in competency-based training (CBT)
3. Skills passport includes basic skills (VHS) and working skills (industry)
4. Student gets a soft skills
5. VHS has assessment centre

WORKING PRACTICE IN INDUSTRY:
1. Student chooses industry has memorandum of understanding with VHS
2. Before working practice in industry, student must be observer in the industry and choose the focus competencies and must be agreed by industry.
3. Assessment must be implemented in real job.
4. Supervisor assesses student.
5. Material of CBA is cluster competencies referring to industry job.
6. Result of CBA must be recorded in the skills passport.

INTEGRATED COMPETENCY-BASED ASSESSMENT:
1. VHS has Institution of Profession Certification First Party (*Lembaga Sertifikasi Porfesi Pihak Pertama/ LSPP-1*).
2. LSPP-1 arranges Competency-Based Assessment and assessment centre appropriate to student choice.
3. LSPP-1 verifies the student competencies in Skills Passport
4. Skills Passport becomes evidence in the determination of student competence.

OUTPUT:
1. Certificates of competence are issued for the competence that student gets.
2. Skills passport and certificate of competence are combined unit.
3. Certificates of competence issued by Profession Certification First Party *(Lembaga Sertifikasi Profesi Pihak Pertama / LSPP-1)*

Figure 1.   ICBA flow chart.

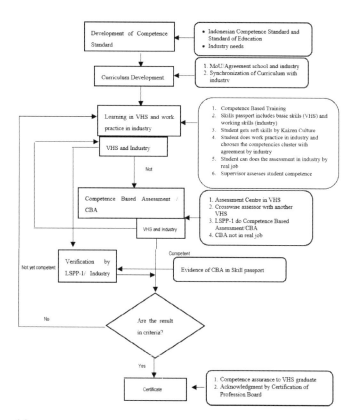

Figure 2.   ICBA model.

Regionalization and Harmonization in TVET – Abdullah et al. (Eds)
© 2017 Taylor & Francis Group, London, ISBN 978-1-138-05419-6

Basic competencies for electrical power engineering in vocational high schools

G. Tjahjono & T. Setiawaty
Program Studi Pendidikan Teknik Elektro, Fakultas Keguruan dan Ilmu Pendidikan,
Universitas Nusa Cendana, Nusa Tenggara Tim., Indonesia

ABSTRACT: This study aims to describe the basic competencies in the electricity sector in the field of electrical power distribution techniques. This study employed the DACUM (developing a curriculum) method of analysis and the Delphi technique. The research sample was the working operatives and technicians of PT PLN (Persero), who were used as a source to obtain data on the technical competence of the electricity sector workforce. The research object was the engineering competencies in the field of electrical energy in the Network Service Area in Yogyakarta Special Territory. The results of the study were that: (1) there are three groups of jobs and 30 components of duty that form the basic field competence in the operation and maintenance sub-competencies of power distribution engineering expertise; (2) there are 150 job tasks that form the basic field competence in the operation and maintenance sub-competencies of power distribution engineering expertise.

1 INTRODUCTION

The Ministry of Energy and Mineral Resources (Keputusan Menteri ESDM Nomor 2053.k/40/MEM/2001, tahun 2001) requires that all professionals in the electricity sector have competency certification. The establishment and enforcement of Power Engineering Competency Standards of Electricity can be described as follows (Keputusan Menteri ESDM Nomor 2052.k/40/MEM/2001, tahun 2001): (1) every technician working in the electricity sector business must have a certificate of competence issued by professional associations and accredited by the Accrediting Commission; (2) to meet the level of competency required, every technician in the electricity sector business needs to take part in education and training carried out by authorized institutions.

As a consequence of these two requirements, it appears that an institution of vocational education (i.e. vocational high schools) should be able to prepare its graduates to compete to achieve jobs in the electricity sector according to the demands of the industry, which means preparing graduates with competency standards in accordance with the demands of labor professionals working in electrification.

Most vocational high school graduates are less able to adjust to changes or developments in science and technology and are not easily retrained in their shortcomings (Depdiknas, 2007). These findings indicate that learning in vocational high school has not seemed to touch on self-development in relation to the adaptability of students. It suggests that the majority of vocational graduates cannot be easily absorbed into the workforce because their capacity is not in accordance with the demands of the working world. It is in terms of the conditions, among other things, that the vocational curriculum needs to be improved, according to the demands of the world of work and national competency standards. Further, it is the need to equip graduates with the ability to adapt to the development of science and technology in the basic competencies of their vocation.

Basic competency is a capability of learners that has to be possessed in certain subjects as an indicator of having developed reference levels of competency (Badan Standar Nasional Pendidikan (BNSP), 2007). The basic competency of vocational high school students is a competency that is required by students in carrying out their studies in order to achieve minimal competence as a graduate in unit-level education. Basic competency includes several components within it, such as tasks, skills, attitudes, values, and the knowledge needed for the success of the task (Finch et al., 1999).

Based on the explanation above, the following issues can be identified: (1) vocational students need a certain level of competency to undertake an internship or a certain expertise in the end unit of vocational education as a preparation to enter the workforce; (2) curriculum or vocational competency standards should be designed in such a way that they address the needs of employment; (3) the industrial world needs a competency in vocational graduates that is in accordance with competency standards in the industrial world, so special concern should be paid to competency in the graduates of vocational schools; (4) vocational high school should be able to prepare its graduates to compete to achieve jobs in the electricity sector according to the demands of the industry, that is, to prepare graduates with competency standards in accordance with the demands of the professional workforce of the electricity sector; (5) an in-depth study of the basic competencies required by vocational high school is required in order to align the learning process more closely and match it with jobs in industry.

2 METHOD

This study used DACUM (developing a curriculum) analysis and in-depth interviews. DACUM analysis is used to carry out a job analysis, while the in-depth interviews were used to deepen the analysis of the work, especially on the subcomponents work activities, through a process of meaningful communication with experts or superiors, which within this case was the manager. To obtain data on the technical competency of the workforce in electrification, the sample for the research were the working operatives and technicians of PT PLN (Persero). The object of the research is the field of engineering competency in electrification expertise in the Service Area Network in Yogyakarta. Data validation was done through validation of the DACUM job analysis tool, which refers to five sets of guidance (Norton & Moser, 2008): (1) the criteria for the participants or expert workers; (2) the criteria for the duty statement; (3) the guidelines for the development of the duty statement; (4) the criteria for the task statement; (5) the criteria for the work activities.

3 RESULT AND DISCUSSION

3.1 Description of basic competence in electricity distribution technical expertise

3.1.1 Occupational cluster
Work on the group profiles for the medium-voltage 20-kilovolt (kV) distribution network showed there are three groups of field work (occupational clusters) that are required to form a basic competence in electricity distribution techniques (see Table 1). These work groups are as follows: (1) operation of the 20 kV network; (2) maintenance of the 20 kV network; (3) handling of medium-voltage network disruption. The symbols for individual work

obligations are A to Z and AA to DD. The group of jobs involved in operation of the 20 kV network are A, B, C, D, E and F. The work group for maintenance of the 20 kV network involves jobs G, H, I, J, K, L, M and N. The work group for handling medium-voltage network disruption involves jobs O, P, Q, R, S, T, U, V, W, X, Y, Z, AA, BB, CC and DD.

3.1.2 Duty components
Group profiling of the field work involved in medium-voltage 20 kV distribution network showed as many as 30 work obligations (duties) being required to establish basic competence in electricity distribution techniques.

3.1.3 Task components
Competency profiles for field engineering on the 20 kV distribution network identified five principal tasks that were needed to form a basic competence in technical electricity distribution as follows: planning the implementation of the work; preparing for the execution of the work; carrying out the work; reporting on the implementation of the work; evaluating the results of the implementation work (see Table 2). The five task components apply to each of the respective obligations of the job (duty); because the field of 20 kV distribution has 30 job obligations, the total number of duties numbers 150 separate jobs that can be assigned and included to form basic competence in electricity distribution techniques.

3.2 Data analysis of basic competence in electricity distribution technical expertise

Analysis of the data refers to the analysis of the content, which is: (1) occupational clusters; (2) duty components; (3) task components.

3.2.1 Occupational clusters
Group work produced as many as three groups of statements of work, building upon ten basic types of equipment used in medium-voltage 20 kV network distribution, which are: (1) medium-voltage networks pole; (2) conductor; (3) insulator; (4) cubicles; (5) air breaker switch (ABSW); (6) load breaker switch (LBS); (7) recloser; (8) sectionalizer; (9) FCO (Fuse Cut-Out); (10) transformer, consisting of 1-phase and 3-phase transformers.

The placement of work groups in column two of Table 1, following the types of equipment used in 20 kV medium-voltage distribution networks shown in column one, produces three main areas of work or groups of job, where each is connected with identified obligations. The obligations identified include: (1) the operation of the 20 kV network— A, B, C, D, E, F; (2) the maintenance of a 20 kV

Table 1. Occupational cluster and duty components of technical skills for electricity distribution competency.

Equipment of medium-voltage 20 kV networks	Occupation cluster	(Job duty/Function)
Medium-Voltage Networks Pole. Conductor. Isolator.	Operation of 20 kV network: A, B, C, D, E, F.	Operation of Cubicle (Outgoing). Operation of Recloser (PBO). Operation of Sectionalizer. Operation of Load Breaker Switch (LBS). Operation of Air Breaker Switch (ABSW). Operation of Fuse Cut-Out (FCO).
Cubicles. Air Breaker Switch (ABSW). Load Breaker Switch (LBS). Recloser. Sectionalizer.	Maintenance of 20 kV network: G, H, I, J, K, L, M, N.	Maintenance of medium-voltage wires without work in a steady-state voltage. Maintenance of ABSW without work in a state-voltage. Maintenance of Isolator without work in a steady-state voltage. Maintenance of Pole (medium voltage). Maintenance of Distribution transformer. Maintenance of Cubicles (Outgoing). Maintenance of Recloser & Sectionalizer. Maintenance of FCO without work in a steady-state voltage.
FCO (Fuse Cut-Out). Transformer: 1-phase; 3-phase.	Trouble-shooting of medium-voltage networks: O, P, Q, R, S, T, U, V, W, X, Y, Z, AA, BB, CC, DD.	Maintenance of Cross Arm without work in a steady-state voltage. Troubleshooting of medium-voltage networks. Troubleshooting of ABSW (air breaker switch). Troubleshooting of distribution transformer without work in a steady-state voltage. Troubleshooting of Breaker Trip. Troubleshooting of SLP (*Saluran Luar Pelayanan – outlet service*) – SMP (*Saluran Masuk Pelayanan – service line*). Troubleshooting of APP (*Alat Pembatas dan Pengukuran – limiting and measuring device*). Demolition of FCO (Fuse Cut-Out) Tap 1 Phase. Substitution of FCO Tap 1 Phase. Demolition of 3-phase Transformer. Replacement of 3-phase Transformer. Installation of 3-phase Transformer. Replacement of CSP (Complete Self-Protection) 1-phase transformer. Demolition of CSP 1-phase Transformer. Installation of CSP 1-phase Transformer. Replacement of Fuse Link.

network—G, H, I, J, K, L, M, N; (3) the handling of disruption to a medium-voltage network—O, P, Q, R, S, T, U, V, W, X, Y, Z, AA, BB, CC, DD.

These three field-derived work groups of the 20 kV medium-voltage distribution network provide a reference to define the components and sub-competency fields of the distribution network. The components refer to the work obligations or job duties. The sub-competencies are the associated work activities, knowledge, tools and work equipment, as well as work attitude.

3.2.2 *Duty components*

The work liabilities produced are built according to the DACUM obligation (duty) guidelines criteria (Norton & Moser, 2008).

There are as many as 30 work obligations in the field of 20 kV distribution network engineering, coded A to DD. The work liability component is part of certain occupational groups. The first working group consists of six work obligations, namely A, B, C, D, E and F. The second work group consists of eight work obligations, namely G, H, I, J,

Table 2. Task components shaping basic employment competence in mechanical electricity distribution expertise.

No.	Plan	Preparation	Implementation	Reporting	Evaluation
1.	Planning for the implementation of the Cubicle (Outgoing) operation.	Preparing for the implementation of the Cubicle (Outgoing) operation.	Implementation of the Cubicle (Outgoing) operation.	Report on the implementation of the Cubicle (Outgoing) operation.	Evaluating the results of the implementation of the Cubicle (Outgoing) operation.
2.	Planning for the implementation of the Recloser operation.	Preparing for the implementation of the Recloser operation.	Implementation of the Recloser operation.	Report on the implementation of the Recloser operation.	Evaluating the results of the implementation of the Recloser operation.
3.	Planning for the implementation of the Sectionalizer operation.	Preparing for the implementation of the Sectionalizer operation.	Implementation of the Sectionalizer operation.	Report on the implementation of the Sectionalizer operation.	Evaluating the results of the implementation of the Sectionalizer operation.
4.	Planning for the implementation of the Load Breaker Switch (LBS) operation.	Preparing for the implementation of the Load Breaker Switch (LBS) operation.	Implementation of the Load Breaker Switch (LBS) operation.	Report on the implementation of the Load Breaker Switch (LBS) operation.	Evaluating the results of the implementation of the Load Breaker Switch (LBS) operation.
5.	Planning for the implementation of the Air Breaker Switch (ABSW) operation.	Preparing for the implementation of the Air Breaker Switch (ABSW) operation.	Implementation of the Air Breaker Switch (ABSW) operation.	Report on the implementation of the Air Breaker Switch (ABSW) operation.	Evaluating the results of the implementation of the Air Breaker Switch (ABSW) operation.
6.	Planning for the implementation of the Fuse Cut-Out (FCO) operation.	Preparing for the implementation of the Fuse Cut-Out (FCO) operation.	Implementation of the Fuse Cut-Out (FCO) operation.	Report on the implementation of the Fuse Cut-Out (FCO) operation.	Evaluating the results of the implementation of the Fuse Cut-Out (FCO) operation.

Table 3. Frequency of key technical skills in electricity distribution competencies.

		Frequency of key competencies						
No.	Job description	01	02	03	04	05	06	07
1	Planning for the implementation of the Cubicle (Outgoing) operation	1	–	66	1	–	1	1
2	Preparing for the implementation of the Cubicle (Outgoing) operation	1	65	1	1	–	–	2
3	Implementation of the Cubicle (Outgoing) operation	1	–	–	2	65	–	2
4	Report on the implementation of the Cubicle (Outgoing) operation	66	–	1	–	–	2	1
5	Evaluating the results of the implementation of the Cubicle (Outgoing) operation	–	–	–	1	–	68	1

Information:
01 – Ability to collect, organize and analyze information.
02 – Ability to communicate ideas and information.
03 – Ability to plan and organize activities.
04 – Ability to work with other people and groups.
05 – Being able to use the ideas and mathematical techniques.
06 – Ability to solve problems.
07 – Being able to use technology.

Table 4. Frequency level of technical skills competency in electricity distribution jobs.

No	Job description	Level		
		01	02	03
1	Planning for the implementation of the Cubicle (Outgoing) operation	2	2	66
2	Preparing for the implementation of the Cubicle (Outgoing) operation	1	68	1
3	Implementation of the Cubicle (Outgoing) operation	3	67	–
4	Report on the implementation of the Cubicle (Outgoing) operation	66	3	1
5	Evaluating the results of the implementation of the Cubicle (Outgoing) operation	2	2	66

Information:
Level 01 – must be able to: (1) implement a process that has been determined; (2) assess quality based on predetermined criteria.
Level 02 – must be able to: (1) manage the process; (2) specify the criteria for evaluating the process.
Level 03 – must be able to: (1) determine the principles and processes; (2) evaluate and remodel process; (3) determine the criteria for evaluating the process.

K, L, M and N. The third work group consists of sixteen work obligations, which are O, P, Q, R, S, T, U, V, W, X, Y, Z, AA, BB, CC and DD.

3.2.3 Task components

The components produced take the form of work tasks built upon statements of the criteria for the duties and the guidelines for the development of the duties (Norton & Moser, 2008).

There are five basic tasks of work in the field of 20 kV medium-voltage distribution networks, which are: planning, preparing, executing, creating reports, and evaluating the implementation of the specific job. The result is 150 component work tasks, coded from A.1, A.2, A.3, A.4 and A.5 through to DD.1, DD.2, DD.3, DD.4 and DD.5.

The frequency of different work levels in the field of 20 kV distribution network competency is shown in Table 4. In general, the planning of the implementation and the evaluation of the results of the implementation operation are the job duties that have the highest frequency of level-03 competencies, which involve: (1) being able to determine the appropriate principles and processes; (2) being capable of evaluating and remodeling the processes; (3) being capable of determining the criteria for evaluating the process.

The job duties that have the highest frequency at the next working level (level-02) are preparing for the implementation, and performing the operation, where operatives should be able to manage the process and determine the criteria for evaluating the process. The job of making a report on the implementation operation has the highest frequency of level-01 competencies, where the operative should be able to implement predefined processes and assess quality based on predetermined criteria.

4 CONCLUSION

The conclusions of this study are that: (1) there are three groups of up to 30 jobs and job liability components forming the basic competences for the fields of operational and maintenance sub-competencies in power distribution engineering expertise; (2) there are as many as 150 job tasks forming the basic competences in the fields of operational and maintenance sub-competencies in power distribution engineering expertise.

ACKNOWLEDGMENTS

The authors would like to thank the work operatives and technicians of PT PLN (Persero), which has provided funding for this research.

REFERENCES

Badan Standar Nasional Pendidikan (BNSP). (2007). *Landasan Pengembangan KTSP.*
Departemen ESDM. (2001). *Keputusan Menteri ESDM Nomor 2052.k/40/MEM/2001, tahun 2001, tentang Standardisasi Kompetensi Tenaga Teknik Ketenagalisrikan.*
Departemen ESDM. (2001). *Keputusan Menteri ESDM Nomor 2053.k/40/MEM/2001, tahun 2001, tentang Penentapan dan Pemberlakuan Standar Kompetensi Tenaga Teknik Ketenagalisrikan.*
Depdiknas. (2007). *Kurikulum KTSP 2007.* http://www.scribd.com/search?cx=007890693382555206581.
Finch, C.R. & Crunkilton, J.R. (1999). *Curriculum development in vocational and technical education.* Needham Heights, MA: Allyn & Bacon.
Norton, R.E. & Moser, J.R. (2008). *DACUM handbook* (3rd ed.). Columbus, OH: Center on Education and Training for Employment.

The Indonesian national competency standards in technical and vocational education and training: An evaluation of policy implementation in Indonesia

M. Sayuti

Ahmad Dahlan University, Yogyakarta, Indonesia

ABSTRACT: To develop the Technical and Vocational Education Training (TVET) system in Indonesia, competency standards have been borrowed globally and implemented as part of the national agenda for skills recognition and qualifications. Little research exists regarding the effectiveness of the implementation of the Indonesian version of competency standards, named Indonesian National Competency Standards (SKKNI), in Indonesian TVET institutions. This study conducted empirical surveys based on comprehensive questionnaires, followed by individual and group semi-structured interviews, as well as the analyses of relevant documents. It involved participants from two types of institutions in Indonesian TVET that were managed by two different ministries, together with implementers from relevant institutions. The first institution type were the Vocational Training Centers (BLKs) of the Ministry of Manpower, which assumed the leadership of the development of the SKKNI policy. The second type were the Vocational Senior Secondary Schools (SMKs) of the Ministry of Education and Culture, which was the main regulator and provider of education and training in education institutions nationally. Our findings revealed that: the policy of SKKNI was poorly established; the resources for implementation of SKKNI (financial, curricular and training workshops) were limited; there was tension and rivalry between the two ministries and a lack of coordination and cooperation in implementation; the commitment of implementers was generally insufficient, although participants from a small number of TVET institutions implementing the SKKNI showed a high commitment to implementation; the support from external stakeholders (industry and the public) was insufficient; teacher disposition was a significant contributor and predictor of teacher performance in implementing two aspects of SKKNI (certification and curricular aspects), with certified teachers showing better disposition and performance in implementing SKKNI.

1 INTRODUCTION

According to the 2003 Act of the National Education System, the basic mission of Vocational Senior Secondary Schools (SMKs) is preparing students for a specific job (Undang-Undang, 2003). However, relevant studies have identified that the unemployment rate of SMK graduates is higher than that of senior high school (*Sekolah Menengah Atas* or SMA) graduates (BPS, 2010, 2013; Chen, 2009; Suryadarma et al., 2007). As a result, the relevance of SMKs have attracted public concern, and the government has been dealing with this challenge for decades (Kemendikbud, 2007, 2011, 2012; Kurnia et al., 2014; Supriadi, 2002). Efforts have been made to improve the relevance of SMK to the jobs market. These efforts have been focused on improving teacher quality, building workshop facilities and developing curriculum relevant to industry demands (Kemendikbud, 2007, 2011, 2012; Kurnia et al., 2014). However, the relevance of SMK to the job market is still problematic. One of the emerging models in improving the relevance

of Technical and Vocational Education and Training (TVET) globally is the introduction of competency standards in its systems (ILO, 2006, 2009; Stanwick, 2009).

In Indonesia, the idea of competency standards was linked to the earlier suggestion of *Paspor Keterampilan* (Skills Passport), which was proposed in 1997 in the document *Keterampilan Menjelang 2020 untuk Era Global* (Skills toward 2020 for a Global Era) from the Ministry of Education and Culture (MoEC) (Supriadi, 2002). However, this proposal was never established or implemented due to the economic and political crisis at the end of the 1990s.

Six years later, a similar agenda of developing the Skills Passport emerged once more, under a different name of 'national competency standards', when the 2003 Manpower Act was promulgated. On this occasion, the resurfacing of the initiative to develop competency standards was led by the Ministry of Manpower (MoM) and not by the MoEC (the ministry that originally proposed the idea of the Skills Passport).

The Ministerial Regulation concerning the Procedure for the Development of the Indonesian National Competency Standards (SKKNI) addresses two main aspects: the first is SKKNI as a framework for certification of profession (also known as certification of competency), and the second is SKKNI as a framework for Competency-Based Education and Training (CBET) (Peraturan, 2012). The 2003 Manpower Act also stipulated the establishment of an implementation agency in the area of SKKNI as an institution responsible for certification of profession (Peraturan, 2007). In August 2004, the Indonesian government put into effect Presidential Regulation No 23 regarding the Indonesian Professional Certification Authority (BNSP) (Peraturan, 2004).

Despite the strong legal standing of the BNSP, which was directly responsible to the Indonesian President, a report by the BNSP noted that the performance of the certification aspect of SKKNI was far from satisfactory. The report showed that ten years after the 2003 promulgation, certification activities involved 19,052 certified assessors across the country, 115 certified master assessors (qualified as a trainer of assessors), and 41 certified lead assessors (qualified as a trainer of assessors and as a chief of certification processes), with a total number of SKKNI certificates awarded of 2,086,688. This number was low compared to the government target of five million certification awards by 2014 (BNSP, 2014a).

In its basic mission of preparing students for a specific job, SMKs have to cope with an unequal distribution in the number of teachers and time allocation for core vocational subjects (the *Produktif* subjects) when compared to the two other subject groups, and the poor quality of training workshops (Kemendikbud, 2012; Wastandar, 2012).

In contrast to SMKs, the *Balai Latihan Kerja* (BLK) vocational training centers established to help senior high school graduates develop specialized skills, which are directly under the auspices of the MoM, have stronger regulations to guide implementation of the two aspects (certification and curriculum) of SKKNI. Government Regulation No 31 (2006) mandates BLKs to implement SKKNI as a resource for CBET and certification of competency as the framework to develop students' competency (Peraturan, 2006). However, reports reveal that the implementation of CBET and certification of competency in BLKs has so far been unsuccessful. Little is known about the factors relating to the failure of the delivery of SKKNI in BLKs, which are under the management of the ministry regulating the policy (the MoM).

The government regulation stated that the development of competency standards in SKKNI should adopt the Regional Model Competency Standards (RMCS) of the International Labour Organization's regional office in Bangkok, Thailand (ILO,

2006). This adoption thereby located the Indonesian SKKNI as part of the regional and global context of the policy. The following section links the development of SKKNI to its international context.

The SKKNI policy has been in place for more than a decade. Regulations for implementation have been developed, implementing agencies have been established and programs related to the curriculum and the certification aspects of the policy have been carried out. Despite these efforts, little is known about its effectiveness because it is very difficult to find reports of how the policy has performed and what the subsequent outcomes of the policy have been.

2 LITERATURE REVIEW

Global interest in National Competency Standards (NCS) and National Qualifications Frameworks (NQF) arose because of a number of political and economic factors. The assumption that employers are in the best position to identify training needs is reflected in the primary role of the private sector in neo-liberal economies (Allais, 2003; Young, 2005). Most of the development of NCS is led by the private sector rather than by unions or governments (Young, 2009). The second political context of the development of NCS/NQF is shown by the initial motive of certifying otherwise unqualified school leavers (Young, 2005); previously, the unqualified workforce only had opportunities for employment in manual jobs. The third political function of the development of NQF is to provide a political instrument to control employers (Young, 2009). The gap between the training sector and the workplace is a persistent problem. NCS/NQF, therefore, switches control from educational providers to employers in the determination of workforce employability (Allais, 2007; Young, 2003).

Much research into NCS/NQF reveals that policy borrowing has extended into the global adoption of NCS (Allais, 2010; Chakroun, 2010; Ernsberger, 2012). The most borrowed model of policy for NQF comes from three countries, England, Scotland and New Zealand, where NQFs have been in place since the 1980s (Young, 2005). Nowadays, more than 138 countries have implemented, or are adopting, NQF into their national policy (Young & Allais, 2013b). Allais (2010) categorizes the adoption of NQF by a country into five stages, which are: (1) a country with official establishment through policy/regulation and a framework for the NQF objective; (2) a country that is in the process of development and implementation of NQF; (3) a country that is exploring how the model of NQF sits within its national context; (4) a country that is considering NQF adoption; (5) a country that has established or is establishing a competency or competency-based framework with different levels and areas.

In Indonesia, as we have already seen, the concept of SKKNI grew from *Paspor Keterampilan* (Skills Passport) that was first proposed in 1997 by the Ministry of Education and Culture (MoEC). The proposal covered four levels of competency, which included international standards, regional standards, national standards and general skills as a passport to work in home and small industries with the emphasis on improving livelihoods in rural and remote areas (Supriadi, 2002, p. 453). However, this proposal did not materialize due to the Indonesian economic and political crisis at the end of the 1990s.

The Indonesian government established a special agency responsible for the implementation of certification of competency under the SKKNI framework. The establishment of the National Authority for Certification of Profession (BNSP) was mandated by the 2003 Manpower Act, Article 18 Paragraph 4. According to a report published in 2014, the BNSP established 113 professional certification bodies (LSPs) in 2013 and increased these to 133 in 2014; the figure was expected to reach 300 in 2015 (BNSP, 2014b). According to the same report, there were 1,715 assessment centers (TUKs), 7,881 assessors and 1,954,858 certificates of competency granted in the period from 2006 to 2013 (Kemenakertrans, 2013).

A study by Allais (2010) identified underlying issues in the implementation of NCS/NQF. The first topic identified was the eminent relationship between competency standards and the qualification framework. In Botswana, there were *'qualifications consisting of parts which could be separately awarded, and which were defined through learning outcomes or competencies'* (Allais, 2010, p. 39). In Sri Lanka, *'there is a seven-level National Vocational Qualification Framework which so far has competency standards for 45 qualifications, based on 63 skills standards'*. In the first instance, the problematic implementation of competency standards as a foundation of qualification was revealed. Thus, in Botswana, the development of competency standards was reported as slow and *'most training providers do not offer courses based on the newly developed standards'* (Allais, 2010, p. 40). A similar problem was reported in South Africa, where *'most of the outcomes-based qualification and unit standards (another term for competency standards) have never been used'*.

In achieving the purpose of the current study, the implementation of SKKNI was evaluated under the lens of the Van Meter and Van Horn (1975) implementation model. In analyzing the implementation process, this model is considered as simpler by virtue of proposing six broad variables, which include standards and objectives, resources, inter-organizational communication, the characteristics of the implementing agencies, the economic, social and political conditions (external factors), and the disposition of implementers (Hill & Hupe, 2002; Van Horn & Van Meter, 1977). In developing their theoretical framework, Van Meter and Van Horn describe themselves as having been 'guided by three bodies of literature' (1975, p. 453). The first is organizational theory, and particularly work on organizational change; the second is studies of the impact of public policy and, in particular, of the impact of judicial decisions and third, some studies of intergovernmental relations (Van Horn & Van Meter, 1977; Van Meter & Van Horn, 1975).

The Van Meter and Van Horn model of implementation analysis extensively utilizes existing studies of policy implementation (Hill & Hupe, 2002; O'Toole, 1986). These include the study by Zeelen et al. (2011) evaluating the implementation of vocational education in South Africa, the study by Harris (2013) evaluating the sport development program in the UK, the study by Webster (2005) of education policy in the USA, the study by Marsh and Walker (2006) of housing policy in the UK, the study of sport policy in Norway by Skille (2008), and the study of Baharom (2008) in evaluating the implementation of human resources development in Malaysian public universities.

3 METHOD OF THE STUDY

The current study consists of quantitative and qualitative components, which provide distinctive approaches in educational policy study. As both components are combined in answering the research questions, the research design can be classified as mixed-method. Creswell and Clark (2011) describe mixed-method research as a mixing procedure for collecting and analyzing quantitative and qualitative research in a single study to understand research problems. The benefit is that mixed methods can provide opportunities for analyzing multidimensional realities through a variety of data resources and data collection techniques (Johnson & Onwuegbuzie, 2004). However, mixed-method research not only combines two different strands of research, it also involves merging, integrating, linking, embedding or mixing quantitative and qualitative data (Creswell et al., 2003).

The quantitative data was collected using questionnaires with teachers at Vocational Training Centers (BLKs) and Vocational Senior Secondary Schools (SMKs). The qualitative data for this study was collected using semi-structured interviews with senior officials in the various relevant institutions (BLKs, SMKs, MoEC, MoM, TUKs, LSPs, BKSP and BNSP) as well as teachers. Interviews were also conducted with the national authorities of the SKKNI in the MoM, the BNSP and a human resources person in the MoEC.

The analysis of the data gathered from the survey method focused on descriptive aspects of samples (descriptive analysis), comparative analyses among the relevant variables, exploratory factor analysis and correlation between the disposition and performance of teachers. The quantitative data analysis for this study included (1) descriptive analysis, (2) exploratory factor analysis, and (3) regression analysis. The four areas of quantitative analysis were facilitated by IBM SPSS (2013, Version 20) statistical software. The analysis of the qualitative data applied thematic analysis using as the coding references the five factors in the implementation process described by Van Meter and Van Horn (1975), and the six conditions of effective implementation conceptualized by Sabatier and Mazmanian.

4 RESULTS

4.1 The macro indicators of implementation performance

At the macro level, the implementation of the SKKNI in two types of TVET institution in Yogyakarta province was found to be ineffective. More than ten years since the promulgation of the policy of SKKNI, only five percent of TVET institutions have established TUKs, all being SMKs and none BLKs. The establishment of a TUK in the TVET sector is regarded as a key indicator of SKKNI policy implementation. There were TUKs in four courses (curriculum clusters of competencies) out of the 45 courses offered in the SMKs (8.89%). Young and Allais (2013) have identified that the success of certification of competency is dependent on the availability of assessment centers and assessors. The limited number of TUKs in TVET institutions in the province indicates that the implementation of SKKNI at institutional level has been ineffective.

The second macro-level indicator for the effectiveness of the implementation was measured by the participation rate of teachers and students in the certification of competency process under SKKNI. After a period of more than ten years since implementation, the number of certified teachers and students was small compared to the total numbers of teachers and students enrolled. The percentage of teachers certified in their area of competency was 37.63% and the percentage of students involved in certification of competency was less than one percent.

4.2 The micro indicator of implementation performance

The effectiveness of the policy at the micro level was measured by assessing teachers' performance in implementing two aspects of SKKNI in their teaching activities. The results from statistical analysis of the questionnaires show that teachers in BLKs and SMKs had, at some level, implemented the certification and curriculum aspects of SKKNI in their teaching activities. However, teachers' performance at this micro level seemed insufficient to facilitate implementation at the institutional (macro) level by, for example, establishing TUKs or sending students for certification. Teachers' performance in implementing SKKNI in the classroom may influence students' competency, but without the establishment of TUKs and professional development/ training courses for teachers, success in implementing the policy is unlikely. Successful implementation of policy requires adequate financial resources, training workshop facilities, and a commitment by teachers/principals/staff to organize these activities and other managerial support.

5 CONCLUSION

The results of the analysis led us to conclude that more than a decade after the promulgation of the SKKNI policy, the implementation has been ineffective. Accordingly, Indonesian TVET sectors have, so far, not received any significant benefit from the promises of the global policy of competency standards, not to mention the impact of the policy on society. Complex problems in the five factors involved in implementation processes have hindered the adoption of SKKNI by the TVET sector as an instrument for improving its relevance to the job market.

The absence of comprehensive study underpinning the policy-making process suggests that the government intended simply to imitate the global trend without making serious commitment and effort to learn how the policy works in other countries. The recent hasty initiative to accelerate the implementation of SKKNI in reaction to the regional free flow of skilled labor under the agreement associated with the Association of South East Asian Nations (ASEAN) Economic Community, which comes into effect in 2015, further demonstrates the frivolous attitude of the government to the policy.

The findings of the current study suggest that policy borrowed from developed countries or an international agency will not be effectively implemented without fulfilling the key implementation factors, including sufficient understanding of the local context and the uniqueness of the policy environment. The analysis of the SKKNI policy implementation process provides an overarching perspective on how a local policy environment affects the ineffectiveness of a borrowed policy.

5.1 Policy implications and recommendations

Given the findings outlined above, three policy recommendations are proposed. First, the conclusion can be drawn from the results reported that the implementation of SKKNI was ineffective because of a poorly formulated policy, inconsistencies in the policy, sectorial ego and inter-ministerial rivalry, and the fragmented authority and management of TVET. The SKKNI policy needs to be reorganized to harmonize with three other interconnected policies (certification of competency, competency-based education and training, and the newly regulated Indonesian Qualification Framework). The reorganization of the four policies may necessitate the development of a prescriptive Law that will harmonize the conflict of interest among the ministries involved and ensure adequate resources are available for successful implementation.

Second, SKKNI policy as an integral part of the four interconnected policies requires review on the basis of research evidence, to address the unique and wide social/cultural/economic/political diversity in Indonesia. A re-established policy could incorporate short- and long-term strategies for implementation which clearly define institutional relationships with authorities in the development of curriculum for training packages, the certification of competency, and the qualification framework too. Third, as in Australia, which has had some success in integrating the management of TVET into TAFE (Technical and Further Education), and the Philippines, which has done the same in TESDA (Technical Education and Skills Development Authority), the integration of the management of Indonesian TVET by 13 ministries into a far simpler management structure is strongly recommended.

5.2 Limitations of the study

The main limitation of this study concerns the attitude of stakeholders from industry in relation to the SKKNI policy. The current investigation did not evaluate comprehension of the policy, intensity of support or industry commitment to it. The second limitation was that the participants in this study were drawn from policy stakeholders of a single Indonesian province and it is unclear whether they were representative of all 34 provinces in Indonesia. The third limitation was the fact that in Indonesia at least 13 ministries and private companies run BLKs and SMKs. This current study, however, only researched the implementation of the SKKNI in BLKs and SMKs, which were run, respectively, by just two ministries, MoM and MoEC.

5.3 Recommendations for future study

With regards to the research findings and the limitations of the study, the following future research is recommended. First, in this study, stakeholders from only two ministries, MoM and MoEC, participated. In fact, 13 ministries manage TVET

institutions in Indonesia. A future investigation should include participants from the other implementing ministries to ensure a more comprehensive picture and a better understanding of their internal policy environments. Second, further research should be conducted to investigate the views from industry in relation to the implementation of SKKNI. Third, further research should be conducted to investigate the implementation of the SKKNI policy in the broader geographical areas of Indonesia that represent great educational and cultural diversity and unique policy environments.

REFERENCES

Allais, S. (2003). The national qualification framework in South Africa: A democratic project trapped in a neoliberal paradigm. *Journal of Education and Work*, 16(3), 305–323.

Allais, S. (2007). *The rise and the fall of NQF: A critical analysis of the South African qualification framework* (unpublished PhD thesis). University of Witwatersrand, Johannesburg, South Africa.

Allais, S. (2010). *The implementation and impact of national qualification frameworks: Report of a study in 16 countries.* Geneva, Switzerland: International Labour Organization.

Baharom, A. (2008). *Organisational determinants of policy implementation: A contextual study of Malaysia and China.* Paper presented at the International Conference on Administrative Experiences and Regional Cooperation in the Era of a Growing China, Institute of China Studies, University of Malaya.

BNSP. (2014a). Status pengembangan & rencana kerja cepat sertifikasi kompetensi profesi [The development status and the rapid plan of certification of competency]. *Sertifikasi Profesi*, 26–33.

BNSP. (2014b). Status pengembangan dan rencana kerja cepat sertifikasi kompetensi profesi [The development status and rapid work plans of certification of profession]. *Sertifikasi Profesi*, 2, 26–33.

BPS. (2010). Keadaan ketenagakerjaan Indonesia Februari 2010 [Indonesia's manpower portrait February 2010]. *XIII*, 1–6.

BPS. (2013). Keadaan ketenagakerjaan Indonesia November 2013 [Indonesia's manpower portrait November 2013]. *XIII*, 1–5.

Chakroun, B. (2010). National qualification framework: From policy borrowing to policy learning. *European Journal of Education*, 45(2), 199–216.

Chen, D. (2009). *Vocational schooling, labor market outcomes, and college entry.* Washington, DC: World Bank. http://dx.doi.org/10.1596/1813-9450-4814

Creswell, J.W. & Clark, V.L.P. (2011). *Designing and conducting mixed methods research.* Los Angeles, CA: Sage.

Creswell, J.W., Clark, V.L.P., Gutmann, M.L. & Hanson, W.E. (2003). An expanded typology for classifying mixed methods research into design. In A. Tashakkori & C. Teddlie (Eds.), *Handbook of mixed methods in social & behavioural research* (pp. 161–196). London, UK: Sage.

Ernsberger, L. (2012). *Implementing national qualification frameworks(s) in India: Challenges of policy planning in the context of human development, the demographic divi-*

dend and the informal sector (MA thesis). London School of Economics, UK.

Harris, S. (2013). *An analysis of the significance of sub-regional partnerships in the community sport policy process* (unpublished PhD thesis). Loughborough University, UK.

Hill, M. & Hupe, P. (2002). *Implementing public policy: Governance in theory and in practice*. London, UK: Sage.

ILO. (2006). *Guidelines for development of regional model competency standards (RMCS)*. Bangkok, Thailand: International Labour Organization Regional Office for Asia and the Pacific.

ILO. (2009). *Making full use of competency standards: A handbook for governments, employers, workers and training organizations*. Bangkok, Thailand: International Labour Organization Regional Office for Asia and the Pacific.

Johnson, R.B. & Onwuegbuzie, A.J. (2004). Mixed methods research: A research paradigm whose time has come. *Educational Researcher*, *33*(7), 14–26.

Kemenakertrans. (2013). *Buku informasi pelatihan dan produktivitas* [*Information book for training and productivity*]. Jakarta, Indonesia: Dirjend Binalattas.

Kemendikbud. (2007). *Rencana strategis Departemen Pendidikan Nasional 2005–2009* [*Strategic plan 2005–2009 of the Department of National Education*]. Jakarta, Indonesia: Pusat Informasi dan Humas Departemen Pendidikan Nasional.

Kemendikbud. (2011). *Rencana strategis Direktorat Jenderal Pendidikan Menengah Kementerian Pendidikan dan Kebudayaan 2010–2014* [*Strategic plan 2010–2014 of the Directorate of Secondary Education, Ministry of Education and Culture*]. Jakarta, Indonesia: Dircktorat Jenderal Pendidikan Menengah.

Kemendikbud. (2012). *Revisi Rencana strategis Direktorat Jenderal Pendidikan Menengah Kementerian Pendidikan dan Kebudayaan 2010–2014* [*The revision of the 2010–2014 strategic plan of the Directorate of Secondary Education, Ministry of Education and Culture*]. Jakarta, Indonesia: Direktorat Jenderal Pendidikan Menengah.

Kurnia, D., Dittrich, J. & Murniati, D.E. (2014). Transferable skills in technical and vocational education and training (TVET) in Indonesia. *TVET@Asia*, *3*, 1–16.

Marsh, A. & Walker, B. (2006). Getting a policy to "stick": Centralising control of social rent setting in England. *Policy & Politics*, *34*(2), 195–217.

O'Toole, L.J. (1986). Policy recommendation for multi-actor implementation: An assessment of the field. *Journal of Public Policy*, *6*(2), 181–210.

Peraturan. (2004). Peraturan Pemerintah tentang BNSP [The Government Regulation about National Certification Authority], Nomor 23, 2004.

Peraturan. (2006). Peraturan Pemerintah tentang SILATKERNAS [The Government Regulation about National Training System for Work], Nomor 31, 2006.

Peraturan. (2007). Peraturan Menteri Tenaga Kerja dan Transmigrasi tentang Tata Cara Penetapan SKKNI [The Decision of the Ministry of Manpower and Transmigration about the Procedure of the Development of National Competency Standards], Nomor 21, 2007.

Peraturan. (2012). Peraturan Menteri Tenaga Kerja dan Transmigrasi tentang Tata Cara Penetapan SKKNI [The Regulation of the Ministry of Manpower and Transmigration about the Procedure of the Development of National Competency Standards], Nomor 8, 2012.

Skille, E.A. (2008). Understanding sport clubs as sport policy implementers: A theoretical framework for the analysis of the implementation of central sport policy through local and voluntary organizations. *International Review for the Sociology of Sport*, *43*(2), 181–200.

Stanwick, J. (2009). Modularization and modular delivery of TVET. In R. Maclean & D.N. Wilson (Eds.), *International handbook of education for the changing world of work: Bridging academic and vocational learning* (pp. 2793–2809). Bonn, Germany: Springer.

Supriadi, D. (Ed.) (2002). *Sejarah pendidikan teknik dan kejuruan di Indonesia: Membangun manusia produktif* [*The history of the Indonesian vocational and technical education: Developing productive manpower*]. Jakarta, Indonesia: Departemen Pendidikan Nasional.

Suryadarma, D., Suryahadi, A. & Sumarto, S. (2007). *Reducing unemployment in Indonesia: Results from a growth-employment elasticity model*. Jakarta, Indonesia: SMERU Research Institute. Retrieved from http://www.eaber.org/sites/default/files/documents/SMERU_Suryadarma_07_2.pdf

Undang-Undang. (2003). *Sistem Pendidikan Nasional* [*National Education System Act*]. Jakarta, Indonesia: Presiden Republik Indonesia.

Van Horn, C.E. & Van Meter, D.S. (1977). The implementation of intergovernmental policy. In S.S. Nagel (Ed.), *Policy studies review annual* (pp. 97–120). London, UK: Sage.

Van Meter, D.S. & Van Horn, C.E. (1975). The policy implementation process: A conceptual framework. *Administration & Society*, *6*(4), 445–488.

Wastandar, W. (2012). *Program Direktorat Pembinaan Pendidik dan Tenaga Kependidikan Pendidikan Menengah* [*The programs of the Directorate of Secondary Teachers*]. Retrieved from http://dikmen.kemdikbud.go.id/rkkal/ARAH%20KEBIJAKAN%20P2TK%20DIKMEN%20-%202015.pdf.

Webster, K.A., Sr. (2005). *Parental involvement: Perception of how Section 1118 of No Child Left Behind is being implemented in New Orleans public schools* (unpublished PhD dissertation). The University of Minnesota.

Young, M. (2003). National qualifications frameworks as a global phenomenon: A comparative perspective. *Journal of Education and Work*, *16*(3), 223–237.

Young, M. (2005). *National qualifications frameworks: Their feasibility for effective implementation in developing countries*. Geneva, Switzerland: International Labour Organization.

Young, M. (2009). National qualifications frameworks: An analytical overview. In R. Maclean & D.N. Wilson (Eds.), *International handbook of education for the changing world of work: Bridging academic and vocational learning* (pp. 2867–2880). Bonn, Germany: Springer.

Young, M. & Allais, S.M. (2013a). Options for designing an NVQF for India. In M. Young & S.M. Allais (Eds.), *Implementing national qualifications frameworks across five continents* (pp. 243–267). London, UK: Routledge.

Young, M. & Allais, S.M. (2013b). Preface. In M. Young & S.M. Allais (Eds.), *Implementing national qualifications frameworks across five continents* (p. 1). London, UK: Routledge.

Zeelen, J., Rampedi, M. & de Jong, G. (2011). Adult education in the Limpopo province of South Africa: Challenges for policy implementation. *International Journal of Lifelong Education*, *30*(3), 385–402.

Regionalization and Harmonization in TVET – Abdullah et al. (Eds)
© 2017 Taylor & Francis Group, London, ISBN 978-1-138-05419-6

An analysis of determinants and obstacles of vocational high school students' internships

R.I. Rokhmawati & S.A. Wicaksono
Fakultas Ilmu Komputer, Universitas Brawijaya, Jawa Timur, Indonesia

ABSTRACT: Vocational high school students find difficulties in applying for standardized professional jobs. The Indonesian government has a program that implements internship called Dual System Education (PSG). One objective of the internship is that students acquire professional skills through practical work in industry, so that they have professional expertise and are able to compete in applying for jobs. Internship placements for vocational high school students often do not match the student's competence. This study invokes person–job matching theory to help students identify their characteristics in accordance with an occupation, in order to achieve a reasonable match between person and career. The exercise of this theory will reveal the determinant factors and obstacles around vocational high school students' internships, which is the main purpose of this study. This study is descriptive research that involves students, teachers and stakeholders.

1 INTRODUCTION

The Indonesian government has a program called Dual System Education (PSG), which is implemented through internships as a joint program between vocational high schools and industry, as is implemented in the industrialized world. The vocational curriculum states, 'internship is a pattern organizer training program run jointly by the vocational high school with industry/professional associations as institutional partners, with planning, implementation, evaluation and certification as an integral program using a variety of alternative forms of execution, such as day release, block release, and so forth'. It means that implementation of Dual System Education is an integral part of the whole implementation of national policy regarding link and match in vocational high school. However, current implementations of internships show that the results are not good enough, with low levels of knowledge assimilation and low relevance (Yani, 2013). Yet, vocational students often face various obstacles in the internship application process. Internship placement often does not match the students' competence (Ningsih et al., 2012). Nevertheless, feedback from carrying out the pilot work of the modern internship system should improve the quality of vocational education and point in the direction of promoting better employment of vocational high school students (Shi & Sun, 2016).

Vocational high school students face the real world after three years of study and they must prepare themselves for getting jobs in industry. Through internships, vocational high schools have a role in ensuring that students' competencies match industry's needs. However, the reality shows that many students admitted to university after graduating from school also had no qualified job target, exacerbated by the structure of the school education and curriculum systems setting unreasonable expectations (Shi & Sun, 2016). They found that after graduation they faced a gap between their knowledge and industry's demands. Consequently, it is hard to find a match for professional work.

Malang is often referred to as a vocational education city because the ratio of vocational and senior high schools is 50:50 in both public and private schools (Pemerintah Kota Malang, 2015). A total of 55.7% of vocational high schools in Malang have at least four ICT skills programs, including Software Engineering (RPL), Computer and Network Engineering (TKJ), Multimedia, and Animation (Direktorat Pembinaan SMK, 2015). Software Engineering (RPL) and Computer and Network Engineering (TKJ) are the most popular ICT skills programs in Malang, and both give Malang the potential to have graduates who are competent in IT. However, stakeholders make a different assessment of the vocational students' competence during their internships.

Students who do not have well-defined career planning during their learning in vocational high school have no goal or motivation. That means that the students' comprehension skills do not mature. This is the reason why this research has involved students, teachers, and stakeholders in examining determinants and obstacles of vocational high school students' internships, seeking to base its conclusions on all three points of view.

The theory of person–job matching is based on personal subjective conditions, which means that individuals have certain possibilities of having jobs. In the matching phase, a person can select a job suitable for their personal career (Shi & Sun, 2016). Person–job matching is also known as person–job fit. Person–job fit is defined as the degree to which an individual's knowledge, preferences, activities and skills match the job requirements (Bhat, 2014). 'Fit' or 'match' can also refer to the individual's fit with their organization, with the work team they are a member of, with the physical and cultural environment they work in, and with the actual work they are required to do (Latham, 2007). Person–job matching helps individuals find their characteristics consistent with an occupation, in order to achieve a reasonable match between people and career. The importance of this theory is that improving person–job matching or fit can improve psychological antecedents of work performance, such as job satisfaction (Latham, 2007) and employee retention (Bhat, 2013). In this case, by the use of person–job matching, students, schools and stakeholders can define what they actually do, what they feel, and what they expect from internship placements. These conditions can be used as the basis for defining the determinants and obstacles that will lead to identification of the system requirements for a decision support system for vocational high school students' internship placements.

Henceforth, the number of students who have lacked the opportunity to select their desired internship places could be considered. It would also be easier for schools to determine criteria for internship placement in accordance with student needs and the internships available. For stakeholders or CEOs, they would be better able to provide jobs that match students' abilities.

2 METHOD

The method used in this research is mixed-method using quantitative and qualitative surveys. Quantitative survey is used to reveal the students' perceptions of internship implementation by using a questionnaire. Qualitative survey is used to reveal teachers' and stakeholders' perceptions of the implementation of internship based on interviews. The results from the questionnaires and interviews are divided into two types, considering the determinants and obstacles of vocational high school students' internships.

The population for this research was all of the vocational high schools in Malang. The study used purposive sampling in relation to two types of internship placement system, one determined by the vocational high school and one by students themselves, so two vocational high schools were selected that were implementing the different systems. The sample for this research was 100 students, two teachers, and two CEOs of a software

house that represents a stakeholder. The students involved in this study were students who had been carrying out an internship.

3 RESULTS AND DISCUSSION

3.1 *Vocational high school teachers' point of view*

Data was produced from two kinds of school: those that are implementing internship placement systems determined by the vocational high school (School A), and those in which the internship placement system is determined by the students (School B). According to the interview with the headmaster, School A places students based on test scores achieved during classes. Usually, there is a separate unit that handles the internship placement. Schools with this system have partnerships with multiple stakeholders. With this system, the school has more flexibility to set the priorities recommended for the students. For those students with less satisfactory test scores, the system is less accommodating of their needs, even though they may have certain preferences and talents that cannot be judged simply by test scores.

The system in School B was similar. However, the difference is that School B still provides an opportunity for students to choose an internship placement. The weakness in this system is that students tend to choose an undemanding internship that lacks challenge. Such a decision was often taken because they did not understand their talents. In this situation, students need the teacher to act in the role of a counselor to help them identify their talents. The result of the students' learning progress is measured according to reports from the internship. These reports do not have any measurement of feedback from the students about their satisfaction and any obstacles encountered during the internship. In order to get more information about this, data were identified and elicited from the students.

3.2 *Vocational high school students' point of view*

Data were gathered for the students' perceptions of the two kinds of majors, Software Engineering (RPL) and Computer and Network Engineering (TKJ), by using questionnaires. There were 50 students from both majors that represented the internship placement system determined by the vocational high school (School A), and 50 students that represented the internship placement system determined by the students (School B). Questionnaires used a 1–4 Likert scale to express their opinions from 'Strongly disagree' to 'Strongly agree'. Table 1 shows students' perceptions of the implementation of internships.

Using Table 1, our analysis was derived from the best practices in each type of system. For School

Table 1. Students' perceptions of internships.

No.	Aspect	School A	School B
1	The process of registering an internship is complicated.	70% disagree (2 on scale) 30% agree (3 on scale)	50% disagree (2 on scale) 50% strongly agree (4 on scale)
2	Basic skill test before internship acceptance.	78% not required (1 on scale) 12% strongly required (4 on scale)	52% not required (1 on scale) 48% strongly required (4 on scale)
3	Internship placement is appropriate to students' expectation.	72% disagree (2 on scale) 28% agree (3 on scale)	64% disagree (2 on scale) 36% strongly agree (4 on scale)
4	Students' competences are appropriate to industry needs.	88% disagree (2 on scale) 12% agree (3 on scale)	86% disagree (2 on scale) 14% strongly agree (4 on scale)
5	Students involved in project during internship.	84% never (1 on scale) 16% always (4 on scale)	86% never (1 on scale) 14% always (4 on scale)
6	Students invited to create product during internship.	90% seldom (2 on scale) 10% often (3 on scale)	86% seldom (2 on scale) 14% always (4 on scale)
7	Students guided on working attitude.	10% disagree (2 on scale) 90% strongly agree (4 on scale)	1% disagree (2 on scale) 86% strongly agree (4 on scale)

A systems, 70% of students found the registration process easy, because their schools organize internship placement. However, in both systems the students wanted to be given the opportunity to choose the internship placement. This is evident from the results of the third question, which indicates that a majority of students are less than satisfied with the results of their placement. Students need to be accustomed to knowing basic skills from the curriculum well. In reality, they face the gap between their own capabilities and the industry needs. Thus, they need to really understand and perform those basic skills from the curriculum well. The lack of ability means that industry rarely involves students in their projects. Instead, students are generally given regular and low-risk jobs, such as entering data, helping pay for the project, etc. Students need ICT basic skills, because some of the industrial placements involve the students in creating useful products. During the internship, students are also taught about working attitude, so this also needs to be prepared in advance. In fact, students have

several considerations in choosing internship places, including whether internships involve jobs that fit their abilities, whether their friends join the same internship, whether the internship location is close to home (Koh & Chew, 2015), and opportunities to be involved in projects. They also hope that if the internship goes well, they could be recruited as an employee. Difficulties include adapting when faced with a project, the challenge of being disciplined, and the lack of information about the job opportunities that are relevant to their basic skills. Students hope that the internships will condition their skills so that they are ready for work, so the parameters of internship placement are not only based on test scores, but other technical matters too.

3.3 Stakeholders' point of view

According to the results of interviews, there are two types of reason why CEOs accept students for internships. First, a software house may require many human resources for a project which is incoming (at Place A). Second, it gives students an illustration of working conditions and challenges (at Place B). Table 2 shows stakeholders' perceptions about the implementation of internships.

In addition to the conditions described in Table 2, the industry wants students to understand their other talents, beyond their basic skills. For example, students of software engineering need not always be programmers, but can also become UI designers. The important thing is that students work with their passion, so that they work without feeling pressured (Latham, 2007). In fact, there are many areas of IT expertise can be tried by the students. But inadequate information means that the students do not have a lot of ideas of how to enhance their skills (Feng & Zheng, 2010).

3.4 Analysis of system requirement

Based on the needs and the activity stream obtained from teachers, students and stakeholders (Kaub et al., 2016), this study can identify several determinants and obstacles which have a role in vocational high school students' internships. There are six determinant factors.

First, the school's procedure to determine internship placement. Several schools implement an internship placement system that is determined by the vocational high school, and several use an internship placement system that is determined by students.

Second, partnerships between schools and multiple stakeholders. Industrial partnerships will affect a school's decision to provide recommendations for their students. The partnership also determines the amount of opportunities available to students to be accepted or otherwise in a company (Ningsih et al., 2012).

Table 2. Stakeholders' perceptions of internships.

No.	Aspect	Place A	Place B
1	Stakeholder preferences	Availability of project that can be done.	CEO's spare time and students' basic skills.
2	The process of registering an internship	Students submit a proposal or portfolio;	CEO got a recommendation from a teacher or school;
		Basic skill test required for certain roles.	Basic skill test required for certain roles.
3	Length of time	Minimum of six months or more.	Flexible and adjust the prescribed time.
4	Student involvement in the project	Involve students in the project or give low-risk/regular jobs.	Does not involve students but invites to create product.
5	Obstacles	Gap between knowledge and industrial demand;	Gap between knowledge and industrial demand;
		Students don't have good attitude to work.	Students don't have good attitude to work.
6	Allocation of internship students	At least two students each year.	No allocation.
7	Opportunities to be employee	Give an opportunity for students who qualified.	Give an opportunity for students who qualified.

Third, the process of registering an internship. This factor can be broken down into parameters such as need proposal or need recommendation, need basic skill test or not, etc.

Fourth, student preferences, such as basic skills and other skills required, involvement in a project or learning to create a product, the location of the internship, and the recommendation of friends recommendation, all of which is relevant to person–job matching theory (Bhat, 2014).

Fifth, the length of time of the internship. Some companies have decided upon a minimum length of time for internships of six months or more. However, some companies were more flexible and adjusted the prescribed time.

Sixth, the opportunity to become a permanent employee. This factor was not directly affected by the placement. However, it can be considered when many graduates of vocational high school become employees of a company (Feng & Zheng, 2010).

All of these factors can be used as a reference in determining the functional requirements of a decision support system for vocational high school students' internship placements.

The obstacles that arise during internships include, among others, students' tendency to choose unde-

manding internships and a lack of challenge because they do not fully understand their other skills. It turns out that students' preferences are diverse. There are students who are willing and capable of being involved in projects. On the other hand, there are students who prefer to work on creative ideas. Students don't have good attitudes to aspects of work such as discipline and good communication with clients. Schools must prepare students' basic skills and attitudes to work before internships are implemented.

4 CONCLUSION

There are six main determinant factors in internship placement: (1) the school's procedure for determining internship placement; (2) the partnerships between a school and multiple stakeholders; (3) the process of registering an internship; (4) student preferences; (5) the length of the internship; (6) the opportunity to become an employee. These six factors can be used as a reference in determining the functional requirements of a decision support system for vocational high school students' internship placement.

Obstacles during internship include students tending to opt for undemanding internships and a lack of challenge, the diversity of students' preferences, and the poor attitude to work of some students.

REFERENCES

Bhat, Z.H. (2013). Examining the relationship between P-O fit and turnover intentions. *PARIPEX—Indian Journal of Research, 3*(5), 158–159.
Bhat, Z.H. (2014). Job matching—The key to performance. *International Journal of Research in Organizational Behavior and Human Resource Management, 2*(4), 257–269.
Direktorat Pembinaan SMK. (2015). Data Pokok SMK Kota Malang.
Feng, S. & Zheng, B. (2010). Imperfect information, on-the-job training, and the employer size–wage puzzle: Theory and evidence. *IZA Discussion Papers, 4998,* 2–48.
Kaub, K., Karbach, J., Spinath, F.M. & Brünken, R. (2016). Person–job fit in the field of teacher education. *Teaching and Teacher Education, 55,* 217–227.
Koh, M.F. & Chew, Y.C. (2015). Intelligent job matching with self-learning recommendation engine. *Procedia Manufacturing, 3,* 1959–1965.
Latham, G.P. (2007). Work motivation: History, theory, research and practice. London, UK: Sage.
Ningsih, P.W., Lusiani, T. & Nurcahyawati, V. (2012). Rancang Bangun Sistem Informasi Praktek Kerja Industri Berbasis Web. *Jurnal Sistem Informasi Komputer Akuntansi, 1*(1).
Pemerintah Kota Malang. (2015). Jumlah SMA dan SMK di Malang Kota.
Shi, H. & Sun, S. (2016). Research on the person–job matching of vocational college students based on Java. *ICASET,* 432–435.
Yani, A.T. (2013). *Pelaksanaan PSG di SMKN 15 Bandung* (S2 thesis, p. 35). Universitas Pendidikan Indonesia.

Skill and personal development

Regionalization and Harmonization in TVET – Abdullah et al. (Eds)
© 2017 Taylor & Francis Group, London, ISBN 978-1-138-05419-6

Life-skill education model for empowering elderly people

A. Hufad, J.R. Pramudia & M.I. Hilmi
Department of Non-formal Education, Education Sciences Faculty, Universitas Pendidikan Indonesia, Jawa Barat, Indonesia

ABSTRACT: A demographic bonus is indicated by the increasing number of elderly people and life expectancy of a community. Having a large amount of experience, skills and wisdom, it is important for the elderly to maintain their productivity. Therefore, a constructive effort is required. This research aims to find ways for the elderly to maintain participation in the community without being a burden to the family. Likewise, a life-skill intervention program was administered to maintain the independence of the elderly. This study discusses the raw food material processing training provided to the elderly people as a lifelong-learning education process.

1 INTRODUCTION

The process of becoming old must be subject to intervention to produce optimal results. In general, there are two categories of behavior in facing the aging process, that is, conscious acceptance of the old age and refusal of the reality of becoming old (Hurlock, 2002). The latter behavior lowers the quality of life, both physically and spiritually, bearing in mind the reducing physical conditions that no longer support the individuals' quality of life. Therefore, positive behavior is important to people who are at a more advanced stage of the aging process. Likewise, attendance at life-skill training that suits the ability and needs of the elderly grows their acceptance and the purposefulness of their old age.

Education and training provide independent learning opportunities that enable individuals to discover their potential and develop their learning needs. In other words, education allows individuals to create their characters. Government Regulation No. 43 of 2004 mandates the development of a life-long learning process for the elderly to be coordinated by the government, along with the community, to empower the elderly so that they maintain their social function and actively participate in the community. Despite the regulation, the current education process pays little attention to the education of the elderly and mainly focuses on the education of young children and women.

Independence is vital to the elderly so that they may conduct their daily activities and maintain their productivity (Surprayogi, 2009). The amount of experience and knowledge that are gained through their productive years are, indeed, examples for the younger generation. To that end, independence (Coombs & Ahmed, 1984) means being able to physically, mentally, emotionally and financially fulfill all aspects of life. Independence is also the freedom to act, not to rely on other people, not to be influenced by other people, and the freedom to determine one's life purpose.

There is a significant amount of research on the empowerment of the elderly. To name a few examples, the Faculty of Sociology and Social Work at the University of Bucharest created an adaptive strategy to empower the elderly socially and medically by studying the trends in the demography of the elderly (Nistor, 2014). Interestingly, the Institute for Health Research at Lancaster University developed an inclusive model of caring for the elderly in which the empowerment of the elderly is gained through the caring itself (Milligan, 2006). Meanwhile, the Department of Nursing, at the Ehime Prefectural University of Health Sciences in Japan, studied the importance of family participation in the empowerment of the elderly (Nomura et al., 2009).

2 METHOD

The study of education models to empower the elderly is qualitative in nature. The condition and behavior of the elderly are described. Likewise, the result of the life-skill training is explained. The data were obtained from field notes, observations, documentation, and interviews.

3 RESULT AND DISCUSSION

The life-skill education model that was implemented in the study was constructed from the need analysis of the Ash-Shoodiq Community Learning Center. Figure 1 depicts the education model.

In a good society, there are strategies to empower each other. (Ife, 2008). The empowering process aims at elevating the ability and power of the unprivileged groups. There are three unprivileged groups. The first group is determined by class (the poor, the unemployed, the low-salaried, and the social security recipients), gender (women), and race (the local minority). The second group consists of the elderly, the young, the disabled, and the homosexual/lesbian community, as well as remote and isolated communities. The last group is those who suffer from personal problems such as losing loved ones, loneliness, dealing with family problems, suffering from identity crises and sexual problems.

Focusing on elevating the ability and power of the elderly, this training model begins with initial research to thoroughly understand the needs of the community and ends with three types of outcome, namely short-term, medium-term and long-term. Initial study of community learning shows that most of the elderly were highly dependent on their family members. This is due to the fact that their education level was low so that they were lacking in knowledge and were not confident in communication. As a result, their productivity was low and insufficient to make ends meet. They have, therefore, been relying on their families for support.

Aside from the aforementioned problems faced by the elderly, there are various amounts of environmental and social potential that support their empowerment. The environment in which this study was conducted was fortunate that it has been producing high-quality natural produce, especially cassava. In fact, cassava has been the staple food of the community. The tradition of consuming cassava has been transferred from generation to generation for decades. Therefore, cassava is highly valued by community members. The environment and surroundings were also suitable as a tourism destination. Meanwhile, a community learning center has been established to initiate and support the empowerment of the community. Moreover, community members were found to have a significant level of empathy and made a contribution to the empowerment process.

As far as the purpose of the study is concerned, the training aims at making the elderly independent, at least enough to meet their basic needs. Therefore, the inputs to this program were: 1) skilled and experienced instructors who have networks to support the learning process; 2) a program manager to manage the conduct of the training program; 3) program liaison to assist with the post-training program in which counseling is given to community members; 4) a suitable budget; 5) infrastructure and facilities, such as classrooms and teaching resources.

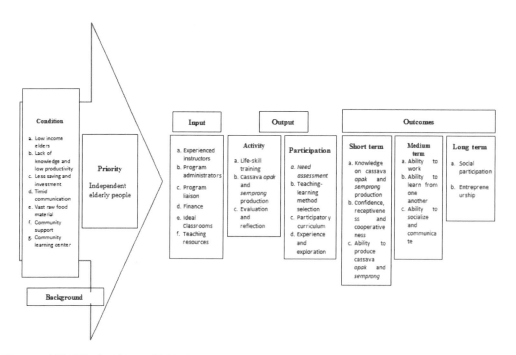

Figure 1.   Life-skill education model for elderly people *(Logic Model Adaptation)*.

Given the presence of high-quality cassavas and the highly valued traditions associated with them, the learning activity focused on innovating around the reputable raw food material to create high-quality traditional snacks. The traditional snacks are the *opak*, or cracker, and *semprong* – a crunchy thin cookie. The community, in fact, have preserved the traditional recipes for generations. The learning activity also focused on the evaluation and assessment of the learning process.

Following the learning activities are the participation aspects which cover the need assessment, the use of suitable learning methods, the curriculum and market potential, as well as the learning activity that explores the community members' learning experience as part of the learning principles of andragogy.

The last component of the education model for the elderly concerns the outcomes. The first of these is the short-term outcome that focuses on cognitive, affective and psychomotor skills. In this case, the cognitive skill is the skill to process the cassava into the *opak* and *semprong*. The affective skills are the confidence, the broad-mindedness, and the ability to cooperate with peers that result from the training.

The second of the outcomes is the medium-term one that results in the ability of the elderly to apply their knowledge, behaviors and skills so that they are able to work, to educate those who are in need, and to interact with their surroundings. The last outcome is a long-term outcome in the form of the active participation of the elderly in social activity. Moreover, the elders are expected to utilize the life skills acquired to develop their own businesses and educate their peers.

4 CONCLUSION

Life-skill education for the elderly is important in creating independence. The education model is constructed according to the community's need and the available local resources to establish independence, reduce reliance, and help make ends meet financially.

REFERENCES

Coombs, P.H. & Ahmed, M. (1984). *Memerangi Kemiskinan di Pedesaan Melalui Pendidikan Nonformal*. Terjemahan. Jakarta, Indonesia: Rajawali Press.

Hurlock, E.B. (2002). *Psikologi Perkembangan: Suatu Pendekatan Sepanjang Rentang Kehidupan*. Surabaya, Indonesia: Erlangga.

Ife, J. (2008). *Community development*. Yogyakarta, Indonesia: Pustaka Pelajar.

Milligan, C. (2006). Caring for older people in the 21st century: 'Notes from a small island'. *Health & Place Journal, 12*, 320–331.

Nistor, G. (2014). New educational strategies regarding quality of life for elderly people. *Procedia-Social and Behavioral Sciences Journal, 142*, 487–492.

Nomura, M., et al. (2009). Empowering older people with early dementia and family caregivers: A participatory action research study. *International Journal of Nursing Studies, 46*, 431–441.

Peraturan Pemerintah Republik Indonesia Nomor 43 Tahun 2004 *Pelaksanaan Upaya Peningkatan Kesejahteraan Sosial Lanjut Usia*. 18 Oktober 2004. Lembaran Negara Republik Indonesia Tahun 2004 Nomor 144. Jakarta.

Suprayogi, U. (2009). *Pendidikan Bagi Masyarakat Lanjut Usia*. Bandung, Indonesia: Rizqi Press.

Developing national core standard for TVET personnel in the Malaysian education system

A. Ismail, R. Hassan, M.M. Mohamad & D.I. Rosli
Faculty of Technical and Vocational Education and Training, Universiti Tun Hussein Onn Malaysia, Batu Pahat, Johor, Malaysia

ABSTRACT: This study centered on the implementation of a national core standard for TVET (Technical and Vocational Education and Training) personnel, especially teachers in Malaysian TVET institutions. Descriptive and open-ended survey methods were adopted for this study from TVET institutions in Malaysia. The findings showed that Malaysia has a unique certification called Vocational Training Operation (VTO) made to purpose for the TVET trainer. The contents of this program encompass both technical and skills training. However, there are certain issues that need to be taken into account in order to propose this certification as a requirement to become a TVET teacher. It was recommended that the government, TVET institutions and other stakeholders should give more recognition to the national core standard for TVET teachers as the main criteria to select a qualified TVET teacher.

1 INTRODUCTION

Teaching standards are simply defined as evaluation points for teachers' performance. Underpinning this idea of teaching standards within literature on teacher education is the notion of teacher competence (Pauline, Noor & Kung, 2012). Research in teacher education has shown that teacher competence is a prerequisite to effective teaching and learning because of its strong relationship to students' learning outcomes, be it academic or otherwise. The Malaysian Teaching Standard (MTS) is based on the assumption that improving teacher competence will ensure that high standards of education are achieved not only academically, but also in other areas of development. The question is whether improving teaching competence alone is enough to achieve educational excellence especially in TVET. This statement forms the center of this paper, and the concerns raised through critical observation of teachers' capability triggers the framework of effective standard.

Based on the MTS, there are three major components: (1) Professional Teaching; (2) Knowledge and Understanding; and (3) Teaching and Learning Skills. Standard 1 consists of three domains which are personal, professional and social. In the aspects of Standard 2, a teacher should be knowledgeable in the objective of the education, the subject's content, Information and Communication Technology (ICT), teaching strategy and the assessment. Standard 3 covers the aspect of teaching preparation, skill to deliver the teaching and learning, assessment skill to increase student achievement and skill in controlling the class. An enhancement to this standard could be made by emphasizing skills relevant to TVET teacher ideal competencies.

The main underlying issues and problems found in this study are: (1) Many instructors lack competency as there is no framework (or competency profile) which has been developed for TVET teachers, (2) the study course for TVET teachers does not provide the practical pedagogical skills required by the teacher during their real job, and (3) there is no current framework or path in training being developed for instructors.

2 OBJECTIVE

The general objective of this study is to identify the practices of the Malaysian current system in developing and implementing their national core standard for TVET personnel which will be used as inputs in developing core standards for TVET teachers. The specific objectives for this study are to identify the development and implementation of national TVET personnel core standards of Malaysia.

3 METHOD

In this study, primary data were gathered from three main TVET providers in Malaysia. Primary data was obtained directly from respondents via a written questionnaire. 101 respondents from these three ministries were successfully traced and responded. This study employed quantitative analysis.

4 CURRENT ISSUE

The teacher or educator is responsible for the development of learners into knowledgeable and able people who are well-equipped and prepared for the nation's development. There are many criteria of a good teacher. In TVET, teachers are sometimes known as trainers, and they should have a certain ability in technical and vocational skills. TVET teaching competencies are defined as an integrated set of technical competency, learning and methodological competency, and human and social competency all of which are needed for effective performance in various teaching contexts and didactic approaches (Spottl, 2009). These three clusters are the basic components of the holistic 'K-worker' produced in Malaysia and were adopted from the above definition.

Ninety-eight competencies were identified in both the literature review and the focus group discussion method. These competencies reflect the range of attitudes, attributes, knowledge, and strategic and tactical skills that were are by electrical instructors (Ali, Kaprawi & Razally, 2010). The concern today is not so much about the value and importance of VTE but how to ensure its relevance, responsiveness and value in an increasingly global economy (Law, 2007).

Norton (1987) describes five essential elements of a CBT system: a) competencies to be achieved are carefully identified, verified and made public in advance, b) criteria to be used in assessing achievement and the conditions under which achievement will be assessed are explicitly stated and made public in advance, c) the instructional program provides for the individual development and evaluation of each of the competencies specified, d) assessment of competency takes the participant's knowledge and attitudes into account but requires actual performance of the competency as the primary source of evidence, and e) participants progress through the instructional program at their own rate by demonstrating the attainment of the specified competencies.

A competency model describes the combination of knowledge, skills and characteristics needed to effectively perform a role in an organization and is used as a human resource tool for selection, training and development, appraisal and succession planning. Identifying and mapping these competencies is rather complex. Skills can range from highly concrete proficiency like the ability to operate a particular machine or to write a sentence, to far less tangible capabilities, such as the ability to think strategically or to influence others (Sanghi, 2007).

5 RESULTS AND DISCUSSION

The respondents for this study were selected from three main ministries that provide TVET training. The details of the respondents are shown in Table 1. Most of them are from an educational background with a specific vocational skill.

There are many standards recommended for each kind of TVET personnel such as teacher, school principal, trainer of trainer and industry trainer. Table 2 shows the respondents' information regarding the development and implementation of TVET personnel.

There are issues of dissemination of these standards to the providers and stakeholders. This is important so that they will understand the criteria and requirements for their competency. Tables 3 and 4 explain the issue and the problems which occur during the process.

Having a single standard that acts as umbrella to TVET personnel could enhance the system that we currently have. In this regard respondents were asked about their opinion (see Table 5).

Table 1. Demography profile.

Institution	Ministry of Education	Ministry of Human Resource	Majlis Amanah Rakyat (MARA)		
Gender	51 Male	19 Female		31	
Working experience	51 <5 years	50 6–10 years		11–20 years	21 > years
Specialization	30 Education	34 Electrical	Engineering	11 Mechanical	26 Other
	86	2	9	3	1

Some of the current standards in TVET consist of a few levels such as beginner, intermediate and advanced. In VTO, certification offered by the Department of Skills Development consists of two levels: (1) Vocational Training Operation, and (2) Vocational Training Management. Table 6 shows the suggested or preferred level for the TVET teacher standard.

Table 2.   Status of the development and implementation of TVET personnel.

Status	Teacher standards	School/college/ Principal Director standard	Trainer of trainers standard	Industry Trainer standard
	Percentage (%)			
Developed	75	76	57	32
Not yet	3	8	15	18
Not sure	22	16	28	50

Table 3.   Issues/problems during dissemination.

Issue	Percentage (%)
1. Limited time	11
2. Unclear guideline	62
3. Limited briefing/capacity Building	19
4. Other	9

Table 4.   Issues/problems during implementation.

Issue	Percentage (%)
1. Limited time	32
2. Unclear guideline	47
3. Limited briefing/capacity Building	16
4. Other	6

The study then focused on the model of the core standard. The components for each part of the model were asked whether it is possible to be employed (see Table 7).

The respondents were asked how they would use the national core standard in their institutions (sometimes the effort made to develop and build a single standard becomes ineffective if people don't make use of it). The response can be studied in Table 8.

The national core standard allows for the establishment of a mechanism and process that signifies professional competence, or formal and full entry to the profession. The standard explains the competency which should be complied with by a teacher. Professionally competent teachers have demonstrated successful teaching experience. They effectively monitor, evaluate and plan for learning and are able to tailor teaching programs to meet the needs of individuals and groups within the class. Professionally competent teachers have a record of effective and ongoing professional learning. They work collegially and in teams to further enhance their professional practice, and take greater responsibility in collaboration with others for identifying and addressing their own learning needs. They are effective members of a school and its broader community and interact effectively with stakeholders.

TVET teachers often assume that trainees will be able to apply what has been taught to them (Feldon, 2007), without realizing that they lack the skill to gain the student's attention. Therefore, an effective model of TVET teachers' standard should be created to be used nationally as a reference. The trainers of TVET teachers, which are the Ministry of Education/Higher Education and the Ministry of Human Resources, should map the criteria found in this study in their syllabus or course content. It is understood that the current system (referred to as MTS) covers the competencies for common teachers but the core standard for TVET teachers is unique and should be enhanced with more practical and hands-on pedagogical skills.

Table 5.   What are the benefits of having national core standards for TVET personnel?.

	Harmonize TVET development in the region	Provide platform for benchmarking	Improve the overall quality of TVET	Strengthen TVET provider integration	Facilitate mobility of human resources
	Percentage (%)				
Strongly Agree	57	62	68	58	51
Somewhat Agree	36	36	29	36	39
Somewhat Disagree	7	2	3	3	10
Strongly Disagree	0	0	0	3	0

Table 6. Leveling competencies: Suggested level for the core standard.

Level	Percentage (%)
1	9
2	60
3	33

Table 7. Preferred model of the core standard.

Level	Percentage (%)
Model 1	44
i) Basic and common (Professional) (Communication, problem-solving, teamwork, etc.)	
ii) Core/functional (teaching, learning and assessment)	
Model 2	44
i) Pedagogical	
ii) Social	
iii) Personality	
iv) Professional	
Model 3	36
i) Educational laws and regulations (institutional and national)	
ii) Pedagogy and pedagogical psychology	
iii) Didactic and teaching methodology	
iv) Subject-based methodology	

Table 8. Proposed dimension of national core standard.

Dimension	Competencies	Training
Professional skill and knowledge	Able to demonstrate technical skills according to teaching requirements	Professional Certification
	Able to assess technical performance in a professional way	
Professional teaching and learning process	Conduct theoretical and practical lesson	Pedagogic Training VTO/CBT
	Able to apply curricula and teaching materials	
	Able to plan a lesson according to curriculum	
	Able to carry out assessment and evaluation of training	
Personal and professional attributes	Equipped with soft skills	Generic Skills Core
	Able to work in teams	Abilities
Professional industries and communities	Able to collaborate with industry	Industry Attachment
	Able to relate the teaching contents to industry needs	

6 CONCLUSION

The development and implementation of a core standard for TVET teachers' in Malaysia is still under enforcement which means each ministry is conducting their own standard. A main and single standard should be proposed for the integration of important competencies needed by those teaching TVET. In conclusion, TVET teachers should comply with the aforementioned dimension being studied in this research as outlined in Table 8.

To conclude, this paper has successfully illustrated the competencies needed by a TVET teacher. For further research it is recommended that the indicators for each of the dimensions should be investigated in a different study that examines the implementation, and even cause-and-effect relationship among those dimensions towards the growth of teachers' competency in teaching and learning.

REFERENCES

Ali, M., Kaprawi, N. & Razzaly, W. (2010). *Development of a New Empirical Based Competency Profile for Malaysian Vocational Education and Training Instructors.* Proceedings of the 1st UPI International Conference on Technical and Vocational Education and Training Bandung, Indonesia, 10–11 November 2010.

Feldon, D.F. (2007). The implication of research on expertise for curriculum and pedagogy. *Educ Psychol Rev, 19*, 91–110.

Law, S.S. (2007). Vocational Technical Education and Economic development—The Singapore Experience. *ITE Paper 2007(9)*, p. 5.

Norton, R.E. (1987). *Competency-Based Education and Training: A Humanistic and Realistic Approach to Technical and Vocational Instruction.* Paper presented at the Regional Workshop on Technical/Vocational Teacher Training in Chiba City, Japan.

Pauline, S.C.G., Noor, S.S. & Kung, T.W. (2012). The 'Voices' of Beginning Teachers in Malaysia About Their Conceptions of Competency: A Phenomenographic Investigation. *Australian Journal of Teacher Education, 37*(7), 58–70.

Sanghi, S. (2007). *Handbook of competency mapping.* Singapore: Sage Publications Asia-Pacific Pte Ltd.

Spöttl, G. (2009). *Standardisation in TVET Teacher Education: Teacher Education for TVET in Europe and Asia: The Comprehensive Requirements.* Frankfurt: Peter Lang.

Regionalization and Harmonization in TVET – Abdullah et al. (Eds)
© *2017 Taylor & Francis Group, London, ISBN 978-1-138-05419-6*

Transferable skills of engineering students and lecturers at universities in Indonesia and Malaysia

A. Setiawan, M. Bukit & I. Kuntadi
Technological and Vocational Program, School of Postgraduate Studies, Universitas Pendidikan Indonesia, Indonesia

J.M. Yunos, K.M. Salleh, L.C. Sern, N.L. Sulaiman & M.F. Mohamad
Faculty of Technical and Vocational Education, Universiti Tun Hussein Onn Malaysia, Parit Raja, Johor, Malaysia

ABSTRACT: A transversal skill is one of the skills needed in every type of workplace setting. There is limited information about the perceptions of which transferable skills are needed in the workplace. The objective of this study is to explore the transferable skills among students and lecturers in TVET higher learning institutions in Indonesia and Malaysia. In the present study, transferable skills consist of communication skills, collaboration skills, problem-solving skills, entrepreneurship, and learning to learn skills. A qualitative research was conducted using survey. The five Likert scale questionnaire was distributed to lecturers and students from selected Malaysian and Indonesian universities who have bachelor program in engineering. Based on the analysis outcomes, it is clearly shown that Malaysian university engineering students yielded significantly higher scores on the perceptions of transferable skill acquisition in all measured components compared to their counterparts in Indonesia. Similar patterns of data distribution have been observed in Malaysian and Indonesian engineering students. Based on the lecturers' perception, Malaysian and Indonesian Engineering Lecturers have comparable perceptions in the aspects of problem solving skills and entrepreneurship skills. In contrast, Malaysian university engineering lecturers gained significantly higher scores on the perception of communication skill, collaboration skill, and learning to learn skill compared to the Indonesian lecturers. The results indicate the need to increase transferable skills of both lecturers and students.

1 INTRODUCTION

To compete in the workplace of today, students in TVET institutions must learn the high-level technical skills that are expected for positions in their field as well as the transferable skills that will allow them to keep these positions or advance to better ones (Echternacht & Wen, 1997). In the past, the term skill solely referred to a specific manual operation. The term now means any practice, form of knowledge, or way of constituting productive labor (Urciuoli, 2008). Raj (2008) stated that hard skills are the technical and administrative skills required in the workplace that are relatively easy to observe and measure. In contrary, transferable skills, including communication, teamwork, problem solving, and other skills, are ingrained behavior patterns that are hard to quantify and to teach. Transferable skills are necessary for university-bound students as well as for those seeking a position in the working world directly out of TVET training institutions. Hard skills and soft skills are both important skills to have in the working world especially in TVET areas.

The concept and definition of transferable skills has been discussed recently. However, the interest in finding the ideal concept and definition across the world is still growing. According to the European Centre for Development of Vocational Training (2008), transferable skills is the skills individuals have which are relevant to jobs and occupations other than the ones they currently have or have recently had. These skills may also have been acquired through non-work or leisure activities or through participation in education or training. Similarly, European Commission (2012) stated transferable skills are generics and directly linked to basic knowledge, to behavioral skills, cognitive skills, and organizational skills. More generally, these are skills which have been learned in one context or to master a special situation/problem and can be transferred to another context. In general, Abbas, Abdul Kadir, and Ghani Azmie (2013) define transferable skill as having a wide variety of basic knowledge, values, and life skills that are necessary to obtain and keep a job it. In contrast, hard skills refer to the more specific, teachable skills, and are usually related to professional knowledge.

Nevertheless, in working world, soft skills complement hard skills and these include capabilities, competencies, and learning outcomes of technical procedures or practical tasks. This is in accordance with Shakir (2009) who suggests that soft and hard skills complement each other. Similarly, a research by Salleh, Sulaiman, and Talib (2010) indicates that soft and hard skills are both demanded by the organizations and industries.

Each country has definition and scope of transferable skills. However, transferable skills found in the majority of examined national policy documents cover communication skills, collaboration skills, problem solving skills, entrepreneurship skills and learning to learn skills (UNESCO, 2014). This scope of transferable skills was used in this research framework.

Unemployment among fresh graduates had become increases as employers expected them to become good in their area and also have positive attitudes with good transferable skills. According to Jelas et al. (2006), students only have average transferable skills level along their studies. In order to solve this issue, an improvement of pedagogy in teaching and learning process should be made. Students being expose with transferable skills by teachers giving talk and demonstrating what to do, but this will not ensure the students to get the skills and apply it in their life. Therefore, students and lecturers perception on transferable skills should be known for improvement.

2 METHODOLOGY

This study explores the transferable skills among lecturers and students in TVET higher learning institutions and examines the gaps between lecturers and students in transferable skills. Consequently, this study allowed the researcher to identify and interpret the transferable skills meaning within the TVET higher learning institutions. Therefore, the objective of this study is to explore the perception and the differences of transferable skills among students and lecturers in Malaysia and Indonesia as well as to compare transferable skills in among students and lecturers between Malaysia and Indonesia.

A qualitative research was conducted using survey (Creswell, 2003). The five Likert scale questionnaire was distributed to students and lecturers from Indonesian and Malaysian University who provide bachelor degree in engineering. Research respondents are from five Indonesian

State Universities (former teacher education institution) including Universitas Pendidikan Indonesia (UPI), Universitas Negeri Malang (UM), Universitas Negeri Semarang (UNNES), Universitas Negeri Surabaya (UNESA) and Universitas Negeri Gorontalo (UNG) and Malaysia Technical University Network (MTUN) comprising of four technical universities; University of Tun Hussein Onn Malaysia (UTHM), University of Technical Melaka Malaysia (UTeM), University of Malaysia Perlis (UniMAP) and University of Malaysia Pahang (UMP). The research respondents are 115 lecturers and 414 students from Indonesian universities and 94 lecturers and 439 students from Malaysian universities. Before the survey was conducted, a discussion on the literature review was carried out. The focus of this research was the perception and different of students and lecturers toward transferable skills from the aspects of pedagogy and assessment.

3 RESULTS AND DISCUSSSION

3.1 Comparison of transferable skills among engineering students between Malaysia and Indonesia

Analysis has been conducted to find out the differences and similarities on perception of transferable skills between Malaysian and Indonesian engineering students. The outcomes are illustrated in Figure 1. Based on the analysis outcomes, it is clearly shown that Malaysian university engineering students yielded relatively higher scores on the perceptions of transferable skill acquisition in all measured components compared to their counterparts in Indonesia. In collaborative skill, for instance, the Malaysian engineering students obtained the mean score of 3.97, whereas Indone-

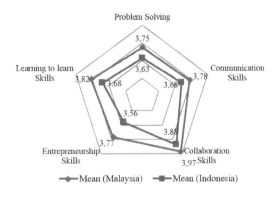

Figure 1. Comparison of transferable skills among engineering students between Malaysia and Indonesia.

sian engineering students only scored 3.88. Likewise, the mean score of 3.75 have been captured in problem solving skill for Malaysian engineering students, whereas the score for Indonesian engineering students was recorded as 3.63. A part from that, the mean scores for learning to learn skill, communication skill, and entrepreneurship skill among Malaysian engineering students were 3.82, 3.78, and 3.77 respectively. For Indonesian students, the mean scores for the aforementioned skills range from 3.56 to 3.68.

T test was conducted to find out if those differences were significantly different. Based on the results, it is clear that the perceptions of transferable skills acquisition between Malaysian and Indonesian engineering students differ significantly. (Problem solving skills: $t(851) = 3.10$, $p < 0.01$; communication skills: $t(851) = 2.21$, $p < 0.05$; collaboration skills: $t(851) = 2.13$, $p < 0.05$; entrepreneurship skills: $t(851) = 5.00$, $p < 0.001$; learning to learn skills: $t(851) = 3.58$; $p < 0.001$).

As far as students' perception is concerned, there are significant perception differences in all measured skill components between Malaysian engineering students and Indonesian engineering students. The Indonesian students have perceived that they have lower level of transferable skills as compared to Malaysian students. The current findings are on a part with the research results from Suarta (2010) who discovered that the Indonesian university students did not have high competency level in transferable skills from the supervisors' perspective. Likewise, a research conducted by Gribble (2014) has also reported that there is a huge room for improvement in terms of transferable skill among Indonesian workforce.

On the other hand, within the context of Malaysia, employers have rated Malaysian university graduates as workers with "moderate" transferable skills level (Hairi, Ahmad Toee, and Razally, 2011). Whereas, from the lecturers' perspective, the Malaysian engineering students have gained satisfactory levels of transferable skills ranging from moderate to higher. This result is in line with what have been perceived by the Malaysian students in the present study.

There are several possible explanations for the current findings. One of the reasons might be that Indonesian students under-estimated their transferable skills acquisition due to their high expectation. According to Williams (2007), expectation may affect the perception of an individual directly or indirectly. If a student has high expectation on herself/himself, s/he tends to presume what s/he has acquired is not sufficient, and thereby rating herself/himself low in self-assessment.

Another possible reason might be attributed to low level of confidence among Indonesian engineering

students due to wrong career choice, lack of industrial exposure, and lack of practical application. Previous research (e.g., Meechan, Jones & Valler-Jones, 2011) has evidenced that self-confidence is positively correlated with skill acquisition. If an individual is not self-confident towards her/his ability, s/he will not perceive herself/himself as competent in every learning domain. Although this research did not put the focus specifically on transferable skills, the finding is plausible to be applied in the sphere of transferable skills.

3.2 Comparison of transferable skills among engineering lecturers between Malaysia and Indonesia

Figure 2 illustrates the mean scores of perception on transferable skills acquisition from the perspective of engineering lecturers in Malaysia as well as Indonesia. Based on the analysis outcome, similar patterns of data distribution have been observed in Malaysia and Indonesia. Generally, both Malaysian and Indonesian engineering lecturers have perceived that they have gained high level of measured transferable skills. In specific, the Lecturers of both countries have relatively low level of perception on entrepreneurship skill acquisition (Malaysia: M = 4.01; Indonesia: M = 3.94), whereas communication skill (Malaysia: M = 4.27; Indonesia: M = 4.09) and collaboration skills (Malaysia: M = 4.27; Indonesia: M = 4.11) yielded the highest mean scores in both countries. In terms of perception differences on the measured transferable skills, huge perception gaps ware not noticed in the present investigation. The smaller perception gap occurred in Problem Solving Skill which is only 0.04, whereas Communication Skill yielded the largest difference which is 0.18.

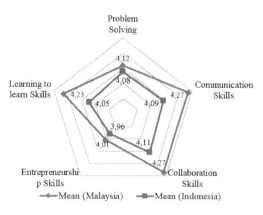

Figure 2. Comparison of transferable skills among engineering lecturers between Malaysia and Indonesia.

T-test was performed to determine if there were any significant differences in perceptions of transferable skills acquisitions between Malaysian and Indonesian Engineering Lecturers. The t-test results revealed that Malaysian and Indonesian Engineering Lecturers have comparable perceptions in the aspects of problem solving skills $(t(230) = 2.08, p > 0.05)$ and entrepreneurship skills $(t(230) = 0.89, p > 0.05)$. In contrast, significant differences were discovered in communication skills $(t(230) = 2.36, p < 0.05)$, collaboration Skill $(t(230) = 2.31, p < 0.05)$, and learning to learn skills $(t(229) = 2.51, p < 0.05)$.

These differences might be caused by several reasons. One of the possible explanations might be that the engineering lecturers in Malaysia Technical Universities (MTU) were compulsory to attend numerous pedagogical courses in which communication, collaboration, and learning to learn skills were embedded in the programs. That might be the reason why Malaysian engineering lecturers rated themselves exceptionally high in those skills.

It is interesting to discuss that entrepreneurship skills showed the lowest score both for students and lecturers. It can be explained that this is due to the lack of facilitation to develop entrepreneurship skills So far, In Indonesia, the development of entrepreneurship skills has been done through 2 credits entrepreneurship course. However, entrepreneurship course tend to be more theoretical and this course is taught, in general, by lecturers who do not have background and experience in practical entrepreneurship In addition, entrepreneurial activities are also less demand by the students. Meanwhile, the acquisition of entrepreneurship skills will affect student's employability (Leary, 2012). Therefore, it is important to develop innovation in pedagogy and assessment to improve entrepreneurship skills both for students and lecturers. The lack of Indonesian entrepreneurship skills also can be caused by cultural factors in which Indonesian people in general are less prepared to compete and are not prepared to accept the risk of failure in business (Indarti, 2008).

4 CONCLUSION

A survey of the perceptions of engineering students and lecturers at universities in Indonesia and Malaysia has been carried out. Based on the research findings, it can be concluded that Malaysian University Engineering Students gained significantly higher scores on the perceptions of transferable skills acquisition in the five measured components of transferable skills compared to their counterparts in Indonesia. We also found that similar patterns of data distribution have been observed in Malaysian and Indonesian engineering students. While based on the lecturer perception, Malaysian and Indonesian engineering lecturer have comparable perceptions in the aspects of problem solving and entrepreneurship skill. In contrast, Malaysian university engineering lecturer obtained significantly higher scores on the perceptions of communication skills, collaboration Skills, and learning to learn skills compared to the Indonesian lecturers. The results indicate the need to increase transferable skills of lecturers and students in Indonesia and Malaysia through improved pedagogy and assessment.

ACKNOWLEDGEMENT

The Authors would like to thank to Post Graduate Studies of Universitas Pendidikan Indonesia for financial support of this research through International Research Collaboration scheme year 2016.

REFERENCES

Abbas, R., Abdul Kadir, F.A. & Ghani Azmie, I.A. 2013. Integrating soft skills assessment through soft skills workshop program for engineering students at University of Pahang: an analysis. *International journal of Research In Social Sciences* 2(1): 33–46.

Cresswell, J.W. 2003. *Qualitative, Quantitative and Mixed Method Approaches*. 2nd ed. London: SAGE publications.

Echternacht, L. & Wen, L.M. 1997. The importance of workplace basic competencies (SCANS) as perceived by beginning business teachers and experienced business teachers. *College Student Journal* 31(1): 37–44.

European Centre for the Development of Vocational Training. 2008. *European training thesaurus*. Luxembourg: Office for Official Publication of the European Communities.

European Commission. 2012. *Transversal skills and best practices*. Retrieved from www.yesme.it/wp-content/uploads/2013/04/documenti-di-lavoro.pdf

Gribble, C. 2014. *Exploring "Employability in Different Cultural Contexts*. Research Report 2014, Society for Research into Higher Education. Retrieved from https://www.srhe.ac.uk/downloads/gribble-cate.pdf

Hairi, F., Ahmad Toee, M.N. & Razally, W. 2011. *Employers' Perception on Soft Skills of Graduates: A Study of Intel Elite Soft Skill Training*. Paper presented on the International Conference on Teaching and Learning in Higher Education 2011. Retrieved from http://eprints.uthm.edu.my/2191/1/EDC243.pdf

Indarti, N. & Rostiani, R. 2008. Intensi kewirausahaan mahasiswa: studi perbandingan antara Indonesia, Jepang dan Norwegia. *Jurnal Ekonomika dan Bisnis Indonesia* 23(4): 1–26.

Jelas Z.M., Azman N., Ali M.M., Nordin N.M. & Tamuri A.H. 2006. *Developing generic skills at graduates: A study of effective higher education practices in Malaysian universities*. Summary report. Kuala Lumpur: Universiti Kebangsaan Malaysia, Faculty of Education.

Leary, S.O. 2012. Industry and Higher Education December. 26: 431–442.

Malaysia Education Blueprint 2015–2025 (Higher Education). 2016. *Risalah Integrated Cummulative Grade Point Average (iCGPA)-versi Bahasa Melayu*. Retrieved from http://www.mohe.gov.my/ms/muat-turun/awam/penerbitan-dan-jurnal/icgpa/126- pamphlet-icgpa-bi/file

Meechan R., Jones H. & Valler-Jones, T. 2011. Students' perspectives on their skills acquisition and confidence. *Bristish Journal of Nursing* 20(7): 445–450.

Ministry of National Education/MoNE. 2003. *Concept of Life Skill Education*. Jakarta: Ministry of National Education.

Raj, R. 2008. Business negotiations: A soft perspective. *ICFA Journal of Soft Skills* 2(1): 7–22.

Salleh, K.M., Sulaiman, N.L. & Talib, K.N. 2010. *Globalization's impact on soft skills demand in the Malaysian workforce and organizations: What makes graduate employable?* Proceedings of the 1st UPI International Conference on Technical and Vocational Education and Training, 210–215.

Shakir, R. 2009. Soft skills at the Malaysian institutes of higher learning. *Asia Pacific Education Review* 10(3): 309–315.

Suarta 2010. *Supervisors' Perceptions of the Employability Skills Needed by Higher Vocational Education Graduates to be Successful in the Workplace*. Paper presented in the 14th UNESCO-APEID International Conference at Bangkok, on 21–23 Oct 2010. Retrieved from http://www.unescobkk.org/fileadmin/user_upload/apeid/Conference/14th_Conference/docs/ppt/I_Made_Suarta.pdf

UNESCO. 2014. *Transferable Skills in Technical and Vocational Education and Training (TVET): Policy Implications*. Education System Review Series No. 8. Unesco Bangkok. 21–23.

Urciuoli, B. 2008. Skills and selves in the new workplace. *American Ethnologist* 35(2): 211–228.

Williams, T. 2007. The effects of expectations on perception: Experimental design issues and further evidence. *Working Paper Series (Federal Reserve Bank of Boston)* 7(14): 1–26.

Work-oriented vocational learning

A. Ana, A.G. Abdullah, I. Widiaty, S. Subekti & Saripudin
Universitas Pendidikan Indonesia, Jawa Barat, Indonesia

ABSTRACT: In recent days human resource quality is still a problem that still requires further improvement in Indonesia. The skill mismatch is still a dominant problem between the world of education and the world of work. In Indonesia the role of vocational education is highly vital to improving quality of labor. This study discusses how the vocational learning is oriented to match the skills required by the world of work. There are three important aspects to improve learning orientation, which are to understand the changes in vocational learning, job skills required by work and TVET teachers' ability needed to improve their vocational learning to be more effective.

1 INTRODUCTION

The ASEAN Economic Community (AEC) implemented in 2015 is a necessity. It is inevitable for Indonesia to involve the global and widespread competition. One of many challenges faced by Indonesia is the quality of its human resource which is still not optimal compared to other ASEAN countries. In 2015, the World Economic Forum released the rankings of Human Capital Index and Indonesia ranks 69 of 124 countries. The index aims to measure the quality of human resources in one country in developing human resource potentials in terms of education and employment, demographics, and performance standards. Ten best rankings are still dominated by European countries.

In the aspect of education and employment, Indonesia still faces the challenges in skills mismatch between the graduates' skills and the skills required in the workplace. Currently, Indonesia ranks 82 of 124 countries, with the literacy rate of basic education and literacy numeracy, and the level of ICT literacy at the age of 15–24 years ranks 62 while the quality of the education system in Indonesia ranks 30 (World Economic Forum, 2015). This condition indicates that in general the quality of human resources is not optimal, especially the gap between the skills required by the workforce and the existing skilled personnel.

The skills gap in ICT is networking skills in which Indonesia has to compete among the ASEAN countries. According to a report of Sandy Walsh Director of Social Innovation Group, Asia Pacific in 2014, Indonesia is predicted to still experience skills gap of 36.5% in 2016 primarily in networking skills that are essential skills required by work today. Indonesia is still lagging behind other countries in Southeast Asia in terms of innovation.

The 2015 Global Innovation Index has reported that Indonesia ranks 97 of 141 countries, indicating a slight drop from 87 in 2014 (Dutta, 2015).

However, Indonesia is predicted to earn a bonus in 2020–2030. It would be a demographics bonus, where the population of productive age would be large, while there would be smaller number of young age people and elderly (www.bkkbn.go.id). The total labor force aged 15 to 64 years in 2020–2030 will reach 70 percent, while the remaining 30 percent is the unproductive population. This condition is a blessing for Indonesia because it will have an impact on economic growth and better welfare. Therefore, Indonesia is expected to prepare themselves in providing jobs, qualified human resources and better quality of education and training.

The commitment on improving the quality of human resources through education in Indonesia is now much better, especially on vocational education. The president of Indonesia, Joko Widodo, reiterated the government's commitment which is to encourage vocational education as an effort to improve the competitiveness of human resources. (Http: //print.kompas.com.2016/03/31). According to the President, vocational education will be a training center for students who will enter certain field of work. However, the main problem is in vocational education in Indonesia is related to graduates' lack of ability to enter the work (Nurharjadmo, 2008). The situation results from the quality of graduates which is far from the market demands, and the discrepancy between the supply of graduates and the small demand. According to the ADB report in 2016, the main priority to solve this problem in the future is to expand productive employment, including improving the quality of labor, increasing employment opportunities, strengthening education and training policy which

43

supports the structural transition from school to work, including strengthening the system of vocational training and apprenticeship (Allen, 2016).

The conditions outlined above indicate the needs for a wide range of vocational education efforts in preparing quality human resources. Volmari (2009), Guthrie (2009), Majumdar (2011), Lucas (2012) agree that an important effort made by vocational education in preparing the quality human resources is to increase the effectiveness of teaching and learning process in vocational education so that graduates of vocational education can play a role as more qualified and competitive workforce.

Effective learning directions in vocational education are urgent and need to be developed to suit the demands of the working world. Considering the importance of effective teaching learning process in vocational education as the main agenda to increase human resources, this study provides an alternative to the idea of learning vocational education oriented towards the world of work. It is hoped that educators are able to create transformation of the knowledge, skills, and attitudes of learners by developing teaching methods that are more oriented on the skills needed in the working world.

2 WORK-ORIENTED VOCATIONAL LEARNING DIRECTIONS

Vocational education started from the social efficiency doctrine conceived by David Sneden and then operationalized by Charles Prosser in the period of rising of the US industry in the twentieth century. The doctrine states that an efficient society is a society that can create a positive living environment by providing prosperity and satisfaction for the majority of its citizens. Education is seen to contribute to the achievement of this efficiency by preparing skilled workforce with appropriate qualifications in accordance with the needs of society (Braundy, 2004). Philosophy considers that vocational education is responsible for preparing people to work and be independent. In Human Capital Theory education is not merely seen as only to bring benefits in economic growth, but also provides benefits to the better welfare, social life and behavior and the improved participation in society (Vila, 2000). In line with the experts' opinion, vocational education provides a solid foundation for the implementation of work-oriented education.

Learning orientation in vocational education is shifting from supply-driven teaching towards demand-led learning. Learning is not only to help students learn academic content and skills alone, but also to train students to be more independent.

Over the past three decades, there is a change in the educational environment which is phenomenal. The changes include a model of learning, the role of teachers and learners, changes in the learning environment, and technology (Majumdar, 2011). The changes in the educational environment are described in Tables 1 and 2 below:

Tables 1 and 2 indicate that learning in vocational education has shifted from teacher-centered to student-centered. The learning approach is not focused merely on a formality-verbal culture, but on a learning approach that allows the integration of human values in personality and behavior during the learning process. Now the learning process

Table 1. The changes in learning environment.

Model	Focus	Learner roles	Technology
Traditional	Teacher	Passive	Chalk and Lecturing
Information	Learners	Active	Personal computer
Knowledge	Group	Adaptive	PC and network

Table 2. The changes in the roles of teachers, learners, curriculum, and media application.

Aspect	From	To
Teacher Roles	Delivering knowledge	Guiding and facilitating
	Controlling learning	Creating joyful learning environment
	Experts	Collaborator and learning partner
	Expository	Interactive/ experiment/ exploration
Learner Role	Passive	Active
	Absorbing knowledge	Producing new knowledge
	Dependent	Autonomy
	Content based only	Continuous learning/creative/ communication/ thinker
Curriculum	Memorizing facts	Discovery
	Teaching practice	Authentic learning
	Stricter time	Flexible/open/ anytime and any place
	Traditional based	Competency based
Media Application	Single simulation	Multi simulation
	Single media	Multi media
	One-way communication	Two-way communication
	Limited sources	Unlimited digital sources

in vocational education is more focused on effective interaction between teachers and learners (Maclean, 2004).

The effectiveness of the learning process is a reflection of the achievement of learning objectives appropriate to the determined learning outcomes. The effectiveness of the learning process relates to some ways, efforts, techniques and strategies used to achieve optimal and precise learning goals.

There are a wide variety of learning methods in teaching work-oriented vocational. Based on research conducted by Lucas (2014) and Perkins (2009), in general there are seven principles of the use of learning methods in vocational learning, namely: 1) The context of authentic learning; 2) Giving freedom to the students to engage in learning; 3) Practice to search something; 4) Providing opportunities for exploration; 5) Giving opportunities for learners to analyze problems; 6) Doing collaborative learning; 7) Providing opportunities to improve on their practices and strategies.

There are a number of vocational learning methods that can be used. Most methods apply the principle of "learning by doing" although many combine the activities of reflection, feedback and theory as in vocational learning the important thing is how students are directed to obtain meaningful learning experiences: 1) Learning by watching; 2) Learning by imitating; 3) Learning by Practicing ('trial and error'); 4) Learning through feedback; 5) Learning through conversation; 6) Learning by teaching and helping; 7) Learning by real-world problem-solving, 8) Learning through inquiry; 9) Learning by listening, transcribing and remembering; 10) Learning by drafting and sketching; 11) Learning on the fly; 12) Learning by being coached, 13) Learning by competing; 14) Learning through virtual environments; 15) Learning through simulation and role-play; 16) Learning through games (Lucas, 2014; Perkins, 2009).

Those learning methods are selected and used to design vocational learning according to the targeted learning objectives to achieve. Effective vocational learning, in my opinion, is how to connect that learning with the real world, where students are actively involved in learning, are capable of learning to learn, and form the characters as good individuals. The changing orientation direction of vocational learning demands TVET teachers to adjust to the labor skills required by the labor market so that there is no mismatch of skills.

Organization for Economic Cooperation and Development (OECD, 2012) published the skill strategy required to prepare vocational education to meet the demands of the 21st century, namely: 1) Knowledge must be more relevant and balanced between theory and practice; 2) high-level skills, called the "4 Cs" (creativity, critical thinking, communication and collaboration) as the skills required to absorb knowledge; 3) Performed characters, including adaptability, perseverance, endurance and moral character: integrity, fairness, empathy and ethics. These characters must be formed either at school or in the workplace to help individuals become active and responsible citizens; and 4) Meta-layer skills, such as learning to learn (continuous learning), building skills, developing creativity and networking skills needed to face the changes in the complexity of the world.

According to Lucas et al. (2012), there are six generic competencies required by world of work in the 21st century, including: (1) being experts in the work procedures in their domains; (2) having the intelligence to act effectively if required, (3) literacy skills, including mastery of ICT, (4) an attitude of commitment and attention to the work, 5) understanding business and (6) having a tough stance. The characteristics of the world of work in the future require labors that have the ability of high-level thinking, problem solving and working collaboratively. It requires the ability to customize applications that articulate with the context of the problems faced (Bound; Solomon, 2003).

Referring to the skills required by the labor market, practitioners should be able to determine "what" should be taught and the "how" to teach it to students and "what" is taught is related to the world of work, technology and professions in the implementation of vocational education. As to this, it is needed to study theoretical frameworks that underlie learning approaches that will be used to fulfill the vision and strategy to prepare the quality and appropriate workforce in that period of time. In short, TVET teachers need to be more qualified.

What are the capabilities required by TVET teachers to encourage the effectiveness of teaching in the changing vocational learning orientation? Majumdar (2011) emphasized that in the 21st century, vocational teachers experience many basic changes in their pedagogical practice. Teachers change their roles in the orientation of determining the strategy and approach to learning. A study conducted by Guthrie (2012) found the TVET teacher skills that are required in the context of the changes are: 1) TVET teachers are now required to acquire pedagogical skills by adapting strategies and learning which are centered on the learners. The teachers are required to apply different pedagogical approaches in guiding and facilitating learners to self-learning and learning in the workplace. 2) Focusing on the learner indicates that a TVET teacher should be able to create a more independent learning; 3) Client-oriented, where TVET teachers are able to establish a relationship with the students and the industries like a client. The teachers are skilled in giving feedback, building and maintaining relationships, developing a network of partnerships with industry, adapting learning to the needs of the industry, and acquiring the ability to monitor and evaluate the results; 4) Acquiring some technical skills to match the skills required by labor market; 5) The ability to use any technology, including acquiring knowledge and expertise in the use of new technologies, particularly to remain "connected" with advances in technology; 6) Understanding the system and how to work on TVET; 7) Having a good quality of personal attributes, such as communication skills, a commitment to self-development, the capacity to deal with change, learn independently, manage time and new knowledge better.

Of the expected capabilities from TVET teachers above, the most important issue is how to develop the abilities of TVET teachers to demonstrate professionalism, develop teaching skills, have the ability to better understand the needs of industries and businesses, apart from their core skills, which are acquiring their pedagogical skills. As a result to this, the development of vocational teachers' capacities is highly necessary and should be directed to achieve the required abilities.

3 CONCLUSION

Vocational education plays a significant role in preparing future skilled workforce. The changes in the era of knowledge-based economy have influenced the direction of vocational learning which is oriented to fulfill the labor market. This direction should address the shift of pedagogical paradigm, current trends and challenges, and current needs to skilled labor. The changes include a shift of teacher and student role, the creation of learning environments which is oriented to curriculum and technology that encourage efforts to improve the quality of vocational education. Therefore, a fundamental change must start from vocational education classes, workshops or laboratories supported by highly-skilled and professional teachers.

REFERENCES

Allen, E.R. 2016. *Analysis of Trends and Challenges in the Indonesian Labor Market.* Manila: Asian Development Bank.

Bound, D. & Solomon, N. 2003. *Work Based Learning.* Buckingham: SRHE and Open University Press.

Braundy, M. 2004. Dewey's technological literacy: past, present, and future. *Journal of International Technical Education* 41(2).

Dutta, S., Lanvin, B. & Wunsch, B. (Editors). 2015. *The Global Innovation Index 2015; Effective Innovation Policies for Development.* Geneva: World Intellectual Property Organization.

Guthrie, H., Harris, R., Simons, M. & Karmel, T. 2009. *Teaching for Technical and Vocational Education and Training (TVET).* New York: Springer International Handbook of Research on Teachers and Teaching.

http://print.kompas.com/baca/2016/03/31/Presiden-Dorong-Pendidikan-Kejuruan

http://www.bkkbn.go.id/Bonus-Demografi

Lucas, B., Spencer, E. & Claxton, G. 2012. *How to Teach Vocational Education: A Theory of Vocational Pedagogy.* London: City & Guilds Centre for Skills Development.

Lucas, B. 2014. *Vocational Pedagogy what it is, why it Matters and What We Can do about it.* http://www.157group.co.uk/sites/default/files/documents/157 g-115-pedagogicleadership.pdf

Maclean, R. 2004. *Importance of Developing and Implementing an International Master Degree Standard for Teacher and Trainer Education in Technical and Vocational Education and Training.* In F. Bunning & Z.-Q.

Majumdar S. 2011. New Challenges in TVET Teacher Education. *UNESCO IICBA Newsletter* 13 (2).

OECD. 2012. *Better Skills, Better Jobs, Better Lives: A Strategic Approach to Skills Policies.* [Online]. Paris: OECD Publishing. Retrieved on Sep. 14, 2012, from http://dx.doi.org/10.1787/9789264177338-en

Perkins, D. 2009. *Making Learning Whole: How Seven Principles of Teaching Can Transform Education.* San Francisco: Jossey-Bass.

Sandy Walsh. 2014. *IDC Skills Gap Study and What We are doing about it.* Cisco.

Vila, L. 2000. The Non-Monetary Benefits of Education: European. *Journal of Education* 35(1): 21–32.

Volmari, K., Helakorpi, S. & Frimodt, R. 2009. *Competence Framework for VET Professions.* Sastalama: Finnish National Board of Education.

Wahyu, N. 2008. Evaluasi Implementasi Kebijakan Pendidikan Sistem Ganda di Sekolah Kejuruan. *Jurnal Spirit Publik* 4(2): 215–228.

World Economic Forum. 2015. *The Human Capital Report 2015.* Geneva: WEF.

Regionalization and Harmonization in TVET – Abdullah et al. (Eds)
© 2017 Taylor & Francis Group, London, ISBN 978-1-138-05419-6

Skills development and employment within the TVET context in Timor Leste

G.S. Ximenes & M.L. Soares
Workforce Development Program Timor-Leste, Timor-Leste

ABSTRACT: The Skills Development and Employment (SDE) project is a 2 1/2 year project funded by Department of Foreign Affairs and Trade (DFAT) to support the Secretariat of State for Vocational Training and Employment Policy (SEPFOPE) from 2016–2018. The project is aimed to improving employment opportunities and quality of life through skills development and expand overseas opportunities. To achieve this goal, SDE is actively engaged industry into the design and development of qualification through industry consultation and qualification development workshops to get their inputs and explore their needs for quality workers. SDE also, works closely with government and training providers to expand employment opportunities and improve the quality of Timorese workers to send and work overseas. This is done through Work Ready Skills (WRS) and English trainings to ensure that the workers with the right skills and rigorous screening and selection process for Timorese youth to work in Australia under Australia Seasonal Worker Program.

1 INTRODUCTION

The Skills Development and Employment (SDE) project is a 2 1/2 year project funded by Department of Foreign Affairs and Trade (DFAT) to support the Secretariat of State for Vocational Training and Employment Policy (SEPFOPE) from 2016–2018 to address skill gaps and low employability of Timorese workers. The SDE project is aimed to improving employment opportunities and quality of life through skills development and expand overseas opportunities.

This paper will give a short introduction of SDE, outline SDE within TVET system (include SWP and TVET) and present some data on Seasonal workers and Work Ready Skills Training in Timor Leste.

2 SKILLS DEVELOPMENT AND EMPLOYMENT (SDE)

SDE component is an investment in Timor-Leste's vocational training and employment and will provide young people with improved access to quality skills, enabling them to enter productive employment, including self-employment opportunities and obtaining employment overseas. The project's main stakeholders are different directorates of SEPFOPE, namely: the directorate of LMIS, (Labour Market Information System), National Institution for Labour Force Development

(INDMO), National directorate for Training Policy (DNAFOP) and overseas employment office.

3 SDE WITHIN TVET SYSTEM

SDE supports DNAFOP and INDMO to held qualification technical working group workshops in September and October to develop both qualification and teacher training frameworks. The development of a TVET framework also enables further implementation with the preparation of curriculum and learning materials, which are essential for technical teachers to deliver skills training at the appropriate levels. The expectation is to have the qualification framework and teacher training ready by December 2016. In addition, the teachers from Accredited Training Providers (ATPs) will be sent to overseas for gaining skills and experience through selected International training providers in 2017. This is to ensure that the teachers have relevant work ethics and experience as well as least one level above the students, certificate IV. This teacher cohort can then deliver Certificate III through apprenticeships in the hospitality industry and through Accredited Training Providers.

4 SWP AND TVET

Seasonal worker program has been a key employment opportunity for Timorese workers to improve

Table 1. Australian seasonal workers 2012–2016.

Area of working	Total 2012–2016		Returned workers 2012–2016		Currently in Australia		Self employed	
	M	F	Male	Female	Male	Female	Male	Female
Agriculture	313	69	219	55	135	28	2	
Hospitality	91	61	69	52				1
Total	534		395		163		3	

Timorese economic growth (Wigglesworth & Fonseca, 2015).

SDE is working closely with the DoE (Overseas Employment Department or Labour Sending Unit) within SEFOPE to improve the selection process around four pillars, physical fitness, attitudes, skills and experience, English level and health checks to send the best Timorese to work in Australia. SDE works closely with DNAFOP and INDMO and to provide Work Ready Skills (WRS) and English Language trainings to equip candidates with industry skills and experience for seasonal workers. This to ensure that the workers with the right skills, good work ethic and experience are in a Work Ready Pool (WRP) and ready mobilize quickly to working in Australia in Australia's Seasonal Worker Program.

From 2012–2016, 582, seasonal workers working in Australia and some have returned to Timor Leste. They now using the knowledge and skills they gained in Australia to improve their lives, help their family and invest in Timor Leste, such as open their own businesses in the country. (See Table 1).

5 CONCLUSION

To sum up, it is clear that SDE program is working together with multiple stakeholders to improve skills and quality human resources through industry and training providers' consultations in the design of qualification framework and training materials for certificate III in food and beverage and accommodation management areas through regular and apprenticeship modes of trainings.

SDE also assist the overseas employment unit and TVET regulatory body to improve the selection process for Australia' Seasonal Workers to provide seasonal workers with the right skills and experience through work ready skills training to better prepare them to work in Australia.

All this enables the Labour Department, SEP-FOPE, to improve the quality of human resources to respond to industry's demand in Timor Leste. Internationally, allow Timor-Leste to compete in Asia Pacific labour market; particularly, in Hospitality and Tourism industry sector.

REFERENCES

Asian Development Bank & International Labour Organization. 2014. *Tracer Study: Technical training graduates 2014*. Available on: http://www.ilo.org/wcmsp5/groups/public/---asia/---ro-bangkok/---ilo-jakarta/documents/publication/wcms_419172.pdf. Retrieved September 16, 2016.

International Labour Organization. 2013. *Timor Leste Labour Force Survey Report*. Jakarta, Indonesia. Available from: http://www.ilo.org/wcmsp5/groups/public/---asia/---ro-bangkok/---ilo-jakarta/documents/publication/wcms_417168.pdf. Retrieved on September 20, 2016.

International Labour Organization. 2013. *Timor Leste Labour Force Survey Report*. Jakarta, Indonesia. Available from: http://www.ilo.org/jakarta/whatwedo/publications/WCMS_152168/lang--en/index.htm. Retrieved September 20, 2016.

The Government of Timor Leste. 2011. *Strategic Development Plan Timor Leste, 2011 – 2030*. Dili, Timor Leste. Available from: https://sustainabledevelopment.un.org/content/documents/1506Timor-Leste-Strategic-Plan-2011–20301.pdf. Retrieved September 19, 2016.

The Government of Timor Leste. 2011. *Timor Leste Technical and Vocational Education and Training Plan 2011–2030*. Dili Timor Leste. Available from: http://www.mlstp.net/uploads/4/8/6/7/48670023/10_timor-leste_tvet_plan_2011–2030.pdf. Retrieved on September 20, 2016.

Wigglesworth, A. & Fonseca, Z. 2015. *Experiences of young Timorese as Migrant workers in South Korea*. Available on: http://devpolicy.org/2016-Australasian-aid-conference/Presentations/Day-2/4c-Migration-Pacific-and-Timor-Leste_Wigglesworth.pdf. Retrieved September 20, 2016.

Developing a culture-based teacher education and training program model: Improving teachers' content and pedagogical knowledge

I.P. Soko, A. Setiawan & A. Widodo
Education Science Program, School of Postgraduate Studies, Universitas Pendidikan Indonesia, Bandung, Indonesia

ABSTRACT: This study investigated whether a teachers' professional development model built around the use of place and culture as the fundamental principles could improve physics teachers' content and pedagogical knowledge. The model was evaluated using formative and summative evaluation and the teachers' knowledge and competences were examined, as well as the understanding of the learners, learning design and implementation, evaluation of learning outcomes, and the development of learners in actualizing their various potentials. The ability of teachers to develop physics learning activities to define the principles and concepts of units, standards and measurements, Newton's laws and their applications, temperature, heat and heat transfer, and sound waves was also studied. This mixed-methods study was carried out with 23 in-service teachers. The resulting model of a culture-based teacher education and training program has four major characteristics: it is a participatory model adaptation; the structure and content of the program are developed by deliberating the perspectives, customs, beliefs and values of local Nusa Tenggara Timur (NTT) culture; the principles of adult learning are applied; the model provides teachers/participants with the ability to develop culture-based physics learning activities for local NTT culture.

1 INTRODUCTION

Physics is a branch of science that empirically, logically, systematically and rationally studies and explains the elements of nature and its phenomena. Learners' success in learning physics can be achieved if they have the ability to understand the three main points: physical concepts, laws or principles, and theories (Siregar, 2003). In order to attain physics learning objectives, the physics learning process should be individualized and contextual; physics learning should occur in students individually in accordance with the students' development and also the environment. In order to achieve meaningful physics learning, the new information needs to be associated with a structure of understanding or students' prior knowledge.

Physics learning should be allied with students' prior knowledge in order to harmonize the new concepts with that knowledge. The knowledge, skills and abilities involved in organizing physics learning are known as Pedagogical Content Knowledge (PCK). Shulman (1987) noted that a professional teacher should have a decent level of knowledge and ability in PCK. A teacher needs to continually develop their quality in designing lesson plans, classroom teaching and learning, and assessment by understanding the PCK. Lave and Wenger (1991) consider these the 'basic building blocks of a social system' as these enable participants to 'define

with each other what constitutes competence in a given context'. Effective professional development of in-service teachers is recognized as fundamental to school success and teacher satisfaction (Education Week, 2004). Regarding PCK as dynamic and affected by changes in multiple social systems suggests there are compelling reasons for taking an explicitly culture-based and place-based approach to professional development in science.

That there are challenges and shortcomings in physics teaching suggests that good PCK is far from being universal. Generally, one of the difficulties that confronts pre-service teachers or even in-service teachers is how to modify theoretical physics material into something that is easy to understand, valuable, and properly fits with the students' daily experiences. Lete's (2012) study showed that conceptual understanding and the ability of senior high school students in Kupang to analyze tables, figures and graphs related to physical phenomena was low. Based on a pre-study interview with one of the physics teachers in Kupang, physics instruction is conducted by utilizing a variety of teaching and learning strategies, but still the students find it difficult to understand physics concepts. Various studies suggest designing contextual learning by illustrating some related problem faced in the students' daily experiences (Skoumis & Hatzinikita, 2009; Guisasola et al., 2009; Hernández et al., 2011; Loukomies et al., 2013).

In recent years, teacher professionalism has been subject to a period of dissatisfaction. Based on the 2015 results of senior high school teacher-competency tests, pedagogical and professional competency scores are generally still below the standard minimum pass criterion, which is 55. The national teacher-competency test average is 53.02, with the average score for professional competency being 54.77, and that for pedagogical competency being 48.94. Only seven provinces (of 33) earned teacher-competency test scores above the average. The test results indicate whether or not the minimum levels of standards, including the knowledge and skills that cover the basic aspects of a subject, are met by the teacher, that is, the results of the test showed how competent they are as teachers.

In Nusa Tenggara Timur (NTT), the teacher association has been organizing *Pengertian Matematika dan Ilmu Pengetahuan Alam* (MIPA) (Understanding Mathematics and Natural Sciences) centers since 2004. MIPA centers contribute to an increase in mathematics and science National Exam (UN) scores and learning quality, but unfortunately this program is not coordinated by the local government and lacks follow-up. This lack of coordination and ongoing support causes teachers to fall back to their teacher-centered and subject-matter-centered approaches. There is another problem in teaching physics: mastering physics. Some teachers only teach certain topics with which they are familiar, while they skip others that they find difficult to teach. Another teaching problem is the ability to provide an interactive, fun and challenging learning process. It is not surprising that the UN score for NTT in 2016 ranks it 29th out of the 33 provinces in Indonesia.

There are institutions in Indonesia with important roles in nurturing and enhancing teachers' professionalism, such as the central government through *Pusat Pengembangan dan Pemberdayaan Pendidik dan Tenaga Kependidikan* (P4TK), the provincial government through *Lembaga Penjamin Mutu Pendidikan* (LPMP), and local government. Based on Winingsih's (2013) study, there was role overlap in the central government, provincial government and local government functions, and there has been no systematic coordination or supportive cooperation in improving the professionalism of teachers. P4TK, LPMP and local governments have a powerful and important role in improving teachers' professionalism, but the defined forms of the roles and the involvement levels of all three institutions differ from each other, as does the authority of each of these institutions. Efforts to improve professionalism through education and training programs organized by P4TK, LPMP and local governments have often been made, but there has not been proficient coordination (Winingsih, 2013).

The autonomy and decentralization of education to local governments opens up opportunities to better orient matters to the changing needs of each region (i.e. bottom up). Local governments need to organize activities through relevant institutions that support the development and improvement of teachers' competences. *Musyawarah Guru Mata Pelajaran* (MGMP) can be a mutual learning exercise and discussion of experiences in which the ability of teachers and the quality of learning is improved. We need to maintain the communication between teachers of physics, so that problems in learning activities, such as the development of teaching materials, instructional strategies, assessment, and others, can be solved together.

The Education Training Union (ETU) (2000) asserts that education and training are an inseparable unity. In general, education and training models consist of three main phases: planning, implementation and evaluation. From the viewpoint of cultural anthropology, to learn science is to acquire the culture of science; students must travel from their everyday life-world to the world of science found in their science classroom. Education through a cultural approach is ideal for environments such as multicultural Indonesia, where education rooted in the nation's cultural values of harmony and peaceful life in a pluralistic state should be a significant aid to comprehension.

Given the importance of integrating culture, two studies provide guidance: Chinn (2012) in her cross-cultural study, *Place and culture-based professional development: Cross-hybrid learning and the construction of ecological mindfulness*, and Triwiyono's (2010) *Development of junior Sentani Papua culture-based physics learning program*. Overall, the literature and some research reviews suggest that carefully designed culture-based physics instruction helped students to harmonize school science with their local culture as their prior knowledge, and empowered teachers to contextualize physics instruction and to teach in ways that supported diverse learning modes. The present study has been conducted to establish: (1) the characteristics of a culture-based teacher education and training program model in *MGMP Fisika* to improve physics teachers' content and pedagogical knowledge; (2) the results in terms of the improvement in teachers' content and pedagogical knowledge that derive from such a program model.

2 METHODS

Four cultural experts (elders) of NTT were interviewed thoroughly as to their knowledge, wisdom, and erudition of local culture. Twenty-three physics teachers from 12 senior high schools in Kabupaten Ende, NTT, were involved to identify the values of NTT local culture. The teachers were heterogeneous,

Table 1. Research instruments and data analysis.

Measured aspect	Instrument	Data source	Data analysis technique
Program need assessment	Program need assessment questionnaire	Teachers	Descriptive statistics
Local culture related to physics	Culture identification questionnaire	Teachers Cultural experts	Data reduction & data display
Education & training program design quality	Guidelines of program structure assessment	Documents (program model blueprint) by expert judgment	Conclusion drawing & verification
	Guidelines of curriculum and syllabus assessment	Documents by expert judgment	Conclusion drawing & verification
	Guidelines of instruments assessment	Documents by expert judgment	Conclusion drawing & verification
Education & training teaching material quality	Guidelines of teaching material substance assessment	Documents by expert judgment	Conclusion drawing & verification
Content knowledge	Multiple choice test	Teachers	N-gain
Pedagogical knowledge	Multiple choice test	Teachers	N-gain
Program success rate	Guidelines of program success assessment	Documents Facilitators Teachers	Data triangulation
	Questionnaire	Teachers	Descriptive statistics

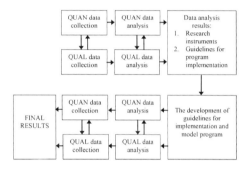

Figure 1. Culture-based teacher education and training program model research design (Adaptation of integrative mixed-methods design (Castro et al., 2011)).

in terms of teaching, professional development experiences, and cultural background. The instruments were validated by a team of experts (expert judgment).

Descriptions of the research instruments and data analysis techniques are shown in Table 1.

This study was mixed-methods research and the research design diagram is outlined in Figure 1.

3 RESULT AND DISCUSSION

3.1 *Program need assessment and culture identification results*

The data were descriptively analyzed and sorted to establish teachers' opinions, teaching experiences and their necessity in terms of enabling teacher professionalism, as shown in Table 2.

The need assessment results suggest that contextual culture-based teaching–learning should be incorporated into program material.

In order to adjust to this requirement, we need to identify the cultural aspects relevant to physics topics. The following subsections identify the elements of traditional NTT culture that can be integrated into various aspects of physics instruction.

3.1.1 *Units, standards and measurements*
The traditional NTT units, standards and measurements of length, mass and time (traditional calendar).

3.1.2 *Newton's laws and their applications*

1. *Pasola*, a thanksgiving ceremony to the ancestral spirits of people from West Sumba. The Alornese still use bows and arrows for hunting tools and war.
2. *Kela Koti* or the traditional spinning top of the Endenese. The traditional *Enene* umbrella dance.
3. The timber panels of the *Ammu Hawu* house (traditional house of Sabunese).
4. *Etu,* a traditional boxing ceremonial of the people of Nagekeo.

3.1.3 *Temperature, heat and heat transfer*

1. *Tatobi* is a series of activities aimed at warming post-partum mothers in rooms where there is a fireplace.

Table 2. Identification results of program need assessment.

Aspects	Indicators	Identification results	%
The needs of education & training program	Program objectives	To improve teachers ability to develop contextual physics learning activities	22.2
	Program material	Learning strategy (approach, model, method & technique)	18.5
		How to develop teaching materials and learning models	30.4
		Teachers' ability to associate concepts with values and examples in students' everyday life	28.3
	The teaching–learning problems to be developed in the program	How to compile contextual physics teaching material (based on students' environment and culture)	34.2
The competences of learning management	The development of teaching materials	Teachers did not develop the teaching material, but took it from textbooks	54.4
		The development emphasizes the close relationship between theoretical and practical aspects of designing the sequence of activities that extend physics learning and relate to other concepts	47.2
	The nature of science implementation	Practicality of teaching material development	26.3
	Practical activities	To develop the concept of laboratory data	33.4
	The development of learning tools	Syllabus and lesson plan	45.2
Experimental activities	Experimental equipment and supplies	Mechanics and optics experiments	74.2
		In order to specify the equipment, teachers need an understanding of how to describe the techniques of measurement to be used	65.3
	Preparation of experimental activities	Guidelines for setting up a practical & conducting a trial experiment	75.4
	Implementation of experimental activities (the obstacles)	Limitedness of lab equipment & time management	82.4

2. *Mbaru Niang* is a traditional house of Wae Rebo village, located within the Rainforest Mountains of Flores.
3. During water boiling, the mother often adding a spoon or other small-sized iron article into a container of cooking water to speed boiling process.
4. *Moke* is a traditional beverage, symbol of brotherhood and unity for the Ngadanese.

3.1.4 *Sound waves*

1. *Sasando* is a traditional stringed musical instrument from Rote island.
2. Traditional musical instrument *Foy Pay* comes from Ngada and is a small double flute of bamboo.

The indigenous cultures of NTT have educational values that can be integrated into learning activities. The integration of indigenous science concepts into physics instruction helps teachers and students to learn better. If students' views and beliefs are in accordance with the concepts of physics, there will be mutually reinforcing interference.

3.2 *Culture-based teacher education and training program model*

A culture-based education and training model was developed by adapting participatory methods (Sudjana, 2000), based on the nine principles of adult learners' learning (Knowles, 1984). The education and training activities ended with review and agreement, so that the knowledge and skills gained from the training activity would be sustainable. The people of NTT uphold collective ordinances and agreements, so by establishing an agreement at the end of the education and training, teachers will be encouraged to obey the agreements they have established and agreed.

The education and training program provided an experiential approach for the participants, who were teachers with more than five years' experience of teaching. The program united teachers' experiences with a number of activities that emphasized real

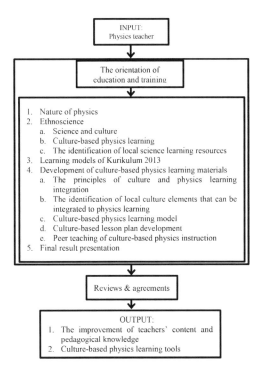

INPUT:
Physics teacher

The orientation of
education and training

1. Nature of physics
2. Ethnoscience
   a. Science and culture
   b. Culture-based physics learning
   c. The identification of local science learning resources
3. Learning models of Kurikulum 2013
4. Development of culture-based physics learning materials
   a. The principles of culture and physics learning integration
   b. The identification of local culture elements that can be integrated to physics learning
   c. Culture-based physics learning model
   d. Culture-based lesson plan development
   e. Peer teaching of culture-based physics instruction
5. Final result presentation

Reviews & agreements

OUTPUT:
1. The improvement of teachers' content and pedagogical knowledge
2. Culture-based physics learning tools

Figure 2. Culture-based teacher education and training program model.

situations and focused on achieving knowledge and skills: pedagogical content knowledge. The facilitators were physics supervisors. They understand the needs and characteristics of teachers. In addition, by choosing well-known facilitators, the teachers could more freely reveal their problems, ideas and opinions. The program implementation began with sharing experiences, followed by the assertion and presentation of knowledge. Physics teachers must socio-culturally contextualize PCK in order to effectively develop learning strategies that meet the diverse needs of students and society.

4 CONCLUSIONS

There is a need to empower MGMPs to act as discussion forums for physics teacher communication. It is often hard to implement a training of trainers (TOT) model for teachers and, therefore, in MGMPs, teachers who have had the opportunity to attend teacher education and training will be able to share their knowledge and information with other teachers. The particular principles, customs, beliefs, views of nature, and daily life experiences which are different in each ethnic group, have the potential to be integrated into physics instruction. The integration of culture into physics instruction

can help students understand physics as modern science based on their prior knowledge through contextual culture-based learning.

The findings from this study indicate that the program was effective in supporting teachers in changing their instructional practices and beliefs because the program's design incorporated theory, demonstration, practice, feedback and follow-up, because participants attended in teams and engaged in peer teaching, and because content was contextualized with the work related and integrated into teachers' learning areas. We can also conclude that there is a continued need to research programs built on this study to provide further evidence to support this claim. The fact that most programs were conducted by central government agencies suggests that there is a challenge in institutionalizing place-based physics teachers' education and training programs while colleges and universities continue to be compartmentalized and discipline-based. This gap suggests that study of culture-based teacher education and training programs might focus on longer-term studies of teacher learning, expertise, and agency in order to capture changes in teachers' place- and culture-based PCK, communities of practice, and student learning.

By providing opportunities for physics teachers' education and training through participation in culture-based communities of learners that address meaningful and relevant physics or science issues in general, there is potential for a path toward educational equity for all learners. A focus on real places and needs empowers teachers as local experts and curriculum developers who are able to contextualize learning in students' communities, practices, and cultural knowledge. It is essential, therefore, to continue to explore, refine and develop our understanding of the design and implementation of teacher education and training to better support the needs of teachers.

REFERENCES

Castro, F.G., Kellison, J.G., Boyd, S.J. & Kopek, A. (2011). A methodology for conducting integrative mixed methods research and data analyses. *Journal of Mixed Methods Research, 4*(4), 342–360.

Chinn, P.W.U. (2012). Developing teachers' place-based and culture-based pedagogical content knowledge and agency. In B.J. Fraser, K. Tobin & C.J. McRobbie (Eds.), *Second international handbook of science education* (pp. 323–335). New York, NY: Springer.

Education Training Union. (2000). *Educational and training guide [Online]*. Retrieved from http://www.etu.org

Education Week. (2004). *Professional development.* Retrieved from http://www.edweek.org/rc/issues/professional-development/

Guisasola, J., Almudi, J.M., Ceberio, M. & Zubimendi, J.L. (2009). Designing and evaluating research-based instructional sequences for introducing magnetic fields. *International Journal of Science and Mathematics Education, 12*(7), 699–722.

Hernández, M.I., Couso, D. & Pintó, R. (2011). The analysis of students' conceptions as a support for designing a teaching/learning sequence on the acoustic properties of materials. *Science Educational & Technolology Journal*, 21, 702–712.

Knowles, M.S. (1984). *Andragogy in action.* San Francisco, CA: Jossey-Bass.

Lave, J. & Wenger, E. (1991). *Situated learning: Legitimate peripheral participation.* Cambridge, UK: Cambridge University Press.

Lete, M.N. (2012). *Identifikasi pemahaman konsep dan kemampuan siswa dalam menganalisis tabel, gambar, dan grafik berkaitan dengan fenomena fisis siswa sekolah menengah atas se-kota Kupang* (Thesis). Universitas Nusa Cendana, Kupang, Indonesia.

Loukomies, A., Pnevmatikos, D., Lavonen, J., Spyrtou, A., Byman, R., Kariotoglou, P. & Juuti, K. (2013). Promoting students' interest & motivation towards science learning: The role of personal needs & motivation orientations. *Research in Science Education, 43*(6), 2517–2539.

Shulman, L. (1987). Knowledge and teaching: Foundations of the new reform. *Harvard Educational Review, 57*(1), 1–22.

Skoumis, M. & Hatzinikita, V. (2009). Learning and justification during a science teaching sequence. *The International Journal of Learning, 16*(4), 327–342.

Triwiyono. T. (2010). *Pengembangan Program Pembelajaran Fisika SMP Berbasis Budaya Sentani-Papua* (Dissertation). Sekolah Pascasarjana, Universitas Pendidikan Indonesia, Bandung, Indonesia.

Regionalization and Harmonization in TVET – Abdullah et al. (Eds)
© 2017 Taylor & Francis Group, London, ISBN 978-1-138-05419-6

English language training in the TVET context in Timor-Leste

J.P. Martins

Workforce Development Program, Timor-Leste

ABSTRACT: Since its independence in 2002, Timor-Leste has declared Tetum and Portuguese to be the official languages, while maintaining English as a working language. Timor-Leste has launched its Strategic Plan for National Development (2011–2030), and as part of this a Technical and Vocational Education Training (TVET) plan has been created and is now being implemented. The National Institute for Labour Force Development (INDMO) was created with the main role of ensuring the quality of training by establishing national qualification standards and supporting training providers in the delivery of accredited qualifications. As Timor-Leste continues to develop, there have been increasing calls for a nationally accredited English qualification to meet specific demands within education and industry nationally, and to provide support for Timorese nationals looking to work overseas. This presentation outlines the work of the Australia Timor-Leste English Language Program, a DFAT-funded partnership working to improve the level of English language teaching in secondary schools in addition to providing an accredited English qualification to all industry sectors within Timor-Leste. In-service English language training in Timor-Leste is now accredited under the National Qualifications Framework and delivered to English language teachers and trainers in schools and accredited training providers across the country. The program aims to deliver in-service English language training to secondary schoolteachers, in cooperation with the national teacher training institute (INFORDEPE), and to TVET trainers in cooperation with INDMO. Teachers and trainers who successfully complete the training have the potential, with some additional training from internationally recognized training providers, to be promoted to higher positions as national master trainers.

1   INTRODUCTION

Timor-Leste is a small country with a land size of 15,000 square kilometers. As of 2015, its population was 1.245 million. It was internationally recognized on the 20th May 2002 through restoration of independence. Timor-Leste has declared Tetum and Portuguese to be its official languages, while English and Indonesian are maintained as working languages. Timor-Leste has launched its Strategic Plan for National Development (2011–2030). The Timor-Leste Strategic Development Plan is a twenty-year vision that reflects the aspirations of the Timorese people to create a prosperous and strong nation. It is built around four pillars:

- Social capital: Health, education and social protection.
- Infrastructure: transport, telecommunication, power, and water supply and sanitation.
- Economic foundations: agriculture, tourism and petrochemicals—to bring growth, jobs and new sources of public revenue beyond oil.
- Institutional framework: macroeconomic management and improvement of the capacity and effectiveness of government institutions.

One of the focuses of the pillar of social capital is vocational education and training and, as part of this, a Technical and Vocational Education Training (TVET) plan has been created and is now being implemented. The TVET plan is the document that provides a clear vision for training and skills development in Timor-Leste. The vision in the TVET plan is that, by 2030, the training system will be characterized by:

- The young people of Timor-Leste following clearly linked pathways that take them from school to training to work and to higher education;
- A skilled labor force driving increased services, industrial development, economic diversification and innovation;
- Training being measured by its quality and how training services match the needs of industry and communities; and
- Industry and civil society working in partnership with Government to increase the skills of all people and to increase opportunities for secure and meaningful work.

Seven elements are recommended in the TVET plan:

1. *Efficient Investment in Training* – securing long-term budget allocations from the Human Capital Development Fund; establishing a managed training market; establishing new funding guidelines and performance measures.
2. *National, District and Industry Needs and Demands* – identifying national priorities; undertaking skill needs analysis of major projects, districts and industries; developing a labor market information system; encouraging enterprise development.
3. *Participation in Training* – promoting the TVET system; establishing equity in participation; implementing the *National Training Commitment*; preparing for a national traineeship scheme.
4. *Building the Capacity of Trainers* – new national teaching and learning materials and training support services; building the capacity of training organizations and community-based training providers.
5. *Business Engagement in Developing Skills* – a National Skills Development Center; building strategic training infrastructure; introducing incentives for business investment in skills development and jobs; implementing a *National Labour Content Policy*.
6. *National Partnerships and Institutions* – creating the *National Skills, Employment and Productivity Council*; better coordinating education, TVET and other government training programs such as Agriculture and Health; removing inconsistencies between TVET laws and other training-related laws.
7. *Governance and Monitoring of Training* – including: making the system work in relation to ensuring effective compliance with contracts; allocating adequate staffing and resources and monitoring; implementing ten key performance measures and the appropriate resourcing to conduct evaluation of the training system on an annual basis.

In response to the implementation of the TVET plan, the National Institute for Labour Force Development (INDMO) has been created. It is responsible for defining the standards of skills and for establishing a vocational training certification system in accordance with national and international standards. It exercises the following responsibilities:

- to define and approve the standards of skills of the various production sectors in Timor-Leste;
- to certify the skills in accordance with the approved standards;
- to certify training centers and companies to act as skills evaluation centers, as well as to certify the relevant trainers.

Within the structure of the newly developed Timor-Leste National Qualifications Framework (NQF) the transformation process is guided by a set of underlying principles, which are: access and equity; quality; proficiency; relevance. It is a system that is intended to be responsive to industry needs, based upon international quality standards, and focused on employment outcomes for Timorese people.

The new TVET system also allows for those already in employment to upgrade their skills and receive national skills recognition. As the system develops, centers of excellence will be established in each trade area. It is envisaged that these centers will have the capacity to conduct skills assessment. This means that people with many years of skills and experience can have their skills assessed against the national standards and receive appropriate qualifications.

The new TVET system provides minimum standards for all training providers in Timor-Leste, whether they are based in civil society, government, church, or private enterprise, to deliver quality training. The regulations also seek to strengthen existing training providers with the capacity and resources to deliver at a higher level, that is, to deliver qualifications registered on the National Qualifications Framework to ensure a skilled workforce for the future.

This paper outlines English language training in Timor-Leste in a TVET context, and covers the following issues:

1. Development of English language qualifications;
2. Partnerships for implementation;
3. English language training and the Timor-Leste National Qualifications Framework;
4. Future implementation of English language training.

2 ENGLISH LANGUAGE TRAINING IN THE TVET CONTEXT IN TIMOR-LESTE

2.1 *The development of English language qualifications for the Timor-Leste National Qualifications Framework*

The English language qualification has been developed by the Timor-Leste English Language Program (ETELP). ETELP was a project funded by the Australian Government through the Department of Foreign Affairs and Trade (DFAT) and managed by the Indonesia Australia Language Foundation (IALF).

The English language qualification is new to the National Qualifications Framework and it has been designed in response to the needs of English language training in Timor-Leste.

This qualification has been developed in consultation with INDMO, the Ministry of Education, and the National Institute for Training of Teachers and Education Professionals (INFORDEPE).

2.2 English language certification levels

Three levels of English language certification have been developed for the National Qualifications Framework:

- Certificate I in General English
- Certificate II in General English and ESP (English for Specific Purposes/Teaching)
- Certificate III in English Language Teaching Methodology

Certificate I is equivalent to the Elementary Level of General English courses and Certificate II is equivalent to the Pre-Intermediate level of General English courses with the addition of specific units for teaching. Certificate III provides an introduction to the concept of communicative English language teaching in the context of English as a Second Language (ESL).

2.3 The partnership for English language training in Timor-Leste

This qualification was developed by ETELP in consultation with INDMO. The Ministry of Education of Timor-Leste and INFORDEPE are partners in the implementation process. The Australia Timor-Leste English Language Program (ATELP) is continuing the partnership and cooperation, and is implementing the training for English language teachers in schools from the districts of Aileu, Ermera and Liquiça.

2.4 English language training in the National Qualifications Framework

The English language training is following the standards of the National Qualifications Framework and can be shown as in Figure 1.

2.5 Future implementation of English language training

There are demands from various sectors and various levels of people for the English language training. Teachers still need in-service training in English to improve their level of English and to develop good methods for teaching English to students. The trainers working within the accredited training providers are required to be competent in English to deliver English as an integrated unit in each qualification provided in the training centers.

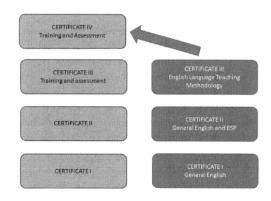

Figure 1. The National Qualifications Framework standards.

Teachers and trainers who successfully complete Certificates I to III in the English language will be provided with further training from abroad in order to qualify as trainers to other teachers and trainers in the future. The government will need to develop a plan and policy for addressing these issues.

3 CONCLUSIONS AND RECOMMENDATIONS

3.1 Conclusions

The English language qualification has been developed and now exists as a national qualification in the Timor-Leste TVET sector. Certificates I and II can be applied to anyone who needs to improve their English or for those who are seeking work in an English language environment. Certificate III is aimed at those who work as English language teachers or trainers or who are willing to become future English teachers or trainers.

3.2 Recommendations

The standard TVET qualification in English is only up to Certificate II, which is equivalent to the Pre-Intermediate level of General English courses. There will be a need for further development of similar qualifications to Certificate III or Certificate IV, which will be equivalent to the Intermediate and Upper-Intermediate levels of General English courses.

This will be a continuing task for all who are involved in the TVET implementations in Timor-Leste. The government of Timor-Leste should play an important role in the development of the qualifications in response to the needs of the global market and state development.

REFERENCES

Department of Foreign Affairs and Trade. (2010). *Australia East Timor English Language Program-Project Design Document*. Retrieved from https://dfat.gov.au/about-us/publications/Documents/australia-timor-leste-language-program-design.pdf.

Government of Timor-Leste. (2008). *Decree Law 8/2008, Creates the National Institute for Manpower Development. Retrieved from* http://mj.gov.tl/jornal/lawsTL/RDTL-Law/RDTL-Decree-Laws/Decree-Law-2008-08.pdf

Government of Timor-Leste. (2011a). *Strategic Development Plan Timor-Leste, 2011–2030*. Dili, Timor-Leste. Retrieved from https://sustainabledevelopment. un.org/content/documents/1506Timor-Leste-Strategic-Plan-2011-20301.pdf

Government of Timor-Leste. (2011b). *Timor-Leste TVET Plan 2011–2030*. Retrieved from http://www.mlstp.net/uploads/4/8/6/7/48670023/10_timor-leste_tvet_plan_2011–2030.pdf

Government of Timor-Leste. (2012). *The New TVET Training System in Timor-Leste-UNESCO-UNEVOC*. Retrieved from http://www.unevoc.unesco.org/fileadmin/user_upload/docs/TVET_in_Timor_Leste_01052012.pdf

Indonesia Australia English Language Program. (2011). *East Timor English Language Program (ETELP)*. Retrieved from http://www.ialf.edu/projects.html

Malaysian teachers' competency in technical vocational education and training: A review

K. Ismail, Z.M. Nopiah & M.S. Rasul
National University of Malaysia, Bangi, Selangor, Malaysia

P.C. Leong
Department of Skills Development, Ministry of Human Resources, Putrajaya, Malaysia

ABSTRACT: Teachers' competency and skills affect their students' progress and are an important component of the TVET institution. A competent teacher is form of quality assurance for students' learning. Malaysia's TVET education system has not escaped the issue of insufficient competence among teachers in the polytechnics, community colleges, vocational colleges and public skills training institutions. The aim of this review is to synthesize the available evidence in the literature about challenges faced by Malaysian teachers in TVET institutions with regards to their competency. Fourteen articles published between 2009 and 2015 have been appraised. The review reveals that concerns about the competency of Malaysian teachers include: the lack of English language usage in teaching; the need to improve skills in technical, ICT and pedagogy; the absence of TVET teacher job profiles and a competency model; and the need to improve TVET teacher skills and knowledge through training.

1 INTRODUCTION

Competent teachers are the driving force behind effective teaching and learning. Scholars (Knight & Elliot 2009; Kömür 2010; Kleickmann et al. 2012; Spöttll 2009; Wesselink et al. 2010) agree that competent and knowledgeable teachers are essential to the processes of teaching and learning. Teachers are a driving force in the implementation of each educational institution's mandate. Therefore, there is a need to ensure that the skills, knowledge, and attitudes of TVET teachers align with technological changes, current job requirements, equipment, machines, processes, and so on (Basu 1997; Chappell 2000).

1.1 *The importance of competency and the competence of TVET teachers*

Competency refers to successful individual performance in applying knowledge and skills in specific activities or tasks performed, while competence refers to a person's success in a specific profession. The concept of competencies comes from David McClelland's 1973 article, "Testing for Competence Rather than Intelligence." He introduces five types of competency characteristics which are knowledge, skills, self-concepts, traits, and motives. Boyatriz (1982), Spencer and Spencer (1993), and

many others used the concept of competence in relation with performance improvement.

Generally, competency is a combination of attitude, knowledge, and skills (ILO 2010; Campion et al. 2011; Chakraborty 2013; Mohd Salleh 2012) and is a prerequisite for workers to carry out a job function (Eraut 1994; Hager & Gonczi 1996; Ellström 1997). Competency, according to Mulcahy (2000); Volmari et al. (2009); Palaniappan (2003); Mulder (2001); and Shippmann et al. (2000), is as an indicator of an individual's level of capacity, capability, and performance in duties/jobs; competency is necessary for an organization to be more competitive. An employee's competency level can be increased through training and core competencies can be developed as a model to benchmark the performance of staff in an organization.

Guthrie (2010) stated that a TVET teacher is someone who has been trained and is competent in the field and in the delivery and evaluation of teaching; has the ability to demonstrate skills; and continuously develops and progresses their career by gaining more knowledge and skills in the field. Other previous studies indicated that the TVET teacher must have social competency (Monnier 2015); knowledge and competency in work processes (Boreham 2002); professional and pedagogical competency (Mirzagitova & Akhmetov 2015; Barbazette 2005); teaching, social, management, technological and technical skills (Othman et al. 2011); leadership and personality competency in classroom organization and student management (Aliakbari & Darabi 2013); personality competency (Blašková et al. 2014); cognitive, behavioural, pedagogic and psychomotor competency (Cakrawati et al. 2015); teaching, educating and professional competency; competency of linking real work processes to a professional learning processes; communication competency; and self-reflection competency (Diep & Hartmann 2016). The purpose of this study is related to the competency of the TVET teachers in Malaysia.

1.2 *Global TVET teacher issues*

Concerns regarding the competence of TVET teachers should not be taken lightly as problems are pervasive in TVET institutions across the country. The report by SEAMEO VOCTECH (2012) states that '...most of the TVET teachers are graduates from different levels but still lacking in industrial practice and exposure ....'. Education Statistics Indicator 2012/2013 reported that teachers in Cambodia have low academic qualifications and teachers did not receive training in pedagogy (Phin 2014). Young-Saing et al. (2010) noted problems related to TVET trainers in countries such as Bangladesh, Cambodia, Sri Lanka, Lao PDR, Vietnam, and Indonesia, where they are facing a shortage of TVET trainers qualified and proficient in pedagogy and technology. Furthermore, expert workers in the industry have lost interest in working as teachers in TVET institutions and prefer to work in other sectors due to the low salaries in the teaching profession (Grollman & Rauner 2007).

TVET teachers in Mongolia are university graduates and they have to undergo additional teaching training to improve the quality of TVET teaching (Duggan 2015). Ahmed (2011) stated that the quality of Sudanese TVET trainers must be enhanced with further skills training in the application of ICT in teaching, as well as industrial training. Rauner & Dittrich (2006) declared that the TVET teaching profession is still considered to be marginal and lacking in prestige, and it offers lower salaries, which prompts teachers to switch to the higher education sector to access more the attractive opportunities.

Two of the weaknesses of TVET teachers are associated with the lack of skills in pedagogy and lesser work experience. Paryono (2015) states that the availability of TVET teachers is a critical issue as teachers' numbers are insufficient and declining, and that quality of teaching staff is inadequate due to their lack of industry experience in teaching. In the Malaysian context, TVET teacher competence has also become an issue. In this regard, the research

question posed is: what are the issues related to the competence of TVET trainers in Malaysia?

1.3 *Background of TVET in Malaysia*

In a nutshell, TVET education in Malaysia began at the end of 1806 to train local young people to work as mechanics and fitters on the national railways (Leong et al. 2010). The educational reform in Malaysia began in the early 1980s, as mentioned in the Cabinet Committee Report in 1979. As part of the development of Malaysia, it promoted a broad range of participation in business and trade. As such, technical and vocational education were expanded and further developed in line with national development (Yahya Emat, 2005). In Malaysia, TVET is led by eight ministries: the Ministry of Human Resources, the Ministry of Works, the Ministry of Youth and Sports, the Ministry of Higher Institution, the Ministry of Education, the Ministry of Regional and Rural Development, the Ministry of Agriculture and Agro-Based Industry, and the Ministry of Defence. The ministries have the common objective and goal to produce a generation of Malaysians with knowledge and skills in their respective fields (Rasul et al. 2015; Ahmad et al. 2015).

The Malaysian Qualifications Agency (MQA) under the Ministry of Higher Education is a government body which gives accreditation to TVET institutions and accredits the training programs implemented in the universities, polytechnics, community colleges, and training institutions under MARA, while the Department of Skills Development under the Ministry of Human Resources is the accrediting body for both public and private institutions for skills development. At present, there are 1369 TVET institutions in Malaysia, including universities, polytechnics, community colleges, vocational colleges, technical schools, and public and private institutions, for skills development (EPU 2015). Thus, teachers play an important role in ensuring the quality of the teaching and learning process in the Malaysia TVET institutions.

2 METHODOLOGY

Articles published between 2009 and 2015 were searched in the databases ScienceDirect and Google Scholar using Mendeley. The following keywords were used in the search: 'Malaysia', 'TVET', 'teachers', 'competence', 'competency' and 'issues'. Titles, abstract, results, and conclusions were screened, and studies were selected to be included if they were relevant to the addressed issues regarding the competencies of teachers in Malaysian TVET institutions. Whittemore & Knafl (2005) mentioned that

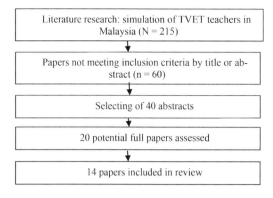

| Literature research: simulation of TVET teachers in Malaysia (N = 215) |
| Papers not meeting inclusion criteria by title or abstract (n = 60) |
| Selecting of 40 abstracts |
| 20 potential full papers assessed |
| 14 papers included in review |

Figure 1.   Flow diagram of the study selection process.

a review involves specifying the review purpose, searching the issues in the literature, evaluating data from the primary sources, analyzing data, and presenting the results are discussed. As shown in Figure 1, the abstracts of studies that are related to Malaysian TVET teachers were examined, resulting in a full review of 20 papers and the final inclusion of 14 articles in this review.

3   RESULTS AND DISCUSSION

The 'key findings' contributing to the issues of Malaysian TVET teachers are lack of ICT knowledge and skills; lack of pedagogical knowledge; lack of English language in teaching; absence of teacher job profiles and competency models; lack of skills training and work experience; and issues related with the unemployment of TVET students.

3.1   Lack of ICT knowledge and skills

Knowledge in ICT is important for the TVET teachers. Using the ICT helps teaching and learning progress smoothly, creates interesting teaching environments, helps the teachers to prepare the teaching materials and allows teachers to explore new knowledge. One issue related to ICT is that the teachers in MARA skills institution can have their knowledge enhanced by providing ICT facilities such as adequate computer and unlimited Internet access (Wahab et al. 2009). TVET institution leaders and teachers should be able to employ technological mechanisms to enhance knowledge integration and view ICT as a powerful force which can revolutionize teaching and learning processes. Saud et al. (2010) said that teachers do not take the time to provide technological materials due to work commitments and lack of the knowledge and skills required to provide ICT-based teach-

ing materials such as video. Alazam et al. (2012) said teachers in public training institutions are not skilled in the field of ICT, especially in programming and simulation. Therefore, teachers need to be trained in ICT-based programming in order to improve their ability to teach using ICT. Teachers should be trained to establish a technology-rich teaching and learning environment and motivated to use the ICT as a powerful tool which can revolutionize teaching and learning processes.

3.2   Lack of pedagogical knowledge

The level of knowledge and practical pedagogy of teachers in TVET public and private institutions with regards to skills training needs to be improved by providing competent teachers (Jabatan Pembangunan Kemahiran 2011). Chua & Jamil (2012) said the level of knowledge for teachers in skills public institutions for Technological Pedagogical Content Knowledge (TPACK) needs to be enhanced. The community colleges are facing the same problem because the level of pedagogical skills, particularly of those involved in problem-solving tasks, is still weak among teachers in the culinary program at the community colleges. Teachers need guidelines in the curriculum for teaching problem-based learning (Techanamurthy, Umawathy Alias & Norlidah DeWitt, 2015). The assessment is part of pedagogy. The absence of specific guidelines for evaluation has resulted in the provision of poor quality lab sheets and a very broad scope of assessment criteria (Rahman et al. 2014).

Knowledge is important to TVET teachers. As (Shulman 1986) suggests, the effective teachers must have seven kinds of knowledge which are general pedagogical knowledge, curriculum knowledge, pedagogical content knowledge, knowledge of learners and their characteristics, knowledge of the educational contexts and knowledge of educational ends. Teachers must regularly update their knowledge about pedagogy to keep abreast with current developments in education.

3.3   Lack of English language in teaching

English is a universal language and most technical references are from English sources. In TVET education, as mentioned by (Sahul Hamed et al. 2010), the issue faced by the teachers at polytechnics is the need to enhance their skills in order to teach in the English language. The transformation of polytechnics requires changes in the organizational working culture leading toward improved quality of high-performance personnel. The teachers should be able to master the English language as a medium of instruction because polytechnics have set the goal to open their intuitions to international students. (Sanmugam 2013) said that technical teachers in polytechnics need training about teaching technical modules in English because they are unprepared to teach technical modules in English, especially in terms of speaking and writing. They also lack confidence and are unable to handle the learning problems of weak students. They much prefer to teach in the Malay language so that the students can understand the content easily. This statement is supported by (Elias et al. 2005), who said that the reason why Malaysian teachers feel that they are not competent in using the English language in teaching is because they do not have enough confidence, lack the vocabulary, are not ready to teach in English, and need a lot of practice before they can teach subjects in English. (Noor & Harun 2015) said that the use of English is lacking among teachers who are serving in the community colleges in subjects other than the Tourism program. Use of English in teaching is subject to the willingness of the teachers.

3.4 Absence of TVET teacher job profiles and competency models

The absence of job profiles, competency models, and frameworks has made it difficult for the teachers to develop profiles and appropriate training (Ali et al. 2010). The competency model and competency profiles also serve as benchmarks to determine the level of competence that each teacher should possess and address the issue of teachers' professional development (Rodolfa et al. 2005). The competency model describes the knowledge, skills, and behaviours that make up the performance criteria which are measured, reviewed, and evaluated (Asumeng 2014). The teacher profiles need to encompass strong subject matter knowledge, pedagogical skills, the capacity to work effectively with a wide range of students and colleagues, the ability to contribute to the institution and the profession, and the capacity to continue developing (OECD 2005).

3.5 Lack of skills training and work experience

TVET teachers face difficulty in teaching technical and practical education because of lack of training. Sulaiman et al. (2014) said that a lack of training in welding and cutting metals among teachers in vocational schools leaves them less skilled. Teachers are advised to get intensive training in the industry and training institutes that offer welding programs. Yusof et al. (2015) said constraints faced by teachers including less exposure to teaching, lack of experience, and overwork have resulted in less diversified methods of teaching. The patterns of teaching are more similar to a typical/traditional classroom teaching approach, but students expect the teachers

to apply more active strategies in teaching. Hence, competency development is an important feature of competency management that encompasses all activities carried out by the organization and helps employees to maintain or enhance the employee's functional, learning, and career competencies (Vos et al. 2011). To ensure that educational goals can be met, teacher training in the key factors seems to be logical. The teachers must undergo training to improve their knowledge and skills in the field.

3.6 Issues related with unemployed students

Unemployment among graduates for nearly 30 percent of TVET skills institutions is due to factors such as the need for a curriculum that is relevant to the needs of the industry, low-quality graduates who do not achieve the standards needed by industry, and poor teaching skills among teachers (Hanapi et al. 2014). The poor teaching skills among the TVET teachers are related to quality and teaching experience. The quality of the teachers is an important factor in determining the quality of the students; and teacher effectiveness is a measure of the teacher quality. A teacher's level of the experience makes the most difference during the early career years. The teacher's effectiveness climbs during the first seven years or so before tapering off, and, by 10 years, experience ceases to be a factor as mentioned by Michael Strong (2011). Inexperienced teachers contribute below-average results.

4 CONCLUSION

The issue of competence is relevant to teachers across TVET institutions in Malaysia. As such, teachers require life-long learning through both formal and informal training methods in order to improve their level of competency. In addition, the provision of relevant ICT tools in teaching, an increase of English language usage in teaching, the preparation of guidelines for assessment, and training in generic teaching skills, as well as creating trainers' job profiles according to fields, are proposed to improve competencies among TVET trainers in Malaysia. The development of a competency model is relevant as a benchmark for the performance of teachers in Malaysia. For future research, researchers would like to propose a competency model for the technical teachers in public skills training institutions.

REFERENCES

Ahmad, M.J., Jalani, N.H. & Hasmori, A.A. 2015. *TEVT di Malaysia: Cabaran dan Harapan.* paper presented to the Seminar Kebangsaan Majlis Dekan-Dekan Pendidikan Awam 2015, Kuala Lumpur. pp. 1–8.

Ahmed, H. a E. 2011. *Building Capacity of Teachers and Trainers in Technical and Vocational Education and Training (TVET) in Sudan Case of Khartoum State.* PhD thesis, University of Dresden-Germany.

Alazam, A., Bakar, A., Hamzah, R. & Asmiran, S. 2012. Teachers' ICT Skills and ICT Integration in the Classroom: The Case of Vocational and Technical Teachers in Malaysia. *Creative Education* 3: 70–76.

Ali, M., Kaprawi, N. & Razzaly, W. 2010. *Development of a New Empirical Based Competency Profile for Malaysian Vocational Education and Training Instructors.* paper presented to the Proceedings of the 1st UPI International Conference on Technical and Vocational Education and Training Bandung, Indonesia, 10–11 November 2010. pp. 10–11.

Aliakbari, M. & Darabi, R. 2013. On the Relationship between Efficacy of Classroom Management, Transformational Leadership Style, and Teachers' Personality. *Procedia - Social and Behavioral Sciences* 23: 1716–1721.

Asumeng, M.A. 2014. Managerial Competency Models: A Critical Review and Proposed Holistic-Domain Model. *Journal of Management Research* 6(4).

Barbazette, J. 2005. *The trainer's journey to competence: Tools, assessments and models.* Pfeiffer, A Wiley Imprint.

Basu, C. 1997. *Challenges of Current Social, Economical and Technological Developments and Need for Reforms/Renovations in Training of Teachers in Technical-Vocational,* viewed on 23 March 2016.

Blašková, M. et al. 2014. Key Personality Competences of University Teacher: Comparison of Requirements Defined by Teachers and/Versus Defined by Students. *Procedia - Social and Behavioral Sciences* 114: 466–475.

Boreham, N. 2002. Work process knowledge, curriculum control and the work-based route to vocational qualifications. *British Journal of Educational Studies* 50(2): 225–237.

Boyatzis, R. 1982. *The Competent Manager: A Model for Effective Performance,* John Wiley & Sons, New York.

Cakrawati, D., Handayani, S. & Handayani, M.N. 2015. Model of Learning Implementation in Preparing Vocational Teachers', *Proceedings of the 3Rd Upi International Conference on Technical and Vocational Education and Training.* pp. 50–53.

Campion, M.A. et al. 2011. Doing competencies well: Best practices in competency modeling. *Personnel Psychology* 64: 225–262.

Chakraborty, R.C. 2013. A model for assessing competency level. *International Journal of Human Resource Management and Research (IJHRMR)* 3(4): 33–40.

Chappell, C. 2000. *The new VET professional: Culture, roles & competence.* http://www.oval.uts.edu.au/working_papers/2000WP/0041chappell.pdf.

Chua, J.H. & Jamil, H. 2012. Factors Influencing the Technological Pedagogical Content Knowledge (TPACK) among TVET instructors in Malaysian TVET Institution. *Procedia - Social and Behavioral Sciences* 69: 1539–1547.

Diep, P.C. & Hartmann, M. 2016. *Green Skills in Vocational Teacher Education – a model of pedagogical competence for a world of sustainable development.* www.tvet-online.asia, issue 6, viewed on 13 March 2016, http://www.tvet-online.asia/issue/6/diep-hartmann

Duggan, S.J. 2015. *Approaches to the quality improvement of TVET teachers in Mongolia: a lost opportunity.* www.tvet-online.asia, issue 5, pp. 1–14, viewed on 15 March 2016, http://www.tvet-online.asia/issue5/duggan_tvet5.pdf.

Elias, H., Lope Pihie, Z.A. & Mahyuddin, R. 2005. *Competencies Needed by Teachers Implications for Best Teaching Practices.* Universiti Putra Malaysia Press, Serdang.

Ellström, P.E. 1997. The many meanings of occupational competence and qualification. *Journal of European Industrial Training* 21(6): 266–273.

EPU, 2015. *Mentransformasi pendidikan dan latihan teknikal dan vokasional untuk memenuhi permintaan industri.* Jabatan Perdana Menteri, Malaysia.

Eraut, M. 1994. *Developing professional knowledge and competence.* Routledge/Falmer: New York.

Grollman, P. & Rauner, F. 2007. Tvet Teachers: An Endangered Species Or Professional Innovation Agents. In Grollman, P. & Rauner, F. (ed.), *International Perspectives on Teachers and Lecturers in Technical and Vocational Education,* Springer, Netherland, pp. 1–26.

Guthrie, H. 2010. *Professional development in the vocational education and training workforce.* National Centre for Vocational Education Research, Australia.

Hager, P. & Gonczi, A. 1996. What is competence? *Medical Teacher* 18(1): 15–18.

Hanapi, Z., Safarin, M. & Che, R. 2014. Unemployment Problem among Graduates of Technical Field: Competencies of the Graduates and Quality of the Education. *Sains Humanika* 2(2): 53–57.

ILO. 2010. *Teachers and trainers for the future – Technical and vocational education and training in a changing world,* International Labour Organization.

Jabatan Pembangunan Kemahiran. 2011. *Level of Acceptance of Skill Training Among Communities in Malaysia,* Report of Jabatan Pembangunan Kemahiran.

Kleickmann, T., Richter, D., Kunter, M., Elsner, J., Besser, M., Krauss, S. & Baumert, J. 2012. Teachers' Content Knowledge and Pedagogical Content Knowledge: The Role of Structural Differences in Teacher Education. *Journal of Teacher Education* 64(1): 90–106.

Knight, J. & Elliot, J. 2009. TVET Teacher Education: A Vision Beyond Tradition. *Journal of Technical Education and Training* 1(1): 73–84.

Kömür, Ş. 2010. Teaching knowledge and teacher competencies: a case study of Turkish preservice English teachers. *Teaching Education* 21(3): 279–296.

Leong, P.C., Narunan, R. & Sim, S. 2010. *Background Paper for Malaysia: Skills Development in the Workplace in Malaysia.* viewed on 24 March 2016, http://apskills.ilo.org/resources/background-paper-for-malaysia-skills-development-in-the-workplace-in-malaysia.

Micheal S. 2011. *The Highly Qualified Teacher. What is teacher quality and how to measure it?* Teacher College Press, Columbia University.

Mirzagitova, A.L. & Akhmetov, L.G. 2015. Self-development of pedagogical competence of future teacher. *International Education Studies* 8(3): 114–121.

Mohd Salleh, K. 2012. *Human Resource Development practitioners' perspectives on competencies: An application of American Society for Training and Development (ASTD) Workplace Learning and Performance (WLP) competency model in Malaysia.* PhD Thesis, The Colorado State University.

Monnier, M. 2015. Difficulties in defining social-emotional intelligence, competences and skills - a theoretical analysis and structural suggestion. *International Journal of Research for Vocational Education and Training* 2(1): 59–84.

Mulcahy, D. 2000. Turning the contradictions of competence: competency-based training and beyond. *Journal of Vocational Education & Training* 52(2): 259–280.

Mulder, M. 2001. Competence development - some background thoughts. *The Journal of Agricultural Education and Extension* 7(4): 147–158.

Noor, F.M. & Harun, H. 2015. Phenomenological Study: Bilingual Teaching Classroom of Malaysian Community Colleges. *Procedia - Social and Behavioral Sciences* 204: 114–118.

OECD. 2005. *Teachers Matter: Attracting, Developing and Retaining Effective Teachers.* viewed on 10 March 2016, http://www.oecd-ilibrary.org/education/teachers-matter-attracting-developing-and-retaining-effective-teachers_9789638739940-hu.

Othman, A., Abdullah, N.H., Sulaiman, M., Shamsuddin, A. 2011. The Emerging Roles of Coaches in the Malaysian Dual Training System. *International Education Studies* 4(1): 154–160.

Palaniappan, R. 2003. *Competency Management : A Practioners's Guide,* Percetakan Suma, Kuala Lumpur

Paryono, P. 2015. Approaches to preparing TVET teachers and instructors in ASEAN member countries. *TVET@Asia,* issue 5, pp. 1–27, viewed on 12 December 2015, http://www.tvet-online.asia/issue5/paryono_tvet5.pdf.

Phin, C. 2014. Teacher competence and teacher quality in Cambodia's educational context linked to in-service teacher training: an examination based on a questionnaire survey. *International Journal of Educational Administration and Policy Studies* 6(4): 62–69.

Rahman, A., Muhamad Hanafi, N., Ibrahim Mukhtar, M. & Ahmad, J. 2014. Assessment Practices for Competency based Education and Training in Vocational College, Malaysia. *Procedia - Social and Behavioral Sciences* 112: 1070–1076.

Rasul, M.S., Mohamed Ashari, Z.H., Azman, N. & Abdul Raof, R.A. 2015. Transforming TVET in Malaysia: Harmonizing the Governance Structure in a Multiple Stakeholder Setting. *TVET-Online.Asia,* issue 4, pp. 1–13.

Rauner, F. & Dittrich, J. 2006. Increasing the Profile and Professionalisation of the Education of TVET. Teachers and Trainers. In Bunning F. & Zhao Z. (ed.), *TVET Teacher Education on the Threshold of Internationalisation*: 35–42.

Rodolfa, E., Bent, R., Eisman, E., Nelson, P., Rehm, L. & Ritchie, P. 2005. A Cube Model for Competency Development: Implications for Psychology Educators and Regulators. *Professional Psychology: Research and Practice* 36(4): 347–354.

Sahul Hamed, A.W., Mohd Amin, Z. & Mohd Ali, J. 2010. 'Transformational of Malaysian's Polytechnic into University College in 2015: Issues and Challenges for Malaysian Technical and Vocational Education. *1st UPI International Conference on Technical and Vocational Education and Training Bandung, Indonesia, 10-11 November.* pp. 544–553.

Sanmugam, S.T. 2013. Technical Instructions in English: Voices of Technical Lecturers. *Journal of Technical Education and Training (JTET)* 5(1): 1–13.

Saud, M.S. et al. 2010. *Teachers' ICT Skills and ICT Integration in the Classroom: The Case of Vocational and Technical Teachers in Malaysia.* vol. 3, pp. 70–76.

SEAMEO VOCTECH. 2012. *TVET Teacher Education in Southest Asia and Nepal Report.* pp. 1–32.

Shippmann, J.S., Ash, R.A., Hesketh, B., Pearlman, K., Sanchez, J.I., Battista, M., Eyde, L.D., Koheo, J, Prien, E.P. 2000. The Practice of Competency Modeling. *Personnel Psychology* 53: 703–740.

Shulman, L.S. 1986. Those Who Understand: A Conception of Teacher Knowledge. *American Educator,* pp. 4–14.

Spencer, L. & Spencer, S. 1993. *Competence at Work: Models for Superior Performance.* John Wiley & Sons, New York.

Spöttll, G. 2009. Teacher education for TVET In Europe and Asia: The comprehensive requirements. *Journal of Technical Education and Training* 1(1): 1–16.

Sulaiman, N.L., Alias, M., Masek, A. & Mohd Salleh, K. 2014. Further training in occupational skills for vocational teachers: the case of metal cutting in Malaysia', *TVET@Asia,* issue. 3, pp. 1–13.

Techanamurthy, U., Alias, N. & DeWitt, D. 2015. *Problem-Solving Skills in TVET: Current Practices Among Culinary Arts Instructors in Community Colleges in Malaysia.* pp. 1–9.

Volmari, K., Helakorpi, S. & Frimodt, R. 2009. Competence Framework For VET professions: Handbook for practitioners. *Finnish National Board of Education, CEDEFOP.* p. 58.

Vos, A. De, Hauw, S. De & Willemse, I. 2011. *Competency Development in Organizations: Building an Integrative Model through a Qualitative Study Competency Development in Organizations: Building an Integrative Model through a Qualitative Study,* pp. 2–38.

Wahab, S.R.A., Shaari, A., Nordin, N.A., Rajab, A. & Isa, K. 2009. *Faktor Persekitaran Organisasi Mempengaruhi Perkongsian Pengetahuan: Satu Analisis Di Institut Kemahiran Mara Johor.* In Amalan Latihan dan Pembangunan Sumber Manusia di Malaysia. pp. 218–236.

Wesselink, R., Dekker-Groen, A.M., Biemens, H.J.A. & Mulder, M. 2010. Using an instrument to analyse competence-based study programmes: experiences of teachers in Dutch vocational education and training. *Journal of Curriculum Studies* 42(6): 813–829.

Whittemore, R. & Knafl, K. 2005. The integrative review: Updated methodology', *Journal of Advanced Nursing* 52(5): 546–553.

Yahya E. 2005. *Pendidikan Teknik dan Vokasional di Malaysia,* IBS Buku Sdn Bhd, Kuala Lumpur.

Young-Saing, K., Ji-Cun, C., Young-Sub, L., Sang-Don, L. & Ki-Rak, R. 2010. TVET Policy Reviews of 8 Asian Countries. In *Korea Research Institute for Vocational Education & Training.* pp. 1–670.

Yusof, Y., Roddin, R. & Awang, H. 2015. What Students Need, and What Teacher Did: The Impact of Teacher's Teaching Approaches to the Development of Students' Generic Competences. *Procedia - Social and Behavioral Sciences* 204: 36–44.

Regionalization and Harmonization in TVET – Abdullah et al. (Eds)
© 2017 Taylor & Francis Group, London, ISBN 978-1-138-05419-6

Needs identification in strengthening the skills of construction workers with the national working competency standards

L. Widaningsih, T. Megayanti & I. Susanti
Universitas Pendidikan Indonesia, Jawa Barat, Indonesia

ABSTRACT: The current paper aims at identifying the needs for strengthening the skills of construction workers involved in a variety of construction jobs in the scale of residential and public buildings. Construction workers in Indonesia are still considered as a low employment which is underappreciated by the community. The skills of the workers are obtained through heredity and self-taught, not through formal or non-formal education and training. This leads to a lack of accessibility of the workers to knowledge and skills required by the National Working Competency Standards (here-inafter referred to as the National Standards). The study used qualitative approach, and data collection techniques were field observation, focus group discussions, and focused interviews. The respondents were 29 construction workers from different expertise in Garut, Indonesia. The needs for strengthening competency were identified at an individual level by analyzing the level of knowledge, skill, and attitude compared to the level required under the National Standards. The results of the study showed a grouping of worker expertise, knowledge and skill level mapping, and the mapping of the needs for strengthening construction workers' skills.

1   INTRODUCTION

Construction workers in Indonesia are still faced with some fundamental problems which include a lack of welfare, the level skills possessed, safety and education, and education and training qualifications. As the technical field workers, their contribution in the construction industry is huge, but in the structure of employment they are a group of informal workers.

Informal workers do not have or subject to labor laws. The income is not taxed, and their social protection or rights to job security is low. The condition causes the difficulty in structuring the construction workforce in an employment scheme that can guarantee their rights, the standardization of wages, and access to education and training to improve job skills. (Rothenberg et al., 2016; Organization, 2015).

This paper is the result of a preliminary study of the construction workers in a district of Garut. The objective is to get an overview of the needs identification results of the workers in strengthening their skills. This is important because job competition in urban, national and even global with the ASEAN economic community demands the construction workers to acquire job skills that meet the qualifications as required by the National Standards.

2   MATERIALS AND METHODS

2.1   *Participants*

The participants of the present study were 29 construction workers from different expertise in Garut, Indonesia.

2.2   *Data collection*

The data were collected from focus group discussion and in-depth interview to 27 construction workers in a district of Garut.

2.3   *Data analysis*

Data analysis was conducted to identify the extent to which the workers know and understand the information about the certification issued by the National Standards, their education and work experience, their involvement in projects in urban areas, their training participation, the knowledge and implementation of occupational and health safety, and the skills of masonry, carpentry, and finishing (painting).

According to their level of education, the research participants who graduated from senior high school, junior high school, and elementary school level accounted for 47%, 29%, and 24% respectively. This can be seen as well according to

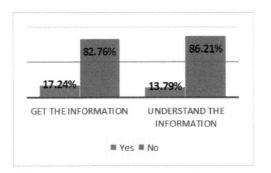

Figure 1. Getting information and understanding work certification.

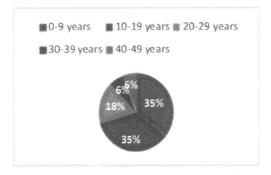

Figure 2. Work experience.

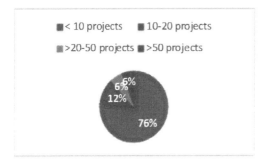

Figure 3. Experience in project involvement in urban areas.

their age groups of 20–29, 30–49, and 50–59 showing 59%, 18%, and 23% respectively. This means that the group of 20–29 years old was the generations who had higher education level.

Figure 3 shows that most participants involved in work projects for more than 10 years (94%) while there were only 6% having less than 10 years of experience. This indicates that the construction workers had experience in small to big construction projects. This experience becomes a way to

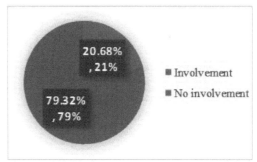

Figure 4. Involvement in training.

Table 1. The skill level of construction workers.

	Level of skills	
Skill aspects	Average (%)	Category
Occupational and Health Safety	56	Fair
Mansory	64.67	High
Carpentry	76.25	High
Finishing	73	High

improve their working skills. They had lack of formal training to develop their working skills. There were about 20.68% of the participants who had some training, while most of them had no experience in work training.

The skill level is assessed based on the existing groups in the community of construction workers (Figure 5). Based on the four skill aspects, the level of their skills based on the requirements and the detailed orders issued by the Construction Services Development Institution was in the category of high. Meanwhile, the level of attitude and culture in occupational and health safety related was in the category of fair.

3 RESULTS AND DISCUSSION

3.1 Job skill mapping

Text The work of construction services consists of the work of architecture, civil, mechanical, electrical and environmental planning (landscape) (Jatnika dkk, 2016). This study focused on the construction workers in the field of architecture set out in the board of national qualification standards. The vocational qualification in the field of architecture is in accordance with BSK accreditation 117/KPTS/LPJK/X/2009 comprising of 26 skill areas of architecture that can be certified.

The construction workers involved as participants in this study were the workers who have ties historically to other workers who were from similar village. Job skills were obtained from self-taught, starting from being an assistant in construction work to self-learning and following the development. They gained the knowledge more from observing, asking questions, and doing things together rather than from obtaining formal education and training. In doing this, their skills improved and this increased their position to be a construction worker, not just an assistant.

Traditionally among their construction worker community, the grouping of expertise/skill was only carpenters or masonry. Other job specifications such as plumbers, electrical, finishing are already considered as part of the skills possessed the two expertise. In a rural community culture, the position becomes a determinant factor in terms of the salary. The salary of each worker is different based on the position. That means that the skill specifications, the skill levels, and the salary are not formally standardized, but are agreed based on the traditions in the society.

3.2 *Knowledge and implementation of Occupational and Health Safety (OHS)*

The construction industry is a heavy industry that employs a lot of manpower manually with high occupational safety risks (Eaves, Gyi, & Gibb, 2016). The problems that often arise in occupational safety and health, among others, are the factors that endanger the health, and protection factor to health and safety work environment.

Research on health and safety in several countries showed an increase in awareness of construction workers about the risks faced. Some substantial aspects have improved although the rate of accidents in the construction industry is still high compared to other industries (Sousa, M. Almeida, Dias, 2014).

The culture formed among construction workers who mostly come from rural areas with low levels of education often neglects the factor of OHS. In fact, one of the characteristics and demands of the current job is an issue related to OHS which is capable of changing the safety culture and regulatory powers governing both at national and local level as an important agenda for both countries (Kim, Park, & Park, 2016).

Participants' knowledge and understanding of OHS were above 50%. This suggests that their experience and involvement in a variety of construction work has provided information and benefits and the importance of OHS. However, their knowledge and understanding of OHS is not necessarily followed by their compliance in applying it in their work.

The use of safety equipment is used only when they work on major projects such as multistorey buildings and if the equipment is available in the workplace. The results of the in-depth interviews confirm that the participants who wear boots, safety helmets, goggles, masks, long-sleeved clothing, gloves and safety belts was below 50%. In fact, they often neglected the maintenance and checking of OHS equipment. The results of focused group discussion showed that the use of OHS tools and equipment is not their priorities because apart from the absence of the equipments and tools, the majority of workers think that the tools and equipment are not necessary.

The factors of habits and work culture that prioritize safety and health become a weakness of the majority of construction workers in Indonesia. They are unaware that wearing OHS equipment and paying attention to work regulations are part of the attitudes and behavior in modern industry. They consider that the use of the equipment at work is still regarded as a burden which just makes them uncomfortable to work.

3.3 *Education and job training*

Formal education does not equip skills that meet the needs of the construction work. Thus, the construction workers are self-taught or learn from their fellow workers and get more job experience. Most of the participants started from being assistants in some construction work, such as building houses or public facilities such as mosques or multipurpose rooms in their own communities. Their involvement in a variety of construction work increases their knowledge and job skills and gradually a group of workers started to work in urban areas.

The principle that has been traditionally developed by the construction workers can be the basis to the concept of lifelong education in accordance with the development of rural communities (Nasdian, 2014). Lifelong education indicates an education approach that is not only related to school or work (formal institutions), but all aspects of daily life and interaction with the environment (Kocak & Baskan, 2012). The program developed through technology and non-formal vocational education emphasizes the empowerment process that is based on the knowledge and practical skills is in accordance with the needs and usefulness (Blaak, Openjuru, & Zeelen, 2013). Non-formal education enables learning model that can touch the individual needs and be an alternative to improve job skills, especially the youth (Tripon, 2014).

The strengthening of job skills for construction workers through non-formal training is tailored to the needs of the field of architectural work which refers to the National Standards. Apart from technical skills, education and training on OHS are also needed by the workers. OHS training serves to increase understanding, attitude and work culture at the individual level. It functions as part of efforts to reduce workplace accidents if they are involved in project work. The training can be conducted by the construction industry that can effectively improve knowledge of OHS, skills and attitudes of the participants (Endroyo, Yuwono, Mardapi, & Soenarto, 2015).

4 CONCLUSION

Strengthening job skills for construction workers is based on mapping skills group, based on a Job Skill Qualification in the Field of Architecture in accordance Accreditation BSK: 117/KPTS/LPJK/X/2009. The skill levels which are identified in three occupational groups such as carpentry, masonry and finishing show the levels of compliance procedures and implementation of the work required by Construction Services Development Board (LPJK) in the high category. Meanwhile, the implementation of OHS is an aspect that still needs to obtain further gains through education and training to instill the attitude and work culture.

An approach to education and training for construction workers who come from rural communities refers to the principle of lifelong education programs and non-formal vocational and technology education. Non-formal vocational and technology education focuses on the empowerment process that is based on the knowledge and practical skills which can touch the fundamental needs of each individual and their technical capabilities.

REFERENCES

Blaak, M., Openjuru, G.L. & Zeelen, J. 2013. Non-formal vocational education in Uganda: Practical empowerment through a workable alternative. *International Journal of Educational Development* 33(1): 88–97.
Eaves, S., Gyi, D.E. & Gibb, a.G.F. 2016. Building healthy construction workers: Their views on health, wellbeing and better workplace design. *Applied Ergonomics* 54: 10–18.
Endroyo, B., Yuwono, B.E., Mardapi, D. & Soenarto. 2015. Model of learning/training of Occupational Safety & Health (OSH) based on industry in the construction industry. *Procedia Engineering* 125: 83–88.
Kim, Y., Park, J. & Park, M. 2016. Creating a culture of prevention in occupational safety and health practice. *Safety and Health at Work* 7(2): 89–96.
Kocak, S. & Baskan, G.A. 2012. Village Institutes and Life-long Learning. *Procedia—Social and Behavioral Sciences* 46: 5937–5940.
Nasdian, T.F. 2014. *Pengembangan Masyarakat*. Penerbit Yayasan Pustaka Obor Indonesia, Jakarta.
Organization, I.L. 2015. *Tren Ketenagakerjaan dan Sosial di Indonesia 2014–2015 Memperkuat daya saing dan produktivitas.*
Paper, C. 2016. *Peningkatan kinerja tenaga kerja konstruksi dengan melakukan restrukturisasi kerangka klasifikasi, kualifikasi dan bakuan kompetensi kerja*, (January).
Rothenberg, A.D., Gaduh, A., Burger, N.E., Chazali, C., Tjandraningsih, I., Radikun, R. & Weilant, S. 2016. Rethinking Indonesia's Informal Sector. *World Development* 80: 96–113.
Sousa, V., Almeida M., Dias N. & Luís A. 2014. Risk-based management of occupational safety and health in the construction industry—Part 1: Background knowledge. *Safety Science* 66.
Tripon, A. 2014. Innovative Technology for Sustainable Development of Human Resource Using Non-formal and Informal Education. *Procedia Technology* 12: 598–603.

The Human Resource Management (HRM) professional competency standard in Indonesia: How should HRM lecturers address it?

M.C. Sondari, H. Koesmahendra & W.O. Zusnita
Universitas Padjadjaran, Bandung, Indonesia

ABSTRACT: Professional training through vocational education in higher education (the diploma program) emphasizes the competency of graduates, which is proven by certification of competency. One important factor required by a diploma program in order to deliver competent graduates is the provision of competent lecturers. Traditionally, a lecturer on a diploma program, especially in the subject of Human Resource Management (HRM), has been an academician who doesn't have any professional experience. Thus, it has been a challenge when they are asked to complement their qualifications with professional certification as requested by the accreditation standard for diploma programs. This paper explains the competency standard for professional accreditation in HRM, based on Indonesian Labour and Transmigration ministerial decree, and discusses how HRM lecturers should address the standard to earn the certificate of competency. Using descriptive analysis, each competency that forms part of the standard for HRM professionals will be described, with an example of the portfolio that should be possessed by HRM lecturers in order to fulfill the standard.

1 INTRODUCTION

Higher Education Institutions (HEI) are expected to play a role in the improvement of a nation's competitiveness, as the knowledge creation process is one of the factors associated with national competitiveness (Sondari et al., 2014). In terms of the quality of education in higher education, much depends on the quality of the lecturers. According to regulation in Indonesia (Republic of Indonesia, 2005), all higher education lecturers in Indonesia should be certified as having a teaching license or permit. For vocational streams, or diploma programs, the lecturers are also obliged to have professional certification in order to demonstrate the possession of the professional competencies related to the subject they teach, besides certification as educators.

The standard of professional competencies is developed under the National Professional Certification Body, in the form of the Indonesian National Work Competency Standard (SKKNI). A competency standard for Human Resource Manager was first created in Ministerial Decree No. 307 in 2014 (Republic of Indonesia, 2014). This standard should be referred to by academicians when developing the curriculum of vocational programs in relation to the subject of Human Resource Management (HRM), as well as informing the standards for lecturer competency.

In order to prove the competency of lecturers in the HRM field, each lecturer should have been certified by the National Professional Certification Body. However, traditionally, a lecturer in diploma programs, especially for the subject of HRM, is an academician who doesn't have any professional experience. Thus, it has become a challenge when they are asked to complement their qualification with professional certification as requested by the accreditation standard for diploma programs. This paper will explain the competency standard for professionals in HRM, and discuss how HRM lecturers should address the standard to earn the certificate of competency.

2 LITERATURE REVIEW

2.1 Competency

HR professionals have very dynamic roles. As increasingly more complex business contexts have raised the bar for HR professionals, it is important for HR professionals to catch up with the competencies needed in current business situations (Ulrich et al., 2009). It is suggested that HR professionals should have competencies that are demonstrated by creating value that positively influences the bottom-line (financial) metrics of their company (Ulrich et al., 1995).

HR competencies include the ability to deliver competitive advantage in order to help a company achieve its goals (Ulrich et al., 1995). It is a blend of values, knowledge and abilities that will take HR professionals to the highest level of performance (Ulrich et al., 2009). It is believed that the competencies of an HR professional have an effect on the effectiveness with which they perform their job (Ulrich et al., 1995).

The possession of HR competencies should be proven by certification. It is an indication that the holder has acquired the knowledge and skills to do their job, and proves that they can carry out the tasks required in their job (Wiley, 1995).

2.2 HR certification

Certification programs started in 1976 in the United States, pioneered by the Human Resource Certification Institute (HRCI). The most famous is that of the Society for Human Resource Management (SHRM), which was founded by the American Society for Personnel Administration (ASPA) (Aguinis et al., 2005).

Most studies argue that both the individual HR professional and the employer (organization) perceive HR certification as a value-added activity that gives benefit to both parties (Lester & Dwyer, 2012). For organizations, it is believed that HR certification can boost organizational commitment (Hsu & Yancey, 2015). It is also believed that certification can create a positive impact with the individual performing better, giving more commitment to their job and contributing more to problem-solving (Hsu & Yancey, 2015).

The benefits of certification for individuals can be seen from at least three perspectives. First, signaling theory suggests that certification can be a signal sent out to potential employers, with regards to the qualifications of the certification holder. Second, it is believed that certification can be a way for individuals to gain power and be more influential. Third, certification can increase self-confidence and satisfaction, from the perspective of intrinsic motivation theory (Hsu & Yancey, 2015).

On the basis of signaling theory arguments, professional certification provides very important information for potential employers to predict the competency of individual job applicants, especially in the fields of information technology (IT) and accounting (Aguinis et al., 2005). However, although the assumptions of signaling theory state that employers need preemptive information about an individual to be provided by professional certification, previous research shows that only 48% of job announcements put certification as a requirement, and only 70% of job announcements express a preference that applicants be complemented by professional certification (Aguinis et al., 2005).

For individuals, HR certification is usually voluntary. It is up to individuals to decide whether they need to be certified (Lester & Dwyer, 2012). The theories that can form the foundation of a certification program and may explain why an individual is motivated to earn a certificate of professional competency include human capital theory and the expectancy theory of motivation (Lester & Dwyer, 2012). Human capital theory suggests that individuals are willing to invest in

their own human capital based on rational considerations. Expectation theory provides a basis for how individuals act to achieve their own self-interest and maximize the utility of their decisions.

In terms of motivation, HR certification seems to be driven by intrinsic rather than extrinsic motivations, such as a commitment to continual learning and career advancement, although indirect extrinsic factors such as the marketable reputation of one's own competence may also be a motivating factor (Lester & Dwyer, 2012). In other research, it was found that HR certification does not correlate with direct financial outcomes (Lester & Dwyer, 2012), although other studies report that there are monetary advantages of HR certification, with certified HR professionals paid more than non-certified ones (Hsu & Yancey, 2015). Such research suggests that in order to promote a certification program, organizations should correlate it with tangible values that can be perceived by employees (Lester & Dwyer, 2012).

2.3 HR certification and education

There is some research that has tried to correlate HR professional certification with educational context. One study attempted to correlate a requirement for HR practice competency with the education curriculum for HR students in the form of learning portfolio guidance (Groenewald et al., 2004). In other research, it was found that, in the case of Malaysian polytechnic lecturers, professional knowledge and skills had become one of the weaknesses that should be developed further through professional development programs (Wan Kamaruddin & Ibrahim, 2010).

3 METHODOLOGY

This study uses descriptive analysis in the delivery of its results and discussion. First, the units of HR competency included in the regulations regarding standards in Indonesia will be illustrated in a table. Then, the detailed elements and key indicators that are expected from each competency unit will be explained, along with the relationships to the portfolio needed to fulfill the criteria.

4 RESULT AND DISCUSSION

4.1 Overview

Based on the National Work Competency Standard (Republic of Indonesia, 2014), HRM practitioners are required to master eight of the basic generic or soft competency prerequisites. Furthermore, a HRM practitioner must score a minimum level of 525 in the Indonesian Language Proficiency Test or *Uji Kemahiran Berbahasa Indonesia* (UKBI).

Following this, HRM practitioners in Indonesia must master nine clusters of technical competence. There are a total of 104 units of competency that are packaged by the occupational Indonesian National Competency Standards clusters scheme (Republic of Indonesia, 2014). In this paper, the package that will be considered is just the occupational scheme that consists of two schemes, HR Manager and HR Supervisor, with a focus solely on the HR Manager scheme. In Table 1, all of the competency units for the HR Manager scheme are shown. These can be divided into five clusters, namely: 1) Strategy and HR Planning or Organizational Development; 2) Learning and Development; 3) Talent Management; 4) Career Management or Performance Management and Remuneration; 5) Industrial Relations (Republic of Indonesia, 2014).

To be certified, individuals must register with a Professional Certification Institution or *Lembaga Sertifikasi Profesi* (LSP). The LSP will provide an online form to be filled in by the individual to acknowledge that she/he is ready to be certified. On that form, individuals must provide a set of evidence that can prove that she/he has competencies as required by SKKNI. The evidence that should be provided is actually the port-

Table 1. Competency elements for HR Manager (source: Republic of Indonesia, 2014).

Competency Unit		
Cluster: Strategy and HR Planning/Organizational Development		
Formulate Policies in line with the Organization of HR Management Strategy (1)	Develop Role of Stakeholders' Position in line with the run of Human Resource Management Functions (6)	Design the Competency Measurement Methods (10)
Make Draft Model/ Organizational Structure (2)	Design the Competency Model (7)	Determine Personnel Information System (11)
Assign the Demand for Workers (3)	Develop Technology Intervention (8)	Conduct Organizational Change Intervention (12)
Formulate the Problems of Organization (4)	Develop Personnel Management Intervention (9)	Make Company or Personnel Regulation at Organization Level (13)
Develop Interpersonal Interventions (5)		

(Continued)

Table 1. *(Continued)*.

Competency Unit		
Cluster: Learning and Development		
Design the Learning and Development Program (14)	Align Learning and Development Strategy in accordance with Organization Strategy (15)	
Cluster: Talent Mangement		
Develop Succession Management in Organizations (16)	Implement Succession Management Program (17)	Determine Talented Employees (18)
Cluster: Career Management/Performance Management and Remuneration		
Structuring and Wage Scale Level Organizations (19)	Design the Follow-Up of Performance Assessment Results (22)	Develop Labor Wage Determination of System-Level Organizations (25)
Design the Remuneration Policy at Organization Level (20)	Manage Performance Indicators Formulation Process (23)	Develop Incentive Program at Organizational Level (26)
Develop Allowances and Benefits System-Level Organizations (21)	Develop Performance Management Strategy (24)	
Cluster: Industrial Relations		
Build Harmonious Communication with Workers at Organization Level (27)	Build Harmonious Industrial Relations with the Labor Deputy or Workers' Union/Trade Unions (29)	Implement Process Termination of Employment at the Organization Level (31)
Implement Effective Industrial Relations Dispute Settlement Mechanism (28)	Make a Collective Labor Agreement at the Organization Level (30)	

folio possessed by the individual as a result of past experience. It may be, for example, a Curriculum Vitae (CV), past training certificate, instructor's certificate and/or letter of assignment.

These competencies should be fulfilled to pass the certification process. For each competency, there are several indicators that should be addressed by the evidence. The evidence could be from past experiences mentioned in the CV or certificates of proficiency or instruction in that skill.

4.2 Competency elements

The first cluster concerns competency in strategic planning and organizational development. For example, 'Formulate policies in line with the Organization of HR Management Strategy' means that the person should be able to identify the organization's objectives as they relate to HR management strategy, formulate the organization's HR policy and obtain approval of the organization's HR policy from the heads of the organization. A portfolio of evidence for this competency might involve the experience of being involved in a corporate planning project team, a HR planning project team or any other matching experiences that would indicate the capability of the candidate in that competency.

The second cluster concerns learning and development. Competencies in this cluster are, in essence, about developing training and development for the organization's workers. To satisfy this cluster qualification or set of competencies, the candidate should present appropriate evidence, including a certificate of proficiency or experience of conducting needs analysis for learning and development (TNA, Training Needs Analysis), formulating learning and development objectives, preparing a syllabus for learning and development and orientation materials, determining the timetable for learning and development, and assigning suitable instructors to implement the learning and development process.

Talent management represents the third cluster of HRM competencies. In this cluster, the competencies are about managing talent that has been identified within the organization, which is a competency that is essential for HR managers. 'Develop Succession Management in Organizations' means that the candidate should be able to design a succession management program and obtain succession management approval. The candidate should provide evidence related to this, as any other, competency.

The fourth cluster of HRM competencies concerns career and performance management and remuneration. The person will be considered to have competencies in this cluster if he or she has experience in developing performance management and remuneration systems.

The last cluster concerns industrial relations. The requirements for passing this cluster are certificates in the field of industrial relations, experience of conducting an employee's termination of employment, or past experience in a job that had the authority to terminate employment. For academicians, this cluster is typically the hardest in which to provide evidence, since it is often difficult, for example, for academicians to have gained experience in terminating people's employment.

5 CONCLUSION

This paper has explained the competency standards for HR professionals and the evidence that should be provided to prove that individual lecturers possess such a qualification.

In the case of the HR Manager scheme, there are 31 units of competency within five clusters. Among these, the last cluster, industrial relations, could become the most challenging cluster, because it is difficult for academicians to gain experience in this area. Therefore, academic institutions should design development programs for lecturers that involve immersion in real industry situations, such as through professional sabbaticals or apprenticeships.

REFERENCES

Aguinis, H., Michaelis, S.E. & Jones, N.M. (2005). Demand for certified human resources professionals in internet-based job announcements. *International Journal of Selection and Assessment*, 13(2), 160–171.

Groenewald, T., Bushney, M., Odendaal, A. & Pieters, M. (2004). Case study regarding the implementation of an innovative experimental learning portfolio in human resource management. *Asia-Pacific Journal of Cooperative Education*, 5(1), 35–44.

Hsu, Y. & Yancey, G. (2015). The benefits of human resources certification. *Emporia State Research Studies*, 50(1), 1–10.

Lester, S.W. & Dwyer, D.J. (2012). Motivations and benefits for attaining HR certifications. *Career Development International*, 17(7), 584–605.

Republic of Indonesia. (2005). *Law Concerning Teacher and Lecturer*.

Republic of Indonesia. (2014). *Labour and Transmigration Minister Decree Concerning Indonesian National Work Competency Standard in Human Resource Management*.

Sondari, M.C., Tjakraatmadja, J.H. & Bangun, Y.R. (2014). Foreign co-authorship phenomenon: A preliminary study of research productivity of higher education institution in Indonesia. In *GTAR Full Paper Proceeding* (pp. 225–235).

Ulrich, D., Brockbank, W., Yeung, A.K. & Lake, D.G. (1995). Human resource competencies: An empirical assessment. *Human Resource Management*, 34(4), 473–495.

Ulrich, D., Brockbank, W., Johnson, D. & Younger, J. (2009). Human resource competencies: Rising to meet the business challenge. *The RBL White Paper Series*.

Wan Kamaruddin, W.N. & Ibrahim, M.S. (2010). Enhancing Malaysian polytechnic technical lecturers' competency through the identification of professional development programs. *Procedia - Social and Behavioral Sciences*, 7(2), 446–454.

Wiley, C. (1995). Reexamining professional certification in human resource management, *Human Resource Management*, 34(2), 295–297.

Social and cultural issues

Regionalization and Harmonization in TVET – Abdullah et al. (Eds)
© *2017 Taylor & Francis Group, London, ISBN 978-1-138-05419-6*

Profile of learning that develops mathematics creativity of junior high school students

Alimuddin & S. Asyari
Universitas Negeri Makassar, Makassar, Indonesia

ABSTRACT: To improve students' mathematics creativity, a comprehensive learning framework is needed. This was an experimental research study with one group pretest/post-test design to study the profile of learning which is effective in developing students' mathematics creativity. The research sample consists of two classrooms, selected using a simple cluster random sampling technique, with six homogenous classrooms of Grade VIII students from State Junior High School 26 Makassar. The instruments used were pretest and post-test related to mathematics creativity. The collected data was then analyzed descriptively and inferentially. The research result showed that the profile of learning which is effective in developing students' mathematics creativity consists of seven phases, that is: (1) Introduction, (2) Understanding, (3) Synthesis, (4) Creation, (5) Interaction, (6) Reflection, and (7) Extension, abbreviated as IUSCIRE. The results of this study enhanced the teachers' Pedagogical Content Knowledge (PCK) and the students' learning process and achievement.

1 INTRODUCTION

1.1 *Definition of mathematics creativity*

Mathematics creativity is defined by many experts differently. In general, experts define mathematics creativity in cognitive aspect which comprises thinking process and thinking product.

Torrance (1988) and Krutetskii (1976) define mathematics creativity as a thinking process which is initiated by formulating hypothesis concerning cause and effect of mathematics problems, hypothesis testing, hypothesis retesting and modification, as well as communicating the results. Parnes (1992) stated that the creative thinking process consists of five stages, that is: collecting facts, investigating problem, finding ideas, getting answer/solution, and finding acceptance. Ervynck (1991) reveals that the creative thinking process in mathematics consists of three stages, that is: initial technique, algorithmic activity, and creative activity (conceptual, constructive).

Haylock (1997) and Kim et al. (2003) stated that mathematics creativity is the result of a thinking process characterized by *fluency*, *flexibility*, and *originality*. Studies in mathematics creativity (Singh, 1988) emphasize more on the measurement of mathematics creativity in mathematics problem-solving and problem-posing by referring to *fluency*, *flexibility*, and *originality* aspects. *Fluency* means the number of correct answers that one shows in mathematics problem-solving, but following the same pattern. *Flexibility* means the

number of approaches or different ways that a student uses in solving a given mathematics problem, or the number of categories of correct answer that a student reveals. Thus, in this case, a student states two answer categories, whereas *originality* means an unfamiliar answer (new answer to student constituting the combination of some mathematics concepts). Within this research, mathematics creativity is considered as the students' ability in finding ways/solutions to mathematics open-ended and non-routine problems fulfilling *fluency* and *flexibility*. The indicators are: 1) ability in formulating problem, 2) ability in producing ideas, 3) ability in synthesizing ideas, 4) fluency in producing way/solution, and 5) flexibility in producing way/solution. Meanwhile, the originality aspect is not included in this research. This is because if a student can reveal a way/solution to a given non-routine problem, then he/she would be considered as having found something new.

1.2 *The importance of mathematics creativity and its issues*

Perception on creativity source also gradually commences, shifting from aptitude inheritance (genius is inherited through the individual with most aptitude) to diverse human ability. Craft (2001), Feldman and Benjamin (2006), and de Bono (2007) state that all individuals possess potential to be creative. Creative thinking always evolves and can be learned, as well as being trained. This view has inspired some countries, such as US, UK, France, Germany, Sweden, Australia, China, Japan, South Korea, Taiwan, Singapore, and Hong Kong, to reform curricula so as to improve students' mathematics creativity (Shaheen, 2010). In fact, the creativity of students in a variety of countries is still low. Many students have high achievement in mathematics at school, but have low performance in social events, either national or international ones, particularly in cases of imagination and creativity (Wu, 2004). Teachers play a great role in developing students' creativity. Teachers with traditional practice become an obstacle for improving creativity in the classroom (Simonton, 2003). Other constraints are the lack of teachers' creativity in developing learning, generating students' imaginations, critics and creativity (Wu, 2004). A comprehensive learning framework must be developed to evolve students' creativity in accordance with subject characteristics.

The question is, what is the profile of mathematics learning which effectively develops students' mathematics creativity? The answer to this question is the main focus of this paper.

After elaborating constructivist views revealed by von Glasersield (Suparno, 1997), Piaget (Slavin, 1994), Vygotsky (Confrey, 1995), and Polya (1973), it is then concluded that the characteristics of constructivist learning are: 1) using students' prior knowledge to construct new knowledge, 2) giving students opportunities to experience, observe, ask, analyze, and draw a conclusion, 3) forming a learning community, 4) providing students with a complex mathematics problem, 5) interacting and communicating, and 6) scrutinizing the thinking process (connecting and synthesizing). These characteristics are highly related to mathematics creativity indicators, namely: formulating a problem, producing ideas, synthesizing ideas, producing ways/solutions fluently, as well as producing ways/solutions flexibly, so that the characteristics would be referenced in developing instruction comprising seven syntaxes, that is: Introduction, Understanding, Synthesis, Creation, Interaction, Reflection, and Extension, which is then abbreviated to the IUSCIRE Learning Model. Meanwhile, the development of its supporting components such as student worksheet and student book refers to scientific, problem-solving, and open-ended problem approaches.

2 RESEARCH METHODOLOGY

The stages for developing IUSCIRE learning which are valid, practical and effective, are: 1) preliminary study, 2) design, 3) construction, and 4) test, evaluation, and revision. This article exposes the research results regarding the stages of testing and

evaluation by administering an experimental research study in the form of one group pretest/post-test design to see the effectiveness of IUSCIRE learning in developing mathematics creativity of grade VIII students. IUSCIRE learning is applied to as many as 25 persons of grade VIII-2 students (Group I), and also as many as 25 persons of grade VIII-5 students (Group II) that are selected using a cluster random sampling technique of six homogenous classrooms of grade VIII at State Junior High School 26 Makassar. There were four meetings, with different teachers and time, in Group I and Group II. Mathematics creativity criteria within this study are: 1) N-Gain score is at least 0.3, 2) there is a significant difference between students' creativity before and after implementing IUSCIRE learning, and 3) mathematics creativity of Group I and Group II is the same. Data was then collected using a mathematics creativity test consisting of five questions, which are developed by referring to mathematics creativity indicators. Meanwhile, the utilized scoring rubric was developed from a creativity rubric defined by Guilford (1971). Next, the quantitatively descriptive analysis used here was aimed at describing students' mathematics creativity, N-Gain analysis was aimed at seeing the enhancement of students' mathematics creativity, and t-Test analysis was aimed at seeing the difference between students' creativity before and after implementing the learning, and to see whether the mathematics creativity of Group I and Group II were the same.

3 RESULTS AND DISCUSSIONS

3.1 Research results

3.1.1 Reviewing analysis of N-Gain average score in each mathematics creativity indicator

Analysis of N-Gain average score for Group I and Group II in each mathematics creativity indicator is presented in Table 1.

Table 1. The results of statistical analysis of N-gain average score in each mathematics creativity indicator of students in Group I and Group II.

| No. | Group | N-Gain average score in each indicator | | | | |
		IN-1	IN-2	IN-3	IN-4	IN-5
1	I	0.58	0.52	0.45	0.38	0.34
2	II	0.60	0.56	0.49	0.39	0.35

Note:
IN-1: Abiility in formulating problem
IN-2: Ability in producing ideas
IN-3: Ability in synthesizing ideas
IN-4: Fastness/smoothness in producing way/solution
IN-5: Fluency in producing way/solution

Table 2. The results of *pretest* and *post-test* concerning students' mathematics creativity.

Pretest		Post-test							
Mean ($\bar{x}_1$)	Standard deviation (s_1)	Mean ($\bar{x}_2$)	Standard deviation (s_2)	Calculated t Value	N	Correlation	f	t-table value	Sig. (2-tailed)
17.59	12.49	67.78	13.79	−16.39	50	0.141	49	1.68	0.00

Table 3. Summary of ANOVA.

Sources of Variation (SV)	Sum Squares (SS)	Degree of Freedom (DF)	Mean Square (MS)
Intergroup (K)	0.09	2	0.045
Inner group (d)	2.32	47	0.032
Total (T)	2.41	49	–

Table 1 shows that: 1) N-Gain average score for all mathematics creativity indicators is more than 0.3, and 2) it is in the moderate category, for either Group I or Group II.

3.1.2 Reviewing two-tailed t-Test of statistical analysis

The results of data analysis with t-Test of Group I and Group II are shown in Table 2.

Table 2 indicates that there is a difference with a significance level 0.05 between students' mathematics creativity, either before or after implementing the IUSCIRE learning.

3.1.3 Reviewing variance analysis

The following is the summary of analysis using one-way analysis of variance (one-way ANOVA). $F_0 = \frac{MK_K}{MK_d} = \frac{0.045}{0.032} = 1.41$, $F_t\ 5\% = 3.13$ which shows that the value $F_0 < F_t\ 5\%$. This indicates that there is significant difference of students' mathematics creativity between Group I and Group II.

From the outline above, it is concluded that IUSCIRE learning is effective in developing students' mathematics creativity.

3.2 Discussions

IUSCIRE learning is developed by referring to constructivism stating that knowledge is not acquired through transfer, but constructed or generated actively by the individual itself. Humans construct knowledge through interaction with object, phenomena, experience, and environment. The supporting components of this learning are evolved by integrating scientific, problem-solving, and open-ended problem approaches. A scientific approach provides students with learning experience to observe, ask, reason, and draw a conclu-

sion. The scrutiny ability in observing would generate quality questions which need answers through imaginative, critical, and creative thinking. Reasoning and drawing a conclusion would train students to make connections in their knowledge divergently before making an appropriate decision, and here is the most essential ability of the creative person. Carrying out an open-ended problem using Polya heuristic would train students to produce distinct ideas and develop their synthesis ability. The typical and essential aspect of this IUSCIRE learning is that the availability of complex problems for students to be solved by themselves in a collaborative way while teachers serve only as a scaffolding provider. Working collaboratively impacts on students' social development, interaction ability and communication. The distinction between students' mathematics creativity before and after implementing IUSCIRE, and its consistency in improving their mathematics creativity in the class taught by different teachers and with different instructional time, indicates that this IUSCIRE learning impacts on the improvement of students' mathematics creativity. Although the impact of this learning is still relatively less, the obtained results with only four meetings show that the direction of IUSCIRE learning is appropriate in developing students' mathematics creativity. Developing this creativity needs a long time and continuous training.

4 CONCLUSION

The profile of IUSCIRE learning which is effective in developing students' mathematics creativity consists of seven phases, namely: (1) introduction. In this phase, the teacher conditions students to be ready to learn, clarifies goals and the importance of the topic, as well as explores students' prior knowledge. Meanwhile, students express ideas, ask questions and answer questions; (2) understanding. In this phase, the teacher presents information in terms of mathematics problem and the problem-solving strategy, facilitates students to brainstorm, formulates the problem and identifies concepts and principles needed to carry out the problem. Meanwhile, students expose ideas, ask questions, answer questions, discuss, and interact with each other; (3) synthesis. In this phase, the teacher facilitates students to intertwine concepts in constructing problem-solving strategies, choose an appropriate strategy, and implement the strategy. Meanwhile, students are exposed to ideas, ask questions, answer questions, discuss, and interact with each other; (4) creation. In this phase, the teacher organizes students into some heterogeneous groups in terms of ability, gives students' worksheet, facilitates the existence of intergroup discussions, and provides scaffolding. Meanwhile, students interact, think, try, reason, and draw a conclusion; (5) interaction. In this phase, the teacher facilitates intergroup discussions and provides reinforcement. Meanwhile, students are exposed to ideas, ask questions, answer questions, discuss, and interact with each other; (6) reflection. In this phase, the teacher facilitates students to identify things they have and they have not known. Meanwhile, students write and draw a conclusion; (7) extension. In this phase, the teacher addresses misconceptions and makes clear what students have not understood. Meanwhile, students scrutinize, ask questions and make notes.

The IUSCIRE learning is supported with lesson plan, students' worksheet, students' book, and assessment sheet. Both students' worksheet and students' book consist of context, an open ended problem, and structured assignments, as well as a problem-solving strategy.

The implication from this research is that the implementation of this IUSCIRE learning leads us to outcomes such as the improvement of teachers' Pedagogical Content Knowledge (PCK), and students' learning process and achievement.

REFERENCES

Confrey, J. (1995). How compatible are radical constructivism, socio-cultural approaches and social constructivism? In L.P. Steffe & J. Gale (Eds.), *Constructivism in education*. Hillsdale, NJ: Lawrence Erlbaum.

Craft, A. (2001). Little c creativity. In A. Craft, B.J. & M. Leibling, *Creativity in Education*. London: Continuum.

De Bono, E. 2007. *How to have creative ideas: 62 exercises to develop the mind*. London: Vermilion.

Ervynck, G. (1991). Mathematical creativity. Advanced mathematical thinking. In D. Tall (Ed.), *Advanced mathematical thinking* (pp. 42–53). Dodrecht: Kluwer.

Feldman, D. & Benjamin, A.C. (2006). Creativity and education: An American retrospective. *Cambridge Journal of Education*, *36*, 319–336.

Guilford, J.P. (1971). *The nature of human intelligence*. New York: McGraw-Hill.

Haylock, D. (1997). Recognizing mathematical creativity in schoolchildren. *International Reviews on Mathematical Education*, *29*(3), 68–74.

Kim, H., Cho, S. & Ahn, D. (2003). Development of mathematical creative problem solving ability test for identification of gifted in math. *Gifted Education International*, *18*, 184–174.

Krutetskii, V.A. (1976). *The psychology of mathematical abilities in school children*. Chicago: University of Chicago Press.

Parnes, S.J. (1992). *Source book for creative problem-solving: A fifty year digest of proven innovation processes*. Buffalo, NY: Creative Education Foundation Press.

Polya, G. (1973). *How to solve it* (2nd ed.). New Jersey: Princeton University Press.

Shaheen, R. (2010). Creativity and education. *Creative Education*, *11*(3), 166–169.

Simonton, D.K. (2003). Human creativity: Two Darwinian analyses. In S.M. Reader & K.N. Laland (Eds.), *Animal innovation*, 309–325. New York, NY: Oxford University Press.

Singh, B. (1988). *Teaching-learning strategies and mathematical creativity*. Delhi, India: Mittal Publications.

Slavin, R.E. (1994). *Using student team learning* (2nd ed.). Baltimore, MD: Johns Hopkins University, Center for Social Organization of Schools.

Suparno, P. (1997). *Filsafat konstruktivisme dalam pendidikan*. Jakarta: Kanisius.

Torrance, E.P. (1988). The nature of creativity as manifest in its testing. In R.J. Sternberg (Ed.), *The nature of creativity* (pp. 43–75). Cambridge, MA: Cambridge University Press.

Wu, J.J. (2004). Recognizing and nurturing creativity in Chinese students. In S. Lau, A.N.N. Hui & G.Y.C. Ng. (Eds.), *Creativity: When East meets West*. Singapore City: World Scientific.

Entrepreneurial intentions: A review of self efficacy of tourism vocational school students

A. Ana, Y. Rostika, Y. Rahmawati & R. Hurriyati
Universitas Pendidikan Indonesia, Jawa Barat, Indonesia

ABSTRACT: The main objective of this study is to provide an overview of the determinants of entrepreneurial intentions using self-efficacy approach. The model used in this study is Bird's Contexts of Entrepreneurial Intentionality model as the application of the Plan Behavior Theory. This study involved 162 students as samples, and data were collected through observations, questionnaires and interviews. The data were analyzed using descriptive statistics. The results showed that the level of self-efficacy of SMK 3 Garut students was much higher than that of the students of SMKN 9 Bandung in some indicators, such as in looking for opportunities in entrepreneurship, achieving maximum results in each task or job, learning on time, resolving the problems successfully, being motivated to others' success, and being passionate to complete the targets.

1 INTRODUCTION

Vocational education programs are reserved for students who have particular interests and are ready to work and create jobs based on their skills and talents. The learners must be prepared to fill job opportunities as workers in some businesses and industries and to acquire better attitude, behavior, and entrepreneurial spirit.

In Indonesia, the learning process in Vocational High School (VHS) is based on the 2013 curriculum which is designed to provide a large amount of learning experience. The curriculum enables learners to develop their attitude, knowledge, thinking skills and psychomotor skills which are packaged in a variety of subjects. In addition, the curriculum structure provides learning materials in the form of entrepreneurship subjects.

Entrepreneurial learning at schools is considered to be one of the important factors to foster entrepreneurial spirit among students. This learning is expected to prepare students to gain knowledge about entrepreneurship, develop entrepreneurial attitude, and develop other skills required to manage a business independently.

One factor supporting entrepreneurship is the desire of the students themselves, and this desire is referred to as intention. Intention is a component within the individual that refers to the desire to perform certain behavior. Intentions are things that are assumed to be able to capture motivating and influential factors on behavior.

One factor that affects entrepreneurial intentions is self-efficacy. The higher the learners' confidence on their ability to be entrepreneurs is, the greater their desire to become an entrepreneur. This is in line with the studies of Bandura (1986) and Nurul Indarti and Rostiani (2008) conducted on students from Indonesia, Japan and Norway suggesting that the most dominant factor which influences entrepreneurship intentions is self-efficacy.

2 METHOD

The study used Entrepreneurial Intention Model developed by Bird (1988), called Model of Bird's Contexts of Entrepreneurial Intentionality. The participants were 162 first grade students of tourism vocational schools in two VHS in Bandung and Garut, namely SMKN 9 Bandung and SMKN 3 Garut. Data collection techniques used in the study were survey and interviews. The data analysis used descriptive analysis.

3 RESULTS AND DISCUSSION

The results show that the level of self-efficacy of SMK 3 Garut students was higher than that of SMKN 9 Bandung students. The indicators include looking for opportunities in entrepreneurship, getting maximum results in each task or job, learning on time, resolving the problems well, being motivated to others' success, and being motivated to meet the targets.

The analysis shows that the average score of self-efficacy of SMK 3 Garut students was higher than that of SMKN 9 Bandung students. The highest average scores for SMK 3 Garut students was 4.79, with standard deviation of 0.41 to the statement of "being motivated to see other people succeed, and the lowest average score was 4.45, with the standard deviation of 0.69 to the statement "do not procrastinate time". SMKN 9 Bandung students got the highest average score of 4.62, with the standard deviation of 0.53 on a statement of "what I do is to hit the targets", and the lowest average score was 4.04, with the standard deviation of 0.98 to the statement "keeps looking for business opportunities".

The analysis results of self-efficacy of SMKN 9 Bandung and Garut SMK 3 students can be seen in Figure 1.

The results showed that SMK 3 Garut students are more superior to SMKN 9 Bandung students in all aspects. The reason is that the maturity level of SMK 3 Garut students is higher that the counterpart. Most of SMK 3 Garut students are over or equal to 18 years compared SMKN 9 Bandung students. The results were supported by the results of research Caecilia Vemmy, S. (2012) showing that (a) the needs for achievement, creativity, independence, taking risks, being tolerant to ambiguous things, parental influence, and self-efficacy has a positive and significant effect to entrepreneurial intentions either partially or simultaneously on VHS students (b) self-efficacy is the most dominant predictor affecting entrepreneurial intentions on VHS students.

One determining factor to entrepreneurial intentions of SMK 3 Garut and SMKN 9 Bandung students is influenced by self-efficacy. The study was supported by the study of Henky Oral S (2010) which suggests that the higher the learners' confidence on their ability to do efforts, the greater their desire to become entrepreneurs. Self-efficacy has a positive effect to entrepreneurial intentions. This is in line with the results of Bandura (1986) and Nurul Indarti and Rokhima Rostiani (2008), who conducted research in Indonesia, Japan and Norway,

showing that the most dominant factor influencing the intention of entrepreneurship is self-efficacy.

SMKN 9 Bandung always maintains the quality of its graduates to meet the profiles of expected graduates. The 2013 curriculum emphasizes on Competency-based which is oriented to the needs of the world of work today. Meanwhile, SMK 3 Garut implements the curriculum with the aim to prepare medium-level workforce who have the competence and work ethic according to the demands of the industry and to prepare workforce that are capable of producing and selling high-standard services or products.

In the implementation of entrepreneurial learning, both schools use a learning model of teaching factory. As stated by Martawijaya D. H (2010), teaching factory is a model of learning through TF-6M consisting of soft skills and hard skills activities which aim to improve students' competence in productive competency skills subjects. One work cycle in this model consists of six steps: receiving orders, analyzing orders, accepting orders, completing orders, performing quality control, and handling services or products.

4 CONCLUSION

The conclusion of this study is that self-efficacy is a decisive factor in the entrepreneurial intentions in both SMKN 9 Bandung and SMKN 3 Garut. The level of self-efficacy of SMK 3 Garut students was higher than that of SMKN 9 Bandung students in such indicators as looking for opportunities in entrepreneurship, achieving maximum results in each task or job, do not procrastinate time and work, trying to solve the problems properly, being motivated when seeing other people succeed, doing best things to fulfill the targets.

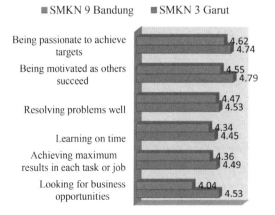

Figure 1. Self-Efficacy level between SMKN 3 Garut and SMKN 9 Bandung students.

REFERENCES

Bandura, A. 1986. *Social foundation of thought and action*, Prentice Hall, Englewood Clift,NJ. Department.
Bird, B. 1988. *Implementing entrepreneurial ideas: the case for intentions*. Academy of Management Review.
Caecilia Vemi S. 2012. Faktor-faktor yang mempengaruhi Intensi berwirausaha siswa SMK. *Jurnal Pendidikan Vokasi* 2(1).
Henky Lisan uwarno & Ida. 2014. *Intensi Kewirausahaan Pada Mahasiswa—Mahasiswa di Indonesia*. Prosiding Seminar Nasional Multi Disiplin Ilmu & Call for Papers Unisbank.
Martawidjaya, D.H. 2010. *Teaching Factory 6 Langkah (Model TF-6M)*. Disertasi Pengembangan Kurikulum SPS Universitas Pendidikan Indonesia.
Nurul Indarti & Rokhima Rostiani. 2008. Intensi Kewiausahaan Mahasiswa, studi perbandingan antara Indoensia, Jepang dan Norwegia. *Jurnal Ekonomi dan Bisnis* 23(4): 369–384.

Photovoice as promotion media to grow empathy leads to a non-discriminating treatment against people living with HIV/AIDS

A. Demartoto, R.B. Soemanto & S. Zunariyah
Department of Sociology, Faculty of Social and Political Sciences, Sebelas Maret University, Indonesia

ABSTRACT: Health promotion copes with HIV/AIDS less optimally. This community-based participatory research emphasized on learning, development and empowerment processes through photographic technique for People Living with HIV/AIDS (PLWHA) in Surakarta, Indonesia. Data collection used observation, in-depth interview, focus group discussion, and documentation. Data analysis was conducted using Habermas's Theory of Communicative Action with interactive model of analysis. PLWHA attended photovoice training about photographic technique, art and ethic, and photograph exhibition. Photovoice is exhibited every Sunday from 6 to 9 a.m. at Solo Car Free Day as a public space for critical dialog about the situation and condition of PLWHA, thereby achieving comprehensive rational validity claims from the public based on truth, precision, and honesty. Photovoice serves to grow the public's empathy, contributing to reducing negative stigma and leading to non-discriminating treatment against PLWHA. Technical ability, sense of art, and limited funds become the obstacles for photovoice to be the media of HIV/AIDS socialization.

1 INTRODUCTION

Since 2000 until today, the number of People Living with HIV/AIDS (PLWHA) has increased rapidly, even in some locations where the transmission of HIV/AIDS has been high (concentrated level epidemic). Many attempts taken in fact have not yet ensured its case reduction effectively (Halmshaw & Hawkins, 2004; Laperrière & Zúñiga, 2006; Alistar & Brandeau, 2012; Mannell et al., 2015; Demartoto et al., 2015). Cumulatively, there are 191,073 people with HIV, 77,112 people with AIDS, and 13,319 of them died in the period April 1, 1987 to December 31, 2015. In Surakarta, there were 1,821 PLWHA up until December 2016.

The epidemic situation leading to the expansion of HIV/AIDS transmission and the recognition of PLWHA's identity within society have become serious problems. On the one hand, we protect the automatic rights of PLWHA on the behalf of humanity, but on the other hand we injure them because of social structure relations, and still-existing conservative religion norm and dogma. For that reason, there should be intervention to change health behavior, both in the group with high risk of being infected with HIV/AIDS and within the wider society, among others, using photovoice.

Photovoice is a technique that can help an individual identify, represent, and reinforce communication through figure, image or photograph. Photovoice can be applied to various areas, communities and age levels from children to adult (Killion & Wang, 2000; Baker & Wang. 2006; Wilson et al., 2007; Gotschi et al., 2009; Ho et al. 2011; Ward et al., 2016). In education and learning fields, photovoice is highly regarded because it can develop the students' creativity through certain photographic techniques, using visual message along with narrative to improve learning effectiveness (Nelson & Christensen, 2012; Warne et al., 2012). Similarly, public health sector targets, and certain disease, either generally or particularly (Catalani & Minkler, 2010; Stegenga & Burks, 2013; Mohammed et al., 2015; Han & Oliffe, 2016; Kingery et al., 2016). Photovoice is also used widely in the attempt of preventing and coping with HIV/AIDS, such as in the United States and such African countries as Uganda and Kenya (Rhodes et al., 2008; Kubicek et al., 2012; Markus, 2012; Fournier et al., 2014).

In attempting to achieve its objective, photovoice has some steps to do: selecting and recruiting a target audience of policymakers or community leaders; recruiting a group of photovoice participants; introducing the photovoice methodology to participants, and facilitating a group discussion about cameras, power, and ethics; obtaining informed consent; posing initial theme/s for taking pictures, distributing cameras to participants and reviewing how to use the cameras; providing time for participants to take pictures; meeting to discuss photographs and identifying themes and plans with participants, and to discuss a format to share photographs and stories with policymakers or community leaders (Wang, 2006).

Photovoice is discussed in the public sphere as discursive space becomes a medium for creating mutual understanding based on validity claim as an ideal precondition, but empirical in nature to determine the validity of a communicative action mechanism (Habermas, 1989). This research aims to develop photovoice to be both the answer and the alternative response of the people caring about HIV/AIDS.

2 METHODS

Community-based participatory research emphasizes on learning processes, development and empowerment of the PLWHA community using photographic technique (Kemmis & Taggart, 2000; Hergenrather et al., 2009; Kindon & Sarah, 2009). At the planning stage, the author conducted need-assessment mapping with PLWHA in Surakarta, affiliated with Solo Plus Peer Support Group, and approved the action plan choice to reinforce the conception and knowledge on photographic technique (Vos, 2005; Ozanira, 2012). After PLWHA have attended photographic training, produced photovoice media and implemented their action by exhibiting photovoice media every Sunday from 6 to 9 a.m. at Solo Car Free Day, the author observed the effect of such PLWHA's actions. The author also participated in a dialogic process between PLWHA and the public concerning the situation and condition of PLWHA. Finally, the author made reflections on the photovoice used as a medium for socializing HIV/AIDS and analyzed it using Habermas's Theory of Communicative Action.

3 RESULT AND DISCUSSION

Identity definition is a vital component of the social interaction process, because it determines an individual's position and role within society. This position recognition is the manifestation of each individual which ensures an individual's existence in his/her social environment, including PLWHA in Surakarta. Photovoice is present as another alternative to socializing the prevention and the coping of HIV/AIDS, because this issue is no longer presented in formal circumstances, requiring the audiences to sit down and to listen to what the resources (informants) explain. Information on HIV/AIDS displayed through photovoice is the picture taken by PLWHA that is interesting to watch. Behind the photographs exhibited, there is certain meaning to be interpreted by those viewing them.

Photovoice is the manifestation of photographic technique; for that reason an ability of using the camera and understanding photographic art and ethic is absolute (Wang & Redwood-Jones, 2001). AIDS Coping Commission of Surakarta City holds training on photographic technique, art and ethics, particularly in relation to informed consent for people with HIV/AIDS, photo-editing and budgeting for exhibition. So there is intensive facilitation for PLWHA in a certain period of time. The training participants also hold discussion and critical dialog in relation to a photograph's concept, execution and editing, and they discuss intensely illustration and the meaning of the photographs taken. This process is an arena for PLWHA to voice their opinion (point of view) and to reflect it (Teti et al., 2012). This attempt is generally known through certain techniques in photovoice, known by the acronym SHOWED: S–What is SEEN here?; H – What is really HAPPENING?; O – How does this relate to OUR lives/work?; W – WHY are things this way?; E – How would this image EDUCATE/EMPOWER people?; D – What can I DO about it?. The presence of acronym SHOWED in photovoice, particularly the points E (EDUCATE/EMPOWER) and D (DO), confirm the presence of the empowerment process (Taboada, 2012).

Solo Car Free Day, on Slamet Riyadi Street in Surakarta, is inclusive in nature and becomes a public space choice to represent and to argue about photovoice, related to the situation and condition of PLWHA. Every Sunday from 6 to 9 a.m. at Solo Car Free Day, PLWHA hold a critical dialog along with the people visiting and watching the photovoice exhibited, and photovoice becomes PLWHA's medium to voice the conditions they encounter. For example, they tell about their health condition dependent on medicines, being avoided by their beloved people, friend or family, and their apathy in realizing the fact that they are infected with HIV/AIDS until they revive and survive. In such a communication, PLWHA attempt to make society understand their intention by trying to achieve validity claims considered as rational because they are supported with truth, accuracy, honesty, and comprehensiveness concerning the situation and condition of PLWHA.

Photovoice successfully grows empathy, contributing to reducing negative stigma against PLWHA. This empathy results in support for PLWHA as well, particularly from family and society. Photovoice opens another opportunity for facilitating the attempt of socializing HIV/AIDS, because it allows for the establishment of partnership network with individuals, community government and Non-Government Organization. The attempt to prevent and cope with HIV/AIDS has a high cost, which often becomes a constraint.

For that reason, photovoice can be a means of collecting funds using both fundraising and sponsorship from those interested in helping. Thus, it is not impossible for photovoice to be a medium for promoting HIV/AIDS that has a wide impact for low cost, and for bringing the people caring about HIV/AIDS into reality.

4 CONCLUSION

Photovoice has empowerment potency that can result in change within society, particularly improving the capacity of PWLHA and the public. The public realizes the danger of HIV/AIDS, and participates actively in preventing and coping with HIV/AIDS. It also builds sensitive culture and empathy to what PLWHA encounter and feel towards non-discriminative behavior against PLWHA.

REFERENCES

Alistar, S.S. & Brandeau, M.L. (2012). Decision making for HIV prevention and treatment scale up: bridging the gap between theory and practice. *Medical Decision Making*, *32*(1), 105–117.

Baker, T.A. & Wang, C.C. (2006). Photovoice: Use of a participatory action research method to explore the chronic pain experience in older adults. *Qualitative Health Research*, *16*(10), 1405–1413.

Catalani, C. & Minkler, M. (2010). Photovoice: A review of the literature in health and public health. *Health Education and Behavior*, *37*(3), 424–451.

Demartoto, A., Soemanto, R.B. & Zunariyah, S. (2015). Supporting and inhibiting factors in the structured peer network among housewives in coping with HIV/AIDS. *Proceedings: 1st UPI International Conference on Sociology Education (UPI ICSE 2015)*, 425–427. Available at http://www.atlantis-press.com/php/pub.php?publication=icse–15.

Fournier, B., Bridge, A., Mill, J., Alibhai, A., Kennedy, A.P. & Konde-Lule, J. (2014). Turning the camera back: A photovoice project with Ugandan children who are orphaned and living with HIV. *Sage Open*, April-June 2014, 1–10.

Gotschi, E., Delve, R. & Freyer, B. (2009). Participatory photography as a qualitative approach to obtain insights into farmer groups. *Field Methods, 21*(3), 290–308.

Habermas, J. (1989). *The structural transformation of public sphere: An inquiry into category of bourgeois society*. Translated by Thomas Burger with the assistance of Frederick Lawrence. Cambridge, MA: MIT Press.

Halmshaw, C. & Hawkins, K. (2004). Capitalising on global HIV/AIDS funding: the challenge for civil society and government. *Reproductive Health Matters*, *12*(24), 35–41.

Han, C.S. & Oliffe, J.L. (2016). Photovoice in mental illness research: A review and recommendations. *Health, 20*(2), 110–126.

Hergenrather, K.C., Rhodes, S.D., Cowan, C.A., Bardhoshi, G. & Pula, S. (2009). Photovoice as community-based participatory research: A qualitative review. *American Journal of Health Behavior*, *33*(6), 686–698.

Ho, W-C., Rochelle, T.L. & Yuen, W-K. (2011). 'We Are Not Sad At All': Adolescents talk about their 'City of Sadness' through photovoice. *Journal of Adolescent Research*, *26*(6), 727–765.

Kemmis, S. & McTaggart, R. (2000). Participatory action research. In K.N. Denzin & Y.S. Lincoln (Eds.), *Handbook of qualitative research*. London: Sage Publication.

Killion, C.M. & Wang, C.C. (2000). Linking African American mothers across life stage and station through photovoice. *Journal of Health Care for the Poor and Underserved*, *11* (3), 310–325.

Kindon, S. & Sarah, E. (2009). Introduction: More than methods-reflections on participatory action research in geographic teaching, learning and research. *Journal of Geography in Higher Education*, *33*(9), 19–32.

Kingery, F.P., Naanyu, V., Allen, W. & Patel, P. (2016). Photo voice in Kenya: Using a community-based participatory research method to identify health needs. *Qual Health Res, 26* (1), 92–104.

Kubicek, K., Beyer, W., Weiss, G. & Kopek, M.D. (2012). Photovoice as a tool to adapt an HIV prevention intervention for African American young men who have sex with men. *Health Promotion Practice, 13*(4), 535–543.

Laperrière, H. & Zúñiga, R. (2006). Sociopolitical determinants of an AIDS prevention program: multiple actors and vertical relationships of control and influence. *Policy, Politics, & Nursing Practice*, *7*(2), 125–135.

Mannell, J., Cornish, F. & Russell, J. (2015). Evaluating social outcomes of HIV/AIDS interventions: a critical assessment of contemporary indicator frameworks. *Journal of the International AIDS Society*, *17*(19073), 11.

Markus, S.F. (2012). *Photovoice for healthy relationships: Community-Based participatory HIV prevention in a rural American Indian community*. American Indian and Alaska Native Mental Health Research Copyright: Centers for American Indian and Alaska Native Health Colorado School of Public Health/University of Colorado Anschutz Medical Campus. Retrieved May 10, 2016 from www.ucdenver.edu/caianh.

Mohammed, S., Sajun, S.Z. & Khan, F.S. (2015). Harnessing photovoice for tuberculosis advocacy in Karachi, Pakistan. *Health Promotion International*, *30*(2), 262–269.

Nelson, E. & Christensen, K. (2012). *In the middle: how our students experience learning at school and beyond*. Retrieved on May 10, 2016 from www.teacherswork.ac.nz/journal/.../nelson.pdf.

Ozanira, M.S. S. (2012). Reconstructing a participatory process in the production of knowledge: A concept and a practice. *International Journal of Action Research*, *1*(1), 102.

Rhodes, S.D., Hergenrather, K.C., Wilkin, A.M., & Jolly, C. (2008). Visions and voices: Indigent persons living with HIV in the Southern United States use photovoice to create knowledge, develop partnerships, and take action. *Health Promotion Practice*, *9*(2), 159–169.

Stegenga, K. & Burks, L.M. (2013). Using photovoice to explore the unique life perspectives of youth with sickle cell disease. *Journal of Pediatric Oncology Nursing, 30*(5), 269–274.

Taboada, A. (2012). *Photovoice: Using photography to reduce HIV stigma and discrimination in Guatemala.* Retrieved May 10, 2016 from http://www.intrahealth.org/blog/photovoice-using-photography-reduce-hiv-stigma-and-discrimination-guatemala#. VsvUtyezvEQ.

Teti, M., Murray, C. Johnson, L.S. & Binson, D. (2012). Photovoice as a community-based participatory research method among women living with HIV/AIDS: Ethical opportunities and challenges. *Journal of Empirical Research on Human Research Ethics: An International Journal, 7*(4), 34–43.

Vos, A.D. (2005). *Research at grass roots: for the social sciences and human service professions.* Pretoria: Van Schaik Publishers.

Wang, C.C. & Redwood-Jones, Y.A. (2001). Photovoice ethics: Perspectives from flint photovoice. *Health Education & Behavior, 28*(5), 560–572.

Wang, C.C. (2006). *Youth participation in photovoice as a strategy for community change.* Retrieved May 10, 2016 from http://www.haworthpress.com/web/COM.

Ward, A.L., Baggett, T., Orsini, A., Angelo, J. & Weiss, H. (2016). Participatory photography gives voice to young non-drivers in New Zealand. *Health Promotion International*, 31/2, 280–9.

Warne, M., Snyder, K. & Gadin, K.G. (2012). Photovoice: an opportunity and challenge for students' genuine participation. *Health Promotion International, 28*(3), 299–310.

Wilson, N., Dasho, S., Martin, A.C., Wallerstein, N., Wang, C.C. & Minkler, M. (2007). Engaging young adolescents in social action through Photovoice: The youth empowerment strategies (YES!) project. *Journal of Early Adolescence, 27*(2), 241–261.

Regionalization and Harmonization in TVET – Abdullah et al. (Eds)
© 2017 Taylor & Francis Group, London, ISBN 978-1-138-05419-6

Finding Sudalarang as an architecture vocational village

D.P. Mulyana, L. Widaningsih & T. Megayanti
Universitas Pendidikan Indonesia, Indonesia

ABSTRACT: The government, in order to improve social welfare, launched a vocational village program in the non-agricultural sector through the Ministry of Education and Culture. There are six requirements for the establishment of vocational villages: that they have abundant natural resources, a market for service/goods, the villages should have potential, have relevant skills, and limited skills and responsivity from the rural community. The approach used in this study is descriptive qualitative with standardized interview, observation, documentation and focus group discussion as the data collection techniques. Research findings in Sudalarang show that five of the six requirements have been satisfied. The requirement for abundant natural resources is not a research focus because it is a non-agricultural sector. Human resources are the greatest potential as 73% of the population are construction workers. Sudalarang village has the potential to become a vocational village, where human resources independently manage rural development as well as forming a community of building workers.

1 INTRODUCTION

Indonesian society is historically known as an agrarian society with subsistence farming, where people live in the village. However, along with globalization and the passage of time, the title of Indonesia as an agrarian society is increasingly disappearing. The views of rural communities to the successful life in the city, change the mindset of those who were initially farmers to become workers. The desire to gain higher income and a better life is the primary motivation for villagers to migrate into cities. The migration of rural communities into the city, or the socalled urbanization, is the new problem for the population in Indonesia.

The government sought to reduce the rate of urbanization by providing solutions through the Ministry of Education and Culture in 2014 to the establishment of vocational villages. The government's goal is to create high-quality jobs in the village, especially in the non-agricultural sector. The establishment of a vocational village aims to achieve the government's target by changing the village that is left behind, yet has potentially advanced society into an independent village that can manage the economy and the prosperity of their community. A construction worker is one example of non-formal employment that has a lot of enthusiasts in Indonesia. Construction workers may be a major milestone in the development of the country although most do not get a formal education in the field of building.

In line with the government's target to create a high-quality job in the village, it is necessary to know the potential of the village to support the creation of employment in the non-agricultural sector. The greatest potential is human resources. There is one community which is the builders' community in Sudalarang village, Garut, named PAKUBA (Pekerja Kuli Bangunan (construction worker)) (Nuryanto, 2012). This community becomes one of the key potentials in the development of an advanced independent village.

Non-formal education outside Indonesia gives positive feedback. The validation allows for more opportunities of more expertise being available in the labor market. Moreover, this validation also facilitates a better relation between skills and labor demand, and stimulates the transfer of skillful employees between companies and economic sectors. It also encourages the mobility of the labor market in the European region (Tripon, 2014).

The success of rural non-agricultural vocational fields also occurred in the state of Turkey after the Second World War. Non-formal vocational education can reach those who are currently alienated from formal education, so that non-formal education can improve their empowerment by completing the basic knowledge and skills that are useful (Blaak, 2013). Education and training in a rural community or vocational training also give many positive results, for instance, one of which occurs in a village in Turkey with the help of an experienced instructor. Asik Veysel contributes in advancing the post-world-war village in Turkey into a musical vocation village which mostly earns a living from music (Erdal, 2014).

Based on the urgency of the establishment of vocational villages to create high-quality jobs in the non-agricultural sector for the rural community, researchers are interested in investigating how the overview of the problems identified are: (1) describing the characteristics of Vocational Village of Architecture developed by Ministry of Education and Culture; (2) explaining the potential of Sudalarang village to be a vocational village in the field of architecture.

2 METHOD AND MATERIALS

2.1 *Research method*

The study used a qualitative approach, specifically a case study. In this kind of study, the results cannot be generalized. This means that the final result of the identification of a Sudalarang village's potential cannot be equated with the potential of other villages. The case study, using qualitative research, focuses only on the potential condition of the Sudalarang village to be a vocational village in the fields of architecture.

2.2 *Object of the study*

Questionnaire research was carried out with the informants, who were 17 people working as construction workers. Their ages ranged from 35–65 years old, and between them they had eight different areas of expertise in the field of architecture.

2.3 *Data collection*

The data was collected by using observation, standardized interview, documentation and focus group discussion as the data collection techniques. Moreover, the observation and interview guides which were in the form of a research questionnaire were given to the selected informants.

3 RESULTS AND DISCUSSION

3.1 *Vocational village characteristic in architecture field*

The characteristics of vocational village developed by the Ministry of Education and Culture can be identified as having potency in some aspects of the research. The potency is the Human Resources (HR) with skills that are relevant to the primary job of most of the inhabitants, which is construction workers. The potency of HR is a good sign to support the establishment of a vocational village in architecture. HR in Sudalarang village has the attitude of mutual cooperation which eases the activities of empowering rural communities to participate in non-formal education and training.

The attitude of mutual cooperation which is held by the villagers unites them for working together to build a village for the better, for example the creation of irrigation channels in the village. The people often go hand-in-hand in the social field. For instance, giving donations to orphans, holding a mass circumcision for the villagers, and helping to renovate damaged houses. The renovation is done with the help of construction workers who are the members of PAKUBA. They help materially and morally. Materially, they donate building materials while morally, they help to complete home renovation.

The motivation of villagers in Sudalarang to develop their village into a self-reliant village is also great. It can be seen from their enthusiasm during the discussion on education and vocational training in the village. The desire to improve living standards and increase economy is the main reason that motivates Sudalarang's villagers to move forward.

Table 1. Findings' characteristics of vocational village in architecture field.

Vocational village requirements	Result of study
Underdeveloped villages but have abundant natural resources	Rural Sudalarang not classified into the village, is left behind in terms of infrastructure, accessibility and facilities of the village.
Have limited skills of citizens	Most of livelihood as a construction worker. Categorized as having spatial limitations in training and empowerment.
Market goods/services	Services market from construction sector quite a lot. Contractor and sub-contractor have been trusted by Sudalarang workers. Building quality was good and tidy.
Village potency	Natural resources are lush. Majority working as construction workers and as a community formed named PAKUBA. Service market mostly comes from construction field.
Have the kind of skills that are relevant	There are seven areas of expertise available in Sudalarang, such as bricklayer, carpenter, stone, finishing, electrician, foreman and mason.
Responsivity of rural community	There is a need to increase level of economy and income. Motivation to continue as a construction worker because the results are promising. Their HR need to get training and to be empowered.

3.2 Non-formal education

The Vocational Village program is intended to develop HR in the rural spectrum with a regional approach, which is the rural areas that are based on the cultural values by utilizing local potential. This is in line with The Constitution of the Republic of Indonesia No. 20 2003 Article 26, paragraph 5, which explains that knowledge, skills, and life skills provided by courses and training (non-formal education) is not only to develop themselves to gain higher education and professional development, but also to assist learners to work in any business units.

To achieve a successful vocation village in which advantages are felt by the villagers, not only is human resource potential required but also other skills, acquired through courses and training as non-formal education. The education level of the majority of construction workers in Sudalarang village is at high school level or equivalent. Skills are obtained independently without following any formal education about how to build. Skills are hereditary and as if ingrained within the villagers. They are used to gaining skills without formal training, and this is the main reason why they are never involved in any formal education to be a construction worker. Informants said that the quality of their work is similar or even higher than those who participate in formal education.

Those successful stories are certainly not going to happen without the power of change of vocational villages. The establishment of vocational villages is needed for the welfare of the villagers on their own. If there is no willingness from the whole village, the establishment of a vocational village will never happen.

3.3 Village potency

Village potency is mentioned in The Constitution of the Republic of Indonesia No. 6 2014 concerning villages. It becomes an opportunity for every village to be able to develop all their potential independently according to the needs of each in order to realize the public welfare. The potency of a village can be seen and discovered as a force for the establishment of vocational villages in the form of physical and non-physical potency. Without potency, the process of the vocational village formation will be hindered.

After the research was conducted in Sudalarang, the aspects of physical potential became one major point that stands out. HR is categorized as supportive, which is mostly construction workers. Non-physical potency that includes Patterns Community Interaction, Social Institutions, Educational Institutions, Organizations Village, Village Apparatus and Officials, are met.

From the description of the village's potency generally associated with Sudalarang village to be used as a vocational village, all potential aspects have been fulfilled, both physical and non-physical potential. The characteristics of vocational villages are also fulfilled. Sudalarang village is identified as having the potential of HR as a construction worker with six priority-of-skill areas from eight skills recorded.

3.4 Data analysis

3.4.1 Sudalarang livelihood
The livelihood of Sudalarang villagers are 148 Farmers (FR), 82 Traders (TR), 633 construction Laborers (LA), 115 Construction Workers (CW), 46 Government Employees (GE) and 7 cops/army (CA). It shows that people mostly work in the construction sector, 748 in total of construction workers and laborers.

3.4.2 Construction workers' skills
Area expertise in architecture of construction workers in Sudalarang were mapped according to the number of active members of PAKUBA

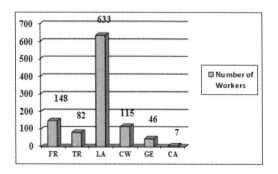

Figure 1. Comparison of construction workers' skills from Sudalarang village.

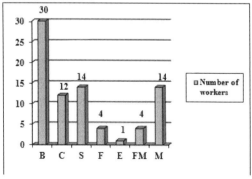

Figure 2. Comparison of construction workers' skills from Sudalarang village.

community with 86 active members, as 79 workers and 7 support staff. There are 7 skills that were identified: bricklayer (B), carpenter (C), stone (S), finishing (F), electrician (E), foreman (FM), and mason (M).

4 CONCLUSION

Research findings in Sudalarang show that five of the six requirements have been met. Terms of abundant natural resources is not a research focus because it is a non-agricultural sector. The biggest village potency from Sudalarang is HR and the greatest potential, with 73% percent of the population being construction workers.

The HR of Sudalarang has the potential to be a good vocational village architecture. They have relevant skills for the majority of the population living as construction workers. The willingness or the request of the villagers became non-physical potential that can help the course of the establishment of vocational villages. Aspects of potential villages have been fulfilled, both physical and non-physical potential. Likewise with the characteristics of vocational villages, Sudalarang is identified as having the potential of HR as construction workers. HR needs training and empowering to improve their skills because they never got formal education as professional construction workers.

REFERENCES

Blaak, M. (2013). Non-formal vocational education in Uganda: Practical empowerment through a workable alternative. *International Journal of Educational Development, 33*(1), 88–97.

Constitution of Republic Indonesia Law Number 20 of 2003 Article 26, Paragraph 5 about Courses and Training.

Constitution of Republic Indonesia Law Number 6 of 2014 on village affairs.

Erdal, G.G. (2014). Aşık Veysel in village institutions and his contributions to music education. *Procedia - Social and Behavioral Sciences, 116*, 1449–1453.

Ministry of Education and Culture. (2014). *Technical instructions social assistance of vocational village.* Jakarta: Kemdikbud.

Nuryanto. (2012). *Improving the competence of construction workers of PAKUBA the worker's community through provision of knowledge in construction sector (located in Sudalarang Village, Garut-Jawa Barat).* LPPM-UPI. Not Published.

Tripon, A. (2014). Innovative technology for sustainable development of human resource using non-formal and informal education. *Procedia Technology, 12*, 598–603.

Perception of vocational high school students on the transformation of local wisdom value

E.E. Nikmawati, I. Widiaty, R. Hurriyati & Y. Achdiani
Universitas Pendidikan Indonesia, Jawa Barat, Indonesia

ABSTRACT: The background of this research is the importance of the transformation process of local wisdom value in the learning process. The purpose of this study is to determine the perceptions of students about the transformation of the local wisdom value in the cookery field of study in a vocational school. The scope of the transformation elements consists of content, process, perspectives, context, and design. The method used is a survey by giving a questionnaire to students who have attended the learning of Iconic Batik Brownies Baking. The results show that the transformation of local wisdom value that gives the most positive impression is on the meaning of learning which has an impact on the appreciation of culture (aspect of the process). Transformation of the local wisdom value also motivates learners to explore the potential of nature in its territory further. Learners assume that the local wisdom-based learning is a fun process of learning.

1 INTRODUCTION

The transformation of local wisdom values which are integrated in the learning process is seen as a process of cultural conservation through the concept of transformative sustainability pedagogy (Burns, 2015). The transformation process is important to do in a way that the learning could be meaningful, because it is rooted in the culture and noble values that are owned and 'close' to the students' environment (Poikela et al., 2015). One of the sources of local wisdom values that can be transformed into the learning comes from the local wisdom value of a community (Jifa, 2013).

The scope of the transformation elements of the local wisdom value in the learning process consists of the content aspect of learning which contains the local wisdom value (content), meaning perceived by students about the local wisdom value (process), to develop the students' paradigm of thinking about the local wisdom value in wider perspective (perspectives), the context of the local wisdom value in a particular community (context), and the design of continuous learning so that the local wisdom value is integrated into daily life (design) which move simultaneously (Burns, 2015).

The value of local wisdom that comes from the community, one of which is reflected in the indigenous village of Cireundeu. Cireundeu region, which is located in Cimahi, West Java, can be used as a source of local wisdom-based learning for students. Cireundeu indigenous villages is the prototype of the nation food security village. Cireundeu has been able to promote its traditional food as a symbol of traditional food with local wisdom value.

Learning with traditional foods is expected to be able to present an alternative to public education to love the food, culture, and noble values in the form of local wisdom based on the traditional food (Frochot, 2003; Hjalager & Corigliano, 2000).

The traditional food is seen not only as a traditional cookery, but also as a room for science and local wisdom (Wurianto, 2008). This space for knowledge and local wisdom can be transformed on learning so that this 'space' does not vanish. There are two strategies that can be applied to the process of transformation of local wisdom value of the Cireundeu Indigenous Village, which are the design of learning made by teachers and the implementation of local wisdom value-based learning process for students.

This study aims to determine the perceptions of students about the transformation of the local wisdom value in the field of cookery learning at a vocational school. More specifically, this study tries to explore the perceptions of students about the transformation elements of the local wisdom value (content, process, perspectives, context, and design) on the pastry learning with the topic of 'Iconic Batik Brownies Baking'.

2 RESEARCH METHODOLOGY

The data collection of students' perception about the transformation of the local wisdom value on learning was done through a survey conducted among students at SMK 3 Cimahi. The choice of location, SMK 3 Cimahi, was based on the consideration that this vocational school is located near the Cireundeu Indigenous Village which is in the same region, namely Cimahi City, Indonesia.

The study was designed with the involvement of culinary practitioners from Cireundeu Indigenous Village, who acted as teacher assistants in the learning process alongside the cookery teacher at SMK 3 Cimahi. The subject of learning for this local wisdom value-based learning was making the 'Iconic Batik Brownies' cake. Brownies was made using the 'rasi' ingredient made from cassava, as a main food of people at Cireundeu Indigenous Village. The brownies was also made using the iconic batik motif, which was derived from Cimahi's specialty batik.

Respondents involved in this research were 32 pastry students from the cookery program, who were students of the culinary expertise program. The study also involved two practitioners as partner instructors from Cireundeu Indigenous Village.

A survey of students' perceptions about the transformation of the local wisdom value was conducted by completing a short questionnaire. The questionnaire consisted of ten statements on the Likert scale three-point. The scope of questions was about the transformation elements of local wisdom values, which are: aspect of content, process, perspectives, context, and design. After filling in the questionnaire by students, the whole learning process was completed. Analysis of the research data was conducted by using Microsoft Excel to calculate the percentage of learners' perceptions about the local wisdom value of Cireundeu Indigenous Village's traditional foods, which was transformed into learning at a vocational school.

3 RESULTS AND DISCUSSION

The results of this research will be described by presenting information about the uniqueness of Cireundeu Indigenous Village as a source of learning the local wisdom value. In this section, there is also an overview of Cimahi's specialty batik motifs that also become an inspirational motif of local wisdom, which will also be assessed in the learning of Iconic Batik Brownies Baking. After that, the perception of students about the learning of Iconic Batik Brownies will be presented, by transforming the local wisdom value of Cireundeu Indigenous Village's traditional food and motifs of Cimahi's specialty batik.

3.1 Local wisdom of Cireundeu Indigenous Village

Cireundeu Village is an area marked by the Government of Cimahi, West Java as a traditional village. Cireundeu community, which is located in Leuwigajah District of South Cimahi, Cimahi, West Java, has a habit of consuming 'rasi' (cassava rice) as a main food.

The Cireundeu community in the region has been consuming 'rasi' as their main food and it has been done for generations since hundreds of years ago. They believe that if things are violated, disasters will happen in their area. This distinction is closely related to the natural history of the food they encountered, which is then used as the basic philosophy of life of the community in Cireundeu Village.

In addition, the eating habit of rasi as the main food (made from cassava) becomes a unique phenomenon in the middle of the government's intensive efforts to find other main foods as alternatives to rice. For its achievement in regard to this, in 2009 the society of Cireundeu received a national award from President Susilo Bambang Yudhoyono as one of the pioneered villages of national food security.

Two main unique features of the Cireundeu community are the cultural aspects and food security, in which the latter is based on the 'rasi' eating habits. It could be used as one of the potential travel/ecotourism educations regarding how communities of Cireundeu can maintain their eating habits of rasi despite the incessant flow of modernization. In addition, the potential for 'rasi' as an alternative main food to rice needs to be developed further and this condition can be used as an alternative educational process for the wider community.

3.2 Cimahi's unique motif of batik on iconic batik brownies

Cimahi's motifs of batik become one of the learning content based on local wisdom in vocational schools. Cimahi's motif of batik used as a study for brownies topping, is the motif of Cireundeu's cassava, depicting the Cireundeu Indigenous Village's local wisdom of value symbolized by Cireundeu's cassava leaf motif (Figures 1a and 1b). Another motif which is as a content of local wisdom on brownies topping, is the motif of Ciawitali bamboo, which is the characteristic plant in the Cimahi area. Bamboo tree is like the tree of life because there is always a source of water around the bamboo tree. Water is the source of human life (Figures 2a and 2b).

Figure 1a. Motif of Inspired Figure 1b. Brownies batik, Cireundeu's by with motif of batik, Cireundeu's cassava leaf. cassava leaf.

Figure 2a. Motif of Inspired Figure 2b. Brownies
batik, Ciawitali by with motif of batik,
bamboo tree. Ciawitali bamboo tree.

Table 1. Perception of students on the transformation of local wisdom aspects of content, process, and perspective.

	Students' answers (%)		
Statement	Agree	Disagree	Do not know
Content			
Making Iconic Batik Brownies teaches values of local wisdom taught in Cireundeu Ingenious village	79	18	3
Making Iconic Batik Brownies teaches about philosophical value of Cimahi's batik	81	19	0
Process			
Making Iconic Batik Brownies provides meaningful experiences in order to appreciate their own culture	94	6	0
Making Iconic Batik Brownies provides meaningful experiences about simplicity of Cireundeu community but have high self-esteem	88	10	2
Perspectives			
Making Iconic Batik Brownies inspires to explore the potential of other local culinary specialties	90	9	1
Making Iconic Batik Brownies provides an understanding/new perspective that it is interesting to learn the local culture	92	8	0

3.3 Perception of students about the transformation of local wisdom values

Table 1 illustrates the process of transformation of the local wisdom value on learning in vocational

Table 2. Perception of students on the transformation of local wisdom on the aspect of context and design.

	Students' answer (%)		
Statement	Agree	Disagree	Do not know
Context			
Making Iconic Batik Brownies provides an overview of the society and social and cultural aspects of Cireundeu	90	10	0
Making Iconic Batik Brownies provides an overview of the potential natural wealth of Cimahi	93	7	0
Design			
Making Iconic Batik Brownies gives motivation so that the local wisdom values of Cireundeu Indigenous villages (simplicity, togetherness, pride in their own products) can be applied in everyday life	89	9	2
Making Iconic Batik Brownies provides guidelines for understanding and applying local wisdom values on education in school, outside of school, and in the family	80	18	2

school. 94% of students agreed the process can provide valuable experience to love their own culture. 92% of students agreed that the process of transformation of the local wisdom value in learning can provide insights/new perspective that it is interesting to learn the local culture, as well as 90% of learners are inspired to explore the potential of other local culinary specialties.

The results of this study indicate that the transformation of the local wisdom value of the 'process' aspect is able to give profound meaning for students through the learning experience. Learners are moved to love the culture and values of local wisdom. Education in this context is seen as an education which is oriented in the cultural formation of students' character. Character education is seen as a solution in strengthening the identity of Indonesia (Alwasilah et al., 2009; Kartadinata, 2010).

The impact of foreign culture, especially in the younger generation today is very worrying. One effort that can be done to fortify the identity of the younger generation is to strengthen the aspects of character-based education. Educational character of a nation is always associated with the value of local wisdom. The rationality of introducing local wisdom in an educational context is based on that value of local wisdom, and has a positive force in shaping the character of learners (Suratno, 2010).

Transformation of the local wisdom value in learning at a vocational school provides a new perspective for students. Learners have the view that learning about the local culture is fun and opens their horizons to explore more local potential in the region that can be made into global products.

Table 2 shows the perception of the students about the transformation of the local wisdom value on the aspects of context and design. 93% of students agreed that the learning of local wisdom can provide a snapshot of potential development of the traditional food and natural resources of Cimahi. 90% of students agreed that the learning is able to describe the typical customs of the people in Cireundeu Indigenous Village. Developing traditional food basically becomes a part of natural resource of the region. As we know, traditional food and beverage generally comes from the richness and potential of local natural resources, which are processed in certain ways to become specialties (Teffler, 2000).

4 CONCLUSION

The process of transformation in the local wisdom value in the learning at vocational school has a positive influence on most of the elements of the transformation, which include the content, process, perspective, context, and design. Transformation of the local wisdom value provides valuable experience for the students to appreciate our own culture better. Learners are more aware of local potential in their region. Learners have a positive perspective on local wisdom-based learning, where such learning is apparently interesting to learn.

ACKNOWLEDGMENT

We acknowledged RISTEK DIKTI (Grant: MP3EI).

REFERENCES

Alwasilah, A.C., Suryadi, K. & Karyono, T. (2009). *Etnopedagogi: Landasan praktek pendidikan dan pendidikan guru*. Kiblat Buku Utama, Bandung.

Burns, H.L. (2015). Transformative sustainability pedagogy: Learning from ecological systems and indigenous wisdom. *Journal of Transformative Education, 133*, 259–276.

Frochot, I. (2003). An analysis of regional positioning and its associated food images in French tourism regional brochures. *Journal of Travel & Tourism Marketing, 14*(3), 77–96.

Hjalager, A.M. & Corigliano, M.A. (2000). Food for tourists—Determinants of an image. *International Journal of Tourism Research, 2*(4), 281–293.

Jifa, G. (2013). Data, information, knowledge, wisdom and meta-synthesis of wisdom-comment on wisdom global and wisdom cities. *Procedia Computer Science, 17*, 713–719.

Kartadinata, S. (2010). *Etnopedagogik: Sebuah resureksi ilmu pendidikan (pedagogik)*. Makalah disajikan pada 2nd International Seminar 2010 'Practice Pedagogic in Global Education Perspective'. PGSD UPI, Bandung, 17 May, 2010.

Poikela, P., Ruokamo, H. & Teräs, M. (2015). Comparison of meaningful learning characteristics in simulated nursing practice after traditional versus computer-based simulation method: A qualitative videography study. *Nurse Education Today, 35*(2), 373–382.

Suratno, T. (2010). *Memaknai Etnopedagogi Sebagai Landasan Pendidikan Guru*. Proceedings of the 4th International Conference on Teacher Education; Join Conference UPI & UPSI Bandung Indonesia, (November), 515–530.

Telfer, D. (2000). Tastes of Niagara: Building strategic alliances between tourism and agriculture. *International Journal of Hospitality and Tourism Administration, 1*(91), 71–88.

Wurianto, A.B. (2008). *Aspek Budaya Pada Tradisi Kuliner Tradisional Di Kota Malang Sebagai Identitas Sosial Budaya (Sebuah Tinjauan Folklore)*. Lembaga Penelitian Universitas Muhammadiyah Malang.

Developing content of curriculum based on local wisdom in a vocational high school

I. Widiaty, I. Kuntadi, Y. Achdiani & A. Ana
Universitas Pendidikan Indonesia, Bandung, Indonesia

ABSTRACT: The purpose of this study was to analyze the content development of a local wisdom-based curriculum in a vocational high school. The scope of the study was focused on the content resources of the curriculum implemented in a vocational high school on a subject called Batik. The analysis unit of the study was a batik pattern from Cimahi, West Java. Data was collected from three batik industries at Cimahi through documentation, observation, and in-depth interview with their owners. The results of the study reveal that the pattern of Cimahi Batik was inspired by the environment and the city icon of Cimahi. The pattern, which contained local wisdom, particularly about loving nature and culture, became an inspiration of the curriculum content development. The development of the curriculum which was 'familiar' with the students actually impacted the meaningful understanding of internalization.

1 INTRODUCTION

Curriculum development leading to 'wisdom' education is becoming a new thing in today's education. A wisdom-based curriculum (Kuhn & Udell, 2010; Halpern, 2010) is a curriculum in which students not only learn knowledge and skills, but also use them in their society (Sternberg et al., 2007). Wisdom values that are integrated in a curriculum are believed to be able to enrich the learner's understanding which is likely to lead to higher-order thinking skills, which lately have been neglected in the curriculum (Sternberg, 2010).

The main recourse of wisdom-based curriculum basically derives from the local culture, which means it has to refer to the local wisdom of each area (Scott, 2010). Some of the possible references include individual wisdom (local heroes) and collective wisdom (local custom, community, environment), which represent the culture of local wisdom (Jifa, 2013). To learn the values of local wisdom, either from individuals or groups, is one of the concepts of transformative sustainability pedagogy; this concept is an attempt to learn and transform it to education (Burns, 2015).

Transforming local wisdom into curriculum plays an important role since local wisdom values are commonly related to nature and environment (Widodo, 2012), environment sustainability, and local knowledge conservation (Barliana & Permanasari, 2014). In addition, local wisdom values integrated into the curriculum also encourage the learners to appreciate their own culture.

This study is aimed to develop the contents of local wisdom-based curriculum, particularly on batik learning in a vocational high school. Developing the contents of the curriculum in the context of this study is a learning strategy of Cimahi batik, integrated in the curriculum of the vocational high school. Developing the curriculum consisting of local wisdom is expected to contribute to character education so that the learners love the culture of Indonesia.

2 METHOD

2.1 Data source

The data source of the study is batik industry in Cimahi, West Java. A survey has been conducted in three Cimahi Batik industries, namely 'Sekar Putri', 'Lembur Batik Cimahi', and 'Batik Anggraeni'.

The data collected from the three industries lead to the idea resources of Cimahi Batik pattern-making, since this pattern reflects the local wisdom. The inspiration of the pattern-making can come from the flora, fauna, nature, local heroes, historical buildings, city icon(s), tourism places, art, and even beliefs.

2.2 Data collection and data analysis

The data collection is carried out through observation, in-depth interview, and documentation study. Observation is conducted by studying and analyzing various Cimahi Batik patterns processed in each industry. An interview is conducted with each leader of the industry to investigate deeply the inspiration of the pattern-making as well as the philosophical meaning behind each pattern. A documentation study, in the meantime, is employed to define the city profile, such as its nature, culture, buildings, arts, tourism places, and also beliefs.

The collected data is analyzed using a descriptive technique that describes the percentage of the inspiration of the batik patterns and also their philosophical meanings. Data presentation of batik patterns is the main signature of Cimahi Batik.

3 FINDINGS AND DISCUSSION

The idea resources (inspiration) of the content of local wisdom-based curriculum in the vocational high school that is inspired by the three batik industries in Cimahi can be seen in Table 1.

Table 1 shows that the main recourses of each industry studied are flora, nature, city icons, tourism places, and local tools.

Developing contents of a curriculum based on local wisdom can make learners have a better understanding, since what they learn is something 'familiar' with their needs and characteristics (Paik, 2015). These types of content are also expected to enable teachers to create more concrete teaching and learning materials. This condition will lead to a meaningful teaching and learning process (Poikela et al., 2015).

Below are some of the pictures of Cimahi Batik patterns inspired by local wisdom.

This pattern, namely Ciawitali (Figure 1a), is one of the Cimahi Batik signature. This pattern is inspired by the huge number of bamboo trees (Figure 1b) in an area in Cimahi called Ciawitali. For people living at Ciawitali, bamboos do not only appear as usual trees, but also have symbolic meanings. They believe that each part of a bamboo tree, such as root, trunk, and leaves, are actually useful. Bamboos are also a sign of a water spring.

The batik pattern of Singkong Cireundeu (Figure 2a), which literally means Cireundeu Cassava, is inspired from the area Cireundeu, whose people have cassava for their meals (Figure 2b). Rice, which becomes most Indonesians' staple food, is considered taboo to eat by the people of Cireundeu. This area has received an award as a national prototype of food sustainability, since they have an alternative food so that they do not need to have rice, which is mostly imported.

Peluru and Kujang (bullets and Kujang, a traditional weapon) pattern is inspired by the fact that the city is known as an 'army' city (Figure 3a). Kujang as a traditional weapon also becomes an inspiration, either for Cimahi Batik or West Java Batik (Figure 3b).

The pattern of Curug Cimahi (Figure 4a) pattern is taken from one of the popular tourism places, namely Curug Cimahi (Figure 4b). This place reflects Cimahi as a city that does not lack water. Cimahi itself literally means adequate water; Ci (water) and Mahi (adequate).

Table 1. Resources of Cimahi Batik patterns.

Idea resources	Percentage
Flora	100
Fauna	66.6
Nature	100
Humans/Important People /Heroes	0
Historical Buildings	33.3
Local Custom	33.3
City Icons	100
Tourism Places	100
Arts/Local Musical Instruments	0
Local Tools	100

Figure 2a. The batik pattern of Singkong Cireundeu. Inspired by Figure 2b. Cireundeu & Cassava.

Figure 3a. The batik pattern of Peluru and Kujang. Inspired by Figure 3b. Bullets and Kujang.

Figure 4a. The batik pattern of Curug Cimahi. Inspired by Figure 4b. Cimahi waterfall.

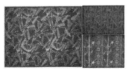

Figure 1a. The batik pattern of Ciawitali. Inspired by Figure 1b. Bamboo trees.

The patterns of Cimahi Batik are rarely inspired by historical building or local heroes since in that area there are few of them, as is also the case with the arts and local musical instruments.

Developing the contents of curriculum based on local wisdom demands teachers to have a better framework in terms of scope and flexibility (Grossman & Thompson, 2008). To cope with it, teachers can develop the framework using the characteristics of educative curriculum materials (Davis & Krajcik, 2005) since it can help them create a framework that is more specific and suitable to the needs of the learners.

4 CONCLUSION

Developing the contents of a local wisdom-based curriculum in a vocational high school is important in developing the love of country education. The contents of the curriculum based on local wisdom can be inspired by nature, city icons, tourism places, culture, arts, and local tools. Finally, the values of local wisdom in the batik patterns appear to be a precious point which creates more meaningful learning.

ACKNOWLEDGMENTS

We acknowledged RISTEK DIKTI (Grant: Penelitian Unggulan Perguruan Tinggi).

REFERENCES

Barliana, M.S., & Permanasari, D.C. (2016). Learning Pattern of Inheritance Tradition of Sustainable Architecture: From Ethno-Architecture to Ethno-Pedagogy. *TAWARIKH*, 5(2).

Burns, H.L. (2015). Transformative sustainability pedagogy: Learning from ecological systems and indigenous wisdom. *Journal of Transformative Education, 133*, 259–276.

Davis, E.A. & Krajcik, J.S. (2005). Designing educative curriculum materials to promote teacher learning. *Educational Researcher, 34*(3), 3–14.

Grossman, P. & Thompson, C. (2008). Learning from curriculum materials: Scaffolds for new teachers? *Teaching and Teacher Education, 24*(8), 2014–2026.

Halpern, D. (2010). Why Wisdom. *Educational Psychologist, 36*(4), 2001–2001.

Jifa, G. (2013). Data, information, knowledge, wisdom and meta-synthesis of wisdom-comment on wisdom global and wisdom cities. *Procedia Computer Science, 17*, 713–719.

Kuhn, D. & Udell, W. (2010). The path to wisdom. *Educational Psychologist, 36*(4), 261–264.

Paik, S. (2015). Teachers' attention to curriculum materials and students contexts: The case of Korean middle school teachers. *The Asia-Pacific Education Researcher, 24*(1), 235–246.

Poikela, P., Ruokamo, H. & Teräs, M. (2015). Comparison of meaningful learning characteristics in simulated nursing practice after traditional versus computer-based simulation method: A qualitative videography study. *Nurse Education Today, 35*(2), 373–382.

Scott, G.P. (2010). Wisdom, snake oil, and the educational marketplace. *Educational Psychologist, 36*(4), 257–260.

Sternberg, R.J. (2010). Why schools should teach for wisdom: The balance theory of wisdom in educational settings. *Educational Psychologist, 36*(4), 227–245.

Sternberg, R.J., Reznitskaya, A. & Jarvin, L. (2007). Teaching for wisdom: What matters is not just what students know, but how they use it. *London Review of Education, 5*(2), 143–158.

Widodo, J. (2012). Urban environment and human behaviour: Learning from history and local wisdom. *Procedia—Social and Behavioral Sciences*.

Developing training and vocational education for achieving gender equality

I.D.A. Nurhaeni
Public Administration Study Program, Universitas Sebelas Maret, Surakarta, Indonesia

Y. Kurniawan
English Department, Universitas Sebelas Maret, Surakarta, Indonesia

Supartiningsih
Department of Education, Youth and Sports, Demak Regency, Indonesia

ABSTRACT: Developing values of gender equality in an Islam-based region is difficult. The objective of this study is to evaluate the implementation of training and vocational education, that is, Gender-Responsive Family Education (GRFE), in actualizing gender equality, embracing variables of Communication, Resources, Disposition and Bureaucratic Structure. This research was conducted in five Community Learning Activity Centers in Demak Regency, Central Java, Indonesia. The data was gathered using *focus group discussion* and *participatory observation*. The analysis technique employs interactive analysis of Miles and Huberman's models. The result reveals that the effective communication between program managers and religious leaders, the availability of human resources understanding religion and gender, the utilization of religion-based preschools, household-based productive economic efforts, and active husbands' involvement in designing programs, are considered good practices of the implementation of GRFE. To make the program more quickly and equally implemented in various religion-based areas, educating and training about gender to religious leaders and preschool teachers become important.

1 INTRODUCTION

Indonesia has developed a program to achieve gender equality in the family since 2006, namely Program *Pendidikan Keluarga Berwawasan Gender* (Gender-Responsive Family Education), then shortened to GRFE program. It was developed by Indonesia's Ministry of Education based on the reality that women's participation in development and the position of women in public organizations are lower than that of men. The GRFE program is an effort to make families understand their rights, obligations, and male and female roles, so that gender equality in families can be achieved. In its implementation, the GRFE program is integrated through life skills education to families.

The family has an important role to shape the good character of individuals and to institutionalize the value equality and equity among the members of the family (Puspitawati, 2012). By having socialization and implementation of this value in the family, they can develop non-discriminative behaviors so that they can achieve a high level of education and choose the various kinds of job without gender stereotyping.

The effort to achieve gender equality in the family is not easy because of culture and religion (Wadud,

1999; Abouchedid, 2007; Self & Grabowski, 2009; Vasi, 2010; Ozcan et al., 2011; Tamuri, 2013; Haghighat, 2014; Pan, 2015). Paternalistic culture and religious faith always position men at a higher position than women. One of the arguments holds implicit gender discrimination, focusing on women's physical personality characteristics and domestic responsibility, related to reinforcing its explanation *'why women cannot compete as successfully as men and why their economic contribution is still lower than men's.'* Another argument states that women's *'emotional characteristic'* is used to rationalize why women are not promoted to the top position requiring many efforts and rational decision-making, which is not women's emotional characteristic (Ozcan et al., 2011). Furthermore, it is stated that women are impacted by discriminative behavior in organizations in various aspects, covering open discrimination, sexual harassment, and the glass ceiling phenomenon. Vasi (2010) stated that Muslim women have more time to become leaders, but in practice they frequently get marginal roles.

In contrast, Sidani (2005) stated that Islam gives higher spiritual, social, political and economic rights to women compared to the previous period. Vasi (2010) stated that women have more possibility to attend religious services more regularly and more possibility to contribute their time and donate their money to religious-based activities. Bala (2010) stated that Islam supports equality on women's rights.

Moreover, Tamuri (2013) stated that the formal education system, especially schools, in most developing countries has overtaken nearly all family roles in educating the young generation. What is more, Islamic educators have become important figures in developing young generations. Therefore, they require sufficient preparation in order to effectively fulfill their responsibility. For these reasons, the implementation of the GRFE program should be done with smart strategy.

This article aims at studying the implementation of the GRFE program in Demak regency, Central Java, Indonesia. Demak regency was intentionally selected because it has strong Islamic religious values. From this study, it is expected that the best practice of the implementation of the GRFE program, within the context of society having strong Islamic faith, can be formulated.

2 METHOD

Demak regency was elected due to three considerations: first, it has a low Gender-related Development Index (GDI) and Gender Empowerment Measure Index (GEM) in Central Java, Indonesia (GDI in 2013 was 88.98 and 89.28 in 2014, whilst GEM in 2013 was 69.33 and decreased to 66.60 in 2014 (KPPA & BPS, 2015)). Second, it has implemented gender mainstreaming in Education since 2012, in accordance with the Regulation of Education Minister Number 84 Year 2008 on Gender Mainstreaming in Education. Finally, Demak regency is one of the cities in Indonesia having high potential to have conflict due to its strong Islamic culture. Five CLACs (Community Learning Activity Centers) in Demak regency were intentionally selected since they had implemented the GRFE (Gender-Responsive Family Education) program, namely *(CLAC) Surya Alam, Nurul Insan, Latansa, Arrafat* and *Ngudimulyo*.

The data was collected by using *focus group discussion* and *participatory observation*. The analysis technique employs interactive analysis of Miles and Huberman's models.

The variables which were used in assessing the implementation of the GRFE program are divided into four categories, that is, communication, resources, the disposition of implementers, and bureaucratic structure (George III, E, 1980).

According to George III, E (1980), the first requirement for effective policy implementation is communication, as those who implement a decision must know what they are supposed to do. Policy decisions must be transmitted to the appropriate personnel clearly, accurately, and consistently. The second is the available resources which facilitate their administration, including staff, authorities and facilities. The third is the disposition of implementers. If implementers are well-disposed towards a particular policy, they are more likely to carry it out as the original decision makers intended. But when implementers' attitudes or perspectives differ from the decision makers', the process of implementing a policy becomes infinitely more complicated. The fourth is bureaucratic structure. Two prominent characteristics of bureaucracies are Standard Operating Procedures (SOPs) and fragmentation. SOP is a routine that enables public officials to make numerous everyday decisions. Fragmentation is the dispersion of responsibility for a policy area among several organizational units.

3 RESULTS

3.1 *Communication*

It was found that CLACs have clear standards and targets in implementing the GRFE program. The standards and targets have been set out since CLACs propose funding to the Ministry of Education and Culture. They then receive some reviews from a gender expert team, and then the reviewed result is determined as the guidance for carrying out the GRFE program.

A number of those things determined in the standard of GRFE are as follows: the first is a target standard, that is, the families are required to be financially disadvantaged, having high risk in gender inequality, and having school-aged children, either living in rural or urban areas. The priority was awarded to participants who had high motivation to participate in the program. Second, that the learning material standard has adhered to the guidance: the embracing of Democracy and Basic Human Rights, Gender Equality and Concept, Life skills (academic, personal, social and vocational), and parenting. Moreover, that learning materials have been suitable for the local potential. Third, that the learning process standard has adhered to the guidance where the learning process was conducted by using an active learning and participation approach to the principles of equality, and more practices than theories. The tutors and the source persons mastered their field of knowledge. The learning groups were divided into two or three groups, and the learning venue was suitable for the local condition. The learning and training activities adhered to the competency standard. Fourth, that the competency standard of the participants has adhered to the guidance.

In the implementation of GRFE, CLACs referred to the developing strategy of the Community Education Program developed by the Directorate of Community Education—the Ministry of Education and Culture of the Republic of Indonesia (2010 and 2014), covering (1) various resources such as facilities, learning materials and research collaborations; (2) process integration, covering data gathering integration, integration of program—socialization activity, assignment integration, acknowledgment and reward.

The clarity of the standards enables program implementers to communicate the program appropriately and consistently.

3.2 *Resources*

The study results found that the educational institutions carrying out the GRFE program have sufficient human resources. They are comprised of religious leaders understanding about gender, parents understanding the necessity of gender equality within the family, husbands getting involved in productive economic effort development, and support of public bureaucrats in accompanying productive economic effort and non-formal institutional support (groups of Islamic religious learning and family welfare groups/PKK). The involvement of human resources actually leads to the use of the existing public facilities, For example, the co-usage of the meeting room in conducting training, and the utilization of public facilities and working equipment.

3.3 *The disposition of implementers*

The disposition of implementers in implementing the GRFE program has been in line with that of the policy makers. This occurred because of the intensive communication pattern and coordination between the central decision maker and decision makers in the local area (between the Ministry of Education and Culture, and the educational institution at the regency level) twice a year. Whereas at the level of implementer the same attitude and perspective of CLAC managers and the target groups have also been developed. With the implementer disposition being in line with that of in the top level, the implementation of the GRFE program became easier.

3.4 *Bureaucratic structure*

It was found that the GRFE program implementers have had SOPs and conducted responsibility fragmentation among the existing organizational units. The SOPs developed by the GRFE program implementers were suited to their own characteristics.

In the CLACs carrying out GRFE which use Productive Economic Effort strategy, the SOPs always start with counseling, practices and assistance in producing productive economic efforts, such as producing nuggets or meatballs. The materials on family and gender were inserted in-between, whereas the religious-based CLACs always begin with Islamic learning activities and then give motivation and endorsement of gender integration within their activities. CLACs which focus on preschool, applied SOPs by teaching children to read the Qur'an whilst their parents were invited to be given some materials on the importance of integrating gender equality in looking after the children in the family. Fragmentation was done by making labor division among the Ministry of Education and Culture of the Republic of Indonesia at the central government level, the educational institution at the regency level, the CLACs carrying out GRFE, and partner institutions such as Gender Studies Centers at universities.

4 DISCUSSION

4.1 *The role of religious figures in Islam*

The success of the implementation of GRFE in Demak regency was highly influenced by the intensive communication among Islamic figures, educational institutions and society. Islamic figures who understand the values of gender equality were very dominant in supporting the success of the program. The importance of religious figures in supporting a program was stated by Tamuri (2013), Arat (2010) and Bala (2010). They stated that the role of religious educators is very important because parents entrust their children's education to them. Meanwhile Islam tenets have not only explicitly endorsed the equality for women but also strongly advocated and stood up for their rights. The insight that Islam actually endorses gender equality has countered the statements of Wadud (1999) and Self and Grabowski (2009), that Islam has negative influence towards gender equality.

4.2 *Parents' role*

Parents have an important role in implementing the GRFE program. Rinaldo (2008) said that Islamic revival has brought democratization of religious knowledge and authority. This enables religious parents to integrate gender equality values into their children's education. Moreover, according to Eirich (2012), parents' religiosity has influence towards children's behavior, even if the children are not religious themselves. This can be done by giving religious advice to their children.

The importance of the parents' role in planting the values of gender equality can be seen from Hannum's studies (2009). According to Hannum et al. (2009), '*A number of rural families think that sons have more reliability on education and capability than daughters.*'

The different supports towards girls and boys were shown in Monin's studies (2008): '*The results supported that people perceive more responsiveness from female family members than from male family members. These associations were mediated by felt and perceived intimacy, dependence, and obligation, but not liking.*' Moreover Monin, et al. (2008) found that '*Women may typically be involved in more mutually responsive family relationships than are men, meaning that they are in relationships characterized by both more communal responsiveness to family members and receiving more communal responsiveness from family members.*' Hoag (2014) found out that '*mothers, communicate more with children than fathers, teach their children how to relate to others socially (including being sensitive), as well as how to manage their emotions.*' In addition, Levin and Currie (2010) found out that '*The parent-child relationship mediates the effects of poverty on child well-being and good parenting practices are believed to lessen the impact of marital conflict.*'

In order to avoid or to lessen discriminative treatment to children in families, mothers' education is very important (Charak & Koot, 2014). Moreover, they stated that '*Parental level of education especially maternal education is another factor which has received much attention in the field of child abuse and neglect.*'

Struffolino et al. (2015) suggested that '*The intersection of gender and education for family life courses is highly context-specific. They further suggest that different patterns of assortative mating play a key role for gender differences in family life courses.*'

4.3 Husband's support

Husband's support has strong influence in the changes of structure of role division leading to gender equality. The research result of Lotfizadeh and Hanzaee (2014) revealed that '*the power of wives in families is significantly greater than previous decades and this issue has influenced and changed family structure.*' Pan's research (2015) in Turkey suggested that '*gender equality remains elusive in a nation where secular and Islamic ideologies compete and produce different solutions to ongoing economic, socio-cultural and political issues. Women's entrepreneurship has emerged as an important solution toward gender equality and economic development.*' Mayrhofer's research (2008) showed that '*The work life of the partners and their career*

orientations are important factors influencing the form of family responsibility.' Moreover, Huffman et al. (2014) discovered that '*Men and fathers suggests that their gender roles are expanding to include responsibilities beyond the workplace to the family domain, it is critical to understand how fathers manage the work-family interface.*' Furthermore, Abouchedid (2007) suggested that '*Socialization (siblings, parents and groups) and life experiences contribute to the formation of gender role attitudes as well as to their transmission across generations in which children model their attitudes and behaviors on those of significant others, particularly, mothers.*'

4.4 Family economic role

Marks et al. (2009) stated that '*women and men who have higher educational attainment and income express more egalitarian gender role orientations.*' Moreover Marks et al. (2009) stated that '*Consistent with a social learning perspective, children from more economically advantaged family backgrounds also have more egalitarian gender attitudes.*' and that '*Non-traditional allocation of housework is likely to promote egalitarian attitudes within the family.*' and '*Child care is stereotypically feminine activity, and marks a less traditional family role for fathers. Fathers react more negatively to crying, fearfulness, or signs of feebleness. Fathers involvement with children generally, reflects more egalitarian gender role orientation.*'

5 CONCLUSION

The result reveals that the effective communication between the program managers and religious leaders, the availability of human resources understanding religion and gender, the utilization of religion-based preschools, household-based productive economic efforts, and the active involvement of husbands in designing the programs are considered good practices of the implementation of the GRFE program. To make the program quickly and equally implemented in various religion-based areas, the education and training about gender given to religious leaders and preschool teachers become important.

REFERENCES

Abouchedid, K. E. (2007). Correlates of religious affiliation, religiosity, and gender role attitude among Lebanese Christian and Muslim college students. *Equal Opportunities International*, 26(3), 193–208.

Arat, Y. (2010). Religion, politics and gender equality in Turkey: Implications of a democratic paradox? *Third World Quarterly*, 31, 869–884.

Bala, H. (2010). Socio-economic status and role of woman in Islam towards gender equality. *Gender & Behaviour, 8,* 3143–3151.

Charak, R. & Koot, H. M. (2014). Abuse and neglect in adolescents of Jammu, India: The role of gender, family structure, and parental education. *Journal of Anxiety Disorders, 28,* 590–598.

Eirich, G. (2012). Parental religiosity and children's educational attainment in the United States. *Religion, Work, and Inequality Research in the Sociology of Work, 23,* 153–181.

George III, E. (1980). *Implementing Public Policy.* Washington DC: Congressional Quarterly Press.

Haghighat, E. (2014). Establishing the connection between demographic and economic factors and gender status in the Middle East: Debunking the perception of Islam's undue influence. *International Journal of Sociology and Social Policy, 34*(7/8), 455–484.

Hannum, E., Kong, P. & Zhang, Y. (2009). Family sources of educational gender inequality in rural China: A critical assessment. *International Journal of Educational Development, 29,* 474–486.

Hoag, A. (2014). Mothers' perceptions of family communication patterns when having an ADHD child. *Family Relationships and Familial to Health Issues, Contemporary Perspectives in Family Research, 8A,* 211–246.

Huffman, A. H. et al. (2014). Gender role beliefs and fathers' work-family conflict. *Journal of Managerial Psychology, 29*(7), 774–793.

Kementerian pendidikan dan kebudayaan Republik Indonesia. (2014). *Profil Direktorat Pembinaan Pendidikan Masyarakat.* Jakarta.

Kementerian Pendidikan Nasional. (2010). *Program pendidikan keluarga berwawasan gender.* Jakarta: Kementerian Pendidikan Nasional.

KPPA & BPS. (2015). *Pembangunan manusia berbasis gender 2015.* Jakarta: Kementerian Pemberdayaan Perempuan dan Perlindungan Anak (KPPA) & Badan Pusat Statstik (BPS).

Levin, K. A. & Currie, C. (2010). Family structure, mother-child communication, father-child communication, and adolescent life satisfaction. *Health Education, 110*(3), 152–158.

Lotfizadeh, F. & Hanzaee, K. H. (2014). Family structure and decision making styles among Iranian couples. *Journal of Islamic Marketing, 5*(2), 241–257.

Marks, J. L., Lam, C. B. & McHale, S. M. (2009). Family patterns of gender role attitudes. *Sex Roles, 61,* 221–234.

Mayrhofer, W. et al. (2008). The influence of family responsibilities, career fields and gender on career success. *Journal of Managerial Psychology, 23*(3), 292–323.

Monin, J. K., Margaret, S. C. & Edward P. L. (2008). Communal responsiveness in relationships with female versus male family members. *Sex Roles, 59,* 176–188.

Ozcan, K. et al. (2011). Discrimination in health care industry: A research on public hospitals. *International Journal of Equality Diversity and Inclusion, 30*(1), 22–40.

Pan, B. O. (2015). Secular and Islamic feminist entrepreneurship in Turkey. *International Journal of Gender and Entrepreneurship, 7*(1), 45–65.

Puspitawati, H. (2012). *Gender dan keluarga: Konsep dan realita di Indonesia.* Bogor: PT. Penerbit IPB Press.

Rinaldo, R. (2008). Envisioning the nation: women activists, religion and the public sphere in Indonesia. *Social Force, 86,* 1781.

Self, S. & Grabowski, R. (2009). Relative gender differentials and Islam in non-Arabic nations: A regional analysis. *International Journal of Development Issues, 8*(2), 102–118.

Sidani, Y. (2005). Women, work, and Islam in Arab societies. *Journal of Women in Management Review, 20*(7), 498–512.

Struffolino, E., Studer, M. & Fasang, A. E. (2015). Gender, education, and family life courses in East and West Germany: Insights from new sequence analysis techniques. *Advances in Life Course Research, 29,* 66–79.

Tamuri, A. H. et al. (2013). Religious education and ethical attitude of Muslim adolescents in Malaysia. *Multicultural Education and Technology Journal, 7*(4), 257–274.

Vasi, J. (2010). Environmentalism and Islam: A study of Muslim women in the United States. *Environment and Social Justice: An International Perspective Research in Social Problems and Public Policy, 18,* 451–484.

Wadud, A. (1999). *Qur'an and women: Rereading the sacred text from a woman's perspective.* New York Oxford: Oxford University Press.

The development of Indonesian textbooks-based collaborative learning to strengthen character education: A case study on vocational education in Sebelas Maret University

K. Saddhono
Universitas Sebelas Maret, Jawa Tengah, Indonesia

P.Z. Diana
Universitas Sarjanawiyata Tamansiswa, Yogyakarta, Indonesia

ABSTRACT: This research examines the importance of textbooks to facilitate students in learning Indonesian subjects. The purpose of this research is to develop Indonesian textbooks-based collaborative learning to strengthen character education on vocational education in Universitas Sebelas Maret (UNS). The researchers adopted the theory of Research and Development (R & D) proposed by Gall, Gall, & Borg. The sampling technique was a purposive technique, and the research sample was determined by researchers based on the objectives and considerations that each sample represented the population of university students in UNS. In this preliminary study, a needs analysis was carried out to prepare a prototype model of Indonesian textbooks-based collaborative learning to strengthen character education in higher education. To improve a prototype of Indonesian textbooks, peer debriefing was conducted with experts in the field of textbooks, experts in the field of learning methods and character education. The improved result was tested further on a limited but wider basis in UNS. The result shows that university students' ability to speak Indonesian using Indonesian textbooks-based collaborative learning to strengthen character education at UNS is better than university students who do not use textbooks (using conventional textbooks).

1 INTRODUCTION

The Indonesian course is a course in college that is mandatory for all students of the university, especially in the beginning of their semester in college. Indonesian is one of the subjects at the college which is expected to train students to acquire Indonesian language skills. The implementation of the Indonesian course has been considered to only provide theoretical material in the form of a monotonous lecture. It is supported by the research conducted by Kurniady (2008) which states that lecturers in general divide the Indonesian course into two terms of lectures. The first term is the provision of course materials that discuss aspects of language. Presentation of these materials is considered boring. The second term presents Indonesian materials science, which is focused on writing scientific papers, techniques used in writing scientific papers, and commonly used techniques for writing scientific papers theoretically. Lectures give the material using lecture method.

Based on the background above, this study used the integrated collaborative learning through Indonesian textbooks. The reason for the use of collaborative learning, as seen from the results of field observations, was that students were not able to work in groups well. In the work group, one or two students tended to do the work, while the other students looked relaxed without taking any responsibility in completing the task. It cannot be separated from the process of teaching and learning.

Based on that phenomena, Vygotsky (in Liu & Matthews, 2005) developed the theory of social constructivism which has the idea that learning for children can be done in the interaction within the social and physical environment. This invention or discovery in learning more easily is obtained in a person's socio-cultural context. Constructivism core according to Vygotsky is the interaction between the internal and external aspects of the emphasis on the social environment in learning.

In addition to the problems described above, the issue of character education was also targeted in this study. Internalized character education is currently a priority in building a generation of the nation's dignity, morals, and good manners. Still seen are low-level characters embedded in students. The development of character education in college can be integrated into education in each course. Educational materials relating to norms or values on each course should be developed explicitly, and associated with the context of everyday life. Character education values are not only on the cognitive level, but touch on the internalization, and real experience in student life in the community. Character education in college is an attempt to develop the character of students as a continuation-character development at the level of previous education.

Trends in the Indonesian language learning during this time are to learn about the language, and less steeped in learning the language and learning through language. Learning through language means listen to learn, talk to learn, read to learn, and write to learn. Practically all the language skills required politeness as a part of character development (Setyawati, 2013).

According to Hidayatullah (2010), young people (students) and the future were equally the hope of the nation. In conjunction with the duties and obligations of students as the next generation ideals of the nation, then the position of the students will increasingly become an important role, especially those students who prepared a position as an intellectual or scholar and a leader in the future. In fact, public opinion has expectations for mainly the students to develop the nation.

2 METHOD

The researchers adopted the theory of Research and Development (R & D) proposed by Gall, Gall, & Borg, 1996. The sampling technique was a purposive technique, and the research sample was determined by researchers based on the objectives and considerations that each sample represented the population of university students in UNS.

3 RESULT AND DISCUSSION

The preparation of the Indonesian course textbook started from the preparation of a prototype model. The preparation of this book is based on studies that have been done before (Saddhono, 2011; Sitepu, 2008; Syamsi et al., 2013). The steps taken were as follows. (a) Analyzing lecturers, students, and stakeholder needs. (b) Developing Indonesian textbook framework. (c) Fixing the Indonesian textbook concept. (d) Asking for consideration and feedback on the expert's judgment. (e) Revising for the improvement. (f) Doing the editing process. The study results of this collaborative learning study are in line with other studies which have been conducted before by different object and media (Elola & Oskoz, 2010; Barkley et al., 2012; Du and Christian, 2011; Kessler, 2009; Lee, 2008).

Effectiveness test was used to analyze the differences between existing teaching materials and newly developed teaching materials. Normality testing was done through two approaches, the namely chart approach (histograms and P-P Plot) or the Kolmogorov-Smirnov test, Chi square, Lilliefors or the Shapiro-Wilk. The normality test in this study used the Kolmogorov-Smirnov test.

Based on Table 1 above, it can be concluded that distribution of the data is normal.

The sample of this study was collected from all vocational programs in Sebelas Maret University with different education, culture, and characteristic. Heterogeneity is expected to be tolerated so that it can be considered as a population unit. Besides, it can also be used as homogeneity assumption fulfillment so that ANOVA test is not bias. The homogeneity test is used to fulfill data variant which is homogenous or heterogeneous based on certain factors. The same applies to normality, and the homogeneity assumption used in some statistic parametric analysis. The homogeneity test in this study was done by using Levene test.

Based on Table 2 above, it can be concluded that the pretest-posttest data difference between the experimental group and the control group had statistically Levene price of 0.091 with a significance of 0.965 > 0.05. Therefore, Ho received and stated that the data has variation between groups is balanced.

Table 1. Kolmogorov-Smirnov normality test.

Data	Research group	Kolmogorov-Smirnov(a) statistic	df	Sig.	Conclusion
Balance test data (Pre-test)	Experiment	0.132	42	0.064	Normal
	Control 1	0.121	39	0.155	Normal
	Control 2	0.133	38	0.089	Normal
	Control 3	0.136	39	0.067	Normal
Experiment test data (Difference between Pre-test-Post-test)	Experiment	0.133	42	0.059	Normal
	Control 1	0.132	39	0.083	Normal
	Control 2	0.129	38	0.114	Normal
	Control 3	0.137	39	0.062	Normal

Table 2. Levene homogeneity test.

Data	Levene statistic	df
Experiment test data (the difference between *Pretest-Posttest*)	1.311	3
Experiment test data (the difference between *Pretest-Posttest*)	0.091	3

Table 3. One way ANOVA test result.

Data	F	Sig.	Conclusion
Balance test data (Pretest)	1.398	0.245	There is no significant difference
Experiment test data (the difference between Pretest-Posttest)	9.775	0.000	There is significant difference

Based on Table 3 data of balance test on the pretest there was no significant difference. Meanwhile the data between groups has significant differences.

Based on the average price of each group, it showed that the control group data are in one column, while the average of data experimental group are in different columns. This shows that the inter-group controls had no significant difference, while the experimental group was significantly different to the three control groups.

Related to the assessment of character, education essentially is an evaluation of the learning process on individual and group in order to understand role and freedom to live with other people in an academic environment for developing moral integrity as human beings. Character education assessment in this study is not to determine graduation in the field of course, but to determine the growth and development of character education internalization in the form of attitudes, knowledge, and action (Samani & Hariyanto, 2013). Assessment of character education is based on Ki Hajar Dewantara's teachings, in the form of the doctrine (operational guidelines practice) Tri Nga: understand *(ngerti),* feel *(ngrasa),* and act *(nglakoni).* The *Tri Nga* in general terms is cognitive *(ngerti),* affective *(ngrasa),* and psychomotor *(nglakoni).* Based on the teachings of Ki Hajar Dewantara the assessment of character education in this study is translated according to the provisions of character education assessment of the National Education Ministry used today. The results showed a positive impact on several aspects of education character. This is in line with the character education raised by experts (Lickona, 2012; Wibowo, 2013).

4 CONCLUSION

Based on the explanation above, it should be reiterated that Indonesian education is directed to achieve some of the goals that should be owned by the students, namely the ability to speak, language gesture, the science of Indonesian knowledge, self-awareness of the importance of literature for self-development, and positive attitude towards literature. The goal of this goal is that students are able to communicate characteristically. The results of this research are the development of the Indonesian textbook based on collaborative learning for strengthening character education in vocational study programs. Universitas Sebelas Maret are having a positive impact in learning Indonesian.

ACKNOWLEDGMENT

The author expressed his gratitude to the Indonesian Endowment Fund for Education (LPDP), the Ministry of Finance, the Republic of Indonesia and LPPM UNS.

REFERENCES

Barkley, E.E., Cross, K.P. & Major, C.H. (2012). *Collaborative learning techniques.* San Francisco: Jossey-Bass.

Du, H.S. & Wagner, C. (2011). Editorial: Collaborative knowledge management and e-learning. *Knowledge Management & E-Learning: An International Journal, 3*(2), 116–118.

Elola, I. & Oskoz, A. (2010). Collaborative writing: Fostering foreign language and writing conventions development. *Language Learning and Technology, 14*(3), 51–71.

Gall, M.D., Borg, W.R., & Gall, J.P. (1996). *Educational research: An introduction.* Longman Publishing.

Hidayatullah, M.F. 2010. *Pendidikan karakter: Membangun peradaban bangsa.* Surakarta: Yuma Pustaka.

Kessler, G. (2009). Student-Initiated attention to form in wiki-based collaborative writing. *Language Learning and Technology, 13*(3), 79–95.

Kurniady, H.K. (2008). *Pemanfaatan model pembelajaran menulis karya ilmiah secara kolaboratif dengan menggunakan teknik portofolio dalam mata kuliah umum bahasa Indonesia.* Bandung: Universitas Pendidikan Indonesia.

Lee, L. (2008). Focus-On-Form through collaborative scaffolding in expert-to-novice online interaction. *Language Learning and Technology, 12*(3), 53–72.

Lickona, T. (2012). *Educating for character: Mendidik untuk membentuk karakter.* Jakarta: Bumi Aksara.

Liu, C.H. & Matthews, R. (2005). Vygotsky's philosophy: Constructivism and its criticism examined. *International Educational Journal, 6*(3), 386–399.

Marsuki. (2015). Pengembangan buku ajar bahasa indonesia berbasis kurikulum 2013. *Lingua, 10*(2), 74–81.

Saddhono, K. (2011). Penyusunan dan pengembangan buku ajar untuk meningkatkan kualitas pembelajaran di perguruan tinggi. *Akademik. III(2)*, 99–106.

Samani, M. & Hariyanto. (2013). *Konsep dan model pendidikan karakter*. Bandung: PT Remaja Rosdakarya.

Setyawati, R. (2013). Peranan bahasa Indonesia sebagai sarana membangun karakter bangsa. Saddhono, dkk. (Ed.). *Proceeding Seminar International Pengembangan Peran Bahasa dan Sastra Indonesia untuk Mewujudkan Generasi Berkarakter*. Surakarta: Universitas Sebelas Maret.

Sitepu, B.P. (2008). Buku teks pelajaran berbasis aneka sumber. *Jurnal Pendidikan Penabur* (10) Tahun ke–7.

Sugiyono. (2012). *Metode penelitian kuantitatif kualitatif dan R&D*. Bandung: Alfabeta.

Syamsi, K., Esti Swatika, S., & Pujiono, S. (2013). *Pengembangan model buku ajar membaca berdasarkan pendekatan proses bagi siswa smp*. Cakrawala Pendidikan. Februari 2013, Tahun XXXII, Nomor 1.

Wibowo, A. (2013). *Pendidikan karakter di perguruan tinggi*. Yogyakarta: Pustaka Pelajar.

English as a second language for an international nursery student in United Kingdom

Mukhaiyar
English Department of the State University of Padang, Padang, Indonesia

S. Utari
The State University of Padang, Padang, Indonesia

R. Mukhaiyar
ISPAI Research Group of the State University of Padang, Padang, Indonesia

ABSTRACT: Practicing different language for adults requires an extra effort, but this is not the case for children. In UK nursery classes, foreign children are exposed to a new language and use those words in sentences so that children are able to express their ideas and feelings. In concept, this learning process purposes four main themes and seven inter-connected shape educational programs in their early years. Those areas are divided into three prime areas and four specific areas to help children experiencing their development stages and acquiring English as their second language. To sum up, children's cognitive development is formed into seven prime and specific areas which give children an opportunity to interact and engage with other people and their environment by playing and exploring, learning actively, and creating and thinking critically to remain as effective and motivated learners.

1 INTRODUCTION

The International School in Newcastle-upon-Tyne, UK, has become a destination school for immigrants and international university students who have brought their families with them to the UK. Classes in the UK start from nursery and reception (years 3–4), and Key Stage 1–4 (years 5–16), where at every level of the classes English is one of the main subjects being taught every day.

Since the students come from different countries, most of them bring their home languages at the very beginning of the school term. But this lasts for only few months because mostly after six months attending the school, the students begin to actively communicate and begin to understand what others are saying in English. One example is a three year old boy who comes from Indonesia. He used to speak in his home language, 'Bahasa' or 'Bahasa Indonesia'.

After almost a year living in the UK, Azzam – the boy's name – cannot speak English since his parents and people surrounding him speak in Bahasa Indonesia. Azzam attended the school and used only a few words of English vocabulary, such as 'pee' and 'poop', the English alphabet, and numbers that he memorized through children song. After the first three months, Azzam still could not communicate in English, but he was already mumbling using intonation that was close to that of a native speaker, even though none of the words he said were understandable. However, he began to memorize some of the words that he learnt from school, and began to recognize a thing and say it in English. In the fourth month, Azzam began to use a few words in English and tried to combine them, yet not in the form of a full sentence. For example, instead of saying "I'm ready," he said, "I'm yes ready", adapting from the "I'm not ready". On the sixth month, Azzam began to make a full sentence into a conversation, for example, "Let me try", or "I want this one", although some of the times he mixed it with the word in Bahasa, for example, "because there are many orang there", instead of saying, "because there many people there". In Bahasa Indonesia, 'orang' means a person.

The example above shows that a three year old boy with no English background knowledge only needs about six months to begin communicating actively in English. Without minimizing the importance of other aspects like peers, or media used at home such as English songs or movies for children, I would like to describe class activities in one of the nurseries in Newcastle, UK. This paper hopes to share information and ideas that can be adapted or adopted by other nursery teachers all over the country for teaching English as a second language.

2 LINGUISTICS FOR CHILDREN

Children as active learners directly and immediately recognizing objects, people, ideas and events, is considered as an important condition in order to reconstruct children's cognitive ability as well as their development. In other words, children learn concepts, form ideas, and create their own symbols through self-initiated activity such as moving, listening, searching, feeling and manipulating, where adults as participant-observers give an opportunity for a child to get involved in interesting experiences that might draw contradictory conclusions and a consequent reorganization of the child's understanding of his/her own world.

Teaching children is different from teaching adults. According to Cameron (2001) there are obvious differences between children and adults:

- Children are more enthusiastic and more lively in learning.
- Children want to be complimented by the teacher, rather than by the peers.
- Children will have a go at doing an activity even they do not understand about why and how.
- Children will easily feel bored and less motivated towards an activity that they found difficult to perform.
- Children do not feel ashamed to speak in a new language.
- Children's lack of inhibition allows them to nearly master the native language.

However, Cameron said that these generalizations cover the details that every child is different, and the difference of skill in teaching the language. Furthermore, she adds that beneath these generalizations, she found that the linguistic and psychological development have an important role for children as active learners.

On the other hand, Piagette (McCloskey, 2002) sees children as scientists, where children as active learners develop by doing experiments on their environments. He sees that thought is derived from action. He also divides cognitive development into assimilation and accommodation. Assimilation is when a child takes new experience without any changes as new information is being processed, while accommodation is adjusting features with other features that exist in the environment. Besides, Piagette also divides child development into four stages;

- Sensorimotor, from birth–2 years. At this stage, the children interact physically with the environment, developing ideas of how things work.
- Pre-operational, ages 2–7. At this stage, children are not able to think abstractly, but need concrete situations to process ideas.
- Concrete operations, ages 7–11. At this stage, children have enough experience to begin to conceptualize and do some abstract problem solving, though they still learn best by doing.
- Formal operation, ages 11–16. At this stage, children are able to use abstract thinking like adults.

While Piagette emphasizes the children as active learners alone in the world of object, Vygotsky emphasizes that the children are active learners in a world full of other people. Vygotsky (McCloskey, 2002) said that language provides children with new tools, opens up new opportunities for doing things and for organizing information by using symbols. Young children sometimes perform private speech, where they are talking to themselves and organizing themselves while doing a task or play.

By considering the early speech of infants and how it develops into language, Vygotsky distinguishes the outward talk and what is happening in the child's mind. First, the infant begins to speak by using single words, for instance, 'water'. The word 'water' might have various meanings—"I want water", or "I just spilt the water". The second is when the child's language is developed; the whole undivided thought message can be broken down into smaller units and expressed by putting together words that are now units of talks. Vygotsky sees the child's learning as developing through interaction with more knowledgeable others, who mediate learning by talking while playing, reading stories, and asking questions. With the help of adults, children can do more than they can do on their own. A concept developed by Vygotsky is called Zone of Proximal Development (ZPD). This is the area where children can nearly do but cannot do alone, where mediation gradually moves this ZPD outwards as learners begin to be able to do more on their own.

Meanwhile, Bruner (Cho, 2009) emphasized the role of language play in children's cognitive growth. In order to mediate the world for the children and to support them in solving problems, Bruner offers the label of 'scaffolding'. Based on Bruner's research with North American mothers and children, the following are ways parents scaffold tasks effectively:

- By helping the children in getting interested in the tasks.
- By simplifying the tasks, often breaking them down into smaller pieces.
- By keeping the children on the tasks by reminding them of the goal.
- By pointing out what was important or demonstrating alternative ways to do the tasks.
- By keeping the children from becoming too frustrated.
- By demonstrating the tasks.

Bruner also emphasizes the formats and routines which are the features of events that allow scaffolding to occur. He describes the routine of parents reading bedtime stories to their children.

At first, they share a large picture together, and then they turn the pages together. The adults do most of the talking, like naming and telling about objects and characters in the book. Later on, parents start to read simple stories, even with rhyme, rhythm and repetition. Parents also begin to ask questions about the book. As the children begin to finish sentences and recite along, children may begin to recite the stories based on what they remember. The familiar and secure routine can also incorporate novelty and change as the child is ready for more challenge. By doing this, the parents help the children to operate the ZPD.

3 METHODOLOGY

There are seven areas of learning and development that shape educational programs in the early years. All areas of learning and development are important and inter-connected. The seven areas are divided into three prime area: Personal, Social, and Emotional Development (PSED), Physical Development (PD), and Communication and Language (CL), and four specific areas: Literacy, Mathematic, Understanding the World, and Expressive Arts and Design. These areas are delivered through topics and themes in the following activities.

3.1 Circle time

The first activity in class is circle time where children sit in a circle form, and the teacher encourages them to discuss about the focusing topic of the term. For example, if the topic of the term is 'people who help us', then the teacher might ask the children about how they can help each other, for example, doctor, policeman, fireman. They also learn to listen and recognize the initial names and objects around them.

There are two prime areas involved in circle time: PSED, and CL. Based on SEAD (Social and Emotional Aspects of Development) guidance for practitioners (Department for Children, Schools, And Families UK, 2008), PSED has an important role to help children to success in their future:

- Personal development (being me) is how children learn to understand who they are and how they can take care of themselves.
- Social Development (being social) is how to understand themselves to relate to others, for example, how to make friends, understand the rules in social environment, and how to behave toward others.
- Emotional development (having feelings) is how children learn to understand how they feel, and other's feelings, by developing the feeling of empathy.

In developing PSED, children need to be able to communicate what they feel. Thus, children's CL skill is also being developed so that children are able to let others know how they feel, what they need, and to ask questions. Moreover, language is a means by which children learn about the world and communicate with their friends and practitioners. This is important to enhance their cognitive development and in solving problems, as well as in building social relationships with others.

Based on development matters in Early Years Foundation Stage (EYFS), here are some of the activities being done by the practitioners in helping children develop their PSED and CL:

- Encouraging children to choose to play with a variety of friends from all backgrounds.
- Labeling emotions such as sadness, happiness, feeling lonely, and being scared, to help children understand the feelings of others.
- Supporting children who have not yet made friends.
- Naming and talking about all feelings that are understandable and acceptable, including feeling angry, however that not all behaviors are acceptable.
- Showing concern and respect to others, living things and the environment.
- Modeling and involving children in finding solutions to problems and conflicts.
- Value and support the decisions that children make.
- Asking for children's ideas of what would they do if someone is sad or has cross feelings.
- Recognizing that children vary in their interests.

and in CL:

- Giving cues to children in changing conversation, especially for those who have communication difficulties. For example, "now we are going to talk about…".
- Saying children's names, particularly for children who find it difficult to 'listen and do', before giving instruction or asking questions.
- Playing games that involve listening for a signal, for example, "ready, steady, go…!"
- Using environmental sounds to talk about environmental sounds, for example, asking the children to stop and listen carefully for the sound around them.
- Explaining that paying attention to others when they are speaking is important.
- Giving opportunities for children to speak and listen to make sure that the needs of children in learning English as a second language are met.
- Giving children clear direction for activities that involve more than one action, for example, "turn the computer off, wash your hands, and get ready for dinner."

- Using mime and gestures in introducing new activities to support language development.
- Giving opportunity for children to start the conversation and follow children's lead to talk about the topic they are interested in.
- Giving children 'thinking time' to put their thoughts into words.
- Introducing new words in context of playing and doing activities.
- Using lots of statements and open questions, showing interest when children are speaking, and helping them expand on what they are saying.

3.2   Adult-led session

Adult-led activity is an activity defined, structured and delivered by an adult to a child or group of children. It focuses on the direct teaching of skills and knowledge with a specific objective in mind (British Association for Early Years Foundation Stage, 2008). An adult-led activity has a specific focus and is planned by the adult to encourage a particular aspect of learning, to discuss a particular topic or to provide an opportunity to learn a particular skill. The adult may introduce the material, skill or idea, initiate the activity, and may direct elements of the learning. However, once introduced the activity may provide an opportunity for children to practice by themselves or to modify it.

Activities in adult-led session:

- Adult-led activities can be one-to-one, in a small group or whole class.
- The length of time involved will be appropriate to the age and needs of the child.
- An adult-led activity can be either objective-led with clear aims linked to EYFS Development Matters, or open-ended, where adults observe and support learning during the activity and consider next steps based on children's responses. It can be either planned or as a result of a spontaneous event. For example:
  - A specific, planned activity initiated by the adult to introduce new ideas, introduce a learning provocation develop and practice skills or revisit, review and consolidate previous learning
  - Adult modeling a skill or behavior
  - Adult involvement in the child's play to extend child initiated learning, support progression, and scaffold play and language.
- During adult-led activities, the role of the adult will be to directly teach, which means to systematically help children to learn so that they can make connections in their learning, are actively led forward and can reflect on their learning.
- Adult-led activities must be delivered by a skilled, knowledgeable and thoughtful practitioner.

- Adult-led activities should be in line with the EYFS ethos and therefore be playful, even when planned, with a specific objective in mind.

3.3   Story session

The prime area involved in this session is literacy which consists of reading and writing. The development involves encouraging children to link sounds and letters and to begin to read and write. Children are given access to a wide range of reading materials such as books, poems, and other written materials, to ignite their interest.

Early language and literacy (reading and writing) development begins in the first three years of life and is closely linked to a child's earliest experiences with books and stories. The interactions that young children have with such literacy materials such as books, paper, and crayons, and with the adults in their lives, are the building blocks for language, reading and writing development. Students with experience in hearing and telling stories such as myths, legends, and folklore are eager to begin creating or writing their own stories. Critical thinking skills, vocabulary, and language patterns are enhanced through the use of stories (Koki, 1998).

In this story session, the children sit together with a teacher in front while reading a book. To help the children remember new words in the book, the teacher uses media such as pictures or miniatures. For example, the new word in the book is 'moon'. So, every time the word 'moon' comes up the teacher show the miniature of a moon to the children. By repeating this step, the children can easily remember new words being introduced.

Based on EYFS, here are other activities being done to develop children's reading and writing skills:

- Discussing similarities and differences between symbols by focusing on meaningful print, such as a child's name, or book title.
- Pointing out words in the environment and in books.
- Discussing the characters in the book being read with the children.
- Encouraging children to predict the ending of the story.
- Noticing the meaning of the marks, symbols that the children made.
- Support the children to recognize their own name and write them.
- Making books with children of activities they have been doing by using their photographs as illustration.

3.4   Math sessions

Prime areas involved in a math session are numbers and shapes. They provide children with opportunities to develop and improve their skills in counting, understanding and using numbers, calculating simple addition and subtraction problem, and to describe shapes, spaces, and measures. Based on National Council of Teachers of Mathematics (NCTM), stresses the importance of an early math education as a high-quality, challenging and accessible mathematics education that provides early childhood learners with a vital foundation for the future understanding of mathematics, where early childhood educators should actively introduce mathematical concepts, methods, and language through a range of appropriate experiences and teaching strategies. Thus, early mathematics education is vital to the development of young children in order to help them to grow as learners.

To develop children's skills in mathematics, the following are some of the activities being done in class:

- Using language numbers such as 'one', 'two', 'lots', 'fewer', 'how many' or 'count' in a variety of situations.
- Supporting children to count things that are not objects such as hops, jumps, clicks, or claps. This is to help children in developing their understanding of abstraction.
- Helping children to understand that one thing can be shared, such as a pizza can be shared into several slices.
- Asking questions while reading number stories or rhymes, for example, "when one more frog jumps in, how many will there be in the pool altogether?"
- Using pictures and objects to illustrate counting songs, rhymes, and numbers stories.
- Supporting children thinking about numbers and simple problems by encouraging them to use mark-making.
- Talking about the strategies they can use, for example, to work out a solution to a simple problem by using fingers or counting out loud.
- Demonstrating the language for shapes position and measures in discussion, for example, 'shape', 'box', 'in', 'on', 'under', 'long', 'longer', 'longest'.
- Encouraging children to talk about shapes they see and use, and how they are arranged and used in constructions.
- Value children's constructions by helping to display or take photographs.

3.5   Circle time session – understanding the world

A prime area involved in this session is understanding the world. Practitioners are guiding the children to make sense of their physical world and their community through opportunities to explore, observe and find out about people, places, technology and the environment. Children are also supported in developing the knowledge, skills and understanding that help them to make sense of the world. Their learning must be supported through offering opportunities for them to use a range of tools safely: encounter creatures, people, plants and objects in their natural environments and in real-life situations; undertake practical 'experiments'; and work with a range of materials.

To help children in understanding the world, there are school visits where children are accompanied to go to public places, such as the post office to introduce the children about posting letters and how letters are posted. There are also times where public officers such as policemen, firemen, and doctors come to visit the school so that children can learn about different people in the community. Besides, the children are also introduced to rhyming books. Nursery rhymes help children to learn positive attitudes, and challenge negative attitudes and stereotypes, based on the story of the rhyme. Moreover, nursery rhymes help children to easily recall and memorize new words; teaches children that events happen in sequence and they begin to learn how to understand a story and follow along; learn simple math skills as they recite them since rhymes use pattern and sequence; and help children to imagine what the characters are doing.

The following are other activities being done in class to help children in understanding the world:

- Practitioners encourage children to talk about their own home and community life, and to find out about other children's experiences.
- Practitioners ensure that children who learn English as a second language have opportunities to express themselves in their home language some of the time.
- Provide children with supplementary experience and information to enhance children learning about the world around them.
- Practitioners help children to be aware of features of the environment in the setting of the immediate local area, for example, making visits to a park or museum.
- Children are introduced to vocabularies to enable children to talk about their observations and to ask questions.

3.6   End of day

The prime area involved in this session is Expressive Arts and Design (EAD). In this session, children are enabled to explore and play with a wide range of media and materials, as well as providing opportunities and encouragement for sharing their thoughts, ideas and feelings through a variety of activities in art, music, movement, dance, role-play, and design and technology (Statuary Framework for the Early Years Foundation Stage, 2012).

In this session, children are given opportunities to be creative where they can express these through movements, making and transforming things, and using a variety of media such as crayons, paints, scissors, and paper. It involves children in initiating their own learning and making choices and decisions. According to Sharp (2004), creativity is an important human characteristic. It is perhaps best thought of as a process, requiring a mixture of ingredients, including personality traits, abilities and skills. Practitioners can help children to develop their creativity through a creative environment, play, behaving creatively and praising children's creative efforts. As an example, practitioners supporting children's response to different textures by touching sections of a texture display with their fingers or feeling it with their cheeks to get a sense of different properties.

The following are other activities that practitioners do to develop children's EAD:

- Introducing vocabularies so that children can talk about their observation and experience, for example, 'smooth', 'shiny', 'rough', 'prickly', 'soft', 'hard'.
- Letting the children choose the colors they are interested in as they begin to find the difference between colors.
- Making suggestions and asking questions to extend children's ideas of what is possible, for example, "I wonder what would happen if….".
- Supporting the children to think about what they want to make, including the process and the materials they need.
- Supporting the children's excursion into imaginary worlds by encouraging inventiveness, offering support and advice on occasions, and ensuring that they have experiences that stimulate their interest.

Another prime area in EYFS is PD. This prime area lies in every activity in class, and covers two aspects: moving and handling, and health and self-care. The aspect of moving and handling allows children to move freely, such as run skillfully, walk downstairs, use one-handed tools or equipment, hold pencils between thumb and two fingers, while the aspect of health and self-care allows children to understand that the tools have to be used safely, manage to wash and dry hands, and attend to toilet needs when needed. The physical development of children must be encouraged through the provision of opportunities for them to be active and interactive and to improve their skills of coordination, control, manipulation and movement. They

are supported in using all of their senses to learn about the world around them and to make connections between new information and what they already know (Statuary Framework for EYFS, 2012). The following are what practitioners do to help children in developing their PD:

- Encouraging children to move with controlled effort, and use associated vocabulary such as 'strong', 'firm', 'heavy', 'reach', and 'floppy'.
- Creating moods through music from different styles and cultures, and talking about how people move when they are sad, happy, or cross.
- Playing games to motivate children to be active.
- Talking to children about why they should take care while moving freely.
- Teaching children to use equipment safely, such as cutting using scissors.
- Encouraging children to rest when they are tired and giving explanation, or explaining, why they need to wear wellingtons when it is muddy outdoors.
- Talking about the importance of hand-washing.
- Helping children who are struggling with self-care by leaving a last small step for them to complete. For example, pulling up their trousers from just below the waist.

Hence, to support children's learning and development, practitioners observe every child by looking, listening, and taking notes that describe every child. The information can also be obtained from parents/carriers about children at home. Further, the practitioners doing assessment analyze the observations they make to help identify where the child may be in their own development pathway. The observations and assessments are needed to make plans to consider ways to support the children strengthen and deepen their current learning and development.

4 RESULTS AND DISCUSSIONS

In general, there are two ways in which children learn a second language. According to McLaughlin et al. (Halgunseth, 2013), children learn a second language through simultaneously second language learning, and sequential second language learning. Simultaneously a second language learner is when children are exposed to more than one language since they were babies. This commonly happens to children whose parents speak separate languages to them at home, for example, a mother speaks English while the father speaks Bahasa Indonesia. In this process, children begin to notice the difference between languages used at the age of six months and then they begin to choose which language they prefer to hear and use. Meanwhile, a sequentially second language learner is when children are exposed to only one language but then are suddenly introduced and having to use another language. For example, it is when a non-English speaking child enters an English-dominant classroom. In this way, children might face four stages in acquiring the second language:

- Home language use, where children are still using their home language.
- Silent period, where children realize that their home language is not working so they choose to be silent and rely heavily on non-verbal means to communicate with others.
- Telegraphic and formulaic speech, where children begin to communicate using the second language in small utterances (for instance, "me down", "me want") or by repeating the words of others.
- Productive language, where children begin to use the second language to express their ideas although in basic and simple sentences and grammatically incorrect.

Children who learn English as a second language in the area where English is the main language on an everyday basis seem to have big advantage to be able to learn and acquire the language faster than children who learn English as a second language in a non-English speaking area, for example, Indonesia, China, or Thailand. An important factor in determining the success in learning a language depends on the amount of comprehensible input to which that learner is exposed so that they understand the meaning of each word based on its context through the use of gestures, examples, illustrations, and experience. This can be achieved by providing them with an enabling environment where children can learn comfortably as well, as well as being suitable for learning activities, either inside or outside of the classroom.

However, to meet children's needs either inside or outside of the classroom, practitioners must know the children's emotional environment so that children will feel comfortable and will be more willing to try things out. Thus, building positive relationships with children is also important in the learning process. With the help of adults, children can do more compared to what they can do without the help of adults. Positive relationships with children are very important because when children have a good relationship with practitioners, they will be less likely to show unwanted behaviors, and develop their language acquisition as they feel confident to talk. Besides, practitioners can also understand each child's needs and give appropriate response because they already understand the children's expressions and emotions.

The positive relationships with children can be noticed through interaction. There are several techniques to interact with children (Halgunseth, 2013). For example, talk about the importance of hand-washing:

- Using sentences that are easy to understand.
- Listening to what children say to show that we are interested.
- Being patient because we might need to explain several times.
- Using eye contact.
- Having a friendly approach; smile, listen.
- Not assuming that children will not understand.

Furthermore, providing children with more opportunities, letting them help, allowing them to explore, informing them about the importance of life, and providing a secure environment, are also important to develop positive relationships with children.

In conclusion, by maintaining positive relationships with children and providing them with an enabling environment, children will find it easier to learn new language and understand the use of it in communication. However, another aspect that is also important to notice in exposing new language to children in nursery is the ratio between the number of staff and the number of students in the class. It is because children who spend six hours in school need to feel individually noticed, thought about, and responded to sensitively and consistently. And it can only be achieved if the number of staff is adequate for the number of students.

5 CONCLUSION

EYFS is the statutory framework that sets the standards that all Early Years providers must meet to ensure that children learn and develop well and are kept healthy and safe, which is mostly adapted by the international primary schools in the UK. It promotes teaching and learning to ensure children are ready for school and gives children the broad range of knowledge and skills that provide the right foundation for good future progress through school and life.

Children learn language through their cognitive development that is formed into seven prime and specific areas; Personal, Social and Emotional Development; Physical Development; Communication and Language; Mathematics; Literacy; Understanding the World; and EAD. In each area, children are given opportunities to interact in positive relationships and enabling environments where children engage with other people and their environment through play and explore, learn actively, and creating and thinking critically in order to support children remain effective and motivated learners. This is in line with theory proposed by Mary

Lou (McCloskey, 2002) about seven instructional principles in teaching English to young learners. She stated that teachers should: offer learners enjoyable, active roles in learning experiences; help student develop and practice language through collaboration; use multi-dimensional, thematically organized activity; provide comprehensible input with scaffolding; integrate language with content; validate and integrate home language and culture; and provide clear goals and feedback on performance.

By maintaining positive relationships and providing children with an enabling environment in every area of development, children are helped in understanding the use of English as a second language and begin to be able to use them in their daily lives.

REFERENCES

British Association for Early Childhood Education. (2008). *Development matters in the early years foundation stage*. London: Early Education UK.

Cameron, L. (2001). *Teaching languages to young learners*. Cambridge: Cambridge University, UK.

Cho. (2009). *Characteristics of Young Learners. Languages and Children*. Chapter 1.

Department for Children, Schools, and Families. (2008). *Social and emotional aspects of development*. London: The National Strategies, UK.

Halgunseth, L. (2013). *How children learn a second language*. Diversity in Education Special Contributor. Education.com

Koki, S. (1998). *Storytelling: The heart and soul of education*. Honolulu: PREL Briefing Paper, Pacific Resources for Education and Learning.

McCloskey, M. L. (2002). *Seven instructional principles for teaching young learners of English*. San Diego: TESOL Symposium, Georgia State University.

Sharp, C. (2004). *Developing young children's creativity: What can we learn from research*. England, UK.

Statuary Framework for EYFS. (2012). *Setting the standard for learning, development, and care for children from birth to five*. Department of Education. UK.

Watkins, C., Carnell, E., Lodge, C., Wagner, P., and Whalley, C. (2002). *Effective learning; NSIN Research Matters*. Institute of Education. University of London, UK.

Regionalization and Harmonization in TVET – Abdullah et al. (Eds)
© 2017 Taylor & Francis Group, London, ISBN 978-1-138-05419-6

Confirmatory factor analysis of trans-adapted generalized trust belief scale in *Bahasa Indonesia* on poor adolescents in vocational high schools

N. Astiyanti
SMKN 1 Kota Sukabumi, Kota Sukabumi, Indonesia

D. Harding & E. Fitriana
Faculty of Psychology, Universitas Padjadjaran, Indonesia

ABSTRACT: Interpersonal trust is necessary for poor adolescents who attend Vocational High School (VHS), especially in dealing with social situations. The most frequently used measuring instrument for interpersonal trust determination is the Children's Generalized Trust Belief (CGTB) scale. This study is aimed to develop and testify construct validity of the Indonesian trans-adapted version of the scale as an age-appropriate scale for poor middle adolescents in their VHS years. Thus the scale can be reliable to be used in other similar research in Indonesia. The original scale has been trans-adapted into Bahasa and after twice piloting, with 591 participants ($M = 16.78$ years) involved in the main study. The scale reaches the high value of internal consistency while Confirmatory Factor Analysis (CFA) modeling has resulted in valid and significant path diagrams, where 4 of 12 loadings are very significant. The differences between this study and those of others may be due to the nature of interpersonal trust as an affect-laden construct.

1 INTRODUCTION

Anecdotally, Indonesia reaches 16.9 point of 100-index in the world map of interpersonal trust. The higher the points, the greater the potential for the country to achieve its population welfare, and *vice versa* (Medrano, 2009). It reinforces the significance of trust in the form of social capital. Countries with high-trust societies achieve legal compliance, social solidarity and high economic prosperity (Fukuyama, 2010). In this case, the study of interpersonal trust with high levels of prosperity and low levels of poverty in a country can be explained.

Statistical data (Badan Pusat Statistika, 2016) showed that the prone-to-be-poor population group in Indonesia tends to decline while the population group in absolute poverty tends to increase annually. Despite the national gini ratio having declined .01 point from .41 (March 2015) to .40 point (September 2015), the West Java Province gini ratio is above the national number at .43 point. It means that the degree of inequality of income and prosperity of the population of West Java is at an alarming level (yellow zone)[1].

Schools in West Java have more diverse students than in any other provinces, accordingly.

This condition leads to a more challenging teaching and learning process. Teachers are required to maintain awareness of both culture of poverty and individual needs of students from low socio-economic background to be facilitated (Pellino, 2007; Yates et al., 2003). In fact, earning tertiary education such as Vocational High School (VHS) for students in poverty is pragmatically offered as one of the effective vertical mobility devices (Prasetyo, 2008). Graduating from VHS is a scaffolding to acquire marketable skills and personality that is suitable for industry employment, continuing education and/or entrepreneurship.

Pellino (2007) proves that a safe and trusting classroom allows learning enhancement for students in poverty. Interpersonal trust is important to study because so many social learning processes take place in the form of formal and informal teaching rather than direct experience. Therefore, individuals must be able to believe that the sources of information or the resources of learning can be relied on (Rotenberg, 2010).

Sen (1999) argues an alternative lens to view poverty as the deprivation of certain basic capabilities within a multidimensional perspective. In this regard, most parents in a poverty context have good intentions to provide sensitive, appropriate, yet consistent caregiving that would strengthen their infants' and children's trust capacity.

---

[1]http://www.neraca.co.id/article/40694

However, they should deal with limited resources that cannot be solved easily and quickly (Yates et al., 2003). Thus, Anthony (1987) suggested that such a situation be as a form of deprivation.

Interpersonal trust issues are still very limited to be investigated from a developmental paradigm, especially among children and adolescents. Nevertheless, interpersonal trust during childhood and adolescence affects individuals by adulthood (Rotenberg, 2010; Szczesniak et al., 2012). Meanwhile, Rotenberg (2010) reviews that the most current psychological literature on childhood or adolescence fails to provide any allusion to interpersonal trust at all.

Starting from 1986, Rotenberg (2010) notes that interpersonal trust among children and adolescents is marked as a highly significant phenomenon for researchers from various nationalities and cultures. After reviewing both preceding measurement tools HCITS (Hochreich, 1973) for sixth grade children and ICTS (Imber, 1973) for fourth grade children, Rotenberg et al. (2005) analyzed construction and validation of Children's Generalized Trust Belief (CGTB) scale for 9-to-11-year-olds. CGTB was developed on Base × Domain × Target (BDT) dimensions framework of interpersonal trust. CGTB is also diversified for late adolescents (Randall et al., 2010) and for 5-to-8-year-olds (Betts et al., 2009).

However, there is no corresponding measure of interpersonal trust for middle adolescents, especially those whom are expected to play a family backbone role immediately after their VHS graduation. In addition, such studies that relate to topic of trust from adolescent-parents relationship primarily focus on European and European American adolescents (Smetana, 2010) who are culturally and socially differed from Indonesian middle adolescents' characteristics and preferences. Therefore, the study is aimed to develop and testify the construct of the Indonesian trans-adapted version of CGTB scale as an age-appropriate scale to assess interpersonal trust for middle adolescents in poverty during VHS years.

Based on the reliability and validity evidences of the measurement instrument in other countries, trans-adaptation and Confirmatory Factor Analysis (CFA) modeling for psychometric analysis need to be performed. Therefore, this study is proposed to translate CGTB from English to Bahasa Indonesia, to perform a transcultural adaptation, and to examine the Indonesian version of CGTB psychometrically through CFA modeling.

2 METHOD

2.1 Trans-adaptation process

Trans-adaptation is concerned with the combination of translation and adaptation required to produce a reliable and valid version of a measurement instrument in a non-English language (Zucker et al., 2005). The *Standards* (American Educational Research Association et al., 1999) concerns trans-adaptation of assessment regarding language proficiencies of an examinee. According to international standard, there are six recognized stages of cross-cultural adaptation procedure, on which the scale in Bahasa Indonesia version has been developed (Beaton et al., 2000).

The CGTB scale consists of 24 items by 3 bases and 4 targets. Optional answers are provided on a Likert five-point scale (1 = very unlikely, 5 = very likely). After single forward translation, another translator made backward translation regarding comparability wording in English to a version in Bahasa Indonesia.

The first adaptation attempt was addressed to alter 18 names of children within scale using person perception with commonly Indonesian names. Some situations of scale that are originally targeted for elementary school children who reside in the UK were also adjusted to Indonesian middle adolescents' developmental preferences. Before being piloted, the Indonesian version scale was read by three representatives of poor middle adolescents and were reviewed by an expert committee of the Faculty of Psychology, Universitas Padjadjaran.

Participants confirmed written informed consent before being involved in the pilot study. Within classroom counseling services hours in both VHSs, participants completed the first form of Indonesian version scale. With a 98.5% response rate, data from 201 completed questionnaires were involved in psychometric properties analysis (Brown, 2011; Suliyanto, 2011; Osterlind, 2010; Freidenberg, 1995). Even though the reliability coefficient ($\alpha = .722$) is at high level (Munro, 2001), the validity ($r = -.245 -.0732$) and item analysis evidences ($r = -.024 -.478$) in average are at a poor level.

To explain those unexpected results, some of the participants were interviewed and the responses were reviewed. The second adaptation attempt was aimed to modify protagonist figures in person perception scale into disposition of self-evaluation scale. Through face validity and expert judgment, the second form of Indonesian version scale was tested with a relatively smaller number of different participants ($n = 49$). The validity and reliability evidences significantly increased ($\alpha = .821$), 18 items were acceptable and all indicators were represented. To support increasing likelihood, eight parallel items for some single-item-indicators were involved in the final form to be applied in the main study.

2.2 Participant

By utilizing stratified random sampling technique (Shaughnessy et al., 2009), there were 643 participants of poor adolescents of both VHS clusters in Kota Sukabumi involved in this main study. With 91.91% response rate, the final form data was obtained from 591 participants. Demographic data is presented in Table 1. The data reach α-Cronbach = .768 which is at a high level of reliability. Besides, 25 of 26 items are considered acceptable (Kaplan & Saccuzzo, 2009; Munro, 2001; Freidenberg, 1995).

2.3 CFA modeling

CFA is based on the assumption that the observed variables are not perfect indicators of latent or constructs variables. In order to be measured, the construct should be operationalized into observable variables or indicators that are drawn up into items of statements or questions to be responded. The response of participants is exactly quantified and analyzed in an effort to represent the construct into defined behavior or a particular profile. Next, the study is designed to produce an empirical result and the measurement validity is assessed (Wijanto, 2008; Hair et al., 2006; Osterlind, 2010).

Conceptually, interpersonal trust refers to a defined set of beliefs about reliability, emotion and honesty of individuals which comprises positive expectation of their behavior (Rotenberg, 2010). Operationally, interpersonal trust is constructed as quantified scores of participants' responses towards a trans-adapted questionnaire designed for individual trust measurement regarding indicators of reliability, emotion and honesty addressed to mother, father, teacher and same-sex peer.

Reliability trust is indicated by sum of mother (RTM), father (RTF), teachers (RTT) and peers (RTP) in keeping the promise. Emotional trust is indicated by sum of mother (ETM), father (ETF),

teacher (ETT) and peer (ETP) in keeping the secret of participants. Finally, honesty trust is indicated by sum of mother (HTM), father (HTF), teacher (HTT) and peer (HTP) in telling the truth.

Based on the interview results during the pilot study, very few of the participants and also their counterparts had some romantic partners. Thus, romantic partner is not determined as one of the trust targets, as had Randall et al. (2010) determined for late adolescent group.

The construct is reflected by indicator formula of $3 \times 1 \times 4$ BDT. There are 3 bases to 4 targets in a domain. Thus, interpersonal trust CFA model (Figure 1) performs 12 measured indicator variables and a latent construct. All parallel item data in each measured indicator is analyzed as an aggregate.

Based on developmental characteristic of adolescents, on one hand they are enduring growth, while on the other hand, they are improving independence. Their ambiguity of autonomy, harmony and conflict dimension during puberty turns to clarity. Healthy development of middle adolescent is indicated by parents' de-idealization as the perfect resources who will provide all he/she needs emotionally as well as behaviorally. They tend to not only realize their parents' weaknesses, but also accept their parents' limitation as human beings. However, healthy middle adolescent is also marked by peer conformity in a more limited group such clique (Steinberg, 2001; Steinberg & Silk, 2011; Vazsonyi et al., 2003; Randall et al., 2010). Therefore, the scale is expected to confirm that the participants would address their trust to mother, father and peer at a higher level than they do to teachers.

Table 1. Demographic data of participants.

Age (years) (Mean, ± SD)	16.78	2.69
Gender distribution	%	n
Girls	44.16	261
Boys	55.84	330
Level of VHS	%	n
XI-graders	48.90	289
XII-graders	51.10	302
Type of settlement	%	n
Legally owned by parents	73.77	436
Extended family house	9.99	59
Rented house	8.21	49
Boarding house	1.32	8
Others	5.41	32
Head of household	%	n
Biological father	71.91	425
Biological mother	15.73	93
Others	10.66	63

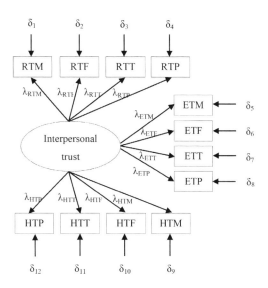

Figure 1. Measurement model of trans-adapted interpersonal trust scale of adolescent living in poverty.

To produce empirical results, the study is designed by determined coefficient of correlation data. The model is estimated using fixed parameter, both factor loading and error estimation. However, free parameter in manner of correlation between indicators is possible. While Maximum Likelihood Estimation (MLE) is determined as estimation technique, the model is estimated using computer program LISREL8.7. The estimation becomes relatively challenging with sample size of 591, because the system with >400 data points tends to be more sensitive in identification for differences (Hair et al., 2014).

The significance and the validity of the CFA empirical model is analyzed using the test criteria for model fitness (goodness of fit/GOF) and specific evidence of construct validity. Firstly, absolute fit measure is used to assess the appropriateness of the overall model. In this study, statistical Chi-Square (χ^2) and degrees of freedom (*df*), probability (p), Goodness of Fit Index (GFI) and RMSEA (Root Mean Square Error of Approximation) are considered to summarize overall fitness. In this case, RMSEA also doubles as the index criteria of badness of fit. And secondly, the incremental fit measure is a measure used to compare the resulting model with other models or baseline models. For this study, Comparative Fit Index (CFI) is used (Hair et al., 2014).

3 RESULTS AND DISCUSSION

Because values of χ^2/df = 399.32/54 = 7.394 in the p-*value* are .0000 and RMSEA .104, the empirical model of CFA is estimated to be not a fit. Due to that, model modification is taken in accordance with the theory. The model is modified by gradually adding 5 of 10 error covariance, suggested in order to obtain the model fitness. Due to the results of these modifications, the value of χ^2/df = 131.84/48 = 2.746. Although the p-value = .00000, the value of RMSEA .054 and CFI and GFI > .90, which overall show that the measurement model is a fit.

Accordingly, the empirical model fits to the theoretical model, and each indicator significantly reflects the construct. Four loadings exceed .50 rule of thumb, that is, HTP, ETT, ETM and ETF factors, while the others are below .50. Even though the loadings estimates statistically are significant, the 8 loadings <.50 are too low for good item qualification. Besides, a value of AVE = .232 confirms that there is inadequate convergence because of more error revealed in the item than variance explained by the construct. However, a value of CR = .697 (Construct Reliability) shows the evidence of reliable or internally consistent construct (Hair et al., 2014; Wijanto, 2008).

Table 2. Standardized factor loadings, T-value, average variance extracted and reliability estimates.

Indicator	Std. factor loadings	T-*value*
RTM	.28	5.75
RTF	.26	5.18
RTT	.31	6.26
RTP	.28	5.61
ETM	.53	11.13
ETF	.53	10.43
ETT	.54	10.52
ETP	.39	8.08
HTM	.33	6.57
HTF	.41	8.34
HTT	.32	6.44
HTP	.60	12.07
Average Variance Extracted	23.2%	
Construct Reliability	.697	

Table 2 displays standardized loadings of factors, T-*value* and also both Average Variance Extracted (AVE) and CR estimation. Entirely T-value ≥ 1.96 of path diagrams.

BDT 3 × 1 × 4 formulation in the construct of interpersonal trust variable consists of 25 items that are aggregated into 1–3 items per indicator. Meanwhile, the item format of the scale is relatively perceived distinguished by participants in spite of relatively suitable content of item.

Poor adolescents in VHS believe that peer honesty is strongly associated with openness regarding peers' financial to look for loan in order to pay daily needs. Further, they tend to devote a strong effort towards providing a loan, even though they should be in debt. They hope that they will be treated the same when common conditions occur. Thus, belief in peer honesty associates to solidarity among poor adolescents with target trusts which usually are their counterpart from poor families.

Meanwhile, teachers are predominantly targeted as resources that are ranked capable to keep poor students' secrets of their parental conflict or friends' deviant behavior. Frequently, telling teachers about their parental conflict is linked to their expectation in stress-relieving and resistance-gaining, so that the conflict would have no effect on their academic activity and concentration. Moreover, telling the teacher about the conflict is meant to invite the teacher into familial conflict resolution.

Unlike teachers whose trust being granted by parents easily, fathers are accountable for more diverse feeling and experience of poor students, that is, feeling of happy/unhappy, appreciation/resentment, and the desire to surprisingly give/be hostile to mother. Randomly, these father reliances are represented by poor students who live with bio-logical parents at home. Fathers also become the target of trust about academic difficulties that are associated whether to lessen content understand-ing or quality of poor students' relationships with a particular teacher.

Specifically, poor students rely on their mothers (Werner, 1993, 2005) as trust target for romantic feelings and experiences because fathers usually forbid them to deal with such experience before they are perceived to be grown up. The interview data shows that poor adolescents propose to dis-close such experience in terms of cultural norm understanding that is applicable for opposite sex relationships around their environment.

Interpersonal trust is one of the affect-laden trust constructs (Rotenberg, 2010). That is, empiri-cal data *per se* is insufficient to explain individual trust dynamic; it is implied to either context or con-tent to finally be considered as interpersonal trust. Most of the poor students in this study, for exam-ple, have been taught earlier to always not only trust their parents as their most significant others but also to have to obey any rule or conduct that their parents determined. Accordingly, they believe that mistrusting parents is unacceptable, thus resulting in negative consequences. In the meantime, they grow up with a rising publication about phenomena of physical as well as professional violence towards teacher figures. This issue potentially leads them to underestimate or avoid teachers as trust target. Such cultural norms and dogmatic values that are grounded and believed by the target group are investigated, to contribute towards the relevance of the construct (Das & Teng, 2004).

Besides, in such a context emerges the possibility to examine a wide array of trust targets in accordance to whether institutional purpose of VHS graduates or socio-political role of adolescents as first voters.

On the other hand, psychometric proper-ties issues in trust belief measurement scale are another concern that actually had been reviewed from previous scales. Some scales that have been used to measure trust belief do not perform ade-quate measurement properties to be rated as a sig-nificant scientific use (Bernath & Feshach, 1995; Rotenberg et al., 2005). It is associated to produce good items of scale that represent accuracy of measurement as the main objective of CFA (Hair et al., 2014). However, the new use and the new evi-dence are collected to support the item likelihood to be valid, if necessary (American Educational Research Association et al., 1999). Therefore, specifically-measured situation, evaluation proc-ess, and psychological exploration are in need of investigation. (Osterlind, 2010).

Nevertheless, performing a trans-adapted meas-urement instrument is regarded to be as expensive as producing a whole new assessment in term of efforts as well as financial cost (Zucker et al., 2005). Nowakowski et al. (2010) offered the more valid and contemporary measurement method in interpersonal trust assessment through neurobio-logical investigation. The study is approximately directed to a biometric approach that required a relatively costly advanced technology.

Finally, interpersonal trust development dur-ing middle adolescence relies on intensively and progressively learning and the facilitation process. Interpersonal trust development sounds like boost-ing competence of an athlete in a particular sport. Poor students who devote some efforts to chal-lenge, strengthen and improve their interpersonal trust development, will gain benefit not only to be more resilient individuals but also to be potential social agents (Resilience Institute, 2014; Luthar, 2003; Werner, 1999, 2005; Sroufe et al., 2005).

4 CONCLUSION

All in all, the theoretical model of interpersonal trust significantly fits with the data. That is, the factor of reliability trust, emotional trust, and honesty trust are believed among poor adoles-cents in VHS as the ability to show trust towards mother, father, teacher and peer. Specifically, qual-ity of item for HTP, ETT, ETF, and ETM factors of a total 12 indicators are at a good level, while the others are below that. Therefore, the four indi-cators employed are determinant factors of the construct.

The CFA of trans-adapted interpersonal trust scale shows that poor adolescents in VHS trust their peer and teacher more than their mother and father. They tend to select their trust target based on their needs in terms of emotional trust that are associated to keeping their secret.

There is no differences of interpersonal trust levels among poor student in VHS based on gen-der, grade level, age, settlement type, and also head of household.

REFERENCES

American Educational Research Association, American Psychological Association & National Council of Measurement in Education. (1999). *Standards for edu-cational and psychological testing.* Washington, DC: American Educational Research Association.

Anthony, E. J. (1987). Risk, vulnerability, and resilience: An overview. In E. J. Anthony & B. J. Cohler (Eds.). *The invulnerable child.* New York: Guilford Press.

Badan Pusat Statistika (BPS). (2016). Rapat Dengar Pen-dapat Komisi XI DPR RI dengan BPS: Pembicaraan Pendahuluan Pembahasaan Asumsi Dasar dalam

RAPBN Tahun Anggaran 2017, Jakarta, July 2016. Jakarta: Badan Pusat Statistika.

Beaton D. E., Bombardier C., Guillemin F. & Ferraz, M. B. (2000). Guidelines for the process of cross-cultural adaptation of self-report measures. *Spine (Phila Pa 1976)*, *25*(24), 3186–91.

Bernath, M. S. & Feshbach, N. D. (1995). Children's trust: Theory, assessment, development and research direction. *Applied and Preventive Psychology*, *4*, 1–19.

Betts, L. R., Rotenberg, K. J. & Trueman, M. (2009). The early childhood generalized trust belief scale. *Early Childhood Research Quarterly*, *24*(2), 175–185.

Brown, J. D. (2011). Likert items and scales of measurement? *SHIKEN: JALT Testing & Evaluation SIG Newsletter*, 15(1), 10–14.

Das, T. K. & Teng, B-S. (2004). The risk-based view of trust: A conceptual framework. *Journal of Business and Psychology*, *19*(1).

Freidenberg, L. (1995). *Psychological testing*. Massachusetts: Allyn & Bacon.

Hair, J. F., Black, W. C., Babin, W. C, Anderson, R. E. & Tatham, R. L. (2014). *Multivariate data analysis*. Seventh Edition. New Jersey: Pearson International Edition.

Hochreich, D. J. (1973). A children's scale to measure interpersonal trust. *Developmental Psychology*, *9*, 141.

Imber, S. C. (1973). Relationship of trust to academic performance. *Journal of Personality and Social Psychology*, *28*, 145–150.

Kaplan, R. M. & Saccuzzo, D. P. (2009). *Psychological assessment and theory creating and using psychological test*. Canada: Wadsworth.

Luthar, S. S. (Ed.). (2003). *Resilience and vulnerability: Adaptation in the context of childhood adversities*. Cambridge: Cambridge University Press.

Medrano, J. D. (2009). Interpersonal trust. Article. [Online]. Retrieved from http://www.jdsurveyMaps.jsp?idioma=%201&SeccionTexto=0404&NOID=104 2 September 2014.

Munro, B. H. (2001). *Statistic method for health care research*. Philadelphia: Lippicott William Wilkins.

Nowakowski, M. E., Vaillancourt, T. & Schmidt, L. A. (2010). Neurobiology of interpersonal trust. In K. J. Rotenberg (Ed.), *Interpersonal trust during childhood and adolescence* (pp. 28–57). Cambridge: Cambridge University Press.

Osterlind, S. J. (2010). *Modern measurement: Theory, principles, and applications of mental appraisal*. Second Edition. USA: Allyn & Bacon.

Pellino, K. M. (2007). *The effects of poverty on teaching and learning*. Article. [online]. Retrieved from http://www.teach-nology.com/Articles/teaching/poverty/27 July 2016.

Prasetyo, E. 2008. *Pelanggaran atas hak pendidikan*. Paper. Yogyakarta: Pusham UII.

Randall, B. A., Roternberg, K. J., Totenhagen, C. J., Rock, M. & Harmon, C. (2010). A new scale for the assessment of adolescents' trust beliefs. In K. J. Rotenberg (Ed.), *Interpersonal trust during childhood and adolescence* (pp. 247–69). Cambridge: Cambridge University Press.

Resilience Institute. (2014). Building trust, building community resilience. Article. [online]. Retrieved from www.resilientus.org/building-trust-building-community-resilience2 September 2014.

Rotenberg, K. J. (Ed.). (2010). *Interpersonal trust during childhood and adolescence*. Cambridge: Cambridge University Press.

Rotenberg, K. J., Fox, C., Green, S., Ruderman, L., Slater, K., Stevens, K. & Carlo, G. (2005). Construction and validation of a children's interpersonal trust belief scale. *Faculty Publications, Department of Psychology. Paper 2. 4/1/2005*. University of Nebraska-Lincoln. [online] retrieved from http://digitalcommons.unl.edu/.

Sen, A. (1999). *Development as freedom*. Oxford: Oxford University Press.

Shaughnessy, J. J., Zechmesiter, E. B. & Zechmeister, J. S. (2009). *Research methods in psychology*. Tenth edition. USA: McGraw-Hill Education.

Smetana, J. G. (2010). The role of trust in adolescent–parent relationship: To trust you is to tell you. In K. J. Rotenberg (Ed.), *Interpersonal trust during childhood and adolescence* (pp. 223–46). Cambridge: Cambridge University Press.

Sroufe, L. A., Egeland, B., Carlson, E. A. & Collins, W. A. (2005). *The development of the person: The Minnesota study of risk and adaptation from birth to adulthood*. New York: The Guilford Press.

Steinberg, L. (2001). We know some things: Parent-adolescent relationship in retrospect and prospect. *Journal of Research on Adolescence*, *11*(1), 1–19.

Steinberg, L. & Silk, J. S. (2011). Parenting adolescents. In M. H. Bornstein (Ed.), *Handbook of Parenting* 1:103–127. Mahwah, New Jersey: Erlbaum.

Suliyanto. (2011). Perbedaan pandangan skala Likert sebagai skala ordinal atau skala interval. *Prosiding Seminar Nasional Statistika, Sewindu Statistika, FMIPA Universitas Diponegoro*.

Szczesniak, M., Colaco., M. & Rondon, G. (2012). Development of interpersonal trust among children and adolescents. *Polish Psychological Bulletin*, *43*(1), 50–58.

Vazsonyi, A. T., Hibbert, J. R. & Snider, B. J. (2003). Exotic enterprise no more? Adolescent reports of family and parenting processes from youth in four countries. *Journal of Research on Adolescence*, *13*(2), 129–160.

Werner, E. E. (1993). Risk, resilience, and recovery: Perspective from the Kauai longitudinal study. *Development and Psychopathology*, *5*, 503–515.

Werner, E. E. (2005). Resilience and recovery: Findings from the Kauai longitudinal study. *Research, Policy, and Practice in Children's Mental Health*, *19*(1), 11–14.

Wijanto, S. H. (2008). *Structural equation modeling dengan LISREL 8.8*. Edisi Pertama. Yogyakarta: Graha Ilmu.

Yates, T. M., Egeland, B. L & Sroufe, L. A. (2003). Rethinking resilience: A developmental process perspective. In S. S. Luthar (Ed.), *Resilience and vulnerability: Adaptation in the context of childhood adversities* (pp. 243–66). New York, NY: Cambridge University Press.

Zucker, S., Miska, M., Alaniz, L. G. & Guzman, L. (2005). *Transadaptation: Publishing assessments in world languages*. Assessment report. September 2005. Pearson Education, Inc.

Regionalization and Harmonization in TVET – Abdullah et al. (Eds)
© 2017 Taylor & Francis Group, London, ISBN 978-1-138-05419-6

Traditional game to educate togetherness by *Anak Bawang Community*

S.H. Pujihartati & M. Wijaya
Department of Sociology, Faculty of Social and Political Sciences, Sebelas Maret University, Surakarta, Indonesia

ABSTRACT: Recently, traditional games such as '*gobak sodor*', '*Engklek*', and '*Dakon*' are no longer known widely among children. They prefer playing with gadgets such as Nintendo, PlayStation and the Internet. Even parents prefer their children playing at home. Thus, children become more individualistic because of their reduced time to play and to interact with their friends. Otherwise, many traditional games are performed collectively. It will affect their social life in the future. Meanwhile, the most appropriate environment for children is playing, as playing is the most effective media for transferring value and knowledge. *Anak Bawang* Community of Surakarta Indonesia is one of the communities actively making traditional games more well known to children. This research employed purposive sampling with a descriptive qualitative approach. The author selected the members of *Anak Bawang* Community, the schools where the traditional games were socialized, and members of the community watching the traditional games playing on the street. *Anak Bawang* Community introduced traditional games every Sunday at 6–9 a.m. by demonstrating them at *Car Free Day (CFD)* on Slamet Riyadi Street, Surakarta, at schools and certain events.

1 INTRODUCTION

Playing is a recreational activity and plays a part to develop children's self-potency, either physically or creatively. To children, playing is an important part and feature of developing in daily life, because through playing children can develop their fantasy, imagination and creativity. Human is *homo ludens*, and even animals are playing. Playing becomes important because it can be an effective education media to transfer value, and it is the core of education (Johan Huizinga in Murtiningsih, 2012).

Instead, a natural educative learning media has been present since thousands of years ago, departing from the traditional and natural root called traditional game synergistically. The traditional kid game is one of the folklore forms constituting the one circulating orally among the members of certain cultural tradition, inherited from one generation to another (Danandjaja, 1987).

Traditional playing contains cultural elements no longer considered as trivial because traditional games affect significantly the mentality, character, and social life of children later (Achroni, 2012). The creation of good character begins earlier. Some self-qualities are reflected on during childhood including care, awareness of their community life, justice, honesty, and respect. Learning while playing is something joyful to children. Thus, transfer of knowledge can run more effectively without making the children feel stressed or suppressed (Lickona in Kurniawati, 2014; Lewis, 2004).

Traditional games contain moral messages with local wisdom content raised from the vocabulary of cultural diversity yielded by the Indonesian nation. The important moral messages for the Indonesian nation's identity are: commonness, and care about their fellows. Traditional games can develop social skills by stimulating the children to build cooperation, helping the children in adjusting themselves, interacting positively and conditioning the children in self-control, and developing empathy to friends. Traditional games can build the understanding of honesty character. Those values should be implanted since childhood because the best character creation occurs in childhood (Kurniati, 2011; Lusiana, 2012). Through traditional games, the children are taught with various cultural values of their nation, so that the identity will precipitate in their subconscious nature because this is the best time to implant the values.

Early character begins to appear since childhood. The research on child development has been conducted since 1987, as a long-term study was conducted by University of Otago in Dunedin, New Zealand on 1,000 children, finding that by the age of three, it can be predicted what the children will be in the future. Even from four years old, a child is able to express discriminative attitude to different individuals (Miller, 1988).

In traditional games, actually the children learn to practice role playing as adults and it helps the children to understand more about their village, so that it will bring understanding of their village identity. From this, self-identity of an individual, a community, and an ethnicity will be created. As one of the cultural elements, *dolanan* (or traditional game) has a positive function in building the national identity (Yuan-Ling, 2010).

For that reason, traditional games should be promoted again as the appropriate environment in which children play. To children, playing has a very important meaning because through playing, children experience development in any aspect of their life. Meanwhile, the development of modern games follows Western bias, the development progress in Western countries and the idea that the entire world has no choice but to imitate the Western countries (Ritzer, 2010: 50). Similarly, the development of modern games is increasingly modern and follows the development of Western countries. Traditional games such as *petak umpet, lompat tali, gobak sodor, engklek,* have been performed rarely by urban people. They are more familiar with, and even play, *games on line, ipod,* and *playstation* more fluently. The informatics world changes the the development of existing culture, not only in game aspect but also in mindset (Dwipa, 2015).

Generally, traditional games need more than one player; they are different from modern games in that they can be played by an individual alone. The ability of interacting with the opponent is not prioritized, because the child basically focuses on the game existing in front of him/her. Thus, modern games tend to be played aggressively because what is needed is the self-winning. Modern games need sophisticated tools, a comfortable place and sophisticated technology. Meanwhile, traditional games need only any tools existing in the surroundings such as bamboo, stone, dry leaves, or even frangipani flower.

Traditional games do not need special maintenance. For that reason, modern games often exist in a mall, while traditional games in the kampong or rural fringe. In fact, technological development has confronted us with a fairly complicated problem, particularly pertaining to the consequence to the children's mentality that is still very vulnerable to diverse foreign culture, and uncertainly consistent with our cultural values (Handayani, 2003).

The effects of modern game development, for example online games, are sexual abuse committed by the six-year child against the four-year-old child, or the thief caught who steals to pay for the online game as he has become addicted to it. Even the children truant, due to playing games in Internet stalls, which affects the development of national mentality and character. Indonesian people, well known for their friendliness, now change into those with violent character.

The swift globalization currently penetrating into all aspects of life also affects the children. The emergence of modern games in the form of concrete objects or massively-produced online ones, affects the children's perspective as the modern products' users, so that the response to traditional games is reduced.

Consumptive society is often defined as society that has just come into a growing cycle and connected to the extravagance (Baudrillard, 2004). If the children use a gadget, currently not for its function but for a game, it indicates extravagance. Playing formerly performed outdoors now is performed more indoors using gadgets. This poor response is primarily affected by an assumption that *dolanan anak* (traditional child game) provides less attraction and challenge compared with the modern game.

Unconsciously, traditional games will strengthen the family bond (kinship). Bengal is one of the poor areas in India. There, parents cannot afford expensive products for their children, so that they recommend the children to play outdoors. Their parents know that playing outdoors will strengthen their children's mentality and physique, so that they insist to encourage their children to play outdoors from 5–7 p.m. Such playing circumstances, according to Ghosh (2015), will strengthen fraternity bonds.

For that reason, the more fading traditional games should be revived within our society, the source of which can actually be the means of developing our cultural values.

This research aimed to describe the *Anak Bawang* Community's attempt to develop traditional games.

2 METHOD

This research employed a descriptive qualitative method to catch a wide range of qualitative information along with its description. The data was more inductive in nature so that the author's errors during developing the research plan could be corrected and adjusted based on the field observation.

This research took place in Surakarta (Solo), an area with much potency in many sectors, including the cultural sector. One community that has poured its creativity into Solo was *Anak Bawang* Community, operating in preserving traditional games. The data was obtained from primary and secondary data sources using interview and observation techniques. The sampling technique used in this research was purposive sampling, particularly maximum variation sampling (Michael Quinn Patton in Muhadjir, 2000). The variation searched for was information from the members of *Anak Bawang* Community and the members of society watching the games including adults, children participating in and watching the games in *CFD* events and those having ever invited the *Anak Bawang* Community, including Al Firdaus Kindergarten.

Data validation was conducted using a source validity test, by means of comparing and cross-checking the confidence level of information obtained from different sources of information.

The technique for analyzing data used in this research was an interactive model of analysis encompassing data reduction, data display and conclusion drawing.

3 DISCUSSION

Anak Bawang Community is the traditional game-lover community, who are attempting to preserve it. This community invites the wider society to replay traditional games to the next generation, including the children spending most of their time on playing. It is because children are the beneficiary and those forwarding the cultural values, modesty, respect, and devotion to parents and respect to others' existence (Danandjaya 1987). *Anak Bawang* Community teaches the society that traditional games are replete with education and noble character values. They not only pursue intellectuality, but also educate the children emotionally and spiritually, and implant tolerance, mutual cooperation, and kinship attitude.

Anak Bawang Community was founded in a National Seminar on traditional games held by Psychological Study Program of Medical Faculty of Sebelas Maret University. The seminar was held on November 10, 2012. Considering the large enthusiasm among the society on the seminar of traditional games, the students of Psychological Study Program of Sebelas Maret University established a traditional game community named *Komunitas Anak Bawang* (*Anak Bawang Community*).

This community invited the society to replay a traditional game in modern or digital era. It is named *Anak Bawang* because every young child considered as minor is called *"Pupuk Bawang"* in Javanese language or *Anak Bawang* in Indonesian language. *Anak Bawang* is always considered as the complement in a game. He/she follows the game but as if he/she is not existent. However, never underestimate *Anak Bawang*. Formerly he/she is indeed considered as minor, but as the time progresses, *Anak Bawang* will develop and be the main player in the game.

The routine activities conducted in introducing traditional games is *CFD* event proceeding at 6–9 a.m., exactly on Slamet Riyadi Street, Surakarta. *CFD* is the public space accessible to everyone, whether adults or youths or children. It is in the public space that dialogue occurs between the *Anak Bawang* Community and the visitors, and sometimes the visitors give some ideas.

Other visiting children state that they love to come to the place because they can play directly with their friends and the ones existing in the exhibition. For that reason, the *Anak Bawang* Community puts itself as the friend, rather than the teacher or coach, of children, and even the children can choose the game they like freely.

In addition, another routine activity done is a workshop on *dolanan*, or called *dolanan* lecture, that is a discussion or sharing between the administrators and the members of *Anak Bawang* Community about the ways and rules of traditional games conducted every Friday afternoon in Psychological Campus of Sebelas Maret University.

The *Anak Bawang* Community also campaigns actively for traditional games through social networks, one of which is Facebook. Hundreds of people have joined the account of *Komunitas Permainan Traditional* (Traditional Game Community). The members affiliated with this community have reached about 500 persons. For those who want to join this community, just join this Facebook Group of *Anak Bawang* Community, and they will automatically become the members.

In addition to the routine activities above, *Anak Bawang* Community also held Traditional Game Olympic on January 21–22, 2014 in Grand Atrium Solo Paragon. Along with the sponsor (a mall) in Solo, this community held *Gobag Sodor* Olympic and *Dolanan Anak* parade.

This community held traditional games activity in Kampong Kemlayan Surakarta on September 21, 2014. The participants in this activity consisted of both children and adults. Traditional games featured were, among others, *Egrang, Bakiak, Dakon, Bekelan*, and *Gasing*.

On March 1, 2015, this community held an activity in Mall Palur Plaza. This community got an invitation to the *"Expo Jadul Event"*. A painting competition, art performance, and singing competition were also held at this event. To attract the visitors, they held a *Bakiak* competition.

Still another activity followed is the one held by the Department of Sociology of Social and Political Sciences Faculty to demonstrate traditional games in Al Firdaus Kindergarten on May 14, 2016. The participants welcomed this activity enthusiastically to attract the Kindergarten B's interest in attending the *Dakon* competition. Meanwhile, some other games were also introduced: *Bakiak, Dakon, Dragon, Kontrakol*, and *Gasing*.

4 CONCLUSIONS

The attempt the *Anak Bawang* Community takes is to hold routine activity in *CFD* in addition to holding an activity in the Psychological Department of

Medical Faculty of Sebelas Maret University every Friday. Other activities are incidental in nature depending on the existing invitation, for example, when it is invited to Kampong Kemlayan to participate in a program in a mall or in the Olympic.

The adults' and children's response to routine activity in *CFD* is very enthusiastic as indicated by the many participants trying to play the game, and it is also even supported by those parents present and accompanying them.

Nevertheless, the competition with modern games should not be forgotten. Therefore, parents should be encouraged to teach the children to participate in preserving traditional games.

REFERENCES

Achroni, K. (2012). *Mengoptimalkan tumbuh kembang anak melalui permainan tradisional*. Yogyakarta: Javalitera.

Baudrillard, J. (2004). *The consumer society. Myths and structure*. Wahyunto, T. & Sumrahadi (Eds.). Yogyakarta: Kreasi Wacana.

Danandjaya, J. (1987). *Folklore Indonesia*. Jakarta: Gramedia.

Dwipa, A.A., (2015). *Pengaruh Permainan Tradisional Terhadap Peningkatan Kemampuan Gerak Motorik Kasar pada Siswa Putra Sekolah Dasar*. Semarang: Universitas Negeri Semarang.

Ghosh, P. (2015). Traditional sports and games culture around West Bengal. *International Journal of Novel Research in Humanity and Social Sciences*, 2(3), 1–5.

Handayani. (2003). *Menghidupkan kembali Dolanan Anak Sebagai Media Pelestarian Budaya. Sarasehan Menggali Nilai-nilai Kebangkitan Nasional*.

Kurniati, E. (2011). *Program bimbingan untuk mengembangkan ketrampilan sosial anak melalui permainan tradisional. Surakarta*. Skripsi universita Muhammadiyah Surakarta: Tidak diterbitkan.

Kurniawati, (2014). Young children character development through Javanese traditional game. *IJECES* 3(1), 54–58.

Lewis, B. A. (2004). *Character building Untuk anak-anak*. Batam: Kharisma Publishing Group.

Lusiana, E. (2012). Membangun pemahaman karakter kejujuran melalui permainan tradisional pada anak usia dini di Pati. *Journal of Early Childhood Education*, 1(1).

Miller, P. & Kim, K. (1988). Human nature and the development of character. The Class of descriptive and normative elements in John Stuart Mills educational theory. *Journal of Educational Thought*, 22(2), 133–44.

Muhadjir, N. (2000). *Metode Penelitian Kualitatif*. Yogyakarta: Rake Sarasin.

Murtiningsih, S. (2012). *Pendidikan multikultural melalui Dolanan Anak*. Proseding Seminar Internasional Multikultural dan Globalisasi, 153–166.

Ritzer, G. (2010). *Teori sosiologi modern. Penerjemah Triwibowo*. Jakarta: Kharisma Putra Utama.

Wahyuni, I. (2009). *Efektivitas Pemberian Permainan Gobak Sodor Terhadap Dwipa, Aristrokrat Agung, th 2015, Pengaruh Permainan Tradisional Terhadap Peningkatan Kemampuan Gerak Motorik Kasar Pada Siswa Putra SD*. Skripsi Jur Ilmu Keolahragaan Fakultas Ilmu Keolahragaan Universitas Negri Semarang.

Yuan-ling, T. U. (2010). The traditional child-rearing in a village of the Northwest China in the perspective of anthropology of education. *Journal of Educational Science of Human Normal University*, 5: 004.

The participation of surakarta children forum in annual community consultations on development planning as democratic education media

S. Yuliani, R. Humsona & R.H. Haryanti
Universitas Sebelas Maret Surakarta, Jawa Tengah, Indonesia

ABSTRACT: This research aimed to find out the participation of the Surakarta Children Forum in Annually Community Consultations on Development Planning and the extent to which the children's participation in development planning can be democratic values learning. This study was a qualitative research with data source taken using a purposive technique. Data analysis was carried out using an interactive model of analysis. The result of the research showed that the participation of Surakarta Children Forum in Annually Community Consultations on Development Planning had not been able to be a learning media for democratic values learning because their participation was still pseudo rather than active. It was because the children did not have bravery and ability to voice their aspiration. Stakeholders or adults, particularly the builder of Children Forum, bureaucratic apparatus, and members of legislative assembly, poorly understood the children's world so that children participation had not yet been considered as important.

1 INTRODUCTION

The 3rd International Congress on Technical and Vocational Education and Training (TVET) entitled *Transforming TVET: Building skills for work and life* in Shanghai, China, confirmed that TVET should contribute actively to the achievement of Education For All (EFA) and the organization of lifetime education. Specifically, this congress also underlines the role of TVET in promoting cultural plurality and distributing local knowledge and skill to help the evolvement of human-oriented development. In addition, TVET provides not only vocational skill but also knowledge, skill and attitude desirable to participate in work and life, such as growing self-awareness and self-esteem, interpersonal ability, citizenship, communication, and entrepreneurial skill.

Democratic education is a part of civic education, important to the evolvement of human-oriented development. Knowledge and democratic decision-making skills are skills for life, very desirable to the state with a plural cultural background like in Indonesia. For that reason, there should be earlier socialization about democratic values embedded through both formal and non-formal education. Democratic education belongs to the non-formal education form and is an integral part of TVET (National Education System Law of 2003; TVETipedia Glossary).

In the attempt to grow democratic awareness and skill in the children, the Indonesian government has created a medium for children participation in development planning named Children Forum. Children participation in development planning is the mandate of the Convention on the Rights of Children, considering that the development program for children should be formulated by listening to the children's aspirations, and organized according to the perspective on children's needs. In Surakarta City, since 2013, Children Forum is one of the society groups involved in Annually Community Consultations on Development Planning (*Musrenbang*). Children participation in *Musrenbang* is intended to base the design of the development program planning for children on the children's needs, voiced actually by the children, rather than formulated according to the adults' perspective. This research studies the extent to which children participation in *Musrenbang* can be the media of democratic value learning and the factors inhibiting it.

2 METHOD

This research was a qualitative descriptive research. Informants were selected purposively, consisting of the Surakarta Regional Development Planning Board (*Badan Perencanaan Pembangunan Daerah*

Kota Surakarta) and the Agency for Community Empowerment, Women Empowerment and Child Protection (*Badan Pemberdayaan Masyarakat, Pemberdayaan Perempuan, Perlindungan Anak*), and some other communities empowering children. In addition, this study also utilized secondary data sources derived from documents, archives, government regulations and data obtained from newspapers, magazines, and Internet-related research themes. Data collection was carried out using observation, in-depth interviews and Focus Group Discussions (FGD) methods. Data analysis was carried out using an interactive model including three components: data reduction, data presentation, and drawing conclusions (Miles and Huberman, 1992).

3 RESULT OF DISCUSSION

3.1 *The profile of surakarta children forum*

Children Forum is defined as a communication forum managed by children, built by the government, and is used as the medium of child participation. Its members are children, either as individuals or as representatives. Since 2013, Surakarta City Government has determined the Child Forum to be part of the community involved in Annually Community Consultations on Development Planning or *Musrenbang* (Surakarta Mayor's Regulation No. 3-B of 2013 about General Guidelines of Child Participation Development in Surakarta City Development). The objective is to base the design of the development program intended for the children on children's suggestions or ideas, rather than on the parent's perspective.

As a medium of child participation in development, Children Forum serves: a) as a medium of monitoring the implementation of children's rights implementation; b) as a medium of socializing activity program related to the children's rights in a peer environment; c) as a medium of voicing children participation; d) to support children's participation in the decision-making process, and e) to support the children to develop their potency actively.

The development of Children Forum in Surakarta City began around 2008 through the establishment of Children Forum at municipal city, Surakarta Children Forum (*Forum Anak Surakarta* = FAS). By 2015, there have been 51 children forums established at village level, five at sub-district level, and one at municipal level in Surakarta City. The membership of Children Forum consists of ordinary members (those aged less than 18 years, domiciling and having activity in Surakarta) and special members containing FAS alumni (ordinary members who are more than 18 years old) who are still needed for their effort and thought by FAS.

Children participation in development planning is very important to bring a child-friendly city development program into reality. A child-friendly city is the one built on the principles of appreciating humanity values and children's dignity as an intact human being, both physically and mentally.

The development planning is connoted as public affairs that can be done by adults only. The development planning process in Surakarta City is so far still dominated by a top-down approach in the sense of being formulated according to the perspective of state official's interest. The participative development planning involving the participation at any levels of society, or by stakeholders, has not been the mainstream. The actors involved in development decision-making are very elitist, only involving local government officials, and stakeholders close to the power so that the budget and policy produced poorly accommodates the aspiration or voice of marginal groups, one of which is the children's voice.

Through establishing Children Forum, the government wants to refer to the children's voice in organizing development programs for children. Children's problems and needs are discussed and the solution is sought by listening first to the children's will. For that reason, in development planning, a room is required to be the place where the sector groups and the Local Government Agency (Satuan Kerja Perangkat Daerah) serving them meet to explore the real problem faced by communities, and to determine the solution more appropriate to their needs.

3.2 *The participation of surakarta children forum in annually community consultations on development planning and democratic education*

Participation is defined by Hart (1992) as "the process of sharing decisions which affect one's life and the life of the community in which one lives". Convention on the Rights of Children (CRC) defines children participation as ongoing processes, which include information-sharing and dialog between children and adults based on mutual respect, and in which children can learn how their views and those of adults are taken into account and shape the outcome of such processes.

It can be concluded that children participation is a process of dialoging and information-sharing between children and adults to make decisions related to the children's needs and interest, in which the children are positioned equally and appreciated for their opinion and aspiration. Children's participation will give the children the opportunity of influencing public policy pertaining to their interests and rights.

Involving the children in development planning is the form of democratic education. Bennis (http://democraticeducation.org) states that democratic education can create the youths skillful in making decisions and thinking critically, which is very desirable in building a democratic and socially just society.

Children's participation in development planning is a form of deliberative democracy. Gutmann (1999:13) stated that deliberative democracy underscores the importance of publicly supported education that develops the capacity to deliberate among all children to have freedom in the future and to be equal citizens.

Democratic education can be conducted out of formal education or in non-formal education learning such as in children's organizations or forums. Participating actively in forums or organizations, the youths can learn to take initiative, responsibility, and learn how to appreciate others. Learning communication and interpersonal skills, conflict resolution, leadership, management, planning, and problem-solving skills, the youths' feelings of self-confidence can improve (http://www.youthforum.org).

Participation as the children's right is closely related to the decision-making process, particularly in relation to development program planning. Children participation in development is a process of dialog and sharing information between children and adults to make decisions related to policy or program pertaining to the need and interest of children. DeWinter (in Roche, 1999) sees the youngster as a fellow citizen with potency and capacity to contribute to development. Thus, children's capacity to be involved in the decision-making process becomes a key to the effectiveness of children participation policy in development planning.

Surakarta Children Forum was established in 2008. The fundamental objective of Surakarta Children Forum is to be the media for children participation in development. Participation is understood not only as children's involvement as the target of the development program, but their active participation in development planning. This definition is in line with the definition of Children Participation in Development Planning as mentioned in Surakarta Mayor's Regulation Number 3-B of 2013 about General Guidelines of Children Participation Development in Development in Surakarta City:

Children Participation in Development Planning is children involvement to express their aspiration and need in decision making process through Annually Community Consultations on Development Planning *(Musrenbang) about everything pertaining to them and conducted based on mutual consciousness, understanding and willing so that the children can enjoy the result or benefit from such the decision.*

Participating in *Musrenbang* becomes a medium of introducing, experiencing and practicing democratic function and values. From the result of interview with the members and administrators of Children Forum, it can be concluded that there are some advantages of Children Forum's participation in *Musrenbang*: *Firstly*, to be a medium of channeling the children's voice and rights. The role of Children's Forum in *Musrenbang* is to convey the aspirations and needs of children to local governments.; *Secondly*, to be more familiar with who and what the government apparatus does. By engaging in *Musrenbang*, children can get to know better the regional officials and what they are doing to develop their regions; *Thirdly*, a more opened mindset on the environment, particularly on politics and government. Most young people have a negative view of politics. By participating in *Musrenbang*, children become more empathetic to the difficulties and problems faced by bureaucratic officials in carrying out government duties; *Fourthly*, to speak and to express opinion bravely. Participation in *Musrenbang* requires children to dare to voice their aspirations and needs, in order to be accommodated in local development planning (Yuliani et al., 2015).

Although *Musrenbang* is considered as important, there are some problems inhibiting the active participation of Children Forum in *Musrenbang*. *Firstly*, not all children understand actually what the function and the role of Children Forum is in development planning (*Musrenbang*). *Secondly*, children have less self-confidence to voice their aspiration and interest. *Thirdly*, the participation of Children Forum in *Musrenbang* is limited to giving suggestion rather than determining priority. *Fourthly*, the builders of Children Forum have not run their function maximally yet. Most of them are recruited from government apparatus, are old, and poorly understand the psychology of youth. *Fifthly*, the government officials of Surakarta City (executive and legislative) have not yet considered the importance of children participation in development planning (Yuliani et al., 2015).

The participation of Children Forum in *Musrenbang* in Surakarta City as a democratic learning media is not yet optimum. It is because the children are still positioned unequally. Adults (Regional Development Planning Board/Bappeda, members of DPRD (Dewan Perwakilan Rakyat Daerah) [Local Legislative Assembly], Builders of Children Forum) are still dominant in formulating development policy and program.

This research's findings are similar to the results of the survey conducted by UN IANYD in 2012, finding that most of the 13,000 respondents coming from 186 countries confirmed that the challenge for the youths is the limited opportunity of participating actively in the decision-making process. To encourage active participation, participatory structure, trust between the youths and the institutions, and larger capacity developments are required (http://www.un.org).

Matthew et al. (in Cavet and Sloper, 2004) argued that adult's lack of trust in the children's ability makes the program "adult focus". Matthews found that non-participatory culture is still very strong, so that there is "invisible control" by adults, making the children not being taken into account for their thinking and decisions. For that reasons, active participation, according to Shier (in Thomas, 2007) can occur if only adults are willing to share their power by means of delegating or giving some of their power to children.

4 CONCLUSIONS

The participation of Children Forum in Annually Community Consultations on Development Planning in Surakarta City is still pseudo-participation or tokenism in nature (Arnstein, 1969; Hart, 1992) rather than active participation, because the children are limited to be present only and to give suggestions rather than to determine priority and formulate their own opinion. The Involvement of Children Forum in Annually Community Consultations on Development Planning as a democratic education media is still limited to introducing procedural democracy rather than embedding and practicing the substantial functions and values of democracy.

REFERENCES

Arnstein, S. (1969). Eight rungs on the ladder of citizen participation. *Journal of the American Institute of Planners*, *35*, 216–224.

Bennis, D. (2016). *What is Democratic Education?* <http://democraticeducation.org/index.php/features/what-is-democratic-education/> Retrieved 15 July 2016.

Cavet, J. & Sloper, P. (2004). *The participation of children and young people in decisions about UK service development*. Social Policy Research Unit, University of York, Heslington, York, UK.

Convention on the Rights of Children. <http://www.ohchr.org/Documents/ Professional Interest/crc.pdf> Retrieved 15 July 2016.

European Youth Forum Position Paper on 'Life-wide Learning for Active Citizenship' <http://www. youthforum.org /assets/2013/12/ 0238-02-Life-wide-learning-for-Active-Citizenship.pdf> Retrieved 4 July 2016.

Gutmann, A. (1999). *Democratic education*. Princeton University Press. Princeton, New Jersey.

Hart, R. A. (1992). *Children's participation: From tokenism to citizenship*. UNICEF International Child Development Centre.

Mile, M. B. & Huberman, A. M. (1992). *Analisis Data Kualitatif*. Jakarta: UI Press.

Peraturan Walikota Surakarta Nomor 3-B Tahun 2013 tentang Pedoman Umum Pengembangan Partisipasi Anak Dalam Pembangunan di Kota Surakarta.

Roche, J. (1999) Children: rights, participation and citizenship. *Childhood* 6(4), 475–493.

Thomas, N. (2007). Towards a theory of children's participation. *International Journal of Children's Rights*, 15(2), 199–218.

TVETipedia Glossary <http://www.unevoc.unesco.org/go.php?q=TVETipedia+Glossary I A-Z&term=Technical+and+vocational+education+and+training>. Retrieved 15 July 2016.

Undang-Undang No. 20 Tahun 2003 tentang Sistem Pendidikan Nasional.

UNESCO. (2012). *Third International Congress on Technical and Vocational Education and Training*. Shanghai, China 14–16 May 2012.

Youth, Political Participation and Decision Making <http://www.un.org/esa/socdev/documents/youth/fact-sheets/youth-political-participation.pdf> Retrieved 14 July 2016.

Yuliani, S., Humsona, R., Haryanti & Herlina, R. (2015). *Strategi Pengembangan Kapasitas Forum Anak Surakarta untuk Meningkatkan Partisipasi Aktif Anak dalam Musyawarah Perencanaan Pembangunan*. Penelitian Unggulan Perguruan Tinggi Research Report.

Towards collaborative governance for conflict resolution of diverse interest groups

Sudarmo
The Study Program of Public Administration, Faculty of Social and Political Sciences, Universitas Sebelas Maret, Surakarta, Indonesia

ABSTRACT: The area around the former monarchy of the Kasunanan Surakarta's palace where thousands of textile vendors traded their commodities in the traditional market attracted numerous street vendors and other non-Solo casual large-scale textile traders. This situation had encouraged the city government or the royal family released actions that affected the traders or street vendors' livelihood. By using ethnographic approach, this research shows that conflict rose because of the inconsistency in decision making created through a top-down approach in the Reform era, economic motives and different interest amongst groups. Conflicts were sometimes resolved by using bottom-up approach through delegation of authority, promises, or forces of powerful groups. Since conflicts were not entirely resolved, powerless groups of traders wanted to have decision making approach, representing collaboration based on inclusive authentic dialogue in governing conflicts.

1 INTRODUCTION

There are some important buildings and land around the former monarchy of the Kasunanan Surakarta's Palace (FMKSP). They include the Klewer Market, the Great Mosque, the Cinderamata Batik Market (CBM), the Northern Square, and the Gladhak—the main entrance gate from Slamet Riyadi Boulevard to the Northern Square. The buildings and/or the land are (partly or totally) believed to belong to the royal family. These strategic areas for textile traders also attracted other large textile traders using cars from outside Surakarta. Hundreds of street vendors have also migrated to areas around the FMKSP from outside Solo. Thus, in addition to the royal family of Kasunanan Surakarta (RFKS) which is a relatively fragmented group, central government and city government of Surakarta's interests, there are many other groups including association of Klewer market traders namely the HPPK; two associations of market traders in the CBM consisting of the HPTPPK and the P3C; groups of street vendors and renteng traders; unorganized illegal occupants; and the Car-Using Large Scale Textile Traders (CULSTTs) from outside the city—they are mainly citizens of Districts of Pekalongan, Jepara, and Kudus. They were living side-by-side in these areas but with different values and preferences and may utilize and compete for similar resources. This heterogeneous situation may lead to conflicts amongst them because of various group demand (Protasel, 1988). Conflict can be

defined as the actions of an individual, a group, or an organization which inhibits at least temporarily another party from achieving its desired goals or maximizing its interest (Okotoni and Okotoni, 2003; Barki and Hartwick, 2004; Botvinick et al., 2001) but its consequences may be constructive (Coser, 1956; Higashiden and Birley, 2002).

There have been many studies on decision making approach in conflict resolution for better public lives. For example, Soltani and Allan (2012), Limapornwanitch and Tanaboriboon (2003), and Sudarmo (2009) focused on the importance of communities' participation in decision making process. A study by Sudarmo (2009) shows that during the New Order era the city government of Surakarta used a top-down approach in which there used to be a lack of street-vendor's participation in the public decision making, because the city government of Surakarta and its local legislative assembly deliberatively overlooked the value of the street vendors' participation and did not provide them with any chances to participate in the process that affected their life. This comes from the reason habituated by established Javanese social hierarchism creating a psychological burden against demanding participation, including obstacles regarding street vendors' socio-economic status, lack of their own organizations that can support them in taking part in the policy process, and lack of back-up from local non-government organizations. These studies suggest that public participation is an efficient way to achieve better results in resolving conflicts. Although top-down approach was believed to be able to make the policy goals clear and consistent (Van Meter and Van Hom, 1975; Mazmanian and Sabatier 1983), it was unproductive due to the ignorance of the local wisdom, traditional customs, socio-economic circumstances and existing resources (Pretty and Shah, 2000). Since the top-down approach fails to consider broader public objectives (Matland, 1995) and ignores needs of grassroots (Tiwari, Bajracharya, and Sitaula, 2008; Michaelsen, 1991) it is ineffective to resolve conflict (Smith, 2014). Because there are many non-state stakeholders with different values and interests in the area while their desires for participation in decision making have been found to be more obvious in larger city (Wang, 2001; O'Toole, Marshall, and Grewe 1996; Ebdon 2000) as it happens in Surakarta due to the transition towards a fuller democracy (Sudarmo, 2009), any decision representing elites' value but ignoring the various grassroots' interest, may create vigorous conflicts.

Conversely, some others suggested bottom-up approach in public decision making claiming that a more accurate comprehension of implementation can be achieved by looking at a policy from the viewpoint of the target population and the service deliverers (Hjern and Hull, 1982; Hjern, 1982; Hjern and Porter, 1981; Berman,1978). However bottom-up approach was still represented as a contradictory tendency producing conflict, and it is also attributed as a source of inefficiency impending the beneficial development of the city (Smith, 2014). Thus, it is likely that an alternative approach for a conflict resolution that is able to accommodate all stakeholders' interest inclusively and appropriate for Surakarta society which is in the transition towards a fuller democracy, called 'collaborative governance' (Booher, 2004; Ansell and Gash, 2007; O'Brien, 2012), instead of just individual top-down, bottom-up or combined the two approaches, is required.

Some studies found that there is no relationship between democracy and conflict (Small and Singer, 1976; Chan, 1984; Weede, 1984; Vincent, 1987) but another study by Gates (1983) found that democracies tend to be more conflict-prone than non-democratic regimes. A Study by Mintz and Geva (1993) shows that democracies do not fight each other because their leaders have very few political incentives to do so. These studies suggest that there is not clear relationship whether democracy causes conflict, and they also suggest that different location and frequent level of interactions between stakeholders may have different contribution to conflicts. These studies imply that causes of conflict may not be a single but complex and need to be managed carefully so that it is constructive. Doucey (2011) contends that 'crisis management

can be successful only when essential human needs are met and collective fears are addressed'.

Despite the insights provided by earlier theoretical, empirical, and case-study work on conflict, the study of public decision making process for conflict resolution involving street vendors, the non-local residents' vendors and traditional market traders and the powerful groups including local government and the aristocracy family during the newly democratic era in the area around the FMKSP has not been studied in a systematic manner.

The purpose of this study is intended to identify actors involved in conflict, reasons for conflicts and the way the conflicts were resolved in the early Reform era in different locations around the FMKSP. It is also intended to discuss whether both top-down and bottom-up approaches in decision making for conflict resolution appropriate in the circumstance. This study finally attempts to find an alternative approach for conflict resolution that is able to accommodate all interests of stakeholders inclusively, called collaborative governance.

2 METHOD

This study was conducted in five main areas around the FMKSP, Surakarta-Central Java, including the Klewer market, the Great Mosque, the CBM, the Northern Square, and the Gladhak. It is a descriptive qualitative research using an ethnographic method, involving several periods of fieldwork using participant observation, spending much time watching people, talking to them about what they were doing, thinking and saying. This approach was designed to gain an insight into viewpoints of street vendors; officials of city government; the Royal family of the Kasunanan Surakarta, the HPPK, the HPTPPK and the P3C; and the CULSTTs; and the way how they understood their circumstances where they interacted to one and the others, including triangulation by using several approaches to people from different directions. Those approaches were selected on the basis of both purposive and snow-ball sampling techniques. This was combined with interviews with local people including parking attendants, pedicab drivers, public transport drivers, and local visitors and customers of the Klewer Market and the CBM, and with detailed content analyses of secondary research and local newspapers.

3 RESULTS

The RFKS initiated to reconstruct the site of the Palace including the front yard of the Great Mosque funded by the Central Government in

2001 but there were more than 50 unauthorized kiosks blocking it. It was intended to return the FMKSP to be a cultural preservation for tourism in Surakarta. Beside the Mosque are the Northern Square and Gladhak where hundreds of street vendors run their informal economy. The traders and street traders were instructed to move into the Pekapalan buildings of the CBM. The traders steered by Sholahudin rejected the relocation to the new place until they got the expected benefits. Due to the RFKS's promise in coordination with the city government to fulfill his demand, the traders were successfully relocated. Soon after they were relocated to the CBM and formed a traders association called HPTPPK, he asked for the Pekapalan buildings to be under his authority and planned to divide it into 65 open kiosks. His request was fulfilled and he was mandated to accommodate all street vendors and any illegal occupant in the area around the FMKSP but the remaining 13 illegal occupants and the other 17 street vendors in the Northern Square who did not have any link to the thug, the HPTPPK leader, the royal family or the city government—were simply ignored whilst all of the kiosks had been sold out by the HPTPPK leader to anybody who could afford to pay (Sudarmo, 2011).

The situation of numerous unmanaged CULSTTs occupying the area around the FMKSP was used by the P3C to offer cooperation with the royal family and the city government to construct new kiosks at the CBM intended to accommodate the activities around the front yard of the market. Since the new kiosks had already been constructed in 2007, the CULSTTs were imposed to buy kiosks they advertised, but they rejected because they only run their business in the area for no more than three days a week. The HPPK, HPTPPK, and the P3C then proposed a humiliating rule; they argued that the CULSTTs have been conducting some violation in trading since 2000 so that they have to be punished by seizing their commodities. The CULSTTs rejected this decision because the punishment had been decided based on one-sidedness, and did not protect them; even this seemed to be like a robbery instead. The CULSTTs needed fair, open and honest face-to-face dialogue inclusively accommodating their interests, not dialogue with pressure and intimidation because it is unfair and it threatened their survival. However, the CULSTTs' expectation was not met. Soon after all kiosks were sold out and obtained profits of hundreds of million rupiahs, the P3C which is basically consisting of several rich men pretending themselves as market traders suddenly disappeared in early 2008; no street vendor could afford the kiosks. Since the number of CULSTTs occupying the area around the FMKSP from outside Solo gradually increased, the HPPK demanded the city government

to protect their business interest in the Klewer Market. The presence of the non-Solo resident traders was strictly controlled not only by three groups of traders including the HPPK, the HPTPPK and the P3C but also by the city government's apparatuses. Since the Pekalongan textile traders were under pressure by city government of Surakarta they asked the District Legislative Councils of Pekalongan to provide protection for them but the councils were not able to help them. Due to vigorous pressure made by the apparatuses of the city government and the HPPK, the CULSTTs traded their textile beyond the area around the FMKSP. Since their transactions declined, they approached the RFKS to obtain authorization for trading in the Northern Square, about 25 meters away from the Klewer market and the CBM with financial compensation provided for the royal family. Since the CULSTTs have been under the Royal family protection since 2012, apparatuses of city government of Surakarta, the HPPK and the HPTPPK is now unable to control the CULSTTs anymore.

4 IMPLICATIONS

It is evident that where there is dynamics of human interaction there will be disagreements among individuals and groups that may lead them to conflicts (Fidelis and Samuel 2011; Ghaffar, 2009). Conflicts in the area around the FMKSP were driven by 'economic motives' among traders and street vendors (Emanuel and Ndimbwa, 2013; Bukari 2013), and by elites' decisions that did not meet other stakeholders' interests (Asadzadeh, 2016; Bernard and Umar, 2014) because it mainly used top-down approach in decision making; and by elites' inconsistency in making decision (Hegre et al., 2001). This approach ignores the needs of powerless traders and street traders and neglects the creativity of individuals, socioeconomic conditions and available resources (Jones, 2009, Sabatier, 1986; Pissourios, 2014). Since the top down approach is a kind of decision making method without the joint contribution of the public (Cernea, 1992), it might create further conflicts.

Although the CULSTTs or street vendors prefer bottom-up approach to top-down, it is complicated because this approach is unable to deal with the provision and the location of facilities and their implementation becomes difficult because of the large size of population of communities (Pissourios, 2014). The 'bottom up approaches in decision making' was also easily abused by the leader of the HPTPPK who received the mandate from the royal family since 'there was lack of control system' from the city government and the RFKS so that it creates unaccountable behavior'

(Adewale, 2014). The bottom-up approach seems to create inconsistency because decision was based on personal rule where powerless traders with more links are more likely to survive but those who are excluded and those who have fewer networks with the powerful elite, RFKS or city government, are the most vulnerable ones (Sudarmo, 2016). Thus, bottom-up approach still 'produced conflict', and is 'inefficient to resolve the problem impending the beneficial development of the city' (Smith, 2014).

Moreover, since the RFKS recently has provided protection for the CULSTTs, this non-Solo traders' business obviously has threatened the future of local Solo textile traders' survival while the city government has responsibility to keep the survival of the later. Since the Northern Square was claimed as part of culturally preserved materials according to the 1992 Act Number 5, both the CULSTTs and the royal family may be accused of breaking the rule of law in relation to materials of cultural preservation. This law states that all culturally preserved materials are under the State's authority of the Republic of Indonesia and nobody is allowed to change and destroy any original form of the construction and nobody is authorized to sell them for economic purposes whilst the royal family used it for maximizing their self-interest. This potential conflict may change into seriously manifested conflict in the area around the FMKSP in the future if attempts to resolve the problem are lacking and if the unfair resource competition amongst the traders sustains (Emanuel and Ndimbwa, 2013; Bukari 2013).

It is likely that combined transparently top-down and bottom-up decision making approaches that represent collaborative governance is critical for the survival and sustainability of the construction of the FMKSP and any culturally preserved buildings around it because this approach allows all the stakeholders to participate so that they get involved in designing, building and governing their communities with different interests (Brugmann, 2009). Although the implementation of this approach raises complex political decisions together with stable social values and a varied set of socio-economic and environmental opportunity costs (Hull, 2005), it enables all groups to have equal opportunities when it comes to a policy formulation that affects their future (El-asmar, Ebohon and Taki, 2012; Ansell and Gash, 2007).

5 CONCLUSIONS

Powerless parties evidently need a certain public decision making approach beyond the conventional top-down approach or bottom-up approach called conflict resolution based on collaborative governance through authentic dialogue (Sudarmo, 2015). It is the approach that is able to accommodate their interest through authentic dialogue; it is a face-to-face dialogue, open and honest, involving the all stakeholders, i.e. the city government, the aristocratic family, market traders, *renteng* traders, street traders, unorganized illegal occupants and the CULSTTs who are non-local. All of them should be seated in a forum with independent facilitators who have accurate data as a part of their assisting in making a fair public decision transparently.

ACKNOWLEDGEMENT

I would like to express my sincere appreciation to the Indonesian Directorate General of Higher Education, DIKTI 2013–2014 fund research project and the Universitas Sebelas Maret for their supports in this study.

REFERENCES

Adewale, O.H. 2014. Internal Control System: A Managerial Tool For Proper Accountability A Case Study of Nigeria Customs Service. *European Scientific Journal* 10(13): 252–267.

Ansell, C. & Gash, A. 2007, Collaborative Governance in Theory and Practice. *Journal of Public Administration Research and Theory* 18: 543–571.

Asadzadeh, N. 2016. How Coercive and Legitimate Power Relate to Different Conflict Management Styles: A Case Study of Birjand High Schools. *Journal of Studies in Education* 6(1): 147–159.

Barki, H. & Hartwick, J. 2004. Conceptualizing the Construct of Interpersonal Conflict. *International Journal of Conflict Management* 15: 216–44.

Berman, P. 1978. The Study of Macro- and Micro-Implementation. *Public Policy* 26(2): 157–84.

Bernard, E.I. & Umar, U. 2014. Authority, Power, and Conflict in Organization: Analysis of the Impact of Their Functional Relationship In Organization Performance. *European Journal of Business and Management* 6(22): 174–184.

Booher, D.E. 2004. Collaborative Governance Practices and Democracy. *National Civic Review* Winter: 32–46.

Botvinick, M.M., Carter, C.S., Braver, T.S., Barch, D.M. & Cohen, J.D. 2001. Conflict Monitoring and Cognitive Control. *Psychological Review* 108(3): 624–652.

Brugmann, J. 2009. *Welcome to the Urban Revolution: How Cities Are Changing the World.* Bloomsbury Press.

Bukari K.N. 2013. Exploring Indigenous Approaches to Conflict Resolution: The Case of the Bawku Conflict in Ghana. *Journal of Sociological Research* 4(2): 86–104.

Cernea, M.M. 1992. *The Building Blocks of Participation: Testing Bottom-Up Planning,* World Bank Publications.

Coser, L.A. 1956. *The Functions of Social Conflict*. New York: The Free Press.

Chan, S. 1984. Mirror, Mirror, on the Wall … Are the Democratic States More Pacific? *Journal of Conflict Resolution*. 28: 617–648.

Doucey, M. 2011. Understanding The Root Causes of Conflicts: Why It Matters For International Crisis Management, *International Affairs Review* 20: 649–664.

Ebdon, C. 2000. The Relationship between Citizen Involvement in the Budget Process and City Structure and Culture. *Public Productivity and Management Review* 23(3): 383–93.

El-Asmar, J.P., Ebohon, J.O. & Taki, A. 2012. Bottom-up Approach to Sustainable Urban Development in Lebanon: The Case of Zouk Mosbeh. *Sustainable Cities and Society* 2(1): 37–44.

Emanuel, M. & Ndimbwa, T. 2013. Traditional Mechanisms of Resolving Conflicts over Land Resource: A Case of Gorowa Community in Northern Tanzania. *International Journal of Academic Research in Business and Social Sciences* 3(11): 214–224.

Fidelis, P.A.E. & Samuel, E.G. 2011. Colonialism and Political Conflict in Contemporary Nigeria: The case of the Niger Delta. *International Journal of Humanities and Social* 1(6): 276–284.

Gates, S. 1983. The war involvement of democratic regimes. Presented at the annual meeting of the Midwest Political Science Assn.

Ghaffar, A. 2009. Conflict in Schools: Its Causes & Management Strategies. *Journal of Managerial Sciences* 3(2): 212–227.

Hegre, H., Ellingsen, T., Gates, S. & Gleditsch, N.P. 2001. Toward a Democratic Civil Peace? Democracy, Political Change, and Civil War, 1816–1992. *American Political Science Review* 95(1): 33–48.

Hjern, B. & Hull, C. 1982. Implementation Research as Empirical Constitutionalism. *European Journal of Political Research* 10(2): 105–16.

Hjern, B. & Porter, D. 1981. Implementation Structures: A New Unit of Administrative Analysis. *Organization Studies* 2: 211–27.

Hjern, B. 1982. Implementation Research-The Link Gone Missing. *Journal of Public Policy* 2(3): 301–308.

Higashiden, H. & Birley, S. 2002. The consequences of conflict between the venture capitalist and the entrepreneurial team in the United Kingdom from the perspective of the venture capitalist. *Journal of Business Venturing* 17: 59–81.

Hull, A. 2005. Integrated transport planning in the UK: From concept to reality. *Journal of Transport Geography* 13: 318–328.

Jones, L. 2009. Development: Bottom up or Top down? *Geography Review* September: 10–13.

Limapornwanitch, K. & Tanaboriboon, Y. 2003. A Bottom-Up Approach to Implement Transportation Demand Management Measures In Developing Countries: Bangkok. *Journal of the Eastern Asia Society for Transportation Studies* 5: 1829–1844.

Matland, R.E. 1995. Synthesizing the Implementation Literature: The Ambiguity-Conflict Model of Policy Implementation. *Journal of Public Administration Research and Theory: J-PART* 5(2): 145–174.

Mazmanian, D. & Sabatier, P.A. 1983. *Implementation and Public Policy*. Glenview III: Scoot. Foresman.

Michaelsen, T. 1991. Participatory Approach in Watershed Management Planning. *Unasylva Watershed Management* 42(164): 1–15.

Mintz, A. & Geva, N. 1993. Why Don't Democracies Fight Each Other? An Experimental Study. *Journal of Conflict Resolution* 37: 484–503.

O'Brien, M. 2012. Review of Collaborative Governance: Factors crucial to the internal workings of the collaborative process, Research Report prepared for the Ministry for the Environment by Collaborative Governance Research Team under sub-contract to Ecologic, April 2010, Publication Number: CR 135, the Ministry for the Environment, Manatu Te Taiao.

Okotoni, O. & Okotoni, A. 2003. Conflict Management in Secondary Schools in Osun State, Nigeria. *Nordic Journal of African Studies* 12(1): 23–38.

O'Toole, D.E., Marshall, J. & Grewe, T. 1996. Current Local Government Budgeting Practices. *Government Finance Review* 12(6): 25–29.

Pissourios, I.A. 2014. Top-Down and Bottom-Up Urban and Regional Planning: Towards A Framework for the Use of Planning Standards. *European Spatial Research and Policy* 21(1): 83–99.

Pretty, J. & Shah, P. 2000. Soil and Water Conservation: A Brief History of Coercion and Control. In: F. Hinchcliffe, J. Thompson, J.N. Pretty, I. Guijt & P. Shah (eds.), *Fertile ground: The impact of participatory watershed management*: 1–12. London: Intermediate Technology Publications.

Protasel, G.J. 1988. Abandonments of the Council-Manager Plan: A New Institutional Perspective. *Public Administration Review* 48(4): 807–12.

Sabatier, P. 1986. Top-down and Bottom-up Approaches to Implementation Research: A Critical Analysis and Suggested Synthesis. *Journal of Public Policy*. 6(1): 21–48.

Small, M. & Singer, J.D. 1976. The war proneness of democratic regimes, 1816–1965. *Jerusalem Journal of International Relations* 1(4): 50–69.

Smith, N.R. 2014. Beyond Top-Down/Bottom-Up: Village Transformation On China's Urban Edge, URL: http://dx.doi.org/10.1016/j.cities.2014.01.006.

Soltani, A. & Allan, A. 2012. Feasibility of Transport Demand Management Policies through a Bottom-Up Planning Approach. *International Journal of Advances in Applied Sciences* (IJAAS) 1(2): 71–76.

Sudarmo. 2009. Participation Efforts of Solo's Street Vendors in Policy Formulation during the Reform Era but without Results. *Action Learning and Action Research Journal ALAR* 15(1): 107–140.

Sudarmo. 2011. Neo-patrimonial Strategies in the Governance of Solo's Street Trader, *Southeast Asian Journal of Social and Political Issues* 1(1): 5–67.

Sudarmo. 2015. *Menuju Model Resolusi Konflik Berbasis Governance: Memuat pengalaman lapangannkonflik pedagang kaki lima dan konflik antar kelompok*, (Towards A Model of Conflict Resolution based on Governance, It Includes field work experience on governance of street vendors and conflicts among groups), UNS Press, Surakarta.

Sudarmo, S. 2016. Social Capital in Dealing with Neo- Patrimonial Governance of Street Vendors. URL: http://www.atlantis-press.com/php/pub.php?publication=icse-15.

Tiwari, K.R. Bajracharya, R.M. & Sitaula, B.K. 2008. Natural Resource And Watershed Management In South Asia: A Comparative Evaluation With Special References To Nepal. *The Journal of Agriculture and Environment.* 9: 72–89.

Van Meter, Donald S. & Van Horn, C.E. 1975. The Policy Implementation Process: A Conceptual Framework. *Administration and Society* 6(4):445–488.

Vincent, J.E. 1987. Freedom And International Conflict: Another Look. *International Studies Quarterly* 31(1): 103–112.

Wang, X. 2001. Assessing Public Participation in U.S. Cities. *Public Performance Management Review* 24(4): 322–36.

Weede, E. 1984. Democracy and War Involvement. *Journal of Conflict Resolution* 28: 649–664.

Teaching innovations in TVET

Regionalization and Harmonization in TVET – Abdullah et al. (Eds)
© 2017 Taylor & Francis Group, London, ISBN 978-1-138-05419-6

Vocational students entrepreneurial personality analysis through application of self-designed project learning model

A. Hamdani, A. Djohar, B. Darmawan & A. Hadian
Universitas Pendidikan Indonesia, Jawa Barat, Indonesia

ABSTRACT: One of the strategic plans that targeted the Directorate of Vocational, is that graduates of vocational school are capable of entrepreneurship in the field. But in reality it is hard to achieve. The purpose of this study is to find out the effect of self-designed project learning model application on entrepreneurial persona by vocational students in the field of lathe complex machining. The method used is a quasi-experiment that uses the sample group and entrepreneurial personality analyzed before and after treatment. The results showed that insightful learning includes planning the manufacture of the product. Based on the calculation of the average score for entrepreneurial personality, there is an increase. This means that there is an increase preparedness of students to plunge into the entrepreneurial world. The implications of this research through this learning model are that students can portray themselves as workers, gain firsthand experience of a working atmosphere in school, and be able to foster the entrepreneurial spirit.

1 INTRODUCTION

Secondary Vocational Schools (SMK) have a role and a strategic function to prepare learners who are ready to work both independently (self-employed) and fill job vacancies in the industrialized world. This means that vocational students are educated to be workers, and should have the knowledge, skills and attitudes in accordance with industry qualifications (Klotz et al., 2014). To be able to work and compete in industry as well as in self-employment, SMK graduates should have the competence as a requirement to complete a particular job in the world of work. Competence should be the official recognition of a recognized institution. Students in vocational education need to integrate knowledge, skills and attitudes, but there is a parallel need to develop a professional identity (Harmen, 2012).

Special-purpose vocational secondary education according to Law No. 20 of 2003, namely: a) preparing students to become productive human beings, be able to work independently, to fill vacancies that exist as a middle-level manpower in accordance with competence in the skills program chosen; (b) to prepare students to be able to choose a career, tenacious and persistent in competent, adapting the work environment and develop a professional attitude in the field of expertise that interested him; (c) provide students with science, technology and art to be able to develop themselves in the future either independently or through higher levels of education; and

(d) provide students with the competencies corresponding to the selected program expertise. On this basis, it is commonly known that vocational school graduates are expected to fill job vacancies in business and industry. SMK graduates are also able to work independently, in this case entrepreneurship. In order for vocational graduates to have entrepreneurial skills, there is a legal requirement for the curriculum to contain the subjects of entrepreneurship.

Entrepreneurship subjects intend that learners can actualize themselves in entrepreneurial behavior. Entrepreneurship subjects focus on entrepreneurial behavior as empirical phenomena that occur in the environment of the learners. In this regard, more active learners are required to study the economic events that occur in the environment. Entrepreneurial learning can generate entrepreneurial behavior and leadership, which is strongly associated with managing the effort to equip learners to be independent. However, in reality more entrepreneurship subjects providing knowledge of entrepreneurship do not deal with how to grow the desire and ability of student entrepreneurs, because in practice, the subjects of entrepreneurship promote more theories rather than practice.

Based on the preliminary survey conducted in several vocational schools in the city of Bandung, 60% of vocational teachers stated that the implementation of learning entrepreneurship subjects was taught in school, it is time to introduce a new theoretical concept of entrepreneurship. Also, based on a search of vocational graduates, some SMK in Bandung said that almost no graduates take part in a self-employment field which they also took during school. These findings indicate that teaching and learning processes in vocational schools are not effective.

According to research Muhadi et al., 2005), there are several factors that allegedly related to the establishment of entrepreneurship students, among others: (a) the background of the work of parents; (b) the culture of the family; (c) the environmental community; (d) the process of education and training in schools; (e) program membership; and (f) gender and others. Besides oriented work, based on PSMK policies, SMK graduates are required to get involved in entrepreneurship so that they need to be exposed to entrepreneurial personality through self-designed and project-based learning.

2 RESEARCH METHODS

The method used is a quasi-experiment. There is a determined sample of one class. On the condition of prior learning analyzed entrepreneurial personality then given treatment through learning the model selected, and measured entrepreneurial personality. Instruments for the analysis reveal the students' entrepreneurial personality using instruments developed by Enterprise Creating models through Forming Entrepreneurs (Marina, 2013).

3 DISCUSSION

Implementation assessment competency improvement is directed to measure and assess the performance of learners (aspects of knowledge, skills, and attitudes), either directly at the time of learning activities, and indirectly through evidence of learning outcomes (evidence of learning) in accordance with the performance criteria being organized in the form of portfolio. The concept of learning that is designed must meet the elements of competence exploration of students able to meet industrial job competence.

After testing and evaluation of the implementation of the scheme implementation model of learning self-design project is shown in Figure 1.

After all the students have carried out the steps in the learning, then the entrepreneurial persona is measured by using the model through Forming Creating Enterprise Entrepreneurs. There are ten competencies that prospective entrepreneurs need to possess namely entrepreneurial personality. The results of the analysis of the entrepreneurial personality can be seen in the following Figure.

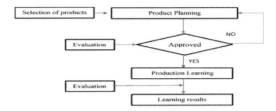

Figure 1. Schematic design self-learning project implementation (Hamdani, 2016).

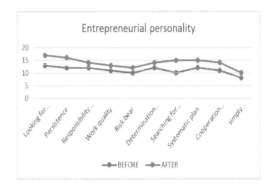

Figure 2. Average entrepreneurial personality.

In step implementation of the learning model based on self-designed project, students are assigned to make the picture work planning products include: 1) The importance of the product to be made; 2) Excellence and functions of the product/service; 3) Sketch/drawing work; 4) Ingredients; 5) Facilities/equipment; 6) The production process (systematic work); 7) Plan budget; 8) Target market/user; and 9) Implementation schedule. Every step of the plan has indicators that are closely related to each competency indicator of entrepreneurial personality. The relationship of both sides of the indicators allows the students to have personal readiness in entrepreneurship.

4 CONCLUSIONS

1. Self-designed project learning model, is one kind of alternative learning that can unlock insights into work, which includes product planning, manufacturing work steps, cost planning, and quality of product control and employment.
2. Increasing the value of the entrepreneurial personality can be achieved through learning to explore the potential of students in both the planning of the product or manufacture of the product so as to stimulate the development of entrepreneurial insight.

REFERENCES

Do Paço, A. & Palinhas, M.J. (2011). Teaching entrepreneurship to children: A case study. *Journal of Vocational Education and Training, 63*(4), 593–608.

Hamdani, A. (2016). *Pengembangan pembelajaran untuk mencapai kompetensi kerja industri siswa sekolah menengah kejuruan, (Disertasi)*, Program Pascasarjana, Univaersitas Pendidikan Indonesia: Bandung.

Harmen, S. (2012). Students' learning processes during school-based learning and workplace learning in vocational education: A review. *Vocations and Learning, 5*(2), 99–117.

Klotz, V.K., Billett, S. & Winther, E. (2014). Promoting workforce excellence: Formation and relevance of vocational identity for vocational educational training. *Empirical Research in Vocational Education and Training, 6*(1), 1–20.

Muhadi, Saptono & Laurentius. (2005). Jiwa kewirausahaan siswa smk: suatu survey pada 3 smk negeri dan 7 smk swasta di DIY. *Indonesian Scientific Journal Database, 16*(1), 15–28.

Marina, Z.S. (2013). Entrepreneurial motivations and intentions: Investigating the role of education major. *Education + Training, 55*(3), 253–271.

Undang-Undang Republik Indonesia Nomor 20 Tahun 2003 Tentang Sistem Pendidikan Nasional.

Teaching factory development model to improve the productive capability of vocational education students

A. Sutopo, A. Rahman & D. Mulyana
Universitas Negeri Medan, Medan, Indonesia

ABSTRACT: Teaching Factory is one of the activities in vocational education to produce products that are managed by teachers and students. The main function of Teaching Factory is: to improve student skills and knowledge in the real job conditions, can substitute industries for being a place for industrial practices and entrepreneurship. The purpose developing Teaching Factory is to increase productive competence abilities of students and school income generation. The productive competence of the students is reflected in the students' ability to finish a job and soft skills. Income generation is intended to supplement school operating expenses and improve the welfare of teachers and schools. The research results showed that the teaching factory development model implemented is based on: 1) oriented to the consumer needs, 2) human resources capabilities, 3) infrastructure and equipment effectiveness, 4) project-based learning and productive development, 5) increased students' ability through training, and 6) development of marketing through print and electronic media.

1 INTRODUCTION

The National Employment census 2007 stated that only five percent of the Indonesian labor force are interested in entrepreneurship (Purna et al., 2016). This is a problem for the SMK graduates. In the meantime, the ratio of SMK graduates is encouraged to reach 70:30 in 2015 (Dikmenjur, 2007). Thus, the activities of vocational education should also be directed so that graduates are capable of entrepreneurship through the program production unit.

Implementation and development of the vocational school is based on the philosophies essentialism, existentialism and pragmatism. Constructivism views that knowledge is not about the world, but rather 'constitutive' of the world. Knowledge is not a fixed object; it is 'constructed by an individual through her own experience of that object' (Hsiao & Lin, 2010). This theory states that the knowledge and skills are obtained through the integration between the transformation and grasping experience.

Vocational education functions as well as a learning center, a business center and business development for the community (Dikdasmen, 2005). It can be done by establishing production units as a means of learning, entrepreneurship and other operating expenses of the school (Direktorat Pembinaan SMK, 2007).

Development of production units uses the theory of workplace learning, situated cognition and constructivism (Engeström & Gröhn; Hsiao & Lin, 2010; Kolb et al., 1999). The actual experience is important in the development of knowledge and skills of students.

Based on the concept of situated cognition, situated learning and experiential learning above, the Teaching Factory in vocational education needed to improve the quality of teaching and learning. Thus, students can learn about real conditions, working in teams, finding and serving the consumer, carrying out activities of production results and market discipline, training, the intensity of student learning and being able to evaluate the quality of the product.

2 RESEARCH METHOD

This research is research development with mix method model. Data collection is using the instrument's observations, inventory, and interview. Data analysis is using the logical framework analysis.

3 RESULTS

The results of research development Teaching Factory model are as follows:

3.1 *Development model of teaching factory*

The implementation of unit development production was done with the following steps:

1. Identified the ability of science knowledge and skills of students and teachers productive in vocational education.
2. Identified community needs against products and services.
3. Identified the availability and adequacy of the school's facilities and infrastructure to be able to carry out activities of teaching factory.

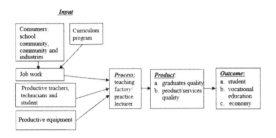

Figure 1. The scheme teaching factory model.

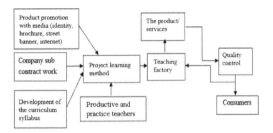

Figure 2. The implementation of scheme Teaching Factory activities.

4. Planned a project-based learning to produce goods/services.
5. Trained students in accordance to specifications expertise in dealing with the possibilities of the problem in the Teaching Factory.
6. Development marketing unit production by developing a media marketing such as bro-chures, banners and more.

Model development of teaching factory is as illustrated in Figures 1 and 2.

3.2 The productive ability of vocational education students

The productive ability of students' educational vocational in the implementation of production units is the ability of hard skills (average value 77.2) and the ability of soft skill-related team work, communication skills, and interpersonal relationship as shown in Table 1.

4 DISCUSSION

Success in the development of the Teaching Factory model in vocational education is indicated by the availability of the following factors: a) the human resources professional, b) means the appropriate infrastructure, and c) results of the marketing product/service. Human resources professionals are associated with the ability to manage and carry out activities of the Teaching Factory. Infrastructure is related to suitability to

Table 1. The ability of soft skill students' executive production units.

No	Aspect	Indicators	Results
1	Communication skills	able to discuss, give opinions and ask questions	Students are able to cooperate well in completing the work, such as in the face of difficulties which cannot be solved yourself then not hesitating to discuss with friends and the teacher's Companion
2	Ability in team work	cooperation in a team in the work	Students are able to conduct cooperation with team in solving problems and finishing the job with a division of tasks and in completing the work
3	Commitment in work	are serious about completing the work	Students trying to finish the job until it is done and as quickly as possible by making use of free time
4	Time management	management of the time, using time effectively	Students are able to do the job in earnest so that it can be completed according to target or consumer needs
5	Leadership	encourage friends to participate actively, helping friends resolve issues	Students' ability in finding friends who can be invited to carry out the activities of the production units and the ability to set the time of activity
6	Creative thinking	find new method to solve the problem	Indication of creativity thinking of students is to find ways of how to find and fix damage to tools/goods
7	Management of stress	manage stress	Yet it appears to be the result because for existing students the job does not have pressures because students feel no difficulty

exercise the process of production. Marketing is very important as it is related to the circulation of products/services produced, so that failure in marketing can make the production process stop. In addition, the ability to market products and services through media such as brochures, banners, and internet is important in order to get noticed.

The ability of teachers in making learning activity design in the form of production became important in integrating between learning activities based on curriculum reference (syllabus) and production activities. A project method was used in teaching activities of the Teaching Factory with the aim of enabling students to become active, independent and responsible in completing the appropriate product/service standards. This is in accordance with the theory of experience learning (Kolb et al., 1999), work place theory (Lin Hsio, 2010) and constructivism philosophy (Engeström & Gröhn, 2004).

Cooperation with industry can be done at the internship program so that Teaching Factory can be promoted together with the production partners. Student success in the activity of production units appears on productive upgrades as well as the cultivation of the students' entrepreneurial soul, because students with mentoring teachers engage fully in the activities of the production process/service, thus providing a real learning experience.

A production system with accompaniment and control by the teacher in the activity of production units is able to produce the product/service standards of consumer products. This indicates that the productive capability of the students becomes better. The results of the production process cannot be separated between discipline, teamwork, time management, creativity, communication with friends and companions, stress management and motivation to produce the best product/service. Based on the Teaching Factory activities that are able to produce the product/service standards, consumers will produce graduates who have the ability of productive, soft skills and entrepreneurial soul.

5 CONCLUSION

Development of Teaching Factory model is adjusted to the capabilities of human resources and infrastructure. Implementation of the activities of the production/service can be done by students with teacher mentoring. Products/services produced students in accordance with the standards that are expected of the consumer. The teaching activities of the factory were able to increase the productive ability and the ability of the soft skills of students. Production Activities in Teaching Learning project using model Factory. Last but not least, it is also dependent upon marketing media used such as brochures, banners, and internet.

REFERENCES

Direktorat Pembinaan SMK. (2007). *Panduan pelaksanaan th 2007, imbal swadaya smk model*. Jakarta: Direktorat Pembinaan SMK Direktorat Jenderal Manajemen Pendidikan Dasar dan Menengah Departemen Pendidikan Nasional.

Engeström, E. & Gröhn, G. (2004). *Workplace learning and developmental transfer*. Diambil pada tanggal 28 Juni 2010 dari www.edu.helsinki.fi/behav/english/index.html.

Hsiao, H. & Lin, W. D. (2010). *CSCL Theories*. Diambil pada tanggal 12 juni 2011 dari http://www.edb.utexas.edu/cscl/Dhsiao/theories.html.

Kolb, D. A, Boyatziz, R. E. & Mainemelis, C. (1999). *Experintial learning theory: Previous research and new direction*. Diambil pada tanggal 8 Agustus 2009 dari http://www.d.umn.edu/~kgilbert/educ5165–731/Readings/experiential-learning-theory.pdf.

Pendidikan Dasar dan Menengah. (2005). *Garis-garis besar program pendidikan menengah kejuruan*. Jakarta. Direktorat Pembinaan SMK Direktorat Jenderal Manajemen Pendidikan Dasar dan Menengah: Depdiknas.

Pendidikan Menengah Kejuruan. (2007). *Panduan pelaksanaan tahun 2007, imbal swadaya smk model*. Jakarta: Direktorat Pembinaan SMK Direktorat Jenderal Manajemen Pendidikan Dasar dan Menengah Departemen Pendidikan Nasional.

Purna, I., Hamidi, H. & Prima, P. (2010). *Mengharmonisasikan Tenaga Kerja dan Pendidikan di Indonesia*. Kamis, 14 Januari 2010.

Regionalization and Harmonization in TVET – Abdullah et al. (Eds)
© 2017 Taylor & Francis Group, London, ISBN 978-1-138-05419-6

The socio-cultural learning in an Indonesian Polytechnic

A. Abduh
Universitas Negeri Makassar, Indonesia

R. Rosmaladewi
Politeknik Pertanian Negeri Pangkajene Kepulauan, Indonesia

ABSTRACT: Research on the socio-cultural has been conducted extensively in higher education in Western contexts. However, few studies have been focused on learning in vocational higher education in Indonesia. This paper aims to address this knowledge gap. This is an in-depth descriptive qualitative study of six lecturers in an Indonesian polytechnic using semi-structure interviews. The finding reveals that there is an integrated socio-cultural learning cycle applied by lecturers in this polytechnic. This research suggests that theoretical, observational, and practice-based learning are implemented as a learning-continuum. This finding provides a unique contribution and significance to the debates on the socio-cultural learning cycle, both locally and globally.

1 INTRODUCTION

The socio-cultural learning practice has been widely acknowledged and investigated. Socio-cultural learning assists learners to integrate face-to-face interaction in the classroom and wider social community contexts (Renshaw, 1992), bridge socio-cultural and cognitive theorizing in situated learning (Billet, 1996), and facilitate the mastery of specific content in particular contexts (John-Steiner & Mahn, 1996). For these reasons, socio-cultural learning is fundamentally important for lecturers and educators.

Socio-cultural learning refers to 'a process of appropriating "tools for thinking", that are made available by social agents who initially act as interpreters and guides in the individual's cultural apprenticeship' (Rogoff cited in Renshaw, 1992, p. 2). Vygotsky (1978) argues that learners learn best through interaction with their environment. This indicates that learners can acquire knowledge and skills through their engagement with particular socio-cultural contexts. For the context of this study, students not only learn in their campus environment, but they also learn through interaction with peers and engagement with people in their workplace.

The socio-cultural learning in the Indonesian context has not developed much. Studies on socio-cultural learning have mostly focused on cultural and economic perspectives of learning of entrepreneurial intention among Indonesian students (Kristiansen & Indarti, 2004), independent language teaching (Lamb, 2004), and empowering learning through informal education (Kindervatter, 1979). None of studies above has focused primarily on the integration of theoretical, nor observational and practiced-based learning, as part of socio-cultural learning perspectives. This research addresses the above gap and contributes to the understanding of how Indonesian polytechnics apply socio-cultural learning in their teaching practice. This research is significant for teachers and educators to help them perform better practice.

2 SOCIO-CULTURAL LEARNING

The socio-cultural learning involves key elements including theoretical input, interaction, collaboration and learning in the workplace, through problem solving and thinking processes (Renshaw, 1992). Karpov and Bransford (1995, p. 61) define theoretical learning as 'a process of supplying the student with general and optimal methods for dealing with certain classes of problems that direct him or her toward essential (not simply common) characteristics of the problems of each class'. A recent study conducted in United States of America school settings suggested that theoretical learning refers to explanatory and descriptive designs of learning that aim to enhance students' academic achievements (Lancer, 2014). This indicates that theoretical learning is a process of constructing student's theoretical knowledge within classroom contexts that aims to improve their learning outcomes.

In terms of observation, a number of researchers indicated that observation is useful to improve subject understanding (Hoover et al., 2012; Renkl, 2014). Observation learning refers to students' abilities to observe other people's behaviors in a variety of academic areas in groups (Bandura & Jeffrey, 1973; Renkl, 2014). Research conducted by Hoover et al. (2012, p. 591) on understanding the benefit of observational learning suggested:

"They [students] benefit from selective observation and the lack of potential distractions produced by behavioral immersion that could confound attentional focus. They suggested that some students engage in role-play simulations, while others observe vicariously."

In relation to the practice-based model, it is a learning process in 'environments in which the knowledge learnt in universities can be practised, refined and honed' (Kennedy et al., 2015, p. 2). Practice-based learning is often associated with different terms: it is a workplace learning because students learn in industrial settings (Kennedy et al., 2015); it is a situated learning (Lave & Wenger, 1991) because students learn in specific programs such as internship programs and work experience placements (Lim et al., 2014); and it is empirical learning (Karpov & Bransford, 1995) because students can provide and confirm authentic experience to their study when dealing with practice setting (Billett, 1996). This implies that practice-based learning is a learning process that occurs in a particular context that aims to provide students with work-related experiences.

3 METHODOLOGY

Descriptive qualitative research was employed in this study. Descriptive qualitative studies relate to 'a comprehensive summary of events in the everyday terms of those events. Researchers conducting qualitative descriptive studies stay close to their data and to the surface of words and events' (Sandelowski, 2000, p. 334). This qualitative study is appropriate to meanings of particular events and activity that occur both inside and outside classrooms (Jensen & Curtis, 2008). In this study, the events occur both inside and outside classroom contexts, where a combination of learning occurs in campus and workplaces.

Data collection method was mainly semi-structure interviews, which lasted between 45 minutes and 1 hour. The interviews were conducted in Indonesian, and the transcriptions were translated into English by a researcher and verified by a competent bilingual researcher and translator. All transcriptions of interviews were sent back to participants in order to provide opportunities for participants to modify and add their comments. The contents of interviews include beliefs and perceptions of learning in a polytechnic.

The participants of this study comprised of six lecturers, three females and three males, with Masters' educational background. Their ages were from 35 to 60. The participants' teaching experiences: 2 were less than 10 years, 2 were about 20 years and 2 were more than twenty years. The participants were coded in P1 (participant one), P2, P3, P4, P5 and P6 respectively. Data was analyzed using thematic analysis procedures (Braun & Clarke, 2006): reading whole data, identifying themes, classifying themes, and identifying core themes.

4 FINDINGS

4.1 Theoretical learning

Most participants in this study argue that theoretical learning is one of the key important elements for their learning. As Karpov and Bransford (1995) suggest, theoretical learning relates to providing optimum input for students. Providing input including concepts and strategies is the first foundational step for learning to master subject matter.

For students in this polytechnic, engagement with key concepts and their characteristics helps to build their knowledge and skills prior to observational and practice learning. There are three important strategies to assists learners get an in-depth understanding of subjects: classroom learning, learners' interaction with peers, and own learning. One lecturer indicates that 'They have to have good understanding of concept through classroom teaching, independent learning and learning through interactions with friends' (P6), and that 'learning is done through videos, tutorial, lecture, and demonstrations' (P2).

The reason why classroom learning is important is due to 'the large number of students enrolled in subject; therefore it is easier to lace them together in a large classroom' (P5). While interaction with peers is done 'through series of structured projects given students conducted in groups of four to six' (P1). In addition, independent learning is done through their 'students' journal of learning' (P4).

Another reason for providing theoretical learning is that 'building good foundation is important so that they can perform better job later' (P2). Another participant stated: 'They [students] have to master theory very well prior to observation and practice' (P3). In this case, students are expected to have solid background knowledge of theoretical concepts prior to proceeding to the following stage, which is observational and practice-based learning.

4.2 Observational learning

Lecturers in this polytechnic aim to bridge students' understanding of theory and practice via observational learning. What they believe important is that students can not directly practice what they have learnt in classroom contexts, but they have to perform structured observation to the subject of their learning. Students have to observe their senior students, lecturers and practitioners. One participant argues that 'every student must have seen the real life of what she or he learns' (P1). By seeing the real-life event, they cognitively perceived the subjects.

There are two important reasons why observational learning is part of their essential element of learning. The first is due to 'students in this polytechnic deal with human' (P3), and the second is 'students have to avoid malpractice or error when they perform real activities' (P4). It indicates that students have to put in their effort to fully understand, for example, how to deal with patients. A student midwife has to observe carefully what the midwife does during the labor.

During the observation, students have to follow several steps: Firstly, students must do structured observation carefully: 'students have to observe carefully before they practice it' (P2). Secondly, students have to write their observational learning via log book: 'They have series of log book from observations' (P5). Thirdly, at the end of their observation, students discuss with each other what they have witnessed and what they have learnt, what went wrong and what were the good points: 'Only after observation, they shared notes with others so that they share and learn from each other' (P3). Finally, all students have to submit their final report of their observational learning to their lecturers: 'all of them have to submit their written report' (P6). During the writing for their report, students consolidate their learning through their observational learning. The observational learning ends when students are fully confident in performing practice learning.

4.3 Practice-based learning

Practiced-based learning refers to the experience of students in the workplace (Kennedy et al., 2015), and learning through internship programs (Lim et al., 2014). Most students at this polytechnic perform their practice learning in the workplace and few of the students through internship programs. Their practice-based learning is supervised by both lecturers and employees in the industry workplace where the practice learning occurs.

The reason why practice-based learning contributes to students is that practice-based learning helps students to connect and build network with industry. One lecturer indicates that 'practice based learning help students to get to know who industry stakeholders are' (P6). In addition, practiced-based learning assists students to build their confidence in their learning, as argued by one lecturer: 'it is important for students to build their confidence' (P1). In addition, students can consolidate their knowledge and their skills through understanding the workplace culture: 'they can improve their knowledge and skills in relation to the culture of workplace' (P3). Finally, practice-based learning facilitates the overarching understanding of the subject matter: 'No-body's perfect, but through a series of practiced based learning they will be able to master it' (P4). For these reasons, practice-based learning becomes one of the important learning elements that is embedded in this polytechnic.

5 DISCUSSION

The analysis of the data shows that the findings were different from earlier studies because previous research focused separately on theoretical, observational, and practice-based learning. For example, Karpov and Bransford (1995) and Lancer (2014) concentrated primarily on theoretical and practical learning; Bandura and Jeffrey (1973), Hoover et al. (2012) and Renkl (2014) focused on observational learning; and Kennedy et al. (2015) and Lim et al. (2014) centered on practice-based learning. While this study identified that theoretical, observational and practiced-based learning were implemented and integrated in sequence. The integration of the three concepts formed a learning cycle. This cycle expands what Hollins (2011) described as the socio-cultural learning. The reason why we call it an expanded socio-cultural learning cycle is that it involves cognitive, behavior and socio-cultural settings (Hollins, 2011). In our findings, the theoretical phase involved the cognitive process which was the learning of concepts. The behavior was depicted in the observational learning cycle. The socio-cultural elements are embedded in practiced-based learning because learners gain direct experience in industry.

These learning cycles have implications for lecturers and students. For lecturers, they were required to master both theoretical knowledge and practical skills in order to be able to deliver effective learning in polytechnic settings. For students, the combination of the theoretical, observational and practical learning assisted them to develop competence in their field of study. We believe that these learning cultures are applied in this polytechnic.

6 CONCLUSION

Despite a small-scale study, the finding of this research provides further understanding of theoretical, observational, and practical (empirical) learning. These elements of learning notions extend understanding of theoretical and practical learning (Karpov & Bransford, 1995) and observational learning (Renkl, 2014). These three stages of learning offer opportunities for students to master theory, further observe how theory works, and gain practical skills in the field. This indicates that the three cycles of learning offer a continuum which is an holistic and overarching approach to learning.

The implication for this finding is that lecturers and educators can apply this finding to help them perform better practice. Thus, this finding is significant for policy makers and educational stakeholders, particularly in relation to polytechnics, so that they can provide appropriate policy and assistance. Thus, this can improve the standard quality of output in polytechnics in particular, and higher education in general. Finally, this finding can be useful for similar settings, in both local and global contexts.

REFERENCES

Bandura, A. & Jeffrey, R.W. (1973). Role of symbolic coding and rehearsal processes in observational learning. *Journal of Personality and Social Psychology*, 26(1), 122.

Braun, V. & Clarke, V. (2006). Using thematic analysis in psychology. *Qualitative Research in Psychology*, 3(2), 77–101.

Billett, S. (1996). Situated learning: Bridging sociocultural and cognitive theorising. *Learning and Instruction*, 6(3), 263–280.

Hollins, E.R. (2011). Teacher preparation for quality teaching. *Journal of Teacher Education*, 62(4), 395–407.

Hoover, J.D., Giambatista, R.C. & Belkin, L.Y. (2012). Eyes on, hands on: Vicarious observational learning as an enhancement of direct experience. *Academy of Management Learning & Education*, 11(4), 591–608.

Jensen, A. & Curtis, M. (2008). A descriptive qualitative study of student learning in a psychosocial nursing class infused with art, literature, music, and film. *International Journal of Nursing Education Scholarship*, 5(1), 1–9.

John-Steiner, V. & Mahn, H. (1996). Sociocultural approaches to learning and development: A Vygotskian framework. *Educational psychologist, 31*(3–4), 191–206.

Karpov, Y.V. & Bransford, J.D. (1995). LS Vygotsky and the doctrine of empirical and theoretical learning. *Educational Psychologist*, 30(2), 61–66.

Kristiansen, S. & Indarti, N. (2004). Entrepreneurial intention among Indonesian and Norwegian students. *Journal of Enterprising Culture, 12*(01), 55–78.

Kindervatter, S. (1979). *Nonformal education as an empowering process with case studies from Indonesia and Thailand.* Amherst, Mass: Center for International Education, University of Massachusetts.

Kennedy, M., Billett, S., Gherardi, S. & Grealish, L. (2015). *Practice-based learning in higher education: Jostling cultures.* New York: Springer.

Lamb, M. (2004). It depends on the students themselves: Independent language learning at an Indonesian state school. *Language, Culture and Education, 17*(3), 229–245.

Lancer, J.R. (2014). The meaning of quality professional learning for school improvement: Articulating a coherent vision rooted in a theoretical perspective on learning. *School Effectiveness and School Improvement (ahead-of-print)*, 1–29.

Lave, J. & Wenger, E. (1991). *Situated learning: Legitimate peripheral participation*: Cambridge University Press.

Lim, C., Chin, L. & Kuek, M. (2014). Unlocking the value of practical learning. *International Committee for University Museums and Collections (UMAC) Proceedings* 6.

Price, B. (2001). Enquiry-based learning: An introductory guide. *Nursing Standard*, 15(52), 45–52.

Renshaw, P. (1992). The sociocultural theory of teaching and learning: Implications for the curriculum in the Australian context. *Annual Conference of the Australian Association for Research in Education*, Deakin University, Geelong, Victoria.

Renkl, A. (2014). Toward an instructionally oriented theory of example-based learning. *Cognitive Science, 38*(1), 1–37.

Sandelowski, M. (2000). Focus on research methods-whatever happened to qualitative description? *Research in Nursing and Health*, 23(4), 334–340.

Schmeck, R.R. (2013). *Learning strategies and learning styles*. Springer Science & Business Media.

Vygotsky, L. (1978). *Mind in society: The psychology of higher mental functions.* Cambridge, Mass: Harvard University Press.

Regionalization and Harmonization in TVET – Abdullah et al. (Eds)
© 2017 Taylor & Francis Group, London, ISBN 978-1-138-05419-6

The development of an android-based English vocabulary introduction education game for early childhood

A.B. Utomo, G.D. Robbani & S. Nurmasitah
Faculty of Engineering, Universitas Negeri Semarang, Semarang, Central Java, Indonesia

ABSTRACT: Early childhood education is an effort to develop newly born children until they reach six years of age. Cognitive behavioral, social, emotional, self-reliance, moral values of religion, and language are some aspects of development at this education level. The process of language learning should be intensive and maximal because they have fast-growing language skills. Moreover, the globalization era expects English to be taught at the early childhood education level. Interactive mobile games in smartphone devices can be selected as an alternative media for children language learning. This research develops an android-based education game for early childhood to introduce English vocabulary. Two material and three media experts evaluated the function and feasibility of the developed media. The implementation of the media was done in an experimental class and then compared to the control class. The feasibility of media and material are 84.52% and 83.33%. The different level of vocabulary mastery in the experimental class is 43.68% compared to the control class. It means that the media significantly supports the learning process.

1 INTRODUCTION

In Indonesia, early childhood education is an effort from the government to develop newly born children until they reach six-years-old. Education stimulation is given to support children's mental and physical growth and development in order to have the readiness to enter further education level (Law No. 20 of 2003). Cognitive behavioral, social, emotional, self-reliance, moral values of religion, and language are some aspects of development in early childhood education.

In early childhood, language needs to be developed because it cannot be separated from the social life. Language is a means of communication to express ideas and knowledge between people. Because of that reason, learning language should be started from early childhood through formal or informal education. Perizade and Suhery (2012) said that kindergarten (TK) or Raudhatul Athfal (RA) is an example of formal early childhood education. Moreover, they also said that play group (KB), child care (TPA), and other similar education formats at the same level are examples of informal early childhood education.

Seefeldt and Wasik (2007) indicated that the language development of three- to five- year-old children is growing very fast. They have already mastered 900 to 8,000 words. There are three scopes of early childhood language development; they are accepting language, revealing language, and literacy. At that age, the children are taught to listen, know the vocabulary, understand the story, express the idea, duplicate the letters, and recognize their surroundings (Rule of Education Ministry No. 58 of 2009).

Learning a second and foreign language has been an important part of the education process. Gass (2013) stated that second language acquisition is the process of learning another language after the native language has been learned. Foreign language learning is different from second language learning. It is most commonly done within the context of the classroom. The second language of the children in Indonesia is Bahasa Indonesia. Bahasa Indonesia acquisition is obtained from the child's environment of life and from school. While English and other languages, such as Japanese, French, Spanish, and Chinese, are the foreign languages for Indonesian people.

From early childhood, English is learned in order to have English skills ability, so they can follow science and technology development. However, the teacher delivers the material using simple media, such as a paper flashcard image, which is less interesting for the students. Children will be more interested in learning if the media is interesting and fun. Because of that reason, teachers should use or provide interesting media for learning, especially when learning language. Learning media is used to convey instructional information and for teaching purposes. Learning using audio-visual is one of the important aspects in the education system. The learning process will be easy, attractive and effective when using audio-visual media (Bal-Gezegin, 2014).

Mobile learning (M-Learning) is one of the audio-visual learning processes that are performed by using a mobile media device (Mehdipour & Zerehkafi, 2013). The learner can learn anywhere and anytime using mobile devices (Crescente & Lee, 2011). A mobile game is an example of M-Learning which is currently developed. It is applied to a smartphone or mobile phone device. In education, mobile games not only stimulate children's interest in learning but also encourage and promote the development of language, critical thinking, emotional development, intelligence and imagination in children. Therefore, education games have an important role to develop children in their play activities (Ni & Yu, 2015). One of the platforms used for developing M-Learning is the Android operating system. The aim of this research is to develop an android-based education game for early childhood to introduce English vocabulary.

Android is an open-source software stack which includes an operating system, middleware and key applications along with a set of Application Programming Interfaces (APIs) that are used to design a mobile application using the Java programming language. Android-based applications can be created, developed independently, easily downloaded, and used in accordance with the user's needs. Android has Linux-based version 2.6. system services such as security, memory management and process management, controlled by Linux (Holla & Katti, 2012).

2 METHOD

The method used in this research is the R&D for developing the education games, while the implementation of the education game in English class in kindergarten uses a quasi-experimental design; the post-test only controls group design.

The process of developing an educational game includes: map-making the material, flow charts, activity diagram, and layout design of the game, which is then processed by using Audacity, CorelDraw, and Adobe Flash CS6 X7 software. Then the results of the educational game are tested for the feasibility of the media and material aspects. The feasibility testing of media and material aspects is based on ISO 9126 and the multimedia quality criteria. The tested education game is revised and improved, and then tested before it is implemented. The stages of the education game development process can be seen in Figure 1.

The purpose of map-making the material is to facilitate the grouping of material in the product creation process of the educational game application. There are two themes, six sub-themes and 24 vocabularies that are incorporated into the education game, which is the introduction of English vocabulary.

Figure 1. The stages of education game development process.

The main menu of the game has four menu buttons: Learn, Let's Play, Hints, and Exit. The 'Learn' menu is for learning the English vocabulary process. Children can learn 24 kinds of English vocabulary in accordance with the themes in the education game. The 'Let's play' menu has three types of games: matching games, puzzle games and guess-the-picture. These three types of the game use the drag and drop concept, moving an object to a predetermined place. If the object is in the correct place, it will proceed to the next level. The 'Hints' menu contains the instructions regarding the usage of applications, and the 'exit' menu is for exiting the applications. The education game application has an easy-to-use design for the children. There are sound and back buttons in each page menu. The sound button is used to turn on and turn off the sound. The back button is for returning to the previous page.

The implementation process was in TK Islam Al Furqon Rembang, using a quasi-experimental method. The experimental design used in this research is the design of experiment Post-test Only Control Design. This quasi-experimental method used a group or class that was used as the experimental group and the control group. The experimental class was treated using the education game application as a media of learning, while the control group did not get the similar treatment. The homogeneity of the control class and experimental class before the learning process is assumed to be equal (zero) because the children had not been taught the same vocabulary in English language learning materials beforehand. Then both classes were given a post-test to determine the level of mastery of the English vocabulary. The post-test is an oral test that relates to the learned vocabulary.

Purposive sampling is used in this research. The consideration for determining the sample in this study is that the sample has the same capabilities and characteristics. The population of this study was 76 six-year-old children. They were divided into five classes (B1–B5). There were 29 children for each control class and experimental class (B1–B4). The determination of control class and experimental class was conducted by a coin toss. The rest of the other children were treated as the initial test responder of the education game.

The data collection technique in this research includes observation, interviews, questionnaires and oral test. The data analysis includes descriptive analysis results of the questionnaire, normality test, homogeneity, independent sample t-test, and the calculation of the difference level of English vocabulary mastery percentage. The normality, homogeneity, and difference test use SPSS version 23. The requirement of normality and homogeneity tests is if p-value or significance value (.sig) is greater than the significance level (α) of 5% (.sig > 0.05), it can be concluded that the data is normally distributed. Moreover, the data variants of the control class and experimental class are similar. While in a different test, if the p-value or significance value (.sig) is smaller than the significance level (α) of 5% (.sig < 0.05), it can be concluded that there are differences in the level of mastery of the English vocabulary between the control class and experimental class.

3 RESULT AND DISCUSSION

By playing the education game, children can learn 24 kinds of English vocabulary with the specific themes. This application provides fun-learning for children with its images and activities. There are several images that belong to each theme. Children can hear or listen to the pronunciation of the object when they touch the image. Moreover, they can do some activities through several games in this application, such as: matching game, puzzle game, and guess-the-picture game. In matching game, children should match the similar object. It trains the children in recognizing some object images. While in the puzzle game, children will arrange a puzzled object image. To check the children's memorizing skill, they can play a guess-the-picture game. In this game, children should guess the object image by arranging letters. Some screenshots of the education game layout can be seen in Figure 2.

The media and material of the education game were tested by the experts: two media experts and three material experts. The media experts tested

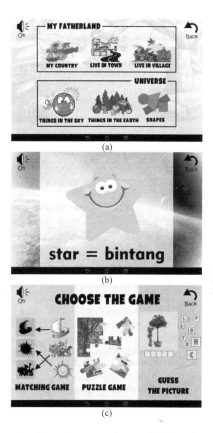

Figure 2. Education game layout (a) "learn" menu; (b) one of learned vocabulary; (c) "game" menu.

the efficiency, usability, reliability, and portability aspects for the media. While for the material test, it consisted of learning, media layout, content, and program aspects. The experts did the evaluation by filling in the questionnaire.

The evaluation result can be seen in Table 1 and Table 2. Both of the tests got a very good result. The usability and program aspects reached the highest score for both media and material tests. The use of the audio-visual concept was easy to understand by the users. So, this applied education game is good to be the alternative learning media in the early childhood education process, especially in learning English.

The education game was implemented in the learning process in the experimental class. While in the control class, the children were treated using a common method of learning. From 24 learned vocabularies, the children in the control class can master 9.55 words per child on average. The result in the experimental class shows that the children mastered 13.72 words per child on average. The difference level of English vocabulary mastery, can statistically be proved by using a different test after normality and homogeneity tests. The result

Table 1. Media test result.

Aspect	Percentage (%)	Category
Efficiency	85.71%	Very Good
Usability	87.50%	Very Good
Reliability	80.00%	Good
Portability	84.38%	Very Good
Average	84.52%	Very Good

Table 2. Material test result.

Aspect	Percentage (%)	Category
Learning	83.33%	Very Good
Media Layout	77.08%	Good
Content	80.56%	Good
Program	90.00%	Very Good
Average	83.33%	Very Good

of normality post-test in the experimental class and control class is that both of the classes have normal distribution. Moreover, both of the classes also have similar variants and homogenies. The different test analysis result shows that the p-value of 0.012 is smaller than a predetermined significance level which is equal to 0.05, so it can be concluded from the results of different test analysis that there are significant differences regarding the mastery of vocabulary between the experimental class and control class. The magnitude of differences in levels of English vocabulary mastery in the experimental class and control class is 43.68%.

The introduction of the English vocabulary education game attracts the attention of the children in learning to improve the mastery of vocabulary. The result of the oral test vocabulary mastery in the experimental class earns a higher average than the control class. It is also reinforced by the record results of observation, interviews and documentation during the process of the research. The children became more enthusiastic in the learning process when they used an education game.

There are some words that still cannot be mastered by the children in the control class and experimental class. Some vocabulary that is difficult to master by children are: traffic light, mountain, square and triangle. The children still find it difficult to master vocabulary that consists of more than one word, like traffic light. It is because of the very limited English language skills of the children. They find it so difficult to master the vocabulary, although assisted by the education game that has been developed. Another vocabulary which still cannot be mastered by the children is that which has two vowels appearing together such as mountain, square, and triangle. In English learning, it is called a diphthong. Pronunciation of words

containing the diphthong is different from writing so that the children have difficulty in spelling the word. Learning about the words that contain the diphthong needs to be done repeatedly so that children can master these words.

4 CONCLUSION

The introduction of an English vocabulary android-based education game with audio-visual for early childhood is eligible for use for early childhood learning media after the test on the media and material by the experts. The results of the media and material tests are 84.52% and 83.33%, with very good category. There are significant differences regarding the vocabulary mastery if the children use the education game. The different level of English vocabulary mastery in the experimental class is 43.68%, compared to the class that uses conventional learning. The use of a smartphone for the learning process has some advantages, such as: it is interactive, can be used everywhere and anytime, and it is an integration of image, animation, graphic, sound and text.

REFERENCES

Bal-Gezegin, B. (2014). An investigation of using video vs. audio for teaching vocabulary. *Procedia-Social and Behavioral Sciences*, *143*, 450–457.

Crescente, M.L. & Lee, D. (2011). Critical issues of m-learning: design models, adoption processes, and future trends. *Journal of the Chinese Institute of Industrial Engineers*, *28*(2), 111–123.

Gass, S.M. (2013). *Second language acquisition: An introductory course*. Routledge.

Holla, S. & Katti, M.M. (2012). Android based mobile application development and its security. *International Journal of Computer Trends and Technology*, *3*(3), 486–490.

Indonesia, P.R. (2003). Undang-Undang Republik Indonesia Nomor 20 Tahun 2003 Tentang Sistem Pendidikan Nasional.

Mehdipour, Y. & Zerehkafi, H. (2013). Mobile learning for education: Benefits and challenges. *International Journal of Computational Engineering Research*, *3*(6), 93–101.

Ni, Q. & Yu, Y. (2015). Research on educational mobile games and the effect it has on the cognitive development of preschool children. *Digital Information, Networking, and Wireless Communications (DINWC), 2015 Third International Conference on*: 165–169.

Perizade, B. & Suhery, T. (2012). *Early Childhood Education in Indonesia*.

Seefeldt, C. & Wasik, B.A. (2007). *Early education: Three-, four-, and five-year-olds go to school*. Recording for Blind & Dyslexic.

Undang-Undang Permendiknas No 58. Tahun 2009 Tentang Standar Pendidikan Anak Usia Dini. *Jakarta: Depdiknas*.

Development of graphic design learning model based on multimedia

A. Huda & K. Rukun

Electronic Engineering Department, Technical Information Education Program, Engineering Faculty,
Universitas Negeri Padang, Padang, Indonesia

ABSTRACT: Based on previous observation, it was found that the implementation of graphic design teaching using lectures and guided practice has not demonstrated independent learning. The purpose of this research was twofold: (1) the development of a multimedia-based learning model for graphic design in an Electronic Engineering Department; (2) to test the validity, practicality and effectiveness of this Multimedia-Based Graphic Design Learning Model. We used a Research and Development (R&D) approach, based on the design principles of Plomp (2013) and consisting of three phases: preliminary research, a prototyping phase, and an assessment phase. The data in this research consisted of quantitative data. The research into the development of a Multimedia-Based Graphic Design Learning Model for an Electronic Engineering Department proved successful, giving rise to the conclusion that its use was more effective than conventional instructional models by improving students' learning results, and their cognitive, affective, and psychomotor skills. The development and implementation of an instructional Multimedia-Based Graphic Design Learning Model was shown to be valid and practical.

1 INTRODUCTION

The Education for All Global Monitoring Report is published by UNESCO every year and contains the results, from 120 countries, of monitoring the education world. In the 2012 report, the Education Development Index (EDI) placed Indonesia in 64th position. A survey by PERC (Political and Economic Risk Consultancy) and UNDP (United Nations Development Program) stated that the education system in Indonesia was the worst in the Asia region (of 12 nations surveyed).

One indication of the low education quality in Indonesia can be seen from the average learning results still being low (Sudrajat, 2009) so that efforts to improve these learning results are needed. One way to improve learning results is through the use of learning media.

Media is anything that can be used to deliver a message from a sender to a receiver, which can stimulate the mind, feelings, concerns, interests and the student's attention to the learning process. Media use in teaching and learning is important, because by using media, educators can be expected to help in delivering material learning. Lecturers should be more wise and precise in selecting media. One of the most effective media is electronic media, such as computers, radio, and OverHead Projectors (OHPs). However, such media can only be used in certain places, such as those areas which have electricity. In rural areas without electricity, the solution must be manual use and simple media.

According to Riyanto (2006), graphic design is a form of applied painting (picture) that gives freedom to a designer to select, create, or adjust the shape of elements such as illustrations, photographs, text, and lines on a surface for the purpose of generating and communicating a message. It involves pictures and signs that use typographical or other media such as photography. Graphic design is generally applied in the advertising world, packaging, and film, among many others. Many occupations are affected by the development of computer technology, and one of the fields that is most affected is graphic design.

In pre-research observations conducted in the Information Engineering Studies Program of the Engineering Faculty of Padang State University, it was found that the learning of graphic design by students is limited by the use of the conventional methods of lecturing and practical guidance (50% lectures and 50% guided practice). That case made the students merely memorize the steps of how to design.

The lecturing method is also not appropriate for subjects which focus on psychomotor skills. The learning process is successful if good results can be obtained and the learning material delivered can be applied. The material delivered in the subject of graphic design is very useful in the supply of student knowledge, and the attitudes and practical skills required for graphic design to be applied in practice.

Recognizing the learning limitations of graphic design instruction in the Information Engineering Studies Program, Engineering Faculty, Padang

State University, a strategy is needed for the development of a learning model for students of graphic design. Various models can be developed to support students of the graphic design subject in the Information Engineering Studies Program, one of them being through the development of a Multimedia-Based Graphic Design Learning Model.

Based on the explanation above, if the two concepts are combined, multimedia learning can be defined as multimedia applications used in the learning process. In other words, a multimedia message is useful to distribute learning (in the form of knowledge, skills and attitudes) and that can stimulate feelings choices, concerns and the willingness to make learning occur intentionally and in control.

Based on the problems of graphic design instruction described, the purpose of this research was to:

1. Develop and produce a Multimedia-Based Graphic Design Learning Model;
2. Determine the validity, practicality and effectiveness of this Multimedia-Based Graphic Design Learning Model.

2 RESEARCH METHODS

The method of this study is Research and Development (R & D), which is included into the "need to do" category. The research results used to assist in the work will also be used to help in the work implementation and if that work is helped by the R&D results it will be more productive, effective and efficient. The development model followed in this research is the general model of design development described by Plomp (2013), which consists of three stages or phases, namely, preliminary research, a prototyping development phase and an assessment phase.

3 RESULTS AND DISCUSSION

3.1 Needs analysis results

The initial investigation in the preliminary research involved a needs analysis of the competencies associated with graphic design learning, based on the achievement level of the respondents.

As shown in Figure 1, it can be seen that of the 16 indicators or competencies associated with graphic design learning, one indicator (i.e. 6.25%) was identified as 'Very needed'. Five indicators (31.25%) were analyzed as 'Required', and ten indicators (62.50%) were placed in the 'Quite needed' category.

3.2 Results of prototype design

To build a model of learning we must pay attention to the basic elements of the model. According to Joyce et al. (2008), there are five basic elements involved in building a model (see Figure 2), namely: (1) syntax, which defines the operational steps of learning; (2) social system, which defines the atmosphere and norms of learning; (3) the principles of reaction, which describes how teachers should regard, treat, and respond to their students; (4) the support system, which is all the facilities, materials, tools, or the learning environment that supports learning; (5) instructional and guidance

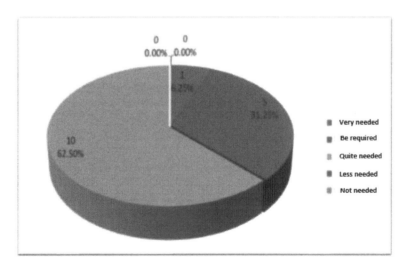

Figure 1. Result of needs analysis of graphic design learning based on the criteria of achievement level of respondents.

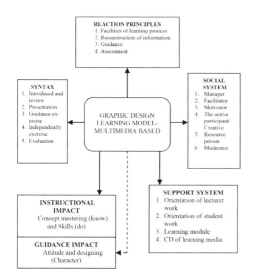

Figure 2. Conceptual framework for Multimedia-Based Graphic Design Learning Model.

Table 1. Results of validity test for the Graphic Design Learning Model.

No.	Assessment aspect	Assessment result		
		Average	TCR	Category
1	Supporting theory	4.56	91.11	Very good
2	Structure of Multimedia-Based Graphic Design Learning Model	4.11	82.22	Good
3	Learning result desired	4.00	80.00	Good
	Final average	4.22	84.44	Good

effects, which are a form of learning result that is obtained directly by meeting goals (instructional effects), and the results of learning beyond simple goals (guidance effects).

This fifth component of the model is constructed from several aspects. More detail about the construction and function of components of the Multimedia-Based Graphic Design Learning Model are explained below.

3.3 Formative evaluation (Validity)

The purpose of this assessment is to conduct a more in-depth assessment about the products revised. The assessment conducted is a summative evaluation, which involves the validity test, the practicality test and an effectiveness test. The focus is on testing that the Multimedia-Based Graphic Design Learning Model that is developed is valid, practical and effective.

1. Validity of the Graphic Design Learning Model Book

The results of the assessment (validity) of the Multimedia-Based Graphic Design Learning Model are shown in Table 1.

Based on the results of the validity test, the Multimedia-Based Graphic Design Learning Model was categorized as very valid. These results were obtained after rating by three validators. The average value for the three aspects of the assessment was 4.22, giving an overall achievement level of 84.44%.

2. Formative Evaluation (Practicalities Test)

The practicalities tests was conducted to assess the practicality of the book aspect of the Multimedia-Based Graphic Design Learning Model. It was completed by a lecturer who teaches the graphic design subject.

Based on Table 2, it can be concluded that the average score for the practicality of the book(s) of the Multimedia-Based Graphic Design Learning Model was 4.23, giving an achievement level of 84.56%, and it was categorized as 'Good' in terms of practical criteria, meaning that the result of the practicalities test is that the book of the Multimedia-Based Graphic Design Learning Model can be applied.

3. Product Implementation Results (Effectiveness Test)

a. Description of data for graphic design learning

In describing the data, the researchers will consider each set of supporting data in turn and address the problems that have been posed in this research. In this section, the data information obtained from the field/respondents is processed, which is used by applying descriptive statistical analysis in order to see the trend in the spread of data.

1. Value of Graphic Design Learning in Control Class

Based on assessment of data for graphic design learning in control class.

Based on the calculations shown in Table 4, 25.00% of respondents obtained an average score in graphic design learning (post-test), 35.00% of respondents obtained a score below the average, and 40.00% of respondents obtained a score above the average.

2. Value of Graphic Design Learning in Experimental Class

Based on values of data from application of Multimedia-Based Graphic Design Learning Model in experimental class.

Based on the calculations shown in Table 5, that 6 (30.00%) of respondent obtained an average

Table 2. Assessment result of practicality of book of Multimedia-Based Graphic Design Learning Model.

No.	Assessment aspect	Assessment result		
		Average	TCR	Category
1	Clarity of instruction used in model	4.42	88.33	Good
2	Competency achievement and purpose of learning	4.17	83.33	Good
3	Student response	4.00	80.00	Good
4	Difficulty level implemented	4.22	84.44	Good
5	The time precision	4.33	86.67	Good
	Average	4.23	84.56	Good

Table 3. Value frequency distribution of graphic design learning in control class.

No.	Interval class	Frequency (absolute)	Frequency (relative) (%)
1	56–59	2	10.00
2	60–63	5	25.00
3	64–67	5	25.00
4	68–71	6	30.00
5	72–76	2	10.00
Total		20	100.00

Table 4. Value frequency distribution of graphic design learning in experimental class.

No.	Interval class	Frequency (absolute)	Frequency (relative) (%)
1	70–73	2	10.00
2	74–77	7	35.00
3	78–81	6	30.00
4	82–85	3	15.00
5	86–90	2	10.00
Total		20	100.00

Table 5. The results of data normality testing.

Variable	Kolmogorov–Smirnov		
	Statistic	N	Sig.
Learning results of control class	0.703	20	0.706
Learning results of experimental class	0.671	20	0.759

score from score learning result Graphic Design (posttest), 9 (45.00%) of respondents obtained score below the average price, and 5 (25.00%) of respondents obtained score above the average price.

3. Testing Requirements Analysis Data

Testing of the research hypothesis used t-test analysis. T-test analysis can be applied if the data are analyzed complete in several condition.

a. Normality Test

The data was processed through a Kolmogorov–Smirnov normality test to obtain an indication of the normality of data distribution in each of the two classes, as shown in Table 6.

As shown in Table 6, the significance value for the variable of the learning results of the control class is 0.706 >0.05. The normality test of the variable learning results of the experimental class produced a significance of 0.759 >0.05; this means that the variable data of the learning results from the experimental class and the control class follow the normal distribution.

b. Homogeneity Test

A homogeneity test is conduct to see if the research data associated with the learning results of the two different classes had the same variance (were homogeneous) or not.

The analysis results in Table 7 show that the significance probability of each variable is more than 0.05, meaning that the data of this research is homogeneous and we can proceed to the analysis of hypothesis testing.

c. Hypothesis Testing

The hypothesis testing in this research was conducted using the t-test. It is used to present the result of the data processing in terms of the difference in learning results between students in a control class and those in an experimental class using the Multimedia-Based Graphic Design Learning Model.

Table 6. The results of homogeneity testing.

Research variable	Sig.	Result
Learning results of control class	0.168	Homogen
Learning results of experimental class	0.221	Homogen

Table 7. T-test of student learning results in control class with student results in experimental class using Multimedia-Based Graphic Design Learning Model.

Variable	Mean	n	SD	t	Sig.
Learning result Class experiment	78,00	20	4,98	10,225	0,000
Learning result Class control	65,30	20	4,78		

From the calculated t test above shows that the t calculate = 10.225 > t table = 1.72 significance level α = 0.000 it means that H0 is rejected and H1 accepted, thus the hypothesis that there is a difference of student learning result in control class with learning result student in learning Experiment Class by used Graphic Design Learning Model—Multimedia Based is acceptable. This is also shown with significant level is 0.000 < 0.05, which means that shows there are significant differences between Student Learning result in Experiment Class of Graphic Design Learning Model-Multimedia Based with learning graphic design in Control Class (Conventional).

4 CONCLUSION

Based on the results from the development and testing of a Multimedia-Based Graphic Design Learning Model for the Information Engineering Studies Program of the Engineering Faculty of Padang State University the following conclusions can be drawn:

1. The development through the design process described by Plomp (2013) consisted of three phases. The Multimedia-Based Graphic Design Learning Model that was created defined a syntax that described five phases of learning: 1. Introduction and Review (expressed the objectives and established motivation); 2. Presentation (Presentation of learning graphic design by using multimedia); 3. Guidance Practice (Practice Guidance by using Graphic Design module); 4. Independent Practice (Independent Practice Learning by using Graphic Design module and Multimedia Applications Help); 5. Evaluation.
2. A valid Multimedia-Based Graphic Design Learning Model was generated that was practical in application and effective in support of the learning process in graphic design.

REFERENCES

Joyce, B.R., Weil, M. & Calhoun, E. (2008). *Models of teaching* (8th ed.). Upper Saddle River, NJ: Pearson Education.
Plomp, T. (2013). Educational design research: An introduction. In Plomp, T. & Nieveen, N. (Eds.), *Educational design research*. Enschede, The Netherlands: Netherlands Institute for Curriculum Development (SLO).
Riyanto, S. (2006). *Bagaimana Memulai Belajar Desain Grafis?* [*How to start learning graphic design?*] Retrieved from: http://www.ilmukomputer.org/wp-content/uploads/2006/12/bagaimana-memulai-desain-grafis-slametriyanto.pdf.
Sudrajat, A. (2009). *Pembelajaran Tuntas* [*Mastery-Learning*]. Retrieved from: http://akhmadsudrajat.wordpress.com/2009/11/02/pembelajaran-tuntas-mastery-learning-dalam-ktsp/.

Regionalization and Harmonization in TVET – Abdullah et al. (Eds)
© 2017 Taylor & Francis Group, London, ISBN 978-1-138-05419-6

Learning computational thinking through introductory programming at the engineering faculty of the State University of Surabaya

E. Hariadi
Universitas Negeri Surabaya, Jawa Timur, Indonesia

ABSTRACT: High-order thinking is a capability that in the 21st century should be owned by every graduate of a college. Computational thinking concerns how to solve the problem with an approach which uses the principles of computer science. The purpose of this research is to apply the concept of computational thinking into the teaching/learning process and produce an assessment model of computational thinking. Computational thinking is a new way to solve problems and can be taught through programming of the visual language Scratch. The basic ideas of computational thinking are: 1) a way of solving problems and designing systems; 2) how to use various abstractions, understand and solve the problems more effectively; and 3) think in algorithms and use the concept of mathematics to solve the problems with more convincing results. The concepts of computational thinking as taught through the visual programming language Scratch are: sequence, variable, conditional, iteration, and procedure. The easiest of these to learn is sequence, while the most elusive concept is procedure. Students' programming abilities consist of two domains, namely, mastery of programming theory and programming practice. The first ability is measured by multiple-choice items, while the second is measured by performance assessment items. To obtain a composite score, the raw scores of multiple-choice and performance assessment are converted to a scaled score.

1 INTRODUCTION

How can we prepare learners to succeed in the 21st century? This is an important question to educators, parents and the community. The quality of life, welfare, and economic competitiveness depends on a better readiness to face the 21st century. In the era of industry with high technology, a change in the types of dexterity and skills will be more complex. The skills needed by students to face the 21st century are communication problem-solving and inter-personal skills. (Partnership for 21st Century Skills, 2003).

In the 21st century, information and communication technology grows rapidly. The development covers various aspects of life. Information and communication technology skills require not only technical skill, but also demand mental and problem-solving skills.

Wing explains computational thinking as solving problems, designing systems and understanding human behavior by drawing on the concept fundamental to computer science (Wing, 2006, p. 33). After Wing articulated this idea, researchers focused on the relationship between computational thinking and other fields (Bundy, 2007). Other researchers tested the implication of computational thinking (Deming, 2007). The computational thinking skill represents an important concept in computer science in general, and in programming language in particular (Howland et al., 2009). The concept is to define instructions specifically and clearly to complete a process. The skills pertain to the writing of step-by-step program instructions to stimulate the way that the programmer solves problems. Computational thinking also relates to the concept of flow control flow such as conditional statement, repetition, and branching in programming language. The skill can be transferred easily to a context outside of computer science.

The definition of computational thinking has evolved from year to year. Wing (2006) introduces computational thinking as a universal skill that should be learned by every person. Computational thinking is not a programming and is not associated to certain software. Wing (2006) defines computational thinking as '*solving problems, designing systems and understanding human behavior that draws on concepts fundamental to computing*'. According to the definition, computational thinking is abstraction and automation. Wing et al. (2011) improve the definition by stressing the role of information-processing: '*Computational thinking is the thought processes involved in formulating problems and their solutions so that the solutions are represented in a form that can be effectively carried out by an information-processing agent*'.

Computational thinking as a process cannot be taught only through memory, but needs to be demonstrated as experience from practice, in the same way that a person becomes proficient in reading and writing through practice. Computational thinking is a combination of some skills: when someone solves problems as computation, he first develops a model of the problem, and then goes through the process of solving the problem; both aspects rely on a model and principles based on a method of computation. Thus, in computational thinking, the thinking process involves two basic skills: computation skills and problem-solving skills.

Computation skill derives from the principle of computing. Reddy and Sarma (2015) identify six categories of computing principles: logical reasoning; algorithm; decomposition; abstraction; pattern and generalization; and evaluation.

Computational thinking is a relatively new approach to solving problems. The basic ideas of computational thinking are: 1) how to solve the problem and design the system; 2) how to use various abstractions, and understand and solve problems more effectively; and 3) how to think in algorithms and use mathematical concepts to solve problems more convincingly (Lu & Fletcher, 2009). Computational thinking is not about asking people to think like computers, but about how to develop a set of the mental skills required to resolve complex human problems (Wing, 2006). Computational thinking looks at the problem in a systematic way, step-by-step, and breaks down a big problem into smaller parts. It is a basic skill that can be learned by everyone, not only computer experts and many educators argue that computational thinking should be part of education, together with other basic skills such as reading, writing, and arithmetic.

Scratch is a visual programming language created by researchers from the Massachusetts Institute of Technology in 2007. The purpose of Scratch is to create animation, games and interactive art. Although Scratch is easily understood by young people, the concept of Scratch cannot be separated from the concept of computational thinking as it is in other programming language. When students compose animation, interactive stories, games, music, or artwork with Scratch, they simultaneously learn about ideas of computing and mathematics. In the creation of Scratch programs, the students learn concepts of computing, such as iteration and conditionals. They also acquire an understanding of important aspects of mathematical concepts such as coordinates, variables, and random numbers. The concepts of computational thinking in visual programming languages are summarized in Table 1. (Malan & Leitner, 2007; Maloney et al., 2008; Ruthmann et al., 2010).

Table 1. Concepts of computational thinking.

Concept	Description	Sample
Sequence	Make programs in sequence	
Iteration	**Forever** and **repeat** used for iteration	
Condition	Check **if** and **if-then** for condition	
Variable	Category variable enables students to make new variables	
Procedure	Make a sub-program called by other programs	

2 METHOD

The research is the implementation of teaching of the visual programming language Scratch to students from the Informatics Education study program at the Engineering Faculty of Universitas Negeri Surabaya. The subject of the research consisted of 39 students. The topics taught are the concepts of computational thinking in the visual programming language Scratch, summarized in Table 1 below.

Every topic was taught for two meetings. Every meeting took 100 minutes. The learning model used was direct instruction. With this model, the teachers firstly conveyed the purpose of students learning a visual programming language and its relation

Table 2. Content of visual programming concepts.

Concept	Content
Sequence	Command of motion, pen, sound, looks
Variables	Data type, operator
Iteration	Iteration block, counter, nested loop
Conditionals	Comparison operations, logical operations, conditional
Procedure	Sending and receiving message, modular programming, and recursion

Table 3. A summary of analysis of performance assessment.

No	Concept	Difficulty index	Discrimination
1	Sequence	0,41	0,42
2	Variables	0,90	0,13
3	Conditionals	0,30	0,55
4	Iteration	0,23	0,39
5	Procedure	0,15	0,11

Table 4. Summary of the analysis of item parameters (β) and difficulty index.

	Parameter (β)	Difficulty index (p)
Mean	0.00	0.48
Std. Dev.	1.49	0.27
Minimum	-3.2	0
Maximum	4.19	0.90

to computational thinking. Next, the teachers presented programs that became models, and finally the teachers gave guidance on how to create programs using the visual programming language Scratch. Students had to implement what they designed. Every session, students developed prototype programs of every topic. The contents of each concept of computational thinking are summarized in Table 2.

3 RESULTS AND DISCUSSION

After completing the course, students undertook a performance assessment and paper and pencil test. The performance assessment consisted of five items, while the paper and pencil test consisted of 50 multiple-choice items. The five items of performance assessment tested the concepts of computational thinking: sequence, variables, conditionals, iteration, and procedure. Similarly, the paper and pencil test measured the same concepts, with each concept being assessed by ten multiple-choice items. The results of both the performance assessment and paper and pencil tests were analyzed. The results of performance assessment were analyzed using classical test theory, while the results of the paper and pencil test were analyzed using Rash model, whose items respond to the theory of one parameter, and classical test theory. The Test Analysis program (Brooks, 2014) was used to estimate index difficulty (p) based on classical test theory, while the Conquest program (Wu, 1998) was used to estimate item parameters (β) based on item test theory. The results of the analysis of the performance assessment are summarized in Table 3.

Table 4 shows a summary of the analysis of item parameters (β) and difficulty index from multiple tests. Item parameter is a point on the ability scale where the probability of answering correctly is equal to 0.5. The parameter is a location parameter, indicating a position on the item characteristic curve in conjunction with the ability scale. The greater a location parameter, the greater the ability required by students to obtain a 50% possibility of answering correctly. The location parameter minimum is -3.20, and location parameter maximum is

4.19. According to classical test analysis, the difficulty index has a range from 0 to 0.90.

The correlation between parameter β and difficulty index is shown in Figure 1. The correlation index was -0.92.

The final task given to students was the five items of performance assessment. Task analysis was conducted to establish which concepts were understood by students as being easy and which were difficult. The analysis was based on a scoring rubric of performance assessment. All items have scoring levels 0, 1, 2, 3, and 4. Level 0 indicates that students could not do their task at all. Level 4 indicates that students were able to perform the tasks very well. The distribution of students' responses to performance assessment is summarized in Table 5.

Figure 2 shows a bar chart of the students' responses in relation to programming tasks. The concept of variables was very easily understood by the students. Around 95% of the students could handle the concept of variables up to Level 4. The concepts of sequence and conditionals were somewhat more elusive than the variables concept with only 23% of students able to handle these concepts to Level 4, while even fewer students (18%) were able to handle the concept of iteration to Level 4. The most elusive concept was procedure: only 3% of students were able to handle this concept to Level 4.

Mastery of programming theory was measured by 50 multiple-choice items. The raw score statistics are summarized in Figure 3.

Mastery of programming practice was measured by five performance assessment items. The raw score statistics are summarized in Figure 4.

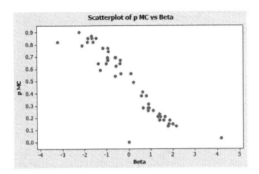

Figure 1. Correlation between β and p.

Table 5. Students' responses (%).

No	Level concept	0	1	2	3	4
1	Variables	5.12	0	0	0	94.87
2	Sequence	46.15	2.56	10.25	17.94	23.07
3	Conditionals	56.41	7.69	12.82	0	23.07
4	Iteration	64.1	12.82	5.12	0	17.94
5	Procedure	64.1	17.94	12.82	2.56	2.56

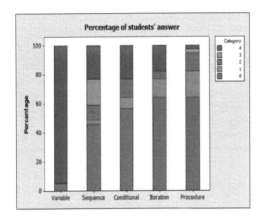

Figure 2. Percentages by level of students' responses.

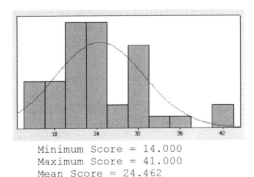

Minimum Score = 14.000
Maximum Score = 41.000
Mean Score = 24.462

Figure 3. Raw score of programming theory.

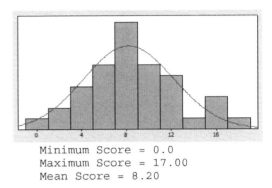

Minimum Score = 0.0
Maximum Score = 17.00
Mean Score = 8.20

Figure 4. Raw score of programming practice.

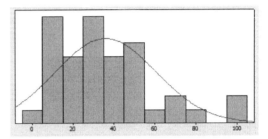

Minimum Score = 0.0
Maximum Score = 100.00
Mean Score = 35.97

Figure 5. Composite score.

The combination of multiple-choice and performance assessment items to form a total score (composite score) needs to be weighted, but as the time taken for the tests of programming theory and programming practice was similar at 90 minutes each, both types of items were weighted equally. To obtain a composite score, each raw score was converted to a standard score. Both standard scores were summed and divided by two. Next the composite score was converted to a 0–100 scaled score. The distribution of the composite score is summarized in Figure 5.

4 CONCLUSION

The concepts of computational thinking taught through the visual programming language Scratch are sequence, variables, conditionals, iteration, and procedure. The easiest concept to learn was sequence, while the most elusive concept was procedure. Students' programming abilities consist of two domains: mastery of programming theory and mastery of programming practice. The first ability was measured by multiple-choice items, and the second ability by performance assessment items. To obtain a composite score, the raw scores of multiple-choice and performance assessments were converted to a scaled score.

REFERENCES

Brooks, G.P. (2014). *Test Analysis Program* (Version 14.7.4).

Bundy, A. (2007). Computational thinking is pervasive. *Journal of Scientific and Practical Computing Noted Reviews*, *1*(2), 67–69.

Lu, J.J. & Fletcher, G.H. (2009). Thinking about computational thinking. *ACM SIGCSE Bulletin*, *41*(1), 260–264.

Malan, D.J. & Leitner, H.H. (2007). Scratch for budding computer scientists. *SIGCSE*, *7*(10), 1–8.

Maloney, J.M., Peppler, K., Kafai, Y.B., Resnick, M. & Rush, N. (2008). Programming by choice: Urban youth learning programming with Scratch. *SIGCSE*, *12*(15), 367–371.

Partnership for 21st Century Skills. (2003). *Learning for the 21st century*. Retrieved from http://www.21stcenturyskills.org/downloads/P21_Report.pdf.

Ruthmann, A., Heines, J.M. & Greher, G.R. (2010). Teaching computational thinking through musical live coding in Scratch. *SIGCSE*, *10*(3), 1–5.

Wing, J.M. (2006). Computational thinking. *Communications of the ACM*, *49*(3), 33–35.

Wu, M.L., Adams, R.J. & Wilson, M.R. (1998). *ConQuest: Generalized item response modeling software*. Camberwell, Australia: Australian Council for Educational Research.

Design and development of animation-based multimedia to illustrate corrosion and coating processes for vocational learners

E. Permana & Y. Sukrawan
Universitas Pendidikan Indonesia, Bandung, Indonesia

ABSTRACT: The purpose of this research is to create an animation-based learning media of *corrosion processes* in the subject of Corrosion and Coating at the Department of Mechanical Engineering Education, Universitas Pendidikan Indonesia, Bandung. The learning media program can be directly installed and accessed on personal computers for learning purposes. The research was conducted in 2016 and started with concept exploration to find the necessary product model, followed by its development through many test steps and correction procedures. The last step was product validation through quasi-experiments on a number of students taking the corrosion class. The result is animation-based interactive media that demonstrates good criteria in terms of a media expert judgment value of 78.3%, students' response of 83.0%, and a subject matter expert judgment value of 89.0%. Validity tests show that the media has a significant effect on the increase in the number of students who reach minimum standard competency.

1 INTRODUCTION

1.1 Research background

Learning media has a significant effect on the achievement of learning objectives. As agreed by almost all education experts, using various kinds of learning media can drive students' motivation and improve their learning achievement. Learning media can be understood as any kind of tool utilized by people to deliver their ideas, opinions, or expressions to other people so that all of the information is completely transmitted.

Nowadays, the use of animation-based multimedia in the learning–teaching process has already been adopted in many education institutions, especially in Indonesia. One of them is animation-based multimedia using Adobe® Flash software. The animation can visually represent abstract concepts to make the subject easier to comprehend.

Corrosion and Coating is one of the subjects that students must take to fulfill their undergraduate program in the Mechanical Engineering Education Department at Universitas Pendidikan Indonesia (UPI), Bandung. The subject deals with the concepts of the corrosion process that occurs with corrosive materials, and the coating processes required to overcome said corrosion. In order to be capable in this subject, students must first have a deep understanding of the concept of corrosion before moving to the coating process, which is delivered after this topic.

An evaluation of the results data, ensuing from a research survey during lecturing processes conducted during the first term of 2015–2016 at the Department of Mechanical Engineering Education, shows that less than 40% of students taking the Corrosion and Coating subject managed to reach the minimum standard grade (Grade B). One of the reasons for this failure was that the students were unable to acquire a deep understanding of the corrosion concept presented by the lecturer.

From the researchers' point of view, it can be concluded that one of the factors affecting the education results is that the lecturer did not make optimal use of learning media in the lecturing process. The abstract concepts involved in corrosion and coating could not be fully understood by the students because they failed to visualize them clearly in their mind.

1.2 Problem statement

Formulation of research problem is as follows:

– How to develop learning media on the subject of corrosion (which has good criteria for corrosion and coating) using Macromedia Flash Pro-8.
– How will using learning media on corrosion and coating using Macromedia Flash Pro-8 on the subject of corrosion affect the learning result?

1.3 Research objective

The objective of the research is to create an animation-based multimedia of corrosion and coating which has good criteria and can be implemented in the learning process. It will be in the form of an executable file which can be directly accessed from a computer. The media should be able to support any kind of learning processes required by educational institutions.

2 LITERATURE REVIEW

2.1 Animation basic concept

The term animation comes originally from 'anima', which means soul or breath of life. Animation is the creation of living objects from dead ones (Harry & Herman, 1992, p. 2).

In the *Kamus Besar Bahasa Indonesia*, the Departemen Pendidikan National (Department of National Education of Indonesia) (2005, p. 53) states that an animation is a television program in the form of texts and pictures which mechanically and electronically brings to life objects on the screen.

Based on the two definitions above, the meaning of animation can be concluded as the technique and process of generating unreal objects to be seen as real-life objects. The motion in animation results from arranging picture frames in a sequential order according to the type of motion. Every frame stores one picture that corresponds to the required motion. By visualizing the frames continuously on the screen, the 'dead' object will be seen as a real-life object. Thus, animation-based multimedia is animated audiovisual media in the form of a series of pictures projected frame-by-frame so as to look 'alive' on the screen.

2.2 Previous research

Some previous research of utilizing animation-based multimedia shows that this media has been proven to help increase vocational students' problem-solving capability (Wahono, 2010); increase senior vocational school students' ability to describe engineering drawings (Choirun et al., 2000); and raise learning results for the subject of braking systems at senior vocational school (Beni et al., 2009).

3 RESEARCH METHOD

The research was started by observation to find out a required research product followed by product development through some testing steps (experts' judgment, limited tests, and field tests), product revision process, and finally validation process.

On the basis of the Research and Development (R&D) method, the following research steps were conducted:

– Undertake a preliminary study of the course syllabus of Corrosion and Coating at the Department of Mechanical Engineering Education at UPI, Bandung.

– Design and develop an animation program according to the course syllabus. This consisted of arranging the selected material course frame-by-frame, storyboard making (setting, organizing, audio planning, editing, and proofreading), computer programming, and product evaluation through the judgment of experts.
– Limited testing of the developed animation-based multimedia. The media was tested by implementing it with a small group of students. Response and feedback from the students was captured and analyzed.
– Validating the media. Validity testing was carried out through quasi-experimental research in which two groups of students were treated in different classes. The first group of 30 students took a course conducted with the animation media and a second group of another 30 students was subjected to the course without using the animation. The evaluation results after the course were compared and analyzed to establish the difference.

4 RESULT AND DISCUSSION

4.1 Nature of the course

The nature of the course of Corrosion and Coating requires students to be able to illustrate the movement of ions on metal that causes the onset of corrosion before they can understand it as a whole. The movement of ions is an abstract idea which cannot be delivered simply by using still images and media, and will be improved if depicted with a movement that resembles the real movement of the ions. For that use, animation as a media could be an alternative learning method.

4.2 Design result

The design phase was composed of three activities: preparation of the flowchart, storyboards, and interface design. The flowchart describes an overall view of the animation. The storyboard is a design of the animation in each part, from sound up to the multimedia animation, and used as a reference for the development of interactive animation-based multimedia design. The interface of the media was made with a simple design that makes it easy for users to find the buttons to navigate from one frame to another.

The interface design consists of two parts, namely the main menu interface design and interface design submission material. The main menu interface design is the main view of the animation that serves as the key navigator to explore multimedia features on the whole, while the material submission interface is displayed simply with a little button, because this material relies on animated movement and sound to make users focus on it.

4.3 Development result

The first stage of development of the interactive multimedia-based animation began by making the interface a reference of the layout of components, and creating a storyboard as a reference for the animation and multimedia navigation in moving from one frame to another. The interface consists of the main menu interface and interface of material in the form of animation.

The main menu display interface on the interactive multimedia-based animation is shown in Figure 1. On this main menu interface, the object that is created is an object in the form of navigation buttons to move to the display according to its name. The subjects assigned to these buttons are: profiles that describe the media creators; objectives which explain the direction of the learning process; material which captures the animated process of metal corrosion; an exercise as a means of evaluation after viewing this multimedia display; and messages from the creators. It also contains graphs and text describing the corrosion of the metal as a background on this interface.

Figure 1.   Main menu display.

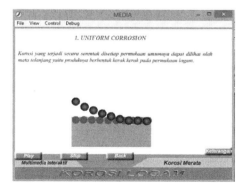

Figure 2.   Material display.

The display interface of material is shown in Figure 2. On this material interface there is an animation of corrosion, complete with sound, that accompanies the animation. When the 'play' button is pressed the animation will begin, and it will stop if the 'stop' button is pressed. A button that will restore preview display was also created, as well as navigation buttons to explain the matter.

4.4 Testing result

4.4.1 Description of media expert judgment
The sheet format used by media experts for the judgment made on this measurement has a scale-shaped research rating consisting of 15 statements. The data results of the judgment by the media experts can be seen in Table 1.

Based on Table 1, the percentage of the feasibility of multimedia animation corrosion is 78.3%. The percentage of this animated multimedia is compared to proprietary percentage to get area eligibility for multimedia animation where a percentage of 78.3% are at the interval with *good criteria*.

4.4.2 Description of user response
User response data in the research was used to assess the students' response description of the media. The student response sheet format created on this scale-shaped research rating scale consisted of ten statements. This statement concerned the use of animation-based interactive multimedia in the development of competence in the corrosion and coating of metals.

The student response data aimed to establish student interest in the media. Response data were taken from 30 students who had seen the animation-based interactive multimedia material on the corrosion and coating of metals. The student response data processing in general is presented in Table 2.

The results of student responses in Table 2 describes the average interest of students toward interactive multimedia-based animation of 83.0%; this percentage is higher than the required number

Table 1.   Data of media expert judgment.

Acqusition	Mark					Total
	4 (SL)	3 (L)	2 (KL)	1 (TL)	0 (STL)	
Summation	2	13	0	0	0	15
Score	8	39	0	0	0	47
				Maximum score		60
				Percentage (%)		78.3

Table 2. Data of user response.

| Acqusition | Remark | | | | | Total |
	4 (SL)	3 (L)	2 (KL)	1 (TL)	0 (STL)	
Respondents	13	15	1	1	0	30
Score	520	450	20	10	0	1,000
				Maximum score		1,200
				Percentage (%)		83.0

in which students are interested. Thus, this percentage is categorized as "interesting".

4.5 Discussion

The animation-based interactive multimedia has proven to drive students' learning interest. They become motivated and able to achieve learning objectives. This is in line with the opinion of Sudjana and Rivai (2005, p. 2) who stated that: '*the media learning function in the learning process will further draw attention so as to cultivate motivation [for] study, and learning materials will [clarify] its meaning so that it can be better understood by students and enable [them] to achieve the goals of learning*'.

The result of the media experts' judgment showed the feasibility of the media reached 78.3%, that is, it deserves to be used as a learning media.

Subject matter expert judgment undertaken before the media expert validation showed that 89% is a worthy percentage. If the matter needed no improvements or additions then the interactive animation-based multimedia is worthy of implementation.

Before the process of application of the media, researchers first tried to test the student response. Response was given after students had looked through the media during the learning process by completing a statement sheet of student opinions. They include: level of media attractiveness, the way to operate the media, and the material contained therein, as well as the look and sound of the narrative. Media response of the students indicated that 83.0% of them had a good opinion of the animation media which means that it attracts students once they have seen it.

After using the multimedia animation in the learning process, the students' learning results improved. The number of students reaching the minimum competency level increased to 73.91% (up from the previous value of 40%), with an average value of 80.43 points. These results indicate that the use of interactive multimedia-based animation can improve the results of study.

Based on the description of the research data, it can be stated that interactive multimedia-based

animation is capable of improving learning results and encouraging motivation.

5 CONCLUSION AND RECOMMENDATIONS

Based on the findings and discussion of the results of the research, the conclusions are as follows:

– The animation-based multimedia of corrosion developed in the research has good criteria and deserves to be used in teaching and learning activities in the vocational institution of engineering.
– The results of the study show that the use of the multimedia animation of corrosion contributed to an increase in the number of students who achieved the minimum standard of competency from 40% to 73.91%.

Some recommendations according to the results of the research are as follows:

– The animation-based interactive media has proved that it can improve student learning outcomes, and therefore its broader use in teaching and learning processes needs to be carried out and optimized.
– Vocational education at secondary level and in colleges needs to be equipped with computers and projector devices, along with the animation-based media, in order to improve students' competency.

REFERENCES

Arsyad, A. (2002). *Media Pembelajaran.* Jakarta, Indonesia: Raja Grafindo Persada.

Beni, H., Soesanto, S. & Samsudi, S. (2009). Perbedaan Hasil Belajar antara Metoda Ceramah Konvensional dengan Ceramah Berbantuan Media Animasi pada Pembelajaran Kompetensi Perakitan dan Pemasangan Sistem Rem. *Jurnal PTM, 9*(2), 71–79.

Choirun, A., Khumaedi, M. & Basyirun, B. (2009). Pembelajaran Ceramah dengan Media Animasi untuk Mengingkatkan Kemampuan Siswa Dalam Membaca Gambar Proyeksi. *Jurnal PTM, 9*(1), 7–13.

Departemen Pendidikan Nasional. (2005). *Kamus Besar Bahasa Indonesia (Great dictionary of the Indonesian language).* Jakarta, Indonesia: Departemen Pendidikan Nasional.

Harry, H. & Herman, H. (1991). *Animasi.* Yogyakarta, Indonesia: Multi Media Training Center.

Sudjana, N. & Rivai, A. (2001). *Media Pengajaran.* Bandung, Indonesia: Sinar Baru Algensindo.

Sugiono, S. (2010). *Research methods.* Bandung, Indonesia: Alfabeta.

Wahono, W. (2010). Pengembangan Model Pembelajaran "Mikir" pada Perkuliahan Fisika Dasar untuk Meningkatkan Keterampilan Generik Sains dan Pemecahan Masalah Colon Guru SMK Program Keahlian Tata Boga (Dissertation). Sekolah Pascasarjana UPI, Tidak Diterbitkan.

A comparative study of learning interest and creativity between male and female students

Farihah & B. Sanjaya
Faculty of Engineering, State University of Medan, Medan, Indonesia

ABSTRACT: The purpose of this study is to find out the difference in learning interest and creativity in handicraft subject between male and female second year students at SMP N 3 Tanjung Pura. The population is 107, and the sampling technique used is proportional random sampling. The average outcome for students' learning interest (Variable X_1) is 78, while the average outcome for X_2 is 84.86. The average outcome for male students' creativity (X_1) is 84.25, while that of the female students' (X_2) is 83.22. From the result of the hypothesis analysis, it is found out that there is no significant difference between X_1 and X_2, either in terms of learning interest or creativity. It can be observed from the result of the statistical analysis in which $t_{sum} = -0.002870846$ for learning interest, and $t_{sum} = -0.00039365$ for creativity. The result is interpreted by t_{table} with 5% significance level as much of 2.038 and 1% significance level as much as 2.741. Since $t_{sum} < t_{table}$, H_0 is accepted.

1 INTRODUCTION

Learning outcomes are the skills possessed by students after receiving their learning experience. Furthermore, Sudjana, as quoted by Horwart (2014), classifies three kinds of teaching and learning outcomes: (1) skills and habits, (2) knowledge and guidance, (3) Attitudes and ideals.

Djaali (2011) asserts the factors that influence the success in the learning process are as follows: 1) Internal factors (that comes from within yourself): health, intelligence, interest and motivation, and learning style, and 2) External factors (from outside), include: family, school, community and environment. According to Caroline Munandar (2014), some of the factors that affect the child's creativity are gender, socio-economic status, birth order, family, environment, and intelligence.

Overall, a few problems that occur in SMP N 3 Tanjung Pura involve the conception that craft subject is not of importance, and that male students see the subject as feminine and thus are meant for females only. Furthermore, students face difficulty in exploring their creativity to complete practical craft tasks despite the previously given demonstration.

Interest is a tendency to pay attention and remember some activities; activities observed by someone, who observes for a considerable amount of time with some extent of delight (Slameto, 2010). According to Muhibbinsyah (2010), interest is high excitement or desire toward something. While the study according to Anderson (2001) distinguishes three scenarios: the first scenario is to help students to gain a complete and clear understanding of the purpose of study, the second scenario is the teacher carries out learning and assesses students in order to assist them in achieving the learning objectives, while the third scenario is to jointly assess how well learning objectives are achieved. Learning has been discussed by a number of educational psychologists, who propose a diverse definition and elaboration of the term. Learning is a common, everyday occurrence. Every man will learn. Mardianto (2009) mentions that: "learning is the absolute requirement to be clever in all things, both in terms of science as well as in terms of the field of skill or proficiency." Creativity is also interpreted as a pattern of thought or idea that occurs spontaneously and imaginatively that reflects the results of scientific discoveries and inventions in the mechanical creation (Purwanto, 2010). According to Moreno, as cited by Daryanto (2010), the important thing in creativity is not the invention of something that has never been known before, but rather the product of creativity it is something new for yourself. Aside from some definitions above, Kao, as cited by Ambarjaya (2012) argues that "we all have a wonderfully creative ability, and creativity can be taught and learned." On the other hand, Campbell states "creativity is an idea or thought of humans who are innovative, powerful, and understandable."

According to Supriadi (2004), handicraft lesson in junior high school aims for learners to have the following skills:

1. Ability to develop the knowledge and skills to make a wide range of craft products and product technologies that are useful for human life.
2. A sense of aesthetics, appreciation of craft products, product technology, and objects from various parts of the archipelago as well as the world.

3. Ability to identify local potential that can be developed through the utilization of technology and craft activities simple.
4. Have professional and entrepreneurial attitude.

Standards of competence and basic competence skills subjects include:

1. Crafts (craft appreciation and craft production),
2. Engineering technology, including its appreciation and work production.
3. Management technology, including technology of cultivation and appreciation of the work and implementing the technology of cultivation.
4. Processing technologies, including appreciation the work of processing technology and applying technology.

2 METHODOLOGY

The study was conducted at SMP Negeri 3 Tanjung Pura in August 2014, in the academic year 2014/2015. The population is all second year students of the school (107 students in total). The sampling technique used is Proportional Random Sampling. The instruments used for data collection are previously tested questionnaires and observation sheets. Steps in data analysis include: preliminary analysis and hypothesis testing analysis.

3 RESULTS AND DISCUSSION

From the result of the analysis of students' learning interest, it is found out that female students have higher level of interest than males. The mean of the outcome of the female students amounts to 84.86 while the average for male students is 78. After being interpreted in terms of both 5% significance (2.038) and 1% significance, it is found that $t_{sum} = -0.002870846$, which means t_{sum} is smaller than ttable ($-0.002871 < 2.038$ and ($-0.002871 < 2.741$). Thus, H_o is accepted and H_a is rejected, that is there is no significant difference between male and female students in terms of learning interest at SMP Negeri 3 Tanjung Pura. The same goes to creativity. The result shows that male students are more creative than females. The mean of male students' learning outcome for creativity is 84.25 while females only reach an average of 83.22. To prove the validity of this result, significance test was conducted. After being tested against 5% and 1% significance tests, the result shows that $t_{sum} = -0.00039365$, which means t_{sum} is smaller than t_{table} ($-0.003937 < 2.038$ and ($-0.003937 < 2.741$). Thus, H_o is accepted and H_a is rejected, and we can say that there is no significant difference in terms of creativity between male and female students at SMP Negeri 3 Tanjung Pura.

From the results of the study, it can be concluded that there is no difference or gap in interest and creativity between male and female second year students in SMP N 3 Tanjung Pura.

4 CONCLUSION

Based on the result and discussion, it can be concluded that:

1. Male students' learning interest with an average score of 78 is in middle category. Whereas female students' average based on the interval is 84.86, and is also in the middle category.
2. Male students' creativity had the average score of 84.25 (middle category). Whereas female students' creativity average score based on the interval is 83.82, also in the middle category.
3. There is no significant difference or discrepancy in terms of learning interest and creativity between male and female students in the school.

In line with the conclusion, some implications of the study are as follows:

1. Learning interest of both male and female students towards crafts subject is in the middle category. Male and female students need to increase their learning interest towards crafts subject, because the higher the learning interest, the better the results obtained.
2. The creativity of male and female students in making woven paper is in the middle category. They need to improve and explore their creativity to do better in making woven paper.
3. That there is no difference or gap in interest and creativity between male and female students. The same result is found in terms of creativity.

REFERENCES

Arikunto, Suharsimi. 2013. *Prosedur penelitian suatu pendekatan praktik*. Rineka Cipta, Yogyakarta.
———. 2012. *Dasar-dasar evaluasi pendidikan*. Bumi aksara, Jakarta.
Daryanto. 2010. *Belajar dan mengajar*. Yrama Widya: Bandung.
Djaali. 2011. *Psikologi pendidikan*. Bumi Aksara: Jakarta.
Lorin W. A. 2001. *Taxonomy for learning, teaching, and assessing: a revision of bloom's taxonomy of educational objectives*. New York: San Fransisco Boston.
Margono. 1990. *Keterampilan anyaman bambu dan rotan*. CV. Aneka Ilmu: Semarang.
Munandar Utami. 2014. *Pengembangan kreativitas anak berbakat*. Rineka Cipta: Jakarta.
Purwanto, Ngalim. 2010. *Psikologi pendidikan*. Rineka Cipta: Jakarta.
Slameto, Drs. 2010. *Belajar dan faktor-faktor yang mempengaruhinya*. PT. Rineka Cipta: Jakarta.
Nana Sudjana. 2014. *Penilaian hasil proses belajar mengajar*. Remaja Rosdakarya: Bandung.
———. 2004. *Dasar-dasar proses belajar mengajar*. Sinar Baru Algesindo Offset: Bandung.
Sugiyono. 2009. *Metode penelitian pendidikan (pendekatan kuantitatif, kualitatif, dan r&d)*. Alfabeta: Bandung.

Peer tutoring as a way of improving students' achievement in the digital drawing subject

H. Juniati, T. Aryanti & T. Megayanti
Universitas Pendidikan Indonesia, Indonesia

ABSTRACT: Teaching is often teacher-centered, resulting in students' low level of cognitive, psychomotoric, and affective achievements, one of which is shown by the low accomplishment of the mastery criteria. This study investigates the effectiveness of peer tutoring learning model in improving students' achievement in the Digital Drawing subject. This is a Classroom Action Research, consisting of three cycles, each of which includes planning, action, observation, evaluation, and reflection. The research subjects were 11th grade students of SMK PU Negeri Bandung specializing in Building Technical Drawing. Employing descriptive statistics, it showed improved learning achievement from the 1st cycle to the 3rd cycle. This study demonstrates that student-centered learning, combined with active student's participation in peer tutoring, effectively improves cognitive, psychomotoric, and affective learning achievements in Digital Drawing subject. This may be applicable to other subjects as well.

1 INTRODUCTION

The Digital Drawing subject at SMK PU Negeri Bandung (PU Vocational High School of Bandung) has previously applied the conventional teaching method, employing the lecture technique. However, a preliminary research showed that 17.65% students had not achieved the minimum mastery criteria of the psychomotoric aspect and 50% students had not achieved that of the cognitive aspect. It also showed that students had low level of cognitive, psychomotoric, and affective achievements.

A number of studies have proven that peer tutoring is an effective way of learning for teens (Suherman dkk, 2003). A teacher-centered learning, on the contrary, is not effective in increasing students' affective, cognitive, and psychomotoric achievements.

Effective learning program is indicated from several achievements, such as the achieved instructional objectives, students' active participation in the class, and the availability of facilities to support learning process (Firman, 1987). Peer tutoring an effective learning method, in which leading students can assist their classmates to grapple with course materials. Peer tutoring method is advantageous because it helps to diminish students' fear and reluctance due to their variety of age, social status, and background, it helps those who serve as tutors to their classmates to attain more self-confidence, and it helps students to overcome their

difficulties efficiently, while allowing the tutors to strengthen their understanding on the discussed topics. However, assisted students are sometimes less serious in learning because they learn with their classmates, some of them may be shy and reluctant to ask questions. Moreover, clever students are not always able to teach their knowledge to their classmates.

We investigated whether or not peer tutoring effectively works to improve students' academic achievement in the Digital Drawing subject. This study was conducted using the AutoCAD two-dimensional drawing software. It examines the affective, cognitive, and psychomotoric aspects in the Digital Drawing subject. The study particularly focuses on students' participation during the peer tutoring process and their individual achievements in the class. The basic competences that are examined in this study include: applying the basic instructions in drawing software (B.C. 3.2), analyzing the instruction to modify drawings using drawing software (B.C. 3.3), and applying drawing supporting facilities in the software (B.C. 3.4), and modifying drawings using the software efficiently (B.C. 4.3).

2 RESEARCH METHOD

This study employed Classroom Action Research, in accordance with Kemmis and McTaggart's model. It contains planning, action, observation, and reflection (Kusumah and Dwitagama 2011:20). Research was conducted in the 11th grade of SMK PU Negeri Bandung, specializing in Building Drawing Technique. The class consisted of 34 students. Data was collected using participant observation to look at the learning process and students' participation in the process; written essay exam to assess students' cognitive ability; and practical assignment guided by job sheets to assess students' psychomotoric skills.

The data on the learning process that was obtained from observations was analyzed using Guttman scale, while data on students' affective skills obtained from observations was analyzed using Likert scale. The results of the exams were analyzed using simple statistics, consisting of average, modus, median, standard deviation, frequency distribution, and the increase of learning achievement. Effectivity of the learning method was assessed using average difference significance test.

3 RESULTS AND DISCUSSIONS

3.1 Description of the classroom action research

The research consisted of three cycles, each of which involves action planning, action, observation and evaluation, and reflection. Each cycle was conducted during two class sessions, each of which comprised 3×35 minutes, taking place in the school's computer lab. Every session was begun with a short opening and introduction, the core lesson, and closing.

The first session of the first cycle focused on drawing a single-floor house plan drawing, while the second session focused on the shop drawing presentation in front of the class. In this cycle, students had begun working in groups but it did not work quite well. Some students did not focus on their assignment and instead conversed with their classmates. The assigned tutors did not do their job to transfer their knowledge and teach their group as well. Students had not demonstrated active participation in either individually or as a group. During class presentations, some students were still dominant, while the others were quiet.

The second cycle was planned based on the evaluation of the first cycle. We also revised the learning plan, the grouping, and supervised the tutors. The first session focused on drawing roof plan and truss details, while the second session was the presentation of the drawings. Although the learning atmosphere was better than that of the first cycle, it was not well enough. Some students did not concentrate on their job and still conversed with others during class. Students also had not grappled with the subject so that they lacked confidence during the class presentation.

The third cycle plan was set based on the evaluation of the second cycle to include the revision of the learning plan and the grouping as well as

the tutor supervision. In the first session, students learned about how to draw a roof plan and truss details; in the second session, they presented their works. During this cycle, students worked better with their tutors and had their confidence to present their works.

3.2 The affective learning achievement

The affective learning aspect was focused on students' participation in the class. This aspect was identified through participation, asking questions, answering questions, presentation, and giving opinions. The research shows that students' affective learning achievement increased on all categories (Figure 1).

In affective domain, students' achievement increases. Their active participation increases from 80% in the 1st cycle to 83% in the 2nd cycle, and 91% in the 3rd cycle.

3.3 The cognitive learning achievement

The cognitive learning aspect was assessed from students' mastery in using basic operations, modification operation, supporting facilities, and their understanding of the given job sheet. The result shows that the number of students who had not achieved the minimum mastery criteria decreased significantly during the research and none of them was under the minimum mastery criteria after the research was done (Figure 2). Their mastery criteria in the cognitive domain increases from 82% in the 1st cycle to 94% in the 2nd cycle, and 100% in the 3rd cycle.

3.4 The psychomotoric learning achievement

The psychomotoric aspect include the mastery of the software, the length of work time, drawing completeness, and drawing consistence. The research result shows that the number of students

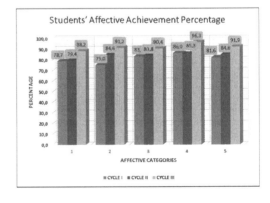

Figure 1. Student's affective achievement percentage.

172

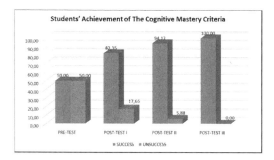

Figure 2. Student's achievement of the cognitive mastery criteria.

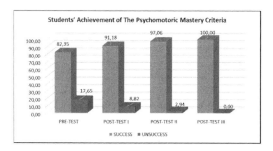

Figure 3. Students' achievement of the psychomotoric mastery criteria.

who had not achieved the minimum mastery criteria decreased considerably from the first to the third cycles and none of them was under the minimum mastery criteria when the research was completed (Figure 3).

Students' achievement of the psychomotoric criteria increases from 91% in the 1st cycle to 97% in the 2nd cycle, and 100% in the 3rd cycle.

3.5 The learning achievement average difference

The significance test employed the significance rate at 95% ($\alpha = 0.05$). There are significant average differences in the results of the affective aspect observation, except for the first and the second cycles. The cognitive average difference is shown by the 0.00 probability (which is smaller than 0.05). This means that students achieved significant average increasement in each cycle. The psychomotoric achievement difference demonstrates significant increasing average, except for the first and the second cycles.

The paired samples test shows that the average score of students' affective achievement using peer tutoring is different significantly from that of learning without peer tutoring. This can be seen in the 0,00 probability, which is smaller than 0,05. This means that the score increases significantly. This demonstrates the effectiveness of peer

tutoring to improve students' active participation in the class.

A similar result is found in the cognitive and psychomotoric domains. Students' cognitive and psychomotoric achievements in learning using peer tutoring significantly increases, based on the 0,00 probability, which is smaller than 0,05.

3.6 Discussions

The increase of teacher's skill to manage the class and students' active participation in the class result in the increase of students' learning achievement. This is indicated by the rise of students' average achievement in cognitive aspect, which increases from 3.18 (in scale 4) in cycle 1, to 3.28 in cycle 2, and 3.43 in cycle 3. The percentage of students' cognitive mastery also rose from 82% in cycle 1 to 94% in cycle 2 and 100% in cycle 3. Students' psychomotoric achievement average increased from 3.44 (in scale 4) in cycle 1 to 3.45 in cycle 2, and 3.54 in cycle 3. Their mastery rose from 91% in cycle 1 to 91% in cycle 2 and 100% in cycle 3. In the third cycle, students showed active participation in the learning process. They asked questions to their presenting classmates, answered questions, and gave their opinions in the class discussions. They also demonstrated more confidence when presenting their group assignment.

The fact that the result of cycle 3, in which tutors are requested to select their own groupmates, are better than cycle 2 and cycle 1 show to us how important are personal and social relationships in learning (Woolfolk, 2007).

4 CONCLUSION

The Classroom Action Research to apply peer tutoring in Digital Drawing subject was conducted through three cycles. The third cycle employed a student-centered learning, in which tutors were to select their own groupmates and tutors were responsible for teaching them. In so doing, students might find their best way of learning and improving their achievements with their peer. This research proved that peer tutoring, which is student-centered designed, effectively improves student's learning achievements in cognitive, affective, and psychomotoric aspects.

REFERENCES

Firman, H. 1987. *Ilmu dan Aplikasi Pendidikan.* Bandung: Penerbit ITB.
Kusumah, W. & Dwitagama. 2011. *Mengenal Penelitian Tindakan Kelas Edisi Kedua.* Jakarta: PT. Indeks.
Suherman, E. dkk. 2003. *Strategi Pembelajaran Matematika Kontemporer.* Bandung: UPI.
Woolfolk, A. 2007. *Educational Psychology.* USA: Pearson Education.Inc.

The effectiveness of web-based interactive blended learning model in programming language courses

H. Effendi & Y. Hendriyani
Universitas Negeri Padang, Padang, West Sumatera, Indonesia

ABSTRACT: This research aims to test the effectiveness of the Web-Based Interactive Blended Learning (WBIBL) model in improving learning outcome in term of cognitive aspect in Programming Language Course. The research was a quantitative experimental model using one group pretest-posttest design which was conducted in Diploma 4 students in Electrical Engineering Department, Universitas Negeri Padang. Data collected by giving a pretest to a group known as the experimental class. Then treatment is given by applying the WBIBL model in teaching and learning, then given a posttest at the end of the lesson. The results of the study in terms of the cognitive aspects indicate that the learning outcomes of the students increased by 0.55 or 55%, where the average of pretest and posttest are 28.80% and 83.40% respectively. The results of this study indicate that the application of the WBIBL model on Programming Language courses could enhance the effectiveness of learning in terms of cognitive aspects.

1 INTRODUCTION

The use of e-learning is viewed as one of the alternatives that might be used to overcome the limitations that exist in the available resources. The use of ICT might improve rapidly especially in universities because technology has been considered as a way of improving learning access to the information source as well as a way of decreasing educational cost (Naidu, 2006, p.2). However, the use of e-learning in the learning process in universities is not as easy as flipping our hands, because e-learning demands multiple prerequisites that might be hard to accomplish.

Since the publication of the regulations, both at the level of Educational Minister and Directorate General of Higher Education, which regulate the implementation of distance learning, the Faculty of Engineering, Universitas Negeri Padang has expanded e-learning. Specifically, it has prepared a sufficient web-based learning system. Through the assistance of Islamic Development Bank, Universitas Negeri Padang has implemented the training programs for lecturers. The university serves as the designer of the e-learning training program so that the lecturers will have sufficient competencies for benefitting all of the available information and communication technologies as their teaching media.

The students and lecturers, for years, have been accustomed to face-to-face learning model. In e-learning model, the interaction in terms of students' control toward the learning process, is very limited. Interaction and interactivity are important things to consider in developing a technology-based learning. In terms of interaction, there are four components of interaction, namely: (a) the learners-instructor interaction; (b) the learners-teaching materials interaction; (c) the learners-learners interaction, and (d) the learners-interface interaction (Jonassen, 1996:407).

Some people argue that the use of ICT for the learning process has caused the occurrence of social isolation due to the decrease in the interaction both between the students and the lecturers and among the students themselves in the classroom. In order to overcome the problem, the researchers would like to use a blended learning model whose characteristics is being interactive. Blended learning or hybrid courses is teaching and learning process which combine the best of face-to-face and online learning (Garrison & Vaughan, 2008:4). It is believed that the combination of two learning methods (in this case, face-to-face and online) will make the learning process more effective (Aggarwal, 2003, p.399).

There are three models used in blended learning: the supplemental, the replacement, and the emporium model (Caraivan, 2011: 4–5). Firstly, the supplemental model is based on the structure of traditional courses and uses technology resources to supplement traditional lectures. Secondly, the replacement model replaces some of the face-to-face classroom meetings with online, interactive activities. Thirdly, the emporium model renounces to all face-to-face meetings, which are replaced with learning platforms or learning portals.

One of the blended learning models that has been developed is Web-Based Interactive Blended

Learning (WBIBL) Model. The model refers to the appropriate learning theory and learning method. Then, the term interactive refers to the fact that the learning will focus on the students (student-centered learning) and will be fully controlled by the students (student-controlled learning). The model also has complete learning components and considers the students' needs and learning styles (Effendi, 2015, pp. 16–17). The model emphasizes the aspect of interaction between the students and learning materials, between the students and lecturers, and among the students themselves. The interaction between the students and learning materials is designed by using the component display theory that is proposed by Merrill (1981). Meanwhile, the interaction between the students and lecturers is designed by using the facility of direct and indirect discussions, which is provided by the model-based online learning system. As a result, the blended-learning model is based on the combination of constructivism paradigm, interactivity principles, and learning styles, which are the aspects given attention in the WBIBL model.

The model has been used for teaching and learning process in Electrical Machineries subjects and it has been proved that the model was effective for used in teaching and learning process in the subject. At this advanced research, the model is used for the effectiveness on other subjects, which is Programming Language subject.

Programming Language course is a basic course which is very important in supporting other subjects. If the student has a good competence in this subject then this expertise can be used to solve engineering problems that exist with using a computer. In fact, this course is considered as a separate subject and is not used to solve various problems for other subjects. At some Study Programs, this course is not taught in the first semester, but in the final semester. Another problem is the lack of time given in the curriculum to achieve the learning competencies. Especially if the method used is teacher-centered. It is therefore necessary to find in order to get students active in learning (student-centered learning) with sufficient guidance from the lecturers.

WBIBL Model, which is an interactive learning model that combine the face-to-face learning in the classroom and e-learning, may be suitable for use in learning Programming Language course. On face-to-face learning in classroom, lecturer and students can discuss problems encountered in learning on particular subject and may be followed by a discussion anywhere and anytime via e-learning between students and other students and between lecturer and students. So that students have enough time in learning and competencies expected in this course can be achieved.

Based on the background of the study, the problem in the study can be formulated as follows:

What is the effectiveness of the Web-Based Interactive Blended Learning (WBIBL) model in improving the learning achievement on Programming Language Course? Therefore, the objective of the study is to test the effectiveness of WBIBL model in improving the learning achievement of the students on Programming Language Course.

2 METHOD

2.1 Research type

The study was quasi-experimental with one group pre-test and post-test design. The design is categorized in the study group pre-experiment. Pre-experimental study has no control group for comparison with the experimental group (Creswell, 2014: 238). It is used to determine if the WBIBL model qualify as an effective model for Programming Language subject. The study might be described as follows:

$$O1 \times O2 \tag{1}$$

Note:
  O1 = Pre-test
  O2 = Post-test
  X = Experiment

2.2 Time and location of the research

This study was conducted in the semester July-December 2015 at Electrical Engineering study programs.

2.3 Research subject

The subjects in the study were a learning group that consisted of 50 students who took the Programming Language subject at the Electrical Engineering Department, Universitas Negeri Padang.

2.4 Instrument of data collecting

The data which were gathered in the study were the scores of the pre-test and post-test in the programming language subject. The data were gathered by means of a learning achievement test which had been initialized by designing the test guidelines. The test guidelines included five topics, namely: (a) introduction of algorithm; (b) flowchart and pseudo code; (c) introduction of programming language; (d) the structure of input and output; and (e) control flow.

2.5 Data analysis technique

In data analysis technique, the following techniques were employed: (1) point-biserial correlation analysis for item validity whose item score is dichotomy (1 or 0); (2) reliabilitas analysis using KR-20; and (3) t-test for testing the effectiveness of the WBIBL model by comparing the results of the pre-test and post-test.

The instrument quality were tested through quality test items. The quality of test items tested with point-biserial correlation analysis. The analysis is used followed the opinion proposed by Mardapi which stated that if the score would be performed under dichotomous manner (1 for correct answers, 0 for incorrect answers) then the implemented correlation technique would be point-biserial (Mardapi, 2004, p.27). The result of the analysis showed that 21 out of 25 items were good. There are four questions (items number 10, 11, 19, and 20) were not good. Internal reliability test is also used to ensure that all questions measure the same thing. The internal reliability test was 0.831 (KR-20). These results suggest that the validity and the reliability of the test has been good.

3 RESULTS AND DISCUSSION

3.1 Findings

The experiment was conducted to a learning group that consisted of 50 students. The learning materials of Programming Language subject that became the example of the experiment consisted of eight sessions. The teaching and learning processes were conducted in the face-to-face learning manner and through e-learning activities.

The initial meeting was used for explaining every single aspect that was related to the e-learning and for administering the pre-test. In addition, the researchers also motivated the students to implement the Web-Based Interactive Blended Learning (WBIBL) model. Sessions two to seven were used for having a class discussion regarding the learning materials that the students had not mastered. Session eight is used for post-test.

The effectiveness test for the WBIBL Model was implemented by comparing the scores of the pre-test and the post-test. The scores of learning achievement in the experiment are shown in Table 1.

In the experiment, it was found that the learning by means of the WBIBL model had achieved

Table 1. The effectiveness of WBIBL model in programming language course.

Test period	Score (%)			Deviation standard	Note
	Max	Min	Mean		
Pre-test	44	16	28.8	1.74	P <
Post-test	100	44	83.4	3.75	0.05
Increase	76	20	54.6	–	

around 83.4% of the learning objectives. In general, the increase from the pre-test results to the post-test results was 54.6%. The difference between the pre-test scores and post-test scores quite high and the value of the two tests differ significantly.

3.2 Discussions

Within the study, the WBIBL model was implemented by combining face-to-face and online learning. The online learning using moodle platform was used as suplement of learning. Students could study the learning materials at home and discusss them with lecturer and other students by using forum discussion that available online. The effectiveness of the WBIBLM was 83.4%. This indicates that the WBIBL model might be used as an alternative for the face-to-face lectures.

Despite the effectiveness, other limitations of the study on the model might not also be avoided. One of the limitation is there was not any control group and this situation had been the consequence of implementing the one-group pre-test and post-test design. The researchers did not have any other choice because there was only one learning group in the Programmming Language subject.

In connection with the application of WBIBL model, it is rather difficult to motivate students to be active in online discussions. This is because students are not familiar with this kind of learning model. There are still many questions that appear on face-to-face lectures, whereas e-learning has provided a forum that can be used to discuss the issue of learning that can be used anytime and anywhere during the lectures. So that lecturers need to find a way to make students want to actively discuss through elearning.

Furthermore, with regard to the validity of the analysis items, it turns out there are four items that are not valid, namely, the question numbers 10, 11, 19, and 20. All of these questions asks a case study of a program code. Most students are not able to answer this question. If anyone can answer this question, perhaps they answered randomly. It can be seen as it turns out this issue was answered very well by the less intelligent students, while students who are good otherwise. Having explored further, from the recognition of students, it turns out they are really do not understand the questions and answer them randomly. So as to further learning, it is necessary to use methods that are able to solve problems like this. Perhaps one of the active learning that is adopted is problem-based learning.

4 CONCLUSION

The effectiveness of the Web-Based Interactive Blended Learning (WBIBL) model was tested by comparing the pre-test and post-test scores. From the experiment, the average pre-test score was 28.8 and the average post-test score was 83.4. The increase in the average score was significant at alpha 0.05. Such result is quite significant; the study on the model has concluded that WBIBL model might be used as an alternative for the face-to-face lectures.

The development of WBIBL model might be continued by creating a stronger design. Probably, future researchers might use control groups, more subjects, longer period and more comparisons between face-to-face learning and e-learning to produce a more effective and reliable WBIBL model.

In connection with the implementation of the WBIBL model in the Programming Language course, maybe it is necessary to add a Problem Based Learning method into the model so that the student can solve a variety of problems according to their field of learning. So that the learning process can be more effective and all the competencies expected in this course can be achieved.

REFERENCES

Aggarwal, A.K. 2003. *Web-based education: learning from experience*. University of Baltimore.

Caraivan, L. 2011. Blended learning: from concept to implementation. *Euromentor Journal* 2(4).

Effendi, H. 2015. Model blended learning interaktif berbasis web mata kuliah mesin-mesin listrik di Fakultas Teknik Universitas Negeri Padang. *Dissertation*, unpublished. Yogyakarta Sate University.

Garrison, D.R. & Vaughan, N.D. 2008. *Blended learning in higher education: framework, principles, and guidelines*. San Fransisco: John Willey & Sons.

Jonassen, D.H. (ed.). 1996. *Handbook of research for educational and communication and technology*. Macmillan library reference.

Mardapi, D. 2004. *Penyusunan tes hasil belajar*. Yogyakarta: Program Pascasarjana Universitas Negeri Yogyakarta.

Mendikbud, *Peraturan Menteri Pendidikan dan Kebudayaan No. 24 Tahun 2012 tentang Penyelenggaraan Pendidikan Jarak Jauh pada Pendidikan Tinggi*. Jakarta.

Merrill, M.D. 1981. *Component display theory*. New Jersey: Educational Technology Publication Englewood Cliffs.

Naidu, S. 2006. *Elearning: a guide book of principles, procedures, and practice*. New Delhi: Creative Workshop.

Pemerintah Republik Indonesia, *Undang-Undang Republik Indonesia No.12 Tahun 2012 tentang Pendidikan Tinggi*. Jakarta, 2012.

Regionalization and Harmonization in TVET – Abdullah et al. (Eds)
© 2017 Taylor & Francis Group, London, ISBN 978-1-138-05419-6

The influence of the vocational learning process on the acquisition of employability skills attributes mediated by performance assessment

I.M. Suarta
Bali State Polytechnic, Bali, Indonesia

ABSTRACT: The main purpose of the study was to assess the acquisition of employability skills attributes, and to predict the effects of the vocational learning process on these when mediated by the implementation of performance assessment. The research was conducted using research and development approaches. The learning innovation product testing was conducted using classroom action research. A total of 77 students participated in the study. The data was analyzed using structural equation modeling. The overall, mean level acquisition of employability skills attributes by students was 3.866. Students had high mean scores in team work and independent skills. The direct effects of the vocational learning process on the acquisition of employability skills attribute is not significant. However, the vocational learning process has a significant indirect effect on the acquisition of employability skills attributes when mediated by performance assessment. The study recommends the implementation of performance assessment in the vocational learning process for assessing the acquisition of employability skills attributes by students.

1 INTRODUCTION

Highly skilled graduates need to develop skills that will enable them to face the challenges of increased competition in both local and global markets. In the 21st century, the employer not only requires graduates with a high knowledge qualification, but that they also have a number of attributes known as employability skills (Archer et al., 2008; Saunders & Zuzel, 2010; European Commission, 2010). Employability skills emphasize the need for graduates to create their own profile so as to prepare them for today's highly competitive marketplace for graduate jobs, for example, the ability to work effectively with others, communication skills, self-management and problem-solving (Archer et al., 2008; Maxwell, et al., 2009). Employability skills—also variously referred to as non-technical, professional, key, core or generic skills—are considered vital in enabling graduates to apply disciplinary knowledge effectively in the workplace (AAGE, 2011). Therefore, vocational education graduates need to be given more opportunities to develop employability skills attributes besides technical skills.

The development of the employability skills of students has become the main concern of higher vocational education—including polytechnic education in Indonesia. There are many factors reported in the literature that might contribute to the successful teaching of employability skills. These include instructional method, teacher attributes, the inclusion of skill acquisition as an explicit learning

goal, student involvement and activity, relevant context and student responsibility and autonomy (Cassidy, 2006). Innovations in vocational curricula, such as learning method and strategies, and assessment method are needed for the development of employability skills. Some studies indicate that a learning method that is (1) learner-centered, (2) work-centered, and (3) attribute-focused can improve the quality of the process and learning outcomes, including the acquisition of employability skills by students (Martin et al., 2008). Klotz et al. (2014) stated vocational learning comprises more than factual knowledge and procedures; the development of a vocational identity is a key aspect and outcome of vocational education provisions and is assumed to play an integral role in how students learn and perform.

The measurement of a student's knowledge is objective as it is about facts, but measuring a student's skills and ability to apply knowledge is subjective. The problem of measuring employability skills is one of the key obstacles in assessing their supply. Theory education goals state that assessment should focus on the achievement of authentic learning outcomes (Cumming & Maxwell, 1999). Based on this theory, authentic assessment can be used to measure the student's acquisition of employability skills. Gulikers et al. (2004) define authentic assessment as: *"An assessment requiring students to use the same competencies, or combinations of knowledge, skills, and attitudes that they need to apply in the criterion situation in professional life*". The strength of authentic assessment is that inferences about student competency are made from performances of a kind similar to the performance for which the students are being educated. The authentic assessment is also called performance assessment or alternative assessment.

Theoretically, authentic assessment follows the constructivist paradigm of teaching and learning. In constructivism, the learner as a whole person is the focus. Many types of authentic assessment practices are reported in the literature, such as portfolios, student logs, and peer- and self-assessment (Mintah, 2003). Student peer- and self-assessment are examples of educational practice that are likely to contribute positively toward the development of employability skills (Cassidy, 2006). Some researchers have indicated self-assessment can be defined as students judging their own work, based on evidence and explicit criteria, for the purpose of improving future performance (McMillan & Hearn, 2008), and it has been identified as a key factor in the effective assessment of learning (Joyce et al., 2009).

The difficulty lies in measuring the acquisition of employability skills and there is a gap between what is required of students in assessment tasks and what occurs in the world of work, the background of this study. In this study, we used self-assessment—as a type of performance assessment—to measure students' acquisition employability skills attribute. The main purpose of the study was to assess the acquisition of employability skills attributes by higher vocational education students. This study also aimed to predict the effects of the vocational learning process on the acquisition of employability skills attributes mediated by performance assessment.

2 RESEARCH METHOD

In this study, authors assumed the performance assessment to be a mediating factor between the vocational learning process and the acquisition of employability skills attributes. The research model is shown in Figure 1.

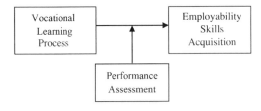

Figure 1. Research hypothetical model.

The following three hypotheses are proposed:

H1. Vocational learning process have a positive effect on the students' acquisition of employability skills attributes.
H2. Vocational learning process have a positive effect on the performance assessment.
H3. Performance assessments have a positive effect on the students' acquisition of employability skills attributes.

This paper is part of the development of an employability skills learning model, conducted using research and development approaches. Learning product testing was conducted using classroom action research. The 'objects' being tested were accounting students from the Bali State Polytechnic who were studying courses in Applied Computer 3. A total of 77 students participated in the study. The research subjects are the vocational learning process, the performance assessment, and the acquisition of occupational skills attributes.

The acquisition of employability skills attributes observation of learning activities in the computer lab. The employability skills attributes were adapted from research conducted by Suarta (2010). The response choices used to assess the level of acquisition of employability skills attributes are: 1 = not competent, student cannot perform this skill; 2 = partly competent, student can perform parts of this skill, but requires considerable assistance and/or supervision; 3 = sufficiently competent, student can perform this skill, but requires some assistance and/or supervision; 4 = highly competent, student can perform this skill satisfactorily without assistance or supervision; and 5 = completely competent, student can perform this skill without supervision and with initiative and adaptability to problem situations. Measurement of the acquisition of employability skills attributes was done by student self-assessment.

The students' responses for the vocational learning process and performance assessment perception were measured using a questionnaire developed and adapted from previous studies (Chappell, 2003; Gulikers et al., 2004; Fisher et al., 2005). A five-point Likert scale from 1 (strongly disagree) to 5 (strongly agree) was used to assess students' response.

The validity of the instrument was tested using the Pearson product moment correlation coefficient with $\alpha = 5\%$. The employability skills consist of seven attributes, with the coefficient Pearson product moment correlation varying from 0.524–0.707, and the value of reliability (Cronbach's Alpha) at 0.757. The construct of the vocational learning process consists of seven observed variables, with the coefficient Pearson product moment correlation varying from 0.440–0.634, and the value of reliability (Cronbach's Alpha) at 0.581. The perceptions of performance assessment consisted of six questions, with the coefficient Pearson product moment correlation varying from 0.520–0.702, and Cronbach's Alpha at 0.700.

Data analysis included confirmatory factor analysis and structural equation modeling, carried out with the SmartPLS 3 program. Confirmatory factor analysis was intended to confirm whether the observed variables are measure of constructs variables. The criteria used is factor loading (λ) $\geq$ 0.50 with a significance level of 5%, Construct Reliability (CR) $\geq$ 0.60, and Average Variance Extracted (AVE) $\geq$ 0.50 (Hair et al., 2006). The structural model describes the linear relationship between the vocational learning process and the performance assessment; the vocational learning process and the employability skills acquisition, and the performance assessment and employability skills acquisition. Evaluation of the relationship between variables is done by using the path coefficient (γ or β) and t-value with a significance level 5%.

3 RESULTS AND DISCUSSION

3.1 Students' perception of employability skills acquisition

Table 1 shows students' perception of employability skills acquisition. The overall, mean level acquisition of employability skills attributes by students was 3.866 (SD = 0.690). Students had high mean scores in only two aspects: team work skills (M = 4.182, SD = 0.575) and independent skills (M = 4.078, SD = 0.504). The other five attributes of employability skills were moderate: written communication skills (M = 3.935, SD = 0.589), self-evaluation skills (M = 3.883, SD = 0.702), self-management skills (M = 3.818, SD = 0.833), analyzing skills (M = 3.597, SD = 0.707) and problem-solving skills (M = 3.571, SD = 0.633).

3.2 Analysis of the structural model

A structural equation modeling technique was used to test the model. The SmartPLS 3 program was employed for this purpose. There are two variables in the construct of the vocational learning process that are not significant, which are implementation strategies that require students' active participation (Voc_LP3), with loading factor (λ) = 0.327 ($p = 0.196$), and providing feedback on the learning process (Voc_LP6), with loading factor (λ) = 0.217 ($p = 0.407$). Figure 2 illustrates the structural relationships between the study variables. Evaluation of the relationship between latent variables is done by using the path coefficient (γ or β) and t-value at a significance level of 5%. The path coefficient and t-value of the relationships exist as hypothesized (previously summarized) in Table 2.

A structural model with a hypothesized mediating effect can produce direct and indirect effect. Direct effects are the relationship linking the vocational learning process construct with the acquisition of employability skills attribute construct. Indirect effects are those relationships that involve a sequence of relationships with performance assessment as an intervening construct. Table 3 shows the direct, indirect and total effect among variables.

3.3 Discussion

The acquisition of employability skills attributes by accounting vocational students is moderately high. This is similar to findings reported by Omar et al. (2012) and Dania et al. (2014). The study conducted by Omar et al. (2012) showed the overall mean of employability skills among community college students was 3.63. Other research by Dania et al. (2014) showed that the overall mean of vocational secondary students' employability skills was 3.81. Based on these studies, we can say that the employability skills of the accounting vocational students at the Bali State Polytechnic were moderate. Students had high mean scores in two attributes, namely: team work skills and independent skills. Both of these skills are employability skills attributes that are needed in the workforce (Saunders & Zuzel, 2010; European Commission, 2010).

Table 1. Students' perception of employability skills acquisition.

Rank	Variable	Employability skills attributes	Mean	SD
1	S_Att6	Team work skills	4.182	.575
2	S_Att5	Independent skills	4.078	.504
3	S_Att3	Written communication skills	3.935	.589
4	S_Att7	Self-evaluation skills	3.883	.702
5	S_Att4	Self-management skills	3.818	.833
6	S_Att1	Analyzing skills	3.597	.707
7	S_Att2	Problem-solving skills	3.571	.633
Overall			3.866	.690

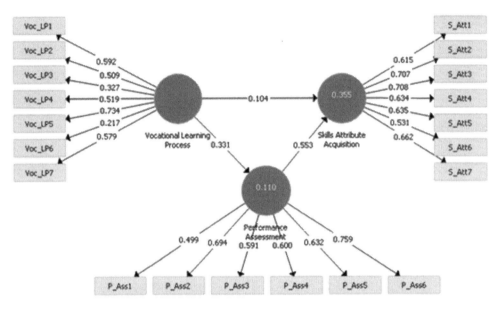

Figure 2. Analysis of structural equation model.

Table 2. Evaluation of path coefficient.

Path	Path coefficient	T-statistic	P-value
Vocational Learning Process → Skills Attribute Acquisition	0.104^{ns}	0.796	0.426
Vocational Learning Process → Performance Assessment	0.331^{**}	2.173	0.030
Performance Assessment → Skills Attribute Acquisition	0.553^{**}	6.034	0.000

Table 3. Direct effect, indirect effect, and total effect.

Path	Direct effect	Indirect effect	Total effect
Vocational Learning Process			
→ Skills Attribute Acquisition	$0.104 (0.426)^{ns}$	$0.183 (0.045)^{**}$	$0.287 (0.043)^{**}$
→ Performance Assessment	$0.331 (0.030)^{**}$	—	$0.331 (0.030)^{**}$
Performance Assessment			
→ Skills Attribute Acquisition	$0.553 (0.000)^{**}$	—	$0.553 (0.000)^{**}$

– Digits in brackets indicate P values.
– ** = significant at 5%.

The results of the structural model are discussed as follows: Hypothesis 1 stated that the vocational learning process has a positive effect on students' acquisition of employability skills attributes. The direct path of vocational learning process to acquisition of employability skills attributes is not significant. This means that the vocational learning process does not have a direct effect on the acquisition of employability skills attributes. These findings are in line with Attard et al. (2010, p. 12) which states that learning outcomes refer to the achievements of the learner and thus do not relate to the perspective of the teacher or of the teaching process as such. One approach in the vocational learning process is the student center. The use of learning outcomes is identified as being the second parameter of student-centered learning.

Hypotheses 2 and 3 postulate that the vocational learning process will have a positive effect on the performance assessment, and the performance assessment will have a positive effect on the students' acquisition of employability skills attributes.

The direct path of the vocational learning process to performance assessment is significant. It means that the vocational learning process has a positive direct effect on performance assessment. Moreover, the direct path of performance assessment to students' acquisition of employability skills attributes is significant. It means that performance assessment has a positive direct effect on the acquisition of employability skills attributes. The role of the teacher in the vocational learning includes creating a trusting classroom culture which promotes meaningful assessment of the learning process. This finding reinforces the assumption that the implementation of performance assessment has a positive impact on learning outcomes (Gulikers et al., 2006). Performance assessment promotes mastery goal orientation, in which the focus is on improving knowledge, understanding, and skill (McMillan & Hearn, 2008), and can measure students' cognitive thinking and reasoning skills, as well as their ability to apply knowledge to solve realistic, meaningful problems (Darling-Hammond & Adamson, 2010).

The vocational learning process has a significant indirect effect on the acquisition of employability skills attributes with an indirect effect coefficient 0.183, and a total effect coefficient of 0.287. These findings indicate performance assessments to be factors that mediate the vocational learning process, and have a significant influence on the level of acquisition of employability skills attributes by students. As stated by Jönsson (2008), an assessment methodology which could assess students' self-assessment skills, and in this way help them to develop those skills, would therefore make a substantive contribution to teacher education. In this research, the vocational learning process and performance assessment accounted for 35.5% of the variance in the acquisition of employability skills attributes. Attard et al. (2010, p. 12) state that the constructivist approaches to learning and teaching are well aligned with this process and develop employability because they encourage exploration, provide feedback and develop reflection, motivation and engagement. It is clear that assessment can be used strategically to motivate and engage students, and carefully chosen assessment tasks can help develop specific employability attributes.

4 CONCLUSION AND RECOMMENDATIONS

The overall mean level of the students' acquisition of employability skills attributes was moderate. In view of the findings from this study, the innovation learning process is necessary to develop employability skills in students. The vocational learning process had a significant indirect effect on the acquisition of employability skills attributes, which was mediated by the performance assessment; thus the latter becomes a very important factor in mediating the learning process in vocational education.

The teacher's role is very important in promoting the meaningful assessment of vocational learning processes. The study recommends the implementation of performance assessments in the vocational learning process for assessing students' acquisition employability skills attributes.

REFERENCES

AAGE. (2011). *2011 AAGE employer survey*. Sydney: Australian Association of Graduate Employers.

Archer, W., Davison, J., Brown, R. & Herrmann, K. (2008). *Graduate employability: The views of employers*. London, UK: The Council for Industry and Higher Education. Retrieved from http://ec.europa.eu/education/higher-education/doc/business/graduate.en.pdf

Attard, A., Di Ioio, E., Geven, K. & Santa, R. (2010). *Student centered learning: An insight into theory and practice*. Bucharest, Romania: The European Students' Union.

Cassidy, S. (2006). Developing employability skills: Peer assessment in higher education. *Education + Training, 48*(7), 508–517.

Chappell, C. (2003). *Changing pedagogy: Contemporary vocational learning*. OVAL Research Working Paper 03–12. Sydney, Australia: Australian Centre for Organizational, Vocational, and Adult Learning (OVAL). Retrieved from http://www.oval.uts.edu.au/publications/2003wp0312chappell.pdf

Cumming, J.J. & Maxwell, G.S. (1999). Contextualizing authentic assessment. *Assessment in education: Principles, policies and practices, 6*(2), 177–194.

Dania, J., Bakar, A.R. & Mohamed, S. (2014). Factors influencing the acquisition of employability skills by students of selected technical secondary school in Malaysia. *International Education Studies, 7*(2), 117–124.

Darling-Hammond, L. & Adamson, F. (2010). *Beyond basic skills: The role of performance assessment in achieving 21st century standards of learning*. Stanford, CA: Stanford Center for Opportunity Policy in Education.

European Commission. (2010). *Employers' perception of graduate employability: Analytical report*. Retrieved from http://ec.europa.eu/public_opinion/flash/fl_304_en.pdf

Fisher, D.L., Waldrip, B.G. & Dorman, J. (2005). *Student perceptions of assessment: Development and validation of a questionnaire*. Paper presented at the Annual Meeting of the American Educational Research Association, Montreal, Canada.

Gulikers, J., Bastiaens, T. & Kirschner, P. (2004). A five-dimensional framework for authentic assessment. *Educational Technology Research and Development, 52*(3), 67–85.

Gulikers, J., Bastiaens, T., Kirschner, P. & Kester, L. (2006). Relations between student perceptions of assessment authenticity, study approaches and learning outcome. *Studies in Educational Evaluation, 32*(4), 381–400.

Hair, J.F., Jr., Black, W.C., Babin, B.J., Anderson, R.E. & Tatham, R.L. (2006). *Multivariate data analysis* (6th ed.). Upper Saddle River, NJ: Pearson Education.

Jönsson, A. (2008). *Educative assessment for/of teacher competency*. Studies in Science and Technology Education No. 18. Retrieved from http://www.mah.se/muep

Joyce, C., Spiller, L. & Twist, J. (2009). *Self-assessment: What teachers think*. Wellington: New Zealand Council for Educational Research (NZCER). Retrieved from http://www.nzcer.org.nz/pdfs/self-assessment.pdf

Klotz, V.K., Billett, S. & Winther, E. (2014). Promoting workforce excellence: Formation and relevance of vocational identity for vocational educational training. *Empirical Research in Vocational Education and Training, 6*(6), 1–20.

Martin, L., West, J. & Bill, K. (2008). Incorporating problem-based learning strategies to develop learner autonomy and employability skills in sports science undergraduates. *Journal of Hospitality, Leisure, Sport and Tourism Education, 7*(1), 18–30.

Maxwell, G., Scott, B., Macfarlane, D. & Williamson, E. (2009). Employers as stakeholders in postgraduate employability skills development. *International Journal of Management Education, 8*(2), 1–22.

McMillan, J.H. & Hearn, J. (2008). Student self-assessment: The key to stronger student motivation and higher achievement. *Educational HORIZONS, 87,* 40–49.

Mintah, J.K. (2003). Authentic assessment in physical education: Prevalence of use and perceived impact on students' self-concept, motivation, and skill achievement. *Measurement in Physical Education and Exercise Science, 7*(3), 161–174.

Omar, M.K., Bakar, A.R. & Rashid, A. (2012). Employability skills acquisition among Malaysian community college students. *Journal of Social Science, 8*(3), 472–478.

Saunders, V. & Zuzel, K. (2010). Evaluating employability skills: Employer and student perceptions. *Bioscience Education, 15*(1), 1–15.

Suarta, I.M. (2010). Supervisors' perceptions of the employability skills needed by higher vocational education graduates to be successful in the workplace. In *14th UNESCO-APEID International Conference: Education for Human Resource Development, Thailand*, 1–14.

Regionalization and Harmonization in TVET – Abdullah et al. (Eds)
© *2017 Taylor & Francis Group, London, ISBN 978-1-138-05419-6*

Integration model of employability skills in vocational education to support competitive industry

I. Hanafi, M. Ma'sum & R. Febriana
Universitas Negeri Jakarta, Indonesia

ABSTRACT: The purpose of this research is to find an implementation model of integration of employability skills into vocational education, especially the three aspects of the most dominant skills which graduates of vocational education must have, namely, those needed by industry such as personal qualities, and basic and interpersonal skills. The research method used was the Research and Development model with analysis, design, development, implementation, and evaluation phases. The results showed that the conceptual model of integration of employability skills into vocational education to build attitudes and behaviors of learners must be comprehensively implemented by using an approach of Action-Oriented Learning (AOL), through learning in the classroom, and practice in the laboratory or workshop. In addition, practice in the industry is controlled through debriefing and the common perception of teaching staff in relation to the aspects and assessment of employability skills, and managed jointly between educational institutions and industry.

1 INTRODUCTION

Vocational education has specific characteristics that are oriented toward preparing students for working as technicians in certain fields. Vocational education cannot be separated from the world of work as it is a chain that should not be disconnected. The world of work and vocational education can be viewed as two sides of a coin; they should be developed by taking into account what the working world needs in order to meet the demands of the labor market. Vocational education cannot be closed to developments in the working world because the demands of knowledge and work skills are dynamically changing. Thus, the working world should always be observed as a reference for developing vocational education in an effort to maintain the sustainability that has a direct impact on the demands of the knowledge, attitudes and skills of graduates.

A nation's competitiveness depends on the knowledge, skills, and work ethic of its workforce. A knowledgeable workforce which has been well-trained and is highly skilled, would be able to increase the added value of products derived through improved productivity, cost production efficiency, and a high quality of production. Vocational education thus makes a big contribution to the improvement of the economy's competitiveness. Wilkins (2001) stated that the paradigm of vocational education is the improvement of the economy to support the modernization of the

industry and to improve economy in society. In addition, vocational education should enhance its role to prepare graduates in the knowledge, skills, and personality which fit the expectations of the world of work. Many industries have complained that the knowledge, skills and attitudes of graduates are still far removed from the needs of industry; even graduates of vocational education were not considered ready for work, because of the demanding attitudes and behavior of employees.

Vocational education should provide adequate provisions for graduates to enter into the world of work through various strategies, both in the classroom and practice in workshops. Graduates of vocational education should have sufficient competence in accordance with the demands of the work environment. However, these graduates will continue to find it difficult to perform in the working world if educational institutions do not anticipate the changes and demands therein and do not equip the graduates with the mental attitude needed to face job competition. The characteristics of the work climate are changing rapidly because of the development of technology. Therefore, the workforce is not only required to understand and perform their jobs well in their chosen fields of work, but they should also have employability skills in order to sustain jobs and improve the quality of production and competitiveness.

The employability skills demanded by the world of work should be used as an umbrella for vocational education institutions in the planning and implementation of the curriculum, as well as an effort to improve and sustain the quality of graduates. The demand for skilled workers should be taken seriously; it is the feedback that gives a correction in the right direction for the development of vocational education, especially with regard to the demands of employability skills. This study aims to develop a vocational education model that integrates the aspect of employability skills through the development of the learning process. The results of previous studies on employability skills suggest that the three main aspects which are most required from graduates of vocational education are: 1) the personal qualities of the individual, such as honesty, responsibility, confidence, social attitudes, self-management, commitment, adaptability, ability to work without supervision, and safety work; 2) basic skills including reading, writing, counting, listening and speaking/communication; and 3) interpersonal, that is, team player, listening to friends, serving customers, leadership, negotiation, and working with different cultures. This indicates that the competence of graduates of vocational education is related to attitudes and behavior. The results of previous research findings illustrate that the order of priority in the world of work has shifted. The interpersonal aspects should receive most attention, while thinking skills is the least emphasized as these are assumed to be less important in comparison to developing the qualities of the individual and their interpersonal skills. Based on these findings, a procedural model of vocational education which integrates employability skills into the learning process is to be developed. The results of this study are expected to be used as a product development model for vocational education in accordance with the demands of the world of work.

2 INTEGRATION OF EMPLOYABILITY SKILLS

2.1 Conceptual model

Based on the results of previous studies, an early conceptual integration model of employability skills in vocational education is shown in Figure 1. The conceptual model is validated and evaluated by industry experts and vocational education through Focus Group Discussion (FGD) to get input on the development of the procedural model in the implementation process that integrates employability skills in the planning and learning process.

The conceptual integration model acts as an overview of the integration of employability skills aspects into the learning process from the first year to third year. Figure 1 shows that aspects of employability skills are an integral part of shaping the attitude and behavior of students in vocational education. All aspects should be an inherent part in the learning process to prepare graduates to not only be competent in a certain job, but also to have the attitude and behavior required to meet the demands of the world of work. Implementation aspects of employability skills in the process of learning need to be structured and organized to provide a significant impact on attitudes and behavior.

The Indonesia Qualification Framework (IQF) requires graduates of vocational school at Level 3 and up to diploma Level 5 to have the required capability, namely, 1) being able to finish the job with a wide scope, choose the appropriate method from the various options that have been offered, being able to analyze raw data and to demonstrate the data in both qualitative and quantitative ways; 2) mastering the theoretical concept of this area of knowledge in general, as well as formulating procedural problem-solving; 3) ability to manage working groups and prepare a written report in a comprehensive manner; and 4) responsibility for the work itself and thus be held accountable for the achievement of the group's work. In addition, some effort is needed for the integration of employability skills at every level to achieve specific skills, and students must also be given the knowledge, understanding and actualizing aspects of employability skills so that they know, understand, and can implement all these aspects in everyday life. It is not easy to implement the program, but through the implementation of a curriculum model and a variety of learning strategies and initiatives of the administrators, it is hoped that aspects of employability skills can be integrated in the individual students.

2.2 Procedural model

The procedural model is the development of a conceptual model to integrate aspects of employability skills in the structuring and implementation of vocational education. The development of vocational education through an implementation model that integrates of employability skills should follow the rules and theory of the research and development method by following the model of Analysis, Design, Development, Implementation, and Evaluation (ADDIE). The next stage is the implementation of the test limited by the sample which has been selected based on certain criteria, such as the diploma program in environmental engineering at the Universitas Negeri, Jakarta. The implementation of trials must be conducted with respect to the factors that have an effect, including site selection, as well as identify the supporting and inhibiting factors.

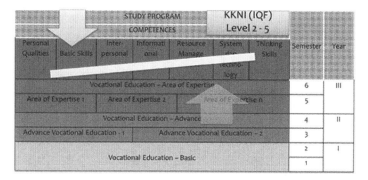

Figure 1. Conceptual model integration of employability skills (source: Hanafi & Ma'sum, 2014).

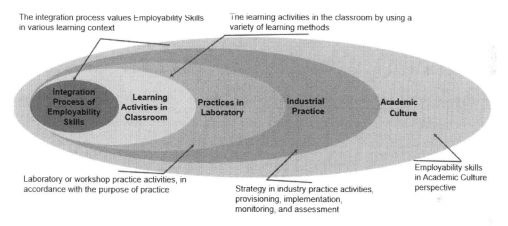

Figure 2. Various approaches.

Based on the characteristics of vocational education that promote an approach of learning by doing, aspects of employability skills can be integrated through three components, namely, 1) learning in the classroom, 2) practical exercises in the workshop, and 3) industry practice, which is managed jointly between institutions and industry. The values of employability skills are instilled in the classroom and in practical workshops conducted using Action-Oriented Learning (AOL) as an approach. The strategy pursued to integrate the values of employability skills is to conduct a workshop to create common perceptions among faculty members, especially the head of the program, and debriefing the students prior to conducting the practice in the industry. With the same perception, the values of employability skills can be realized as a foundation of the integration process and thus change the behavior of the learners. Various approaches are described in Figure 2.

By using the approach of AOL to gain knowledge and skills, students will also acquire a positive attitude and behavior toward the work.

The AOL approach allows learners to gain knowledge from experience and share it with a group of friends. Peer group input provides feedback and constructive criticism to help complete the job, and learners gain knowledge of the advantages of cooperation within the group. Action-Oriented Learning can provide a significant impact on the behavior of learners, because they are able to see how problems can be solved by working together, sharing knowledge, listening to others, and being responsible for each task mandated to them. It can provide enough space to instill the values of employability skills that are demanded in the world of work to learners. Lindemann (2002) states that Action-Oriented Learning is not just a method of learning, but is about the principles of learning. Another important aspect that should be emphasized in vocational education is as a form of activity for understanding the employment situation in the industry. Vocational education is geared to generating employment for multi-skilled, multi-function, knowledgeable people who are willing to learn continuously, and have the ability to acquire and apply their knowledge, as well as technology. Therefore, there needs to be an effort to encourage and establish learners to be workers who value knowledge as their main capital, that is, knowledge workers.

In an effort to instill employability skills into the learning process, the important thing is that they must be explicitly stated in each unit of competency in any subjects that are given to the students. This means that the aspect of employability skills is part of the performance requirements that would form the competencies that will be generated as a whole. Aspects of employability skills must be clearly defined and written into each unit of competency to ensure that aspects of the employability skills do exist and can be measured and evaluated as an important component of job competence. In instilling aspects of employability skills into the learning process, the principles of adult learning should be used, namely to give the relevant subject and learners a set of concepts that emphasize that commitment, responsibility and openness are conducted continuously (Cleary et al., 2006).

Employability skills need to be integrated with competencies that will be produced at every level of qualification and necessary support provided to the process of learning and assessment of learning outcomes. In addition, we need an approach to learning and assessment strategies for the integration of employability skills in any learning activities in the classroom, in the workshop, or in industry. The results of FGD with a number of education experts, as well as continued discussions with the vocational education study program, have produced a picture of the scope of activities that can be associated with the implementation of the integration aspects of employability skills to embed these aspects. The results of the discussion suggest that there should be dissemination to the faculty members who administer related subjects, and to instructors in industry, to form shared perception of employability skills aspects.

Using the AOL approach will provide a deep understanding of the values of employability skills, so that the values occur naturally and have an impact on the attitudes and behaviors of learners. Thus an AOL approach can provide corroboration for: 1) technical capabilities, the ability to perform the task technically well and properly and monitor the work independently and critically; 2) social skills, the ability to work both in a team and independently, and monitor and consider the factors of the environment and safety; and 3) the ability to learn and use the methodology to continue to learn independently and be the best in field. The third ability is a demand for the skills required by the world of work in the form of values contained in employability skills.

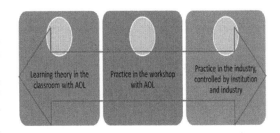

Figure 3. Integration model of employability skills in vocational education.

Based on the results of FGD, preparation needs to be done to equip learners to build a system that controls industrial practice and that will ensure learners are ready to adapt to the practical working environment. Industrial environments along with a different educational environment will give a new experience to the students, not only in the atmosphere and work situation that requires readiness of learners, but in the industry which also requires changes in attitudes and behavior in the face of every task and the work which is the responsibility of each worker. Through the implementation of industry practice, students will acquire knowledge and skills that will be a provision for work in the future. Industry practice provides an opportunity for learners to carry out activities in accordance with their expertise, and more importantly students can apply social interaction and the employability skills which have been obtained in educational institutions in practice activities. The results of the evaluation provided feedback to the analysis phase to obtain a model of the ideal integration of employability skills which can be implemented by educational institutions. The final result is an implementation model that integrates employability skills values into the learning process as part of a response to the needs of the working world, as well as efforts to improve the quality of vocational education graduates. The analysis of integration model employability skills in accordance with the purpose of vocational education is shown in Figure 3.

3 CONCLUSION

In an effort to develop a model of vocational education that integrates aspects of employability skills into learning, some steps must first be taken, such as identifying aspects that are needed by the world of work and placing them in the learning design, and implementing learning by using the AOL approach and control of industry practice, including shared perception and understanding of employability skills values by the parties responsible for the implementation of vocational education. Vocational education institutions – as a form of education that prepares learners for employment – should always be responsive to the demands and needs of the increasingly dynamic environment of the workplace. The process of integrating and cultivating the aspects and values of employability skills should be done gradually and continuously, starting with the process of perception and debriefing of the learner, then going through the learning process, and finally to the process of assessment. To that end, the right strategy needs to be in place so that vocational institutions can respond to the development of the world of work and the demands of industry – especially in the aspect of employability skills – in order to enhance the contribution of vocational education to support competitive industries.

REFERENCES

Bakar, A., Mohamed, S. and Hanafi, I. (2007). Employability skills: Malaysian employers perspectives. *The International Journal of Interdisciplinary Social Sciences*, 2(1), 263–274.

Cleary, M., Flynn, R. & Thomasson, S. (2006). *Employability skills: From framework to practice*. Melbourne, Australia: Precision Consultancy.

Cotton, K. (2005). *Close-Up #15 – Developing employability skills* (School Improvement Research Series VIII). Portland, OR: Northwest Regional Educational Laboratory.

Hanafi, I. & Ma'sum, M. (2014). Integration of the employability skills into TVET curricula: Proposed by demand perspectives. In *Proceedings of 10th International Conference of AASVET (Asian Academic Society for Vocational Education and Training), Tokyo, Japan* (pp. 31–38).

Lindemann, H.-J. (2002). *The principle of action-oriented learning*. Retrieved from http://www.Halindo.de/html/docde/HOL-prinzip02002.pdf.

Lowden, K., Hall, S., Elliot, D. & Lewin, J. (2011). *Employers' perceptions of the employability skills of new graduates*. Research commissioned by the Edge Foundation. University of Glasgow SCRE Centre and Edge Foundation.

SCANS. (2001). *About SCANS*. Baltimore, MD: SCANS2000 Center, Johns Hopkins University. Retrieved from http://www.scans.wpmc.jhu.edu

Wilkins, S. (2001). Human resource development through vocational education in the United Arab Emirates: The case of Dubai Polytechnic. *Journal of Vocational Education and Training*, 54(1), 5–26.

Regionalization and Harmonization in TVET – Abdullah et al. (Eds)
© 2017 Taylor & Francis Group, London, ISBN 978-1-138-05419-6

Vocational learning tools based on scientific learning

J. Kustija
Fakultas Pendidikan Teknologi dan Kejuruan Universitas Pendidikan Indonesia, Bandung, West Java, Indonesia

D. Fauziah
Sekolah Tinggi Elektro dan Informatika Institut Teknologi Bandung, Bandung, West Java, Indonesia

ABSTRACT: Based on preliminary studies it was found that the learning tools of Basic and Power Measurement for scientific-based learning that are suitable for use in Vocational High School (VHS) are not available. This research aims to develop a scientific learning tool for Basic and Power Measurement at VHS by adopting the steps of discovery learning. This research used the mixed method with sequential exploratory design and stages conducted through the procedural approach of Research and Development (R&D) presented by Borg and Gall. The research produced 128 pages of teaching material equipped with learning media. Based on the results obtained, it was shown that the product was effective in improving student learning outcomes.

1 INTRODUCTION

Vocational education-based schooling is different from that in public schools. The learning principle of this schooling is the combination of theoretical knowledge with technical competences. Currently, curriculum 2013 (K13), with a scientific approach, has been applied in Indonesian Vocational High School (VHS). In this curriculum, students are expected to study more actively so they can better implement the learning material.

Curriculum changes have an impact on teaching and learning components. Each component related to the curriculum change must be adapted so it does not obstruct implementation. The components are learning tools consisting of syllabus, lesson plans, teaching materials and learning media that must be integrated and prepared before the teacher instructs the material in class. Based on preliminary studies conducted by the researchers, it was found that the learning tools for Basic and Power Measurement with scientific-based learning that are really suitable for use in VHS are not available so the students' learning outcomes are lower than expected.

For all levels, K13 is implemented using a scientific approach that puts students' activity at the center of the learning process. The characteristics of scientific learning are: (1) place student at the center; (2) involve science process skills in constructing the concept, law or principle; (3) involve cognitive processes to stimulate development of students' intellect, especially for high-level thinking skills; and (4) develop the students' character (Hosnan, 2014).

One of the learning models contained in K13 is the discovery learning model, which emphasizes the importance of students' activity in understanding the key structure or ideas of a study subject. Students are encouraged to learn mostly through their own active involvement with the concepts and principles, and teachers encourage the students to get experience and conduct experiments which allow them to find principles by themselves. The three main characteristics of discovery learning that relate to cognitive theory are: (1) an emphasis on active learning, (2) the development of meaningful learning, and (3) the capacity to change attitudes and values toward the subject and the self as problem solver (Svinicki, 1998). If the students find the meaning of the lesson by themselves, it is expected that their comprehension will persist for a longer time (Dean & Kuhn, 2006).

There exists previous research on learning tools development based on scientific learning in vocational high schools. For example, Said et al. (2016) developed the scientific approach-based co-operative learning tool for vocational students' program of automotive electronic engineering, which consisted of an interactive multimedia program, group-sheet, photo viewer and learning scenarios. In addition, Rasyidi et al. (2015) developed teaching material based on scientific learning with the help of information technology; Fauziah (2013) developed a scientific-based RPP (Rencana Pelaksanaan Pembelajaran (lesson plan)) through Problem-Based Learning model in vocational high school, and Wirasari et al. (2016) developed learning material of business principles using a scientific approach to improve students' achievement. The research products have been tested and proven to increase students' learning outcomes.

After reviewing previous research, the researchers found that there is no research that has developed learning tools for Basic and Power Measurement as teaching material in vocational high school, so from the needs analysis the researchers decided to conduct such research.

In this study, the researchers developed learning tools in the form of teaching materials and learning media with scientific discovery learning as the learning model. This research is expected to result in a product that can enhance the learning process of vocational students thus improving their learning outcomes.

2 METHOD

This research was conducted using Research and Development (R&D) as outlined by Borg and Gall (1983). To collect the data, the study employs mixed-method promoting one-group pre-test post-test design (pre-experimental). This method is called sequential exploratory design (Creswell, 2013).

The research was conducted in VHS 6 Bandung. Testing and validation of the product is conducted by a test team that consists of experts and practitioners. The expert judges comprise two lecturers from the study subject and the practitioner judges consist of two teachers from the study subject. There were 30 students involved as the user sample. For more detail, information about the research subjects can be seen in Table 1.

Figure 1 shows the flow chart of the research conducted.

The research started with a preliminary study and needs analysis to ascertain the field conditions,

Table 1. Process and orientation of the product validation.

Judges	Process and orientation of the product
Expert	Qualitative, questioner, interview, preliminary draft product; suitability of methodology, language, graphical design.
Practitioner	Suitability of material and evaluation learning method with the main and basic competencies.
User	Suitability with students' needs, clarity of instructions and learning steps, informative, interactive, and capability of increasing the learning motivation of the students.

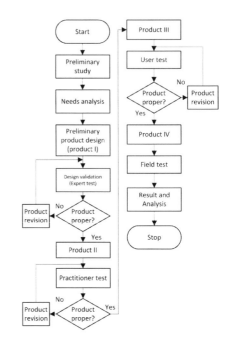

Figure 1. Research flow chart.

after which a preliminary product was made and validation processes conducted until final product was complete. Following that, a field test was conducted to check how effectively the product could increase students' learning outcomes.

3 RESULT AND DISCUSSION

3.1 Preliminary study and needs analysis

Based on the preliminary study and needs analysis conducted by the researchers, it was found that the learning tools for Basic and Power Measurement with scientific-based learning that are really suitable for use in VHS are not available and the learning outcomes of students are lower than expected and below the target for K13.

3.2 Preliminary product (Product I)

Based on the analysis in the preliminary study and needs analysis, the researchers decided to adopt discovery learning as the learning model for the development of teaching materials and the presentation of content to be presented by using a scientific approach to suit the demands of K13.

The scientific activities contained in the teaching materials include: (1) observing, (2) asking, (3) reasoning, (4) trying, and (5) communicating activity/forming a network.

192

The learning steps presented in the teaching materials include: (1) stimulating, (2) problem identifying, (3) data collecting, (4) data processing, (5) evidencing, and (6) drawing conclusions. For presentation, the teaching materials are equipped with discussion sheets, assessment sheets, and evaluation sheets to establish the learning outcomes.

The teaching materials developed consist of three sections: (1) introduction, (2) body, and (3) additional sections. The introduction section consists of the outer cover, the inside cover, copyright page, development team page, preface, table of contents, a brief description of K13, a brief description of the discovery learning model, syllabus, and Lesson Plans I, II and III. The body section consists of three chapters, namely, the complex numbers, the alternating current and a series RLC circuit. Each lesson was developed using a model of discovery learning by adopting scientific learning activities contained in K13.

Specification of the product developed consists of three chapters with a total of 128 pages of A4-size paper (210×297 mm). The total of 128 pages does not include a brief description of K13, a brief description of the discovery learning model, syllabus and lesson plan for each chapter. The researchers originally intended to include brief descriptions of the curriculum and the discovery learning model, the syllabus, and lesson plans in the teaching materials because the investments in these parts are considered to be essential in order to meet the needs of teachers and students in VHS regarding the implementation of K13. The design and presentation of teaching materials have been created in such a way that students can extract the information and organize their learning experience. The cover of the product design is displayed in Figure 2.

The validation process was conducted to test the feasibility of product content, presentation, language and visual. In order to obtain a value for the feasibility of the teaching materials developed,

Figure 2. Product design.

validation of the product was conducted by the expert and practitioner teams. Collecting data at every stage of product validation is done by giving questionnaires that include the checklist and a qualitative advice column. The development of a checklist questionnaire and qualitative advice column is in accordance with the provision of teaching materials for student assessment issued by Kemendikbud (2013).

3.3 Expert test (Result Product II)

Based on suggestions and feedback improvements from the experts, the researchers conducted several fixes on errors in certain parts of the teaching materials. The Product I revision of teaching materials is described in Table 2.

3.4 Practitioners test (Result Product III)

Based on suggestions and feedback improvements from the practitioners, the researchers conducted several fixes on errors in certain parts of the teaching materials. The Product II revision of teaching materials is described in Table 3.

3.5 User test (Result Product IV)

Collecting data on the user tests was carried out by giving questionnaires that included the checklist and qualitative advice column. This questionnaire follows the same principle as the expert judgment

Table 2. Description of Product I revision.

Category	Revision
Content feasibility	• Enhancing the completeness of teaching materials • Adding further implementative problems • Developing further concept of life skills-based learning • Developing further learning steps • Adding of a glossary
Presentation feasibility	• Adding the image corresponding to the content of the material • Improving the referral source or reference studies' instructional materials • Developing further learning steps • Including actual images of the components described
Language feasibility	• Improvement in terms of conformity with the perspective of material that really motivates students • Improving accuracy of spelling
Visual feasibility	• Repairing on step material at chapter or sub-chapter

Table 3. Description of Product II revision.

Category	Revision
Content feasibility	• Fixing the addition of material • Adding example problems • Adding a reference source adapted to the material presented • Improving the stage content of material starting from the basics material until complex material • Adding more images to support explanation of the learning materials
Presentation feasibility	• Fixing color elements in order to clarify the function of illustrations • Adding some real image of the material explained
Language feasibility	• Improving accuracy of spelling usage according to EYD (Ejaan Yang Disempurnakan (Proper Grammatical Language)) • Fixing the use of terms and vocabulary
Visual feasibility	• Improving the cover

Table 4. Description of Product I revision.

Category	Revision
Content feasibility	• Adding more interesting information • Providing explanation of foreign words
Presentation feasibility	• Adding motivating illustrations • Improving sharpness and clarity of the images
Language feasibility	• Fixing a typo • Changing the style of language to be easily understood
Visual feasibility	• Improving the layout of the image • Improving the quality of the binding covers

but uses simpler language to enable users to more easily understand the information that is explored in the questionnaire.

The results of product validation by the user test is used to see the extent of the feasibility and whether it meets the needs of students for instructional materials in the learning process for Basic and Power Measurement. The test result shows that the teaching materials developed are proper to implement.

Based on suggestions and feedback given by the users, some improvements were made and are described in Table 4.

3.6 Field test

After the teaching materials had been declared feasible, a field test was performed to determine their effectiveness. The field test tested the normalized gain of learning outcomes by comparing before-and-after uses of the teaching materials developed by the researchers; it appears that the normalized gain was 0.51.

4 CONCLUSION

The research resulted in a product that can enhance the learning process of vocational students and, in particular, improve the learning outcomes of the students, and on the basis of expert judgment conducted on the product, it is categorized as proper.

REFERENCES

Borg, W.R. & Gall, M.D. (1983). *Educational Research.* New York, NY: Longman.

Creswell, J. (2013). *Research Design* (Translated by Achmad Fawaid). Yogyakarta, Indonesia: Pustaka Pelajar.

Daryanto, D. & Dwicahyono, A. (2014). *Pengembangan Perangkat Pembelajaran (Silabus, RPP, PHB Bahan Ajar).* Yogyakarta, Indonesia: Gava Media.

Dean, D. & Kuhn, D. (2006). Direct instruction VS discovery: The long view. *Journal of Science Education,* 91, 384–397.

Fauziah, R. (2013). *Pembelajaran Saintifik Elektronika Dasar Berorientasi Pembelajaran Berbasis Masalah.* INVOTEC (Innovation of Vocational Technology Education), 9(2), 165–178.

Hosnan, M. (2014). *Pendekatan Saintifik dan Konstektual dalam Pembelajaran Abad 21.* Bogor, Indonesia: Ghalia Indonesia.

Kemendikbud. (2013). *Modul Pelatihan Implementasi Kurikulum 2013.* Jakarta, Indonesia: Kementerian Pendidikan dan Kebudayaan.

Muslich, M. (2010). *Text book writing.* Yogyakarta, Indonesia: Ar-ruzz Media.

Rasyidi, M., Supartono, S. & Yuniastuti, A. (2015). Development of teaching materials scientific approach with help of information technology. *International Conference on Mathematics, Science, and Education,* SE14-SE17.

Said, I., Sutadji, E. & Sugandi, M. (2016). The scientific approach-based cooperative learning tool for vocational students vocation program of autotronic (automotive electronic) engineering. *IOSR Journal of Research & Method in Education,* 6(3), 67–73.

Sugiyono, S. (2013). *Metode Penelitian Kombinasi (Mixed Method).* Bandung, Indonesia: Alfabeta.

Svinicki, M. (1998). A theoretical foundation for discovery learning. *Journal of the American Physiological Society,* 20(1), S4-S7.

Wirasari, Y. & Churiyah, M. (2016). Developing learning material of business principles using scientific approach to improve students' achievement. *IOSR Journal of Research & Method in Education,* 6(3), 7–13.

Regionalization and Harmonization in TVET – Abdullah et al. (Eds)
© *2017 Taylor & Francis Group, London, ISBN 978-1-138-05419-6*

Learning building construction based on local wisdom in Sundanese traditional buildings with SETS vision and mock-up media

J. Maknun, I. Surasetja, T. Busono & R. Mardiana
Departemen Pendidikan Teknik Arsitektur, Universitas Pendidikan Indonesia, Jawa Barat, Indonesia

ABSTRACT: This research aims to develop the formulation of the learning program for building construction based on the local wisdom of Sundanese traditional buildings and the SETS (Science, Environment, Technology and Society) vision by using mock-up media, and to explore the impact of the implementation on the improvement of students' learning outcomes in architecture education. It employs the Research and Development (R&D) method. The research produced a product which is of good quality in terms of theory, methodological procedure, and empiricism. The development of learning materials is based on lecture materials developed by lecturers in the subject of building structure and construction. The researchers incorporated the concepts of structure and construction based on local wisdom. The concepts of structure and construction of Sundanese traditional buildings can be applied to some materials, such as wooden blocks, wooden boards, construction of doors and windows, construction of stairs and wooden floors, and the wooden frames of roof construction. The implementation of teaching building construction based on the local wisdom of Sundanese traditional buildings using SETS vision and mock-up media can improve the learning outcomes of architecture students on the building structure and construction course. This indicates that learning with a SETS vision using mock-up media affects the students' learning outcomes according to the characteristics of both the learning and the media. It also suggests that the use of mock-up media for delivering teaching material should be considered by lecturers. If the media can be used well, it will improve students' learning outcomes.

1 INTRODUCTION

Local knowledge is everything that characterizes an area, be it food, customs, dances, songs or ceremonies. Local potential cannot be separated from local culture. Culture is not just the potential that is directly related to arts and culture, but it is everything about the way of life of local communities related to confidence, productivity, employment, basic food, creativity, values and norms (Arowolo, 2010).

Local wisdom in the form of Sundanese traditional building is not fully understood by the students at the college as a richness, especially in terms of the structure and construction of buildings. This is due to various perceptions by students, such as lack of knowledge of a typical house of the Sundanese people, glorifying modern architecture over local, and so on. Therefore, understanding and awareness of the importance of studying the structure and construction of traditional buildings is to be implemented, one of them through the learning process that promotes the structure and construction of local buildings.

Selection of visionary learning in SETS leads learners to maximum learning. This allows learners to gain a clearer picture of the conceptual linkages to other elements in SETS, either in the form of excess or deficiency. According to Rusilowati et al. (2012), every learner has the ability to vary the basis on which they learn; through the implementation of constructivism, learners can start learning with something they are familiar with to things they never knew before.

The use of media in teaching and learning is a very important tool for use by lecturers because it helps students to better understand the material presented by the lecturers. One example is to use a media mock-up in the building construction education program for students of architecture. Media mock-up is a simplification of the arrangement of that principal part of a process or system that is otherwise complicated.

2 METHOD

The method used in this study is a pre-experimental one, studying the implementation of learning the structure and construction of buildings with Sundanese local wisdom. Implementation of the study begins by providing a pre-test before the intervention and ends with provision of a post-test after the intervention. The test instrument takes the form of a test of building construction materials.

Increased mastery of concepts before and after the learning activities is calculated with the normalized gain score:

$$\langle g \rangle = \frac{(\% < S_f > - \% < S_i >)}{(\% < S_m > - \% < S_i >)} \tag{1}$$

where

$\langle g \rangle$ is a normalized gain score;

S_f is the average post-test score;

S_i is a pre-test mean score;

S_m is the maximum score.

Normalized gain score $\langle g \rangle$ is a suitable method for analyzing the outcome of pre-test and post-test results. Normalized gain score $\langle g \rangle$ is also a better indicator as it shows the level of effectiveness of the intervention in the post-test score (Hake, 1998). The rate of normalized gain score is categorized into three groups (Hake, 1998):

Gain-high: $(\langle g \rangle) > 0.7$;

Gain-being: $\geq 0.7 (\langle g \rangle) \geq 0.3$;

Gain-low: $(\langle g \rangle) < 0.3$.

3 RESULT AND DISCUSSION

3.1 Visionary learning implementation of SETS with media mock-up

Education based on local wisdom involves education as a process that interacts with its environment. This study is based on the view that the cultural background of students has a greater effect on the education process than those contributed by the provision of learning materials. The way a person understands, an individual's relationship with the environment, as well as one's perspective on causality, space and time, is influenced by their origins and culture. Accordingly, the approach selected for the instruction of construction building is based on the Science, Environment, Technology and Society (SETS) vision using media mock-ups.

The development of learning materials is based on lecture material developed by the lecturer. The researchers inserted concepts of local wisdom related to structure and construction into materials developed by lecturers. The material developed concerns wooden construction, and wooden construction is part of building construction. Having adequate knowledge on timber is believed to be helpful to understand the connection and relationships of buildings made of wood. The compilation

of a wooden construction generally consists of two or more bars each connected into one piece until solid. To qualify for this robustness, the connections and relationship between the wooden parts must meet the following requirements:

• The connection should be simple and robust to avoid large or deep indentations because that could lead to weakness and the wooden logs needed are large, which would be a waste of money.
• Must pay attention to the properties of the wood, especially its nature (shrink, swell and pull).
• A connection of relationships in the wood construction should be established that is resistant to the forces that work on the structure.

The learning implementation envisions building construction using SETS with media mock-up as described in the following section. The introduction to buildings is presented in the traditional village environment. This stage can be called 'the initiation', and could also be called 'the invitation', as an invitation to the students to focus on learning. Since students are considered to have prior knowledge on it, it appears that it makes the second phase easy to implement.

The second phase of learning about construction of buildings through SETS with media mock-up is the process of concept formation, which begins by introducing the media mock-up. Learning is initiated with the explanation of the essential concepts, followed by charging students with completing a worksheet to reinforce the essential concepts, before concluding with a discussion group.

In the concept formation event, researchers provided the material and described the types of wood connections for the wooden frame of a stable roof using the medium of mock-up for approximately 60 minutes. It has been shown that students give positive responses in answering questions related to the provision of material progress. Once the

Figure 1.   Instructional media mock-up.

processing of material was complete, the researchers asked the students to demonstrate and try the roof props directly. Almost all of the students tried disassembling one of the mock-up props.

Furthermore, armed with the correct understanding of the concepts, the students performed the analysis of issues or solving problems by the so-called application of the concepts to real-life. The concepts which have been understood by students can be applied in their daily lives. During the process of concept formation, problem-solving and/or analysis of the issue, professors need to correct any misconceptions which arise during the learning activities. This activity is called the 'consolidation concept'. If during the process of forming the concept there do not seem to be any errors occurring for the students (as well as after completion of issue analysis and problem-solving), the faculty still needs to conduct this stabilization exercise with an emphasis on key concepts that are important to know in the specific study of the materials. In the final stages of the building construction instruction, the researchers carried out an assessment of the learning outcomes that have occurred and the learning process that has taken place.

Based on the observation of the students' responses to SETS learning, it was proven that 90% of them agree. Thus, the figure of the interval scale is well-shaped. It can be concluded that learning in the context of a SETS vision using mock-up media can add to the appeal of learning, as this elicited a positive response from students during the learning process.

3.2 Building construction concepts mastery

The level of mastery learning concept is expressed by the building construction category applicable upon assessment, and the improvement in mastery of concepts is based on the score of normalized gain (g). A general overview of the level of mastery of concepts is shown in Table 1.

Based on the graduation rate categories for the pre-test results, the majority (66.7%) of students graduate in the 'Less' category, and 33.3% of students did not even pass. After the learning intervention, most students graduated in better categories, with only 7.1% of students graduating in the 'Less' category and only 2.4% not graduating at all.

The improved learning outcome for building construction is based on the normalized gain values. The average value of the pre-test was 55; the average post-test value was 79, with a normalized gain of 0.55 for the medium category. This shows that the implementation of the building construction learning approach based on a SETS approach of local wisdom using media mock-ups has been

Table 1. Overview of mastery of the concept of building construction.

No	Range	Categories	% pre-test	% post-test
1	86–100	Very Good	0	21.4
2	76–85	Good	0	40.5
3	66–75	Sufficient	0	28.6
4	55–65	Less	66.7	7.1
5	<55	Much Less	33.3	2.4

successful in increasing the mastery of concepts included in this category.

The results of this study are also consistent with the results of research conducted by Ferawati et al. (2012), which states that students who experience learning envisioned in a SETS context find it more meaningful than students who did not. This is because the SETS approach can facilitate the explanation of the abstract through real phenomena and events in the environment around students. Thus, a SETS approach which is integrated in the media mock-up managed to improve students' understanding of the concept of building construction.

Another reason for learning excellence is the way that SETS envisions building construction so that students are able to connect their real world life as a member of society with the building construction study class. This is in line with the opinion of Widyatiningtyas (2009), which states that the learning process envisioned with SETS can provide learning experiences for students in identifying potential problems, collecting data related to the problem, considering alternative solutions, and considering the consequences of their decisions.

Increasing mastery of the concept of building construction is proof that media mock-ups help students more easily understand concepts by providing direct and concrete experience. Furthermore, Furman (2007) states that media mock-ups improve students' ability to remember material presented over a longer period of time. Their direct concrete experience as well as the memory of the material can facilitate students' ability to connect the material with technology, the environment and society.

4 CONCLUSION

The implementation of building construction learning based on local wisdom of Sundanese traditional building with mock-up media as envisioned by SETS can improve learning outcomes in the building structure and construction course in architectural engineering education. This shows that learning to use media needs to consider several factors, such as the appropriateness of media, characteristics of the students, and learning objectives. The study proves that media use of concrete objects should be considered by the faculty for other presentations too, because if the media is used properly it will maximize student learning outcomes.

REFERENCES

Arowolo, D. (2010). The effects of western civilisation and culture on Africa. *Afro Asian Journal of Social Sciences, 1*(1), 2229–5313.

Ferawati, F., Rusilowati, A. & Supriyadi, S. (2012). Keefektifan pembelajaran bencana alam bervisi sets terintegrasi dalam ipa dengan media animasi dan lembar pertanyaan. *Jurnal Pendidikan Fisika Indonesia, 8*(2), 184–189.

Furman, O. (2007). They saw a movie: Long-term memory for an extended audiovisual narrative. *Cold Spring Harbor Laboratory Press, 14*, 457–467.

Hake, R. (1998). Interactive-engagement vs traditional methods: A six-thousand-students survey of mechanics test data for introductory physics courses. *American Journal of Physics, 66*(1), 64–74.

Rusilowati, A., Supriyadi, S., Binadja, A. & Mulyani, S. (2012). Mitigasi bencana alam berbasis pembelajaran bervisi science environment technology and society. *Jurnal Pendidikan Fisika Indonesia, 8*(1), 51–60.

Widyatiningtyas, R. (2009). Pembentukan pengetahuan sains, teknologi dan masyarakat dalam pandangan pendidikan IPA. *EDUCARE. Jurnal Pendidikan dan Budaya*, 1(2), 34–45.

Regionalization and Harmonization in TVET – Abdullah et al. (Eds)
© *2017 Taylor & Francis Group, London, ISBN 978-1-138-05419-6*

Instructional model to improve problem solving, creativity and team working skills for TVET student teachers

M. Samani
Department of Mechanical Engineering, Universitas Negeri Surabaya, Jawa Timur, Indonesia

Suparji
Department of Civil Engineering, Universitas Negeri Surabaya, Jawa Timur, Indonesia

R. Rahmadian
Department of Electrical Engineering, Universitas Negeri Surabaya, Jawa Timur, Indonesia

ABSTRACT: Problem solving, creativity and team working are very important skills, yet TVET student teachers' capability on those skills is low. The purpose of this research was to develop instructional model that able to improve those skills. The problem solving concept was developed using a combination of Polya's theory and expert-novice theory. Creativity concept was developed based on an inside-box theory integrated with Piirto's creativity system. Team working concept was developed based on sociotechnical approach in cooperated with co-creation. Instructional model was developed based on project-based learning. The instructional model was developed using 4-D method. Quasi experiment used to test the instructional model. The research was conducted at Faculty of Engineering-State University of Surabaya in 2014–2015, with 126 students participated. The result shows by using the instructional model developed, student's score on problem solving: 3.26, creativity: 3.12 and team working: 3.65. On the other hand score on problem understanding aspect: 2.84, originality aspect: 2.98, commitment to team success and shared goals: 2.91 and commitment to team processes, leadership and accountability: 2.97. The research shows that the instructional model can increase problem solving, creativity and team working skills, but it needs to be improved so that can to increase students' capability in problem understanding, originality, commitment to team success and shared goals and commitment to team processes, leadership and accountability aspects.

1 INTRODUCTION

The fast development of science and technology forces changes in our work and life patterns. To efficiently deal with these changes, people are required to possess some essential competencies such as problem solving skill, creativity and team work. (The Economist Intelligence Unit, 2015; Trilling & Fadel, 2009, Wagner, 2008). Problem solving and creativity is the most important skills in higher order thinking, while team working is the most important of social skills. All these three skills are often considered as future competences (Samani, Cholik, Suparji, Ismawati, 2015) and are essential for Technical and Vocational School (TVET) graduates. However, research data showed that the students' ability in these three skills are far from proficient (Unesa, 2011).

To create a teaching-learning process that can nurture those essential competencies, the teachers themselves will need to have them. Unfortunately, a study of Samani, Nurlaela and Ismayanti (2014) shows that the student teachers of TVET are not yet competence in those competencies. The study

observed teaching-learning process and conducted discussions with lecturers; and it found out that the teaching-learning emphasized more on practical applications and emphasize less on the development of the three competencies. As a result, students' ability in problem solving and creativity is low. The lecturers also tend to give individual tasks, so it was not enough to give the students the opportunity to cultivate team work skill.

This research aims at developing instructional model that develops problem solving, creativity and team working ability, especially for student's teachers in TVET.

2 THEORETICAL FRAMEWORK

2.1 Problem solving skill

Problem-solving skill is an ability to transform an initial state into a prospective goal, so it is an important indicator of human intelligence required at a high level activity (MacLellan Langley and Walker, 2012: 1). It requires analytical thinking, creativity as well as the skill to be able to strategically prioritize tasks in order to ensure that the problem solving steps can be effective. (Samani, 2014).

In the expert-novice theory, Hardin (2003: 228) explains that experts can crystallize several relevant information to solve the problem, while those who are still learning may only collect information separately. Therefore Hardin (2003) and Samani, Nurlaela, Widodo and Inzanah (2016) consider understanding problem correctly is the most important stage in problem solving. In contrast, Polya (in Berkeley, 2014) states the problem solving strategy is the most important key for problem solving expertise.

Many experts propose problem solving concepts. Polya (in Berkeley, 2014) proposes four steps, they are: understand the problem, devise a plan, carry out the plan and look back. Restructuring Associates (2008) proposes six steps, they are: define the problem, determine the root (s) of the problem, develop alternative solutions, select a solution, implement the solution, and evaluate the outcome. While MacLellan, Langley and Walker (2012) describe that problem solving consists of five steps: problem selection, termination check, intention generation, failure check, and intention application. The three concepts are similar, the difference lies at certain aspect emphasized.

2.2 Creativity

Thinking creatively means to think in a new way that is different from the existing ones and it needs an ability and courage to think freely regardless of the existing thinking trap (Adair, 2011). By thinking creatively, it will get a different perspective, so as to produce different solutions (Shelter & Bentley in Craft, 2001). Liu & Schonwetter (2004: 801–803) mentions creativity has hierarchy ranging from expressive creativity, technical creativity, inventive creativity, innovative creativity, and emergent creativity. While Boyd and Goldenberg (2013) proved that creative thinking should not always be out of the box but also inside the box.

Liu & Schonwetter (2004: 802) mention four aspects in creative thinking: fluency, flexibility, originality, and elaboration, while Filsaime (in Nurlaela and Ismayati, 2015) names originality, adaptability, appropriateness, and contribution to domain. Pirto (2011: 3) describes thinking creatively for the 21st century covers the use wide range of idea creation techniques, creation of new and worthwhile ideas, and elaboration, refining and evaluating their own ideas.

Boyd and Goldenberg (2013) proves thinking inside the box can be taught through Systematic Inventive Thinking. However, originality remains the most difficult aspect, especially for those who are still learning, therefore the development of this aspect requires encouragement to dare to think freely and to be different from others (Samani,

Nurlaela and Ismayati, 2014). Liu & Schonwetter (2004: 803–804) found ten barrier of blocks to creativity, they are: fear of the unknown, fear of failure, reluctance to exert influence, frustration avoidance, resource myopia, custom-bound, reluctance to play, reluctance to let go, impoverished emotional life, and over certainty, These are known barriers that should be removed to allow originality.

2.3 Team working

Team work is very important, because 81% of the Fortune Company developed based on team work organization (Kennedy & Nilson, 2008: 5). If the analogy of vectors are used, the energy accumulation of team work will be optimal if all members of the team have the same vision (Northouse, Peter G, 2016). In practice, it turns out equating vision is not easy, especially if the team members have different expertise background or point view (Mental Health Commission, 2006; Nazaro & Stazzabosco, 2009).

A team work has always gone through five stages; forming, storming, norming, performing, and transforming (Nazaro & Stazzabosco, 2009: 6). Team work can only works effectively if it is able to go beyond the stage of norming and at least reach the performing stage. According to the sociotechnical theory, the success of team work in reaching performing and transforming stage is influenced by interaction and relationships between members of the team (Sycara and Sukthankar, 2006). Therefore, the co-creation principle, which emphasizes on experience mind-set, context of interaction, engagement platforms and network relationships, could be applied (Ramaswamy & Gouillart, 2010).

Tarricone & Luca (2002: 641) says that there are six aspects should be considered in building team work, namely the commitment to team success and shared goals, interdependence, interpersonal skills, open communication and positive feedback, appropriate team composition, commitment to team process and leadership and accountability. Meanwhile, Mickan and Rodger (2000: 202) states team work process effectiveness includes coordination, communication, cohesion, decision making, conflict management, social relationships, and performance feedback. Although these two theories are using different terms and emphasizing on different terms, conceptually both propose very similar aspects.

2.4 Project-Based Learning (PjBL)

Which instructional model could develop problem-solving skills, creativity and team working simultaneously? Since ability grows in line with learning experience, a necessary instructional model is needed to solve problems creatively in team work (Fry, Ketteridge & Marshall, 2009).

One of the instructional models that can provide experiences for the three abilities is a project-based learning (PjBL) which is characterized by long-term activities, interdisciplinary, student centered, and integrated with real world issues and practices (Education Technology Division-MoE, 2006). Similarly, Harmer and Stokes (2014) describes key features of PjBL are learning by doing, real-world problems, role of the tutor: "a guide in the side", interdisciplinary, collaboration and group work, and an end product.

For student activities, the National Academy Foundation (2009: 4) states that PjBL will ask students to tackle real problems and issues beyond the classroom, to actively engage in their learning, to make important choices during the project, and to demonstrate in tangible ways that they have learned the key concepts and skills.

3 METHODS

Instructional models was developed using the 4-D method (Thiagarajan, Semel and Semel, 1974), but only until the third D stage (develop). One study was designed to test the effectiveness of the model. A pre-test was determined not to be relevant since creativity and team working are something new, due to a significant difference between PjBL and the existing instructional models. A control group cannot be implemented, because it is potentially confounding (McNamee, 2003).

The research was conducted in 2014 and 2015, involving 126 student teachers in the Faculty of Engineering-State of University of Surabaya. Structured observation and open-ended interviews were conducted to determine the ability of students to apply team work, as well as their responses during the PjBL models. At the end of PjBL process, problem solving ability and creativity was also measured by a test.

4 FINDINGS

Using 1–4 score system, Table 1 shows that the students' overall ability in problem solving is high, with score of 3.26. While their ability in understanding problem is significantly low, with a score of 2.84. This is in line with Hardin's (2003) research finding which states that understanding problem is the most important but at the same time the hardest aspect.

Observation and open ended interviews with students found that the difficulty lies in their ability to dissect the problem, finding relevant variables and causal relationship among them.

Table 2 shows the students' ability to think creatively. As a whole, the students' creativity scores well with 3.28, which is a little better than the previous year research achievements at 3.12. However, aspects of originality is still considerably low with a score of 2.98. These results repeat last year's result of a score of 2.78. Indeed, there has been

Table 1. Students' achievement on problem solving.

No	Aspects	Score
01	Understanding the problem	2.84
02	Devise a plan	3.43
03	Carry out the plan	3.76
04	Look back	3.31
	Mean	3.26

Table 2. Students' achievement on creativity[*].

No	Aspects	Score
01	Fluency	3.34
02	Flexibility	3.54
03	Originality	2.98
04	Elaboration	3.26
	Mean	3.28

[*] The 1st year result was presented on TVET International Conference at Bremen University, September 2–4, 2015.

an increase of 0.20 but it still has not been able to achieve a score of 3.0 (good).

Observation and interviews with students and lecturers reveal that students' firm habit of thinking "what if" makes them dreading to stray away from the law, formulas, of rules that have been understood; hence the difficulties for students to form original ideas. It seems PjBL that was developed in 2015 still has not been fully able to release students from block to creativity (Liu & Schowetter, 2004).

After attending teaching-learning process using PjBL, students' ability to work together as a team is good with a score of 3.35 as showed in Tabel 3. However, there are two aspects that have not been good, namely, commitment to team success and shared goals with a score of 2.91 and a commitment to team processes, leadership and accountability with a score of 2.97.

Synchronizing work objectives and targets was not easy for the students. The observations indicate that they need a longer time to agree on a workable targets and objectives, because of the differences on their point of views. To reach the storming phase as stated by Nazaro & Strazzabosco (2009), the students also took a lengthier time. However, once the norming stage was reached it was immediately followed by a performing stage.

Students' free and unstructured lifestyle makes them feel unbound by the team work, thereby inhibiting the onset of commitment to leadership and team accountability. The different ways of working also brings disharmony in working together, so that the engagement platform as stated by Ramaswamy & Gouillart, (2010) did not immediately occur.

Table 3. Students' achievement on team working.

No	Aspects	Score
01	Commitment to team success and shared goals	2.91
02	Interdependence	3.84
03	Interpersonal skills	3.48
04	Open communication and positive feedback	3.08
05	Appropriate team composition	3.82
06	Commitment to team processes, leadership and accountability.	2.97
	Mean	3.35

5 CONCLUSION

Based on the finding described, it can be concluded that PjBL improves students' ability on problem solving, creativity and team work. However it still needs a follow up research to increase the four aspects (problem understanding, originality, commitment to team success and shared goals, and commitment processes, leadership and accountability) of the three competencies which found to be significantly low.

REFERENCES

Adair, John. 2011. The Art of Creative Thinking. http://www.cflo.com.cn/UploadFile/File/201302/63495566 8500676000389.pdf. Downloaded on February 2014: 09.27 pm.

Berkeley. 2014. *Polya's Problem Solving Techniques.* https://math.berkeley.edu/~gmelvin/polya.pdf. *Downloaded on September 12, 2015: 9.12 pm.*

Boyd, Drew & Jacob Goldenberg. 2013. *Inside the Box: Why the Best Business Innovation are in Front of You.* London: Profile Book Ltd.

Fry, Heather, Steve Ketteridge & Stephanie Marshall. 2009. "Understanding Student Learning" in *A Handbook for Teaching and Learning in Higher Education.* Editors: Heather Fry, Steve Ketteridge & Stephanie Marshall.

Harmer, Nichola & Alison Stokes. 2014. *The Benefit and Challenge of Project-Based Learning: A Review of the Literature.* Plymouth: Pedagogic Research Institute and Observatory.

Hardin, Laura E. 2003. Problem Solving Concepts and Theories. *Journal of Veterinary Medical Education* 30(3).

Kennedy, Frances A. & Linda B. Nilson. 2008. *Success Strategy for Teams.* Clemson, South: Office of Teaching Effectiveness and Innovation.

Liu, Zhiqiang (Eric) & Dieter J. Schonwetter. 2004. Teaching Creativity in Engineering. *International Journal of Engineering Education* 20(5).

MacLellan, Christopher J., Pat Langley and Collin Walker. 2012. A generative theory of problem solving. *First Annual Conference on Advance in Cognitive Systems*: Poster Collection 1–18.

McNamee, R. 2003. Confounding and Confounders.http://www.ncbi.nlm.nih.gov/pmc/articles/PMC1740493/pdf/v060p00227.pdf. Downloadeb on June 08, 2016: 10.07 pm.

Mental Health Commission. 2006. *Multidisciplinary Team Working: From Theory to Practice.* https://www.google.com/search?q=multidiciplinary+team+working&ie = utf-8&oe = utf-8&client = firefox-b-ab. Downloaded on July 5, 07:58 pm.

Mickan, Sharon & Sylvia Rodger. 2000. Characteristics of effective teams: a literature review. *Australian Health Review* 20(3).

National Academy Foundation. 2009. *Project-Based Learning: A Resource for Instructors and Program Coordinators.* http://www.hazlet.org/cms/lib05/NJ01000600/Centricity/Domain/635/PBL_Guide.pdf. Downloaded on July 5, 08:14 pm.

Nazzaro, Ann-Marie & Joice Strazzabosco. 2009. *Group Dynamics and Team Building: Second Edition. Montreal:* World Federation of Hemophilia.

Northouse, Peter G. 2016. *Leadership: Theory and Practice.* Seventh Edition. London: SAGE Publications Ltd.

Nurlaela, Lutfiyah & Euis Ismayati. 2015. *Strategi Belajar Berpikir Kreatif.* Surabaya: Universitas Negeri Surabaya Press.

Ramaswamy, Venkat & Francis Gouillart. 2010. *The Power of Co-Creation: Build It with Them to Bost Growth, Productivity and Profits.* New York: Free Press.

Restructuring Associates. 2008. *Six Step Problem Solving Model.* https://www.academia.edu/ 8229711/Problem_Solving_Overview_SIX-STEP_PROBLEM_SOLVING_MODEL. *Downloaded on September 12, 2015: 9.37 pm.*

Samani, Muchlas. 2014. *Rethinking Education for 21st Century: An Indonesia Case.* Paper presented at Asaihl Conference, NTU Singapore December 4–5, 2014.

Samani, Muchlas, Luthfiyah Nurlaela and Euis Ismayati. 2014. *Penelitian dan Pengembangan Strategi Belajar Mengajar untuk Mengembangkan Keterampilan Berpikir Kreatif dan Perilaku Berkarakter.* LPPM Universitas Negeri Surabaya: Laporan PUPT.

Samani, Muchlas, Moch Cholik, Suparji and Euis Ismawati. 2015. *Teaching-Learning Strategy for Developing Critical Thinking and Creativity for Engineering Student Teachers.* Paper presented on TVET International Conference at Bremen University-Germany, September 2–4, 2015.

Samani, Muchlas, Lutfiyah Nurlaela, Wahono Widodo & Inzanah. 2016. *Berpikir Tingkat Tinggi: Problem Solving.* Surabaya: Sarbikita Publishing.

Tarricone, Pina & Joe Luca. 2002. *Successful Teamwork: A Case Study.* Higher Education Research Development Society of Australasia 2002. https://www.google.com/search?q=Successful+Teamwork%3A+A+Case+Study&ie=utf-8&oe=utf-8&client=firefox-b-ab. Downloaded on June 28: 15, 2014: 03.12 pm.

The Economist Intelligence Unit Limited. 2015. Driving the Skill Agenda: Preparing Students for the Future. The Economist-Intelligence Unit.

Trilling, Bernie & Charles Fadel. 2009. *21st Century Skills: Learning for Life in Our Times.* San Francisco: Jossey-Bass.

Unesa-Universitas Negeri Surabaya. 2011. *Penelitian Pengembangan Mutu Pendidikan.* Surabaya: Laporan Penelitian.

Wagner, Tony. 2008. *The Global Achievement Gap: Why Even Best Schools Don't Teach the New Survival Skills Our Children Need-and What We Can Do About It.* New York: Basic Books Group.

The learning model development of higher order thinking on electronics system subject

M. Anwar, N. Jalinus & Pardjono
Padang State University, Padang, Indonesia

ABSTRACT: The 21st century skills becomes the key of human resources' competitiveness in the future, essentially about mastery of thinking skills. Therefore, a valid, effective and efficient learning model to improve students' Higher Order Thinking (HOT) skills and also their specific competences is very significant. This study was a developmental research by using Richey & Klein procedures of Type Model II (model research) that was conducted in two phases: model development and model validation. Model design was accomplished by in-depth literature review and Focus Group Discussion (FGD) with the experts and senior lecturers related. Model validation was formed with expert judgement, pre-experimental design, and applying confirmatory factor analysis procedures to assess the design of higher order thinking skills construct. The study results shows that the learning model developed, factually, fulfills the appropriate validity, effectiveness, and efficiency criteria. However, the model implementation to the subject sample confirms that students' HOT skills and electronics competences can be improved outright.

1 INTRODUCTION

The concept of higher order thinking skills becomes the main agenda after the Bloom's publication regarding the taxonomy of educational objectives. Bloom established a workgroup that discussed three aspects and taxonomies namely the cognitive aspects, the affective aspects and the psychomotor aspects. These aspects or categories have been the taxonomy classification from the simple range until the complex behavior and from the real construction until the abstract construction (Bloom, 1956, p.30). Based on these results, the Bloom taxonomy in the cognitive aspects is differentiated into six levels (knowledge, comprehension, application, analysis, synthesis and evaluation). The last three levels are categorized into the HOT skills and are inputted into the taxonomy after the taxonomy has been revised in 2001 by Anderson-Krathwohl (Kratwohl, 2002).

Krathwohl, through several revisions upon the Bloom taxonomy, views the learning objectives from two dimensions namely the knowledge dimension and the cognitive process dimension. The cognitive process dimension follows the six levels of verb format in the previous section namely to remember, to understand, to apply, to analyze, to evaluate and to create. Each thinking level might be categorized into four levels of knowledge, including the HOT skills. Thereby, the researcher might state that the create block is the highest HOT level in the most abstract knowledge (meta-cognitive knowledge).

Based on the main ideas, the researcher might comprehend that the main concept of the HOT skills is the complex thinking. The term complex refers to the interconnection among several basic thinking skills with the balanced combination and composition. The term complex also refers to the fact that the thinking process might be applied into the context of real life within the problem solving activities, the planning activities and the other activities that demand more than simple thinking skills. Thereby, the complex thinking skills also refers to the sequential, the logical and the systematic thinking skills with more cognitive process. In addition, such individuals in general will be able to overcome the real problems and situations in their life.

Haladyna (King et al., 2009, p.27) mentions that the thinking complexity and the learning dimension might be stated into four levels of mental process (understanding, problem solving, critical thinking and creativity) that might be implemented into four types of content namely facts, concepts, principles and procedures. Brookhart (2010, p.3) views the HOT in three terminologies namely the HOT as transfer, the HOT as critical thinking and the HOT as problem solving. As transfer, the HOT encourages the learners more to understand, to benefit and to implement what they have learned (King et al., 2009, p.34). Then, as critical thinking, the HOT "… is reasonable, reflective thinking that is focuses on deciding what to believe or do." On the contrary, as problem solving the HOT includes the thinking process for recognizing the appropriate path in order to achieve the desired objectives.

The HOT skills such as the creative-critical thinking skill and the problem-solving thinking skill are the skills that the university students should master as a teacher candidate. Carroll (2007) explains that teachers should have the critical thinking ability and should deliver such capacity to their students. Similarly, Snyder & Snyder (2008) reveal that a business educator should have the critical thinking ability by considering that the students are not information receiver but, instead, the students are information user. The teachers who have such ability will encourage the students to learn independently and to be able to solve the real problems in their life. Beers (2012) quotes that "Exemplary science education can offer a rich context for developing many 21st century skills, such as critical thinking, problem solving and information literacy. These skills not only contribute to a well-prepared workforce of the future but also give all individuals life skills that help them succeed."

Recalling the challenges of 21st century and the internal condition related to the quality of nowadays graduates, the researcher is interested to develop an innovative learning model that focuses on the improvement of HOT skills. The study is to find an effective and efficient design, the mechanism and the stages of learning model development, especially for the teachers education of electronics engineering. The study is also to discover the feasibility of the learning model developed for improving the students' HOT skills and the effectiveness of the HOT learning model for the domain of electronics engineering.

2 METHOD

The development model formed by R&D study was the type II model design and development (model research) proposed by Richey & Klein (2007, p.8). The model research was intended to construct a new model or to develop an existing model along with the requirements that facilitated the model use. There were 2 main stages that should be conducted in developing a new model by means of this approach namely: 1) the model development, consisting of comprehensive model development and process development within the model components; 2) model validation, consisting of internal validation toward the model components and external validation toward the model impacts. Each stage would be outlined in the section of development procedures that had been designed, including preliminary study. This stage had been an inseparable part from the efforts of designing and developing the model comprehensively.

2.1 Experiment design of product

The objective was to define whether the initial draft of model that had been developed would be feasible or not for the implementation. The activity in the stage was performing a practical-evaluative experiment toward the good initial draft. In the expanded experiment that was conducted after the revision upon the model based on the analysis of limited (small group) experiment results. In order to identify the model effectiveness, there should be several tests toward the improvement of thinking skills and electronics competences... The measurement on the results of experiment was conducted according to the experiment design (Creswell, 2009, p.160) as in the following Figure 1.

2.2 Data collecting and instrument

The data collecting was conducted under multiple techniques namely by means of literature study and documentation, interview with multiple parties and questionnaires distributed among the students or research subject (especially the learning groups of Electronic Circuit Innovation Engineering course). The experts and senior lecturers by means of Focus Group Discussion (FGD) was conducted to elaborate and to validate the model guidelines, the thinking skills instrument and learning design, the cognitive test on the mastery of electronics competences and certainly the students' HOT skills.

2.3 Data analysis

The results of data analysis were implemented in order to define the further stage within the model development. The data analysis that the researcher implemented referred to the research process in each stage namely the descriptive analysis, the analysis toward the coefficient of inter-rater correlation (inter-rater agreement) by means of intraclass coefficient correlation (ICC), the analysis of Pearson correlation, the analysis of Spearman correlation, the analysis of Alpha Cronbach and the comparative analysis toward the results of differential test along with the factorial analysis toward the fitness between the theoretical structure and

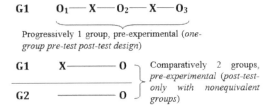

Figure 1. The experiment design of model effectiveness.

the empirical structure for the higher order thinking skills construct.

3 RESULTS

3.1 *HOT skills construct*

Based on the literature review, the researcher would like to emphasize three main components of the HOT skills. The three kinds of thinking skills were believed to be the key skills in dealing with the 21st century competition. In order to measure in a more detailed manner, the thinking skills then would be outlined skills into several aspects as having been displayed in the Figure 2 below.

In general, the experts assessed that the scoring concept and guideline that had been implemented in designing the HOT skills instrument had been very good although there should be revision. The mean score of the experts in all items had been good, namely 3.80, in accordance with the coefficient of content validity (Aiken's V) namely 0.93. The coefficient implied that each item had very good content validity and supported the content validity of the instrument in overall.

Based on the test of reliability, the researcher found that the intraclass correlation coefficient had been equal to 0.859 and the individual coefficient had been equal to 0.550. According to the criteria provided by Fleiss and Cicchetti & Sparrow in Barrett (2001), the researcher might state that the inter-rater agreement index belonged to the excellent category (very good, > 0.74) while the individual index (consistency) belonged to the fair category (moderate range of 0.40–0.59). Then, the significance rate had been significant where the P-value < 0.05. Thereby, the researcher might state that the conceptual design of HOT skills learning model had been valid and reliable.

3.2 *Model development*

Based on the conceptual model constructed via FGD, the researcher designed the HOT skills learning model hypothetically as having been displayed in Figure 3.

The hypothetical model was designed by applying the aspects of input, process and output. In the input level, the materials that would be used consisted of the learners' initial information (with 3 main variables; cognitive structure, CS; prior knowledge; PK; and trait thinking, TT), the desired learning outcome (Electronic Engineering Study Program, EESP's LO) and 3 components of HOT skills that would be strengthened. The input then would decide the options of pre-condition, the learning strategy and the type of assessment that would be applied in the process level. The options of strategy that would be proposed were experiment, fault-finding and mini-project design; these options would be outlined more tactically in the stages of learning model implementation further. The measure of successful model implementation would be apparent in the output level in the form of vocational competences based on the LO and (mainly) the improvement of HOT skills. The hypothetical model was designed in such way in order to pay attention to all aspects and variables

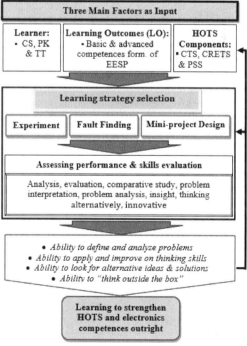

Figure 3. The HOT learning model final hypothetically.

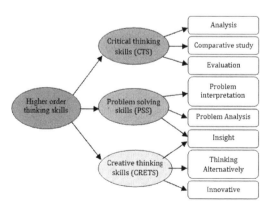

Figure 2. Higher order thinking skills components.

Table 1. The results of differentiation test for the model group and the control group.

Aspects	U test* Z_0	Z	t test t_0	t	Significance P-value	Sig.2tailed
HOTS	2.056		2.546		0.05	0.017
EEC	−1.960		−2.345		0.05	0.019

*By using Mann-Whitney U test.

that had been disclosed theoretically and conceptually in the stages of model development.

3.3 Results of experiment and effectiveness test

For the model implementation in the expanded experiment, the researcher performed 3 tests of electronics competences in accordance with the design of one-group pre-test post-test. The score of the test results were correlated to the students' GPA to ensure the validity and the reliability of the instrument. The progressiveness described that there had been quite significant improvement on the capacity in terms of percentage toward all individuals. With these results, the researcher might state that both individually and collectively the HOT learning model had been effective to improve the students' cognitive capacity in the electronics realm.

In order to identify the effectiveness of the learning model, the researcher performed a differentiation test by means of Mann-Whitney U Test toward the data of Electronic Engineering Competences (EEC) and of t-test toward the HOT skills data. The results of both test, as having been displayed in Table 1, achieved after the variance of the model group had been similar to the control group (homogenous).

Based on the t test and the Mann-Whitney U test in Table 1, there had been significant improvement on the HOT skills and the cognitive competence in the domain of electronic engineering. The results also implied that the HOT learning model had empirically been effective in improving both aspects altogether in the same time.

4 CONCLUSIONS

The development of HOT learning model was started from the study of exploration to many models (that focuses on strengthening the thinking skills) in the appropriate group of theories. The elaboration by means of comparative and integrative approach, furthermore, delivered the strengths and the weaknesses of the existing models. The developed model offers 3 optional learning strategies that can be selected. The strategies have demonstrated the strengths to effectively improve HOT skills and its components rather than existing model like problem-based learning. However, the three main factors (inputs), especially on learner factor, become the key of success in model implementation and outcomes. The feasibility of the model, in terms of learning aspects based on the lecturers' and the students' perception, belongs to the very good category. In terms of mastery toward the electronic engineering realm, the model has also proved to be effective in improving the electronics competences significantly. The progress on the results of electronics cognitive competence measurement has good improvement especially after the final stage of model implementation.

REFERENCES

Barrett, Paul. 2001. Assessing the reliability of rating data-revised. From http://www.liv.ac.uk/~pbarrett/programs.htm.

Beers, Sue Z. 2012. 21st Century skills: preparing students for their future. Diambil pada tanggal 5 August 2013 dari https://www.mheonline.com/glencoemath/pdf/21st_century_skills.pdf.

Bloom, B.S., Engelhart, M.D., Furst, E.J., Hill, W.H. & Krathwohl, D.R. 1956. Taxonomy of educational objectives, the classification of educational goals: handbook 1 cognitive domain. London: Longmans, Green & Co Ltd.

Brookhart, Susan M. 2010. How to assess higher order thinking skills in your classroom. Virginia, USA: ASCD Member Book.

Carroll, Robert Todd. 2007. Teaching critical thinking. The article was presented Critical Thinking Workshop: The Amazing Meeting V di Las Vegas.

Creswell, John W. 2009. Research design: qualitative, quantitative, and mixed methods approaches (3rd Ed.). London, UK: SAGE Publications Ltd.

King, F.J., Goodson, L. & Rohani, F. 2009. Higher order thinking skills: definition, teaching strategies, assessment. Florida, USA: Educational Services Program, FSU.

Krathwohl, D.R. 2002. A revision of Bloom's taxonomy: an overview. Taylor & Francis Ltd: Theory into Practice 41, 4, 212–218.

Ramsden, Paul. 2003. Learning to teach in higher education (2nd Ed.). London: Taylor & Francis Group.

Richey, Rita C. & Klein, James D. 2007. Design and development research. New Jersey, USA: Lawrence Erlbaum Associates, Inc.

Snyder, Lisa G. & Snyder, Mark J. 2008. Teaching critical thinking and problem solving skills. The Delta Pi Epsilon Journal, L, 2, 90–99.

Regionalization and Harmonization in TVET – Abdullah et al. (Eds)
© 2017 Taylor & Francis Group, London, ISBN 978-1-138-05419-6

The implementation of multimedia animation to improve the mastery of material about crystal defects in engineering courses

M. Komaro, A. Djohar, A. Setiawan, B. Hasan & A. Wibi
Universitas Pendidikan Indonesia, Bandung, Indonesia

ABSTRACT: The most recent data from the lecturer of engineering materials indicates that only 41.6% of the students could solve Crystal Defects-related problems. Therefore, this research was conducted on the implementation of multimedia animation on Crystal Defects material. This study aims to obtain information on the students' ability of concept mastery and responses after they experienced the learning process using multimedia animation on Crystal Defects material in engineering materials course. The research method used is pre-experimental design in the form of One group Pre-test Post-test design. Data collection was conducted using tests, namely pretest and posttest. The results showed that the students from lower group who used MMA in the learning of Crystal Defect material in Engineering Materials course are better than those from upper group. The implementation of MMA also helps the students to better understand the material content and facilitates their learning process.

1 INTRODUCTION

Education has an importantmeaning in life, that is, improving the quality of human resources in any field, therefore the quality of education must be continuously improved. In the world of education, the advancement of education is not only the responsibility of the government but also the responsibility of teachers, parents and students. To improve the quality of education, refinement needs to be conducted in the field of education in order to produce high quality students.

Prospective teachers are not only equipped with pedagogical and solid professional knowledge, but they also have to master subject competence that will be taught when teaching. The weaknesses of prospective teachers are learning happening globally everywhere caused by the limitation of humans that have separate visual and verbal information processing system. Human visual and auditory working memory systems are very limited, so learning that only involves visual and verbal information does not last long and is not effective to absorb much information (Mayer, 2009).

One of the difficulties encountered by students in understanding Crystal Defects material, besides the learning process, is allegedly caused by the abstract, complex and dynamic characteristics of the material. With such characteristics, the students are required to master the material concept in order to understand it.

Weaknesses in learning certainly happen in every field, on the problems people work at that are related to students/prospective teachers' weaknesses in Engineering Materials course, where all material properties are determined by its atomic structures in micro or determined by its microstructures. The explanations of these concepts are represented in pictures and theories that generally describe abstract events since these events cannot be observed by unaided eyes because of the small size of the atoms. The difficulty in understanding abstract, complex and dynamic concepts is a problem in the learning of engineering materials.

Based on the fact above, in order for prospective teachers to master engineering materials course that is considered difficult, refinement in learning needs to be conducted so that it is no longer difficult. Even though it is still not easy, at least it is not boring if it is repeated or studied alone, thus it can finally be mastered. A type of technology that can be utilized for this purpose is Information and Communication Technology (ICT), with consideration that nowadays students are generally able to easily access computers, which are utilized in learning or courses. One the alternative of its utilizations is in the form of e-learning, virtual reality and interactive multimedia (MMI). The use of interactive multimedia is more effective than the use the media presented through printed media with face-to-face activity and is also more effective than the use of the media presented through web with online learning.

2 METHOD

Two groups are required to see the extent of the improvement of concept mastery in learning usingmultimedia animation. The first group is lower group, consisting of students who have low pretest results and the second group is upper group, consisting of students who have high pretest results. The division of this thinking groups was determined by the result of the initial pretest conducted on the students before the treatment-was given. The research design used in this study is Pre-Experimental Designs in the form of One-Group Pretest-Posttest Design. The underlying reason for the selection of this research design is because the sample was not selected randomly, so this research design is suitable with the author's research (Sugiyono, 2014).

In this design there is pretest before treatment, so the result of the treatment can be known more accurately because it can be compared with the situation before being given treatment. The design pattern used in this study can be seen in Table 1.

In this research design pattern, there are two groups consisting of lower group and upper group that were not chosen randomly. These twogroups were divided through a pretest to determine differences in their ability in the population. After being given a pretest, they were divided into two groups: lower group and upper group, which were subsequently given treatment, which is the learning using multimedia animation. Furthermore, they were given post test to determine the difference in learning outcomes between the two groups. The questions in pretest and post test are the same.

The difference of two averages of two samples wasused to determine whether the lower group and the upper grouphave difference in N-Gain (normalized gain) based on Hake (2002), namely:

$$(N-Gain) = \frac{\% \; actual \; gain}{\% \; potential \; gain}$$
$$= \frac{\% \; skor \; postes - \% \; skor \; pretes}{100 - \% \; skor \; pretes} \quad (1)$$

In this study, descriptive analysis of N-Gain was also performed using N-Gain criteria based on

Hake (2002), namely: 1) increase with "high-gain", if (N-Gain) > 0.7; 2) increase with"medium-gain", if $0.7 \geq$ (N-Gain) ≥ 0.3; and 3) increase with "low-gain", if (N-Gain) < 0.3.

3 RESULT

The result of preliminary study showed that the students who took engineering materials course encountered difficulty on the material about abstract calculation and movement of atoms. Considering the importance of engineering materials course, and based on the data showing that students encountered difficulty on Crystal Defect material, an effort of improvement is required in order to make the process easy to understand. One attempt to do it is using media that is not only theoretical, but also practical, economical, accessible, and teachable, thus allowing the material to be studied repeatedly. The efforts to meet the accessible criteria will be performed by manipulating the theoretical model (pictures) into realistic model so that it will be teachable in the form of multimedia.

Development of science aims to understand how students learn. In the efforts to apply the science of learning, the challenge in education is the development of instructional science that aims to understand how to present materials in a way that helps students to learn (Mayer, 2008). Animation multimedia on atomic Crystal Defects was created in order for the learning to be representative enough to realistically explain the concepts of a system so it will be accessible by learners, which in turn creates the effect of learning experience. Meanwhile, the data of pretest and posttest in control and experiment class was used to calculate N-Gain values which are the improvement of students' ability. N-Gain values are presented in Table 2.

The increase of Concept Mastery ability on Crystal Defects material in the lower group using MMA reached an average of 83% or high category. This is higher than the increase of Concepts Mastery ability using MMA in the upper group,

Tabel 1. One-group pretest-posttest design.

Group	Pretest	Treatment	Posttest
Lower	O_{L1}	X	O_{L2}
Upper	O_{U1}	X	O_{U2}

Keterangan:
O_{L1} = Result/condition of concept mastery of lower group;
O_{U1} = Result/condition of concept mastery of upper group;
X = Treatment using multimedia animation;
O_{L2} = Result of lower group after being given treatment X;
O_{U2} = Result of upper group after being given treatment X.

Table 2. Results of the calculation of pretest, posttest, and n-gain of concepts mastery on crystal defects.

Class group		Pretest	Posttest	N-Gain
Upper	Highest	65	95	0.91
	Lowest	45	75	0.50
	Average	55.71	85.71	0.68
Lower	Highest	40	95	0.93
	Lowest	10	80	0.71
	Average	29.12	87.94	0.83

which reached the average of 68% or medium category.

Development of science aims to understand how students learn. In the effort to apply the science of learning, the challenge in education is the development of instructional science that aims to understand how to present materials in a way that helps students to learn. To achieve the purpose above, educational experts created various educational media with different emphasis and with corresponding principles. For researches and creation of multimedia, Mayer formulated seven principles of multimedia design, namely: multimedia, spatial closeness, temporal closeness, coherence, modalities, redundancy, and individual differences (Mayer & Mayer, 2001).

Meanwhile specific principle which characterizes the engineering materials multimedia animation-based e-bookies accessible or affordable by students' reason. This becomes a major emphasis related to the characteristics of Engineering Materials course whose characteristics are determined by micro properties, namely: structure of atoms, dynamic movement of atoms and abstract properties. The micro size that is extremely small and abstract requires an appropriate media to understand, and for that, MMA has become a medium that can meet these needs. Meanwhile the procedure of MMA development includes the steps generally performed, namely: analysis, early development, limited testing and final product testing.

Basic principle of MMA as research result in the form of findings is the involvement of students in giving opinions and in the simulations of thinking. MMA on engineering materials was created for active learning that produced student-centered media, even though it is not yet available for all materials. Narration was created in the form of questions to be answered in students' mind and the students are given time to think. The purpose is to involve the students in giving opinions, and it is expected that the students will achieve the learning outcome of 70%. Subsequently the answers are displayed in the form of animation to correct the result accuracy of students' thinking. This is also meant to involve students in thinking simulation, so the learning outcome is expected to increase to 90%, as the result of the involvement in simulation. Basic principles of creation and production of MMA result in better and lasting learning outcome, that combines text read, voice heard, and still and moving images or animation seen.

Current development of learning tools is available and easier to use, so the trend of teachers designing and implementing the animation they make themselves will continue. This development trend is easy to combine with wider understanding about how these tools can help the learning process, thus the implementation of animation and simulation in classrooms will continue to grow (Falvo, 2008). Learning outcome related to concept mastery is deeper because of the existence of long term memory as stated by Berk (2009). This is influenced by almost all interesting aspects of multimedia project features. Multimedia is not only interesting to see, but should also be beautiful/aesthetic, enjoyable and entertaining (Chorianopoulos, 2008). Signaling can be made to highlight important materials, as well as improving concentration, by giving different colors and making it blinking (Harp & Mayer, 1998). Another thing that is also performed to gain attention is the addition of redundancy, that is, adding text to the screen for the animation narrated by only displaying the text narrated (Moreno & Mayer, 2002).

Crystal Defects MMA has the following advantages:

– Displaying information that is not only in text and images, but also concretizing abstract materials, clarifying messages so the messages are not too verbalistic, and overcoming the limitation of space and senses.
– Accommodating students/learners in: providing interactive process and the easiness of feedback, easiness of systematic control in learning process and freedom in determining learning topic.
– Increasing students' learning passion and spirit, because: there is direct interaction between students and learning source, learning can be more interesting, learning process can happen anytime and anywhere, it is possible to learn independently based on students' talents and abilities, and there is uniformity in: stimulation, experience and students/learners' perception.
– Learning is shorter and the outcome is better, as a result of: learning time that can be shortened, the limitations can be overcome, which include: space, time, energy, and senses. Students' positive attitude on learning materials and learning process can be increased. Consequently learning quality can improved.

4 CONCLUSION

MMA is more interesting, easier and faster in improving the ability of concept mastery. The improvement of Concept Mastery ability on Crystal Defects material in lower groups using MMA reached high category. It is higher than the increase of Concept Mastery ability in upper group using MAA which reached medium category. Therefore, atomic Crystal Defects MMA has been proven to improve the ability of Concept Mastery better and is more suitable for students with low early ability.

REFERENCES

Berk, R.A. 2009. Multimedia teaching with video clips: TV, movies, YouTube, and mtvU in the college classroom. *International Journal of Technology in Teaching and Learning.* 5(1): 1–21.

Chorianopoulos, K. 2008. User interface design principles for interactive television applications. *International Journal of Human-Computer Interaction* 24(6): 556–573.

Falvo, D.A. 2008. Animations and simulations for teaching and learning molecular chemistry. *International Journal of Technology in Teaching and Learning.* 4(1): 68–77.

Hake, R.R. 2002. Relationship of individual student normalized learning gains in mechanics with gender, high-school physics, and pretest scores on mathematics and spatial visualization. *The Physics Education Research Conference; Boise, Idaho*: http://www.physics.indiana.edu/~hake. [14 Juni 2015].

Harp, S.F. & Mayer, R.E. 1998. How seductive details do their damage: A theory of cognitive interest in science learning. *Journal of Educational Psychology* 90(3):414–434.

Moreno, R. & Mayer, R.E. 2002. Verbal redundancy in multimedia learning: When reading helps listening. *Journal of Educational Psychology* 94(1): 156–163.

Mayer, R.E. 2008. Applying the science of learning: evidence-based principles for the design of multimedia instruction. *The American psychologist* 63(8): 760–769.

Mayer, R. & Mayer. 2001. Principles of Multimedia Design. *Multimedia Learning.* pp. 5–10.

Mayer, R. E. 2009. *Multimedia learning (2nd ed.).* New York: Cambridge University Press.

Regionalization and Harmonization in TVET – Abdullah et al. (Eds)
© 2017 Taylor & Francis Group, London, ISBN 978-1-138-05419-6

Students' competence with reasoning ability using problem-based instruction modules in 'building materials science'

N.F.D.B. Pakpahan
Universitas Negeri Surabaya, Surabaya, Indonesia

ABSTRACT: This study aims to determine the effect of student competence in terms of the reasoning ability between using problem-based instruction modules and jobsheets in a 'Building Materials Sciences' course. The method used is experimental with factorial design (2×2). The study population consisted of students of Civil Engineering. The research samples in the experimental and control groups were each formed from 30 students in the Civil Engineering Education Department at the Universitas Negeri, Surabaya. The research instrument used was a test of both cognitive competence and reasoning ability. Reasoning ability tests are intended to determine the level of logical thinking in formal and concrete terms. The results obtained are: 1) overall, there are differences in student competence between using Problem-Based Instruction (PBI) modules and jobsheets on a 'Building Materials Science' course; 2) overall, there are differences in student competence between formal reasoning and concrete reasoning in a 'Building Materials Science' course; 3) there are differences in student competence for both the formal and concrete reasoning groups between using PBI modules and jobsheets on a 'Building Materials Science' course, with those students using PBI modules showing higher competence.

1 INTRODUCTION

Learning Building Materials Science requires a learning process carried out continuously from the most basic to the highest of concepts. Understanding and controlling the fundamental concept is believed to be able to determine the success of the students to develop their competence.

Regarding teaching and learning activities, the researcher found the following: first, student results show that subject mastery by students in Building Materials Science has still not been achieved. Second, the results of the competency test show that out of an average of 35 students, two students (5.71%) obtained score D (fail), and six students (17.14%) obtained score C. Third, implementation of learning uses jobsheets. Teaching materials to practice learning or practicum in a workshop or in the laboratory are printed on these jobsheets. The jobsheet contains a practicum that includes measures of operational work, working drawings of the material that is to be practiced and includes the results of the evaluation sheet of the students' practice.

Based on these facts, maximum effort is needed to implement learning to develop students' formal reasoning so as to improve their mastery of competence. Lessons need to be implemented in formal reasoning in the form of getting used to thinking from the most basic concepts through to the highest concepts. If the student's formal reasoning is high then competence will be high anyway, likewise the reverse applies. Thus, in applying a model of learning we need to pay attention both to the material being taught and the level of formal reasoning of which the students are capable.

Piaget (1964) explains that the intellectual system of children at the stage of cognitive development that illustrates the level of reasoning consists of four phases: 1) sensory motor (0–2 years), 2) pre-operational (2–7 years old), 3) concrete operational (7–11 years old), and 4) formal operational (11 and over).

Nur (1991) defines formal reasoning as the ability to think correctly in reaching the truth, and distinguishing between accepted reality and desired expectations. Students who are aged 11 and over have formal reasoning; they are able to think in both symbolic and abstract ways regarding the object being observed, systematic, purposeful, and achievable, in addition to being able to think in terms of inductive, deductive and empirical rational reasoning. Aspects of formal reasoning include combinatorial reasoning, correlational reasoning and proportional reasoning.

Lawson (1980) describes five characteristics of formal reasoning: 1) identifying and controlling variables as an ability to identify the most significant variables, especially for solving the problem;

2) the ability to think in combinatorial terms—to combine multiple factors and then reach a conclusion as a result of the merger, especially in solving a problem; 3) the ability to think of correlation—to analyze problems by using relationships or causal aspects; 4) the ability to think of probability—a way of thinking to resolve the matter through identifying probability trends; 5) the capacity to think proportionately—the ability to solve problems in a proportional way. Thus, a child has formal reasoning when he or she has these five characteristics.

Learning based on problem-based instruction uses syntax to stimulate students to think at a high rate in steps. The teacher: 1) explains the purpose of learning and the logistics required, and motivates students engaged in selected problem-solving; 2) helps students define and organize study duty pertaining to the issue (set topic, duty, schedule); 3) gets students to collect appropriate information, experiment to obtain an explanation for problem-solving, collect data, form a hypothesis, problem-solve; 4) helps students in planning prepared work in accordance with the report their fellow students make; 5) helps students to reflect upon and/or evaluate their investigation and the processes they used.

Student competency standards can be achieved according to learning objectives when students conduct testing of these materials. Testing of various building materials can be achieved to the maximum when the lesson is conducted from the most basic concepts to the highest concepts using modules. Students have to perform a series of tasks in carrying out the tests, solving problems and analyzing the test results, to draw appropriate conclusions based on logical principles. Troubleshooting the topics of matter is closely related to aspects associated with reasoning. Modules are teaching materials arranged in a systematic and interesting way that includes content, methods and evaluations that can be used independently to achieve the expected competencies.

Based on this, it is important to implement learning materials science based on Problem-Based Instruction (PBI) by using modules with which students can develop formal reasoning. Formal reasoning skills are needed in practical learning, especially in problem-solving tests materials.

Thus the study was conducted to answer the following problems: 1) What, as a whole, was the difference between the students' competence using PBI modules and jobsheets in Building Materials Science study; 2) What was the overall difference in student competency between formal reasoning and concrete reasoning in Building Materials Science study; 3) What are the differences in students' competencies for the formal reasoning group, between using problem-based instruction modules and jobsheets in Building Materials Science study;

4) What are the differences in students' competencies for the concrete reasoning group between using problems-based instruction modules and jobsheets in Building Materials Science study?

2 RESEARCH METHODOLOGY

2.1 Location and time research

The research was conducted at the Department of Civil Engineering, Faculty of Engineering, at the Universitas Negeri, Surabaya. The research commenced in March 2016 and continued until July 2016.

2.2 Population and sample

The population for the research is students of Building Engineering education in the Civil Engineering department, Universitas Negeri, Surabaya. The samples were collected using a technique of purposive sampling where both the experimental class and control class consisted of 30 students each.

2.3 Research method

This study is a quasi-experimental study that aims to determine the effect of student competency in reasoning ability between using modules and using jobsheets. This study uses two factors with two levels (groups). The design was a factorial design (2×2) using an experimental group that was taught through the use of PBI modules, while the control group learned through the use of jobsheets.

Table 1. Factorial design: learning using PBI modules and jobsheets according to level of reasoning ability as indicator of student competence.

Student competence (Y)	Reasoning ($X_2 = B$)	
	Formal (B_1)	Concrete (B_2)
Learning PBI module (A_1)	$A_1 B_1$	$A_1 B_2$
($X_1 = A$) Jobsheet (A_2)	$A_2 B_1$	$A_2 B_2$

Explanation:
  A1 = student competence using PBI modules;
  A2 = student competence using jobsheets;
  B1 = formal reasoning of student;
  B2 = concrete reasoning of student;
  A1B1 = student competence with formal reasoning using PBI modules;
  A1B2 = student competence with concrete reasoning using PBI modules;
  A2B1 = student competence with formal reasoning using jobsheets;
  A2B2 = student competence with concrete reasoning using jobsheets.

2.4 Instruments

Reasoning ability tests were used to measure the level of students' formal reasoning (controlling variables, and proportional, combinatorial, probabilistic and correlational reasoning). This test is a standard test adapted from a Test Of Logical Thinking (TOLT). The competence test is a test of cognition that determines a student's competency in Building Materials Science.

Implementation of learning in the experimental class used PBI modules (modules 'Tile Testing', 'Testing Stone-Brick' and 'Testing Ceramics') that were feasibility-tested by an expert in his field and then tested on 30 students. In the control class, learning was conducted as usual using jobsheets (jobsheets 'Tile Testing', 'Testing Stone-Brick', and 'Testing Ceramics').

2.5 Analysis technique

Before testing the hypothesis, initial tests are a prerequisite and included tests of normality and homogeneity. Hypothesis testing was performed using Analysis Of Variance (ANOVA) two-way tests and continued with Scheffé's test. The test results of normality using a chi-square test on the competence of each student learning group was as shown in Table 2.

The results of the students homogeneity test using problem-based learning show that the F value is 2.63. In Table 3, it is shown that $F_{table} = 4.00$ with error level $\alpha = 0.05$. Because $F = 2.63 < F_{table} = 4.00$ then both of these learning otherwise homogeneous.

Table 2. Normality test results summary of student competency in learning module–jobsheet group (A) and formal–concrete reasoning group (B).

No.	Group	χ^2	$\chi^2_{table\ (\alpha=0.05)}$	$\chi^2_{table\ (\alpha=0.01)}$	Sum
			Value		
1	A_1	6.703	11.1	15.1	normal
2	A_2	10.884	11.1	15.1	normal
3	A_1B_1	6.092	9.49	13.3	normal
4	A_1B_2	5.383	7.81	11.3	normal
5	A_2B_1	2.495	9.49	13.3	normal
6	A_2B_2	5.226	9.49	13.3	normal

Table 3. The result of ANOVA calculations (2×2) between learning with PBI modules and jobsheets in formal and concrete reasoning.

Competence (Y)		Learning ($X_1 = A$)		
		Module (A_1)	Jobsheet (A_2)	Σb
		A_1B_1	A_1B_2	Row 1
	F	$n_{11} = 21$	$n_{12} = 16$	$n_{b1} = 37$
	(B_1)	$\Sigma Y_{11} = 1760$	$\Sigma Y_{12} = 1265$	$\Sigma Y_{b1} = 3025$
		$M_{11} = 83.81$	$M_{12} = 79.06$	$M_{b1} = 162.87$
Reason- $X_2 = B$		$\Sigma Y^2_{11} = 148000$	$\Sigma Y^2_{12} = 100475$	$T_{b1} = 248475$
		$A_2 B_1$	$A_2 B_2$	Row 2
	C	$n_{21} = 9$	$n_{22} = 14$	$n_{b2} = 23$
	(B_2)	$\Sigma Y_{21} = 660$	$\Sigma Y_{22} = 995$	$\Sigma Y_{b2} = 1655$
		$M_{21} = 73.33$	$M_{22} = 71.07$	$M_{b2} = 144.4$
		$\Sigma Y^2_{21} = 48650$	$\Sigma Y^2_{22} = 71275$	$T_{b2} = 119925$
		Column 1	Column 2	TOTAL
		$n_{k1} = 30$	$n_{k2} = 30$	$n_T = 60$
Σk		$\Sigma Y_{k1} = 2420$	$\Sigma Y_k = 2260$	$\Sigma Y_T = 4680$
		$M_{k1} = 157.14$	$M_{k2} = 150.13$	$M_T = 307.27$
		$T_{k1} = 196650$	$T_{k2} = 171750$	$T_T = 368400$

3 RESULTS AND DISCUSSION

Description of data students' competence between using PBI modules and jobsheets in formal reasoning and concrete reasoning on Building Materials Science. The research hypothesis testing was conducted using ANOVA harmonics, by using the average method is not balanced or the method of unweighted means for n each sub-class (self) is different.

The first hypothesis proposed is: overall, the students' competence using PBI modules (A_1) is higher than those using jobsheets (A_2). In the ANOVA calculation of the significance test of the mean differences in student competence for those using PBI modules (A_1) and those using jobsheets (A_2), the value obtained is $F = 36.98 > F_{table} = 7.08$, at significance level $\alpha = 0.01$ and dk = 1; 58.

Thus the null hypothesis (H_0) is rejected and the alternative hypothesis (H_1), which stated that overall the competence of students in the group using modules based on PBI is higher than the group using jobsheets, is accepted.

The second hypothesis proposed is: overall, the competence of the students in the group with formal reasoning (B_1) will be higher than the group with concrete reasoning (B_2).

In the result of the ANOVA test on the significance of the mean difference in student competence between the group who have formal reasoning (B_1) and the group with concrete reasoning (B_2), the value obtained was $F = 5.33 > F_{table} = 7.08$, at significance level $\alpha = 0.001$ and dk = 1; 58.

The result of the calculation of the mean difference in student competence using Scheffé's method obtained the value of $F = 153.51 > F_{table} = 7.08$, at a significance level $\alpha = 0.001$ and dk = 1; 58. This means that the difference in the competence of students in the group who have formal reasoning (81.76), which was higher than the group with concrete reasoning (71.96), was very significant.

213

Table 4. Summary ANOVA (2 × 2) results of group learning module–jobsheet (A_1–A_2) and formal–concrete reasoning (B_1–B_2).

Source of variation	Sum of squares	dk	Average SS	F-count	F_{table} $\alpha = 0.05$	$\alpha = 0.01$
Rows (A)	1165.66	1	1165.66	36.98**	4.00	7.08
Columns (B)	167.91	1	167.91	5.33*	4.00	7.08
Interact (A × B)	21.19	1	21.19	0.67 n.s.	4.00	7.08
In group	1765.10	56	31.52			
Total	3119.86	59				

The result of the calculation of the mean difference in student competence using Scheffé's method obtained the value of $F = 23.39 > F_{table} = 7.08$, at significance level $\alpha = 0.01$ and dk = 1; 58. This means that the competence of students using PBI modules (80.67) was higher than those using jobsheets (75.33), which is very significant.

Table 5. The result of comparison test with Scheffé's method: difference between students' competence in module–jobsheet and formal–concrete reasoning learning groups.

Variation source	Square total	dk (k–1); k (n–1)		F-count	F_{table} $\alpha = 0.05$	$\alpha = 0.01$
A_1-A_2	23.39	2	1; 58	23.39**	4.00	7.08
B_1-B_2	153.51	2	1; 58	153.51	4.00	7.08
A_1B_1-A_1B_2	6.50	4	1; 56	6.50*	4.00	7.08
A_2B_1-A_2B_2	0.89	4	1; 56	0.89	4.00	7.08
A_1B_1-A_2B_1	21.95	4	1; 56	21.95**	4.00	7.08
A_1B_2-A_2B_2	15.12	4	1; 56	15.12	4.00	7.08

Thus the null hypothesis (H_0) is rejected and the alternative hypothesis (H_1), which stated that overall the competence of students who have formal reasoning is higher than the group with concrete reasoning, is accepted.

The third hypothesis proposed is: in the students who have formal reasoning (B_1), the competence of students in the group using modules based on PBI (A_1B_1) was higher than the group using jobsheets (A_2B_1).

The calculation results average for student competence in learning groups using modules based on PBI with formal reasoning (A_1B_1) was 83.81. The average student competence in the learning group using jobsheets with formal reasoning (A_2B_1) was 79.06.

Based on the calculation of the mean difference in student competence using Scheffé's method, the value obtained was $F = 21.95 > F_{table} = 7.08$, at a significance level $\alpha = 0.001$ and dk = 3; 56. This means that for the students with formal reasoning, the difference between the competence of students in the group using modules based on PBI (83.81) and the group using jobsheets (79.06) is very significant.

Thus the null hypothesis (H_0) is rejected and alternative hypothesis (H_1), which stated that for

students with formal reasoning, the competence of the students in the group using modules based on PBI was higher than that of the group using jobsheets, is accepted.

The fourth hypothesis proposed is: for the students who have concrete reasoning (B_2), the competence of students using PBI modules (A_1B_2) was higher than those using jobsheets (A_2B_2).

From the calculations, the average score of student competence in the learning groups using PBI-based modules with concrete reasoning (A_1B_2) was 73.33. The average score of student competence in the learning group with jobsheets with concrete reasoning (A_2B_2) was 71.07.

Based on the ANOVA calculation, which was continued with Scheffé's method, to test the difference between the average competence of the students lie on the lines $A_1B_1 - A_2B_2$ (concrete reasoning group), which obtained the value of $F = 15.12 > F_{table} = 7.08$, at significance level $\alpha = 0.01$ and dk = 3; 56. This means that for the students with concrete reasoning, the difference between student competence when using PBI modules (73.33) and using jobsheets (71.07) is very significant.

Thus the null hypothesis (H_0) is rejected and the alternative hypothesis (H_1), which stated that for the students with concrete reasoning, the competence of those using PBI modules was higher than those using jobsheets, is accepted.

4 CONCLUSIONS AND RECOMMENDATIONS

4.1 Conclusions

The conclusions of this study are: 1) the competence of students using PBI modules was higher than those using jobsheets in 'Building Materials Science' study, and was statistically significant; 2) the competence of students with formal reasoning was higher than those with concrete reasoning, which was also statistically significant; 3) for the students with formal reasoning, the competence of students using PBI modules was higher than that of those using jobsheets, and was statistically significant; 4) for the students with concrete reasoning, student competence when using PBI modules was higher than when using jobsheets, and this was statistically significant.

4.2 *Recommendations*

Advice for the implementation of learning that uses PBI modules: (1) see the guidance that contains all necessary information such as the purpose of the learning, the modules, etc; 2) understand every teaching material; 3) do all exercises and tasks provided; 4) examine reading materials whose originality can be checked by both teachers and students; and 5) sort out website addresses in the reading materials to broaden knowledge in relation to the materials.

The preparation of PBI modules are based on subjects taught at the faculty of Civil Engineering of UNESA (Universitas Negeri Semarang) which implies that those modules can also be implemented in other relevant places. But in the application to be in accordance the contents of material based on field of study.

ACKNOWLEDGMENT

The author would like to thank all those who have assisted directly or indirectly in the completion of the study and this article: Prof. Dr Warsono, MSi (Rector of UNESA); Prof. Dr Ekohariadi, MPd (Dean of the Faculty of Engineering, UNESA); Prof. Dr I Wayan Susila, MT (Head of Research and Community Service of UNESA); Hendra Wahyu, C, ST, MT (Head of Civil Engineering, UNESA).

REFERENCES

Bloom, B.S. (Ed.) (1984). *Taxonomy of education objectives: Book I, Cognitive domain.* New York, NY: Longman.

Departemen Pendidikan Nasional. (2003). *Pedoman Penulisan Modul:* Direktorat Jendral Pendidikan Dasar dan Menengah.

Ibrahim, M. & Nur, M. (2000). *Pembelajaran Berdasarkan Masalah.* Surabaya, Indonesia: UNESA University Press.

Jackson, N. (1978). *Civil engineering materials.* Hong Kong: ELB & MacMillan.

Lawson, B. (1980). *How designers think.* London, UK: The Architectural Press.

Nur, M. (1991). *Pengadaptasian Test of Logical Thinking (TOLT) dalam Seting Indonesia.* Surabaya, Indonesia: IKIP Surabaya.

Ringsun, I.N.. (2004). *Ilmu Bahan.* Surabaya, Indonesia: UNESA University Press.

Robbins, S.P. & Judge, T.A. (2007). *Perilaku Organisasi.* Jakarta, Indonesia: Salemba Empat.

Singh, G. (1979). *Materials of construction.* Delhi, India: Standard Book Service.

Supriyadi, E. (1997). *Pedoman umum pengembangan bahan ajar Sekolah Menengah Kejuruan (SMK).* Fakultas Pendidikan Teknologi dan Kejuruan Institut keguruan dan ilmu pendidikan Yogyakarta.

Tobin, K.G. & Capie, W. (1981). *Patterns of reasoning: Controlling variables.* Columbus, OH: Educational Resources Information Center (ERIC).

Attention cueing in developing Simplified Data Encryption Standard (SDES) simulation

P.W. Yunanto, A. Diamah & Soeprijanto
Universitas Negeri Jakarta, Jakarta, Indonesia

ABSTRACT: The Data Encryption Standard (DES) was one of the most widely used modern algorithms particularly in financial applications. DES is no longer considered a secure algorithm. However, DES remains important to study as it has similar encryption principles to its successors triple DES and the Advanced Encryption Algorithm (AES). One approach to help students learn the DES algorithm is through simulation. This paper aims to identify the effective type of attention cueing for DES simulation. Two mock-ups designed using color and animated arrows as cueing were demonstrated to students for feedback. The result shows that both color and animated lines cueing used in the mock-ups helped students understand one of the DES processes represented by the mock-ups. Although the students' preferences split as half students prefer color cueing while the rest likes animated lines better, our observation indicates that animated lines were the better cueing at guiding the students in learning.

1 INTRODUCTION

Data Encryption Standard (DES) is one of complex modern cryptography algorithms. Although most of the building block operations in DES are linear, DES is still difficult to understand because of its lengthy process. Examples of DES applications are the PIN encryption in ATMs and the authentication of transactions over certain amount limit. DES is considered breakable since the 1990s and has been replaced with triple DES and AES. However, DES maintains an important algorithm to learn because it is the key to understanding the new encryption standard AES and triple DES (Tao et al., 2011).

Computer simulation has been long used to help replicate the real-world process in a classroom setting (Michael, 2002). According to Mills (2002), computer simulation provides students the opportunity to acquire knowledge and construct their understanding. Simulation allows students to repeat and explore the process of interest and consolidate learning (Hennessy et al., 2007; Windschitl, 1998). For example, if they don't understand a process when running the simulation for the first time, they can re-run the simulation many times, with different pace or different parameters. Therefore their knowledge and comprehension build up each time the simulation is run. Various courses have incorporated computer simulation in teaching, to name a few: statistics (Mills, 2002), nursing (Kaveevivitchai et al., 2009) and

physics (Jimoyiannis and Komis, 2001). However, there have been very few simulations developed for learning cryptography. To the best of the authors' knowledge, there is only one literature on DES visualization by Tao et al., (2011). There are other simulations available online, one is available at ("animation," n.d.), however, it was very lengthy and contain errors. The other one which simulates simplified DES can be found at ("Simplified DES Simulator," 2008). However, this simulation serves more like a calculator with no further description on how each encryption process is performed. In addition, the work of Tao et al. (2011) did not discuss the design aspects that make their simulation effective for learning.

To address this gap, this paper describes the development process of DES simulation to help students understand DES algorithm using effective simulation principle. Specifically, this paper focuses on attention cueing, which is one of such principles. This paper is one part of our ongoing study on developing and evaluating a DES simulation.

2 RELATED WORK

2.1 *How simulations can support learning*

According to Jimoyiannis & Komis (2001), computer simulations provide an open learning environment and allow students to: develop their understanding of a topic by making hypothesis and testing ideas, isolate and manipulate parameters which help them comprehend relations between parameters and variables, use different types of representations such as pictures, graphs, numerical data to understand the underlying concept and processes they are learning and investigate complex, dangerous, happens-too-fast or time consuming phenomena in classroom settings. In real world settings, DES happens very fast, depending on the size of data being encrypted and the computer computing power. A study by Elminaam et al. (2010) found that a set of text, audio, and video data ranging from 33 Kbytes -139 Mega-Bytes were all decrypted under 2 seconds using a 2.4 GHz CPU laptop. This finding by Elminaam et al. (2010) demonstrates that encryption using DES happens very fast, making it impossible for students to observe, let alone to learn DES real time. With a simulation, students can learn DES at their own paces.

2.2 *Principles of effective simulation*

A research conducted by Wieman et al. (2008) revealed that students who spent two hours with "Circuit Construction Kit" simulation were better at understanding the current and voltage concepts than students who conducted laboratory exercise with real electrical equipment. Such result, according to Wieman et al. was attributed by the engaging simulation. In addition, Wieman et al. identified several characteristics of an engaging simulation: (i) dynamic visual environments that allow users to control them, (ii) moderate challenges which are neither too easy nor too hard and (iii) complex visualization that ignites curiosity without being overwhelming. To achieve these characteristics, students should be involved in the simulation development and testing.

In line with point (i) suggested by Wieman et al., Plass, Homer & Hayward (2009) are of the view that users should be provided with features that allow them to control the simulation.

Plass et al. also point out that a simulation should not place too much cognitive load on students. Dynamic visualization often requires more mental effort to understand. One way to reduce an extraneous load of an animation is with the attention cueing (Amadieu et al., 2011). They used cueing to guide students' attention to key information. In addition, effectively designed dynamic visualization can help students focus their attention to key information and minimize the need to process too much information when such cueing does not exist (de Koning et al., 2007; Mayer, 2005). Moreover, dynamic visualizations are more effective than static information when they are meant to be a representational rather than a decorative aspect of the topic (Höffler and Leutner, 2007).

As simplified DES consists of many encryption processes, we applied the effective design principles discussed above to support better comprehension of simplified DES. In this paper we only focus on the attention cueing principle.

3 SIMPLIFIED DES

Compared to the straightforward classic cryptography algorithms, DES is regarded as a complex and hard to understand encryption because of its lengthy process. In 1996 Prof. Schaefer from the Santa Clara University created a much simpler version of DES, called the Simplified DES (SDES) (Schaefer, 1996). The simplified DES is not a secure algorithm, but it is intended for educational use. Instead of sixteen stages of encryption used in DES, the simplified DES only has two stages. It also operates with 8-bit keys instead of 56-bit keys used in DES. The structure of SDES is shown in Figure 1.

4 METHOD

In developing the simplified DES simulation, the iterative software development lifecycle (SDLC)

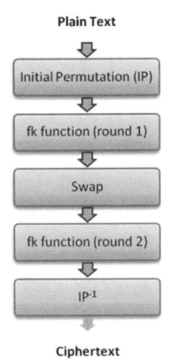

Figure 1. Simplified DES stages.

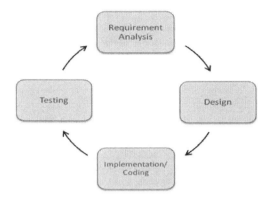

Figure 2. The iterative software development cycle.

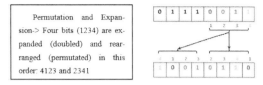

Figure 3. Mock-up 1 with color code cueing.

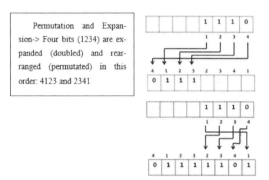

Figure 4. Mock-up 2 with running lines cueing.

(Ruparelia, 2010) was used as presented in Figure 2.

As seen in Figure 2, the initial stage of the iterative SDLC is the requirement analysis. This involves analyzing what platform the simulation will be running on. The design stage defines what components should be in the simulation, how the simulation interface looks like and what features the simulation should have. Following the design stage is the implementation, in which codes are written before testing is conducted to find errors with the program (functional testing) or get feedback from users (usability testing). This paper focuses on the initial design involving attention cueing. Two mock-ups were created using one of the principles of effective simulation design: attention cueing. Before deciding what kind of cueing to be applied to the mock-ups, we chose the encryption process that appears most often in DES to be represented by the mock ups. Permutation takes place at the beginning and the end of the DES encryption, as well as in the fk function (as seen in Figure 1), making it the most frequent operation in DES. Therefore, the permutation and expand process was selected to be represented by the mock ups.

One mock-up was designed with color cueing (as shown in Figure 3) and the other with animated running arrows (as depicted in Figure 4). A total of ten students participated in the mock-ups demonstration and feedback. We first showed the mock-ups to each student. They were asked to read a text containing the concept of expands and permutation before each mock-up was demonstrated. After the students had viewed each mockup, we asked the students to explain the expand and permutation concept using the mockup and requested their opinion individually on how well each mock-up illustrates and explains the expand and permutation concept.

5 RESULTS AND DISCUSSION

Table 1 lists the opinion of each student on the mock-ups and which one is their preference.

The result presented in Table 1 shows that in general, both cueing with color and running lines help students understand one of the processes in the DES encryption, the expand and permutation. However, observing more closely, students took more time learning with color cueing than with running lines. When presented with mock-up 1 where bit positions are illustrated with color, half of the students had to focus and they seemed to require more mental effort with color cueing to decode the bits arrangement. When presented with running lines, the majority of students immediately associate the lines with the position of bits in the permutation. However, their choice of which cueing they prefer is evenly distributed between color code and running lines. Considering that there were more students who had difficulties with understanding color codes than the students who were confused with running lines presentation, we decided that cueing with running lines is easier to understand. Therefore running lines will be used in the development of DES simulation for illustrating bits arrangement. This result suggests that when dealing with changes of position in the permutation, animated lines are better than color code in focusing students' attention on how bits are rearranged.

Table 1. Students' opinion on mock ups with cueing.

	Does the mock up help them understand the concept given?		
Student	Mock up 1 (color)	Mock up 2 (running lines)	Preferences
1	x	√	Running lines
2	√	√	Running lines
3	√	√	Color code
4	√	√	Color code
5	√	√	Running lines
6	√	√	Color code
7	√	√	Color code
8	x	x	Running lines
9	x	√	Running lines
10	√	√	Color code

This result is in line with the result of the experiment conducted by Finkelstein et al. (2005). In their study, students who used the electrical circuit simulation performed better at concept questions than the students who conducted laboratory practice with the real equipment. According to Finkelstein et al., the use of the visual flow of electrons helped students understand the concept of current flow. The use of explicitly moving electrons serves as a cue of current flow. In our case, by visually indicating how bits are repositioned with moving lines, the majority of students grasped the permutation and expand concept better than using the color code.

6 CONCLUSION

This paper has presented one part of our ongoing research to develop and evaluate a simplified DES simulation. In the initial design phase of the SDLC, two mock ups representing the permutation and expand process were created with attention cueing. Attention cueing is one of the design principles for effective simulation. One mock-up accentuates the bits arrangement in permutation with the color code. The other mock up applies running lines to help students focus on how permutation moves bits. Feedback from ten students reveals that both cueing helped them understand the permutation process. Although their preferences were evenly distributed between color and animated arrows cueing, a closer observation of how fast and well each mock-up was understood by the students indicates that animated lines are better visual cueing in helping students understand permutation concept.

This study has given an insight that when dealing with a movement or position ordering simulation, cueing involving visual movement helps students to focus on the position aspect of a simulation. The result of this study also helped us deciding animated lines are the cueing to use in our subsequent stages of SDES simulation development.

REFERENCES

Amadieu, F. Mariné, C. & Laimay, C. 2011. The attention-guiding effect and cognitive load in the comprehension of animations. *Comput. Hum. Behav.* 27: 36–40.

Animation [WWW Document], n.d. URL http://kathrynneugent.com/animation.html (accessed 9.13.16).

De Koning, B.B., Tabbers, H.K., Rikers, R.M. & Paas, F. 2007. Attention cueing as a means to enhance learning from an animation. *Appl. Cogn. Psychol.* 21: 731–746.

Elminaam, D.S.A., Abdual-Kader, H.M., Hadhoud, M.M. 2010. Evaluating the performance of symmetric encryption algorithms. *IJ Netw. Secur.* 10: 216–222.

Hennessy, S., Wishart, J., Whitelock, D., Deaney, R., Brawn, R., La Velle, L., McFarlane, A., Ruthven, K. & Winterbottom, M., 2007. Pedagogical approaches for technology-integrated science teaching. *Comput. Educ.* 48: 137–152.

Höffler, T.N. & Leutner, D. 2007. Instructional animation versus static pictures: A meta-analysis. *Learn. Instr.* 17: 722–738.

Jimoyiannis, A. & Komis, V., 2001. Computer simulations in physics teaching and learning: a case study on students' understanding of trajectory motion. *Comput. Educ.* 36: 183–204.

Kaveevivitchai, C., Chuengkriankrai, B., Luecha, Y., Thanooruk, R., Panijpan, B. & Ruenwongsa, P. 2009. Enhancing nursing students' skills in vital signs assessment by using multimedia computer-assisted learning with integrated content of anatomy and physiology. *Nurse Educ. Today* 29: 65–72.

Mayer, R.E. 2005. Principles for reducing extraneous processing in multimedia learning: coherence, signaling, redundancy, spatial contiguity, and temporal contiguity principles. *Camb. Handb. Multimed. Learn.* 183–200.

Michael, K.Y. 2002. The Effect of a Computer Simulation Activity versus a Hands-on Activity on product Creativity in Technology Education. *J. Technol. Educ.* 13.

Mills, J.D. 2002. Using computer simulation methods to teach statistics: A review of the literature. *J. Stat. Educ.* 10: 1–20.

Plass, J.L., Homer, B.D. & Hayward, E.O. 2009. Design factors for educationally effective animations and simulations. *J. Comput. High. Educ.* 21: 31–61.

Ruparelia, N.B. 2010. Software development lifecycle models. *ACM SIGSOFT Softw. Eng. Notes* 35: 8.

Schaefer, E.F. 1996. *A simplified data encryption standard algorithm.* Cryptologia 20: 77–84.

Simplified DES Simulator. 2008. Hardw. Side Cryptogr.

Tao, J., Ma, J., Mayo, J., Shene, C.K. & Keranen, M. 2011. DESvisual: A visualization tool for the des cipher. *J. Comput. Sci. Coll.* 27: 81–89.

Windschitl, M.A. 1998. A practical guide for incorporating computer-based simulations into science instruction. *Am. Biol. Teach.* 92–97.

Regionalization and Harmonization in TVET – Abdullah et al. (Eds)
© *2017 Taylor & Francis Group, London, ISBN 978-1-138-05419-6*

The effectiveness of Student Team Achievement Division (STAD) on academic achievement and social behavior

R. Febriana, Z. Akbara & Mahdiyah
Universitas Negeri Jakarta, Jakarta, Indonesia

ABSTRACT: An effective learning process is capable of improving the results of study and effecting a positive change in student behavior. This research aims to establish the effectiveness of Student Team Achievement Division (STAD) on academic achievement and social behavior. This research uses the quasi-experimental method by performing the treatment on a student group. The research design used was a pre-test/post-test control group design. Data collection was done using post-test and questionnaire. Data analysis for student learning outcomes used a Mann-Whitney test, while an analysis of the cooperative behavior of students used descriptive analysis. The results of this research indicate that: (1) learning with STAD can improve student behavior including motivation, activity, cooperation, responsibility, requests for help, mutual respect, and confidence; (2) student learning outcomes in cognitive improvement are also quite significant. The implications of the application of this model are the increased cognitive and effective aspects of students.

1 INTRODUCTION

Sekolah Menengah Kebangsaan (SMK) is one of the types of vocational education in Indonesia and is aimed at preparing the participants to enter employment.

This study looked at competence as a result of learning in the perspective of escalation, which covers three aspects, namely, knowledge, skills and attitude to work. In addition to demands for basic skills, as well as skills in the areas of a specialty, the world of work requires the skills in terms of the labor candidate's temperament. Employability skills are the abilities to manage behavior and attitudes in the workplace to match those expected by industry (McLeish, 2002).

The Secretary's Commission on Achieving Necessary Skills (SCANS) conducted a study to identify and outline the skills required in the workplace (Kane, 1990). Based on the review and deep verification, SCANS defined two groups of skills: foundation skills and workplace competencies. Foundation skills are basic and thinking skills, and personal qualities. Workplace competencies concern resources, interpersonal interactions, information, systems, and technology.

In this study, the component's behavior refers to research (Andreas in Samani, 2007). It can be categorized in employability skills. These skills can be obtained from the learning process in schools, one of them through the study of Cooperative Learning (CL).

The main contributions of this paper are: (1) implementation of cooperative learning with the Student Team Achievement Division (STAD) technique, (2) improvement of the social behavior of students, and (3) enhancement of student learning outcomes.

The initial assumption in this study (H1) is that there will be an improvement in student learning outcomes with the application of the STAD cooperative learning technique.

2 LITERATURE REVIEW

2.1 *The skills gap*

The term 'skills gap' has been identified by previous researchers, and can be defined as 'the disparity between the quality and adequacy of skills possessed by IS graduates and required by the IS/IT industry' (Scott et al., 2002). There have been a number of explanations and causes for this skills gap: one is that rapid changes in technology make it difficult for individuals to obtain the requisite level of experience in these skills before they skills become outdated, and the other is a mismatch between the academic perceptions of needs and requirements (curriculums) and the actual skill requirements of industry (Scott et al., 2002; Milton, 2000).

Success in the learning process is often measured by the achievement of competence of students in terms of the cognitive aspect Jordan et al.

(2008) describe competency as the ability to perform a set of tasks that requires the integration of knowledge, skills, and attitudes.

The research results of Burnett and Jayaram (2012) found that employers are looking for three key types of skills: cognitive, non-cognitive, and technical. Cognitive skills include critical thinking and basic functions like literacy and numeracy. Non-cognitive skills are variously called 'life skills' or 'behavioral skills' and include interpersonal communication skills, while technical skills are usually geared toward a specific occupation. In addition to this skills gap, the problem is compounded by the very limited interaction between teachers and industry (Burnett & Jayaram, 2012). A more detailed explanation of the results from such research can be seen in Figure 1.

UNESCO (2012) identified issues related to effectiveness in the field of education. The problem here is the gap created by a teacher who is only concerned with the structure and content of learning without providing an effective learning process.

2.2 Student Team Achievement Division (STAD)

Cooperative learning is a model system where learning, studying and working is conducted collaboratively in small groups of 4–6 people to induce more passion for learning. In general, all learning techniques in this emphasize the cooperation of students in learning, both in presenting an idea, or in completing tasks in the hope that a learning atmosphere is created that is more active and effective, bringing about the achievement of learning objectives (Slavin, 1995). The cooperative learning model has many techniques in its application, and one is STAD.

Salehizadeh and Behin-Aein (2014) concluded that there is a positive difference in the results of study and the attitude of students to study as a result of cooperative learning by the inquiry method.

The implementation of this learning requires the participation and cooperation of group learning. Cooperative learning can improve the attitude of students toward learning better too, improving some social behaviors (Rahmawati, 2013).

2.3 Social behavior

Krech and Crutchfield stated that, according to Ballachey (in Ibrahim, 2001), a person's state of behavior appears in the pattern of response between humans, which is manifested in segmented interpersonal relationships. Social behavior is also synonymous with the person's reactions toward others. Behaviors are associated with feelings, actions, attitudes, believes, memories, and respect for other people. A person's social behavior can also be defined as their attitude in response to others' attitude and each person's attitude is different to one another.

Baron and Byrne (in Ibrahim, 2001) stated that there are four major categories that make up an individual's social behavior, namely: (1) the behavior and characteristics of others; (2) cognitive processes; (3) environmental factors; (4) culture.

Previous studies at international level show that CL can enhance Tim's work and the social abilities of students (Cohen, 1994; Yang & Zheng, 2010). CL can also improve cooperation within a team (Kern et al., 2007; Smith, 1995). Group activities improve students' belief that success can be gained through positive dependence on others (Erdem, 2009; Smith, 1995).

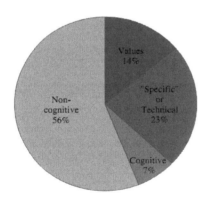

Figure 1. Skills needed in South Asia (source: Burnett & Jayaram, 2012, p. 10).

Table 1. Indicators to be assessed in the teaching–learning.

Indicators							
Numbers assigned	Knowledge	Comprehension	Application	Analysis	Synthesis	Evaluation	No. assigned
	1, 4, 5, 11	2, 3, 6, 12, 15	9, 14, 30	8, 10, 13		–	15
	17, 21, 23, 24	16, 18, 19, 22	20, 25, 26	27, 28	29	7	15
	Total						30

3 METHOD

This research used the quasi-experimental method. In this study, an intervention is applied to students in the form of a model of cooperative learning using the STAD technique. The class taught using STAD techniques is called experimental class, whereas the other class is called control class in which teaching and learning processes take place using conventional method. Both classes are then evaluated to see whether there is difference between class promoting the treatment and the class that does not. Both classes, namely, the experimental class and the control class, were evaluated so as to see the differences induced after the application of the STAD form of CL.

The social behavior of students is measured using the following indicators: motivation, activity, collaboration, responsibility, requests for help, mutual respect, and confidence.

In the experimental class using CL-type STAD methods (Y), the students are given a pre-test rating (Y_1) at the outset, and after the learning intervention ends the students are awarded a post-test score (Y_2). The data results of the study are indicated by the difference (delta) in values obtained from the scores of the pre-test (Y_1) and

those of the post-test (Y_2). The same test regime is applied to the control class that is taught with conventional methods. This design can be described as summarized in Table 2 and the procedures in this research are as shown in Figure 2.

The measurement of social behavior is performed by an instrument in the form of a questionnaire about attitude acceptance. This questionnaire uses the Likert scale (Ridwan, 2007) as an alternative to the answers of each respondent's statements and the students must select the single answer that best fits. Every item has its value scored between 1 and 5 in accordance with the level of the possible answers, which were Strongly Agree, Disagree, Undecided, Disagree, and Strongly Disagree.

4 RESULTS AND DISCUSSION

4.1 *Average score of pre-test and post-test*

The average score results of the pre- and post-tests of both control and experimental groups are listed in Table 3.

Based on the results of the descriptive analysis of public behavior, 75.2% of students agreed that the application of CL can improve community behavior, 9.8% of students stated that this learning model cannot improve social behavior, while 15% were unsure if this model improved social behavior.

A Mann-Whitney test was applied to the data as follows:

$$U_A = n_A.n_B + \frac{nA(nA+1)}{2} - R_A \qquad (1)$$

where $U_A = U_A$ test statistics; R_A = number of samples with N_A; and n_A = the number of members of the A sample.

Table 2. Research design.

Class	Aspects of knowledge		Difference in value
	Pre-test	Post-test	
Conventional methods (X)	Y_1	Y_2	Y_2-Y_1
Methods of CL-type STAD (Y)	Y_1	Y_2	Y_2-Y_1

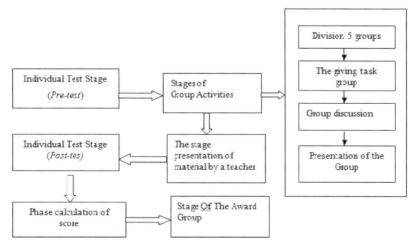

Figure 2. Flowchart applicability CL-type STAD.

Table 3. The average score of pre- and post-tests for experimental and control classes.

Class	The average score		
	Pre-test	Post-test	Delta (Δ)
Conventional methods (X)	70.43	74.78	4.35
Methods of CL-type STAD (Y)	71.20	79.00	7.80

$$U_B = n_A.n_B + \frac{nB(nB+1)}{2} - R_B \qquad (2)$$

where $U_B = U_B$ test statistics; R_B = number of samples with N_B; and n_B = the number of members of the B sample.

The Mann-Whitney test was calculated by using the formula 'U' for large samples because the sample size is greater than 20. U_A is U for group A (experiments); from Equation (1) we obtain the value of $U_A = 391.5$. U_B was U for the control group (B). U used in this analysis is the smallest, that is, U = 183.5, so:

$$z = \frac{U - \frac{nA.nB}{2}}{\sqrt{nA.nB \frac{(nA+nB+1)}{12}}} = \frac{183,5 - 287,5}{\sqrt{575 \frac{49}{12}}} \qquad (3)$$
$$= -\frac{104}{\sqrt{2347,9}} = -\frac{97}{48,45} = -2,14$$

It is shown based on the statistical calculation that the value of z is 2.14v.

Since the z is higher than the z table; therefore, according to the Mann-Whitney criterion, the H1 is accepted. $z = 2.14 > z$-table = z ($\alpha = 0.05 = 5\%$) = 1.96. This means that the H1 hypothesis is accepted. In other words, the application of STAD-type cooperative learning can improve the results of learners, who do significantly better than those taught with conventional methods.

According to Table 3, the delta in the scores of the STAD group was 7.80. The mean delta of the scores from the control group is 4.35. Based on this explanation, the mean scores of the learners using a STAD method were higher than the average score of the students who were using conventional methods.

Table 3 also shows that the pre-test scores of the experimental and control classes were almost the same (71.20 vs. 70.43). This suggests that learners in both classes had the same initial ability. If one class received an intervention and a differential change

in ability was observed, then it can be concluded that this happened as a result of the intervention.

The post-test score for the experimental class is 79.00 with a delta of 7.80. The mean post-test score for the control class is 74.78 with a delta from the average pre-test scores of 4.35. Based on this, the average scores of the learners using a STAD-type method of CL were higher compared to the mean score of the students who were taught with conventional methods. Statistical tests need to be done to find out if the sample data can be used to generalize the data population.

In other words, the application of the STAD method of CL can improve the learning outcomes of students significantly.

The results from this research were reinforced by the liveliness of the learners. This is because the idea of STAD is that learners work together to learn about and take responsibility for their own lessons and also learn from others. In addition, it can increase the confidence of learners (Apriayani et al., 2000).

The advantage of CL is a positive interdependence among learners. The teacher created an atmosphere that encouraged learners to feel a need for each other. The occurrence of interpersonal interaction forces the learners to engage in personal dialog, and this makes the learners more flexible, and makes it easier for them to learn with peers. Such conducive atmosphere created by the teacher leads to the existence of personal responsibility where students are responsible for themselves and at the same time help other fellow students. (Bennett, 1995).

Models like cooperative learning can improve skills in solving problems (process group). The main objective of all STAD learners is accelerating understanding (Slavin, 1995). So it can be said that these methods influence student learning outcomes.

This research shows that the application of CL-type STAD helps students who are individually unable to understand the lessons. This learning encourages students to work together and each student is responsible for what is studied by other students.

5 CONCLUSIONS

The results showed that CL-type STAD can improve student learning outcomes and are significantly better than conventional methods. The experimental classes had an average increase of 7.80 in their scores while the class to which conventional method were applied had a lower average increase of 4.35.

The conventional learning model is still centered on the teacher so that students lack experience in learning for themselves. Students become passive and unenthusiastic in learning because everything has already been provided by the teacher. The class that experimented with the application of the STAD-type model of cooperative learning was more centered on students. Learning through STAD is helping students to become more active, work in teams, and take more responsibility for their education.

REFERENCES

Altun. S. (2015). The effect of cooperative learning on students' achievement and views on the science and technology course. *International Electronic Journal of Elementary Education, 7*(3), 451–468.

Burnett, N. & Jayaram, S. (2012). Skills for employability in Africa and Asia. ISESE Skills Synthesis. In *Innovative secondary education for skills enhancement*: *Phase 1 synthesis reports* (pp. 5–30). Washington, DC: Results for Development Institute.

Cohen, E. (1994). Designing group work strategies for the heterogeneous classroom. New York, NY: Teachers College Press.

Erdem, A. (2009). Preservice teachers' attitudes towards cooperative learning in mathematics course. *Procedia: Social and Behavioral Sciences, 1*(1), 1668–1672.

Jayaram, S. & Engmann, M. (2014). Developing skills for employability at the secondary level: Effective models for Asia. *Prospects, 44*, 221–233.

Jordan, A., Carlile, O. & Stack, A. (2008). *Approach to learning: A guide for teachers*. New York, NY: Open University Press.

Kane, M. (1990). *The secretary's commission on achieving necessary skills (scans): Identifying and describing the skills required by work*. Washington, DC: Pelavin Associates.

Kern, A.L., Moore, T.J. & Akillioglu, F.C. (2007). Cooperative learning: Developing an observation instrument for student interactions. In *Proceedings of the 2007 IEEE Frontiers in Education Conference (FIE 2007), Milwaukee, WI* (pp. T1D1–T1D6).

McLeish, A. (2002). *Employability skills for Australian small and medium sized enterprises: Report of the interviews and focus groups with small and medium enterprises*. Canberra, Australia: Department of Education, Science and Training.

Purwanto. (2010). *Evaluation of the results of the study*. Yogyakarta, Indonesia: Pustaka Pelajar.

Rahmawati, D. (2013). *The influences are cooperative learning model to make a match against the results of the student learning process on subjects in the Senior High School 31 Jakarta* (Thesis). Faculty of Economics, Universitas Negeri Jakarta, Jakarta, Indonesia.

Ridwan, S. (2010). *Introduction to statistics* (3rd ed.). Jakarta, Indonesia: Alfabeta.

Salehizadeh, M.R. & Behin-Aein, N. (2014). Effects of cooperative learning plus inquiry method on student learning and attitudes: A comparative study for engineering economic classrooms. *European Journal of Engineering Education, 39*(2), 188–200.

Sharan, S. (2012). *The handbook of cooperative learning*. Yogyakarta, Indonesia: Familia.

Slavin, R.E. (1995). *Cooperative learning: Theory, research, and practice* (2nd ed.). Boston, MA: Allyn & Bacon.

Smith, K.A. (1995). Cooperative learning: Effective teamwork for engineering classrooms. In *Proceedings of Frontiers in Education Conference, Atlanta, GA* (pp. 2b5.13–2b5.18).

UIS. (2011). *Global education digest 2011: Comparing education statistics across the world*. Montreal, Canada: UNESCO Institute of Statistics. Retrieved from http://www.uis.unesco.org/Education/Pages/ged-2011.aspx

UNESCO. (2012). *Youth and skills: putting education to work. Education for all global monitoring report*. Paris, France: UNESCO. Retrieved from http://www.uis.unesco.org/Education/Documents/gmr-2012-en.pdf

Yang, D. & Zheng, H. (2010). Research on the framework of new college English teaching mode integrating cooperative and autonomous learning in the network multimedia environment. In *Proceedings of 2nd International Conference on Education Technology and Computer (ICETC)* (pp. V3-256-V3-259).

Self-directed learning skills in a study program of agroindustry education technology using portfolio-based advice

S. Handayani, M.N. Handayani & D. Cakrawati
Universitas Pendidikan Indonesia, Bandung, Indonesia

ABSTRACT: The study was designed to investigate whether the use of portfolio-based advice can over-come students' difficulty with self-directed learning skills in work-based simulation learning. The study was conducted using a descriptive method with a quantitative approach. Students were divided into four groups, each student in each group was given a task according to manufacture organization and asked to prepare food from an animal product such as yogurt or ice cream. Each student was required to create a portfolio in the form of a log book as a guide for working in the laboratory. Questionnaires were given to the students to establish their opinion about using portfolios in self-directed learning. The result shows that 78% of students agreed that the use of portfolios helped them to understand the flowchart process of making ice cream and yogurt, as well as the importance of standard operational procedure in preparing food products. Eighty-four percent of the students agreed that creating a portfolio could improve their skills in food preparation. They also agreed that the use of a portfolio helped them to improve their skills in self-directed learning.

1   INTRODUCTION

Nowadays learning is based on real life, and education itself needs to stimulate learners into combining knowledge, skills and attitude. The alumni of the Study Program of Education on Agro-industry Technology are expected to have several competencies including psychomotor skills, as they have had to train vocational students in the processing of food. Vocational teachers are considered having dual professions. Universities that prepare vocational teachers should consider curricula and learning methods that will develop their teaching competencies and professional competencies related to particular vocational practice (Andersson & Köpsén, 2015).

Learning activities at university are important for producing excellent teachers. Learning at different places, such as the laboratory, classroom and workplace, provides possibilities to develop students' knowledge and skill, as well as improve their attitude toward many situations (Onstenk, 2009). Students in higher education such as university and college are encouraged to be responsible and independent as they are considered to be adults (Silén & Uhlin, 2008). This condition is called Self-Directed Learning (SDL). The concept of self-directed learning is considered to be at the core of learning concepts in national curricula since it stresses student-centered learning. It supports the scientific learning method.

To improve students' self-directed learning, teachers need to develop not only learning methods but also means of assessment. Many researchers use SDL terminology in explanation of problem-based learning. SDL itself refers to students' motivation and willingness to engage in learning activities defined by themselves rather than a teacher (Loyens et al., 2008). Silén and Uhlin (2008) proposed the development of problem-based learning—called 'problem-based learning with inquiry' – in tutorial sessions. This could overcome students' difficulties by providing them with the opportunity to discuss their problems with teachers in tutorial sessions.

Increasing demands to provide work-ready graduates have challenged universities to provide teaching methods that could change dynamically according to work-demand (Smigiel et al., 2015). One of the learning methods that can be implemented in preparing vocational teachers is work-based simulation learning. In this learning method, students are given tasks to help them improve their performance. In this study the task was specific to vocational practice which is food technology. In work-based simulation, the learning process is a simplified manufacturing process which nonetheless keeps the same principles. Work-based simulation learning also develops self-directed learning since this learning method improved students' ability to work independently and develop their competencies while they were working on food manufacturing simulation.

However, self-directed learning does have disadvantages. Sometimes, students do not know where or when to start, or what was the first step, while at times when the task is too difficult for some students, it needs to be supervised to make sure the learning process is on the right track. The writer proposes the use of a portfolio to overcome students' difficulties in developing self-directed learning. Using a portfolio, which consists of monitoring, evaluating and planning, will help the learning process.

2 METHODS

2.1 Participants

The participants were 32 students (30 females and two males) in their third year of study who took the course Technology Processing of Animal Products. Five supervisors participated in the study: three lecturers and two laboratory staff.

2.2 Research methods

The research was conducted using the descriptive method with a quantitative approach describing and interpreting the data.

2.3 Data collecting and analysis

The data were collected and analyzed through the following procedures:

1. Development of guided portfolio. A portfolio was created to help students design their steps for preparing a food product specific to the task and take responsibility for their learning process. The portfolio was assessed using a Standard Operational Procedure (SOP) composed by students that included purchasing raw material, production, and quality control procedures, as well as their daily working journal.
2. Questionnaires to the students. The questionnaires focused on the emotions students experienced during the learning process, such as motivation and preparedness. There were five indicators that were divided into the 14 questions asked using 1–4 Likert-scale questions (0 = disagree; 4 = strongly agree). These indicators were:
   1. Students' perception of the importance of the subject.
   2. Students' feeling about work-based simulation learning.
   3. Students' understanding of the subject.
   4. Students' commitment to the tasks.
   5. Students' competencies development.

3 RESULT AND DISCUSSION

Many learning methods have been implemented to develop meaningful learning that supports student-centered learning as required in Indonesia's 2013 curriculum. Student-centered learning has both a positive and negative impact: the approach not only stimulates students' intrinsic motivation but also develops their SDL skills; on the other hand, research has shown that students whose background learning has been based on conventional teaching methods have difficulties choosing learning tasks, which impedes their progress in becoming independent learners (Kicken et al., 2009). Silén and Uhlin (2008) proposed that students need to be facilitated through tutorials where they can discuss their problems with their teachers. Kicken et al. (2009) proposed the use of a web portfolio which could help students design their future learning, and thus develop SDL skills.

The authors of this study propose that self-directed learning can be developed by using a portfolio in the form of a log book. Students had to fill out the log book before and after they worked in the laboratory. Prior to doing the work, the students were required to fill out their log book with the procedures they believed were required to do the work. They were given the chance to discuss the working method with the supervisors who could advise them or propose an alternative procedure. After the work was completed, they wrote the results in the log book which helped them to evaluate their work. The result was also reported to the supervisors to be assessed. This is called portfolio-based advice.

Aside from discussion of log book content, meetings with the supervisor were scheduled once a week to discuss problems which occurred or simply to share knowledge with other groups. Research conducted by Kicken et al. (2009) showed that students who received advice developed self-directed learning better than those who did not. Meetings are also important to discuss students' problems in the subject. An example of a product flow chart can be seen in Figure 1.

Questionnaires were given to students to determine students' perception as to whether the learning method and portfolio were effective in developing their SDL skills. Questionnaires grouped by indicators are shown in Figure 2.

Students discussed the flow chart and then revised it, as shown in Figure 2.

The graph shows that the first indicator has the highest percentage while the fourth has the lowest. All students agree that the subject of processing technology of an animal product was important. Students in higher education have already developed self-awareness regarding the importance of study.

About 94% students agreed that they felt excited to experience work-based simulation learning.

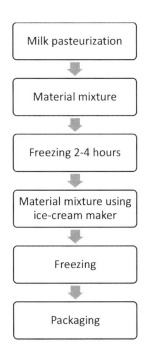

Figure 1. Flow chart of ice-cream product.

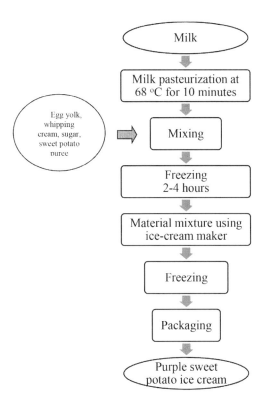

Figure 2. Revised flow chart of ice-cream product.

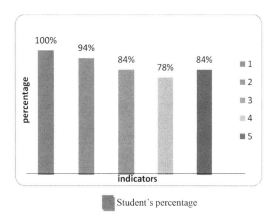

Student's percentage

Figure 3. Questionnaires grouped by indicators.
1. Students' perception of the importance of the subject.
2. Students' feeling about work-based simulation learning.
3. Students' understanding of the subject.
4. Students' commitment to the tasks.
5. Students' competencies development.

Students might have different styles of learning. Supervisors should consider the learning types of learners whether visual, auditory or kinesthetic so that supervisor and students can devise a strategy for study (Cort, 2009).

Some students disagreed that the use of portfolio-based advice can improve their understanding of the subject. To have meaningful learning, it is important for the students to be engaged in learning activities that are supported by students' motivation toward learning. Supervisors (or lecturers) play the role of partner in learners' problem-solving, as students' guide, consultant and coach (Chung 2015).

Students' commitment to the task was the lowest percentage of all indicators. The use of the portfolio was to help students to improve self-directed learning, including being responsible for their report deadline. According to Loyens et al. (2008), SDL skills should help students set goals in their learning process. About 16% students disagreed that the use of a portfolio can develop their competencies.

4 CONCLUSIONS

There are two conclusions in this study:

1. The use of a portfolio can improve students' skills in the subject of processing technology of an animal product
2. The use of a portfolio helps students to improve their SDL skills.

REFERENCES

Andersson, P. & Köpsén, S. (2015). Continuing professional development of vocational teachers: Participation in a Swedish national initiative. *Empirical Research in Vocational Education and Training, 7,* 7.

Cort, P. (2009). The EC discourse on vocational training: How a "common vocational training policy" turned into a lifelong learning strategy. *Vocations and Learning, 2,* 87–107.

Kicken, W., Brand-Gruewel, S., van Merriënboer, J.J.G. & Slot, W. (2009). The effects of portfolio-based advice on the development of self-directed learning skills in secondary vocational education. *Education Technology Research Development, 57,* 439–460.

Loyens, S.M.M., Magda, J. & Rikers, R.M.J.P. (2008). Self-directed learning in problem-based learning and its relationships with self-regulated learning. *Education Psychology Review, 20,* 411–427.

Onstenk, J. (2009). Connections of school- and work-based learning in the Netherlands. In Stenstorm, M.L. & Tynjala, P. (Eds.), *Towards Integration of Work and Learning.* Available at http://www.springerlink.com

Silén, C.L. & Uhlin, L. (2008). Self-directed learning. *Teaching in Higher Education, 13*(4), 461–475.

Smigiel, H., Macleod, C. & Stephenson, H. (2015). Managing competing demands in the delivery of work integrated learning: An institutional case study. Kennedy, M., Billett, S., Gherardi, S. & Grealish, L. (Eds.), *Practice-based learning in higher education* (pp. 159–172). Dordrecht, The Netherlands: Springer.

Upgrading student creativity in computing subjects by synectics application

S.C. Wibawa, R. Harimurti & B. Sujatmiko
Informatics Engineering, Universitas Negeri Surabaya, Surabaya, Indonesia

F.I. Sari
Universitas Negeri Surabaya, Surabaya, Indonesia

S. Dwiyanti
Cosmetology Education, Universitas Negeri Surabaya, Surabaya, Indonesia

ABSTRACT: Creativity is a process that produces something new. The student needs to produce a portfolio of work creativity by integrating their enjoyment of the lecture subject, which compels the student to practice the computer. The synectics learning model leads to learning that can develop the creativity of students. Synectics learning management consists of a six-phase study: (1) a phase of real conditions at the time, (2) a phase of direct analogy, (3) a stage of direct analogy, (4) a stage of compressed conflict, (5) direct analogy to the stage, (6) stage trials of the original task. Classroom action research deals with several stages that are interrelated and continuous, namely: (1) planning, (2) the implementation (of acting), (3) observation (observing), and (4) reflection (reflecting), carried out in two cycles. In our study, the average data yield of Cycle 1 was 77.08%, which included good progress to 79.16% in Cycle 2. Synectics learning can enrich the creativity of students. The average percentage of a cycle starts at around 67.9% in Cycle 1 and increases to 70.6% in Cycle 2. In Cycle 1, practice photography techniques scored 78.1%, and the technique of pre-wedding photography with the concept of beauty increased to 89.6% in Cycle 2. The percentage of completeness of cognitive learning outcomes increased from Cycle 1 to Cycle 2. In cycle one, the completeness is 82.45% while in cycle 2 it is 88.3%. In terms of classroom action research, it can be concluded that synectics learning can enhance student creativity and improve a student's learning outcomes (both cognitive and psychomotor).

1 INTRODUCTION

Creativity is the ability to produce original work and ideas. Creativity can be defined as the ability to produce original ideas and new items. It also includes the combining of existing work, objects, and ideas in different ways for new purposes (Barry & Kanematsu, 2006). The creative process is the emergence of a new product in action which grew out of the uniqueness of the individual, from experience that emphasizes the new product, and the interaction of individuals with their environment or culture (Johnson & Johnson, 2002).

A model of the teaching and learning process characterized by an increase in critical and creative thinking skills and generated through education or training, proves to be conducive and effective to improve both creative and critical thinking of students. Good teaching traditionally makes ingenious use of analogies and metaphors to help students visualize content. A synectics session,

referred to by Gordon (1961) as an 'excursion', is a group problem-solving activity wherein a person is stimulated to think creatively under a loosely structured system. The process, in brief, begins with a problem introduced by a leader who conducts an 'excursion' of the group through a series of steps which attempt to determine a solution to the problem. This procedure deliberately stimulates creative thinking rather than leaving it to chance (Gordon, 1961).

The synectics approach relies on bringing the three keys of Climate, Thinking and Action together (see Figure 1). Foremost is a supportive climate, which is made up of the behaviors we use to work with others, to give and receive ideas and to build the trust environment for speculative ideas to be offered. Thinking requires pushing out our idea boundaries using the spectrum of 'Thinking and Developmental Thinking', which takes promising but speculative ideas, and builds feasibility into them. Synectics' emphasis on developmental

Synectics© Process to Innovative Work
the intersection of climate, thinking, action

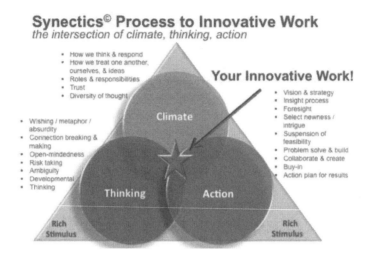

- How we think & respond
- How we treat one another, ourselves, & ideas
- Roles & responsibilities
- Trust
- Diversity of thought

- Wishing / metaphor / absurdity
- Connection breaking & making
- Open-mindedness
- Risk taking
- Ambiguity
- Developmental
- Thinking

Your Innovative Work!
- Vision & strategy
- Insight process
- Foresight
- Select newness / intrigue
- Suspension of feasibility
- Problem solve & build
- Collaborate & create
- Buy-in
- Action plan for results

Climate

Thinking

Action

Rich Stimulus

Rich Stimulus

Figure 1. Synectics process: climate, thinking and action (adapted by Nolan & Williams, 2010).

thinking is a key differentiating feature compared to brainstorming and other creative problem-solving techniques. Finally, there is a set of action steps which move the process along with an emphasis on creative problem-solving to get to actionable execution.

Unfortunately, sometimes the ideas are not interesting. It takes a learning model to generate a portfolio of creative works of students to combine their enjoyment with the lecture material, so that they practice applied computer task subjects with pleasure and attempt to generate good work.

It can be concluded that a characteristic of the learning acquired under the synectics teaching model is student creativity.

As one learning model, synectics has several advantages, such as, 1) increasing the ability to live in an atmosphere which appreciates differences, 2) to be able to stimulate creative thinking abilities, 3) to be able to activate both hemispheres, and 4) to be able to create new ideas. The basis of the synectics model is to enrich the creativity of learning outcomes.

2 METHOD

2.1 Procedures

Data was obtained from the observation of 32 students studying the bachelor degree Educational Makeup in 2013. A synectics strategy was applied in this study. The first strategy is that teachers create something new. The experiment is conducted in two cycles. The actions in the procedure for Cycle 1 are planning, implementing action, observation

and evaluation, and reflection within each Cycle 1 as follows:

1. Planning—this step is done through an observation sheet discussing all the learning activities to carry out.
2. Phase action and observation implementation of teaching and learning activities carried out by researchers who created the teaching plan (RPP). At this stage the application is similar to learning synectics. Observations were carried out simultaneously with the implementation of teaching and learning activities. In this case, the observer used guidelines to fill out the observation sheet in accordance with established practice.
3. Phase reflection—based on observation of the learning process. Students' learning outcomes are the necessary information that relates the advantages and disadvantages for the implementation of learning in one week.

2.2 Data collection technique

This study uses data collection methods as follows:

1. Observation method—the student uses observation to measure creativity and learning outcomes of the students on the computer subject.
2. Achievement test—the test carried out after the teaching and learning activities to determine student mastery and understanding of the material, and the extent of creative thinking of students after receiving a referral from a teacher/lecturer as to the purpose of the synectics learning model.
3. Rating for work—rating for psychomotor assessment work. It performs students' learning

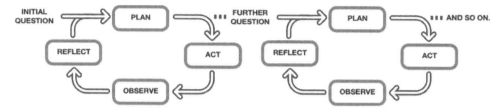

Figure 2.   The cycle of classroom action (source: Kemmis & McTaggart, 1982).

outcomes in the forms of their creativity and class participation. Assessment is carried out by observing the students in expressing the results of their creative thinking, in order to improve the quality of the photos that are expected by doing something different like laboratory processing or outdoor shooting.

2.3   Data analysis technique

This study uses data analysis techniques as follows:

1. Learning observation data analysis—teachers manage data analysis of lecturers/the classroom on the application of this learning model. Synectics are analyzed by calculating the average category of learning undertaken.
2. Analysis observation on student creativity—data analysis of student creativity is measured by using a Likert scale and percentages. Formulas and tables combine to make the analysis of observational data of learning.
3. Test data analysis of student results—at this stage, analysis of the achievement test aims to identify students' learning outcomes in terms of completeness of student learning. The analysis is performed by calculating the evaluation value and converting into a percentage.
4. Analysis of student work—the analysis of the performance of students or lab aims to find out the results of the evaluation of creative thinking that have been previously theorized in groups. The analysis is performed by calculating the value of the performance which is then modified in a percentage calculation.

2.4   Indicators of success

The measure of the success of this class action research process is as follows:

1. Student creativity—indication of success is if 80% or more of the students were categorized with a creative performance score above 65%, and also whether the students have increased their creativity from Cycle 1 to Cycle 2, as measured by the change in the average score of the

students from the observation sheets in terms of creative attitude and creative thinking.
2. Learning outcomes—student results will be measured by tests. Tests will be performed on the final results of each action. There is an indication of success if 85% or more of the students are categorized by an evaluation value of 78 or more in the first and second cycles, when referring to the *Sekolah Menengah Kebangsaan* (SMK) secondary school.

3   RESULTS AND DISCUSSION

The data used in this study are an assessment of the creativity of the students, and the results obtained by the students. Based on the actions that took place in Cycle 1, observations of management learning, creativity of students and student results were obtained. KKM (Kriteria Ketuntasan Minimal) is a minimum score for students to reach.

3.1   Cycle 1

Data obtained in Cycle 1 were as follows:

1. Data observation of synthetic learning management shows that both teacher and students perform the learning management well at every stage in Cycle 1. This can be seen from the percentages, as follows: Stage 1 describes the real situation at that time was 62.5% in either category; Stage 2 by 75% direct analogy with excellent category; Stage 3 direct analogy of 62.5% with good category; Stage 4 conflicts compressed by 100% with a very good category; Stage 5 direct analogy by 75% with excellent category; Stage 6 tests on the original task of 87.5% with very good category.
2. Observations of student creativity at Cycle 1 (theory) – the observation of the creativity of students in Cycle 1. On average, the creativity of students in the Cycle 1 observation is 67.9%. This indicates that the success of the action in Cycle 1 has been reached as the percentage of student creativity is more than 65%. The highest

percentage of student creativity is the indicator of curiosity. It is shown by the high percentage of the indicator (63.% and 74.3%).

3. Data on student results in Cycle 1 – 28 students completed Cycle 1 with the remaining six students not finishing. The percentage mastery of learning outcomes in Cycle 1 was 82.45%, which shows that the minimum score requirement was reached because it is greater than that of the KKM secondary school at 78%.

4. Observations of student creativity at Cycle 1 (practice) – the average of student creativity obtained through observation is shown in cycle 1. This indicates that the success of the first cycle action on a given theory has been achieved because the percentage of student creativity is more than 65%. The highest percentage of student creativity (87.5%) was the indicator of curiosity about the teaching method, followed by having original ideas and problem-solving, and asking good questions.

5. Data learning outcomes practice Cycle 1 – 81.25% of students practiced thoroughly. The data shows that the minimum requirement standard is reached (KKM 78).

3.2 Cycle 2

Data obtained in Cycle 2 were as follows:

1. Data observations of synectics learning management in Cycle 2 – in the results of the observation of the learning management synectics, two cycles can be seen that the teacher has managed the teaching and learning processes well in every stage in cycle 2. This can be seen from the percentages of each stage as follows. Stage 1: 62.5% (good), stage 2: 87.5% (very good), stage 3: 75% (very good), stage 4 compression con-

flicts was 87.5% (very good category); Stage 5 direct analogy with 75% (great category); Stage 6 tests on the original task of 87.5% (highest category). It was concluded that the learning process that was carried out already reflects the learning activities with synectics models.

2. Data observations of student creativity in Cycle 2 (theory) – the development of student creativity is reflected in cycle 1 and 2. In Cycle 1, the average percentage of creativity was 67.9%, and in Cycle 2 it rose to 70.6%. This indicates that success of the action has been achieved because the percentage of Cycles 1 and 2 ≥ 65%.

3. Data student results Cycle 2 – 30 students completed Cycle 2 while two students did not. The percentage of completeness is 88.3%, which indicates that classical completeness has been reached for more than 78%.

4. Observations of student creativity in Cycle 2 (practice) – the average of student creativity in cycle 2 was 79.7% for both categories. The successful teaching is in two cycles that provide

Table 2. Percentage of student creativity Cycle 2 (practice).

No.	Creativity indicators	Percentage
1.	Curiosity about the theme being taught	75.7
2.	Often ask good questions	75.7
3.	Offer plenty of ideas to a problem	72.1
4.	Freedom of opinion	68.4
5.	Look at the problem from different angles	69.1
6.	Power of imagination	68.4
7.	Having original ideas & problem-solving	68.4
8.	Having a sense of "beauty" to appreciate things around them	66.9
	Average	70.6

Table 1. Percentage of student creativity Cycle 2 (theory).

No.	Creativity indicators`	Percentage
1.	Curiosity about the theme being taught	62.5
2.	Asking good questions	75
3.	Offering good ideas to solve problem	87.5
4.	Freedom of opinion	75
5.	Looking at the problem from different angles	87.5
6.	Power of imagination	87.5
7.	Having original ideas & problem-solving	87.5
8.	Having an idea to solve problem	75
	Average	79.7

Figure 3. Product result in Cycle 1.

Figure 4. Product result in Cycle 2.

theory. Student creativity of more than 65% is achieved.
5. Data for Cycle 2 learning outcomes practice – all students have completed the practice of learning outcomes. This shows that the classical completeness is reached because KKM has exceeded 78%.

4 CONCLUSION

On implementation of action Cycles 1 and 2, the stages which were dominant in eliciting student creativity were Stages 3, 5, 6 and 7. At these stages, the students worked in small groups, discussions, and mutual digs, and they bounced ideas and expressed their creativity, and, combined with the theory and practicals, it proved that students show creativity in modifying the basic techniques of photography and beauty of pre-wedding photography, in applied computing subjects.

The conclusion of the research is that the implementation of learning management increased. Synectics learning can enhance the creativity of students and improve learning outcomes of both cognitive and psychomotor students. Students can use their creativity by using synectics learning. The first step in synthetic learning is that students need to learn the subject well to earn good results. The synectics teaching model requires a lot of time, effort and well-organized planning. Therefore, the implementation should focus on the time and the stages of learning.

ACKNOWLEDGMENTS

The authors wish to thank Muhammad Arsyad, PhD (Hasanuddin University) his suggestions to find more research findings on synthetic learning to enrich the discussion of the current study. The authors would also like to thank Dr Yuni Sri Rahayu, Deputy Chancellor for Academic Affairs, Universitas Negeri Surabaya for supporting the research grant.

REFERENCES

Barry, D.M. & Kanematsu, H. (2006). International program to promote creative thinking in chemistry and science. *The Chemist*, 83(2), 10–14.
Cruse, E. (2006). *Using educational video in the classroom: Theory, research and practice.* West Conshohocken, PA: Library Video Company. Retrieved from http://www.libraryvideo.com/articles/article26.asp
Gordon, William J.J. (1961). *Synectics: The Development of Creative Capacity.* Harper Publisher.
Johnson, D.W. & Johnson, R.T. (2002). *Meaningful assessment: A manageable and cooperative process.* Boston, MA: Allyn & Bacon.
Joyce, B.R. & Weill, M. (2003). *Models of teaching* (7th ed.). Boston, MA: Allyn & Bacon.
Kemmis, S. & McTaggart, R. (1982). *The action research reader* (3rd ed.). Victoria, Australia: Deakin University.
Kozbelt, A., Beghetto, R.A. & Runco, M.A. (2010). *Theories of creativity.* In Kaufman, J.C. & Sternberg, R.J. (Eds.), *The Cambridge handbook of creativity* (pp. 20–47). New York, NY: Cambridge University Press.
Nolan, V. & Williams, C. (Eds.) (2010). *A visual overview of the synectics invention model* (From a contribution by Heinz Prekel). In *Imagine that! Celebrating 50 years of synectics* (pp. 32–41). Waltham, MA: Synecticsworld.
Seligmann, E.R. (2007). *Reaching students through synectics: A creative solution.* University of Northern Colorado. Retrieved from http://ellieseligmann.com/essays/SYNECTICS_Seligmann.pdf
Silverman, F. (2006). Learning styles. *District Administration*, 42(9), 70–71.
Wibawa, S.C. (2014). Students' creative e-portfolio: Using Android cellphone cameras for inventive beauty photography. In *Proceedings International Conference on Advances in Education Technology (ICAET 2014)* (pp. 121–124).
Wibawa, S.C. & Schulte, S. (2015). Beauty media learning using Android mobile phone. *International Journal of Innovative Research in Advanced Engineering (IJIRAE)*, 2(11), 20–26.

Regionalization and Harmonization in TVET – Abdullah et al. (Eds)
© 2017 Taylor & Francis Group, London, ISBN 978-1-138-05419-6

Developing project-based CAD teaching–learning module to improve the vocational competence of mechanical engineering students

T. Wiyanto
Universitas Negeri Surabaya, Surabaya, Indonesioa

ABSTRACT: Vocational education aims to develop performance (psychomotor) skills in addition to knowledge (cognitive skills) and attitude (affective skills). This study aimed to improve the competence of vocational students majoring in Mechanical Engineering in Computer-Aided Design (CAD) using Project-Based Learning (PBL) modules. The study adopted the Research and Development (R&D) method of *Four-D Thiagarajan* in four stages (define, design, develop, and disseminate). The CAD module was validated by CAD experts, design experts and linguists. The module was tested on students by conducting post-test performance and obtaining students' responses when applying the module. The research results indicated that the CAD module was viable, with an average validation score of 90% from CAD experts, design experts, and linguists. Based on the results of module testing, 91.33% of students considered that the module was good, while the results of testing student performance showed improvement in the vocational students' competence of 88% for the psychomotor skills domain and 80% for the cognitive domain.

1 INTRODUCTION

It is undeniable that the success of the learning process of students depends on the competence of teachers/lecturers. The teacher/lecturer competence affects how the learning process is conducted and the teaching–learning process will affect students' learning outcomes. Competent lecturers are able to manage class according to the students' needs. One of the more important competences possessed by lecturers in managing their subject is the development of teaching materials (Roesminingsih, 2011). Developing teaching materials is important in order to optimize the teaching–learning process. Less appropriate teaching materials may cause interruption in students' acceptance and may also show less effect if not in line with learning objectives that have previously been formulated.

Ideally, the competence of lecturers in developing teaching materials has been mastered, but in fact, there are many lecturers who have less suitable instructional materials for their subjects. As a result, the teaching–learning experience is less attractive, boring, monotonous, and does not meet learning objectives.

The results of student learning outcomes in the Department of Mechanical Engineering for the academic year 2014/2015 on Computer-Aided Design (CAD) using learning media in worksheet form were satisfactory. An A was received by 24.5% (22 students), 20% (18 students) received a B, 42.2% (38 students) a C, and the remaining 13.3% (12 students) a D. However, the scores mean that the formulated learning outcomes are not optimal as 55.5% of students had a score below B. This situation led the researcher to create a learning process by developing a project-based module for direct learning.

According to Mulyasa (2006, p. 34), a module is a formulated learning package systematically designed to help students achieve learning objectives. The system is aimed at improving the modules and learning activities efficiently in the classroom, be they time, funds, facilities, or personnel, in order to achieve the objectives. The module was expected to assist students to become more independent learners and improve their readiness before classes.

1.1 *Aims of the study*

The questions that the study set out to address were:

1. What are the experts' opinions on the feasibility of modules?
2. How different are students' learning outcomes after the implementation of CAD learning-based modules?
3. How different are students' responses after the implementation of CAD learning-based modules?

1.2 Objectives of the study

Based on the problems above, the objectives of this study are to improve learning outcomes and competences of vocational students majoring in Mechanical Engineering who take the subject of CAD Drawing.

1.3 Significance of the study

The results of this study provide information, especially for lecturers in CAD Drawing, on the development of CAD-based learning modules.

2 RESEARCH METHODOLOGY

The method used was a development model adopted from *Four-D Thiagarajan* (Thiagarajan et al., 1974). It was selected because the model explains the detailed operational steps of software development systematically. The Four-D model has four stages, namely, the definition stage (*define*), design stage (*design*), development stage (*develop*), and dissemination stage (*disseminate*).

2.1 Define

This stage has five steps, namely: (1) front-end analysis; (2) students' analysis; (3) conceptual analysis; (4) task analysis; and (5) learning objectives formulation.

2.2 Design

This stage has four steps, namely: (1) arranging reference tests; (2) selecting media; (3) selecting forms; and (4) initial design.

2.3 Develop

This stage has two steps, namely: (1) evaluations by CAD and media experts and by linguists; (2) limited tests.

2.4 Disseminate

The last stage in developing the module is student implementation.

3 RESULTS AND DISCUSSION

3.1 Definition stage (define)

At this stage, the activities are carried out by analyzing several aspects to formulate learning objectives according to the learning materials. Analyses of these aspects are divided into five stages, namely,

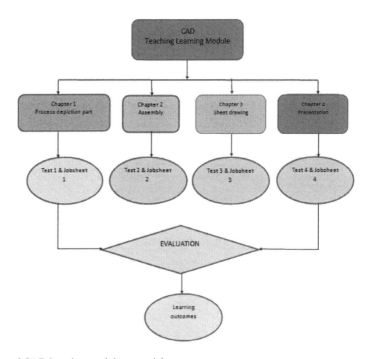

Figure 1. The map of CAD learning modules material.

front-end, student, task and conceptual analyses, and learning objectives formulation.

The material taught in the CAD module includes four aspects, as shown in Figure 1.

3.2 Design stage (design)

The function of this stage is to design or plan the CAD learning module. It has three steps that should be followed, namely: (1) arranging reference tests, (2) selecting media, and (3) selecting forms.

3.3 Development stage (develop)

After the design stage, the next stage was to produce a module prototype based on curriculum and material analyses. After being validated by the experts, the prototype might need to be revised as advised by the evaluators. In the development stage, there are two steps in producing the product, namely: (1) evaluation of the media experts, linguists, and lecturers who teach CAD (it is considered viable if scored at 90%), and (2) limited tests.

A limited testing stage was carried out to determine students' learning outcomes when using CAD learning modules, especially in their understanding and skills improvement of learning activities, in addition to the positive responses of students regarding the use of CAD learning modules. The limited test results showed that the learning outcomes were 80% for the cognitive test and 88% for the psychomotor tests.

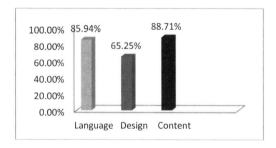

Figure 2.   Module evaluation results.

Table 1.   The result of the limited test trial in both cognitive and psychomotor skills.

Cognitive Test		
1.	Percentage of learning mastery	80%
Psychomotor Test (*Jobsheet*)		
2.	Percentage of learning mastery	88%

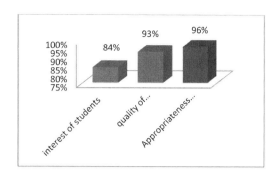

Figure 3.   Percentage of votes of student response.

3.4 Dissemination stage (disseminate)

The dissemination stage is the final stage of product development. Here, the products have been previously revised in the development stage and implemented for the target. However, due to various limitations, the dissemination stage was carried out in the Department of Mechanical Engineering of the State University of Surabaya, and articles were prepared for participation in educational seminars.

3.5 Students' responses to CAD-based learning

At the end of the test, students were asked to give feedback on the CAD learning modules. Students' responses to the module can be seen in the closed questionnaire. The results, as shown in Figure 3, gave an average score of 91.33% (excellent).

4   CONCLUSION

Based on the analysis, it can be concluded that:

1. Module eligibility showed that the average feasibility of the module met 90% of the criterion, considered as eligible.
2. The learning outcomes of vocational students in cognition showed 80%, with 88% for psychomotor skills. It was proved that CAD learning modules help students to improve both cognitive and psychomotor skills.
3. The students' response to the CAD learning modules was good, as shown by the average score of 91.33%.

REFERENCES

Arikunto, S. (2013). *Prosedur penelitian suatu praktik pendekatan*. Jakarta, Indonesia: PT Rineka Cipta.

Ganjar, D. (2012). *Pemrograman CNC & aplikasi di dunia industri*. Bandung, Indonesia: Informatika Bandung.

Gintings, A. (2008). *Efisiensi belajar dan pembelajaran*. Bandung, Indonesia: Humaniora.

Hidayat, N. & Shanhaji, A. (2011). *Autodesk inventor mastering 3D mechanical design*. Bandung, Indonesia: Informatics Bandung.

Mulyasa, E. (2006). *Kurikulum yang disempurnakan pengembangan standar kompetensi dan kompetensi dasar*. Bandung, Indonesia: PT Remaja Rosdakarya.

Roesminingsih, D.V. & Susarno, L.H. (2011). *Teori dan praktek pendidikan*. Surabaya, Indonesia: Fakultas Ilmu Pendidikan Unipress.

Sanjaya, W. (2008). *Strategi pembelajaran berorientasi standar proses pendidikan*. Jakarta, Indonesia: Kencana Prenada Media Group.

Sugiyono. (2013). *Statistika untuk penelitian*. Bandung, Indonesia: Alfabeta.

Thiagarajan, S., Semmel, D.S. & Semmel, M.L. (1974). *Instructional development for training teachers of exceptional children*. Minneapolis, MN: Leadership Training Institute/Special Education, University of Minnesota.

Tian Belawati (2003). *Pengembangan bahan ajar*. Jakarta, Indonesia: Pusat Penebitan UT.

Trianto. (2007). *Model pembeljaran terpadu dalam teori dan praktek*. Surabaya, Indonesia: Pustaka Ilmu.

Warsita, B. (2008). *Teknologi pembelajaran landasan dan aplikasinya*. Jakarta, Indonesia: Rineka Cipta.

Regionalization and Harmonization in TVET – Abdullah et al. (Eds)
© 2017 Taylor & Francis Group, London, ISBN 978-1-138-05419-6

The development of critical thinking ability through the implementation of a Technological Pedagogical Content Knowledge (TPCK) framework in vocational secondary schools

T. Busono, E. Krisnanto, T. Aryanti & J. Maknun
Department of Architecture Education, Faculty of Technology and Vocational Skills Education, Universitas Pendidikan Indonesia, Jawa Barat, Indonesia

ABSTRACT: Current learning in a *Sekolah Menengah Kebangsaan* (SMK) vocational secondary school is centered on teachers with lectures and assignments as the principal methods. To further enhance the learning process and the level of understanding of students toward the subject matter and the development of Higher-Order Thinking Skills (HOTS) or ability needs a learning innovation. Integrating technology in learning is a challenge for teachers. A productive integration model in teaching enables students to be more active in the learning process as long as the component of the technology is used proportionately and effectively. It is also believed to be able to improve their ability to think critically and solve problems. One integration model is the framework for Technological Pedagogical Content Knowledge (TPCK). This model is optimal for all three main components, namely, subject matter, pedagogy and technology. The learning process can be managed well if students are invited to take advantage of all sensory tools. The more senses which are used for receiving and processing information, the more likely the information is to be understandable and understood, and thus maintained in memory. Direct experience will give the most complete impression and the most meaningful information and ideas contained in that experience and, therefore, vision, hearing, feeling, smell, and touch should all be involved. Information and Communication Technology (ICT)-based learning demands the ability to think at a high level or possess HOTS. HOTS include aspects of: critical thinking, logic, reflection, creativity, and metacognition. ICT in lessons can be used as a tool to engage students in thinking. The use of ICT is closely related to the components of analysis, synthesis and evaluation in Bloom's taxonomy.

1   INTRODUCTION

Use of computers in education is the first step toward realizing the tech community. Educational institutions need to harness the potential of ICT optimally. With the rapid development in the field of telecommunications technology, multimedia, and information, listening to lectures, or reading those recorded on paper is certainly outdated. Merging aspects of technology in learning is one effort to grow and nurture interest and a positive attitude toward the development of technology.

Integrating technology in learning is a challenge for teachers. A productive integration model in teaching can connect and devise optimally from all three main components namely, the subject matter, pedagogy and technology.

The technology component should be utilized proportionately and effectively to construct and improve the ability of students to think and solve problems so that they will be more active in the learning process. One model is the framework for the integration of TPCK (Sutrisno, 2012).

An understanding of integrated ICT is much more important than just to understand ICT as a learning tool. A developing paradigm in technology can support learning, collaboration and repositioning inquiry in carrying out the learning process (Sutrisno, 2012). There are various models of ICT integration in the framework of learning, one of which is the TPCK framework. According to Mishra and Koehler (2008), the development of the framework is based on the three essential components of knowledge held by an educator who should have mastery of the subject material in accordance with qualifications, and competencies in the curriculum, pedagogy and technology. Thinking is a process of cognition, a mental activity to gain knowledge. The thought process can be grouped into basic thinking (rational thinking) and complex thinking (high-level thinking). Basic thinking covers the following concepts: memorize, visualize, classify, generalize, compare, evaluate, analyze, synthesize, deduce and infer. Complex thought processes consists of four types: problem-solving, decision-making, critical thinking and creative thinking (Costa in Liliasari, 2002). According to Walker (1998), critical thinking is a process that allows learners to gain new knowledge through problem-solving and collaboration. Critical thinking focuses on the learning process rather than just acquiring knowledge. Critical thinking involves activities such as analyzing, synthesizing, making judgments, and creating and applying new knowledge in real-world situations. Critical thinking is important in the learning process as it provides an opportunity for learners to learn through discovery. Learners think critically when they are responsible for an active learning.

2 RESEARCH METHODS

The method used in this preliminary study is content analysis. Content analysis is research that consists of in-depth discussion of the content of written information.

Content analysis can be used to analyze all forms of communication. The results of content analysis are descriptive, that is, the description of the contents of communication.

3 RESULTS AND DISCUSSION

3.1 Critical thinking skills

The development of critical thinking skills of learners has been a goal of education for the last decade. Beyer (in Walker, 1998) stated that it is very important for the teaching of critical thinking to be applied by teachers in order to develop learners' reasoning power. He maintained that to successfully live in a democracy, one must think critically in order to make the right decisions. If learners learn to think critically, then they will be able to use this more generally to cope with life. Critical thinking is a basic process that allows learners to cope with and reduce uncertainty in the future. With critical thinking skills, learners are able to determine when important information is acquired, converted or transformed, and maintained. The learning objectives of critical thinking in science and other disciplines are to improve thinking skills and prepare learners to successfully cope with life. Meanwhile, Dumke (in Jones, 1996) states that learning to think critically is designed to achieve an understanding of the relationship of logical language, which should result in the ability to analyze, criticize, and suggest ideas to reason inductively and deductively and to reach a conclusion factually based on rational considerations.

Critical thinking is one of the life skills that must be owned by the learner for life, in the family, school, and community. Learners who think critically usually appear to be problem solvers. Critical thinking is widely recognized as a valuable skill in everyday life (Verlinden, 2005). It is also very much needed in today's age of science and technology development, because technology sometimes comes with problems for humans and the environment. (Winocur in Costa, 1985).

Studies of the critical thinking skills of learners have revealed that these skills will not flourish without explicit and deliberate effort planted in development (Zohar, 1994). A learner will not be able to develop critical thinking skills well without being challenged to practice using them by teaching. Learners are not born with critical thinking skills, they cannot naturally develop the ability to think for life. As critical thinking is a skill that can be learned, it should be taught. Most individuals rarely study it.

Critical thinking can be developed through a meaningful experience; that is, an experience or learning provides the opportunity for learners to acquire skills in solving problems which can stimulate the critical thinking skills of learners. This experience is necessary so that the learner has the structure of a concept that is useful in analyzing and evaluating a problem. With critical thinking, the learner can adjust, adapt, modify, or repair his thoughts so that the learner can act more quickly. People who think critically will think and act in a more relatively normal way, ready to reason about things they see, hear, or think.

Ennis (1985) positioned critical thinking as consisting of, among others: 1) looking for a clear statement of a hypothesis or question, 2) looking for an excuse, 3) insightful, 4) using credible resources, 5) considering the total situation, 6) looking for alternatives, 7) open thinking, 8) determining the position when there is evidence or arguments in favor (or against), and 9) sensitive to the feelings of others.

3.2 TPCK framework for fostering critical thinking skills

Constructivism learning theory holds that media can be used as a tool that provides the possibility of students actively constructing knowledge. Media can be distinguished from technology (mechanics, electronics, physical form), symbolic systems (numerical characters, objects, images, sound) as well as the means used (radio, video, computers, books). One medium of learning is ICT. Integrating ICT into learning can improve the competence of teachers in teaching and improve the quality of learning for learners. One lesson that integrates ICT is TPCK.

The basic concept of TPCK described by Mishra and Koehler (2008) emphasizes the relationship between the subject matter, technology and pedagogy. The interaction between these three components has the strength and appeal to foster active learning which is focused on the learner. It can also be interpreted as a form of learning that originally centered on the teacher but which has shifted to learners.

The relationship between the components of TPCK is shown in Figure 1.

Sutrisno (2012) explains the concepts of which TPCK consists: (1) Content Knowledge (CK) – the knowledge of the material to be learned; (2) Pedagogy Knowledge (PK) – describes in depth the theory and practice of teaching and learning, and the goals, processes, methods and strategies for learning and assessment; (3) Technology Knowledge (TK) – is the basics of technology that can be used to support learning, such as the use of software, animation programs and virtual labs.

TPCK encapsulates a cycle in which an integrated ability to master technology cannot be separated from its constituent components, namely the content (C), pedagogy (P) and technology (T). TPCK requires multiple interactions between components, and the combination of the subject matter, pedagogy and technology are unique and synergy-based and include Information and Communication Technology (ICT) (Mishra and Koehler, 2006).

Implementation of the TPCK framework is also in line with the theory of knowledge acquisition. Rusman (2012) argued that the acquisition of knowledge, and changing attitudes and skills, occurs because of the interaction between new experiences. Bruner (in Rusman, 2012) suggests there are three main levels in the learning mode: direct experience, the experience and the experience of abstract images.

ICT developments allow the use of the function of various learning media by using a tool called multimedia, which is capable of delivering information and learning materials in the form of text, images, sounds, animations, movies, and even interactions. Computers are one of the main multimedia tools, because the computer is able to present the information and learning materials in all forms, even to perform seemingly complicated and expensive situations in simpler ways (e.g. a chemical reaction process, the impact of a nuclear explosion, trips to the solar system, etc.). Through multimedia, abstract concepts can be presented in a more tangible manner in the learning process to help students understand.

The concept of integration in TPCK is the involvement of the various components of matter and pedagogy to support teachers in implementing technology-based learning. Sutrisno (2012) states that in TPCK, ICT will interact with pedagogy and can increase high-level thinking skills. Based on the exposure, TPCK, through comprehensive research activity, can increase certain concepts to promote high-level thinking skills.

The demand of ICT-based learning is the ability to think critically or demonstrate HOTS. HOTS includes critical thinking, logic, reflection, metacognition and creativity. ICT in learning can be used as a tool to engage students in thinking. The use of ICT is strongly associated with the components of analysis, synthesis and evaluation in Bloom's taxonomy (Sutrisno, 2012).

4 CONCLUSION

There are various models of the framework of the integration of ICT in learning, one of which is the TPCK framework. The development of this framework is based on three essential components of the knowledge that is held by an educator such that mastery of subject material is in accordance with qualifications and competencies in the curriculum, pedagogy and technology.

In TPCK, ICT will interact with pedagogy and can increase high-level thinking skills or HOTS. ICT in learning can be used as a tool to engage students in thinking.

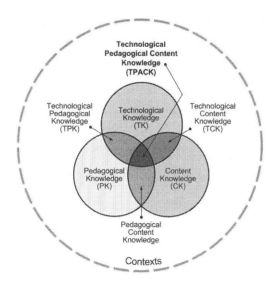

Figure 1.   TPCK (source: TPACK.ORG, 2012).

REFERENCES

AACTE. (2008). *Handbook of technological pedagogical content knowledge for educators.* New York, NY: Routledge.

Binanto, I. (2010). *Multimedia Digital: Dasar Teori dan Pengembangannya*. Yogyakarta, Indonesia: Andi.

Costa, A.L. (1985). Goals for a Critical Thinking Curriculum. Dalam Costa A.L. (ed). *Developing Mind: A Resource Book for Teaching Thinking*. ASCD: Alexandria, Virginia.

Dale, E. (1969). *Audio visual methods in teaching*. New York, NY: Dryden Press.

Ennis, R.H. (1985). Goals for critical thinking curriculum. In A.L Costa (Ed.), *Developing of minds. A resource book for teaching thinking*. Alexandria, VA: Association for Supervision and Curriculum Development.

Jimmoyianis, A. (2010). Developing a technological pedagogical content knowledge framework for science education: Implications of a teacher trainers' preparation program. In *Proceedings of Informing Science & IT Education Conference (InSITE) 2010*.

Jones, D. (1996). *Critical Thinking* in an Online Word untangling the web. http://www.Library.ucsb.edu/untangle/jones.html.

Kemdikbud. (2013). *Kerangka Dasar dan Struktur Kurikulum Sekolah Menengah Kejuruan/Madrasah Aliyah Kejuruan*. Jakarta, Indonesia: Kemdikbud.

Liliasari, L. (2002). *Pengembangan model Pembelajaran Kimia untuk Meningkatkan Strategi Kognitif Mahasiswa Calon Guru dalam Menerapkan Berfikir Konseptual Tingkat Tinggi*. Laporan Penelitian Hibah Barsaing IX Perguruan Tinggi Tahun Ajaran 2001–2002. Bandung, Indonesia: FPMIPA UPI.

Luther, A.C. (1994). *Authoring interactive multimedia*. Boston, MA: AP Professional.

Mishra, P. & Koehler, M.J. (2006). Technological pedagogical content knowledge: A framework for teacher knowledge. *Teachers College Record, 108*(6), 1017–1054.

Mishra, P. & Koehler, M.J. (2008). *Handbook of Technological Pedagogical Content Knowledge (TPACK) for Educators*. New York: Routledge for the American Association of Colleges for Teacher Education.

Munir. (2008). *Kurikulum Berbasis Teknologi Informasi dan Komunikasi*. Bandung, Indonesia: Alfabeta.

Poerbo, H. (1992). *Utilitas Bangunan: Buku Pintar untuk Mahasiswa Arsitektur Sipil*. Jakarta, Indonesia: Djambatan.

Rusman. (2012). *Belajar dan Pembelajaran Berbasis Komputer: Mengembangkan Profesionalisme Guru Abad 21*. Bandung, Indonesia: Alfabeta.

Schmidt, D.A., Baran, E., Thompson, A.D., Mishra, P., Koehler, M.J. & Shin, T.S. (2009). Technological Pedagogical Content Knowledge (TPACK): The development and validation of an assessment instrument for preservice teachers. *Journal of Research on Technology in Education, 42*(2), 123–149.

Sukiman. (2012). *Pengembangan Media Pembelajaran*. Yogyakarta, Indonesia: Pedagogia.

Sukmadinata. (2005). *Metode Penelitian Pendidikan*. Bandung, Indonesia: Remaja Rosdakarya.

Sumarsono, M. & Sutrisno. (2012). *Penerapan Kerangka Kerja TPACK dan Konten Pembelajaran Blended Learning untuk Meningkatkan Aktivitas Pembelajaran Mahasiswa*. Makalah Seminar Nasional Cakrawala Pembelajaran Berkualitas di Indonesia, Jakarta, 25–27 September 2012.

Sutrisno. (2012). *Kreatif Mengembangkan Aktivitas Pembelajaran Berbasis TIK*. Jakarta, Indonesia: Referensi.

Thiagarajan, S., Semmel, D.S. & Semmel, M.L. (1974). *Instructional development for training teachers of exceptional children*. Minneapolis, MN: Leadership Training Institute/Special Education, University of Minnesota.

TPACK.ORG. (2012). *TPACK* (Online). Retrieved from www.tpack.org

Verlinden J. (2005). *Critical Thinking and Every day Argumen*. Balmont. CA: Wadsworth/the msou learning, Inc.

Walker, G.H. (1998). *Critical thinking*. Retrieved from http://www/utr.edu/administration/walkerteaching resoursecenter/facultydevelopment/criticalthinking

Zohar, A. (1994). The Effect of Biology Critical Thinking Project in the Development of Critical Thinking. *Journal of Research in Science Teaching*. 31(2), 163–196.

Regionalization and Harmonization in TVET – Abdullah et al. (Eds)
© *2017 Taylor & Francis Group, London, ISBN 978-1-138-05419-6*

Interactive multimedia-based learning to improve students' creative thinking skills

Y. Irawati, L. Nurlaela & M. Wahini
Faculty of Engineering, Universitas Negeri Surabaya, Surabaya, Indonesia

ABSTRACT: Interactive multimedia is very useful because it is able to create student-centered teaching and learning activities. The collaboration of creative thinking and interactive multimedia-based learning not only enables students to think using multiple scientific disciplines, but also provides for their intellectual needs and development of effectiveness. This research will discuss the development of interactive multimedia-based learning to improve students' creative thinking skills on culinary business management courses. This research applied quantitative descriptive methodology. The research subjects were ten students of Diploma III in the Home Economics department in the Engineering Faculty of UNESA in 2013. The research instrument used was the creative thinking skills test. The test used students' worksheets which contain some issues of creative thinking skills indicators such as: (1) fluency, (2) flexibility, and (3) novelty. Data analysis techniques used a normalized-gain (N-gain) formula. The results showed that the students' creative thinking skills score in post-test improved by 0.33 points after interactive multimedia-based learning had been applied during teaching and learning activities. The improvement of the post-test score by 0.33 points was categorized as 'Mediocre'.

1 INTRODUCTION

Education is an essential role for the development of a country as a good quality education will create high-quality human resources. Indonesian Law No. 20 in 2003 (Depdiknas, 2003, Ch. 3), in respect of the National Education System, states that 'national education aims to develop learners' potency thus they are able to become a human with some personalities such as faithful, devoted, noble, healthy, knowledgeable, skillful, creative, independent, democratic have high responsibility'.

Based on the goal and vision of the Home Economics Department in UNESA, the students are required to master some basic competencies in several courses. The culinary business management course is categorized into working skill courses and contains some theories and practices. This course is quite complex because of its connection to other courses. Thus, it requires multidimensional abilities.

One of the solutions to solving that problem is to develop an attractive learning media that would draw students' attention. An interactive multimedia utilizing computer software may provide the answer for that problem. Multimedia-based learning is a learning activity which utilizes computers to create and combine any text, graphic, audio,

video, or animation. The process of creating interactive multimedia uses links and tools to enable users to navigate, interact, create, and communicate (Rusman, 2012).

Therefore, effective learning activities can be achieved through the use of interactive multimedia-based learning especially for students in the culinary business management course. It is relevant for Setemen (2005) who stated that the application of interactive multimedia-based learning to teach students of culinary business management is very effective for the improvement of students' scores. The use of interactive multimedia in teaching and learning activities is very useful to create student-centered learning activities.

Creative thinking, using the implementation of interactive multimedia-based learning, can help students to think using multidisciplinary perspectives. It also helps to support the students' intellectual skill and development of effectiveness so they are more ready to manage their working life (Rolling & Adams, 2003). Warsita (2008) also added that interactive multimedia can help students to study faster. Students who have fast-thinking ability can learn optimally, while students with average ability are still able to understand the concepts.

Based on those facts, lecturers should be more active in developing other learning models to improve students' scores in creative thinking skills. Silver (1997) stated that to assess creative thinking in children and adults the Torrance Test of Creative Thinking (TTCT) must be applied.

Three important components of creative thinking skills assessment in TTCT are: (1) fluency (the total number of ideas in responding to an order), (2) flexibility (some changes approach in responding to a command), and (3) novelty (originality of ideas in responding to a command). This is similar to Haylock (1997), who gave examples of creative thinking skills criteria: (1) fluency (total number of responses), (2) flexibility (total number of differing responses), and (3) originality (the uniqueness of the response).

This research uses the rubric assessment which focuses on three creative thinking criteria or indicators, that is, flexibility, fluency and novelty, which are adapted to measure students' thinking ability (Siswono, 2007). One of the ways to improve creative thinking skills is the use of an interactive multimedia-based learning model.

Furthermore, Mettas and Constantinou (2007) stated that problem-based learning can help teachers to solve their problems. Riyanto (2010) added that problem-based learning is designed to develop students' ability to solve problems. So the researchers used problem-based learning because it provides authentic material or issues which are close to students' reality (Nur, 2008).

The culinary business management course requires students to have complex thinking, hence problem-based and interactive multimedia-based learning is implemented as it is effective in improving students' thinking ability.

2 RESEARCH METHOD

This research aims to establish the improvement of students' creative thinking skills. The learning activities used problem-based and interactive multimedia-based learning. The research subjects were ten students from the Home Economics department in the Engineering Faculty of UNESA in 2013. The instrument of creative thinking test used to measure the students' creative skills was the students' score for cognitive processing.

The students' creative thinking test used an essay test. The assessment rubric used the Torrance Test of Creative Thinking, adapted from Silver (1997). The rubric used three components to assess the students' creative thinking skills, namely, (1) fluency, (2) flexibility, and (3) novelty. Data analysis determined the improvement of students' creative thinking skills with the pre- and post-tests.

Students' creative thinking skills will be categorized as 'improved' if the result of the post-test average score is higher than the pre-test average score, since the post-test is administered after the implementation of interactive multimedia-based learning activities (Novianti, 2011).

Rating for creative thinking tests was based on the formula of Siswono (2007):

$$\text{Total score} = (3 \times Novelty) + (2 \times Flexibility) + (1 \times Fluency) \quad (1)$$

There are a total of five questions, so the maximum possible rating according to this formula is $(5 \times 3) + (5 \times 2) + (5 \times 1) = 30$.

Thus:

1. The students will get 1 point if they fulfill the fluency component, and 0 if they do not fulfill it.
2. The students will get 2 points if they fulfill the flexibility component, and 0 if they do not fulfill it.
3. The students will get 3 points if they fulfill the novelty component, and 0 if they do not fulfill it.

The novelty component is granted three points because this component is the most important and it is the main feature of the assessment of a product. A creative product must be different from the others. The next most important point is the flexibility component. It is important because it shows the productivity of an idea in completing the task. The last point is the fluency component. It is placed in last position because it shows the students' fluency in producing different ideas, and it is based on the required way of completing the task. (Novianti, 2011).

The pre-test and post-test scores of this adapted test are analyzed by calculating the mean, using the gain calculation given by Hake's formula (Savinem & Scott, 2002):

$$(g) = \frac{S_{post} - S_{pre}}{S_{max} - S_{pre}} \quad (2)$$

Then, the score of gain calculation is categorized into certain criteria with the interval gain factor. Its interval gain criteria is shown in Table 1.

Table 1. Criteria of gain interval factor.

No.	Gain interval factor	Criteria
1	$g < 0.3$	Low
2	$0.3 \leq g \leq 0.7$	Mediocre
3	$g \geq 0.7$	High

Source: Savinem & Scott, 2002.

3 RESULTS AND DISCUSSION

This research aimed to determine the improvement of students' creative thinking skills. To test the students' improvement of creative thinking skills, both pre- and post-tests were administered to them before and after learning activities. The test itself is an essay and interactive multimedia-based test.

The creative thinking skills criteria of Diploma III students of culinary business management in 2013 were categorized in terms of fluency, flexibility, and novelty, as shown in Table 2.

The calculation of the creative thinking skills scores of Diploma III culinary business management students is shown in Table 3.

The average pre-test score of creative thinking skills for Diploma III culinary business students in 2013 before they were taught using interactive multimedia-based learning was 4.80. Their average post-test score of creative thinking skill increased to 13.30. So, the average of the normalized-gain score (N-gain) was 0.33; it was categorized into 'Mediocre' level.

The research findings showed that the interactive multimedia-based learning which was developed by the researcher was only able to improve the students' thinking skills up to a mediocre level. It happened because during learning activity students were asked to answer some question based on given allocation time and plan. In addition, students also had to answer essay test in pre-test and post-test, which obliged them to use creative thinking skills.

Table 2. The calculation of students' creative thinking skills scores in pre-test and post-test.

No.	Pre-test scores			Total pre-test	Post-test scores			Total post-test
	K1*	K2*	K3*		K1*	K2*	K3*	
1	3	0	0	3	5	5	0	15
2	5	1	0	7	5	3	0	11
3	5	1	0	7	5	4	0	13
4	4	0	0	4	5	5	2	21
5	4	0	0	4	5	5	1	18
6	5	1	0	7	5	4	0	13
7	3	0	0	3	5	5	0	15
8	3	0	0	3	5	2	0	9
9	5	0	0	5	5	2	0	9
10	5	0	0	5	5	2	0	9
Total	42	3	0	48	50	37	3	133
Percentage (%)	84	6	0	16	100	74	6	44.3

Note:
*K1 = Fluency;
*K2 = Flexibility;
*K3 = Novelty.

Table 3. The calculation of creative thinking skills scores of Diploma III culinary business management students.

No.	Students' creative thinking scores		N-gain	Criteria
	Pre-test	Post-test		
1	3	15	0.4	Mediocre
2	7	11	0.2	Low
3	7	13	0.3	Mediocre
4	4	21	0.7	High
5	4	18	0.5	Mediocre
6	7	13	0.3	Mediocre
7	3	15	0.4	Mediocre
8	3	9	0.2	Low
9	5	9	0.2	Low
10	5	9	0.2	Low
Average scores	4.80	13.30	0.33	

Note: (Maximum score = 30).

Ruggiero, in Siswono (2009), stated that thinking is a mental activity used to formulate or solve a problem, make a decision, or simply to answer curiosity. It means that when someone formulates and solves a problem, or when they try to understand something they have actually had 'thinking' activity.

Creative thinking can also be called 'a process' when someone brings up a new idea. The new idea could be a combination of previous ideas which have never been discovered before (Infinite Innovations Ltd, 2001). During learning activity, there are many learning strategies and learning models which can be developed to help students understand the material and improve their scores. One of them is a problem-based learning model using interactive multimedia.

4 CONCLUSION

The results showed that the post-test score of students' creative thinking skills after the implementation of interactive multimedia-based learning had improved to 0.33, which falls into the 'Mediocre' category.

REFERENCES

Depdiknas. (2003). *Undang-Undang RI no. 20 tahun 2003 tentang sistem pendidikan nasional*. Jakarta, Indonesia: Depdiknas.

Haylock, D. (1997). Recognizing mathematical creativity in schoolchildren. *Zentralblatt für Didaktik der Mathematik*, 29(3), 68–74.

Infinite Innovations Ltd. (2001). *Creativity and creative thinking* (Online). Retrieved from http://brainstorming.co.uk/

Mettas, A.C. & Constantinou, C.C. (2007). The technology fair: A Project-based learning approach for enhancing problem solving skills and interest in design and technology education. *International Journal of Technology and Design Education, 18*(1), 79–100.

Novianti, D.E. (2011). *Pembelajaran berbasis pengajuan dan pemecahan masalah untuk meningkatkan kemampuan berpikir kreatif siswa pada materi persanaan linear dua variabel di kelas X SMK* (Unpublished Masters thesis). Universitas Negeri Surabaya, Surabaya, Indonesia.

Nur, M. (2008). *Model pembelajaran berdasarkan masalah*. Surabaya, Indonesia: PSMS Unesa.

Riyanto, Y. (2010). *Paradigma baru pembela-jaran sebagai referensi pendidik dalam implementasi pembelajaran yang efektif ber-kualitas*. Jakarta, Indonesia: Kencana Perdana Media Group.

Rolling, A. & Adams, E. (2003). *Game design*. Indianapolis, IN: New Riders Publishing.

Rusman. (2012). *Belajar dan pembelajaran berbasis komputer, mengembangkan profesionalisme guru abad 21*. Bandung, Indonesia: Alfabeta.

Savinem, A. & Scott, P. (2002). The force concept: A Tool for monitoring student learning. *Physics Education, 39*(1), 42–45.

Setemen, K. (2005). Media pembelajaran pengetahuan alat dapur berbasis multimedia pada jurusan boga perhotelan. *Paper in Proceedings of National Seminar*. JPTK ISSN 0216-3241, Vol. 4.

Silver, E.A. (1997). Fostering creativity through instruction rich in mathematical problem solving and thinking in problem posing. *Zentralblatt für Didaktik der Mathematik, 29*(3), 75–80.

Siswono, T.Y.E. (2007). *Model pembelajaran matematika berbasis pengajuan pemecahan masalah untuk meningkatkan kemampuan berpikir kreatif*. Surabaya, Indonesia: UNESA University Press.

Warsita, B. (2008). *Teknologi pembelajaran landasan & aplikasinya*. Jakarta, Indonesia: Rineka Cipta.

Innovations in engineering and education

Sprint device development using an infrared laser with a computer interface system

A. Rusdiana

Sport Science Study Program, Faculty of Sport Education and Health Education,
Universitas Pendidikan Indonesia, Jawa Barat, Indonesia

ABSTRACT: With the ever-growing needs and society demands of today, technology has become a necessary component in each aspect of life. The field of sports science has adopted technology applications as an integral part of improving performance and athletic achievement. In developed countries, different kinds of sports science centers and laboratories have been set up with advanced test and measurement devices which are supported by reliable human resources. This study aimed to develop software and hardware for measuring running speed using a microcontroller with a personal computer interface. The assembly of the device comprises a circuit-based electronics microcontroller, phototransistor sensors and laser beams to collect signals from athletes and send them to a microcontroller for processing on a personal computer interface for display via connector cabling. In the process, a Research and Development (R&D) approach was used to help assemble the system's components. The system consisted of eight sensors spread over 100 meters, intended to detect running speed during a 100-meter sprint race. The device was designed to operate automatically in synchronization with the race-start buzzer, monitoring the sprint from start to finish, and then display the results of the race time and speed to a computer interface.

1   INTRODUCTION

In this modern era, technological advances in all areas and disciplines have become an integral part of society and daily life. These advances have also influenced fields like that of sports science, where technology is said to have contributed to its improvement tremendously. For instance, the use of technology in an effort to improve performance in sports has been carried out in developed countries in Asia such as Japan, China and Australia. This is proven by pursuits in various laboratories of science which can be found around the world, among others, the Japan Institute of Sport Science, the Australian Institute of Sport Science, and the Beijing Institute of Sport Science in China. Experts in such sports centers and laboratories collaborate to diagnose, evaluate, and provide scientific input to the coaches and athletes about various sports components. Speed, as one component of the physical sports condition, is very important and it has been measured using various tools and advanced technologies. Examples of such technology are sensors attached to the shoes of athletes, Global Positioning System and the Differential Global Positioning System (Slawinski et al., 2010; Vescovi, 2012).

Besides this there are other tools including radar, photo finish, kinematic analysis, photocells and opt jump, which are normally used to measure the speed when running; these tools are made to diagnose, evaluate and analyse the performance of athletes for performance enhancement. Running is a sport that takes speed as a benchmark of evaluation, especially sprinting. Electronic technology is already being used to measure time, velocity, and acceleration both during practice and in competitions. During training, measurement results are used for analysis and evaluation of athletes. One tool that is frequently used to measure speed in athletes is a photo cell, a kind of sensor mounted on the edge of the track that can detect the running time when an athlete passes the sensor, but this is only used in developed countries that have either developed or sourced the tool at great expense. Contributions from sports analysis, especially running speed in sprints, is very desirable to conduct research and evaluation of athletes. In Indonesia, the development of test equipment and measurement, especially for sprints, is still undeveloped; this is because because there is insufficient technology, and this is further exacerbated by poor collaboration between experts in sports, especially regarding the development and implementation of technology in sports. So, there is a lack of scientific problem-solving solutions to analyze various situations and conditions in sport. Indonesia still has many products used as testing and measurement instruments that use technology from abroad.

Indonesia itself has electronics experts who, when they collaborate with others, can give birth to a variety of tools that can support an increase in an athlete's performance. The potential is immense if the men and women involved in sport work with electronics experts to create a technology-based means of testing and measurement, as well as high-tech learning in sport. Problems still occur in the measurement of running speed due to the use of manual tools in measurement, such as stopwatches. The use of a stopwatch presents problems of accuracy in the capture of data because of the differences in the time interval in keystrokes. It can, therefore, be the cause of errors due to the sensitivity, reflexes and reactions of the operator. Thus, a need for an automatic timer and runner-speed detecting system is very important. One solution for such problems would be the development and manufacture of innovative measuring devices for the measurement of athletes' running speed based on a microcontroller with a personal computer interface system. Innovations required include, first, a tool that can measure running speed over 100 meters with an option of adjusting the distance; depending on the desired distance of the user, it could be intervals of every five, eight or ten meters, or other distances. To make the system cost-effective but with the same function will require the use of phototransistor sensors and the display of results to a personal computer that has been installed with a monitoring software application instead of an expensive Liquid Crystal Display (LCD). A software application created using Visual Basic 12 enables display of the measurement results to the computer. The tool might not only be used for the measurement of running speed in races but, in addition, the data collected while using the tool could be used in other analyses when studying outcomes of sports activities; such data could include running speed, endurance at a specific running speed, maximum running speed, running speed per meter, or running speed in other measurement quantities.

1.1 Running speed measurement

According to Bergamini et al. (2012) and Dolanec (2009), velocity measurements can be carried out using various commercial tools that have been developed, such as devices affixed to shoes of athletes like Garmin Foot Pod, Polar and Suunt, Global Positioning System (GPS), differential GPS radar, photo finish, kinematic analysis, photocells and Optojump. Different ways of measuring the speed with different tools vary in terms of accuracy, complexity and price. In the measurement of running, the most frequently used tool is the photocell. This tool can be used to measure running speed based on distance and time.

Running speed can also be measured through Dias Frame IV software, which provides an object trajectory tracking system, either automatically or manually. Dias Frame can be used to analyze the variation of motion in two or three dimensions. It uses video of the runner as input data to be analyzed. In the 100-meter sprint, the sprint technique can be broken down into several phases as proposed by Dunn and Kelley (2015) who explained that, 'there are five phases in a sprint, among others: (a) start techniques, (b) acceleration techniques, (c) maximum speed techniques, (d) technical maintenance of speed, and (e) technical finish'. There are four phases an athlete goes through in a 100-meter race: the starting position, the starting action, the sprinting action, and the finishing action. The starting position is the attitude or position of the runner at start time. The starting action has aspects that include the rapid reaction on leaving the starting block, and the time between the sound of the gun, with explosive muscle reactions to encourage movement on pushing off from the block (Exell et al., 2012; Miller et al., 2012a).

The sprinting action has technical specifications, including maximizing the horizontal speed of movement and movement prop overpass. According to Kugler and Janshen (2010), Miller et al. (2012b) and Rumpf et al. (2013), the finishing action has aspects that include movement of the upper body and coordination of the upper and lower body. A 100-meter race can be divided into three parts, namely the acceleration at 0–30 meters, the maximum speed from 30–60 meters, and the speed maintenance from 60–100 meters. Acceleration speed increases after the start reaction in order to achieve maximum speed; the transition from acceleration to maximum speed is the directionality of technical coordination to the maximum speed until the beginning of the decline of speed down to the maintenance speed, because of fatigue in the muscles.

1.2 Visual programing C

The microcontroller, in relation to the programming language C, is now beginning to displace the language first used for programming microcontrollers, that is, assembler language. The use of the C language is very efficient, especially for programs that are relatively large on a microcontroller. Compared with assembler language, the use of the C language in programming has several advantages including accelerating the development time (both modular and structured), while its weakness is that the compiled source code is larger and consequently it will sometimes reduce the speed of execution. CodeVisionAVR software is basically a software programming language-based family of C language components for microcontrollers. There are three essential components integrated in this software: a C compiler, an Integrated Development Environment (IDE), and a program generator. The Visual Basic program is software that is suitable for creating an application program that can work within the Windows system application environment. The language used in Visual Basic is very easy to learn, with visual programming techniques that allow users to create more intuitive application programs; the user can set the display form which is then executed by a script which is very easy. Visual Basic 6.0 is the result of the development of previous versions, with several additional components that reflect current trends, such as a capability of Internet programming with DHTML (Dynamic HyperText Markup Language), and additional features such as multimedia databases. At the time of writing, it can be said that Visual Basic 6.0 is still the leading programming language in creating application programs that exist on the software market internationally. This is due to the ease of the process of development of an application. A phototransistor sensor device is a type of transistor that works in association with light. In general, infrared light is needed to activate a phototransistor; when seen in terms of the way it works, a phototransistor is similar to a light switch, and if a phototransistor is exposed to infrared rays then collector foot-emitter connects and serves as a switch. However, if the phototransistor is not exposed to infrared light or is simply exposed to ordinary light-emitters the collector legs do not connect. Its application in a phototransistor is easy, by simply adding a resistor at the collector foot before being connected to Vcc, while the emitter is connected to the ground feet, and the output is taken from the leg collector.

A laser works by amplifying light that has been emitted by the stimulation of a source of radiation. In laser technology, the light produced has its own characteristics, namely: monochromaticism (one specific wavelength), coherence (at the same frequency), and unidirectionality, so that the light becomes very strong, concentrated and well-coordinated.

Figure 1. Phototransistor device system.

Figure 2. Diagram illustrating the R&D procedure (Sugiyono, 2011).

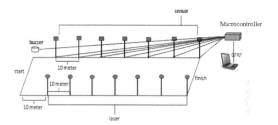

Figure 3. Product design schematic.

2 METHODS

The research methodology employed in this study is the Research and Development (R&D) method used to test effectiveness of the product. Before products are produced for general use, there is a need to test the effectiveness of these products. The results of this study are to be applied in producing a measuring tool for running speed which is based on a microcontroller with a personal computer system interface. Figure 2 is a step-by-step illustration of the Research and Development method.

The product design model for the assembly of the running speed measurement tool comprises a system of phototransistors and sensors that sends signals to the microcontroller, which processes the signals into data of running time and speed which are displayed on a computer screen. The electronic circuit works as an automatic timing system while simultaneously recording the running speed and time of the athlete. Figure 3 shows an illustration of the whole system.

3 RESULTS AND DISCUSSION

3.1 Sensors and lasers

These components work automatically as timing controllers; as runners obstruct/disrupt to laser rays each sensor receives signals that trigger the phototransistor sensor, which are then read and sent to the microcontroller for processing.

The processed data is sent to a computer that uses the installed software to display readable results on the monitor. The main objective of this research is to produce hardware and software products for measuring the running speed of athletes using a microcontroller for processing and a personal computer interface. The main function of this tool is to record the sprint speed of athletes. The system consists of several main components; the following section explains the components and their functions:

The main function of phototransistor sensors is to send signals to the microcontroller circuit when there are runners who cut the laser light emitted at this sensor. When the laser beam is interrupted by the passing of the runner the sensor sends a signal to the microcontroller that then sends the processed data to the computer. The main function of the laser is to emit light to the phototransistor sensor; these light beams are the ones runners cut when running and signals generated after are sent to the microcontroller circuit, which can be regarded as the brains of the system. This circuit consists of several electronic components that are assembled into a single piece of hardware. The main function of this tool is to receive signals sent by the sensor, which are indicated by the cutting of Light-Emitting Diode (LED) lights on the microcontroller circuit.

After signals are received, they are forwarded through the microcontroller to the software program already installed on the computer. The signal received by the computer from the microcontroller is interpreted by the software on the computer. To create an application that displays data for speed results on a personal computer, a Visual Basic 12

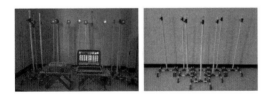

Figure 4. Components running-speed measuring device.

Figure 5. Network microcontroller and LED indicator.

Figure 6. Software personal computer system.

Figure 7. Running sensor setting at running track.

Table 1. Result of running time sprint of 40 m.

Distance (m)	Time (sec)	Time/5 m (sec)	Velocity/5 m (m/s)
5	1.6	1.6	3.1
10	2.3	0.7	6.8
15	3.1	0.8	6.1
20	3.9	0.7	6.6
25	4.6	0.7	6.9
30	5.3	0.7	6.5
35	6.1	0.7	6.7
40	6.9	0.8	5.7
Total time	6.9 sec		
Average velocity	5.7 m/s		
Maximum velocity	6.9 m/s		
Distance	25 m		

program is used. The researcher named the computer application 'Monitoring Applications Running Sprint 100 meters'. In the application, the data recorded is the running time of each line, the speed of each line, total running time and average speed. Figure 6 shows a view of the application interface.

3.2 Field testing product

At this trial the researchers conducted measurements of the speed over a distance of 40 meters. A total of eight sensors were mounted every five meters to determine the speed the athletes were running every five meters.

4 CONCLUSION

A running-speed measuring system based on a microcontroller and interface on a personal computer can be constructed using available electronic components. Costs are reduced in the production of this system because the expensive LCD board component is absent. The system could go a long way in measuring and recording vital sporting data useful in training athletes and as reference in further sports science studies. This, in turn, would improve the way sport is managed and studied in Indonesia, putting the country on the road to modern sports science management and study to match that of more developed countries.

REFERENCES

Bergamini, E., Picerno, P., Pillet, H., Natta, F., Thoreux, P. & Camomilla, V. (2012). Estimation of temporal parameters during sprint running using a trunk-mounted inertial measurement unit. *Journal of Biomechanics, 45*(6), 1123–1126.

Dunn, M. & Kelley, J. (2015). Non-invasive, spatio-temporal gait analysis for sprint running using a single camera. *Procedia Engineering, 112*, 528–533.

Dolanec, A. (2009). Comparison of photocell and Opto-jump measurements of maximum running velocity. *Kinesiologia Slovenica, 15*(2), 16–24.

Exell, T.A., Gittoes, M.J.R., Irwin, G. & Kerwin, D.G. (2012). Gait asymmetry: Composite scores for mechanical analyses of sprint running. *Journal of Biomechanics, 45*(6), 1108–1111.

Kugler, F. & Janshen, L. (2010). Body position determines propulsive forces in accelerated running. *Journal of Biomechanics, 43*(2), 343–348.

Miller, R.H., Umberger, B.R. & Caldwell, G.E. (2012a). Limitations to maximum sprinting speed imposed by muscle mechanical properties. *Journal of Biomechanics, 45*(6), 1092–1097.

Miller, R.H., Umberger, B.R. & Caldwell, G.E. (2012b). Sensitivity of maximum sprinting speed to characteristic parameters of the muscle force–velocity relationship. *Journal of Biomechanics, 45*(8), 1406–1413.

Rumpf, M.C., Cronin, J.B., Oliver, J.L. & Hughes, M.G. (2013). Vertical and leg stiffness and stretch-shortening cycle changes across maturation during maximal sprint running. *Human Movement Science, 32*(4), 668–676.

Slawinski, J., Bonnefoy, A., Ontanon, G., Leveque, J.M., Miller, C., Riquet, A., ... Dumas, R. (2010). Segment-interaction in sprint start: Analysis of 3D angular velocity and kinetic energy in elite sprinters. *Journal of Biomechanics, 43*(8), 1494–1502.

Sugiyono. (2011). *Metode Penelitian Kuantitatif, Kualitatif dan R&D*. Bandung, Indonesia: ALFABETA.

Vescovi, J.D. (2012). Sprint speed characteristics of high-level American female soccer players: Female Athletes in Motion (FAiM) study. *Journal of Science and Medicine in Sport, 15*(5), 474–478.

Network planning software development for wireless communication system subject learning media

A.B. Pantjawati, E.A. Juanda, B. Mulyanti & M. Mutasimbillah
Universitas Pendidikan Indonesia, Bandung, Indonesia

ABSTRACT: During the learning process of Wireless Communication Systems in the Electrical Engineering Education Program of Indonesia University of Education, students generally face difficulties due to the number of transmission path parameters that need to be calculated through many formulas. These parameters are still calculated manually using a calculator, which means that the learning process requires a relatively long time. Therefore, it is necessary to develop a learning innovation that can shorten and simplify the calculating process. In this paper, the development of Network Planning Software and its use as a learning media in Wireless Communication Systems will be discussed. The research was conducted through three phases, that is, software development, software performance testing and limited implementation. The results show that the use of this Network Planning Software enhances the learning process quality. Students can learn more quickly, more interactively and can improve their analytical skills.

1 INTRODUCTION

The learning process is one of the most important elements in preparing our students to answer the challenges of the current technological advances. The unstoppable rush of information requires the development of a learning model that can explore the ability of students to learn more quickly, logically analyze the situation and look for creative solutions for any problems encountered (Rose, 1995). Nowadays, conventional learning models are generally still applied in Indonesian schools. This learning model is more teacher-centered. The learning is only in one direction, from teacher to students. Students are positioned as objects who accept passively what the teacher gives to them. This reduces the ability of students to learn the subject matter quickly. Students also find it difficult to develop their creativity. The Department of Electrical Engineering Education, Indonesia University of Education, has a mission to generate vocational schoolteachers that are able to encourage their students to become superior students who can learn more quickly and become more active and creative in finding solutions to any problems encountered. This is in line with the government program to improve the quality of education that is stated through the Decree of Minister of Education and Culture No. 70 of 2013 on the Basic Framework and Curriculum Structure Vocational School, which brings a pattern

of interactive and student-centered learning. Students are encouraged to be active, be able to work together and utilize multimedia to develop their abilities (Permendikbud, 2013). One of the subjects in the Electrical Engineering Education Program is Wireless Communication Systems. This subject is given to students who take a concentration of Telecommunications Engineering Education. One of the given topics is Cellular Communication Systems Network Planning. In this case, students are required to be able to calculate all the parameters of the signal transmission path. The problems faced by both students and lecturer in the learning process are that there are so many parameters that need to be calculated with a lot of formulas that need to be used. Currently, the calculation of these parameters is still done manually by using the calculator. This inhibits the students from understanding and resolving network design cases quickly, as most of the learning time is used for calculation activities. Frequently, because there are so many formulas to be used, calculation error is inevitable, so it must be recalculated and, therefore, more time is needed. That led to students being unable to develop their analytical skills and creativity in designing a wireless network. Therefore, learning innovation that can shorten and simplify the process of calculating the transmission path parameters needs to be done, so that the learning process can take place more quickly and interactively and can improve the analytical skills of students.

2 METHOD

This research was conducted through three phases, that is, software development, software performance testing and limited implementation. Software development includes a Link Performance Calculation program and a Profile Path program development using MATLAB 7.5.0. Software performance testing is used to determine the level of confidence and effectiveness of the programs that have been made. In this case, the test was performed by comparing the calculation results of the Network Planning Software and PathMW software with the Microsoft excel platform (Subali, 2001) and manual calculation result. Limited implementation was carried out on four students who took a course of Wireless Communication Systems.

2.1 Software development

The program contains the calculation of losses during signal transmission, the received power level, fading margin, outage time, availability, azimuth angle, antenna tilting, 1st Fresnel zone and the representation of the Path Profile (Stuber, 2011; Singh & Kaur, 2016). The design was created using a GUI (Graphic User Interface) Designer or GUIDE on MATLAB. Figure 1 shows the Link Performance Calculation design. Parameters required in the calculation were filled into the input part, while parameters as a result of the calculation will appear in the output part.

The presentation of the Path Profile design is shown in Figure 2. Input parameters were obtained from terrain data and the calculation results of the Link Performance Calculation program. This software was also equipped with features to describe each parameter. Using this feature, students can quickly get an explanation of each parameter used in the calculation by clicking the desired button.

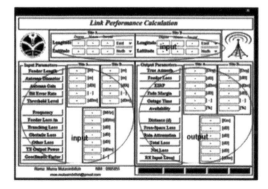

Figure 1. Link Performance Calculation design presentation.

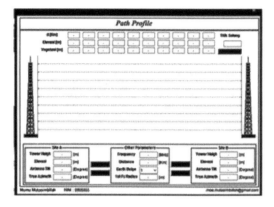

Figure 2. Path Profile design presentation.

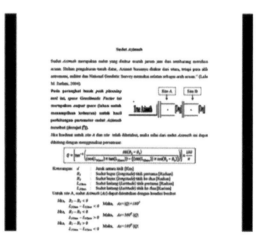

Figure 3. 'True Azimuth' description in pdf file.

For example, if students want to know the explanation of the 'true azimuth', they can just click on the button, then automatically the description of 'true azimuth' in the pdf file will appear on the computer screen. This description is also equipped with the formula needed to calculate the parameter. This is shown in Figure 3.

2.2 Software performance testing

On this test, the Microwave Worksheet - MSC079-MKS_02N021, PKU_02N208 - PKU_02N207 and SUM-NAD-0009-H-P - MAS018 data are used as input parameters (Exalt, 2002). These parameters are then used for calculating output parameters by using Network Planning Software, PathMW software and manual calculations. The calculation results were then compared with each other to find the level of confidence of the software developed. Table 1 shows the Microwave

Table 1. Link Performance Calculation input data.

No.	Parameter		Site A (MSC079)	Site B (MKS_02N021)
			Value	
1.	Coordinate:	Longitude	119° 26" 32.09' E	119° 27" 28.80' E
		Latitude	05° 08" 16.98' S	05° 06" 18.36' S
2.	Feeder Length		0 m	0 m
3.	Antenna Diameter		0.6 m	0.6 m
4.	Antenna Gain		35.60 dBi	35.60 dBi
5.	BER		10^{-6}	10^{-6}
6.	Threshold Level		−81.50 dBm	−81.50 dBm
7.	Frequency		13,000 MHz	
8.	Feeder Loss/m		0.075 dB/m	
9.	Branching Loss		0.40 dB	
10.	Obstacle Loss		0 dB	
11.	Other Loss		0.08 dB (Atmospheric absorption loss)	
12.	Transmitter Output Power		15 dB	
13.	Geoclimatic Factor		1.42×10^{-4}	

Table 2. Link Performance Calculation results.

No.	Parameter	Link Perform. Calculation		Pathmw-v4i		Manual Calculation	
		Value					
		Site A	Site B	Site A	Site B	Site A	Site B
1.	Azimuth	25.6117°	205.6117°	25.61°	205.61°	25.612°	205.612°
2.	Feeder Loss	0 dB	0 dB	0 dB	0 dB	0 dB	0 dB
3.	EIRP	50.20 dBm	50.20 dBm	50.20 dBm	50.20 dBm	50.20 dBm	50.20 dBm
4.	Fade Margin	37.3367 dB	37.3367 dB	37.35 dB	37.35 dB	37.3 dB	37.3 dB
5.	Outage Time	6.7059×10^{-6}	6.7059×10^{-6}	6.68×10^{-6}	6.68×10^{-6}	6.63×10^{-6}	6.63×10^{-6}
6.	Availability	99.9993%	99.9993%	99.9993%	99.9993%	99.9993%	99.9993%
7.	Distance (d)	4.0408 Km		4.04 Km		4.04 Km	
8.	Free-Space Loss	126.8583 dB		126.85 dB		126.856 dB	
9.	Rain Attenuation	2.625 dB		2.625 dB		2.625 dB	
10.	Total Loss	130.3633 dB		130.35 dB		130.361 dB	
11.	Net Loss	59.1633 dB		59.15 dB		59.161 dB	
12.	Rx Input Level	−44.1633 dB		−44.15 dBm		−44.161 dBm	

Worksheet - MSC079-MKS_02N021 input data for Link Performance Calculation. The results are shown in Table 2. Data from the same source are used for Path Profile calculation input data and can be seen in Table 3. The results are shown in Table 4. The comparisons showed that the three methods of calculation gave almost the same results. A level of confidence of 90.3% was also obtained. From these results, it can be concluded that the calculations using the Network Planning Software provide a high level of confidence.

2.3 Limited implementation

The implementation was carried out for 100 minutes (2 credits). In this case, four students were asked to resolve some calculation problems, either by using

Table 3. Path profile calculation input data.

No.	Point to Point Distance (d)	Elevation (h)	Vegetation (veg)
1.	0.000 Km	9.85 m	0 m
2.	0.160 Km	7.4 m	30 m
3.	0.404 Km	3.7 m	30 m
4.	0.808 Km	4.9 m	30 m
5.	1.212 Km	−1.0 m	30 m
6.	1.616 Km	0.0 m	30 m
7.	3.232 Km	4.5 m	30 m
8.	3.636 Km	3.9 m	30 m
9.	3.880 Km	3.3 m	30 m
10.	4.040 Km	2.97 m	0 m
Antenna height		Site A = 45 m	Site B = 47 m
k-factor for Earth bulge = 4/3			

259

Table 4. Path Profile Calculation results.

No.	Parameter	Value					
		Path Profile		Pathmw-v4i		Manual Calculation	
		Site A	Site B	Site A	Site B	Site A	Site B
1.	Elevation	9.85 m	2.97 m	9.85 m	2.97 m	9.85 m	2.97 m
2.	Ant. Tilting	−0.069903°	0.069903°	−0.069°	0.069°	−0.069°	0.069°
3.	Ant. Height	45 m	47 m	45 m	47 m	45 m	47 m
4.	k-Factor	4/3	4/3	4/3	4/3	4/3	4/3
5.	1st Fz	4.8036 m		4.8253 m		4.828 m	

Table 5. Students' response.

Question	Student			
	A	B	C	D
1. The time required to calculate manually	60 minutes	90 minutes	75 minutes	78 minutes
2. The time required to calculate using Network Planning Software (NPS)	4.5 minutes	7 minutes	6 minutes	7 minutes
3. Probability of making mistakes when using manual calculation	High	High	High	High
4. Probability of making mistakes when using NPS	Low	Low	Low	Low
5. The number of input parameters that are able to analyze their effects on the output parameters when using manual calculation	None	None	None	None
6. The number of input parameters that are able to analyze their effects on the output parameters when using NPS	4	2	2	3
7. Search for description of the parameters when using manual calculation	From textbooks or internet	Lecture notes or internet	Lecture notes or internet	From textbooks or internet
8. Search for description of the parameters when using NPS	Clicking the buttons	Clicking the buttons	Clicking the buttons	Clicking the buttons
9. Method that make learning easier and more interactive	NPS	NPS	NPS	NPS

the Network Planning Software or manually. They were also asked to analyze the effect of changes in the input parameter values to the output parameters by using both methods. They then elaborated on their experiences during the implementation. There were five types of questions given to them, that is, the time required to calculate, possibility of making mistakes, the number of parameters that they explored, their attempts to find an explanation of the parameters and the method that made the learning process easier and more interactive.

3 RESULT AND DISCUSSIONS

Table 5 shows the students' response to the two methods used. It was found that students required a much shorter time for completing the calculations when using the Network Planning Software. They also did not have to worry about making a mistake and could repeat the calculation process. Using this software allowed them to have more time to explore the parameters and enhanced their analytical skills. From the table, it can be seen that all the students explored at least two parameters. In this case, Student A explored more parameters than the other students. This was because he required less time to compute using the Network Planning Software. Student B took the longest time to calculate manually, since he had made some mistakes and the counting process had to be repeated. Significant improvements were seen when he used Network Planning Software. He only required seven minutes to insert all input parameters and get the result. The software helps students when they do not understand or need a deeper explanation about the parameters. They just have to click a button for the desired parameter, then the explanation of the parameters and how to calculate them will immediately appear on the computer screen. The learning process becomes more enjoyable and interactive.

4   CONCLUSION

The Network Planning Software has been made as a learning media for the Wireless Communication System subject. This software provides a high level of confidence, as seen in the software performance testing results. Students required a much shorter time to get the output parameter results, which gave them more time to explore the parameters and enhance their analytical skills. This software helps the students to get a quick explanation of each parameter. The learning process becomes more enjoyable and interactive.

REFERENCES

Exalt. (2002). Antenna alignment for terrestrial microwave system. *Technical White Paper*. Exalt Communication.

Permendikbud no.70. (2013). *Kerangka Dasar Dan Struktur Kurikulum Sekolah Menengah Kejuruan/Madrasah Aliyah Kejuruan. Mentri Pendidikan dan Kebudayaan Republik Indonesia*. Jakarta: Permendikbud.

Rose, C. (1995). *Accelerated learning, action guide.* Buckinghamshire: Accelerated Learning Systems Ltd.

Singh, H.R. & Kaur, H. (2016). Automated alignment of microwave antenna of base transceiver station by utilizing hybrid sources. *The Research journal,* 2(2), 2–3.

Stuber, G.L. (2011). *Principles of mobile communication.* New York: Springer.

Subali, E. (2001). *PathMW-v4i.* Bandung: Treetech Engineering.

Regionalization and Harmonization in TVET – Abdullah et al. (Eds)
© 2017 Taylor & Francis Group, London, ISBN 978-1-138-05419-6

Model of instructional thematic game to improve understanding of children with intellectual deficiencies using voice kinect sensor

D. Kuswardhana
School of Information Science, Japan Advanced Institute of Science and Technology, Ishikawa, Japan

S. Hasegawa
Research Center for Advanced Computing Infrastructure, Japan Advanced Institute of Science and Technology, Ishikawa, Japan

ABSTRACT: Children with intellectual deficiencies have diverse limitations, particularly in understanding and expressing a certain object verbally in communication. To resolve these limitations, this paper is oriented to improve their understanding using speech related to the real object. Therefore, we propose a model of the instructional thematic game based on a voice Kinect sensor to detect their speech. This model has an attribute that represents a certain theme for each part of the game topic and a strong relationship to the curricula in improving the learning process at school. It gives them a rule to learn diverse things from a single topic of a real subject by associating it with diverse viewpoints from the abstract subject. Based on the expert and teacher questionnaires to the 13 people involved, most of them answered that such a model would support the children in getting better results in their understanding of the object and in improving their articulation.

1 INTRODUCTION

Communication is one of the important things for the children with Intellectual Disabilities (ID) to learn from the school material from the entire curricula as a part of the central learning component. The children with ID have limitations in communication, either in receptiveness, such as complexity of language adversity in organizing and categorizing information gained from subsequent retrieval, adversity in abstract concepts and adversity in interpreting information (understanding); or in expressiveness, such as word processing, which is often under cognitive ability, a similar but slower developmental path than typical peers, a tendency to use more immature language forms and a tendency to produce shorter and less elaborated utterances (Prelock et al., 2008; Miller et al., 1981; Owens et al., 2003; Boudreau & Chapman, 2007). Therefore, we need an assistive technology system that enables the children to enhance their potential. It would also stimulate them to enjoy training, in order to get much better results (Standen et al., 2001).

On the other hand, according to some researchers, they expressed that the children with ID could be trained (Seay, 2006; Kuswardhana & Hasegawa, 2015) and could also particularly improve their non-verbal communication using Augmentative and Alternative Communication (AAC), such as picture exchange systems (Bondy & Frost, 2001) and speech generating devices (Cheslock et al.,

2008). However, without the children being sufficiently engaged, their learning process could not be established to create proper pedagogical opportunities (Hsu, 2011), specifically when the children with ID have to face an abstract concept that must be understood. Therefore, this paper is oriented to propose the model of the instructional thematic game, which will enhance their understanding.

2 PROPOSED DESIGNS

We propose the system design formed in the assistive technology system. It helps them to increase their learning skills and, moreover, to gain understanding in an easy, simple and fun way.

2.1 Instructional thematic game model

The Instructional Thematic Game (ITG) model gives a rule of thumb for the children. It facilitates the opportunities for them to learn everything from the real object by associating it with the other abstract subject without ignoring the meaning of the subject (Kuswardhana & Hasegawa, 2016). The model consists of three elements, as shown in Figure 1. First, understanding abstract is the solution for the children with ID who are not able to recognize abstract things. They do not know the meaning of the abstract subject, such as mathematics, science, interaction, problem solving, etc. Therefore, they will only understand

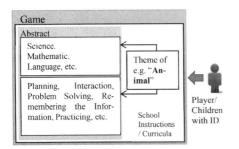

Figure 1.   Model of the instructional thematic game.

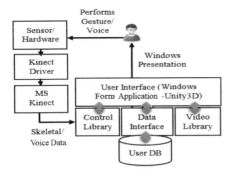

Figure 2.   Architecture system design.

something appearing in front of them visibly or in the concrete existence. Second, school instruction/ curricula are the substance of the game topic, having a strong relation to the curricula in improving the learning process at school. Third, the game delivers the requirements of the instructional theme to the children with ID in the game application form.

2.2   *Architecture system design*

Figure 2 shows a block diagram of the whole environment, which contains the main functions of the system. The children receive some instructions from the user interface application, which is constructed by unity 3D in a windows form. Concurrently, such activities are detected by the sensor, through spelling or gesturing as inputs, by sending the skeletal/voice data to the system. The control library picks up the data sent by sensor to deliver it to the application. On the other hand, the user data are able to be stored in the user database through the data interface, including the result of the game. And also, the video stemming from the library will come up to the user through the user interface before the game section (each scenario) starts.

2.3   *Design game application*

The design of the game refers to the ITG model described in Section 2.1. The topic related to the

curricula is about the animal. Stemming from this topic, we create four types of game design. Namely, the animal name, the animal body name, the number of animals and the direction of the animal. Also, a video that teaches spelling related to the animal will encourage the children to learn more. In addition, the abstract element reached by the game relates to understanding, remembering the information, interaction and problem solving.

3   RESEARCH METHODOLOGY

The method used in this research was single subject research (Zhan & Ottenbacher, 2001). It was carried out generally within two steps: namely, baseline and treatment. This paper was definitely limited to the baseline step, which was oriented to the teacher exploration regarding the children with ID and to endorse and evaluate a proposed design before it would be used by the children. The procedure to carry out the research is shown in the following picture.

The procedure of the baseline stage was explained as follows:

1. Discussion with the teacher. This step was undertaken to gather information in detail from the teacher about the children with ID who would have rehabilitation. These data are regarded as a consideration point for making the system design.
2. Pre-identification. This process was undertaken to identify a model of the proposed design that would be used by the children. The procedure would be done in the following three steps. First, assessment was needed to identify the children's condition by using the proposed snip system design through the teacher. Second, analysis was oriented to analyze the data acquired previously. Third, need was oriented to reveal the analysis result for being used as a model for the children to improve.

3.1   *Participants*

The participants for the research were the teachers and involved 13 participants from the two different areas of the school. Namely, SLB Cipaganti Bandung and SLB Al-Barkah Garut.

3.2   *Questionnaire*

We made a questionnaire, as shown in Table 1, for the participants to explore the condition of the target children, particularly related to their difficulties, which consisted of 10 items with five alternative answers. Namely, scores from 5 to 1 are equal to strongly agree to strongly disagree respectively. The topics of the questions were categorized

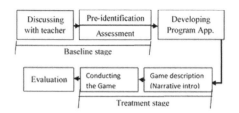

Figure 3. Single subject research.

Table 1. Questionnaire.

No	Question	Score Level
1	Do they need such equipment to improve their ability to learn?	
2	Would it be fine if this equipment is presented in a game application based on the computer?	
3	Should this game application exercise children in having planning aspects?	
4	Should this game application exercise children in having interaction aspects?	
5	Should this game application exercise children in having the problem-solving aspects?	
6	Should this game application exercise children in having a recalling memory of information aspects?	
7	Should this game application tend to particular thematic aspects related to their environment?	
8	Should this game application topic have concurrency to their learning material?	
9	Will their understanding in cognitive aspect be able to be improved?	
10	Will their speech articulation aspect be able to be improved in particular time?	
11	How do you think to improve or optimize their understanding and speech articulation?	

into three types. First, the questions related to the necessity of the equipment. Second, the questions related to the ITG model. And third, the questions related to the children's target to improve their understanding and speech articulation. On the other hand, question number 11 needed a description answer and this was specifically related to the recommendation of activities for improving understanding in cognitive aspects and speech articulation.

The Likert scale was used to analyze the data resulting from the questionnaire. In addition, we tested the questionnaire using a validation (Correlation) test to accurately measure the children's condition through an appropriate questionnaire and also a reliability (Cronbach's alpha) test to get the consistency of each item over different participants.

Table 2. Validity and reliability test.

Question (Q) number	Corrected item-total correlation (r calculating)	Cronbach's alpha if item deleted
Q1	0.933	0.780
Q2	0.875	0.762
Q3	0.886	0.768
Q4	0.796	0.767
Q5	0.891	0.769
Q6	0.880	0.769
Q7	0.849	0.764
Q8	0.902	0.768
Q9	0.886	0.768
Q10	0.924	0.761

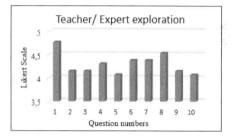

Figure 4. Assessment data.

4 RESULT AND DISCUSSION

Based on Table 2, it was proved that each of the questions is valid due to the logic $r\ table < r\ calculating$, since N = 13 and the level of significance for 2 tail of $r\ table\ (0.05) = 0.55$. Also, all the items are reliable since the Cronbach's alpha test are satisfied, Cronbach's alpha > 0.7.

The data resulting from the assessment were shown in Figure 4. The graph shows that all the items are above the standard level, which means that the participants expressed a high positive argue. The discussions of the results are divided into three categories, as follows:

1. Question for number 1 is related to the necessity of the equipment for the children. The Likert scale value is 4.8, which is almost close to perfect. That means that each of the schools really needs such equipment to improve the children with ID.
2. Questions for numbers 2, 3, 4, 5, 6, 7 and 8 are classified as the ITG model. The Likert scale values of these categories are an average of 4.3. This shows that they gave high positive responses. Therefore, according to them, the model can give enhancement to their difficulties by undertaking a game relating to the learning material in their school.
3. Questions for numbers 9 and 10 are classified as the children's targets relating to improving their

understanding and speech articulation. Their Likert scale values are an average of 4.1. In these categories, they also gave high positive responses. This means that the children can be enhanced to get better understanding and speech articulation in a particular time. In addition, it was also proved and supported by previous research (Seay, 2006).

On the other hand, the question for number 11 is related to the teacher recommendations as follows:

1. The game application designed has already met the requirements of the children, because it related to the methods of articulation, such as Visual, Audio, Kinaesthetic and Tactic.
2. Classification of the animal pronunciation should be started from the easy syllables, such as *ku-da* (horse), *sa-pi* (cow), etc., then moved to the next step, such as three of a syllable, *ha-ri-mau* (tiger), *ke-lin-ci* (rabbit).
3. The children keep practicing routinely using various assisted devices.
4. Practicing should be facilitated by interesting media to make the children interested.
5. The basic ability and character of the children should be considered.
6. We should create a conducive climate/environment around the children.

5 CONCLUSION

The proposed ITG model has three elements: abstract, curricula/school instruction (thematic topic) and game. It can be referred to those children with ID having adversity in abstract concepts and interpreting information (understanding) and expressing certain objects verbally, as the solution for them by training or conducting the game based on the ITG model. Moreover, it was supported by the results that the participants gave high positive responses to the ITG model.

So far, we have just taken the baseline stage. We will then go through the subsequent research methodology called the treatment stage. In this stage, the research will be oriented to implement the ITG model to some of the children with ID, in order to recognize the effectivity of the model and also the enhancement of the children with ID.

ACKNOWLEDGMENT

We would like to thank the Directorate General of Resources for Science, Technology, and Higher Education, Ministry of Research, Technology and Higher Education and the Republic of Indonesia for supporting and funding the doctoral course at Japan Advanced Institute of Science and Technology. And also, the Indonesia University of Education as my Affiliation for your trusted support. The work is supported in part by Grant-in-Aid for Scientific Research (C) (No. 26330395) from the Ministry of Education, Science, and Culture of Japan. We also want to say many thanks to SLB Al-Barkah Samarang Garut and SLB Cipaganti Bandung Indonesia for facilitating us in conducting the research.

REFERENCES

Bondy, A. & Frost, L. (2001). The picture exchange communication system. *Journal of Behaviour Modification, 25*(5), 725–744.

Boudreau, D.M. & Chapman, R.S. (2007). The relationship between event representation and linguistic skill in narratives of children and adolescents with Down syndrome. *Journal Speech Lang. Hear Res, 43*(5), 1146–1159.

Cheslock, M.A., Barton-Hulsey, A., Romski, M. & Sevcik, R.A. (2008). Using a speech-generating device to enhance communicative abilities for an adult with moderate intellectual disability. *Journal of Intellectual and Developmental Disabilities, 46*(5), 376–386.

Hsu, H.J. (2011). The potential of kinect in education. *Journal of Information and Education Technology, 1*(5), 365–370.

Kuswardhana, D. & Hasegawa, S. (2015). Animal thematic game based on kinect sensor for mental retardation rehabilitation. In *Proceedings of the 23rd International Conference on computers in education. China: Asia-Pacific Society for Computers in Education Animal.* 509–514.

Kuswardhana, D. & Hasegawa, S. (2016). A conceptual model of instructional thematic game for children with intellectual deficiencies. Human-computer interaction international 2016 - posters' extended abstracts (Part II). *Communication in Computer and Information Science, 618*, 243–248.

Light, J. & Drager, K. (2007). AAC technologies for young children with complex communication needs: State of the science and future research directions. *Augmentative and Alternative Communication, 23*(3), 204–216.

Miller, J.F., Chapman, R. & MacKenzie, H. (1981). Individual differences in the language acquisition of mentally retarded children. *Proceedings of the 2nd Wisconsin Symposium Research Child Language.* Madison, Wis: University of Wisconsin.

Owens, R.E., Metz, D.E. & Haas, A. (2003). *Introduction to communication disorders: A life span perspective* (2nd Ed.). Boston: Allyn & Bacon.

Prelock, P.A., Hutchins, T. & Glascoe, F.P. (2008). Speech-language impairment: How to identify the most common and least diagnosed disability of childhood. *The Medscape Journal of Medicine, 10*(6), 136.

Seay, O.J. (2006). Evaluating mental retardation for forensic purposes. *Applied Psychology in Criminal Justice, 2*(3), 52–81.

Standen, P.J., Brown, D.J. & Cromby, J.J. (2001). The effective use of virtual environments in the education and rehabilitation of students with intellectual disabilities. *British Journal of Educational Technology, 32*, 289–299.

Zhan, S. & Ottenbacher, K.J. (2001). Single subject research designs for disability research. *Disability and Rehabilitation, 23*(1), 1–8.

Regionalization and Harmonization in TVET – Abdullah et al. (Eds)
© 2017 Taylor & Francis Group, London, ISBN 978-1-138-05419-6

Performance improvement of a domestic refrigerator using parallel expansion device

D. Supriawan, E.T. Berman, M.M. Al Gifari & M. Mutaufiq
Departemen Pendidikan Teknik Mesin, Universitas Pendidikan Indonesia, Jawa Barat, Indonesia

ABSTRACT: The purpose of this study was to determine the performance improvement of a domestic refrigerator that used a parallel expansion device compared to one using a single expansion device. The experiment was conducted by replacing the single expansion device with a parallel expansion device on a domestic refrigerator with a capacity of 120 liters and using R-134a as working fluid. To get the experimental data, measurements were performed on the cooling load through various temperatures (from 30°C to −30°C). The experimental result showed that the use of parallel expansion generated an increase of 17% in the Coefficient of Performance (COP). The pressure ratio was also lower, so that it caused the compressor to work more efficiently and saved electrical power consumption required by the refrigerator.

1 INTRODUCTION

The high cost of electricity in Indonesia has driven electronics manufacturers to create efficient appliances and equipment. The refrigerator is the household object that has the second largest energy consumption after an air conditioner, as the refrigerator works for 24 hours (Geppert & Stamminger, 2010). Furthermore, Negrao and Hermes (2011) have estimated that worldwide there is one household refrigerator for every six people, which corresponds to approximately 6% of the total electrical energy produced. Thus, the effort to improve the energy efficiency of electrical equipment is crucial.

In recent years, the researchers have implemented various ways to reduce energy consumption and have improved the efficiency of the refrigeration system. For example, Yoon et al. (2013) conducted the improvement of insulation inside a refrigerator. They had investigated the bypass of the two-circuit cycle and the dual-loop cycle. The results showed that the energy consumptions of the bypass of the two-circuit cycle and the dual-loop cycle were reduced by 5.7% and 6.1%, respectively. Next, Visek et al. (2014) and Yoon et al. (2011) studied the use of a dual/parallel evaporator for a domestic refrigerator-freezer and showed that the energy consumption dropped by 5.6% – 7.8%, respectively. In addition, Berman et al. (2016) presented and enhanced the performance of a domestic refrigerator with a hot gas injection to the suction line. The results revealed that the injection of hot gas to the suction line generated an increase in the COP of 7% and caused the compressor to work more efficiently. Furthermore, the method for improving the performance of a domestic refrigerator can be done by using hydrocarbons as refrigerants. The experimental results show that the hydrocarbons could reduce the energy consumption and improve the actual COP (Sekhar et al., 2004; Wongwises & Chimres, 2005; Sattar et al., 2007). Recently, the other relevant studies on the system performance of a domestic refrigerator have also demonstrated that modifying the cooling system using a heat exchanger could improve energy efficiency and performance (Klein et al., 2000; Mastrullo et al., 2007; Lee et al., 2010; Rahman & Anthony, 2015). This study is focused on using a parallel expansion device to improve domestic refrigerator performance.

In general, a refrigeration system uses a single expansion device. The parallel expansion device is an engineering method on the refrigeration system to reduce the throttling loss of the refrigerant liquid as it flows through the liquid line to the evaporator. When the liquid passes through the expansion device, a part of the liquid vaporizes. The pressure of the liquid is reduced to the evaporator pressure so that the saturation temperature of the refrigerant entering the evaporator will be below the temperature of the refrigerated space. The refrigerant is discharged from the expansion device into the evaporator as a liquid-vapor mixture. Obviously, only the liquid portion of the liquid-vapor mixture will vaporize in the evaporator and produce useful cooling (Klein et al., 2000). Therefore, the application of this engineering method to domestic refrigerators is expected to improve performance and to decrease the energy/power required as the driving force of the compressor.

2 MATERIALS AND METHODS

Figure 1 shows the schematic installation of the parallel expansion device used for the experiment. The main components of the domestic refrigerator consisted of an evaporator, compressor and condenser (Sanyo). Components of the parallel expansion device were made from copper capillary tubing with a diameter of 0.97 mm. In this study, the working fluid used was R-134a. Two pressure gauges (Robin Air) and two temperature sensors (Lutron) were placed on the inlet and outlet of the compressor to measure the suction and discharge pressures-temperature. On the inside of the refrigerator, a container of the brine (salt water) concentration of 12% was kept, serving as a cooling load. A thermometer (Beuer) was placed in the brine container to determine the changes in temperature. every 1°C.

The experiment was conducted under two conditions. In the first, the system was operated in a normal mode to obtain baseline data of the refrigerator performance. In the second, the system operated with a parallel expansion mode. Data retrieval was conducted four times under each condition. At the beginning of the study, calibration of all the measurement equipment was carried out. Then the vacuum process removed the water content and other substances in the cooling system. After that, checking was done to find any leaks from all the parts and installation of the pipe. The system was then filled with R-134a weighing 100 g

in accordance with the recommendation of the manufacturer. For the next stage, the refrigerator was operated for about one hour to reach a steady condition and then a container of brine was placed into the freezer. Data capture started when the temperature of the brine was 3°C, with the assumption that the system was in a steady condition. Next, the changes were observed until the temperature of the brine reached –3°C. During the study, the temperature of the environment was kept at 28°C ± 2°C.

3 RESULT AND DISCUSSION

3.1 Refrigerating effect

Figure 2 shows the results of the refrigerating effect of a domestic refrigerator under two testing conditions. In general, the refrigeration effect generated by the system using a parallel expansion mode has a higher value than that of the normal mode. In parallel expansion mode, the refrigerating effect generated when the brine was 3°C was 136.4 kJ/kg. Then it increased slightly to 138.52 kJ/kg when the brine temperature reached –3°C. On the other hand, in the system that used the normal mode, the refrigerating effect generated when the brine solution reached 3°C was 131.40 kJ/kg. Further, this slowly decreased to 131.01 kJ/kg when the temperature of the brine was –3°C.

Based on the results, there had been a 6% increase of the refrigeration effect in the system using a parallel expansion device. The effects of the use of the parallel expansion device on the domestic refrigerator resulted in the evaporation process in the expansion device becoming shorter, followed by more liquid refrigerant flowing into the evaporator to absorb heat from the cooling load (brine). Furthermore, the ratio between the discharge pressure and the suction pressure generated by the system becomes lower so that the work of compression needed to compress the refrigerant

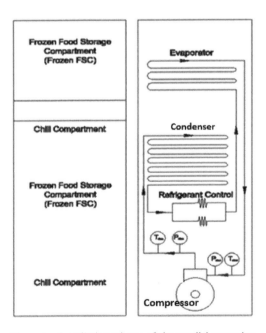

Figure 1. Installation scheme of the parallel expansion device on a domestic refrigerator.

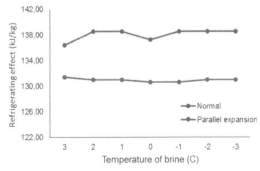

Figure 2. The refrigeration effects value of a domestic refrigerator under normal mode and parallel expansion.

268

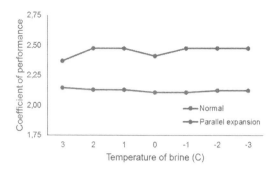

Figure 3. The COP of a domestic refrigerator system under normal mode and parallel expansion mode.

from condensing pressure to evaporating pressure becomes shorter. The achievement of this value will contribute to a smaller energy consumption being needed to operate the compressor.

3.2 Coefficient of Performance (COP)

Figure 3 presents the Coefficient of Performance (COP) systems of the two mode conditions of the domestic refrigerator testing. In the normal mode, the COP decreased along with the decreasing temperature of the brine. At first, the obtained COP was 2.15 when the temperature of the brine was 3°C; a COP of 2.12 was obtained when the brine temperature was –3°C. Further, when the system employed parallel expansion, COP increased significantly. When the temperature of the brine was 3°C, the obtained COP was 2.37. Then, the value fluctuated to 2.48 when the brine temperature was –3°C. These results indicate that the use of parallel expansion on the refrigeration system led to an increased 17% value of COP. The high value of COP indicates that the system worked properly.

The value of COP is influenced by the amount of heat that can be absorbed by the refrigerant flowing in the evaporator (refrigeration effect), and the compression work performed by the compressor when it compressed the low temperature-pressured refrigerant vapor to high temperature-pressured refrigerant vapor. If the value of the refrigeration effect is big and the value of the compression work is small, the COP obtained will be large. The bigger the value of the refrigeration effect and the smaller the value of the compression work, then this will result in a better value of COP being obtained.

4 CONCLUSION

Research on the use of parallel expansion devices to improve the performance of domestic refrigerators has been conducted. To demonstrate the perform-

ance improvement of the refrigerator, the refrigeration system was tested in two different conditions. The results indicate that the installation of a parallel expansion device on the domestic refrigerator generates an increased 17% value of the Coefficient of Performance (COP) and lowers the pressure ratio compressor so that it performs more efficient work and saves on the power consumption required by a refrigerator.

ACKNOWLEDGMENTS

The authors would like to thank the Rector of Universitas Pendidikan Indonesia for funding this research through PPDKI program 2016 (Persatuan Pegawai Dalam Kesehatan Indonesia (Association of Indonesian Health Employees)), on research scheme *penguatan kompetensi*.

REFERENCES

Berman, E.T., Hasan, S. & Mutaufiq. (2016). Enhancing the performance of the domestic refrigerator with hot gas injection to suction line. *IOP Conference Series: Materials Science and Engineering, 128*: 012028.

Geppert, J. & Stamminger, R. (2010). Do consumers act in a sustainable way using their refrigerator? The influence of consumer real life behaviour on the energy consumption of cooling appliances. *International Journal of Consumer Studies, 34*(2), 219–27.

Klein, S.A., Reindl, D.T. & Brownell, K. (2000). Refrigeration system performance using liquid-suction heat exchangers. *International Journal of Refrigeration, 23*(8), 588–96.

Lee, M., Kim, Y., Lee, H. & Kim, Y. (2010). Air-side heat transfer characteristics of flat plate finned-tube heat exchangers with large fin pitches under frosting conditions. *International Journal of Heat and Mass Transfer, 53*(13–14), 2655–61.

Mastrullo, R., Mauro, A.W., Tino, S. & Vanoli, G.P. (2007). A chart for predicting the possible advantage of adopting a suction/liquid heat exchanger in refrigerating system. *Applied Thermal Engineering, 27*(14–15), 2443–48.

Negrao, C.O.R. & Hermes, C.J.L. (2011). Energy and cost savings in household refrigerating appliances: A simulation-based design approach. *Applied Energy, 88*(9).

Rahman, M.A. & Anthony, M.J. (2015). Experimental study on frosting/defrosting characteristics of microgrooved metal surfaces. *International Journal of Refrigeration, 50*, 44–56.

Sattar, M.A., Saidur, R. & Masjuki, H.H. (2007). Performance investigation of domestic refrigerator using pure hydrocarbons and blends of hydrocarbons as refrigerants. *Waset, 23*,223–8.

Sekhar, S., Joseph, D., Mohan, L. & Renganarayanan, S. (2004). Improved energy efficiency for CFC domestic refrigerators retrofitted with ozone-friendly HFC134a/HC refrigerant mixture. *International Journal of Thermal Sciences, 43*(3), 307–14.

Visek, M., Joppolo, C.M., Molinaroli, L. & Olivani, A. (2014). Advanced sequential dual evaporator domestic refrigerator/freezer: system energy optimization. *International Journal of Refrigeration, 43*, 71–79.

Wongwises, S. & Nares, C. 2005. Experimental study of hydrocarbon mixtures to replace HFC-134a in a domestic refrigerator. *Energy Conversion and Management, 46*(1), 85–100.

Yoon, W.J., Jung, H.W., Chung, H.J. & Kim, Y. (2011). Performance optimization of a two-circuit cycle with parallel evaporators for a domestic refrigerator-freezer. *International Journal of Refrigeration, 34*(1), 216–24.

Yoon, W.J., Seo, K. & Kim, Y. (2013). Development of an optimization strategy for insulation thickness of a domestic refrigerator-freezer. *International Journal of Refrigeration, 36*(3), 1162–72.

Internship program in higher vocational education: Students' performance evaluation

D. Zakaria, A.G. Abdullah, M. Somantri & A.A. Danuwijaya
Universitas Pendidikan Indonesia, Bandung, Indonesia

ABSTRACT: The study was conducted to evaluate the students' performance in the internship program in higher vocational education, especially in the Department of Electrical Engineering Education FPTK UPI (Faculty of Technology and Vocational Education, Universitas Pendidikan Indonesia). It provides suggestions about how to perform an appropriate internship program based on previous studies. The respondents were 160 students (graduates or undergraduates) who have undertaken the internship program from 2000–2013. There were only four external variables that were studied, including the procedure of internship program performance, the role of the workplace supervisor, the role of the lecturer supervisor and the student's job description. The study used a quantitative method. The findings of this research showed that the procedure of internship program performance and the role of the lecturer supervisor were not sufficient, while the role of the workplace supervisor and the student's job description in the internship were appropriate.

1 INTRODUCTION

Internship has been an integral part in vocational education. It serves as a bridge between vocational education and the workplace, so that students will have a better understanding of their industrial work when actually entering the workplace after graduation.

Internship is a student placement in the workplace that can have positive impacts for both the owner of the workplace (getting a new employee) and for the student (to get new experience about their future work based on their competency) (Coco, 2000). With the internship program, students will get direct field experience related to the competencies that have been learned in college, learn how to adapt to the workplace and be trained in their responsibilities for performing the job (Gamboa et al., 2013). To get the maximum results of internship program implementation, an internship program for students should be coordinated between universities and industries (Polat et al., 2010; Liviu & Ana-Andreea, 2013).

Vocational education is higher education that is established with the aim of training prospective workers to perform jobs in an organization or workplace (Hadi et al., 2015). Vocational education has the objectives of providing information to individuals about the field of the selected job, initial preparation of individuals regarding the development of capabilities and training in the field of the selected job, to develop individuals in the workplace as a requirement for performing continuously changing work and to give experience to individuals if later there is a transition of work in the workplace, either

by his own choice or requested by the company/workplace (Billett, 2011).

Based on the objectives of vocational education above, it is undeniable that the internship program must be conducted by each vocational student. The students' real experience in the field of the workplace will be invaluable for the students' future work.

A problem that is commonly encountered in the internship program is the mismatch between the internship place (industry or company) and the competencies learned by the students during the learning process at the university. It occurs due to the absence of structured agreement between educational institutions and industries or companies regarding the internship program. When signing up for the internship program, students are positioned as job seekers with a letter of introduction from the educational institutions to apply for internships in a particular company. If accepted in industry, students must be willing to follow the programs given by the company, without any coordination with the educational institution. As a result of this, an agreement between universities and companies/industries regarding the internship program is a necessity, so that the program runs in accordance with the competencies that students have learned during the learning process at university (Liviu & Ana-Andreea, 2013).

Another problem is the ineffective monitoring process of the internship students. It is common that there are a large number of students who follow the internship program. However, the proportion of students and lecturers is imbalanced. The lecturers who guide and evaluate the students are limited, and this results in the poor monitoring process of the students by the lecturer (Koc et al., 2014). During the internship program (1–3 months) the lecturer visits the industry a minimum of three times to discover the progress of the students. However, if the distance from the campus to the industry is too far, there will be another problem. To solve these problems, the use of an Online Diary is required for students. The diary must be filled out by students once a week to share what they learn during the internship program. This would help the assessment process to be more effective (Koc et al., 2014). The results of the study from 70 students who have already implemented the "Online Internship Journal System" indicate that most interns react positively to the learning and the reflective processes embedded in journal writing (Chanlin & Hung, 2015).

According to Alkin in 1969, evaluation is a process of ensuring that the correct decision is made, selecting the right information and collecting and analyzing the information in order to report useful data summaries to the decision makers when choosing alternatives (Arifin, 2010). Alkin offers five kinds of evaluation, including assessment system, program planning, program implementation, improvement program and certification program. This present study used Alkin's model of the improvement program. The improvement program provides information on how the program functions, how the program works and whether unexpected issues or new problems arise when achieving the goals. In other words, the evaluators identify the problems that arise, collect and analyze data and submit this to the decision makers to make improvements to the program implementation immediately

According to some references, good practice for internships is characterized by certain aspects. In the aspect of working practice, students are facilitated to work in groups so that the weakest students will have increased competency (Binder et al., 2015). In addition, students complete a routine journal that can provide guidance to students in achieving the goals of internship (Gaba, 2015).

In terms of the program itself, the internship program should have cooperation between educational institutions and related industries, so that the implementation of the internship runs on track (Liviu & Ana-Andreea, 2013). Besides, a good practice of the internship program is the existence of internship information systems that allows students, lecturers and supervisors from the industry to communicate with each other so that the guidance process becomes effective (Chanlin & Hung, 2015; Chopvitayakun, 2015).

2 METHODS

This study uses a quantitative approach. It involved students/alumni from the classes of 2000–2013 of the Electrical Engineering Education Department

FPTK UPI that have conducted the internship program. Data were collected through questionnaires, literature reviews and interviews. The examined variables were only from external factors, including internship implementation procedures, the role of the Supervising lecturer the role of the supervisor from industry and the students' job description during internship.

The procedure in this research is shown in Figure 1.

The questionnaire has been compiled and then shown to the supervisor for revision. Furthermore, to test the validity, the questionnaire was tested by distributing questionnaires to 40 students who have carried out the internship program. The questions that pass the validity test are then compiled into the questionnaire used in the study, which was then distributed to 160 students and alumni. The data collected from the questionnaire were processed, presented and analyzed. The results of the analysis are used to provide conclusions and recommendations.

A literature review was conducted by reviewing international journals related to the internship program to provide basic and sufficient insights concerning the implementation of internship programs on colleges throughout the world, before conducting further research on the evaluation of the internship program in Electrical Engineering Education in FPTK department.

Field study was conducted by interviewing a few students who had already conducted the internship, regarding the implementation of the internship in

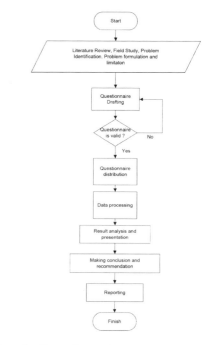

Figure 1. Research procedure.

terms of service satisfaction aspects, process guidance with the supervisor, guidance process with the supervisor from industry and the final evaluation. The interview results can be included in the questionnaire and formulation of the problem.

3 RESULTS AND DISCUSSION

The data collection is conducted by using the Google Forms. Researchers sent a questionnaire to each respondent. From the results of the questionnaire distribution, there were 160 data collected, with the number of respondents as shown in Table 1:

In Table 1, the majority of the respondents were from the classes of 2009–2013, with the highest number of respondents in the class of 2012, which reached 50.625% of the total respondents. This is because the classes of 2009–2013 are still active

Table 1. Number of respondents from every class.

No	Class	Number of respondents	Percentage (%)
1	2000	0	0
2	2001	1	0.625
3	2002	2	1.25
4	2003	0	0
5	2004	0	0
6	2005	1	0.625
7	2006	4	2.5
8	2007	1	0.625
9	2008	4	2.5
10	2009	10	6.25
11	2010	20	12.5
12	2011	26	16.25
13	2012	81	50.625
14	2013	10	6.25
Total		160	

Table 2. Result of data processing for variable: Implementation procedure of internship.

No	Questions	Score 1	2	3	4	5	Value	Mean	SD
1.	Internship implementation procedures in Electrical Engineering Education Department was clear	12	37	55	50	6	60.13%	3.01	1.000
2.	Socialization of the internship procedure has been good	21	57	54	24	4	51.63%	2.58	0.981
3.	Department provide a list of companies or industries that receive the students to carry out internship	72	52	22	8	6	51.63%	1.90	1.059
4.	There has been a cooperation agreement between the company/industry with the department on the implementation of internship	64	50	28	12	6	40.75%	2.04	1.104
5.	Students communicate with the supervisor before deciding the place of internship	30	23	46	40	21	59.88%	2.99	1.296
6.	Making sure letter of internship from faculty is on time	23	29	55	43	10	58.50%	2.93	1.130
7.	Students do internship based programs that have been agreed by the department with industry/company	20	44	36	43	17	59.13%	2.96	1.215

Table 3. Result of data processing for variable: The role of industry supervisor.

No	Questions	Score 1	2	3	4	5	Value	Mean	SD
1	Guidance process with supervisor from industry is progressing well	2	11	29	70	48	78.88%	3.94	0.933
2	Students are given certain performance targets by supervisor from industry	7	20	40	61	32	71.38%	3.57	1.079
3	Students doing work in groups	13	31	39	51	26	65.75%	3.29	1.189
4	Students create a daily journal to find out the achievements of the work presented by the supervisor from industry	15	37	54	38	16	60.38%	3.02	1.119
5	Implementation of internship improves student's competency	1	8	34	66	51	79.75%	3.99	0.890
6	Internship assessment is given objectively by supervisor from industry	3	4	45	73	35	76.63%	3.83	0.863

273

Table 4. Result of data processing for variable: The role of lecturer supervisor.

No	Questions	Score					Value	Mean	SD
		1	2	3	4	5			
1	Guidance process with the lecturer supervisor went well	7	11	56	60	26	70.88%	3.54	0.990
2	Lecturer supervisor visited the internship place	91	40	17	8	4	34.25%	1.71	1.012
3	Lecturer supervisor knows the routine achievement of student	31	46	60	17	6	50.13%	2.51	1.040
4	There is good communication between the lecturer supervisor and supervisor of industries related to the implementation of students' internship	59	42	40	9	10	43.63%	2.18	1.176
5	Students can easily interact with the lecturer supervisor if got into trouble during internship	19	31	59	35	16	59.75%	2.99	1.138
6	Internship assessment is given objectively by lecturer supervisor	5	13	54	59	29	71.75%	3.59	0.980
7	Internship seminar conducted in accordance with procedures	8	11	60	55	26	70%	3.50	1.009

Table 5. Result of data processing for variable: Student job description during internship.

No	Questions	Score					Value	Mean	SD
		1	2	3	4	5			
1	Students are given a clear job description from lecturer	14	51	56	30	9	56.13%	2.81	1.025
2	Students get the materials/practices in accordance with their competency	6	16	44	69	25	71.38%	3.57	0.994
3	Tasks/target given by the supervisor of industry in accordance with time length of internship	5	15	65	60	15	68.13%	3.41	0.899
4	Supervisor from industry explained job description to students during the internship	3	8	43	64	42	76.75%	3.84	0.938

on campus so that, when asked for help to fill out a questionnaire, they responded immediately. In contrast, the classes of 2000–2008, when asked for help in completing the questionnaire, do not quickly respond to it because they are already busy at work or with other activities.

Tables 2 to 5 show the results of the respondents' data processing from four research variables:

Based on the data in Table 2, the procedures for implementing the internship in the Electrical Engineering Education Department still need some improvement. Also, there is no cooperation between the department and industry regarding the internship program. Based on the data in Table 3, the role of the industry supervisor is good.

Based on the data in Table 4, the role of the lecturer supervisor needs some improvement. There is no communication process between the lecturer supervisor and the industry supervisor. Based on the data in Table 5, the students' job description given to students in the internship has been good.

4 CONCLUSION

Based on respondent data and internship evaluation standards, the procedures for implementing

the internship in the Electrical Engineering Education Department still need some improvements due to lack of socialization of internship programs to students and the absence of cooperation between the department and industry regarding the internship program. From the results of the respondent data, the supervising role of the industry is good. One thing lacking was that there were supervisors who required their students to make a regular journal, while others did not. The role of the lecturer supervisor needs to be improved because they lacked information about the students' achievements during the internship, missed visits to the internship places and did not have sufficient communication with supervisors from industry. Based on the respondent data collected, students' job descriptions in the internship have been sufficient.

REFERENCES

Arifin, Z. (2010). *Model-model evaluasi program*. Bandung: UPI Press.
Billett, S. (2011). *Vocational education*. Brisbane, Australia: Springer.
Binder, J.F. et al. (2015). The academic value of internships : Benefits across disciplines and student backgrounds. *Contemporary Educational Psychology, 41*, 73–82.

Chanlin, L.. & Hung, W. (2015)..Evaluation of an online internship journal system for interns. *Procedia—Social and Behavioral Sciences, 191,* 1024–1027.

Chopvitayakun, S. (2015). Android application to enhance performance of internship program implementing cloud computing platform and infrastructure. *Procedia—Social and Behavioral Sciences, 197,* 2530–2538.

Coco, M. (2000). Internships: A try before you buy arrangement. *SAM Advanced Management Journal, 65*(2), 41.

Gaba, A. (2015). Development and evaluation of an e-portfolio for use in a dietetic internship program. *Procedia—Social and Behavioral Sciences, 174,* 1151–1157.

Gamboa, V. et al. (2013). Internship quality predicts career exploration of high school students. *Journal of Vocational Behavior, 83*(1), 78–87.

Hadi, M.Y.A. et al. (2015). Application of thinking skills in career: A survey on Technical and Vocational Education Training (TVET) qualification semi-professional job duties. *Procedia—Social and Behavioral Sciences, 211,* 1163–1170.

Koc, E. et al. (2014). Leisure, sport & tourism education Are internship programs encouraging or discouraging?—A viewpoint of tourism and hospitality students in Turkey. *Journal of Hospitality, Leisure, Sport & Tourism Education, 15,* 135–142.

Liviu, N.M. & Ana-Andreea, M. (2013). Issues on improving internships in technical universities in Romania. *Procedia—Social and Behavioral Sciences, 84,* 1757–1762.

Polat, Z. et al. (2010). Internship education analysis of vocational school students. *Procedia—Social and Behavioral Science,* 3452–3456.

Regionalization and Harmonization in TVET – Abdullah et al. (Eds)
© 2017 Taylor & Francis Group, London, ISBN 978-1-138-05419-6

Effect of installation of a T-junction on the performance of an air-conditioning system

E.T. Berman, A. Setiawan, S. Hasan & M. Mutaufiq
Department of Mechanical Engineering Education, Universitas Pendidikan Indonesia, Jawa Barat, Indonesia

ABSTRACT: This study aims to determine the effect of the installation of a T-junction on the performance of an air-conditioning system. The T-junction is installed to separate the phase of the refrigerant liquid and vapor that flows to the evaporator. Tests are carried out on an air-conditioning system of air-cooled water with a chiller capacity of 9495 kJ and whose working fluid is R-22. Data is collected during the time when the water temperature is at a steady state of T = 14°C to T = 10°C and the superficial velocity of the water is set to a constant of 0.5 m/s. The experimental results showed that the T-junction installation on the air-conditioning system generates an increase in the refrigerating effect and Coefficient of Performance (COP) systems by 4% and 10%, respectively. The pressure ratio is also lower, causing the compressor to work more efficiently and reducing the electric power needed by the air-conditioning system.

1 INTRODUCTION

Air-conditioning systems (AC), which play an important role in creating the comfort of occupants, are among the largest energy consumers in buildings. Furthermore, as most people spend more than 90% of their time inside (Qi et al., 2012), the development of an energy efficient AC system will play a key role in reducing energy consumption.

Normally, more than 50% of the energy used in buildings is consumed by the AC system (Yau, 2008; Enteria & Mizutani, 2011). In Indonesia, the largest electric energy consumption is dominated by the air-conditioning system, especially in areas that have hot and humid climates, such as Jakarta (Kubota et al., 2014). The conditions in other places are not very different. In the United States, the energy consumption of AC systems uses about 50% of the energy in buildings (Pérez-Lombard et al., 2008). In Europe, around 40% of energy consumption is represented in commercial and residential buildings (Balaras et al., 2007). More than 70% of building energy consumption is to support cooling systems in the Middle East (El-Dessouky et al., 2004). The growing reliance on AC systems in residential, commercial and industrial environments has resulted in a huge increase in energy usage, particularly in the summer months. An understanding of the energy efficiency of the air-conditioning system is very important, both to protect consumers from the high costs of basic electricity and to protect the environment from the negative impacts of greenhouse gas emissions generated by the use of electrical equipment.

The method of improving the performance of an air-conditioning system can be achieved by managing the distribution of the two-phase state of refrigerant flowing to the evaporator (Cho et al., 2003; Zou & Hrnjak, 2014). The two-phase refrigerant generated in the expansion process is separated into saturated vapor and a liquid stream. The liquid phase is supplied into the evaporator, in which it vaporizes and provides the cooling capacity, while the refrigerant vapor will produce superheat vapor. Therefore, it is important to improve refrigerant distribution to the evaporator. The method of phase separation using a T-junction was first introduced by the Oranje in 1973, which examines the separation of the two-phase flow of gas-liquid (Wang et al., 2008). Then, Tuo and Hrnjak (2012a, b) presented the study of vapor-liquid refrigerant (R-134a and R-410 A) separation in vertical impact T-separators for use in Flash Gas Bypass (FGB) vapor compression systems. His research states that by using FGB, a COP of 4% - 7% higher is achieved than by using a system with Direct Expansion (DX).

This study aims to determine the effect of the T-junction installation on the performance of an air-conditioning system that uses the working fluid R-22. A T-junction was installed after the expansion device, wherein only the liquid refrigerant was supplied to the evaporator, while the refrigerant vapor in the bypass went directly to the suction line. The implementation of the reconfiguration of the traditional system is expected to reduce the load of the compressor when doing the work of compression, which will impact on the increase of the Coefficient of Performance (COP) system and decrease the value of the compressor power required as its driving force (Berman et al., 2016).

2 MATERIALS AND METHODS

Figure 1 shows the schematic of the experimental setup. This experimental setup was designed to evaluate the effects of the T-junction installation on the performance of the air-conditioning systems. The experimental setup consisted of a refrigeration circuit, a water circuit and a control measurement system. The refrigeration circuits consisted of a reciprocating compressor, an air-cooled condenser, an evaporator, an accumulator, an expansion device and a T-junction. The water circuits consisted of a cooling coil, a water pump and two hand valves. The control measurement system included the pressure gage, the temperature sensor and a flow meter. R-22 is used as a primary working fluid, while water is used as a secondary heat transfer fluid at the evaporator.

The experiment will be conducted under two conditions. At the beginning of the research, the system was operated under normal conditions (without a T-junction) to obtain baseline data on the performance of an air-conditioning system. After that, the T-junction was installed to the refrigeration circuits. Before the second data retrieval, the system was flushed using nitrogen to eliminate dirt, moisture and other substances in the system that might affect its performance. Then, the system was filled with R-22 weighing 0.76 kg in accordance with the recommendation of the manufacturer. Data capture started when the temperature of the water was 14°C, with the assumption that the system was steady. Next, changes were observed until the temperature of the water reached 10°C. During the study, the superficial velocity of the water to a cooling coil is set constant at 0.5 m/s and the temperature of the environment was kept at 28°C ± 2°C. The research procedure was implemented three times to obtain the average value.

3 RESULTS AND DISCUSSION

3.1 Refrigerating effect

Figure 2 shows the results of the refrigerating effect of the air-conditioning system under two testing conditions: with a T-junction and under normal conditions (without a T-junction).

In general, the refrigerating effect generated by the system operating with a T-junction has a higher value than that of the normal system. In the normal system, the refrigerating effect generated when the water was 14°C was 164.48 kJ/kg. Then, it fell to 163.44 kJ/kg when the temperature of the water was 10°C. On the other hand, in the system that operated with a T-junction, the refrigerating effect generated when the water was 14°C was 167.6 kJ/kg. Further, this increased to 169.72 kJ/kg when the temperature of the water was 10°C. Based on the results, there had been a 4% increase in the refrigerating effect of the system operating with a T-junction. The effects of the use of the T-junction on the air-conditioning system resulted in a smaller ratio of discharge and suction pressures, causing the compression work that compresses vapor from condensing pressure to evaporating pressure to become shorter. Such results/values will contribute to the energy consumption of the compressor, which becomes smaller.

3.2 Coefficient of performance

Figure 3 presents the Coefficient of Performance (COP) data of two conditions of the air-conditioning system testing.

In the normal system, the COP decreased along with the decreasing temperature of the water. At first, the obtained COP was 5.05 when the temperature of the water was 14°C; the COP of 4.85 was obtained when the water temperature was 10°C. Further, when the system employed a T-junction, the COP increased slowly. When the temperature

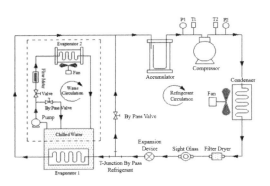

Figure 1.   The schematic of the experimental setup.

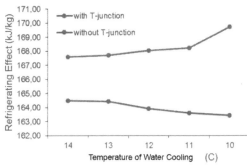

Figure 2.   The results of the refrigerating effect of the air-conditioning system under two testing conditions: with a T-junction and normal (without a T-junction).

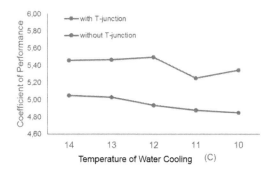

Figure 3. The Coefficient of Performance (COP) system of two conditions of the air-conditioning system testing.

of the water was 14°C, the obtained COP was 5.46. Then, the value fluctuated and rose to 5.50 when the water temperature was 12°C. Next, the COP fell to 5.34 when the water temperature was 10°C. These results indicate that the use of a T-junction on the refrigeration system results in an increased value of COP of 10%. The greater value of COP indicates that the system worked properly. The value of COP is influenced by the amount of heat that can be absorbed by the refrigerant flowing in the evaporator (refrigerating effect), and the compression work performed by the compressor when it compressed the low temperature-pressured refrigerant vapor to high temperature-pressured refrigerant vapor. If the value of the refrigerating effect is big and the value of compression work is small, the COP obtained will be large. The bigger the value of the refrigerating effect and the smaller the value of the compression work, the better will be the value of COP obtained.

4 CONCLUSIONS

Research on the installation of a T-junction to improve the performance of the air-conditioning has been conducted. To demonstrate the performance improvement of the air-conditioning system, we tested the refrigeration system in two different conditions. The results indicate that the T-junction installation on the air-conditioning system generates an increased value of the refrigerating effect and the coefficient of performance system, respectively by 4% and 10%. This has a significant implication for the lighter work of the compressor and low electrical power needed by the air-conditioning systems.

ACKNOWLEDGMENT

The author would like to thank the KemenRistekDikti for funding this research through the research program of decentralization, on research scheme *penelitian hibah bersaing*.

REFERENCES

Balaras, C.A., Grossman, G., Henning, H.M., Ferreira, C.A.I., Podesser, E., Wang, L. & Wiemken, E. (2007). Solar air-conditioning in Europe-An overview. *Renewable and Sustainable Energy Reviews, 11*(2), 299–314.

Berman, E.T., Hasan, S. & Mutaufiq, M. (2016). Enhancing the performance of the domestic refrigerator with hot gas injection to suction line. *IOP Conference series: Materials science and engineering, 128*, 012028.

Cho, H., Cho, K. & Kim, Y.S. (2003). Mass flowrate distribution and phase separation of R-22 in multi-microchannel tubes under adiabatic condition. In *ASME 2003 1st International Conference on Microchannels and Minichannels (pp. 527–533)*. American Society of Mechanical Engineers.

El-Dessouky, H., Ettouney, H. & Al-Zeefari, A. (2004). Performance analysis of two-stage evaporative coolers. *Chemical Engineering Journal, 102*(3), 255–66.

Enteria, N. & Mizutani, K. (2011). The Role of the thermally activated desiccant cooling technologies in the issue of energy and environment. *Renewable and Sustainable Energy Reviews, 15*(4), 2095–2122.

Kubota, T., Surahman, U. & Higashi, O. (2014). *A comparative analysis of household energy consumption in Jakarta and Bandung*. 30th International PLEA Conference, no. December: 1–8.

Pérez-Lombard, L., Ortiz, J. & Pout, C. (2008). A Review on buildings energy consumption information. *Energy and Buildings, 40*(3), 394–398.

Qi, R., Lu, L. & Yang, H. (2012). Investigation on air-conditioning load profile and energy consumption of desiccant cooling system for commercial buildings in Hong Kong. *Energy and Buildings, 49*, 509–18.

Tuo, H. & Hrnjak, P. (2012a). Experimental study of refrigerant two phase separation in a compact vertical T-junction. *In ASHRAE Transactions, 118*, 672–80.

Tuo, H. & Hrnjak, P. (2012b). Flash gas bypass in mobile air-conditioning system with R134a. *International Journal of Refrigeration, 35*(7), 1869–1877.

Wang, L., Wu, Y., Zheng, Z., Gua, J., Zhang, J. & Tang, C. (2008). Oil-water two phase flow inside T-junction. *International Journal of Multiphase Flow, 20*, 147–153.

Yau, Y.H. (2008). The Use of a double heat pipe heat exchanger system for reducing energy consumption of treating ventilation air in an operating theatre-A full year energy consumption model simulation. *Energy and Buildings, 40*(5), 917–25.

Zou, Y. & Hrnjak, P.S. (2014). Single-phase and two-phase flow pressure drop in the vertical header of microchannel heat exchanger. *International Journal of Refrigeration, 44*, 12–22.

Regionalization and Harmonization in TVET – Abdullah et al. (Eds)
© 2017 Taylor & Francis Group, London, ISBN 978-1-138-05419-6

Analysis of computer science curriculum development to improve competency of graduates for global workforces market

F. Purwani & Y. Desnelita
Universitas Negeri Padang, Padang, Indonesia

ABSTRACT: Development of the curriculum requires particular attention to educational goals by looking at the needs of industries. This research aims to analyze the qualifications of the computer science curriculum in Indonesia and compare it with the ACM-IEEE Computing Curricula 2013, as well as the actual needs of industries. The research results showed that there is no significant difference between the computer science curriculum in Indonesia and the ACM-IEEE Computing Curricula 2013. Many graduates are considered to have low competency, which is mainly caused by poor synchronization between the curriculum taught and the needs of industries. It also found that there has been no consistent collaboration between curriculum development in universities, stockholders and relevant government bodies. The study proposes a curriculum development model that enables better collaboration between the parties using cloud technology, which will reduce the competency gap between graduates and what industries need.

1 INTRODUCTION

1.1 Background

The inclusion of Indonesia in the Asean Economic Community (AEC) has significantly increased competition in the labor market, because every citizen of AEC countries is free to move and work throughout ASEAN.

On the other hand, the impact of globalization and rapid technology evolution demands that graduates have suitable competencies in both knowledge and technology application. The condition above is becoming more challenging as there is also an indication of a loss of employment opportunity due to minimum employment information. There is no curriculum portal that is developed and integrated to support the labor market (Baumgartner, 2013), which results in a reduced chance of obtaining jobs (Fardoun et al., 2014). Research in Japan reported that there is a gap between the skills required by industries and those that the graduates obtained from the educational institutions (Kobata et al., 2014).

The above gap also occurs in the field of information technology. The demand for ICT specialists is not in line with the computer science curriculum, in particular for the ICT industry in Europe (Milosz & Lukasik, 2015). In this case, steps were taken by the educational institutions to redesign the curriculum to better meet the needs of industries and the global market.

1.2 The research objective

This research was done to analyze the current computer science curriculum and compare it with ACM-IEEE Computing Curricula 2013 in view of the demands of the global labor market. Additionally, this research aimed to develop a common platform for information systems for the labor market and the computer science curriculum in universities.

1.3 Framework theory

Computer science is concentrated into three major fields: software design and implementation, development of effective methods to solve computation problems and development of a new way of using computers. Curriculum development of computer science, information engineering, information system, computer engineering and their derivatives should be in alignment with the joint task force ACM Association for Computing Machinery, which has established the standard curriculum.

Based on Indonesian government regulation no. 8 in 2012, curriculum development should follow KKNI (Kerangka Kualifikasi Nasional Indonesia (Indonesia National Qualification Framework)). In addition to that, the computer science curriculum also needs to refer to APTIKOM as the association of higher education for information and computers in Indonesia. APTIKOM has been appointed to standardize the curriculum based on KKNI. So far, APTIKOM has mapped the competency of graduates in five domains: computer engineering, computer science, software engineering, information systems and information technology (APTIKOM, 2015).

ACM (Association for Computing Machinery) was established in 1942. ACM has developed methodologies and standard processes, including a software engineering Body of Knowledge (BoK) following global evolution of research and technology.

Software engineering has evolved into a new subject where students of computer science are aiming to become software engineers, as reported in Computing Curricula 2005 (CC2005) published by IEEE (Institute of Electrical and Electronics Engineers).

The CC2005 has been updated and additional reports with updated versions were attached: in 2008, the Computing Curricula Information Technology was approved; in 2010, the Computing Curricula Information Systems was completed and published; Computer Science 2013 (CS2013). (Force, 2013).

The employment market in Indonesia continued to grow in 2014 and 2015. In August 2014 it was estimated that the Indonesian population had reached

Table 1. Computer science branches.

Subject	BoK
Mathematic Science	DS- Discrete Structure
	CS- Computation Science
Algorithms and Programing	AC- Algorithms and Complexity
	PL- Programing Languages
Intelligent System	IS- Intelligent System
Software Engineering	SE- Software Engineering
	IM- Information Management
	SIPP- Social Issues and Professional Practice
	HCI- Human-Comp Interaction
	PBD- Platform-based Development
Architecture Computer	GV- Graphics and Visualization
	AO- Architecture and Organization
	OS- Operating System
	SF- Systems Fundamentals
	IAS- Information Assurance and Security
Distributed System	PDC- Parallel & Distributed Computing
	NC- Network and Communication

Source: (APTIKOM, 2015)

Table 2. Number of core lecture hours CS2013 in comparison with previous curricula.

Knowledge area	CS2013		CS2008	CS2005
	Tier1	Tier2	Core	Core
AC- Algorithms and Complexity	19	9	31	31
AO- Architecture and Organization	0	16	36	36
CS- Computation Science	1	0	0	0
DS- Discrete Structure	37	4	43	43
GV- Graphics and Visualization	2	1	3	3
HCI- Human-Comp Interaction	4	4	8	8
IAS- Information Assurance and Security	3	6	–	–
IM- Information Management	1	9	11	10
IS- Intelligent System	0	10	10	10
NC- Network and Communication	3	7	15	15
OS- Operating System	4	11	18	18
PBD- Platform-based Development	0	0	–	–
PD- Parallel & Distri- buted Computing	5	10	–	–
PL- Programing Languages	8	20	21	21
SE- Software Engineering	6	22	31	31
SF- Systems Fundamentals	18	9	–	–
SP- Social Issues and Professional Practice	11	5	16	16
Total Core Hours	165	143	290	280

All Tier1 + All Tier2 Total	308
All Tier1 + 90% of Tier2 Total	293.7
All Tier1 + 80% of Tier2 Total	279,4

Source: (Force, 2013)

252.7 million, with 121.9 million in the workforce. The number of jobs recorded an increase of 1.7% from August 2013 to 2014, while the workforce recorded an increase of 1.4% in the same period. This trend indicates a reduction of the unemployment rate within the workforce (Ilo, 2015).

According to the Head of Research and Development of Human Resources—Ministry of Communication and Information, Indonesia is still short of the number of information technology professionals needed. This is mainly because information technology graduates only have limited skills as operators and programmers. On the other hand, those who have more comprehensive skills tend to work abroad. Up until 2015, Indonesia was estimated to require 6 million IT related employees who needed to be properly trained.

A study done on five national news media within a 126 day period found that there were 5 IT related vacancies out of 678 jobs vacancies. If the trend continues, there will be 1,800 vacancies in the near future (Wahid, 2006).

Cloud computing is a technology evolution that combines the utilization of computational technology and internet based development. Cloud computing is a kind of computing that is highly scalable and uses virtualized resources that can be shared by the users. Users do not need any background knowledge of the services (Ograph & Morgens, 2008). A user on the internet can communicate with many servers at the same time and these servers exchange information among themselves. Cloud computing is becoming an adoptable technology for many organizations, with its dynamic scalability and usage of virtualized resources as a service through the internet (Ercana, 2010).

2 RESEARCH METHODOLOGY

This study begins with a literature study and the results are then compared with the computer science curriculum in Indonesia and ACM-IEEE 2013, as well as literature on labor market information in Indonesia.

Furthermore, the portal designs curriculum models are integrated with the work market and the government use of cloud computing technology.

3 RESULT

3.1 Computer science curriculum in Indonesia (APTIKOM) and ACM-IEEE 2013

Comparative analysis done between the computer science curriculum in Indonesia as per APTIKOM and ACM-IEEE 2013 suggested that there is no significant difference, which means that our curriculum can be used internationally.

However, the implementation of the above curriculum is not directly improving the competitiveness of the graduates nationally or internationally due to the lack of monitoring and evaluation of contents independently done by each institution. For that reason, it is important to develop a curriculum that is suitable for the actual labor market.

3.2 ICT labor market in Indonesia

Almost all aspects of work require information technology. The Ministry of Communications and Information indicates that there are 300,000 IT graduates from 250 study programs of various educational institutions in Indonesia annually. However, Indonesia is still struggling to meet industries demands, since 75% of those graduates were absorbed by non-IT industries (Kompas.com, 2013). Similar data was reported by the Economist Intelligence Unit (EIU). The above fact needs to be properly addressed so that the graduates can be more competitive and able to work in the field that is in line with their majors.

3.3 Model of information system curriculum with cloud computing integration

It is important to have government participation in order to bridge the gap between universities and

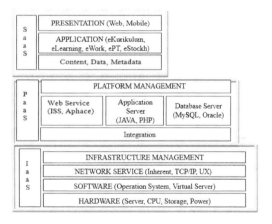

Figure 1. The model of IT development using cloud computing picture.

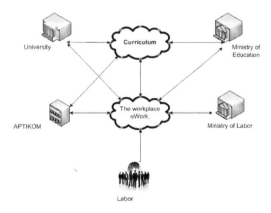

Figure 2. Architecture of workforce IT cloud.

industries as stakeholders, so that the curriculum can better fit the requirements. For that reason, a new model of information system curriculum with cloud computing needs to be developed. The study found that an architecture of information technology can be implemented for universities' curricula, industries, related government bodies, as well as job seekers in Indonesia.

Universities: Educational institutions that develop curricula to build students' knowledge and produce qualified professionals.

APTIKOM: The association of curriculum standardization as per government regulation, in this case the Ministry of Education.

Ministry of Workforce: Government body that provides information on the labor market's requirements. The data is processed based on input from industries as stakeholders for the specific skills needed. This institution is also specialized in providing training for participants.

Worker-Job seeker: The subject that can take the job offer based on their core competency and curricula.

4 CONCLUSIONS

Based on the analysis, the computer science curricula applied by APTIKOM in Indonesia is in agreement with ACM-IEEE Curricula 2013, even though the focus of study and skills development depend on each educational institution. Therefore, the graduates produced should be able to compete in the global labor market.

It is important to have a new feature and cloud computing service in educational institutions based on the requirements of industries as stakeholder, as well as design and strategy from each of the institutions with support from the government. Therefore, it is important to prepare the internal cloud for information system curricula and workforces so that job seekers can understand the required skills offered and minimize the skill gaps.

Government regulation is also critical in order to fully apply IT cloud computing and ensure smooth implementation in all elements, such as education institutions, stakeholder organizations and the public. Therefore, IT division should be placed and monitored by the government, in this case the Ministry of Workforce.

REFERENCES

Asosiasi Perguruan Tinggi Informatika dan Komunikasi (APTIKOM). (2015). *Naskah Akademik Kerangka Kualifikasi Nasional Indonesia (KKNI) Rumpun Ilmu Informatika dan Komputer.*

Baumgartner, I. (2013). Using enterprise level software for a large scale compulsory course in an information systems undergraduate program—An example from singapore. *Proceedings—2013 Learning and Teaching in Computing and Engineering,* 162–166.

Ercana, T. (2010). Effective use of cloud computing in educational institutions. *Procedia Social and Behavioral Sciences, 2.*

Fardoun, H.M., Cipres, A.P. & Alghazzawi, D.M. (2014). Centralizing students curriculums to the professional work. *Procedia—Social and Behavioral Sciences, 122,* 373–380.

Force, A.J.T. (2013). *Computer Science Curricula 2013: Curriculum guidelines for undergraduate degree program in computer science.* Technical report, Association for Computing Machinery (ACM) IEEE Computer Society.

Ilo, K. (2015). *Tren Ketenagakerjaan dan Sosial di Indonesia 2014–2015 Memperkuat daya saing dan produktivitas.*

Kobata, K., Uesugi, T., Adachi, H. & Aoyama, M. (2014). A curriculum develop method for professional software engineers and its evaluation. *In Teaching Assessment and Learning International Conference on,* 480–487.

Kompas.com. (2013). *Indonesia Kurang Tenaga Ahli Teknologi Informasi.*

Milosz, M. & Lukasik, E. (2015). Reengineering of computer science curriculum according to technology changes and market needs. *IEEE Global Engineering Education Conference,* 689–693.

Ograph, B.T. & Morgens, Y.R. (2008). Cloud Computing. *Communications of the ACM, 51*(7), 9–11.

Peraturan Presiden Republik Indonesia Nomor 8 Tahun 2012 tentang Kerangka Kualifikasi Nasional Indonesia.

Wahid, F. (2006). Keahlian Teknologi Informasi yang di Butuhkan di Indonesia: Hasil Pemindaian Media Massa dan Survey, 554–561. *KNSI.*

The implementation of radio frequency identification as a learning tool to increase a student's creativity

G.R. Dantes, K. Sudarma, G. Nurhayata & N. Dantes
Universitas Pendidikan Ganesha, Indonesia

ABSTRACT: The aim of this research was to increase the quality of the learning process through Radio Frequency Identification (RFID) implementation. This technology was implemented in early childhood education programs (PAUD) at Universitas Pendidikan Ganesha as a pilot study. The product provided the flexibility for students to identify the objects around them. The object was given a RFID card as an identification number, while the information was saved in the database server as text. The communication that is used in this process is radio frequency transmission. Algorithm of conversion from text to audio was also implemented in this research. This research used a prototyping methodology to produce a RFID as a learning tool. The research revealed that the use of RFID as a learning media helped to build creativity and courage, while at the same time provided an exercise to develop listening skills and the ability to communicate ideas, although it was not very suitable for students who learn visually and kinesthetically.

1 INTRODUCTION

The rapid development of Information and Communication Technology (ICT), which is in line with the current progress in this era, impacts on several aspects, such as: education, economy, tourism, industry, social, culture and art. The use of ICT becomes more and more inevitable for educators and teachers in order to achieve a better quality of education. This is expected to have significant effects on the improvement of national character, which will lead to the golden year in 2045.

Some of the latest ICT implementations to support the teaching and learning process are electronic learning (e-learning), mobile learning (m-learning) and ubiquitous learning (u-learning). E-learning is one of the most rapidly developed ICT implementations, but this system has been mostly implemented as the content management system, into which educators upload the learning content for the students to access without being limited by time or space. A recent development of e-learning, however, has led to adaptive learning. Adaptive learning is a model of e-learning that tries to incorporate the role of teachers in the traditional learning process. It is designed to identify the students' prior ability and to recognize the students' characteristics: learning style, motivation, etc. In this case, e-learning acts as an agent of learning because it can respond to the students' characteristics in order to optimize the learning process and the achievement of the learning goals.

One of the many ways to improve e-learning as an agent of learning is Radio Frequency Identification (RFID) technology, which allows automatic detection of objects through radio waves (Pathak & Joshi, 2009). Some of the advantages of using RFID in communication are: (1) RFID does not require line-of-sight to be operated, (2) RFID has a high memory capacity, (3) RFID can communicate with many tags at the same time without collision, (4) RFID requires more affordable tags and (5) it enables data encryption (Samekta Hadi, 2008).

Compared to barcodes, RFID allows the process of identification from a considerable distance with a longer unique ID that can be combined with manufacturing, product types and environmental conditions, such as temperature and dampness (Want, 2006). This is the reason behind the rise of RFID in many business processes, such as goods tracking, toll payment, machines able to read running documents, identity tracking, airport baggage tracking, animal tracking and libraries. RFID can identify goods quickly, it is more resistant to interference compared to barcode identification and it is not influenced by the reading angle. In the automation of a library system, for example, RFID can automatize the process of book loans, book returns and reports (Saputra et al., 2010). Further, Pathak and Joshi (2009) integrated RFID features with mobile devices for various future possibilities of detection from mobile phones, while Dantes et al. (2013) implemented RFID for optimizing tourism services in terms of providing guided tours in museums.

Taking into account the many benefecial features of RFID for the detection and retrieval of information, the present study implemented RFID as a learning tool that can increase students' creativity, in searching relevant media to develop e-learning.

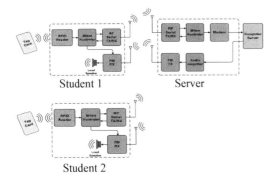

Student 1   Server

Student 2

Figure 1.   The design of RFID-based learning tools.

A RFID-based learning tool was developed to be used in early childhood education (PAUD). The tool consisted of hardware design and software design. Client hardware was used by the students to find out the information needed about an object, while the server hardware kept the information from each object in the form of text.

The components contained in the client hardware consisted of (1) RFID reader that reads the id tag attached to each object; (2) microcontroller that connects the client device and the server and acts as an audio file receiver that contains information about the object; (3) Radio Frequency (RF) serial (Tx/Rx) that sends and receives information from the server and receiver.

The server consists of (1) Radio Frequency (RF) serial (Tx/Rx), which sends and receives information to and from the client; (2) microcontroller that connects the server and the client, through which the data about the tag numbers of the objects are received and sent; (3) modem that connects the microcontroller to the server; and (4) audio amplifier that plays the audio file describing the specific object detected by the RFID reader. Figure 1 describes the design of the learning tools based on RFID in both the client and server.

2   RESEARCH METHOD

2.1   *Subject of study*

This study was conducted at PAUD of Universitas Pendidikan Ganesha (Undiksha). The subjects were the students of PAUD Undiksha, who were chosen purposively, while the samples were randomly selected.

2.2   *Data collection and analysis procedure*

The research instruments of the collecting data used in this study consisted of several instruments, namely: (1) observation sheet, (2) questionnaire, and

(3) interview guide. The data obtained were used in the preliminary evaluation of the product implementation. The data were collected through observation, interview and document study, where the questionnaire and rubrics of evaluation had been validated by expert judgments. Related to the aims of the research to improve students' creativity, the learning process that was observed in this study was themed "My Favorites", in which the students' creativity was observed and evaluated through a creativity test in the form of an oral test.

The learning process was designed as discovery learning, where the students become the center of the learning process and in which the students actively acquire knowledge through experiments in order to gain experience and principles of knowledge (Bruner, 1990). This model was adopted because it could support the development of the students' creativity.

Creativity is a mental process in the form of an idea or new product (Departemen Pendidikan dan Kebudayaan, 1995). It is the ability to show fluency, flexibility and originality and the ability of developing, enriching and specifying an idea (Munandar, 2009), which consists of aptitude and non-aptitude traits. Aptitude traits include fluency, flexibility, originality and elaboration, while non-aptitude traits include self-confidence, hard work, aesthetic appreciation and independence.

Munandar's (2009) definition of creativity was adopted in this study to form the rubric for assessing the students' creativity. The rubric was designed only to assess students' aptitude traits, thus the rubric was designed to measure five dimensions of students' creativity on a scale of 1 to 4, namely (1) fluency, which covers students' ability to deliver information fluently and clearly; (2) originality, which includes students' ability to add new information from their own repertoire; (3) imagination, which observes the students' ability to imagine events, processes and objects; (4) flexibility, which measures students' ability to provide alternatives for problem-solving; and (5) elaboration, which assesses students' ability in structuring specific information in their explanation.

2.3   *Data analysis*

The data analysis was conducted in the preliminary evaluation of the implementation of the research product. The data obtained were both quantitative and qualitative, thus the analysis was conducted statistically and non-statistically. The statistical analysis was used for describing the quantitative data, so it could be formulated into a qualitative meaning in order to make it easier to analyze and revise the product when it was deemed necessary. The non-statistical analysis was used to give meanings to the data description about the content, inferential logic, the process and the product (output).

3 RESULTS AND DISCUSSION

3.1 Result

This research was conducted at PAUD Undiksha Singaraja on Group B1 with a total number of 10 students. This study was conducted in three meetings. The first meeting was on 10th December, 2015; the second meeting was on 11th December, 2015; and the third meeting was on 12th December, 2015.

3.1.1 The summary of students' creativity scores on the first meeting

The data exposed that the total average score of the students' creativity in the first meeting was 60.5. Viewed from the creativity dimension, the fluency dimension (K1) was placed in first position with a total score of 28 and an average score of 70.0, then it was followed by imagination and flexibility (K3 & K4), which both gained total scores of 24 with average scores of 60.0. Meanwhile, the originality dimension (K2) gained a total score of 23 with an average score of 57.5 and the elaboration dimension (K5) gained a total score of 22 with an average score of 55.

3.1.2 The summary of students' creativity scores on the second meeting

The total average score of the students' creativity in the second meeting was 72.5. The dimension of flexibility (K4) was placed in first position with a total score of 32 and an average score of 80.0. Then, it is followed by the dimensions of fluency and originality (K1 & K2), which both had total scores of 30 and average scores of 75. Meanwhile, the dimension of imagination (K3) gained a total score of 29 with an average score of 72.5 and the dimension of elaboration (K5) gained a total score of 24 with an average score of 60.0.

3.1.3 The summary of students' creativity scores on the third meeting

The total average score of the students in the third meeting was 85.0. It can be seen from several dimensions showing creativity in which the dimension of fluency (K1) was placed in first position with a total score of 39 and an average score of 97.5. It is followed by the dimensions of flexibility and elaboration (K4 & K5) with total scores of 37 and 32 and average scores of 92.5 and 80.0. Furthermore, the dimensions of imagination (K3) and originality (K2) showed the same total score of 31 with an average score of 77.5.

3.1.4 The summary of the average percentage of the students' creativity from the first meeting to the third meeting

The analysis revealed an increasing score from the first meeting to the third meeting. At the first meeting, the average percentage of the students' creativity was 60.5, then at the second meeting it was 72.5 and at the third meeting it was 85. There was a 12% increase between the first meeting and the second meeting, and an increase of 24% between the first and third meetings. Figure 2 below describes the recapitulation of the average percentage of the students' creativity at the first, second and third meetings.

3.2 Discussion

3.2.1 RFID as learning tool

The RFID-based learning tool designed in this study was expected to help students to identify the objects around them and to explain them effectively, as a support to conventional teaching methods. During the data collection, the students were asked to identify the objects around them, such as fruits, vegetables and side dishes, with

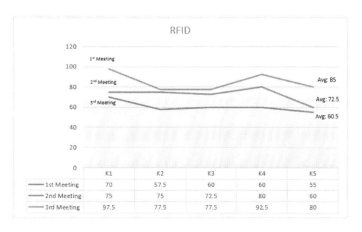

Figure 2. Summary of the average percentage of the students' creativity from the first, second and third meetings.

the theme of "My Favorite", and then they presented the information related to the object they detected. The way they presented the information reflected the students' creativity and they had to tell the information that they got from this tool in front of the class. The data analysis revealed that the RFID-based learning tool facilitated student-centered learning that allows students to experiment and experience the knowledge that they tried to acquire.

3.2.2 Students' creativity

The data analysis revealed that there was a different average percentage for each meeting (meetings 1–3). In the first meeting, the average of the students' creativity was quite low (60.5), because the students seemed to be unprepared for using the RFID learning tool. Because the tool relied on the students' listening skills, they were then directed to focus on listening to the information provided by the RFID-based learning tool. Furthermore, some students were reluctant to speak in front of the class, hence their low score.

In the second meeting, most students started to get used to the RFID-based learning tool. Furthermore, the students started to show more confidence in speaking in front of the class. Thus, the average score of this second meeting increased, especially in the dimensions of fluency, originality, imagination, flexibility and elaboration. Most students were able to explain and describe the information fluently; although some of the information was not very coherently delivered. However, some students covered this weakness with the ability to explain their own ideas and several problem-solving ideas were expressed, although the points were not too specific.

In the third meeting, the students looked very enthusiastic and they actively and confidently posed questions to find out more information. The rise in their confidence further supported their confidence in explaining the object they observed using the RFID-based learning tool. This explains why the third meeting resulted in the highest score in the students' creativity.

The increase in the average scores of students' creativity from the first to the third meeting can be associated with the student-centered design of the teaching and learning process. Discovery learning was adopted in this research, which helps the students to not only experience the process of knowledge acquisition, but also to facilitate the building of long-term knowledge. This is highlighted by Silberman (1996), who states that a good learning process is learning that involves students' mental physical actions. This kind of learning can activate the students' physical activity and is able to maximize the students' ability to think (Meier, 2002). This is in line with the Theory of Confucius that was well known

in the year of 450 BC, which states that 'Tell me and I will forget, Show me and I remember, and Involve me and I understand' (Neill, 2004).

4 CONCLUSION

This study concludes that (1) the use of RFID as a learning tool in the learning process facilitates the students' creativity, bravery and the ability to listen and communicate; (2) the listening media used by the RFID technology is effective for the students whose learning style is the audio type but less effective for those whose learning style is of the visual and kinesthetic type.

The study also found some limitations in terms of the quality of the prototype and the learning cycle. Therefore, further studies are expected to refine the RFID-based learning tool so that the information gained by the students will be clear, interesting and memorable. It is also expected that future studies will cover more meetings in order to gain a more reliable assessment on the impact of the RFID-based learning tools on the students' creativity.

REFERENCES

Bruner, J. (1990) *Acts of meaning*. Cambridge, MA: Harvard University Press

Dantes, G. R., Lasmawan, I. W. & Nurhayata, G. (2013). *Optimalisasi Layanan Pariwisata melalui Implementasi Model Panduan Wisatawan Otomatis Berbasis Radio Frequency Identification (RFID)*. Seminar Nasional Riset Inovatif ke-1, Bali, Indonesia, 21–22 November 2013. ISSN: 2339-1553.

Departemen Pendidikan dan Kebudayaan. (1995). *Program Kegiatan Belajar Taman Kanak-kanak*. Jakarta. Depdikbud.

Meier, D. (2002). *The Accelerated Learning Handbook: Panduan Kreatif dan Efektif Merancang Program Pendidikan dan Pelatihan*. Saduran. Bandung: Kaifa.

Munandar, U. (2009). *Pengembangan Kreativitas Anak Berbakat*. Jakarta: PT Rineka Cipta.

Neill, J. (2004). *Experiential learning cycle*. (Online), http://www.wilderdom.com/experiential/elc/ExperientialLearningCycle.htm diakses tgl 20 oktober 2008.

Pathak, R. & Joshi, S. (2009). *Recent trends in RFID and a java based software framework for its integration in mobile phones*. AH-ICI. First Asian Himalayas International Conference.

Samekta Hadi, R. A. (2008). *Implementasi Radio Frequency Identification (RFID) Pada Supply Chain*. Konferensi dan Temu Nasional Teknologi Informasi dan Komunikasi untuk Indonesia. Jakarta.

Saputra, D., Cahyadi, D. & Krisdalaksana, A. H. (2010). Sistem Otomasi Perpustakaan Dengan Menggunakan Radio Frequency Identification (RFID). *Jurnal Informatika Mulawarman, 5*(3), 1–7.

Silberman, M. L. (1996). *Active learning: 101 strategies to teach any subject*. Boston: Allyn and Bacon.

Want, R. (2006). An introduction to RFID technology. *IEEE Pervasive Computing, 5*(1), 25–33.

Regionalization and Harmonization in TVET – Abdullah et al. (Eds)
© 2017 Taylor & Francis Group, London, ISBN 978-1-138-05419-6

Face-expression detection: Detection of facial expression for optimizing the role of the e-learning system

G.R. Dantes, N.K. Suarni, P.H. Suputra, N.K.A. Suwastini & I.N. Jampel
Universitas Pendidikan Ganesha, Indonesia

ABSTRACT: The aim of this study was to produce the prototype of face-expression detection which was implemented in e-learning, to enable e-learning to recognize students' response and reaction toward the content and thus allowing it to provide proper feedback and stimulus for the students in e-learning. This is an effort to incorporate the active role of the teachers in the traditional learning, which is deemed crucial to be maintained in the learning process. The present study used prototyping methodology in which a prototype of facial detection system was developed and integrated to the existing e-learning systems. By applying Facial Action Coding System and Support Vector Machine (FACS & SVM) method to detect the facial expression, the prototype developed in this study showed an ability to detect the student's facial expression and then to give an automatic respond that suited the students' emotions and response as reflected through their facial expression. However, the present study has not evaluated the effectiveness of e-learning with the facial expression detection as compared to e-learning as content management system only, thus future research on such evaluation is still needed.

1 INTRODUCTION

The use of information and communication technology (ICT) has been widely developed in every field of study, including education. In the field of education, ICT has been extensively implemented for supporting the teaching-learning process. E-learning is one of the implementations of ICT in education, in both formal and informal context alike. However, most of the time e-learning is implemented only content management system (CMS). Therefore, research continues to pursue the development of e-learning that is more actively involved in students' learning process, a function of a traditional teacher in conventional classroom that is severely missing from the use of e-learning as CMS. Some of these crucial roles of an involved learning agent is the identification of students' emotion, expression, and motivations during the learning process though e-learning. In line with this development, the present study was aimed at developing e-learning model with the ability to detect students' facial expression for optimizing the role of e-Learning System through the integration of facial expression into the existing e-learning system.

This quest was made possible by the developments in technology, especially in the field of computer vision, image processing and artificial intelligent for human emotion detection (Shan et al., 2009; Awcock and Thomas, 1996; Chang et al., 2001; Liu and Yamda, 1997). The human expressions such

as smiling, sad, surprised or normal was detected through the features of human's eyebrows, eyes and mouth (Ekman and Friesen, 1978).

Raheja and Kumar (2010) further developed a system to detect human expression from the movements of the eye mouth and hand using Viola Jones method, with the incorporation of add-boosted classifier and simple token finding and matching through propagation neural network for web media. Anurag (2015) applied Eigen Face approach to build HSV (Hue-Saturation Value) color model for detecting facial expressions from picture and dataset generic in training process through which shocked, angry, happy or sad expressions were detected. Meanwhile, Zhu and Xiao (2015) successfully developed a system of human facial expression detection by using ASM (Active Shape Model) to do feature extraction by using optical flow technique to obtain information and characteristic of human facial expression with the implementation of multi-instance boosting model for detecting facial expression through video.

Closely related to the present study was a previous research for developing a prototype of Student Centered Learning as a learning paradigm, which emphasizes online learning to complement the existing learning model. However, this system did not function as expected as it failed to recognize students' motivation and response toward the course material (Dantes, 2009). A further study was conducted to develop a model of Intellectual

Dynamic Learning that enabled the students to explore the learning material and to choose the level of difficulties that suited their level of competence (Dantes and Suarni, 2010).

In the present study, a model was developed using Facial Action Coding System and Support Vector Machine (FACS & SVM) method to detect the facial expression as initiated by (Ekman and Friesen, 1978; Tian, 2001; Zhu and Xiao, 2015).

2 RESEARCH METHOD

This study was pilot study conducted in Guidance and Counseling Department of Universitas Pendidikan Ganesha. The students of Guidance and Counseling Department was purposefully determined with 100 students were randomly selected as the samples of the study. Students were photographed in different expression, i.e.: happy, sad, surprise, angry, and afraid. The data were divided into two groups, namely: 70% for data training and 30% for data testing.

3 RESULT AND DISCUSSION

3.1 *System description*

The model for facial expression in e-learning developed in this study was developed using Action Unit (Ekman & Friesen, 1978; Tian, et al., 2001), with the Facial Action Coding System (FACS) method applied for standardizing the procedures. FACS recognizes the specific nodes on the human face to mark the movement of the facial muscles. There are approximately 76 nodes affecting human facial expression, which are interconnected to form CANDIDE. CANDIDE is a face mask with parameters for encoding human facial expression.

The Action Unit Concept was firstly introduced by Hjortsjö (1970) in his book entitled Man's Face and Mimic Language. This concept was further developed by Ekman and Friesen (1978). The development of CANDIDE so far covers 4 stages. Original version was developed by Ridfalk with 75 vertices and 100 triangles. CANDIDE 1 was developed based on this original version with 79 vertices and 109 triangles. Bill Wels developed CANDIDE 2 with 160 vertices and 238 triangles, covering the front part of a head including hair, teeth and shoulder. CANDIDE 3 was advanced specifically to facilitate the animation of MEG-4 Facial Animation Parameter.

Support Vector Machine system was applied for categorizing the facial expressions detected into six classes of facial expressions: happy, sad, surprised, angry, afraid, and disgust. The classification was conducted by refering to the latest frame of capturing video (camera) through the CANDIDE

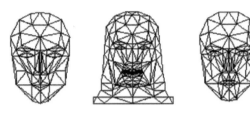

Figure 1. Left: Candide 1; Middle: Candide 2, and Right: Candide 3.

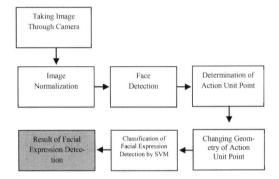

Figure 2. The classification of facial expression by using FACS dan SVM system.

coordinate points, where the the changes of geometical points in each coordinate between the first frame and the last frame become the input of multi class SVM system. The following figure describes the steps of the facial expression detection and classification adopted from Tian (2001).

3.2 *Prototype's design and implementation*

The following figures represent the pseudocode used to determine the beginning of Action Unit points.

```
#include <stdio.h>
#include <stdlib.h>
#include "opencv/highgui.h"
#include "stasm_lib.h"
Static void error(const char* s1, const char* s2){
   Printf("stasm version %a: %s %s\n",
stasm_VERSION,s1, s2);
   Exit(1);}
   Int main() {
      If (!stasm_init("../data", 0/*trace*/))
      Error("stasm_init_failed:", stasm_lasterr());
      Static const car * const path =
"../data/testface.jpg";
      Cv::Mat_<unsigned char> img (cv::imred(path,
CV_LOAD_IMAGE_GRAYSCALE));
      If(!img.data)
         Error ("Cannot load", path);
      If(!stasm_open_image((const char*)img.data,
img.cols, img.rows, path,1/*multiface*/,
10/*minwidth*/))
         Error("stasm_open_image failed:",
stasm_lasterr());
      Int foundface;
      Float landmarks[2*stasm_NLANDMARKS]; //x,y
cords (note the 2)
```

```
     Int nfaces = 0;
     While (1) {
     If(!stasm_search_auto (&foundface,
landmarks))Error("stasm search auto failed: ",
stasm lasterr());
     If (!foundface)
     Break;    //note break
     // for demonstration, convert from stasm 77
point to XM2VTS 68 points stasm_convert_shape
(landmarks, 68);
     // draw the landmarks on the image as white
dots
Stasm_force_points_into_image(landmarks, img.cols,
img.rows);
     For(int i=0;i<stasm_NLANDMARKS;
i++)Img(CVRound(Landmarks[i*2+1]),
CVRound(landmarks[i*2])) = 255;
     Nfaces++;}
     Print("%s:%d face(s)\n", path, nfaces);
     Fflush(stdout);
     Cv::imwrite("minimal2.bmp", img);
     Cv::imshow("stasm minimal2", img);
     Cv::waitKey();
     Return 0;
}
```

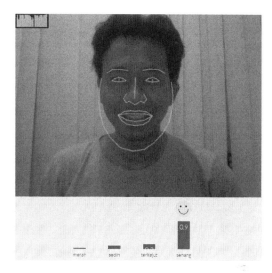

Figure 5.   The classification of happy expression.

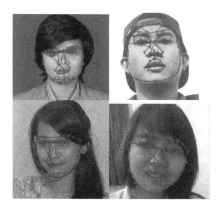

Figure 3.   The determination of the action unit points.

Figure 4.   The determination of action unit point through real time.

The code above were used to detect the marking Facial Action Units where the pictures taken was the images which had been applied using normalization and face detection.

The next step covered the classification of the class using Support Vector Machine. The output produced from the image above resulted form the identification of the face object, followed by initiation of the Action Unit from the model face. Figure 4 below displays the capture of the unit points of the face from a user when the user made eye contact with a computer through

camera installed on the computer for the e-learning. The capture shows that the prototype of the facial expression detection showed the ability to recognize happy, sad, angry and surprised facial expressions.

Figure 5 below displays an example of facial detection by the prototype, classifying the facial expression as happy.

3.3 *Implementation of face expression detection on e-learning system*

In order to optimize the role of the existing e-learning systems, a prototype of face expression detection was integrated into e-learning system. Face expression detection was used to detect and record the learners' facial expressions when they were using the e-learning. The facial expressions detected were then classified into six different types of emotions, according to which the students' response toward the e-learning material were categorized, which were then used by the system to give the appropriate response or treatment for the students. The process of face expression detection was done on the background, thus the interface was not displayed on the screen. The system started the detection of learners' facial expression as soon as the students opened the learning material on e-learning.

When the data on the students' facial expression were collected, the mean was calculated. The expression with the largest mean score was summed up as the dominant expression of learners when they were studying the material shown on the screen as used as the reference for determining the students' emotions and response toward the e-learning. When the system has decided the dominant expression of the learners', then it

291

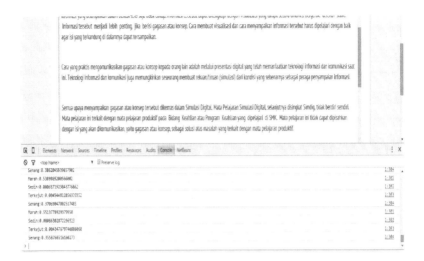

Figure 6.　The implementation of face-expression detection on e-learning system.

made decisions on what response and stimulus is deemed appropriate to respond to the students' emotion and reaction toward the content.

Figure 6 below is the samples of Face Expression Implementation on e-learning system.

4　CONCLUSION

This study developed a prototype of expression detection system by using Facial Action Coding System and Support Vector Machine (FACS and SVM), in which the facial expression detected through real time by considering the dominant facial expression along the process of detection. The study successfully integrated the prototype into the e-learning system for optimizing the existed e-learning system. It was intended to adopt the advantages of conventional learning, in terms of the identification of the students' response and emotions toward the learning process through their facial expressions as a reference for providing relevant response toward the students' emotions as expressed through their facial expression.

However, further studies are needed to precisely compare and evaluate the integration the effectiveness of e-learning as a content management system and e-learning system that had been integrated with facial expression detection.

REFERENCES

Anurag De, Ashim Saha & M.C. Pal. 2015. A Human Facial Expression Recognition Model Based on Eigen Face Approach. *International Conference on Advanced Computing Technologies and Applications (ICACTA)* 45: 282–289.

Awcock G.J. & Thomas R. 1996. *Applied Image Processing.* International Edition, McGraw-Hill, Inc.

Chang, Jyh-Yeong, Chen, Jia-Lin. 2001. *Automated Facial Expression Recognition System Using Neural Networks.* Department of Electrical and Control Engineering National Chiao Tung University Hsinchu:Taiwan 300, R.O.C.

Dantes, G.R. & Suarni, N.K. 2010. *Model Dynamic Intellectual Learning: Pergeseran Paradigma e-Learning menuju Adaptive Learning.* Prosiding Konferensi Nasional Sistem dan Informatika.

Dantes, G.R. 2009. *Dari e-Learning menuju Adaptive Learning: Pergeseran Paradigma Pembelajaran.* Seminar Nasional Universitas Negeri Jakarta.

Ekman, P. & Friesen, W.V. 1978. *The Facial Action Coding System: A Technique for The Measurement of Facial Movement.* San Francisco: Consulting Psychologists Press.

Hjortsjö, Carl-Herman. 1970. *Man's Face and Mimic Language.* Student litteratur Lund Sweden.

Liu Y. & Yamda Li. 1997. *Image Feature Extraction and Segmentation using Fractal Dimension.* International Conference on Information, Communication and Signal Processing.

Raheja, J.L. & Kumar, U. 2010. Human Facial Expression Detection From Detected In Captured Image Using Back Propagation Neural Network. *International Journal of Computer Science & Information Technology (IJCSIT)* 2(1).

Shan, C., Gong, S. & McOwan, P.W. 2009. Facial expression recognition based on local binary patterns: A comprehensive study. *Image and Vision Computing* 27: 803–816.

Shaoping Zhu & Yongliang Xiao. 2015. Intelligent Detection of Facial Expression Based on Image. *International Journal on Smart Sensing and Intelligent Systems* 8(1).

Tian, Y-I., Kanade, T. & Cohn, J.F. 2001. Recognizing action units for facial expression analysis. *PAMI* 23: 97–115.

Regionalization and Harmonization in TVET – Abdullah et al. (Eds)
© *2017 Taylor & Francis Group, London, ISBN 978-1-138-05419-6*

Performance investigation of an air-cooled chiller system using pure hydrocarbons as refrigerant

K. Sumardi, E.T. Berman & M. Mutaufiq
Departemen Pendidikan Teknik Mesin, Universitas Pendidikan Indonesia, Jawa Barat, Indonesia

ABSTRACT: An Air-Cooled Chiller system (ACCs) that is designed to work with R-22 was used as a test unit to assess the possibility of using hydrocarbons as a refrigerant. Pure propane, namely R-290, was used as a refrigerant. The purpose of this study was to determine the performance of air-cooled chiller systems using hydrocarbon R-290, which contains pure propane. The performance of the ACCs using hydrocarbons as a refrigerant was investigated and compared with the performance of ACCs when R-22 was used as a refrigerant. The effect of the discharge pressure and suction pressure on the refrigerating effect, a heat of compression and Coefficient of Performance (COP) were investigated. Finally, the COP and other results obtained in this experiment can provide a positive indication of using hydrocarbons as a refrigerant in the ACCs.

1 INTRODUCTION

R-22 has been widely used as the working fluid in the systems of Air-Conditioning (AC) and refrigeration. This is acceptable because R-22 has suitable qualifying properties, such as non-flammability, non-toxicity, stability and good materials compatibility (Powell, 2002). Unfortunately, it belongs to the family of Hydrochlorofluorocarbon (HCFC) refrigerants, which were considered as harmful to the environment and controlled by the Montreal protocol. HCFC refrigerants will be phased out by 2020 in developed countries and 2030 in developing countries (Park & Jung, 2009; Bolaji, 2010).

Since 1st January 2015, the Government of Indonesia determined that the types of refrigerant HCFC-22 and HCFC-141b are prohibited for use in the filling process of AC production and other refrigeration appliances. Therefore, it needs to be replaced with environmentally friendly refrigerants to protect the environment (Devotta et al., 2005a). The alternative refrigerants for R-22 for air-conditioning systems are grouped into three categories: (i) natural refrigerants, such as HydroCarbons (HC) and carbon dioxide; (ii) a mixture of HFC refrigerants; and (iii) a mixed refrigerant HFC/HC (Mohanraj et al., 2009).

Previous researchers had attempted to replace the refrigerant R-22 in air-conditioning systems with various types of alternative refrigerants. The use of HFC mixtures such as R-404 A, R-407C and R-410 A were leading substitutes for replacing R-22, based on the suitability of compression refrigeration systems, air-conditioning and heat pumps (Yang & Wu, 2013). Out of these three substitutes,

R-404 A is a good replacement for R-22 low-temperature applications (Ge & Cropper, 2008; Bolaji, 2011). Similarly, R407C was reported as a possible alternative to R-22 for compression based systems used for refrigeration, air-conditioning and heat pump systems, by changing the lubricant (Devotta et al., 2005b; Liu et al., 2008). Experiments using R-410A on air-conditioning and heat pump systems as a replacement for R-22 give greater hope, but require some changes and replacement of components (Zaghdoudi et al., 2010).

The refrigerant type of hydrocarbons, such as R-290, R-1270 and R-600a, have been identified as possible alternatives to R-22 for air-conditioning and heat pump systems (Chang et al., 2000; Palm, 2008; Corberán et al., 2008). However, some problems were still found. There is no working substance that could be called an ideal replacement for the different R-22 applications. Therefore, manufacturers are presenting R-22 substitutes for each application.

The purpose of this study was to determine the performance of air-cooled chiller systems using hydrocarbon R-290, which contains pure propane. The performance of systems that use R-290 will be investigated and the results will be compared with the performance of ACCS that use R-22. The results obtained from this study are expected to provide a positive indication to the use of hydrocarbons as refrigerants in air-conditioning systems. So that the process of refrigerant replacement is recommended for old equipment that still works. This involves the pure exchange of the refrigerant without any modifications to the refrigerating system and keeping the existing lubricant oil.

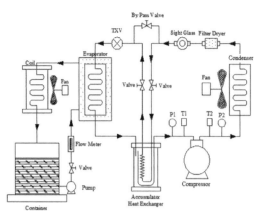

Figure 1. Schematic installation of air-cooled chiller as an experimental apparatus.

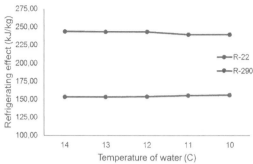

Figure 2. Data of the refrigerating effect of an air-cooled chiller system using R-22 and R-290.

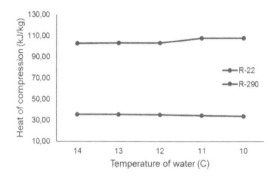

Figure 3. The heat of compression of the air-cooled chiller system using R-22 and R-290.

2 MATERIALS AND METHODS

Figure 1 shows a schematic diagram of the experimental apparatus. It includes a refrigerant circuit and a water circuit. Also, necessary instrumentation and safety and operational controls are installed. R-22 or R-290 is used as a primary working fluid, while water is used as a secondary heat transfer fluid at the evaporator.

The test was conducted on an air-conditioning system (Sanyo) with a capacity of 9495 kJ and the flow rate of the water flowing into the cooling coil was kept constant at 0.4 m/s by regulating the valve opening and this was measured by a flow meter (Mueller). Both sides, high and low pressure and two temperature sensors, are placed in the inlet and outlet parts of the compressor. During the study, the temperature of the environment was kept at 28°C ± 2°C. At the beginning of the research, the system was operated using R-22 to obtain baseline data of the performance of the ACCs. Before the second data retrieval, the system was flushed using nitrogen to eliminate dirt, moisture and other substances in the system that might affect its performance. Then, the system was filled with R-290. Data capture started when the temperature of the water was 14°C, with the assumption that the system was steady. Next, changes were observed until the temperature of the water reached 10°C.

3 RESULTS AND DISCUSSION

3.1 Refrigerating effect

Figure 2 shows the results of the refrigerating effect of an air-cooled chiller system using R-22 and R-290. In general, the refrigeration effects generated by R-290 had a higher value than those of R-22. In the R-22 system, the refrigerating effect generated when the water temperature was 14°C is 153.43 kJ/kg. This then increased slowly to 155.85 kJ/kg when the water temperature was 10°C. On the other hand, in the system which used R-290, the refrigerating effect generated when the water temperature reaches 14°C is 244.02 kJ/kg. Further, this decreased slowly to 239.78 kJ/kg when the water temperature was 10°C. Based on the results, there had been a 50% increase of the refrigeration effect in the system using R-290. The highest value of the refrigerating effect was on systems using R-290, due to it having a high latent heat of vaporization and so resulting in better cooling capacities.

3.2 Heat of compression

Figure 3 shows the heat of compression of the air-cooled chiller system using R-22 and R-290. In general, the heat of compression generated by the system using R-290 was higher than that of the system using R-22. In the R-290 system, the heat of compression generated when the water temperature was 14°C was 102.92 kJ/kg. Then, this

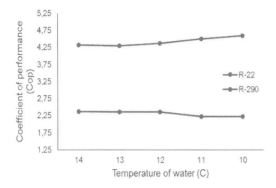

Figure 4. Data Coefficient of Performance (COP) systems that use R-22 and R-290.

increased gradually to 107.90 kJ/kg when the temperature dropped to 10°C. On the other hand, in the system that used R-22, the heat of compression generated when the water temperature was 14°C was 35.56 kJ/kg. Further, this gradually decreased to 33.88 kJ/kg when the water temperature reached 10°C. Based on the results, the heat of compression increased by approximately 68% when R-290 was used as the working fluid in the system ACCs. This is due to the high pressure ratio of the refrigerant and an increase in the enthalpy of the refrigerant at the inlet and outlet of the compressor.

3.3 Coefficient of Performance (COP)

Figure 4 presents the Coefficient of Performance (COP) for the systems that use R-22 and R-290. In general, the COP of R-22 is higher than that of R-290. The obtained COP in the use of R-22 was 4.32 when the temperature of the water was 14°C. Then, a COP of 4.60 was obtained when the water temperature was 10°C. Further, when the system used R-290, the COP decreased significantly. When the temperature of the water was 14°C, the obtained COP was 2.37. Then, the value slightly decreased to 2.22 when the water temperature was 10°C. The COP difference between the uses of R-22 and R-290 was approximately 50%. It is clearly shown in this figure that when the water temperature decreases the COP reduces for R-290. COP is inversely proportional to the heat of compression, therefore, an increase in the heat of compression reduces the COP of the system.

4 CONCLUSION

Research investigations on the use of R-290 as an alternative to R-22 have been implemented. In general, R290 is a promising alternative refrig-

erant to R22 because it has the ability to absorb more heat than the R-22 (the refrigerating effect is higher). However, the COP value for R290 is slightly lower, but this can be improved by specially designing a refrigeration system for it.

ACKNOWLEDGMENTS

The authors would like to thank the Rector of UPI for funding this research through PPDKI program 2016, on research scheme *penguatan kompetensi*.

REFERENCES

Bolaji, B.O. (2010). Experimental analysis of reciprocating compressor performance with eco-friendly refrigerants. Proceedings of the Institution of Mechanical Engineers, Part A. *Journal of Power and Energy, 224*(6), 781–786.

Bolaji, B.O. (2011). Performance investigation of ozone-friendly R404 A and R507 refrigerants as alternatives to R22 in a window air-conditioner. *Energy and Buildings, 43*(11), 3139–3143.

Chang, Y.S., Kim, M.S. & Ro, S.T. (2000). Performance and heat transfer characteristics of hydrocarbon refrigerants in a heat pump system. *International Journal of Refrigeration, 23*(3), 232–242.

Corberán, J.M., Segurado, J., Colbourne, D. & Gonzálvez, J. (2008). Review of standards for the use of hydrocarbon refrigerants in A/C, heat pump and refrigeration equipment. *International Journal of Refrigeration, 31*(4), 748–756.

Devotta, S., Padalkar, A.S. & Sane, N.K. (2005a). Performance assessment of HC-290 as a drop-in substitute to HCFC-22 in a window air conditioner. *International Journal of Refrigeration, 28*(4), 594–604.

Devotta, S., Padalkar, A.S. & Sane, N.K. (2005b). Performance assessment of HCFC-22 window air conditioner retrofitted with R-407C. *Applied Thermal Engineering, 25*(17–18), 2937–2949.

Ge, Y.T. & Cropper, R. (2008). Performance simulation of refrigerated display cabinets operating with refrigerants R22 and R404A. *Applied Energy, 85*(8), 694–707.

Liu, Z., Li, X., Wang, H. & Peng, W. (2008). Performance comparison of air source heat pump with R407C and R22 under frosting and defrosting. *Energy Conversion and Management, 49*(2), 232–239.

Mohanraj, M., Jayaraj, S. & Muraleedharan, C. (2009). Environment friendly alternatives to halogenated refrigerants: A review. *International Journal of Greenhouse Gas Control, 3*(1), 108–119.

Palm, B. (2008). Hydrocarbons as refrigerants in small heat pump and refrigeration systems: A review. *International Journal of Refrigeration, 31*(4), 552–563.

Park, K.J. & Jung, D. (2009). Performance of heat pumps charged with R170/R290 mixture. *Applied Energy, 86*(12), 2598–2603.

Powell, R.L. (2002). CFC phase-out: Have we met the challenge? *Journal of Fluorine Chemistry, 114*(2), 237–250.

Yang, Z. & Wu, X. (2013). Retrofits and options for the alternatives to HCFC-22. *Energy, 59*, 1–21.

Zaghdoudi, M.C., Maalej, S., Saad, Y. & Bouchaala, M. (2010). A comparative study on the performance and environmental characteristics of R410A and R22 residential air conditioners for Tunisian Market. *Journal of Environmental Science and Engineering, 4*(12), 37–56.

Regionalization and Harmonization in TVET – Abdullah et al. (Eds)
© 2017 Taylor & Francis Group, London, ISBN 978-1-138-05419-6

Evaluation of the learning program in the building construction materials course in vocational education

K. Wijaya
Engineering Faculty, Medan State University, North Sumatra, Indonesia

ABSTRACT: The aim of this study is to evaluate the quality of the learning program in the building construction materials course and its effectiveness in the workplace. This evaluation uses the four-level Kirkpatrick evaluation model, with a quantitative descriptive approach. Data collection was done through questionnaires, interviews, and tests on the mastery of the subject matter on building construction materials. The level of student mastery of the subject matter prepared by the lecturer needs to be evaluated in a sustainable manner because it is closely related to the quality of education generated. Results show that learning activities in the building construction materials course were done properly and effectively. Policies to be considered next include providing facilities to support mini-research in the course, focusing subject matter of building construction materials on concrete building materials, and allocating more time and restrictions on mini-research tasks.

1 INTRODUCTION

The definition of learning according to Law No. 20 of the 2003 Act of the National Education System is a process of interaction between students, teachers, and learning resources in a learning environment. The learning environment is established based on a learning design educators make before learning begins in order to create a good learning environment for the achievement of learning goals. The success of the learning program may be seen from the results of learning (Mardapi, 2003). However, other experts argue that teaching is a process of organizing the environment around the students so as to foster and encourage students to perform learning activities (Sudjana, 2002). This means that the success of the learning program is judged not only on the outcomes of learning but also on the quality of the draft learning program prepared by educators. Measuring the success of the learning program is very important for evaluation. Daniel L. Stufflebeam said that evaluation should be more than an academic exercise (Brandt, 1978) because it can provide continuous information for determining the quality of something that is evaluated based on certain criteria to make a decision.

Evaluation of the learning program is an assessment of the quality of ongoing learning. Evaluation of students is important for a teacher, whether it is in the workplace (training), school, or university. Results of the evaluation of the learning program can help and encourage teachers to impart better learning and improve the quality of education, as a teacher is required to produce graduates who are competent. Education plays a major role in the process of learning, knowledge development, and acquiring life skills. So, the quality of education should continue to be explored and improved and its usefulness may follow and meet human needs.

The building construction materials course in civil engineering is essential knowledge for civil engineering students. Students learn about the classification of natural and artificial building materials, the basic characteristics of building materials, and advances in building materials. In studying the characteristics of building materials, students are introduced to the calculation basis for determining the characteristics of building materials through the testing of these materials to determine the physical properties and mechanics (Haimei, 2011). The content of this course includes the knowledge and skill required in selecting and describing construction materials according to prevailing standards. The learning model used is a Research-Based Learning (RBL) approach applied to the Student Learning Center (SCL). SCL is widely used in building engineering education majors at UNIMED (Universitas Negeri Medan (Medan State University)), because this can reduce the waiting period of graduates in obtaining employment (Wijaya & Lubis, 2015). Selection of the learning model is based on the 2003 Stern B. model that defines the structure of the development of vocational education at the college level as fundamental skills (basic skills) and generic work skills (Sudira, 2011). Therefore, students are trained and encouraged to identify opportunities in environmental conditions that can be used as building materials that would be useful and can be expanded up to industrial levels. There are five different types of RBL models: these teach the research that has been done by lecturers or other people, make research known, show the meaning of the research, help conduct research, and provide research experience (Gerda et al., 2010). This course uses the RBL model of teaching the research that has been done by lecturers and other people.

Knowledge of building materials in civil engineering requires specific competencies that must be mastered to be able to classify, plan, test, analyze, and report on building materials and building material products. The curriculum of the Diploma-III Civil Engineering Department includes the course of building construction materials. Based on a survey, Diploma-III Civil Engineering workers must meet competency in the skills of communication, collaboration, problem solving, initiative and enterprise, planning and organizing, and self-management, and have knowledge of and skills in technology. Knowledge of building materials is part of the employment skills required for competency in technology. Therefore, this study is conducted to determine the quality of the learning program in building construction materials course in supporting the development of science, knowledge, and technology.

2 METHOD

This study is an evaluation model that aims to determine the quality of the learning program in building construction materials course by means of direct observation, questionnaires, and interviews and analysis of data using descriptive methods. The data collected are classified and analyzed based on related theories that provide conclusions and suggestions (Detty et al., 2008). The evaluation model used is a four-level Kirkpatrick model to assess the reaction of students, student skill improvement, implementation skills acquired in college for the workplace, and the impact of the implementation of these skills in the work unit. The reason for choosing this model is to assess the effectiveness of this learning program in the workplace. The research samples were Diploma-III Civil Engineering students and alumni of Civil Engineering at Unimed, totaling 150 people.

The Kirkpatrick model of evaluation is used because there is a relationship between the levels, so the reaction of students provides behavioral change data, and behavioral change leads to obtaining learning outcomes. This evaluation model has four levels to ensure an effective program runs (Kirkpatrick & Kirkpatrick, 2009). The model is usually used to assess training programs where training is an effort to improve performance in a particular job (Gomes, 2005). So, while there is a change of behavior among students, the learning program is an attempt to make students learn that there is a change of behavior.

2.1 *Evaluation level 1: Reaction*

This level measures the satisfaction of students with the learning program subject of building construction materials. Satisfaction value is assigned to the lecturer, teaching method, subject matter, facilities, and the overall organization of the learning program. If the satisfaction value is small then it is assumed that students are not seeking to use or apply the knowledge obtained at work. Therefore, evaluation level 1 is the basis for learning motivation.

2.2 *Evaluation level 2: Learning*

This level measures mastery of the subject and skills and the change in attitudes of students. Measurements are made by administering a pre-test and a post-test to students who take this course. If the score increases, it is assumed that the learning is successful. If the learning is successful, then there will be a change in the behavior of students.

2.3 *Evaluation level 3: Behavior*

This level ascertains whether students use the knowledge and skills and whether there is a change in attitude of learners that has been acquired during the course. It is expected that the learning program has a positive influence on the performance of learners currently entering the working world.

2.4 *Evaluation level 4: Results*

This level measures the impact of the learning program. The impact measurement assesses the quality and effectiveness of the learning program in the workplace and helps institutions achieve purpose in other subjects during the next semester.

3 RESULTS AND DISCUSSION

3.1 *Evaluation level 1: Reaction*

Results revealed that the quality of the learning program subject matter in the construction materials course is categorized as "good," as seen from the responses of learners (Table 1). In the views of the students, the component that has the lowest score is facility. Learners stated that the facilities are

Table 1. Evaluation level 1 results.

Evaluation component	Evaluation results (%)		
	Poor	Average	Good
Subject matter	2	27	71
Facility	20	40	40
Model and learning method	3	15	82
Learning quality	0	8	92

Table 2. Evaluation level 2 results.

Test	N	Mean
Pre-test	50	45.35
Post-test	50	83.50

Table 3. Evaluation level 3 results.

Evaluation component	Evaluation results	
	Value (%)	Quality
Suitability of the learning matter, duties and responsibilities in the workplace/advanced courses	78	Good
Upgrading skills and knowledge	85	Very good
Application of the learning matter in the workplace/ advanced courses	82	Very good
Increased cooperative attitude, responsibility, and independence	78	Good
Dissemination of knowledge in the workplace/advanced courses	75.6	Good

considered "poor" as the availability of materials and equipment used is limited for fulfilling the task of mini-research. Learners expressed difficulty in ordering raw materials for research, and expected ease of ordering materials, which is managed by the laboratories and universities. Equipment limitation in the realization of the RBL model is a major problem because the cost of procurement of equipment for all testing is indeed very expensive.

Another component is the lecture material (subject matter). There are too many building construction materials that need to be learned, so this RBL model encourages students to learn the material that is not described in the lecture through mini-research. However, the result of research takes a long time to reach the standard of quality as the lecture material.

Assessment of the other components revealed that generally students claimed that the learning program of this course is "good."

3.2   Evaluation level 2: Learning

Results revealed that students' knowledge on the subject increased. This can be concluded from changes in the average pre-test and post-test scores of the students (see Table 2).

The pre-test score obtained is relatively low because learners were first-year students and most students are from high schools that do not teach courses on building construction materials. However, after the implementation of the learning program in building construction materials, the knowledge of students increased significantly.

3.3   Evaluation level 3: Behavior

Questionnaires were administered and interviews were conducted at this level. Questionnaires were

sent to the students who attended the learning program in building construction materials and to lecturers of the advanced courses. Table 3 shows results obtained from questionnaires returned by the respondents.

Results of the data show that in general the learning program of this course is of good quality, which means that it is beneficial for students because it can be implemented both in the workplace and at the level of further advanced courses, and it is able to change the behavior of former students.

Interviews with former students revealed that the tasks given required very basic knowledge in the workplace. Interviews with lecturers of advanced courses revealed that the learning program needs to include subject material that is more focused on concrete building materials. This is based on the competence of graduates from the Diploma-III Civil Engineering Department at Unimed. Assessment of the attitude of students who have gone through this course remains average, as some still lack competency targets.

3.4   Evaluation level 4: Results

Questionnaires were distributed to graduates of Diploma-III Civil Engineering at Unimed, lecturers for the next semester of the building construction materials course, and the company where students practice fieldwork.

Results obtained in general showed that former students of this course feel satisfied with the knowledge and skills relating to building construction materials. However, the attitudes of former students varied, especially for those who are lecturers on the next semester.

4 CONCLUSIONS

Based on the results of this study, it can be concluded that the learning activities in the building construction materials course are properly and effectively supported by the statements of students, former students, advanced course lecturers, and the workplace/industry. Policies to be considered next include increasing raw material procurement to service mini-research, focusing subject matter on concrete building materials, and allocating time and restrictions on mini-research.

ACKNOWLEDGMENTS

The author would like to thank the Ministry of Research, Technology, and Higher Education that has been supporting the funding of doctoral learning programs.

REFERENCES

Brandt, R. (1978). On evaluation: An interview with Daniel L. Stufflebeam. In Leadership, E. (Ed.), *On evaluation: An interview with Daniel L. Stufflebeam* (pp. 249–254). San Francisco: JRA Publisher.

Detty, R., Christin & Istiharini (2008). Evaluasi Ke-Efektifan Program Pelatihan "Know your customer & money laundering" di Bank X Bandung (Evaluation of the Effectiveness of Training Programs "Know your customer & money laundering" At Bank X Bandung). Paper presented at the National Conference on Management Research, Makassar. ISBN: 979-442-242-8.

Gerda, J.W., Jan, H.D., Roeland, M.R., Nico, V. & Anthonya, V. (2010). The ideal research-teaching nexus in the eyes of academics: Building profiles. *Higher Education Research & Development, 29*(2), 195–210.

Gomes, F.C. (2005). *Manajemen Sumber Daya Manusia.* Yogyakarta: Andi.

Haimei, Z. (2011). *Building materials in civil engineering* (S. Ma & Y. Wu, Eds.). India and China: Woodhead Publishing Limited and Science Press.

Kirkpatrick, D.L. & Kirkpatrick, J. (2009). *Evaluating training programs.* Oakland, CA: Berrett-Koehler Publishers.

Mardapi, D. (2003). *Kurikulum 2004 dan Optimalisasi Sistem Evaluasi Pendidikan di Sekolah. Pada Seminar Nasional Kurikulum 2004 Berbasis Kompetensi, 8.* Yogyakarta: Universitas Ahmad Dahlan.

Sudira, P. (2011). VET curriculum, teaching and learning for future skills requirements. Paper presented at the International Seminar on Vocational Education and Learning (pp. 1–11).

Sudjana, N. (2002). *Dasar-dasar Proses Belajar dan Mengajar.* Bandung: Sinar Baru Algesindo.

Wijaya, K. & Lubis, A. (2015). Analysis of vocational learning system in Department of Education building technique. Proceedings of the 3rd International Conference on Technical and Vocational Education and Training (pp. 213–215). Padang: Universitas Negeri Padang.

Regionalization and Harmonization in TVET – Abdullah et al. (Eds)
© 2017 Taylor & Francis Group, London, ISBN 978-1-138-05419-6

Long-term power load forecasting in the Java–Bali electricity system using neural network backpropagation

L. Anifah, S.I. Haryudo & R. Ardian
Electrical Engineering, Faculty of Engineering, State University of Surabaya, Indonesia

ABSTRACT: Forecasting is an attempt to predict what happens in the future with the data from the past, based on scientific methods and quantitative systematic review. This study reviews Neural Network backpropagation algorithms for long-term power load forecasting for every province in the Java–Bali electricity system. The purpose of this paper is to predict the power load of each province in the Java–Bali electricity system and to compare the results with the electric load forecasting using backpropagation algorithms with conventional methods for the 2015–24 Electricity Supply Business Plan RUPTL *(Rencana Umum Penyediaan Tenaga Listrik)* of the state-owned power utility firm PT Perusahaan Listrik Negara (Pesero). The results of electric power load demand calculation and simulation of long-term forecasting for 2015–24 were not much different from forecasting RUPTL data. Average annual growth of electricity load for Daerah Khusus Ibu Kota Jakarta is 8.98%, Banten Province 8.74%, West Java Province 8.76%, Central Java Province 8.73%, Daerah Istimewa Yogyakarta 8.05%, East Java Province 8.09%, and Bali Province 8.13%.

1 INTRODUCTION

The Java–Bali electricity system is the largest electricity interconnection system in Indonesia, connected to each other through power transmissions of 500, 150, and 70 kV. The Java–Bali electricity system is divided into four service areas that are a unit of the state-owned power utility firm PT Perusahaan Listrik Negara (PT.PLN) Pusat Pengatur and Penyaluran Java–Bali (P3B-JB, Distribution and Load Control Java–Bali Center): APB Daerah Khusus Ibu Kota (DKI) Jakarta–Banten, APB West Java, APB Central Java–Daerah Istimewa (DI) Yogyakarta, and APB East Java–Bali.

Every event in the power system affects the entire interconnected system. As the electricity demand in the Java–Bali electric power system is growing, it needs additional capacity-generating units, transmission lines, transformers, and other infrastructure. Thus, PLN P3B-JB continues to strive to achieve the power system operating goals of reliability, quality, and security (Tresna, 2013).

According to Handoko (2009), electricity consumed in a period of time cannot be calculated exactly. Thus, it is important to predict the electricity demand because the demand for electric power is increasing. The imbalance of demand and supply can cause widespread disturbances or, even worse, extinguish supply completely. On the plant side, it can be a waste if the power generated is greater than the electricity consumption.

On the consumer side, outages can occur if the power generated is smaller than the electricity needs of consumers. Therefore, it is necessary to predict electricity demand (Handoko, 2009).

Forecasting is a process of estimating an incidence/case in the future. Forecasting is usually classified based on the time horizon in the future. In electric power, forecasting is usually load forecasting and includes forecasting peak load (megawatts) and electricity needs (demand forecasting) (megawatt-hours). Forecasting based on time span can be categorized into three types: short term, medium term, and long term (Hamidie, 2009; Heizer and Render, 2009).

Electricity demand forecasting methods nowadays have grown rapidly. Intelligent systems (artificial intelligence) are among the most widely applied by experts to estimate or predict the need for electricity in the future (Son, 2011).

Neural Network (NN) is an intelligent system that can be used in forecasting. Artificial NNs can be used to predict what happens in the future based on the patterns formed in the past. This can be done because of the ability of artificial NNs to remember and make a generalization of what was there before (Yahya, 2012).

Artificial NN is a problem-solving algorithm that imitates the human NN. One type of artificial NN is backpropagation. This method is selected because when output is not equal to the expected target, the output is propagated backward in the hidden layer to be forwarded to the unit in the input layer. So, there is feedback to validate the output of artificial NN (Setiabudi, 2015). In addition, the artificial NN backpropagation method can also be applied in forecasting (Siang, 2009). In this paper, the NN backpropagation method is used to predict electric power demands. Forecasting is done to calculate the total cost per year for each province in Indonesia. The data used in this research are data available from the Electricity Supply Business Plan (*Rencana Umum Penyediaan Tenaga Listrik*, RUPTL) of PT.PLN (Persero) and statistics data of PT.PLN (Persero) in the Java–Bali electricity system.

2 METHOD

This study developed a model of long-term power load forecasting of the Java–Bali electric power system for the period 2015–24. The results of the 2015–24 Java–Bali load forecasting for each area were obtained by multiplying the load forecasting for Indonesia with the forecasting results of the percentage of energy units sold in Java–Bali (Figure 1).

NN backpropagation was used to obtain the electrical load forecasting for the next few years. Figure 2 shows the training process to get the best weight with the smallest error.

After obtaining the best weight, the next step is the testing process. In the testing process, two data types were tested: the Indonesian electricity demand data and data of the percentage of energy units sold in each area.

The data used in this study are the data of annual electrical energy demand in the Java–Bali electricity system for 2009–14, expressed in percentage terawatt-hours (TWh), and energy units sold per customer group of PLN/province, expressed in percentage. Data were sourced from RUPTL and PT.PLN statistics, respectively. Both sets of data—annual sale of electrical energy in the Java–Bali electricity system and energy units sold per customer group of PLN/province—were divided into training data (training) and data testing (testing).

Table 1 shows a data pattern used for electricity load forecasting in Indonesia. There are six patterns for the training process and three patterns

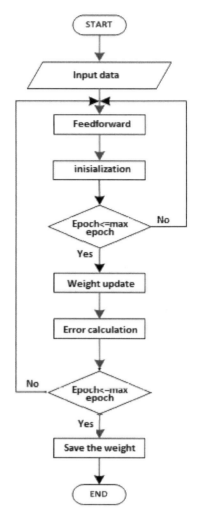

Figure 2. Training process using artificial NN backpropagation.

Figure 1. Forecasting calculation schemes of electricity demand in Java–Bali.

Table 1. Training and testing data load forecasting.

Data	Pattern	Input			Target m
		m-3	m-2	m-1	
Training	1	90.54	100.10	106.09	111.48
	2	100.10	106.09	111.48	119.97
	3	106.09	111.48	119.97	127.63
	4	111.48	119.97	127.63	133.11
	5	119.97	127.63	133.11	145.66
	6	127.63	133.11	145.66	156.30
Testing	1	133.11	145.66	156.30	172.20
	2	145.66	156.30	172.20	185.70
	3	156.30	172.20	185.70	198.60

for the testing process. For each training and testing process, there are three inputs and one target. Input data are m-3, m-2, and m-1; target data is m. Table 2 shows the NN architecture for forecasting electricity loads in Indonesia.

Table 3 shows a pattern of data used to forecast the percentage of energy units sold for each PLN/province. There are two patterns for the training process and one for the testing process. Each training and testing process has three inputs and one target. Input data are m-3, m-2, and m-1; target data is m. Table 4 shows the NN architecture for forecasting percentage of energy sold in the Java–Bali electric power system.

Table 2. NN architecture for forecasting electricity loads in Indonesia.

Layer	2
Neuron layer 1	5
Neuron layer 2	1
Layer function 1	tansig
Layer function 2	purelin
Training function	traingdx
Maximum epoch	5000
Error target (mean square)	0.001
Learning rate	0.01
Momentum	0.08

Table 3. Data of energy demand percentage forecasting in the Java–Bali electric power system.

Province	Data	Pattern	Input m-3	m-2	m-1	Target m
DKI	Training	P1	22.58	22.38	22.19	21.94
Jakarta		P2	22.38	22.19	21.94	21.30
	Testing	P1	22.19	21.94	21.30	20.78
Banten	Training	P1	4.48	4.83	4.60	4.47
		P2	4.83	4.60	4.47	4.85
	Testing	P1	4.60	4.47	4.85	4.23
East Java	Training	P1	21.09	20.86	21.55	21.07
		P2	20.86	21.55	21.07	20.73
	Testing	P1	21.55	21.07	20.73	21.59
Middle	Training	P1	9.95	9.77	9.69	9.54
Java		P2	9.77	9.69	9.54	9.71
	Testing	P1	9.69	9.54	9.71	9.88
DI Yogja-	Training	P1	1.25	1.23	1.18	1.17
karta		P2	1.23	1.18	1.17	1.18
	Testing	P1	1.18	1.17	1.18	1.19
West Java	Training	P1	15.65	15.25	15.20	15.47
		P2	15.25	15.20	15.47	15.31
	Testing	P1	15.20	15.47	15.31	15.37
Bali	Training	P1	2.07	2.10	2.04	2.04
		P2	2.10	2.04	2.04	2.09
	Testing	P1	2.04	2.04	2.09	2.18

Table 4. NN architecture for forecasting percentage of energy sold in Java–Bali.

Layer	2
Neuron layer 1	5
Neuron layer 2	1
Layer function 1	tansig
Layer function 2	purelin
Training function	traingdx
Maximum epoch	500
Error target (mean square)	0.001
Learning rate	0.001
Momentum	0.5

After going through the process of training and testing, the NN backpropagation produces electricity load forecasting for each PLN/province. The results of this forecasting are compared with those of 2015–24 RUPTL PT.PLN (Persero). The comparison is not to determine which one is better but to look at differences between the two forecasts.

3 RESULTS AND DISCUSSION

3.1 Area 1 (DKI Jakarta and Banten)

The smallest difference between NN and RUPTL forecasting data was recorded in 2016 and amounted to 15.2331 TWh or 45.8083% of RUPTL. The largest difference between NN and RUPTL forecasting data was recorded in 2023 and amounted to 41.0460 TWh or 79.1355% of RUPTL. The average difference between NN and RUPTL forecasting data is 63.9864%. On average, NN forecasting results were higher than RUPTL results because differences in the data produce a positive value (+).

Figure 3 shows that the differences started from the beginning of 2015. Data discrepancies are seen in 2023 and the smallest differences in 2016. The result of electricity load demand calculation and simulation of long-term load forecasting for DKI Jakarta is 8.98% per year.

Figure 4 shows that the differences began in early 2015. Data discrepancies are seen in 2024 and the smallest differences in 2015. The result of electricity load demand calculation and simulation of long-term load forecasting for Banten is 8.74% per year.

3.2 Area 2 (West Java)

The smallest difference between NN and RUPTL forecasting data was recorded in 2015 and amounted to 1.3234 TWh or 2.8559% of RUPTL. The largest difference between NN and RUPTL forecasting data was recorded in 2023

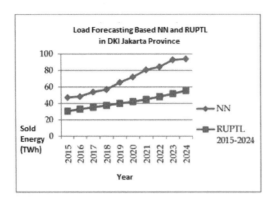

Figure 3.   Graph of forecasting for DKI Jakarta using NN and RUPTL data.

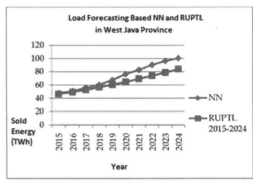

Figure 5.   Graph of forecasting for West Java using NN and RUPTL data.

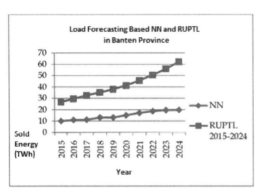

Figure 4.   Graph of forecasting for Banten using NN and RUPTL data.

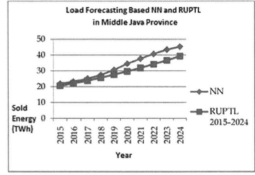

Figure 6.   Graph of forecasting for Middle Java using NN and RUPTL data.

and amounted to 17.5288 TWh or 22.2199% of RUPTL. The average difference between NN and RUPTL forecasting data is 13.0876%. On average, NN forecasting results were higher than RUPTL results because differences in the data produce a positive value (+).

Figure 5 shows that the differences start in 2019 and the largest difference is seen in 2023. Data discrepancies remain low in 2015–18. The result of electricity load demand calculation and simulation of long-term load forecasting for West Java is 8.76% per year.

3.3   *Area 3 (Middle Java and DI Yogyakarta)*

The smallest difference between NN and RUPTL forecasting data was recorded in 2016 and amounted to 1.1306 TWh or 6.2819% of RUPTL. The largest difference between NN and RUPTL forecasting data was recorded in 2023 and amounted to 6.8263 TWh or 18.6053% of RUPTL.

The average difference between NN and RUPTL forecasting data is 12.2968%. On average, NN forecasting results were higher than RUPTL results because differences in the data produce a positive value (+).

Figure 6 shows that differences start in 2019 and the largest data differences occur in 2023. Data discrepancy is still small in 2015–18. The result of electricity load demand calculation and simulation of long-term load forecasting for Central Java is 8.73% per year.

Figure 7 shows that differences start in 2019 and the largest difference is seen in 2022. The result of electricity load demand calculation and simulation of long-term load forecasting for DI Yogyakarta is 8.05% per year.

3.4   *Area 4 (East Java and Bali)*

The smallest difference between NN and RUPTL forecasting data was recorded in 2018, with

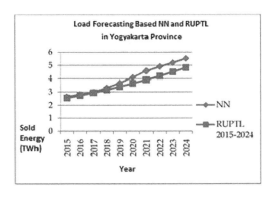

Figure 7. Graph of forecasting for Middle Java–DI Yogyakarta using NN and RUPTL data.

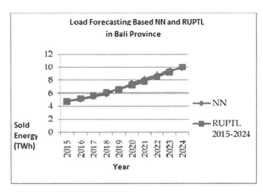

Figure 9. Graph of forecasting for Bali using NN and RUPTL data.

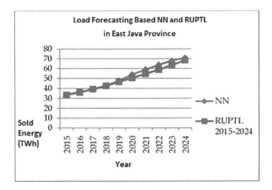

Figure 8. Graph of forecasting for East Java using NN and RUPTL data.

electricity load −0.0068 TWh or −0.0159% of RUPTL. The largest difference between NN with RUPTL forecasting data was recorded in 2022 and amounted to 4.8522 TWh or 8.2221% of RUPTL. The average difference between NN and RUPTL forecasting data is 3.7995%. On average, NN forecasting results were higher than RUPTL results because differences in the data produce a positive value (+).

Figure 8 shows that differences start in 2020 and the largest difference is seen in 2022. Data discrepancy is still small in 2015–19. The result of electricity load demand calculation and simulation of long-term load forecasting for East Java is 8.09% per year.

Figure 9 shows that there is a small difference between NN and RUPTL forecasting data. The result of electricity load demand calculation and simulation of long-term load forecasting for Bali is 8.13% per year.

4 CONCLUSIONS

Average annual growth per unit of electricity load for DKI Jakarta is 8.98%, Banten 8.0506%, 8.74%, West Java 8.76%, Central Java 8.73%, DI Yogyakarta 8.05%, East Java 8.09%, and Bali 8.13%.

Comparison of the electrical load forecasting using NN backpropagation and RUPTL PT.PLN 2015–24 data resulted in an average percentage difference in the data of −4.8320%. The average percentage difference to produce a negative value (−) indicates NN backpropagation forecasting lower than RUPTL PT.PLN 2015–24 data.

REFERENCES

Binoto, M. & Kristiawan, Y. (2015). Peramalan Energi Listrik yang Terjual dan Daya Listrik Tersambung Pada Sistem Ketenagalistrikan Untuk Jangka Panjang di Solo Menggunakan Model Artificial Neural Network. (Forecasting Electrical Energy Sold and Electricity Connected to Electrical Power System For Long Term in Solo Using Artificial Neural Network Model). *Jurnal Prosdiag SNATIF ke-2*. Universitas Muria Kudus.

Hamidie, K.A. (2011). *Metode Koefisien Energi Untuk Peramalan Beban Listrik Jangka Pendek pada Jaringan Jawa-Madura-Bali, Tugas Akhir tidak diterbitkan (Energy Coefficient Method For Forecasting Short-Term Electric Burden on Java-Madura-Bali Network, Unpublished Final Project)*. Jakarta: Universitas Indonesia.

Handoko, B. (2009). Peramalan Beban Listrik Jangka Pendek Pada Sistem Kelistrikan Jawa Timur Dan Bali Menggunakan Fuzzy Time Series (Forecasting Short-Term Electricity Expenses In East Java and Bali Electrical Systems Using Fuzzy Time Series). *Jurnal Surabaya*, November. Surabaya: Institut Teknologi Sepuluh.

Handoko, T.H. (2011). *Dasar-Dasar Manajemen Produksi Dan Operasi (Fundamentals of Production and Operations Management)* (1st ed.). DI Yogyakarta: BPFE.

Heizer, J. & Render, B. (2009). *Manajemen Operasi. Edisi 9. Terjemahan Chriswan Sungkono.* Jakarta: Salemba Empat.Kusumadewi, S. (2004). *Membangun Jaringan Syaraf Tiruan Menggunakan MATLAB & EXCEL LINK.* Yoyakarta: GrahaIlmu.

Laksono, H.D. & Fajira, N. (2014). Peramalan Beban Listrik Daerah Sumatera Barat Jangka Panjang Dengan Menggunakan Integrasi Jaringan Syaraf Truan dan Sistem Fuzzy. *Jurnal Teknologi Informasi & Pendidikan*, 7(1), 8.

Masarrang, M. dkk. (2014). Peramalan Beban Jangka Panjang Sistem Kelistrikan Kota Palu Menggunakan Metode Logika Fuzzy. *Jurnal EECCIS*, 9(1), 13–18.

Maulidin, M.S. (2014). Jaringa Syaraf Tiruan Sebagai Metode Peramalan Beban Listrik Harian di PT. PIS-MATEX Pekalongan. *Jurnal Media Elektrika*, 7(2), 36–44.

Nurmahaludin, N. (2014). Perbandingan Algoritma Particle Swarm Optimization dan Regresi Pada Peramalan Waktu Beban Puncak. *Jurnal POROS Teknik*, 6(2): 55.

PT.PLN (Persero) (2014). *Rencana Usaha Penyediaan Tenaga Listrik PT.PLN (Persero) 2015–2024.*

Purnomo, M.H. & Kurniawan, A. (2006). *Supervised Neural Networks dan Aplikasinya.* DI Yogyakarta: Penerbit Graha Ilmu.

Putra, I.P. (2011). *Aplikasi Logika Fuzzy Pada Peramalan Kebutuhan Energi Listrik Jangka Panjang Di Provinsi Sumatera Barat.* Tugas Akhir tidak diterbitkan. Padang: PPs Universitas Andalas.

Setiabudi, D. (2015). Sistem Informasi Peramalan Beban Listrik Jangka Panjang di Kabupaten Jember Menggunakan JST Backpropagation. *Jurnal SMARTICS*, 1(1), 1–5.

Siang, J.J. (2009). *Jaringan Syaraf Tiruan & Pemrogramannya Menggunakan MATLAB.* DI Yogyakarta: ANDI.

Son, H. (2015). Forecasting Short-term Electricity Demand in Residential Sector Based on Support Vector Regression and Fuzzy-rough Feature Selection with Particle Swarm Optimization. *Procedia Engineering, Procedia Engineering* 118(2015), 1162–1168.

Tresna, W.M. (2013). *Study under Frequency Relay Sistem Tenaga Listrik Jawa Bali.* Telaahan Staff—Executive Education IV. PT.PLN P3B-JB.

Yahya, A. (2012). Material Removal Rate Prediction of Electrical Discharge Machining Process Using Artificial Neural Network. *Journal of Mechanics Engineering and Automation,* 1(2011), 298–302.

Regionalization and Harmonization in TVET – Abdullah et al. (Eds)
© 2017 Taylor & Francis Group, London, ISBN 978-1-138-05419-6

Vocational education with multi-competency based on community needs

Mukhidin, S. Prihartiningsih & A. Mustikawanto
Universitas Pendidikan Indonesia, Bandung, Indonesia

ABSTRACT: Indonesia is a developing country that is trying to solve main issues in education. Indonesian people are heterogeneous and Indonesian society has established vocational high school with various competencies/skills. However, the number of LPTKs (Lembaga Pendidikan Tenaga Kependidikan: Teacher Education Institution) as providers of teacher-candidates are still limited. As a result, there is no balance between the number of vocational teacher-candidate providers and vocational high school users of LPTK graduates. In reality, a number of vocational high schools in certain provinces do not have productive teachers. The government has made many efforts with various programs but they still do not overcome the problems. Thus, it is necessary to have alternative models of community-based vocational education. The development of these models starts from the real needs of the community and proceeds to curriculum planning based on multi-competence and skills. As a result, the LPTK must integrate its curriculum with various skills/competencies to solve imbalance issues between teacher-candidate providers and vocational high schools as users of university graduates. Vocational education using this model will yield graduates who have not only one competence but also value-added competencies/skills based on society's needs.

1 INTRODUCTION

Indonesia is an archipelago with many tribes and cultures. Historically, Indonesia is a nation that has a multi-cultural society. As a developing country, the middle and lower strata of society hopes that their children get jobs soon after they finish studies. Government efforts to promote vocational high schools has yielded some result; there is a saying in Indonesia that "if you want to have a job, you just go to SMK." The government has tried to balance the number of general high schools (SMUs) and vocational high schools (SMKs), with 70% SMKs and 30% SMUs, and this has been successful.

The construction of school buildings is completed sooner than the provision of productive teachers. Development of human resources needs more time and to provide productive teachers requires 4–7 years. Almost all SMKs in Indonesia complain about the shortage of productive teachers. The number of LPTKs (FPTKs, PTKs, and JPTKs), which is jointly with APTEKINDO, is not sufficient for providing SMK teachers in Indonesia.

LPTKs like FPTKs provide productive teachers for SMKs. However, the competence spectrum in SMKs grows very fast. SMKs need more teachers who have specific skills in the spectrum of more than 120 competencies. The number of LPTK graduates for vocational high schools is limited. Multi-competence education is one of the alternatives to solve the imbalance problem. Taba (1962) states that this crisis occurred first after the cold war, where the differences between technological and economic development among and within countries was unequal and urbanization of education occurred from the poor countries to developed countries such as America, European countries, and Australia.

Therefore, it is necessary to have innovation in vocational education. The problems will be overcome if there is cooperation among educational institutions, the industrial world, and local society. The society needs mid-level skillful workers to build their environment. The industrial world and manufacturers are the users of these workers to help the development of areas. Universities are suppliers of vocational teachers. SMKs connect directly with society and prepare the skillful worker who will work in local government and companies.

2 METHOD

Multi-competence education is developed using a collaborative FPTK and PTK/JPTK model with the development of vocational education, industry, SMKs, and local government. This model is conducted inter-faculty in APTEKINDO. This coordination yields the agreement to work together to develop vocational education.

The necessary skills needed are determined after local government describes the geographical condition, economic situation, and available human resources and provides an estimation of vocational-level workers needed in the future. Because the needs of workers in each area is different, there must be a comprehensive plan. Several FPTKs should join

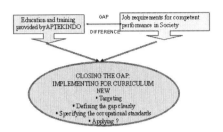

THE COMPETENCY-BASED APPROACH SOCIETY

Figure 1. Gap between educational institution's curriculum and society's needs.

together in fulfilling the needs of workers. It is not sufficient if one graduate has only one skill. It is better if one graduate has more than one skill.

The development of curriculum should refer to Taba's (1962) model that consists of need analysis, determines the need priority, and designs the tree of skills needed by the area. To run the program, of course, there will be some obstacles but these can be overcome through good cooperation.

A standard of competency is established after finding the gap between society's needs and the competency/skills that educational institutions possess. This gap is managed by reformulating the curriculum owned by institutions and involving the industrial world.

3 DISCUSSION

To close this gap between society's needs and the existing curriculum in institutions, a new curriculum needs to be developed. We can identify the gap specifically and determine the standard of competence that is needed. Then, it is about how we apply this information to Taba's (1962) model for developing a new curriculum. The model is called the up-side model, and includes the following steps:

1. Needs diagnosis
2. Formulation of objective
3. Selection of content
4. Organization of content
5. Selection of learning experience
6. Organization of learning experience
7. Determination of what to evaluate and of the ways and means of doing it.

Using these seven steps, a curriculum developer can determine the gap between the educational institution and society's needs. From this gap we can find out the competence that is needed by an area. The standard of competence is in the form of a tree of skills. This tree of skills is then broken down into information that can be organized to become the syllabus or curriculum. The curriculum components consist of purpose/goal/

objective, material, teaching strategy and evaluation (Zais, R.S, 1976). These components must be arranged systematically so that it can be a sequence that becomes a model of community-based competence. As discussed, it is clearly seen that the new curriculum needs a specific purpose so that it is easy for the curriculum developer to organize it, whether it is a separated curriculum, integrated curriculum, or correlated curriculum.

4 CONCLUSIONS

1. In Indonesian society, development in economy, education, agriculture, society, technology, and culture does not progress at the same pace. In contrast, the Island of Java has developed better because of the history and development of its education and culture, which was developed earlier by foreign countries (Dutch, Portugal, Japan, and England).
2. Regarding teacher professionalism, graduates of electronics will teach based on the electronics discipline, whether it is machinery or architecture. It is the job of the curriculum developer to formulate solutions. The developer should develop a curriculum where the graduates from vocational institutions become productive vocational teachers. If these teachers have only one competency with one skill, then it seems that society's need will be fulfilled at a slow pace.
3. Regarding the problem of competence for teacher certification, when a graduate is tested the certification indicates the form of competence but not the skill or competence to teach; the issue relates to the authorization of teachers to teach.
4. From the institutional perspective, it is not easy to ensure cooperation related to existing regulations, financials, resources, and understanding of each area.

REFERENCES

Bloom, B.S., Hasting, J.T. & Madaus, G.F. (1971). *Handbook of formative and summative evaluation of student learning.* New York: McGraw-Hill.

Munir (2008). *Kurikulum berbasis teknologi informasi dan komunikasi.* Bandung: Alfabeta.

Oliva, P.F. (1962). *Developing the curriculum.* New York: Harper Collins.

Saylor, J.G. & Alexander, W.M. (1974). *Planning curriculum for schools.* New York: Holt Rinehart & Winston.

Sukmadinata, N.S. (2005). *Landasan Psikologi Proses Pendidikan.* Bandung: PT Rosda Karya.

Taba, H. (1962). *Curriculum development theory and practice.* New York and Chicago: Harcourt, Brace & World.

Undang-Undang Republik Indonesia Nomor 20. (2003). *Sistem Pendidikan Nasional.* Jakarta: Depdiknas.

Zais, R.S. (1976). *Curriculum: Principles and foundations.* Ty Crowell Company.

Regionalization and Harmonization in TVET – Abdullah et al. (Eds)
© 2017 Taylor & Francis Group, London, ISBN 978-1-138-05419-6

"*Memetri Kali*" as transformative learning model for sociology students to care about environmental issues

S. Zunariyah & A. Ramdhon
Department of Sociology, Faculty of Social and Political Sciences, Universitas Sebelas Maret, Surakarta, Indonesia

ABSTRACT: The degradation of urban rivers is a serious problem and community participation is required to maintain and take care of rivers. This research aims to describe the practice of a transformative learning model among sociology students in taking care of Pepe River in Surakarta, Indonesia. The authors employed participatory action research with sociology students as the subjects of research. Data were collected using observation, in-depth interviews, focus group discussion, and documentation. Data collected were then analyzed using Freire's theory on critical education. Transformative learning for sociology students was conducted for two semesters in the course on environment sociology and social change and results of research showed that transformative learning connects cognitive, affective, and psychomotor aspects. Through workshop, training, and public campaign, this model played a very significant role in building students' care toward problems of river surroundings, helping the community produce information about the river, and facilitating the community in taking care of the river.

1 INTRODUCTION

Urban river degradation has become a main issue throughout the world because it is a serious threat to sustainable development attempts (Campana, 2014; Chen, 2017). River degradation affects energy circulation and earth materials because rivers host 40% of the world population (Jansky et al., 2004; Ching & Mukherjee, 2015; Miao et al., 2016). Since 2012, the quality of water has been degrading constantly. Republic of Indonesia's Living Environment and Forestry Ministry reported that, in 2015, nearly 68% of river water quality in 33 Indonesian provinces has a "severely polluted" status. The main source of river pollution is domestic and industrial wastes. The Surakarta Living Environment Agency reported that, in 2016, river water pollution is found in nearly all rivers and exceeds the threshold of standard quality, is contaminated with *Escherichia coli* bacteria, and not potable.

The factors causing river degradation include human population growth, urbanization, and behavior toward the river surroundings (Xianzhao & Shanzhong, 2011; Salazar et al., 2012; Zhao et al., 2016). The participation of all community elements is required in preventing river contamination and restoring it to preserve the resource (Jingling et al., 2010). One of the forms of participation is to encourage the students to actively take part in developing a transformative learning model. Transformative learning is conducted widely to survive and to adapt to disaster and other environmental changes. In this context, learning is conceived as changing knowledge, trust, behavior, and attitude. Transformative learning leads to change in individual reference and can be identified as the series of concepts, values, feelings, and responses to conditions and the result of experience determining an individual's life all at once. Individual reference consists of cognitive construct supporting the fundamental change of values, attitude, and conduct important in developing life strategy in dealing with threat of disaster and other environmental changes (Sharpe, 2016).

The effect of transformative learning is the individual's ability to reflect on any challenge and problem encountered. The learning outcome can be seen from the change in an individual's values and behavior relevant to the learning experience, what an individual learns, and how to reinforce it. Transformative learning enables students to question their present and previous assumptions, which potentially change as the result of experience. So, the outcome of transformative learning is building an individual's freedom, autonomy, and responsibility to the ability of moving from critical study of an experience to real action (Armitage et al., 2008; Mezirow, 2009).

Freire (1986), in his book entitled *Pedagogy of the oppressed*, stated that in the transformative learning approach, students learn to have active abilities of planning direction, choosing beneficial material, thinking of the best learning method, analyzing and concluding, and taking the benefits of learning so that a critical space can be established in economic and political structures, ideology, gender, environment, and human rights. The transformative learning process is put into the framework of social change and functions as an independent process for social transformation.

Departing from such assumption, this research aims to describe the practice of transformative learning model among sociology students in taking care of ever degrading rivers in Surakarta. Transformative learning is conducted to enable the students to produce information about rivers, to reflect on their experiences of seeing the river problems, and to change their attitude and behavior toward rivers, thereby preserving rivers. Most importantly, students can share their experience and their attitude and behavioral changes with others. Thus, the attempt to connect cognitive, affective, and psychomotor aspects can be brought into reality.

2 METHOD

This research was part of a transformative learning process in the course on environmental sociology and social change, attended by 40 sociology students serving as the subjects of research. The learning process was conducted inside and outside the classroom along the Pepe River in Surakarta, Indonesia from September 2015 to June 2016. The authors employed participatory action research consisting of investigating, acting, and reflecting (Kemmis and McTaggart, 2005). The knowledge production stage was conducted in the form of field observations, including mapping and recording the condition of Pepe River from both physical and non-physical aspects using a transect walk technique, in-depth interviews with 40 people living around the river, focus group discussion with six communities caring about the river, and a document study relevant to Pepe River.

In the knowledge distribution stage, three kampongs existing on the banks of Pepe River were selected: Gandekan, Sangkrah, and Jagalan. A series of education and training programs, workshops, and campaigns about caring for Pepe River were held in the three kampongs by involving youths, children, housewives, and adult men. The knowledge production process was conducted in an attempt to improve knowledge and understanding about the river, followed by reflecting on it to guide the social action process in the form of knowledge distribution (Greenwood & Levin, 2003).

3 RESULTS AND DISCUSSION

Knowledge is an important aspect of encouraging change. The knowledge production phase is the phase in which the students learn theory and the reality of experience, so they learn not only inside but also outside the classroom. The learning outside the classroom invites the students to learn from real conditions within the society. Knowledge production was conducted along with the people living around Pepe River, using a transect walk technique from upstream to downstream, covering a length of 7.8 km. The students recorded and documented all physical conditions of the river, and social, economic, and cultural conditions of the society surrounding Pepe River.

Monitoring and evaluation were conducted in each group, and information was communicated and discussed with each other in order to become collective knowledge and learning. The mapping of the river's physical condition consisted of water flow rate, water quality, and animal and plant types existing around the river. The data obtained confirmed the theory obtained in the classroom regarding environmental sociology. The students respond to the physical condition of rivers differently from what the ecosystem condition should be. As such, critical reasoning can be built into learning systems in colleges that tend to be dominated by rationalistic perspectives and non-critical reasoning (McFarlane, 2006; Gulrajani, 2010).

The mapping of non-physical conditions consisted of social, economic, political, and cultural conditions; for example, the livelihood of people living on the riverbank, river utilization pattern, domestic waste and rubbish processing, cultural and societal values related to rivers, population settlement condition, disaster history, and various government policies related to taking care of and maintaining rivers. In this phase, the most important point is the mapping of citizens' expectation about the future of the river in their area. Their expectation becomes the starting point for developing a change agenda for them and their environment. As such, citizens are invited to analyze the knowledge-based problem to build collectively. Thus, the knowledge production process becomes the initial stage for encouraging social transformation and change facilitated by students.

Citizens' knowledge of the river is gathered by growing the caring attitude and sense of belonging toward the river, existing surroundings, and their residence. Knowledge is the basis of belief and belief is the basis of consideration that defines attitude. The attitude of caring for the living environment is not only determined by the knowledge possessed but is also the basic capital for an individual to care more about the living environment. This is related to the change in attitude and behavior toward the river as water civilizations begin to be abandoned.

The knowledge production phase is the one in which one individual's knowledge authority is not higher than another's. So far, knowledge about the river has been dominated by the government through a series of policies not stemming from the society's will and aspirations. Knowledge derived from the ruler is often considered truer and more important than the knowledge that citizens possess. The mapping of the river resulted in the production of new knowledge about the river based on the social reality of citizens and constituted society's process of recognizing its surrounding environmental condition. This supports the citizens' process of designing need and interest related to kampong or village planning programs. The result of river mapping can be the basis of the citizens' process of building aspirations based on data rather than on interest.

The knowledge production phase was conducted through interaction and dialog between citizens and students. It is the process through which the students listen to citizens' experience and knowledge about the river. In the context of education, dialog is an important part of the emancipator knowledge model. The emancipator knowledge model is based on a dialectical relationship that aims to criticize knowledge, explain ideological interest behind social reality, and contribute to creating a form of reality based on principles of democracy and justice. Emancipatory knowledge aims to deal with mechanistic perspectives of technical knowledge and to reflect on them in order to elicit transformation. This process builds on critique and action, and meaning contained in the historical process of criticizing social reality and taking action to change it. A learning process designed to improve critical concern and personal freedom is needed for individual self-establishment and is the way for students to be empowered.

In the knowledge distribution phase, data collected by the students and the citizens were discussed together to determine the collective need and interest concerning the problems existing in river surroundings. In this phase, the students were divided into three kampongs: Gandekan, Sangkrah, and Jagalan. The consensus-building process to determine the program to deal with the river problem in their area was conducted interactively. The students served as facilitators, whereas the citizens, in this case the kampong's Karang Taruna youth group, became decision-makers.

The knowledge distribution process equips the students to be facilitators for society's diverse needs and interests. There are some workshops as part of the action approved by the kampong's citizens: comic workshop for kids, mural for youths, waste processing for adult women, and disaster response for adult men. The comic workshop for children is intended to educate them early about the importance of maintaining the environment; the mural and documentary movie workshops encourage youths to care about environmental problems in their surroundings; the waste management workshop is intended to enable the citizens to process waste and not to dispose them into the river; and the disaster response workshop is intended to make the citizens alert to flood disasters due to an overflowing river. All of the processes are conducted from, by, and for the citizens, so a democratic process is developed between them.

Change or transformation is the goal of workshops organized in each kampong. Appreciation of the students' interests and abilities becomes a matter of consideration in facilitating the existing process of change. The process of building dialog and interacting with the society is a part of being together and constitutes a prerequisite for transformation. This becomes the new innovative learning process because the conventional learning system relying on meeting in the classroom only deprives the students of social reality. As a result, the transformation process is conducted with difficulty. Transformative learning can connect the cognitive, affective, and psychomotor aspects of students, so that the learning process can run more completely and the social transformation to take care of and to maintain the river can be realized.

4 CONCLUSIONS

The transformative learning model through knowledge production and distribution processes create a participatory space for sociology students in taking care of the river. The collaboration between students and citizens living around the river can create mutual awareness of the importance of maintaining and taking care of the river and of changing society's perception and behavior toward river surroundings.

REFERENCES

Armitage, D., Marschke, M. & Plummer, R. (2008). Adaptive co-management and the paradox of learning. *Global Environmental Change, 1*: 86–98.

Campana, D., Marchese E., Theule, J.I. & Comit, F. (2014). Channel degradation and restoration of an Alpine river and related morphological changes. *Geomorphology, 221*: 230–241.

Chen, E.Y. (2017). Environmental externalities of urban river pollution and restoration: A hedonic analysis in Guangzhou (China). *Landscape and Urban Planning, 157*: 170–179.

Ching, L. & Mukherjee, M. (2015). Managing the socio-ecology of very large rivers: Collective choice rules in IWRM narratives. *Global Environmental Change, 34*: 172–184.

Freire, P. (1986). *Pedagogy of the oppressed.*, New York: Continuum

Greenwood, D.J. & Levin, M. (2003). Reconstructing the relationships between universities and society through action research. In Denzin, N. & Lincoln, Y. (Eds.), *The landscape of qualitative research: Theories and issues* (pp. 131–136). London: Sage Publications.

Gulrajani, N. (2010). New vistas for development management: Examining radical-reformist possibilities and potential. *Public Administration and Development, 30*: 136–148.

Jansky, L., Pachova, N.I. & Murakami, M. (2004). The Danube: A case study of sharing international waters. *Global Environmental Change, 14*: 39–49.

Jingling, L., Yuna, L., Liya, S., Zhiguoa, C. & Baoqiang, Z. (2010). Public participation in water resources management of Haihe river basin. China: The analysis and evaluation of status quo. Paper presented at the Annual Conference of the International Society for Environmental Information Sciences (ISEIS).

Kemmis, S. & McTaggart, R. (2005). *Participatory action research: Communicative.*

McFarlane, C. (2006). Crossing borders: Development, learning, and the North-South divide. *Third World Quarterly, 27*: 1413–1437.

Mezirow, J. (2009). Transformative learning theory. In J. Mezirow, E.W. & Taylor Associates (Eds.), *Transformative learning in practice: Insights from community, workplace, and higher education* (pp. 18–32). San Francisco: Jossey-Bass.

Miao, C., Kong, D., Wu, J. & Duan, Q. (2016). Functional degradation of the water–sediment regulation scheme in the lower Yellow River: Spatial and temporal analyses. *Science of the Total Environment*, pp. 551–555.

Salazar, C.G., Coll, M. & Whitehead, H. (2012). River dolphins as indicator ecosystem degradation in large tropical rivers. *Ecological Indicators, 23*: 19–26.

Sharpe, J. (2016). Understanding and unlocking transformative learning as a method for enabling behavior change for adaptation and resilience to disaster threats. *International Journal of Disaster Risk Reduction, 17*: 213–219.

Xianzhao, L. & Shanzhong, Q. (2011). Wetlands environmental degradation in the Yellow River Delta, Shandong Province of China. *Procedia Environmental Sciences, 11*: 701–705.

Zhao, Y., Wang, S. & Zhou, C. (2016). Understanding the relation between urbanization and the eco-environment in Shina's Yangtze River Delta using an improved EKC model and coupling analysis. *Science of the Total Environment, 571*: 862–875.

Implementation of the learning model of Team-Assisted Individualization (TAI) to improve student activity and student learning outcomes

S. Siregar

Universitas Negeri Medan, Medan, Sumatera Utara, Indonesia

ABSTRACT: This research aims to implement the learning model of Team-Assisted Individualization (TAI), to streamline the learning process, enable students who excel in concrete technology as a companion to the learning process, and improve student results. The research was conducted on 40 students. Results of the first cycle revealed different average scores of 20.9 (Meeting I) and 25.50 (Meeting II). Results of the second cycle continued to rise to an average final score of 84.25. Before TAI, the student learning model gained an average activity level score of 37.72 (pre-test). After TAI, the average activity level score of 42.22 in the first meeting increased to 46.67 in the second meeting of the first cycle, and 53.05 in the first meeting increased to 67.42 in the second meeting of the second cycle. Overall, there is learning results increase by using TAI.

1 INTRODUCTION

Concrete technology is a universal science that underlies the development of modern technology, is important in a variety of disciplines, and develops the power of human thought. In everyday life, the role of concrete technology is increasing, especially for civil engineering. However, concrete technology teaching in vocational high schools is still far from achieving the goal of preparing students to be skilled and to be able to react to and cope with changing circumstances. In this case, applied concrete technology teaching in vocational high schools is fundamental and very important in the intellectual life of the nation's participation in learning activities. In fact, today the subject of concrete technology is not so attractive to most students, except a few students who like the subject.

The learning model of Team-Assisted Individualization (TAI), developed by Slavin (1984), combines the advantage of a cooperative model and individual learning. This model is designed to address individual student learning difficulties; that is, learning activities more widely used for troubleshooting (Megawati, 2012). According to Slavin (1985), the primary helpful extensive learning model created and analyzed was TAI, a system that combines agreeable learning with individualized direction to address the issue of various classrooms.

2 METHOD

Cooperative learning might be characterized as a classroom learning environment in which students work together in heterogeneous gatherings on scholastic errands (Agus, 2011). Cooperative learning is seen as a method for enhancing understudy accomplishment and other intellectual abilities (Slavin, 1984a, b; Parker, R.E, 1985; Brophy, J, 1986). In cooperative learning, every understudy serves as a noteworthy learning asset for each other, sharing and assembling data required. Additionally, it cultivates the highest inspiration and more interpersonal connections, helps youngsters to accept grown-up responsibilities and take care of the earth inventively, reduces uneasiness and ethnic pressures, and expands self-regard among students (Sathyprakasha et al., 2014).

The TAI cooperative learning model is very different from other learning models. This model is developed not only to achieve academic learning but also to develop the social skills of students (Nneji, 2011). Some experts argue that this model is more efficient than other models in helping students understand difficult concepts. Slavin et al. (1985) have been trying to develop TAI cooperative learning models with optimal results.

The steps of the TAI cooperative learning model are as follows (Ekowati, 2004): 1) Lecturers prepare teaching materials to be completed by the student group. 2) Lecturers administer a pre-test for students or monitor average daily assessment of students on lectures to evaluate the weaknesses of students in a particular field (adopting the Placement Test component). 3) Lecturers teach the material briefly (adopting Teaching Group component). 4) Lecturers form small groups of heterogeneous but harmonious students, based on the daily tests of students. Each group consists of four to five students (adopting Teams component). 5) Each group performs some tasks in the form of worksheets designed by the lecturers, and lecturers provide individual assistance to those who require it (adopting the Study Team component). 6) The leader of the group reports the group's success by presenting the group's work ready to be replicated by lecturers (adopting the Creative Student component). 7) Lecturers administer a post-test to be done individually (adopting the Fact Test component). 8) Lecturers group students from the best to the least successful (if any) based on the results of the tests (adopting Team Score and Team Recognition components). 9) Lecturers provide formative tests in accordance with the prescribed competence.

The understudies are helped with comprehension of the subject matter as there is no opposition among them and they cooperate to take care of issues in managing distinctive methods of learning. Understudies do not just expect additional help from the teacher to propel them to grasp all the material quickly and precisely. The instructors could utilize 50% of their time to do this, so it is simpler to give individual help to the understudies who require extra support (Tinungki, 2005).

The research was conducted on students of the Department of Civil Engineering, Faculty of Engineering, University State of Medan, Medan, Sumatra, Indonesia. Study participants were 40 students who were taking a course in concrete technology in the first semester (6 months) in the academic year 2015/16. Research was conducted during lectures in the classroom of the Department of Civil Engineering.

This study aims to improve the quality of learning outcomes of the concrete technology course through the TAI learning model. The study was conducted in four cycles with a timeframe of 2 months. Here, the researcher is the originator of the idea and also serves as an observer and active participant as a tutor. The achievement of quality of learning through TAI cooperative learning strategies uses systematic measures that include students actively.

3 RESULTS AND DISCUSSION

The results of the implementation of the research activities outlined are in accordance with the stage of learning cycles performed in the learning process in the classroom. Two cycles are performed in this study, where each cycle consisted of two meetings. The first cycle consists of four stages: planning, implementation, observation and reflection, and re-planning. The planning stage involves the plan preparation process before learning, including preparation of learning tools and determination of the group and materials. The implementation stage

consists of two meetings for providing study material on concrete technology and is divided into the preliminary stage, the core stage, and the concluding phase. The preliminary stage involves conducting a pre-test on students. The core stage involves giving the material prepared by researchers and explaining the learning model. Students form groups of four people. Each group is appointed a tutor by the lecturer who acts as the leader of the group and as a facilitator for group members.

The observation phase, in which researchers record all the activities, takes place during the lecture. Lessons on concrete technology are given four times; post-tests are conducted every two meetings. Furthermore, from the results of the pre-test and post-tests I and II from the first cycle, reflection and re-planning are done. The planning stage starts Cycle II, which has the same stages as Cycle I. The results are as follows.

The aspects measured to determine the activity of students (presented in Table 1) show a significant increase, especially the involvement of students regarding explanation of lessons by teachers (from 50% to 77.50%). The activity level of students, measured by communication and participation in groups, also increased from 15% to 70%. This shows that students are more comfortable and happy to converse with fellow students because it can increase their confidence. This can be seen in

Table 1. Percentage of the level of activity of students.

No.	Aspect measured to students	Before TAI	After TAI/meeting			
			I	II	III	IV
1	Noting explanation of lecturers	50.0	60.0	72.5	72.5	77.5
2	Asking questions	27.5	32.5	40.0	45.0	50.0
3	Doing the questions with confidence/not relying on others	45.0	45.0	47.5	50.0	57.5
4	Communicating and participating well in the group	15.0	20.0	20.0	47.5	70.0
5	Providing ideas/ opinions	20.0	27.5	27.5	40.0	57.5
6	Responding to the opinions of others	48.5	57.5	57.5	60.0	72.2
7	Receiving opinion/ input of others	20.0	27.5	27.5	32.5	60.0
8	Paying attention to fellow members of other groups	32.5	45.0	57.5	57.5	77.5
9	Making a summary of the study	45.0	65.0	70.0	72.5	85.0
Mean		37.5	42.2	47.7	53.0	67.4

the increase in Aspect 8, which is the level of awareness of students toward other members of the group, from 32.5% to 77.50%. This concern is characterized by group members helping each other to solve engineering problems. Overall, the aspect that is measured in the TAI learning activity increased.

TAI learning models have shown success in implementation because one of the advantages of TAI is to improve communication and activity of students in the learning process (Perihan, 2009). The results of the activity distribution of students who studied concrete technology are shown in Table 2.

Concrete technology is a compulsory subject in the first semester of the civil engineering study program. This course is often considered a difficult subject because of the low graduation rate (preliminary observations: <55%). At the beginning of the first meeting, the students were shy and scared, with a low level of activity and participation in the learning process. With the implementation of the TAI learning model, an increasing activity level for students was observed. During the first meeting, out of 40 study participants, 36 students were passive, only listening and recording, and 4 students were active. Furthermore, when the TAI instructional model that involves students actively learning (with the lecturer as facilitator) appeared at Meeting IV, most of the students became active. Out of 40 students, as many as 33 students were active and very active. Increased activity of the students is expected to have implications on the outcome of the final required value.

Table 3 presents the frequency generated from the first and second cycles with pre-test and post-test results of each cycle. The average pre-test score is 45.50, with a minimum of 0.00 and a maximum of 80.00. The average of this pre-test was associated with a low level of activity (15.00% as in Table 1). In the first cycle of the first meeting, the average score increased to 66.09, with a minimum of 20.00 and a maximum of 100.00. Despite the increase, the result is still lower than the minimum passing score of 70.00. The average, minimum, and maximum scores continued to increase at the first and second post-tests. The second cycle saw an increase in the aver-

age score of 73.88 to 84.25, with the minimum and maximum scores also increasing. Table 1 shows that the level of activity of communication/participation among group members was 70% and Table 2 shows a total of 33 students were active and very active during the learning process.

Results in Table 4 show that the model significantly improves student learning outcomes. The low graduation rate (<55%), noted in preliminary observations of researchers, increased by implementing the TAI learning model. Table 4 presents the recapitulation of the learning outcomes of students studying concrete technology. At the first meeting, 18 students were not competent; at the second meeting, 11 student were not competent; at the third meeting, eight students were incompetent; and at the final fourth meeting, five students remained incompetent. Thus, overall, there are increases in the process, content, and activity of students.

Table 3. Results of the frequency of the first and second cycles.

		Cycle I		Cycle II	
	Pre-test	Post-test I	Post-test II	Post-test I	Post-test II
Valid, N	40	40	40	40	40
Missing	0	0	0	0	0
Mean	45.50	66.09	71.00	73.88	84.25
Standard error of mean	3.06	3.35	2.77	2.71	2.57
Median	50.00	70.00	70.00	75.00	85.00
Mode	50.00	70.00	70.00	70.00	100.00
Standard deviation	19.34	21.16	17.51	17.11	15.91
Variance	374.10	447.85	306.67	292.93	253.27
Range	80.00	80.00	70.00	70.00	50.00
Minimum	0.00	20.00	30.00	30.00	50.00
Maximum	80.00	100.00	100.00	100.00	100.00
Total	1820	2643.75	2840	2955	3370

Table 2. Total activity level of students.

	Number of students/meetings			
Indicator	I	II	III	IV
Not active	12	9	6	0
Less active	24	13	13	7
Active	4	18	21	27
Very active	0	0	0	6
Total number	40	40	40	40

Table 4. Recapitulation of learning outcomes.

		Number of respondents/meeting			
Indicator	Pre-test	I	II	III	IV
Not competent	35	18	11	8	5
Less competent	4	10	13	12	3
Competent	1	4	8	12	15
Very competent	0	8	8	8	17
Total	40	40	40	40	40

4 CONCLUSIONS

The results of the study in the first cycle show changes in cognitive understanding (competence) of students with regard to the subject of concrete technology by applying the TAI learning model. The different average post-test and pre-test scores of the first cycle are 20.59 (post-test I) and 25.50 (post-test II). The difference on this score does not show major changes when associated with the expected minimum passing score. To improve these scores through the TAI learning model, the model was applied not only inside the classroom but also outside the classroom in the form of tasks (individual and group), training, and student discussion. By implementing the TAI guided learning model, in which each student is actively communicating and participating in solving a problem (question), student understanding is much improved compared with individual learning. In the second cycle, there is a significant increase in the difference in value between the pre-test and post-test scores, where the average final score obtained was 84.25.

Furthermore, in addition to evaluating the results of the study TAI also evaluated the level of activity of students during the learning process. Before TAI, the average learning activity level of students was 37.72 (pre-test). After TAI, the average activity level scores were 42.22 (Meeting I, Cycle I), 46.67 (Meeting II, Cycle I), and 53.05 (Meeting I, Cycle II), eventually rising to 67.42 (Meeting II, Cycle II).

REFERENCES

Agus, S. (2011). *Cooperative Learning Teori & Aplikasi Paikem (Cooperative Learning of Paikem Theory & Aplication)*. Yogyakarta: Pustaka Pelajar.

Brophy, J. (1986). Teaching and learning mathematics: Where research should be going. *Journal for Research in Mathematics Education*, 323–346.

Ekowati, E. (2004). *Model-Model Pembelajaran Inovatif Sebagai Solusi Mengakhiri Dominasi Pembelajaran Pendidik*. Makalah Workshop Rencana Program dan Implementasi Life Skill SMA Jawa Timur.

Megawati (2012). Y. D. N., & Sari, A. R. (2012). Model Pembelajaran Kooperatif Tipe Team Assisted Individualization (TAI) dalam Meningkatkan Keaktifan Siswa dan Hasil Belajar Akuntansi Siswa Kelas XI IPS 1 SMA Negeri 1 Banjarnegara Tahun Ajaran 2011/2012. Jurnal Pendidikan Akuntansi Indonesia, *10*(1): 162–180.

Nneji, L. (2011). Impact of framing and team assisted individualized instructional strategies students' achievement in basic science in the north central zone of Nigeria. *Knowledge Review*, *23*(4): 1–8.

Parker, R.E. (1985). Small-group cooperative learning—Improving academic, social gains in the classroom. *Nassp Bulletin,* *69*(479), 48–57.

Perihan, D.A. (2009). Experimental evaluation of the effects of cooperative learning on kindergarten children's math ability. *International Journal of Educational Research*, *48*: 370–380.

Sardiman (2011). *Interaksi dan Motivasi Belajar Mengajar*. Jakarta: PT Grafindo Persada.

Sathyprakasha et al. (2014). Research on cooperative learning: A meta-analysis. *International Journal of Informative & Futuristic Research*, *1*(10): 139–150.

Slavin, R. (1984a). Team assisted individualization: Cooperative learning and individualized instruction in the mainstreamed classroom. *Remedial and Special Education*, *5*: 33.

Slavin, R. (1984b). Effects of team assisted individualization on the mathematics achievement of academically handicapped and no handicapped students. *Journal of Educational Psychology*, *76*(5): 813–819.

Slavin, R. (1985). *Learning to cooperate, cooperating to Learn*, (Part III, pp. 177–209). New York: Springer Science & Business Media.

Slavin, R. et al. (1990). Cooperative learning models for the 3's R. *Educational Leadership*, *47*(4): 22–28.

Tinungki, G.M. (2015). The role of cooperative learning type team assisted individualization to improve the students' math communication ability in the subject of probability theory. *Journal of Education and Practice*, *6*(32): 27–31.

Regionalization and Harmonization in TVET – Abdullah et al. (Eds)
© 2017 Taylor & Francis Group, London, ISBN 978-1-138-05419-6

Management of cooperation and partnership in vocational high schools for improving graduate competencies

T. Setiawaty & G. Tjahjono
Jurusan Pendidikan Teknologi dan Kejuruan, Fakultas Keguruan dan Ilmu Pendidikan,
Universitas Nusa Cendana, Indonesia

ABSTRACT: Vocational High Schools (VHSs) have the appearance of a superior (high-performing) school. To achieve superior performance, VHSs require cooperation and partnership with various parties, such as institutions, individuals, and groups. This study aims to describe the implementation of cooperation and partnership in VHSs to prepare graduates for work. This study uses qualitative research methods with a case study approach. Data were collected using in-depth interviews, participant observation, and documentation. The aim of research is the implementation of cooperation and partnership management in VHSs. Research subjects are all indicators of school plus alumni and industry partners. This research resulted in a model consisting of the plan of operation for quality objectives, socialization and online image creation of the school, development of networking and partnership, cooperation and partnership programs, the implementation of cooperation and partnership, and cooperation in the form of production.

1 INTRODUCTION

The Association of Southeast Asian Nations (ASEAN) created the Asian Economic Community (AEC) in 2015. The purpose of the AEC is to improve economic stability in ASEAN and to be able to overcome economic problems between ASEAN countries. The AEC integrates 12 priority sectors: free flow of skilled labor for health care, tourism, logistics services, e-ASEAN, air travel transport, agro-based products, electronic goods, fisheries, rubber-based products, textiles and apparels, automotive, and wood-based products (http://www.academia.edu/11907160).

One of the AEC's priority sectors is wood-based products. VHS PIKA produces wood-based products and has been known for its furniture products since 1968. Since the establishment of VHS PIKA, this school has been preparing students as ready labor for the wood industry, with expert skills of operator and supervisor. VHS PIKA has many accomplishments that are improved annually. For improved performance, the alumni association also provides information, knowledge, and skills in furniture production technology being developed in companies for which alumni work. Information obtained from alumni and the industry enables VHS PIKA to continuously improve and make adjustments so that practical learning can adapt to the demands of the furniture industry (Setiawaty, 2011).

Based on its achievements, VHS PIKA is able to create superior prospective labor for the furniture industry; they are qualified and able to compete with other labor from other countries. To create superior human resources, good quality schools are required. An effective school is a good quality school (Sallis, 1993). Townsend (1994) classifies the quality of schools into four quality dimensions: the quality of individual students, the quality of the curriculum used, the quality of the teacher, and the quality of graduates produced. Quality can be achieved if the school is able to perform as an effective school. To achieve effective school status, schools must have high absorption in employment, low dropout rates, and the chance for students to go on to higher education (Caldwell & Spinks, 1988) and high-performing schools (Shanon & Bylsma, 2003).

To achieve effective school status, it is time for VHSs to build cooperation and partnership with industry. This will ensure that the schools know about the world of work and are able to accommodate the possibility of a joint venture to develop concepts of learning and adjust to the needs of the working world. Forms of cooperation in the implementation of school programs are adapted to the conditions and needs of the school and also to the associated partner. School partnerships with industry aims to bring skilled and trained labor to the workplace.

Partnership becomes a clear facilitator and is an approach to improve sustainable development, especially in vocational education. The basic principle in establishing partnerships include: mutual benefit, mutual trust, and mutual give and take for the

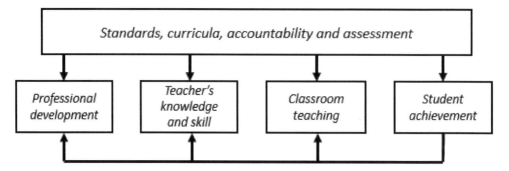

```
┌─────────────────────────────────────────────────────────────────┐
│        Standards, curricula, accountability and assessment        │
└─────────────────────────────────────────────────────────────────┘
     │              │                    │                 │
     ▼              ▼                    ▼                 ▼
┌──────────┐  ┌──────────┐       ┌──────────┐      ┌──────────┐
│Professional│ │ Teacher's │       │ Classroom │      │ Student  │
│development │ │ knowledge │       │ teaching  │      │achievement│
│          │  │ and skill │       │          │      │          │
└──────────┘  └──────────┘       └──────────┘      └──────────┘
     ▲              ▲                    ▲                 ▲
     └──────────────┴────────────────────┴─────────────────┘
```

Figure 1.   How to develop student achievement professionally (Regional Educational Laboratory (REL) Southwest, 2007: 4).

partnership. Some of the collaborative activities and partnerships that can be developed by the school and the workplace are: 1) managing joint activities and programs between providers of educational institutions; 2) utilization of infrastructure owned by partner institutions; 3) program funding to realize a program to be implemented; and 4) the placement of graduates from educational institutions into the expanding sectors or commodity areas required by the partner agency (Bambang & Budi, 2016).

The Regional Educational Laboratory (REL) Southwest (2007) explains that school development in a professional manner will result in student achievement. Development of student achievement in a professional manner is capable of producing outstanding students in the educational system. Figure 1 shows how to develop student achievement in a professional manner.

2   METHOD

This study uses qualitative research methods with a case study approach. The study was conducted in VHS PIKA Semarang, Indonesia. Data were collected using in-depth interviews, participant observation, and documentation. The aim of research is the implementation of cooperation and partnership management in the school. The subjects of research are the principal, vice principal, the curriculum in practice, instructors, students, alumni, partner industries, and administrative personnel. Data were analyzed using the qualitative data analysis interactive model of Miles and Huberman (2007) involving four research stages: data collection, data reduction, data display, and drawing conclusions.

3   RESULTS AND DISCUSSION

3.1   *VHS PIKA*

VHS PIKA has a vision for young people to excel in the wood industry, particularly in the field of

furniture. The school's education motto is competence, conscientiousness, and compassion. The school's vision is to become a center of technical vocational education for the furniture industry, with graduates who are competent, humanist, live noble values, and care for the environment (VHS PIKA, n.d.).

VHS PIKA has a four-year learning program, consisting of Level I (Class X), Level II (Class XI), Level III (Class XII), and Level IV (Class XIII). The school uses the government curriculum combined with the PIKA curriculum. The curriculum is 30% theory and 70% practice. At Level 1, students are taught a sense of quality and learn about: 1) how to make a good product; (2) how to work in a professional manner; and 3) how to be an artisan using manual tools, such as pegs, saws, and chisels. At Level 1, students make the products individually. At Level 2, students learn about the sense of efficiency that governs the way to work, time management, and production processes. At Level 2, students start using the workbench and standard machines, such as graders, planer machines, drilling machines, thickeners, and chainsaws, and make products individually.

Level 3 students learn about the sense of teamwork, that is, how to complete a product in groups of two to three people; for example, making table bureaus and cabinets is done in groups. The goal is that students are trained how to cooperate with each other. Level IV students learn a sense of entrepreneurship, where they apply the knowledge obtained from Levels 1–3 and begin to work with other employees to complete the project. At Level IV, students start to learn how to finish a project, either independently or in groups, and to be responsible for managing a project.

3.2   *Curriculum of VHS PIKA*

VHS PIKA is a place to educate students in the technical skills of furniture making, and continuously improves its quality management system using ISO 9001:2008. This improvement of quality management is the response of VHS PIKA to demands, expectations, and wishes of the customer who comes first and overrides priorities. The curriculum used is a combination of the government curriculum and the PIKA curriculum. It is made jointly by teachers of VHS PIKA, alumni, and the industries that employs PIKA graduates. Inputs from alumni and the timber industry strengthen the PIKA curriculum that is constantly evolving.

3.3 Quality objectives of VHS PIKA

VHS PIKA has five work units: vocational education workshops, curriculum, facilities and infrastructure, student work, and educators and guidance counseling (Setiawaty, 2011). Each unit devises a plan of the quality objectives based on the current strategic plan of the school, an analysis of the internal strengths and weaknesses and external opportunities and threats (i.e., a SWOT analysis), and strategic plans that have not been achieved in the previous year. Determination of quality objectives is set at the beginning of the school year based on PIKA's management coordination meeting and evaluated at the end of the school year. The quality objectives of each unit and the achievement indicators are outlined in the activity plan.

The achievement of quality targets is constantly evaluated by the vice principal during the coordination meeting every week. Management reviews are conducted to evaluate achievement of quality objectives when monitoring learning outcomes at the end of the school year. Management reviews are led by the director of PIKA and attended by representatives of the quality management system and the principal of PIKA.

3.4 Cooperation model for VHS PIKA and the industry

Education in VHS PIKA is fully supported by the timber industry, both financially and through experience. PIKA vocational graduates and VHS PIKA products are ready to compete in the wood industry. These products are recognized as upper-middle class products, as PIKA products are known to be exclusive. PIKA products use good quality wood and are durable. Also, PIKA furniture product design is very interesting and has perfect finish, making PIKA products very well known to the public.

Cooperation between the school and the industry occurs because of: 1) students who not only practice in vocational workshops but also studied at PIKA; 2) PIKA–industry collaboration on products that have to be produced by students; 3) continuous collaboration between the school and the industry to produce graduates who are ready to work and have no trouble during the course of work; 4) information from the industry about what competencies are required nowadays; 5) industrial help in the form of machines to assist student learning; 6) internships in the industry; 7) scholarships made available for outstanding students; 8) the common commitment of VHS PIKA and the industry to promote the Indonesian economy, especially the wood industry; 9) regular training provision for instructors about the technological development of the wood industry; 10) invitations from VHS PIKA to teams of experts if there are new technologies in the furniture industry; and 11) the opportunity for instructors and VHS PIKA staff to upgrade their knowledge and skills regarding the latest developments in the wood industry.

3.5 Developing cooperation and partnership

Cooperation and partnership agreements between the school and industry are carried out directly by the principal. VHS PIKA conducts cooperation and partnership with the furniture industry, related industries such as ironmongery (industrial paints, portable machines, handheld machines), the Employers' Association of Furniture and Handicrafts of Indonesia (ASMINDO), industrial users of PIKA furniture (e.g., hotels, hospitals, institutions), and the Ministry of Labor and Transmigration. Cooperation and partnership with institutions is implemented through several activities: 1) socialization and online image creation of the school; 2) development and expansion of the network of cooperation among industry and government agencies; 3) compilation of collaboration and partnership programs; 4) producing the memorandum of understanding (MOU); 5) implementation of the cooperation plan; and 6) evaluation of cooperation and partnership previously achieved.

3.6 Cooperation and partnership programs

VHS PIKA make cooperation and partnership programs in three forms: 1) Seminars and training for students are carried out by the furniture industry or another related industry. Seminar materials are in accordance with agreements between the school and the industry partners. Training and seminars are conducted after students complete general tests and before they receive their report cards. 2) Students are given industrial work practice opportunities, where activities are carried out in keeping with the MOU between the school and the industry partners. MOU is conducted by the industry and the school. VHS PIKA's industrial work practices are conducted during the first year. The content of the agreement include the rights and obligations of students, the school, and the industry. 3) Placement of orders for furniture products is done with the collaboration of the production divisions of the industry and PIKA.

3.7 Implementation of cooperation and partnership in industrial working practices

VHS PIKA implements industrial working practices for 1 year for students in Level IV. It aims at providing work experience to students to help them apply theory and practice skills in real conditions in the industry. Industrial working practices also provide students technical knowledge, workplace attitudes, mental strength, and managerial experience in an industrial environment and its accompanying problems. Implementation of industrial working practices during the first year gives students more experience while working in the industry. During the work experience, students are asked to observe problems that occur in each industry and these problems become the topic of scientific papers by the students. How students solve problems faced during the practice of industrial work is critically examined in students' papers. Industrial practice is evaluated by assessing the student's performance during the first practice and the results of industry tests conducted before a team of examiners from the school and the industry.

3.8 Implementation of cooperation and partnership in production

VHS PIKA builds programs of cooperation and partnership based on the form of cooperation agreed between the school and the industry. Industries that want to work with VHS PIKA grow annually, in terms of orders and number of students in industrial work practices in the furniture industry. The industry tends to benefit from such cooperation because VHS PIKA students are recognized as being of superior quality.

4 CONCLUSIONS

VHS PIKA has autonomy in managing work and partnerships with industry and government agencies. Implementation of cooperation and partnership management is done effectively using ISO 9001:2008. By standards of quality, WMM (Wakil Manajemen Mutu) requires all heads of units to make quality objectives that contain targets to be achieved during the school year. The quality objectives of each unit of work are outlined in the activity plan, which contains achievement indicators of quality objectives and the implementation of implementing each of the indicators so that the target can be achieved in accordance with the objectives that have been defined. The achievement of these targets is monitored every month and WMM coordinates monitoring with the school in monthly meetings. Obstacles or problems identified during the implementation of the activities are sought to

be solved so that they do not become an obstacle to implementation of activities in the following month.

VHS PIKA has used the management model of cooperation and partnership to achieve quality objectives of the school. This model includes: 1) making each unit of work meet quality objectives, where to achieve quality objectives, each unit makes an activity plan of operation and work is based on that plan; 2) socializing and image creation of VHS PIKA, church activities, and continuous cooperation with the alumni; 3) developing a network of cooperation and partnership; 4) creating cooperation and partnership programs; 5) implementing cooperation and partnership in the form of industrial practice; and 6) implementing cooperation and partnership in the form of production.

ACKNOWLEDGMENTS

The authors would like to thank the principal and all personnel of VHS PIKA that has provided funding for this research.

REFERENCES

Bambang, I. & Budi, S. (2016). Kemitraan Sekolah Menengah Kejuruan Dengan Dunia Usaha dan Dunia Industri (Kajian aspek Penhgelolaan Pada SMK Muhammadiyah 2 Wuryantoro Kabupaten Wonogiri). *Jurnal Pendidikan Ilmu Sosial*, 26(1): 1412–3835.
Caldwell, B.J. & Spinks, J.M. (1988). *The self-managing school* (p. 12). London: Taylor and Francis. Http://www.academia.edu/11907160.
Miles, M.B. & Huberman, A.M. (2007). *Analisis Data Kualitatif (Qualitative Data Analysis)* (pp. 16–17). Jakarta: UI Press.
Regional Educational Laboratory (REL) Southwest (2007). Reviewing the evidence on how teacher professional development affects student achievement. REL 2007-No. 033 (pp. 3–4). National Centre for Education Evaluation and Regional Assistance, Institute of Education Sciences, U.S. Department of Education. Website: http://ies.ed.gov/ncee/edlabs/regions/southwest/pdf/REL_2007033.pdf.
Sallis, E. (1993). *Total quality management in education* (pp. 50–51). London: Kogan Page Education Management Series.
Setiawaty, T. (2011). Manajeman Sekolah Menengah Kejuruan yang efektif. Disertasi (pp. 220, 222, 243). Yogyakarta: Universitas Negeri Yogyakarta.
Shanon, G.S. & Bylsma, P. (2003). *Nine Characteristics of High Performance School*. Olympia, Washington: Office of the School Superintendent of Public Instruction.
SMK PIKA (n.d.). PIKA-Semarang. Website: http://www.pika-semarang.com.
Townsend, T. (1994). *Effective schooling for community. core-plus education* (p. 29). London: Routledge.

Regionalization and Harmonization in TVET – Abdullah et al. (Eds)
© 2017 Taylor & Francis Group, London, ISBN 978-1-138-05419-6

Technical and vocational education and training in the secondary stage: A case study

V.A. Shamsudeen

State Institute of Technical Teachers Training and Research, Kalamassery, Kochi, Kerala, India

ABSTRACT: Being the most literate state in India, Kerala is a forerunner in vocational education and training at all levels. Engineering graduate education started before independence, as also polytechnic education. Industries were in need of qualified people at that time for increasing productivity by diversifying outputs. It was the golden age of industries within and outside Kerala, contributing to the nation's growth. The manpower so utilized resulted in record productivity both internally and externally. This further necessitated training manpower at young age for those who can exhibit their skill as per the design of the engineers. The skill gap could be filled with the manpower produced from secondary stage education by giving proper training. Technical High Schools (THSs) were started in Kerala with an aim to impart skill-oriented technical/vocational training at young age, enabling people to acquire proper jobs after further education. This is a unique system practiced in Kerala and can achieve good results in the country. This paper aims to study the attributes of the THS system in Kerala and its implications in the industry and in society, on the basis of which recommendations are made to other states and countries to follow this unique system in Kerala.

1 INTRODUCTION

1.1 *The Hunter commission, 1882*

In 1882, the Government of India appointed the Hunter Commission to suggest reforms to be brought to the education system at that time. With regard to vocational and technical education, this Commission recommended that in the particular category of high schools there should be two avenues, one leading to the entrance examination of the university and the other of a more practical character intended to empower the youth for commercial, vocational, and non-literary pursuits.

Students in their early teens show a profound inclination toward doing things on their own. This age is best suited for them to grasp more by doing things in practice rather than learning something orally. Studies have shown that the practical knowledge imbibed by teenagers can be exhibited with expertise throughout their life. However, the curriculum should be designed in such a way that necessary and sufficient information in the areas of science, mathematics, language, and social science is optimally imparted. This will aid them to become productive citizens when they reach adulthood.

1.2 *The secondary education commission, 1952*

The All India Commission for Secondary Education was appointed in 1952 under the chairmanship of Dr. A. Lakshmanswamy Mudaliar. This Commission offered a number of suggestions to make the secondary education comply with the new goals and needs of independent India. The aim was to train youth for intermediate leadership and for democratic citizenship. Secondary education was to be the terminal stage for a large majority of the nation's youth, who would take up their place in society after their school education and provide leadership to the general masses. The Commission was equally concerned with qualitative improvement of schools. To develop individual talent, curricular offerings were extended and diversified. To achieve the new aims of education, changes in methods of teaching were suggested. New trends in examination, guidance, and extracurricular work were brought into the school programs. Multipurpose secondary school was a new concept recommended by the Commission. Craft, social studies, and general science was included in the curriculum with the aim to orientate students toward an industrial and science-centered democratic life.

1.3 *Government initiatives*

Kerala, being the most literate state, is a pioneer in school education. With the formation of the state in 1956, visionary leader Prof. Joseph Mundassery, the then Minister for Education, took the lead in bringing forth reforms in general education. School education was made compulsory for all. To ensure this, necessary and sufficient schools were opened even in difficult rural and tribal areas. Mid-day meal schemes were introduced to encourage student attendance and to minimize dropout rates. The state of Kerala has the lowest school dropout rate in India.

2 CONCEPT OF TECHNICAL HIGH SCHOOLS (THS)

2.1 *Requirements of the industry*

Although a state not rich in industries, Kerala had some of the major central public sector industries, such as Fertilizer and Chemicals Travancore Ltd, Hindustan Machine Tools Ltd, Cochin Refineries, and Indian Rare Earth Ltd, working in full swing in the 1960s. Also, state-owned industries, such as Travancore–Cochin Chemicals Ltd, Transformers and Electricals Kerala Ltd, and Kerala Agro Machinery Corporation Ltd, and major private industries, such as Apollo Tyres, Indian Aluminium Company, Madras Rubber Factory, and Mavoor Rayons, flourished to their zenith. A number of scientific and commercial establishments, such as the Indian Space Research Organization, Bharat Sanchar Nigam Limited (BSNL), and Kerala State Electricity Board (KSEB) Ltd, also were in full swing. The manpower requirements of these establishments were large. In agreement with the Secondary Education Commission's suggestion of vocationalization of education, enabling students to obtain a job at a young age which in turn will provide skilled workers for the industry, the Government of Kerala decided to start THSs throughout the state and to attract youth to these establishments. Kerala was a pioneer in this regard also. In the 1960 s, seven schools were started and the outcome was really astonishing. Except a few students, most of them got absorbed in various industries and government. establishments when they reached adulthood. The number of technical institutions were increased to 24 in the 1970 s and to 39 in the 1980 s.

2.2 *The winning strategy*

At present, 4000 students are studying in 39 THSs of Kerala. The students are given training in their selected trade with emphasis on practical knowledge. At present, there are 15 trade specializations in THSs. The trades are selected in such a way as to ensure job opportunities or opportunity for higher studies. The students do practical workshops with much enthusiasm. This not only leads to jobs or higher studies but also equips them for entrepreneurship in the connected areas. Practical knowledge given at young age helps to deliver more productivity in the trades concerned.

The following are trade specializations leading to skill training as per industry and agricultural standards:

1. Welding
2. Fitting
3. Turning
4. Electroplating
5. Maintenance of two- and three-wheeler
6. Motor mechanic
7. Agriculture
8. Printing
9. Refrigeration and air-conditioning
10. Electronics
11. Electrical wiring and maintenance of domestic appliances
12. Surveying
13. Plumbing
14. Rubber technology
15. Masonry and concrete work.

Students undergoing the training in the abovementioned fields are able to achieve competence at the craftsman level, which is obtained from the Industrial Training Institute (ITI) after matriculation. But THS students are able to get the skill and competence by completing matriculation. In addition, efficacy of the THS holders shoots up since they are getting the training at the proper young age.

Recently the THS curriculum has been revised in order to reflect the state of the art knowledge and skill. Both the general studies and technical studies are revamped so that the students are able to grasp the latest developments in science, Technology and Environment.

3 IMPLEMENTATION OF THE NATIONAL SKILLS QUALIFICATIONS FRAMEWORK (NSQF) IN THE THS

3.1 *New initiative by the government of India*

The Government of India proposed implementation of the National Vocational Education Qualifications Framework (NVEQF), later changed to the NSQF, from IX standard onward in general schools, in order to inspire school dropouts to change their general stream to the vocational stream. Levels I to X in the vocational stream leads to award of a vocational certificate, degree, or diploma on completion of the appropriate levels.

When implementation of the same came up for discussion in Kerala, it was suggested that this be implemented in THSs so that students are able to acquire multiple skills through the opportunity to undergo both trade and NVEQF (NSQF) specializations.

The decision was taken at appropriate levels to implement the initiative in THSs across the state. Now, the THSs are taking it as a challenge to train students in both trade and NVEQF (NSQF) specializations (Table 1).

Table 1. NVEQF (NSQF) sectors and specializations implemented in THSs in Kerala (www.aicte-india.org/vocationaleducation).

SECTORS	SPECIALIZATIONS
Agriculture	1. Renewable Energy
	2. Green House Technology
Automobile	1. Automobile
	2. Auto Electrical and Electronics
Communication	1. Mobile Communication
	1. Construction and Building
Construction	
	Technology
Printing	1. Printing and Packaging Industry
	1. Electrical Equipment
Service	
	Maintenance
	2. Electronic Equipment
	Maintenance
Infrastructure	1. Refrigeration and Maintenance
	2. Air-conditioning
Power and Energy	1. Solar Energy
Manufacturing	2. Product and Manufacturing

Table 2. Number of subject periods per week.

SI. NO.	Subject	Period/week VIII	IX	X
1	Malayalam I	4	4	4
2	English	5	5	5
3	Mathematics	5	5	5
4	Physics	2	2	2
5	Chemistry	2	2	2
6	Social Science	4	4	4
7	Information Technology	2	2	2
8	General Engineering	–	2	2
9	Eng. Drawing	2	3	3
10	Enrich your English I & II	2	1	–
11	General Workshop	12	–	–
12	General Workshop Trade Specialization	–	5	5
13	Trade Theory	–		
	Total	40	35	34

Table 3. Scheme of studies in NVEQF (NSQF) sections.

SI. NO.	Subject	Periods/week VIII	IX	X
1	NQSF	—	5 Hrs.	5 Hrs. & 50 Minutes

3.2 Advantages

Students are able to grasp two skills simultaneously. They can select any of the trades to pursue for higher studies. If they select trade specialization, they can choose higher studies in the technical stream of general education. If they select NSQF specialization, they can undertake higher studies in vocational education in a different skill sector. They can seek employment either in the trade specialization as a skilled craftsman or in the NSQF specialization. They can perform jobs in both specializations in the industry as and when required. They can also find self-employment in any of the specialized fields or by utilizing both skills.

The competency level is high in both specializations as students practice skills at the most appropriate young ages (Table 2).

There are eight periods per day, with a duration of 50 minutes each. The total number of periods per week for each class is 40. The working time is 9 a.m. to 4.30 p.m. The distribution of periods in the THS for each subject for classes VIII, IX, and X is given in Table 3.

3.3 Advantages of THS education

Through THSs, students who are really interested are getting an opportunity to pursue their studies in technical and vocational education. Even those who are forced to stop their studies at matriculation are able to obtain a job when they reach adulthood. Those completing THS education get equal opportunity for higher studies in the general/technical/vocational stream, with 10% seats reserved for THS students in polytechnic colleges. On completion of THS education, students can become skilled workers with ITI qualifications. Those who pursue higher studies on the basis of THS education show more aptitude and practical know-how. Students are able to obtain multiple skills with the introduction of NSQF in THSs, as it provides multiple pathways for higher education and employment. Students are largely absorbed in central and state public sector undertakings and also in government establishments such as KSEB, Public Works Department, Kerala Water Authority, and BSNL. Students with adequate technical training and who have innovative ideas can pursue entrepreneurship mostly in the technical/vocational field. Thus, technical education at young age makes individuals more competent in further education and employment.

4 RESULTS AND CONCLUSIONS

The studies on THS education are based on statistics collected from teachers, students, alumni, parents, industries, and higher/technical institutions. Most of the institutions are not able to admit even 20% of applicants because of low sanctioned intake and the lack of proper upgrade of facilities. However, a few institutions in the fringe areas are not able to get sufficient students. Industries and parents expressed satisfaction in the performance of students finishing THS education and who joined a job. Higher/technical institutions are confident that THS students exhibit good competence in the area of training.

Most of the institutions that implement technical/vocational education at the high school level introduce specialized topics as optional or as a work experience subject receiving only internal assessment marks. Students may or may not show interest in studying these technical/vocational subjects.

However, in the THS education system students learn the specialized subject as a core subject that is evaluated in the Board examination like other general subjects.

Kerala, a pioneer in school education in India and with the lowest rate of school dropouts, provides equal opportunity for students who have technical aptitude. Such training obtained at young age will help individuals to conquer heights by further studies/employment. This also helps youth identify their technical/vocational aptitude and makes them capable of getting involved in the reconstruction of the nation by introducing valuable ideas and skills.

REFERENCES

Chaube, S.P. *History of Indian education.*

Naik, J.P. & Nurullah, S. (1973). *A Student's History of Education in India.*

NIEPA (1986). *Indicators of educational development: Report of technical workshop.* New Delhi: National Institute of Educational Planning and Administration.

State Institute of Technical Teachers.

Training and Research (2012). *Proposal for revision and restructure of the technical high school curriculum incorporating NVEQF specializations.*

www.aicte-india.org/vocationaleducation

www.dtekerala.gov.in.

www.sitttrkerala.ac.in.

Multimedia learning to increase student achievement in metal corrosion and coating subject material

Y. Sukrawan, R.A. Hamdani & M. Komaro
Departemen Pendidikan Teknik Mesin, Universitas Pendidikan Indonesia, Bandung, Indonesia

ABSTRACT: Multimedia Animation (MMA) in teaching metal corrosion and plating on the electroplating course material remains largely unused. There are many students who do not understand the electroplating process, despite having attended lectures. This study aims to discover the effect of MMA on students' achievement. This study applied a quasi-experimental method on two classes, consisting of a control class using image media and an experimental class using MMA. Instruments used for measuring learning are pretest and posttest. So, are the learning results obtained by using MMA better than those using image media? The results showed that the use of MMA is better than the use of image media. The average N-gain value for MMA is 0.75, whereas the average N-gain value for image media is 0.26.

1 INTRODUCTION

In the learning process, learning media is one of the important determinants of the quality of learning outcomes. Learning media is needed so that teaching materials presented can be understood by learners. Computer-based learning media developed over time is appropriate for assisting the learning process in order to produce optimum quality learning. Computer-based learning media, with a variety of images, text, sound, and video (multimedia), is expected to stimulate learners and to improve learning quality.

The use of CD-ROM interactive multimedia, with a variety of learning activities, is more effective than print media, with face-to-face activity, and online learning media (Dikshit et al., 2013). Use of interactive multimedia has been proved to improve scientific generic skills and problem-solving skills of prospective vocational teachers (Widodo, 2010). Use of multimedia animation (MMA) has been shown to improve the reading skills of vocational students (Anam and Khumaedi, 2009) and the outcomes of learning on the assembly and installation of the brake system (Harsono and Samsudi, 2009).

Multimedia in learning is widely used because it has many advantages. Twenty learning values that can potentially be produced using multimedia or video in the classroom include: 1) drawing students' attention; 2) focusing students' concentration; 3) being interested in learning in the classroom; 4) creating a sense of anticipation; 5) providing energy for the students for learning practice; 6) adding to students' imagination; 7) enhancing the

attitude of supporting the materials and learning; 8) building relationships with other students and instructors; 9) increasing memory of the materials; 10) improving understanding; 11) helping develop creativity; 12) stimulating the flow of ideas; 13) helping developing deeper learning; 14) providing opportunity for freedom of expression; 15) helping collaboration; 16) inspiring and motivating students; 17) making learning fun; 18) setting the right/comfortable mood; 19) reducing anxiety and tension while studying difficult topics; and 20) making visual images impressive (Berk, 2009).

Development of learning tools is currently easy, so the trend of teachers designing and implementing their own homemade animation will continue. This development trend is easily combined with a broader understanding of how these tools can help the learning process, so the use of animation and simulations in the classroom will continue to grow (Falvo, 2008). The use of multimedia in learning is very helpful for learning processes (Munir and Zaman, 1998). As a complete media, multimedia technology is able to develop the power of imagination, creativity, fantasy, and emotions of students in a positive direction. Students' learning outcomes after the use of macromedia flash-based multimedia applications for the learning of computer network topology increase compared with outcomes of students' learning without the use of macromedia flash-based multimedia applications (Bisono, 2013).

When a media can explain electroplating in detail, it is expected that the media can facilitate the students to understand the topic. Learning using MMA aims to illustrate the actual electroplating conditions, especially in the case of simulation. In this study, the use of multimedia is applied to the electroplating course to determine changes in students' learning achievements.

2 METHOD

The increase of concept mastery can be seen from pretest and posttest results between the experimental class and the control class. Empirical or observed data with a valid criterion are obtained through the research. This study uses an experimental research method in the form of the quasi-experimental design.

This quasi-experiment is considered to have the ability to provide an estimate of information correctly, approaching real experimental analysis in educational research. This is because subjects of the research are humans and the variables affecting the subjects are difficult to control.

Students of Departemen Pendidikan Teknik Mesin, Universitas Pendidikan Indonesia, Bandung, Indonesia were selected for this study using the cluster sampling technique.

With the existence of a control group, it becomes much easier to know the extent of differences in concept mastery for students in both the control group and the experimental group. Table 1 tabulates the research design.

Both classes were given a pretest and a posttest with the same questions to discover the effects of different treatments applied. If there are significant differences between the experimental group and the control group, then the treatment conducted can be considered significantly influential.

3 RESULTS

Research was conducted on students from the Class of 2014 in the Departemen Pendidikan Teknik Mesin, Universitas Pendidikan Indonesia, and the control and experimental classes had 36 students each. Data were obtained in the form of value data of the results of the pretest and posttest conducted on the control and experimental groups. These data

Table 1. Research design.

Class	Pretest	Treatment	Posttest
Experiment	O_1	X_E	O_3
Control	O_2	X_K	O_4

* Information:
X_E = Treatment using animation media;
X_K = Treatment using image media.

were used to describe results quantitatively, so that conclusions resulting from this research could be drawn. The format for multimedia judgment created by the researcher is intended for assessment by the experts. Multimedia judgment consists of physical assessment of media and subject content of multimedia. Description of the data is as follows.

Data judgment by media experts in this study assessed multimedia design; this assessment was rated by the evaluators or expert lecturers of media. Judgment by media experts is intended to test the construct validity of animation multimedia design. Feasibility percentage indicating the feasibility of using MMA for teaching corrosion amounted to 61.25%. This means that it is feasible to use this media for learning about metal corrosion and plating on the electroplating course material.

The minimum computer specification to run the MMA is: Windows XP/Vista/7, 1 GHz processor, 1 GB RAM, 700 MB of free hard disk drive, and a resolution of 1024×768.

A draft discussion of material was prepared that would be presented in MMA as a tool to help students understand the material. Multimedia presentation of the material in the animation was based on the subject of electroplating. Once the subject matter for this MMA was obtained, it was presented in the form of a storyboard that was used as the initial design of the production of this MMA.

The development stage is the stage to create the MMA to be used. There are several steps to create this MMA, namely, making interfaces, making animation, making audio, and testing. This stage consists of designing the multimedia display by combining colors, text, animation, and audio so that it is easy to understand and it can make students interested in using MMA in the learning process. This multimedia development is separate from encoding. Encoding was performed for several things in this animation, including voice storage and animation creation. Encoding was performed using action script 2.0. Voice storage is intended to provide voice narration and sound effects that support MMA, whereas animation creation connects and creates animation that moves according to what would be explained using the multimedia. The MMA generated is shown in Figures 1–3.

In the testing process, the animation was tested to identify errors in the multimedia that can be repaired immediately. In the implementation phase the students were able to use this MMA in the learning process. To help understand its use in learning the subject material, MMA was applied to the experimental class.

Data of pretest results of the control and experimental groups were used to determine the homogeneity of the sample, because the pretest was used to investigate whether the second sample was

Figure 1.   Front display of MMA screen.

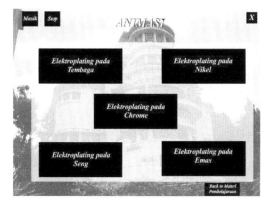

Figure 2.   MMA material of electroplating.

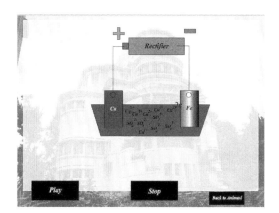

Figure 3.   MMA of copper electroplating.

homogeneous whereas the posttest was used to determine the value of N-gain. N-gain value indicates an increase in the student's ability to solve problems (Figure 4).

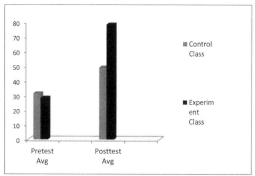

Figure 4.   Comparison of pretest and posttest average scores.

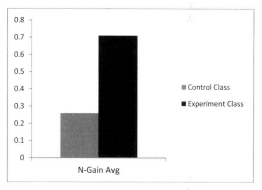

Figure 5.   Comparison of n-gain average scores.

The increase in learning outcome using MMA (experimental class) is found to be high with an N-gain value of 0.75, whereas the N-gain of the control class is low at 0.26. Based on the earlier description, it can be concluded that the average N-gain of the experimental group is greater than that of the control group and improves learning outcomes significantly (Figure 5).

4   CONCLUSIONS

The use of MMA has many advantages because it is interactive and lets users imagine and visualize the subject material. MMA uses narration and animation to help illustrate the actual simulation of the electroplating process.

The use of MMA can improve learning outcomes on metal corrosion and coating on electroplating course material, with the average N-gain value of 0.75.

REFERENCES

Anam, C. & Khumaedi, M. (2009). Pembelajaran Ceramah dengan Media Animasi untuk Meningkatkan Kemampuan Siswa dalam Membaca Gambar Proyeksi (Learning Lecture with Media Animation to Improve Student's Ability in Reading Projection Image). *Jurnal Pendidikan Teknik Mesin, 9*(1): 7–13.

Berk, R.A. (2009). Multimedia teaching with video clips: TV, movies, YouTube, and MTVU in the college classroom. *International Journal of Technology in Teaching and Learning, 5*(1): 1–21.

Bisono, I.C. (2013). *Penggunaan Aplikasi Multimedia Pembelajaran Topologi Jaringan Komputer Berbasis Macromedia Flash Untuk Meningkatkan Hasil Belajar Mata Pelajaran Tik Siswa Kelas XI SMA N 1 Godean* (Doctoral dissertation, UNY).

Dahlqvist, P. & Ramburg, R. (1998). Using animations in educational software. A pilot study of 7th grade students. Paper presented at the Second Swedish Symposium on Multimodal Communication (LUCS).

Dikshit, J., Garg, S. & Panda, S. (2013). Pedagogic effectiveness of print, interactive multimedia, and online resources: A case study of IGNOU. *Online Submission, 6*(2): 193–210.

Falvo, D. (2008). Animations and simulations for teaching and learning molecular chemistry. *International Journal of Technology in Teaching and Learning, 4*(1): 68–77.

Harsono B.S. & Samsudi (2009). Perbedaan Hasil Belajar antara Metoda Ceramah Konvensional dengan Ceramah Berbantuan Media Animasi pada Pembelajaran Kompetensi Perakitan dan Pemasangan Sistem Rem. *Jurnal Pendidikan Teknik Mesin, 9*(2): 71–79.

Hasruddin. 2009. Peran Multi Media Dalam Pembelajaran Biologi. *Jurnal Tabularasa PPS UNIMED, 2*(6): 149–160.

Munir & Zaman, H.B. (1998). Aplikasi Multimedia Dalam Pendidikan. *Jurnal BTP*. Fakulti Teknologi dan Sains Maklumat Universiti Kebangsaan Malaysia 1, 1–16.

Widodo, W. (2010). Pengembangan Model Pembelajaran "Mikir" pada Perkuliahan Fisika Dasar untuk Meningkatkan Keterampilan Generik Sains dan Pemecahan Masalah Calon Guru SMK Program Keahlian Tata Boga (Unpublished Disertasion). Bandung: Indonesia University of Education.

Author index